THE WAY TO OUR
HEAVENLY FATHER

THE WAY TO OUR HEAVENLY FATHER

A Contemplative Telling of
The Lord's Prayer

Revised and Expanded Edition
Compiled and Edited by

G. John Champoux

First published in the USA
by Semantron Press 2007
Second Revised Edition
© 2013 G.John Champoux

Semantron Press is an imprint of Angelico Press

Douay-Rheims Bible throughout except Psalm 22. *Revised Standard Version* (in 'The Sheepfold of the Lord's Prayer'). Excerpts from *The Ladder of Divine Ascent* by Saint John Climacus, translation Archimandrite Lazarus Moore © 1959 and Holy Transfiguration Monastery, Brookline,, MA © 1979, Revised Edition © 2001. Used by permission of the Holy Transfiguration Monastery. Excerpts from *The Lamentations of Matins of Holy and Great Saturday*, translation Holy Transfiguration Monastery, Brookline, MA © 1981. Used by permission of the Holy Transfiguration Monastery. Excerpts from *Orthodox Daily Prayers*, translation St. Tikhon's Seminary Press, South Canaan, PA, © 1982. Used by permission of St. Tikhon's Seminary Press. *Deisis* icons by Monk Gregory Kroug, p. 117. Used by permission of Father Andrew Tregubov.

Library of Congress Cataloging-in-Publication Data
The way to our Heavenly Father : a contemplative telling of the
Lord's prayer / compiled and edited by G. John Champoux.—2nd rev. ed.
p. cm.
Includes bibliographical references and index.
ISBN 978-1-62138-052-8
(pbk. : alk. paper)
1. Lord's prayer—Criticism, interpretation, etc.
I. Champoux, G. John,
1946–
BV230.W33 2007
226.9'606—dc22   2008003031

Cover design: Michael Schrauzer
Cover image: *The Transfiguration* by unknown artist
(second half 15th c., Crete)
Benaki Museum, Athens, Greece

...till we all come in the unity of the faith,
and of the knowledge of the Son of God,
unto a perfect man,
unto the measure of the stature
of the fullness of Christ.

Ephesians 4:13

The mere fact of being able to grasp,
all at once, a multiplicity of points
of view concerning one and the same
object makes the soul happy.

Simone Weil, *Seventy Letters*

THE LORD'S PRAYER

~ LUKE 11:2–4 ~

When you pray, say:
Father, hallowed be thy name.
Thy kingdom come.
Give us this day our daily bread.
And forgive us our sins,
for we also forgive every one that is indebted to us.
And lead us not into temptation.

~ MATTHEW 6:9–13 ~

Thus therefore shall you pray:
Our Father who art in heaven, hallowed be thy name.
Thy kingdom come.
Thy will be done on earth as it is in heaven.
Give us this day our supersubstantial bread.
And forgive us our debts, as we also forgive our debtors.
And lead us not into temptation.
But deliver us from evil. Amen.

~ THE LITURGY OF ST JOHN CHRYSOSTOM ~

And vouchsafe, O Master, that with boldness and without condemnation we may dare
to call upon thee, the heavenly God and Father, and to say:
Our Father, who art in heaven, hallowed be thy name.
Thy kingdom come;
thy will be done on earth as it is in heaven.
Give us this day our daily bread,
and forgive us our trespasses as we forgive our trespasses.
And lead us not into temptation,
but deliver us from evil.
For thine is the kingdom, and the power and the glory, of the Father, and of the Son,
and of the Holy Spirit, now and ever, and unto ages of ages. Amen.

CONTENTS

II. THE SACRAMENTS

The Heavenward and Heavenly Will

Between Heaven and Earth, the Ways of the Way

The Angelic Life

...

Death, Resurrection and Ascension into Triune Glory

Unto Ages of Ages

GENERAL INTRODUCTION

My beloved is like a roe, or a young hart. Behold he standeth behind our wall,
looking through the windows, looking through the lattices. Song of Solomon 2:9

AT FIRST SIGHT this book, with its schematic and interlocking meditations on the Lord's Prayer, might seem more outline than finished work. And in fact it is not a finished work, but rather a lattice-work as in the *Song of Songs*, a pattern of repose and effort, insight and silence, remembrance and direct experience drawn from Christian scripture, tradition and practice. My hope is that this contemplative method will convey, better than exhaustive commentary, the deep coherence and meaning—the vitality—of a prayer seemingly extemporized by Christ at the behest of his disciples (Luke 11:1).

Irenaeus of Lyons (c.130–c.208), the spiritual grandson of John the Evangelist, has challenged us to prove those things contained in Scripture by the Scriptures themselves.[1] These thematic meditations seek to do just this by drawing together Christian ascetic and liturgical practice, the virtues and the life of prayer all within the seemingly narrow compass of the Lord's Prayer. How many the words of Scripture, how few the words of the Lord's Prayer! And yet, using the simple 'proving Scripture by Scripture' method of Irenaeus, we will see how this deceptively familiar prayer holds within itself the entirety of Old and New Testaments, an idea fostered by Tertullian (c.155–c.225): This prayer's "very brevity… supported on the substance of a great and blessed interpretation… [is] diffuse in meaning as it is compressed in words. For it has embraced not only the special duties of prayer, be it veneration of God or petition for man, but almost every discourse of the Lord, every record of his discipline; so that, in fact, in the Prayer is comprised an epitome of the whole Gospel."[2]

But more than a simple correlation of scriptural, liturgical and ascetic texts with the words of the prayer, this book is also an attempt to flesh out or 'incarnate' that ascent spoken of by Gregory of Nyssa (c.330–c.395) in a homily on the Lord's Prayer: "For this is the force of his words, that we should learn by them not to pronounce certain sounds and syllables, but the meaning of the ascent to God which is accomplished through a sublime way of life… learn the Divine discipline through the words of the prayer itself."[3] Taken together, the words of Tertullian and Gregory indicate the dual path followed throughout this book about the way to our heavenly Father. First there is the *lateral* path of a "great and blessed interpretation": seeing the Lord's Prayer repeated in so many different settings leads to a sense of the prayer's all-inclusiveness; gradually or suddenly it becomes something common (to be shared and partaken of)

---

1. "But that all his [Paul's] Epistles are consonant to these declarations, I shall, when expounding the apostle, show from the Epistles themselves. But while I bring out by these proofs the truths of Scripture, and set forth briefly and compendiously things which are stated in various ways, do thou also attend to them with patience, and not deem them prolix; taking this into account, that proofs [of the things which are] contained in the Scriptures cannot be shown except from the Scriptures themselves." *Adversus Haereses* III, 12, 9.

2. *On Prayer*, Chap. I. In 1891, as if to substantiate Tertullian's claim, F. H. Chase drew attention to the similarity between the Lord's Prayer and the 'High Priestly Prayer' of Jesus in John 17:1–26. A striking parallel between the Lord's Prayer and a passage from the Old Testament was also noticed: in 1906, G. Klein saw a nearly perfect rendering of it in Ezechiel 36:23–31 (cf. Jean Carmignac, *Recherches sur le 'Notre Père'*, pp. 351–352 and 369–370). More recently, G. J. Brooke has drawn up two suggestive 'tables of correspondences' out of Johannine and Pauline material ('The Lord's Prayer Interpreted Through John and Paul,' *Downside Review*, 98 (1980) pp. 298–311).

3. *The Lord's Prayer, The Beatitudes*, p. 36.

and no longer common-place, something both old and new (Matt. 13:52). And then there is the the *upright* path of an "ascent to God accomplished through a sublime way of life", an ascension descried in each succeeding chapter: approached in this way the Lord's Prayer becomes *anaphora*, a sacred 'lifting up' of all things to God.

Paradoxically the first chapter, *The Commandments*, dwells on the last and negative petitions of the Lord's Prayer, the commandments being those 'barriers' set up both for protection, for keeping the hostile elements—the world, the flesh and the devil—at bay, and for retaining vital warmth–the love of God, the love of self, the love of neighbor and the almost inexplicable love of enemies. *And forgive us our trespasses as we forgive those who trespass against us, and lead us not into temptation, but deliver us from evil*—these words may be the last said in the prayer, but, as the sound of our own voice dies away, they are the first to be accomplished… so this is where to start.

But followers of Christ do not start unprovided for on this pilgrimage to the summit of the Lord's Prayer. In the *Give us this day our daily bread* of the second chapter they are given for the asking what they need as wayfarers, for it is God's gracious will that they are lavished with the Sacraments; not just one, even though that would surely be enough, but seven.[1] The sacraments are there for whichever way we might turn for help, with Baptism to the left and Chrismation to the right, Repentance behind and Marriage before, Unction below and the Priesthood above, and lastly the Eucharist within, at the center. Not only does the thematic approach to the Lord's Prayer used in this chapter and throughout the book hearken back to the mystagogical catecheses of the early Church, to those instructions bestowed on the catechumens and newly baptized for a full and 'graced' understanding of the Paschal mysteries, this approach also represents a 'sacred geography' of the world that coexists and is coextensive with the Eucharist: the liturgy. When applied to the liturgy, this unifying exegesis by the Lord's Prayer brings out how 'one' are the time, space, and acts of the liturgy: "Let us commend ourselves and each other and *all* [my emphasis] our life unto Christ our God."[2] But not only does the Lord's Prayer 'interpret' the liturgy into oneness, it is *there* in the liturgy. Its recitation is timed to take place at that stillpoint equidistant between two most awesome moments: the changing of bread and wine into the Body and Blood of Christ accompanied by the invoking of the Holy Spirit and the partaking of this holy mystery, in Communion, by those who dare to do so in faith, hope and love.

The petition *Thy will be done on earth as it is in heaven* is a 'shortcut' through the virtues, the topic of the third chapter, for, as we are told by Gregory of Nyssa: "The word 'will' contains generically all the virtues."[3] To the ancient Greeks virtue was that hewing to a 'middle way' that was neither deficiency nor excess. Christianity has accepted this delicate balance, but allows 'deficiency' and 'excess' a place too. Deficiency is welcomed back in a thorough recognition of our limitations as creatures, as partial beings who do not stand isolated and alone, and in this is the virtue of humility; excess is welcomed back in a burning zeal for the will of the living

---

1. Although seven are widely accepted in practice, the monastic tonsure might also be included (cf. Father Michael Pomazansky, *Orthodox Dogmatic Theology*, p. 263) and Augustine speaks of "the sacrament of the Lord's Prayer" (*Sermons on the Liturgical Seasons*, p. 200). Olivier Clément is more generous still; he extends this sacramentality to Scripture as a whole, calling it "the First Sacrament" (*The Roots of Christian Mysticism*, p. 97).

2. From the *Liturgy of St. John Chrysostom*.

3. *Op. cit.*, p. 60.

God who loved us first, and in this is the virtue of charity. Romano Guardini calls *Thy will be done* "a gateway into the structure of these sentences [of the Lord's Prayer], an entrance into their vital core."[1] Then what does *on earth as it is in heaven* represent if not the palpable entry of Name and Kingdom into this world, and, in the form of the virtues, the entry of this world into Name and Kingdom? And so another definition for the virtues might be: enactments of the world of glory. But still we have no idea of what in the virtues is God's and what is our's— this is one of humility's enigmas—, except that Christ begins his prayer with 'Our'—and this is the enigma of charity.

A contemplative reading of the chapters on the commandments, sacraments, and virtues represents a full preparation for turning to the fourth chapter and initial phrases of the Lord's Prayer: *Our Father who art in heaven, hallowed be thy name, thy kingdom come.* Although the use of Scrtpture has been constant throughout the book, here Scripture 'comes into its own', as it were, in the consecutive telling of the Gospel account. Here the Gospel itself becomes prayer. Here true prayer, both our own and the 'prayer' of God in us, the latter also known as 'grace' or 'deification', is the way to union with Christ, this union a living synergy between God and man: "By the Word becoming man, the universal Providence has been known, and its Giver and Artificer the very Word of God. For he was made man that we might be made God; and He manifested Himself by a body that we might receive the idea of the unseen Father."[2] With the Gospel account of the Incarnation and all its consequences, we have the supreme teacher of prayer showing us what to pray and how to pray.

But the end is not yet. Taking the above reading of the Gospel for a pattern, chapters five and six, as denouement, seek to glimpse the Lord's Prayer in the Apocalypse and Psalms; the Lord's Prayer showing itself equally now in the welter of visionary images and battle-din of the Apocalypse, as in the plain-spokenness, inner sorrow, and bursting joy of the Psalms. Chapter seven stands as summary and seal of this book, gathering all things into a smaller and smaller compass until there remains only Christ Jesus, the fulfillment of the Lord's Prayer. And His are the final words in the last, indivisible section: *Amen, Amen and Amen*, where, whether out-of-doors or in the Upper Room, we stand beyond the lattices. Ultimately, this is a book of worship, written for worshippers in the language of worship, the measured, almost breathless diction of the spirit, and, in seeing the Lord's Prayer as universal analogue or metaphor, it also becomes a book of theological poetry.

Although I occasionally make use of Western Christian sources, such as the Christmas carol 'O Come, O Come Emmanuel' and some pertinent gleanings from Bonaventure,[3] this is a work steeped in the contemplative tradition of the Christian East, especially the thought of Maximus the Confessor which has presided over the inception of this book.[4] Also with regard

---

1. *The Lord's Prayer*, p. 4.

2. Athanasius, *On the Incarnation*, 54.

3. A theologian in the era of scholasticism who continued to advocate the 'monarchy' of the Father, as does the Christian East to the present time.

4. Beside the well-known commentary by Maximus on the Lord's Prayer, there is also a more succinct commentary imbedded in the first nine chapters of *Theology and the Incarnate Dispensation of the Son of God*'s second century: Our Father who art in heaven, § 1; hallowed be thy name, § 2 and 3; thy kingdom come, § 4; thy will be done on earth as it is in heaven, § 5; give us this day our daily bread, § 6; and forgive us our trespasses as we forgive those who trespass against us, § 7; and lead us not into temptation, § 8; but deliver us from evil, § 9 (*The Philokalia*, vol. 2, pp. 137–139).

to West and East, Kenneth W. Stevenson has pointed out that the Latins, initially in the persons of Tertullian and Augustine, tend to see the Lord's Prayer structured into seven petitions, while the Greeks, by way of John Chrysostom and Cyril of Alexandria see six.[1] Much of the time I use seven as does Maximus the Confessor, but also six, and even less, but in every instance it is not hard and fast correspondences that are sought, but rather working hypotheses leading not to a theory but to *theoria*,[2] the science of the saints.

NOTICE TO THE SECOND EDITION

This edition contains a number of revised and reformatted meditations, as well as more than forty entirely new ones. The concluding essay, while examining a first century Latin cryptogram found to yield a hidden allusion to the Lord's Prayer, also contains an instruction on how to read *The Way to Our Heavenly Father*. This book was written—over the course of more than twenty years—by a convert to Orthodoxy in the very progress of his conversion. And yet it harbors an ecumenical intent that is not so much a wish as a prayer. With relations between Christian bodies so fraught with controversy at every turn and, alas, beset with the enigma of our own hardened hearts, the Lord's Prayer seems that minimal place where—however fleetingly—all can be one. It might even prove to be a miraculous and maximal place. The Lord's Prayer is, after all, holy words and… holy *common* ground.

Feast of the Protecting Veil of the Theotokos, 2013

---

1. *The Lord's Prayer. A Text in Tradition*, p. 222.
2. I.e. contemplation. Not passive contemplation, but the 'participatory' or 'deified' insight born of grace.

PSALMIC BLESSINGS

BLESSINGS FOR THOSE WHO OPEN THIS BOOK

OUR FATHER WHO
ART IN HEAVEN
HALLOWED BE
THY NAME

May God, our God bless us,
May God bless us: and all the ends of the earth fear him.
Psalm 66:7–8

THY KINGDOM COME

How lovely are thy tabernacles, O Lord of hosts!
My soul longeth and fainteth for the courts of the Lord.
My heart and my flesh have rejoiced in the living God.
For the sparrow hath found herself a house, and the turtle
a nest for herself where she may lay her young ones:
Thy altars, O Lord of hosts, my king and my God.
Blessed are they that dwell in thy house, O Lord:
they shall praise thee for ever and ever. Psalm 83:2–5

THY WILL BE DONE
ON EARTH AS IT IS
IN HEAVEN

Give glory to the Lord, for he is good:
for his mercy endureth for ever.
Who shall declare the powers of the Lord?
Who shall set forth all his praises?
Blessed are they that keep judgment,
and do justice at all times. Psalm 105:1–3

GIVE US THIS DAY
OUR DAILY BREAD

Blessed is he that understandeth concerning the needy and the poor:
the Lord will deliver him in the evil day.
The Lord preserve him and give him life,
and make him blessed upon the earth. Psalm 40:2–3

AND FORGIVE US OUR
TRESPASSES AS WE
FORGIVE THOSE
WHO TRESPASS
AGAINST US

Blessed are they whose iniquities are forgiven,
and whose sins are covered.
Blessed is the man to whom the Lord hath not imputed sin,
and in whose spirit there is no guile. Psalm 31:1–2

AND LEAD US NOT
INTO TEMPTATION

Blessed is the man who hath not walked in the counsel of the ungodly,
nor stood in the way of sinners, nor sat in the chair of pestilence:
But his will is in the law of the Lord,
and on his law he shall meditate day and night. Psalm 1:1–2

BUT DELIVER
US FROM EVIL

I will not fear thousands of the people surrounding me:
arise, O Lord; save me, O my God.
For thou hast struck all them who are my adversaries without cause:
thou hast broken the teeth of sinners.
Salvation is of the Lord:
and thy blessing is upon thy people. Psalm 3:7–9

A SCRIPTURAL EPITOME OF THE LORD'S PRAYER

OUR FATHER WHO ART IN HEAVEN	And no one knoweth who the Son is, but the Father; and who the Father is, but the Son and to whom the Son will reveal him. Luke 10:22 Philip saith to him: Lord, shew us the Father; and it is enough for us. Jesus saith to him: Have I been so long a time with you and you have not known me? Philip, he that seeth me seeth the Father also. John 14:8–9 I and the Father are one. John 10:30
HALLOWED BE THY NAME	Father, glorify thy name. A voice therefore came from heaven: I have both glorified it and will glorify it again. John 12:28
THY KINGDOM COME	The kingdom of God cometh not with observation. Neither shall they say: Behold here, or behold there. For lo, the kingdom of God is within you. And he said to his disciples: The days will come when you shall desire to see one day of the Son of man. And you shall not see it. And they shall say to you: See here, and see there. Go ye not after, nor follow them. For as the lightning that lighteneth from under heaven shineth unto the parts that are under heaven, so shall the Son of man be in his day. But first be must suffer many things and be rejected by this generation. Luke 17:20–25 Jesus answered: My kingdom is not of this world… Pilate therefore said to him: Art thou a king then? Jesus answered: Thou sayest that I am a king. For this was I born, and for this came I into the world… John 18:36–37
THY WILL BE DONE ON EARTH AS IT IS IN HEAVEN	…that he might make known unto us the mystery of his will, according to his good pleasure… to reestablish all things in Christ, that are in heaven and on earth, in him. In whom we also are called by lot, being predestinated according to the purpose of him who worketh all things according to the counsel of his will. Eph. 1:9–11
GIVE US THIS DAY OUR DAILY BREAD	Moses gave you not bread from heaven, but my Father giveth you the true bread from heaven. For the bread of God is that which cometh down from heaven and giveth life to the world. They said therefore unto him: Lord, give us always this bread. And Jesus said to them: I am the bread of life. John 6:32–5
AND FORGIVE US OUR TRESPASSES AS WE FORGIVE THOSE WHO TRESPASS AGAINST US	What I have pardoned, if I have pardoned any thing, for your sakes have I done it in the person of Christ; that we be not overreached by Satan. For we are not ignorant of his devices. 2 Cor. 2:10–11
AND LEAD US NOT INTO TEMPTATION	Blessed is the man that endureth temptation; for, when he hath been proved, he shall receive the crown of life which God hath promised to them that love him. James 1:12

He saved others; himself he cannot save. If he be the king of Israel, let him come down from the cross… He trusted in God: let him now deliver him if he will have him. For he said: I am the Son of God. Matt. 27:42–43

Jesus of Nazareth, a man approved of God among you by miracles and wonders and signs, which God did by him, in the midst of you… this same being delivered up… crucified and slain… God hath raised up, having loosed the sorrows of hell, as it was impossible that he should be holden by it. Acts 2:22–24

I

THE COMMANDMENTS

AND FORGIVE US OUR TRESPASSES
AS WE FORGIVE THOSE WHO TRESPASS AGAINST US
AND LEAD US NOT INTO TEMPTATION
BUT DELIVER US FROM EVIL

INTRODUCTION

God's commandments are beyond man's conception and beyond his power to fulfil. We are humbled from the moment we come into contact with them. The commandments of God have the specific effect of crushing the arrogance of our darkened minds and hearts so as to clear the way for grace to dwell within us.
—Archimandrite Zacharias, *Remember Thy First Love*

To begin our way through the Lord's Prayer by considering its last petitions first, this would be to defy its providential course. We must take the initial petitions of the Lord's Prayer as those commands dictated to the Israelites by God to insure their safe passage out of Egypt, the land of slavery. Although we can only prepare in haste to confront and endure the worst in ourselves, such is the holy wisdom of God—and it is enough for us. But what has He given us to confront the Pharaoh of our bondage to sin, to endure the long years of wandering through the sin-purging wilderness? Behold: in the 'Our Father who art in heaven hallowed be thy name', He gives us, as from the Burning Bush, his own all-powerful name of which the entire universe is not even the faintest of reverberations, and by which the truth of His jealousy for Israel and ourselves is established; in 'Thy kingdom come', He gives not only the promise of a Land flowing with milk and honey, but also the Moses of our holy Church and its saints to be a guidance; in 'Thy will be done on earth as it is in heaven', He charges us to 'eat in haste', with reins girded, shoes on our feet and staves in our hands (Exod. 12:11), ever-attentive to the decrees of Heaven, ever-vigilant to tread upon the whole power of the enemy and ward off temptation with prayer and the bitter herb of fasting; and lastly, in 'Give us this day our daily bread', in the very midst of our fasting, He lavishes upon us the feast of the Paschal Lamb to sustain us on the way and to mark our foreheads with the Blood of the Cross, the sign of our own repentance which turns away the death-dealing angel, a repentance which stuck in our throats along with the Old Adam in Paradise, but a repentance dislodged by the sorrows of the New Adam on Calvary, so that, along with Him, we might utter the all-consuming words: 'Father, into thy hands I commend my spirit'.

WISDOM, LET US BE ATTENTIVE

'Wisdom, let us be attentive!' With this acclamation we are liturgically prepared to receive the word of God in the Epistle and Gospel readings; with this acclamation we are suddenly present before the Lord in the midst of our daily labors, called upright to render an account for all the 'little things' in our life; and with this acclamation we take upon ourselves the Lord's Prayer and stand recollected before the Tree of the Knowledge of Good and Evil which stood in the midst of Paradise. This tree, the subject of God's first commandment and the first object in the exercise of human freedom, is 'summarized' in the two wisdoms mentioned in the letter of James. But what of the Tree of Life which also stood in the midst of Paradise? Is it not reflected in the mirror of wisdom to be found in the Book of Wisdom? Again and again we read the passages in Genesis about these trees and suddenly we are overwhelmed, for, crucified between a good thief and a bad thief, we gaze upon one whose name is Meekness of Wisdom. The God who once tested Adam and Eve with the fruit of the Tree of the Knowledge of Good and Evil, tests us yet with the wood of the Cross: what is it that we do with our freedom?

As the very words of Christ teach, the entirety of the Old Testament is both an anticipation and an exegesis of His life and our own, for in His holy mysteries He has made us one with Him. And so to the Old Testament we turn to descry the best and the worst of our own life before the coming of Christ in the flesh to our own flesh in the Eucharist. From the creation of the world to the last prophecies before His advent, how long and yet already spent—how short a span of years! And, for us, will there be time enough to search both the Scriptures and the scripture of our lives to recognize Him…? What is it that we do with our freedom?

PURIFYING THE DEEP FONT OF THE WORLD

If we have been baptized into Christ, there is no abyss too deep for us, even the abyss of our own sins where the waters are come in even unto our soul (Psalm 68:1). If we are purified in Christ, every abyss has become a font of regeneration, the font where an ever-resplendent light shines as brightly at the greatest depth as it does on the surface, the light by which we not only recognize what sins are ours, but even their very names; we name our sins as Adam named the animals in Paradise (Gen. 2:19) and, repenting as we do so, a new and sparkling cosmos emerges before our eyes. Only a single step separates us from the plunge: we go down into an abyssal dimness of sin and come up from the primal font of Light Incarnate. And what is it that we do with our freedom?

A LAMP ON THE FURTHER SHORE

O love of the Father and the Father's love! O merest of lamps more mighty and intense and inextinguishable than the noonday sun (Apoc. 21:23)! Because of you our poor hearts burn within us (Luke 24:32). What commandment but love have you given us, lest we go blindly wise with perplexity? See how from the throne of God to the 'mustard seed' of conscience charity measures heaven and earth with its instructions! And what is it that we do with our freedom?

WISDOM, LET US BE ATTENTIVE

Howbeit we speak wisdom among the perfect; yet not the wisdom of the world, neither of the princes of this world that come to naught. But we speak the wisdom of God in a mystery, a wisdom which is hidden, which God ordained before the world, unto our glory. 1 Corinthians 2:6

THE TWO WISDOMS

JAMES 3:5–15

OUR FATHER WHO
ART IN HEAVEN
HALLOWED BE
THY NAME
THY KINGDOM COME

Behold how small a fire kindleth a great wood. And the tongue is a fire, a world of iniquity. The tongue is placed among our members, which defileth the whole body and inflameth the wheel of our nativity being set on fire by hell. For every nature of beasts and of birds and of serpents and of the rest is tamed and hath been tamed, by the nature of man. But the tongue no man can tame, an unquiet evil, full of deadly poison. By it we bless God and the Father; and by it we curse men who are made after the likeness of God.

THY WILL BE DONE
ON EARTH AS IT IS
IN HEAVEN

Out of the same mouth proceedeth blessing and cursing. My brethren, these things ought not so to be.

GIVE US THIS DAY
OUR DAILY BREAD

Doth a fountain send forth out of the same hole, sweet and bitter water? Can the fig-tree, my brethren, bear grapes? Or the vine, figs? So neither can the salt water yield sweet.

AND FORGIVE US OUR
TRESPASSES AS WE
FORGIVE THOSE
WHO TRESPASS
AGAINST US

Who is a wise man and endued with knowledge among you? Let him shew, by good conversation, his work in the meekness of wisdom. But if you have bitter zeal, and there be contentions in your hearts; glory not and be not liars against the truth.

AND LEAD US NOT
INTO TEMPTATION
BUT DELIVER
US FROM EVIL

For this is not wisdom descending from above; but earthly, sensual, devilish.

JAMES 3:15

THE WISDOM
DESCENDING
FROM ABOVE

Our Father who art in heaven
Hallowed be thy name
Thy kingdom come
Thy will be done on earth as it is in heaven
Give us this day our daily bread

THE WISDOM THAT
IS EARTHLY
(THE WORLD)

And forgive us our trespasses as we
forgive those who trespass against us
(the corrective for the 'outer' world)

SENSUAL
(THE FLESH)

And lead us not into temptation
(the corrective for the 'inner' word)

DEVILISH
(THE DEVIL)

But deliver us from evil
(the corrective for the 'self ', both inner and outer)

FEAR OF GOD, BEGINNING OF WISDOM

Holy and terrible is his name. The fear of the Lord is the beginning of wisdom. Psalm 110: 9–10

Fear is twofold; one kind is pure, the other impure. That which is pre-eminently fear of punishment on account of offenses committed is impure, for it is sin which gives rise to it. It will not last for ever, for when the sin is obliterated through repentance it too will disappear. Pure fear, on the other hand, is always present, even apart from remorse for offenses committed. Such fear will never cease to exist, because it is somehow rooted essentially by God in creation and makes clear to everyone His awe-inspiring nature, which transcends all kingship and power.
—Maximus the Confessor, *Various Texts*, First Century, 69

SACRED FEAR[1]

OUR FATHER WHO ART IN HEAVEN
And when I had seen him, I fell at his feet as dead. And he laid his right hand upon me, saying: Fear not.[2] I am the First and the Last, And alive, and was dead, and behold I am living for ever and ever, and have the keys of death and of hell. Apoc. 1:17–18

HALLOWED BE THY NAME
And they went out quickly from the sepulcher with fear and great joy, running to tell his disciples. And behold Jesus met them, saying: All hail. But they came up and took hold of his feet, and adored him. Then Jesus said to them: Fear not.[3] Matt. 28:8–10

THY KINGDOM COME
And Jesus found a young ass, and sat upon it, as it is written: Fear not,[4] daughter of Sion: behold, thy king cometh, sitting on an ass's colt. John 12:15

THY WILL BE DONE ON EARTH AS IT IS IN HEAVEN
Wherefore, my dearly beloved, (as you have always obeyed, not as in my presence only, but much more now in my absence,) with fear and trembling work out your salvation. For it is God who worketh in you, both to will and to accomplish, according to his good will. Phil. 2:12–13

GIVE US THIS DAY OUR DAILY BREAD
Servants, obey in all things your masters according to the flesh, not serving to the eye, as pleasing men, but in simplicity of heart, fearing God. Whatsoever you do, do it from the heart, as to the Lord, and not to men: knowing that you shall receive of the Lord the reward of inheritance. Serve ye the Lord Christ. Col. 3:22–24

AND FORGIVE US OUR TRESPASSES AS WE FORGIVE THOSE WHO TRESPASS AGAINST US
Fear is not in charity: but perfect charity casteth out fear, because fear hath pain. And he that feareth, is not perfected incharity. Let us therefore love God, because God first hath loved us. If any man say, I love God, and hateth his brother; he is a liar. For he that loveth not his brother, whom he seeth, how can he love God, whom he seeth not? And this commandment we have from God, that he, who loveth God, love also his brother. 1 John 4:18–21

---

1. By ourselves we cannot overcome or even attenuate this sacred fear; only by divine initiative ('Fear not') are we invited to a humble and festal confidence (παρρησία, parrhesia) before God (cf. Heb. 4:15–16 and 1 John 2:28).

2. *Parrhesia* from the Father with whom the Son is one in essence.

3. *Parrhesia* from the Son who arose again on the third day.

4. *Parrhesia* from the Spirit who spoke by the prophets.

AND LEAD US NOT
INTO TEMPTATION
BUT DELIVER
US FROM EVIL

And fear ye not them that kill the body, and are not able to kill the soul: but rather fear him that can destroy both soul and body in hell. Matt. 10:28

And another came, saying: Lord, behold here is thy pound, which I have kept laid up in a napkin. For I feared thee, because thou art an austere man: thou takest up what thou didst not lay down: and thou reapest that which thou didst not sow. He saith to him: Out of thy own mouth I judge thee, thou wicked servant. Thou knewest that I was an austere man, taking up what I laid not down and reaping that which I did not sow. And why then didst thou not give my money into the bank, that at my coming I might have exacted it with usury? Luke 19:20–23

FEAR OF GOD, FULLNESS OF WISDOM

ECCLESIASTICUS 1

OUR FATHER WHO
ART IN HEAVEN
HALLOWED BE
THY NAME

All wisdom is from the Lord God, and hath been always with him, and is before all time. Who hath numbered the sand of the sea, and the drops of rain, and the days of the world? Who hath measured the height of heaven, and the breadth of the earth, and the depth of the abyss? Who hath searched out the wisdom of God that goeth before all things? Wisdom hath been created before all things, and the understanding of prudence from everlasting. The word of God on high is the fountain of wisdom, and her ways are everlasting commandments.

THY KINGDOM COME

To whom hath the root of wisdom been revealed, and who hath known her wise counsels? To whom hath the discipline of wisdom been revealed and made manifest? and who hath understood the multiplicity of her steps? There is one most high Creator Almighty, and a powerful king, and greatly to be feared, who sitteth upon his throne, and is the God of dominion. He created her in the Holy Spirit, and saw her, and numbered her, and measured her. And he poured her out upon all his works, and upon all flesh according to his gift, and hath given her to them that love him. The fear of the Lord is honor, and glory, and gladness, and a crown of joy. The fear of the Lord shall delight the heart, and shall give joy, and gladness, and length of days. With him that feareth the Lord, it shall go well in the latter end, and in the day of his death he shall be blessed.

THY WILL BE DONE
ON EARTH AS IT IS
IN HEAVEN

The love of God is honorable wisdom. And they to whom she shall shew herself love her by the sight, and by the knowledge of her great works. The fear of the Lord is the beginning of wisdom, and was created with the faithful in the womb, it walketh with chosen women, and is known with the just and faithful. The fear of the Lord is the religiousness of knowledge. Religiousness shall keep and justify the heart, it shall give joy and gladness. It shall go well with him that feareth the Lord, and in the days of his end he shall be blessed.

GIVE US THIS DAY
OUR DAILY BREAD

To fear God is the fullness of wisdom, and fullness is from the fruits thereof. She shall fill all her house with her increase, and the storehouses with her treasures. The fear of the Lord is a crown of wisdom, filling up peace and the fruit of salvation: and it hath seen, and numbered her: but both are the gifts of God.

AND FORGIVE US OUR TRESPASSES AS WE FORGIVE THOSE WHO TRESPASS AGAINST US	Wisdom shall distribute knowledge, and understanding of prudence: and exalteth the glory of them that hold her. The root of wisdom is to fear the Lord: and the branches thereof are long-lived. In the treasures of wisdom is understanding, and religiousness of knowledge: but to sinners wisdom is an abomination. The fear of the Lord driveth out sin: for he that is without fear, cannot be justified: for the wrath of his high spirits is his ruin.
AND LEAD US NOT INTO TEMPTATION	A patient man shall bear for a time, and afterwards joy shall be restored to him. A good understanding will hide his words for a time, and the lips of many shall declare his wisdom.
BUT DELIVER US FROM EVIL	In the treasures of wisdom is the signification of discipline: but the worship of God is an abomination to a sinner. Son, if thou desire wisdom, keep justice, and God will give her to thee. For the fear of the Lord is wisdom and discipline: and that which is agreeable to him, is faith, and meekness: and he will fill up his treasures. Be not incredulous to the fear of the Lord: and come not to him with a double heart. Be not a hypocrite in the sight of men, and let not thy lips be a stumblingblock to thee. Watch over them, lest thou fall, and bring dishonor upon thy soul, and God discover thy secrets, and cast thee down in the midst of the congregation. Because thou camest to the Lord wickedly, and thy heart is full of guile and deceit.

THE MIRROR OF WISDOM

WISDOM 6:17–24, 7:21–30

OUR FATHER WHO ART IN HEAVEN	And all such things as are hid and not foreseen, I have learned: for wisdom, which is the worker of all things, taught me. For in her is the spirit of understanding: holy, one, manifold, subtile, eloquent, active, undefiled, sure, sweet, loving that which is good, quick, which nothing hindereth, beneficent, gentle, kind, steadfast, assured, secure, having all power, overseeing all things, and containing all spirits, intelligible, pure, subtile. For wisdom is more active than all active things: and reacheth everywhere by reason of her purity.
HALLOWED BE THY NAME	For she is a vapor of the power of God and a certain pure emanation of the glory of the almighty God: and therefore no defiled thing cometh into her.
THY KINGDOM COME	For she is the brightness of eternal light, and the unspotted mirror of God's majesty, and the image of his goodness.
THY WILL BE DONE ON EARTH AS IT IS IN HEAVEN	And being but one, she can do all things: and remaining in herself the same, she reneweth all things and through nations conveyeth herself into holy souls. She maketh the friends of God and prophets.
GIVE US THIS DAY OUR DAILY BREAD	For God loveth none but him that dwelleth with wisdom. For she is more beautiful than the sun, and above all the order of the stars: being compared with the light, she is found before it.

AND FORGIVE US OUR TRESPASSES AS WE FORGIVE THOSE WHO TRESPASS AGAINST US AND LEAD US NOT INTO TEMPTATION BUT DELIVER US FROM EVIL	For after this cometh night: but no evil can overcome wisdom.
BUT DELIVER US FROM EVIL	For [wisdom] goeth about seeking such as are worthy of her: and she sheweth herself to them cheerfully in the ways and meeteth them with all providence.
AND LEAD US NOT INTO TEMPTATION	For the beginning of her is the most true desire of discipline.
AND FORGIVE US OUR TRESPASSES AS WE FORGIVE THOSE WHO TRESPASS AGAINST US	And the care of discipline is love; and love is the keeping of her laws;
GIVE US THIS DAY OUR DAILY BREAD	and the keeping of her laws is the firm foundation of incorruption; and incorruption bringeth near to God.
THY WILL BE DONE ON EARTH AS IT IS IN HEAVEN	Therefore the desire of wisdom bringeth to the everlasting kingdom.
THY KINGDOM COME	If then your delight be in thrones and sceptres, O ye kings of the people, love wisdom, that you may reign for ever. Love the light of wisdom, all ye that bear rule over peoples.
OUR FATHER WHO ART IN HEAVEN HALLOWED BE THY NAME	Now what wisdom is, and what was her origin, I will declare. And I will not hide from you the mysteries of God, but will seek her out from the beginning of her birth, and bring the knowledge of her to light, and will not pass over the truth.

THIS ANTICIPATORY LIFE

OUR FATHER WHO ART IN HEAVEN—*Creation, On Sinai's Height*
HALLOWED BE THY NAME—*The Burning Bush, The Exploits of Elijah*
THY KINGDOM COME—*Messianic Prophecy Fulfilled*
THY WILL BE DONE ON EARTH AS IT IS IN HEAVEN—*Jacob's Dream*
GIVE US THIS DAY OUR DAILY BREAD—*Abraham and Isaac*
AND FORGIVE US OUR TRESPASSES AS WE FORGIVE THOSE WHO TRESPASS AGAINST US
—*The Ten Commandments, Adam, First and Fallen*
AND LEAD US NOT INTO TEMPTATION—*Scrutiny by the 'Deep Things of God'*
BUT DELIVER US FROM EVIL—*Exodus, The Dividing of the Waters*

CREATION

GENESIS 1:1–2:3

AND LEAD US NOT
INTO TEMPTATION
BUT DELIVER
US FROM EVIL

In the beginning God created heaven and earth. And the earth was void and empty, and darkness was upon the face of the deep. And the spirit of God moved over the waters. And God said: Be light made. And light was made. And God saw the light that it was good; and he divided the light from the darkness. And he called the light Day and the darkness Night. And there was evening and morning one day.

AND FORGIVE US OUR
TRESPASSES AS WE
FORGIVE THOSE
WHO TRESPASS
AGAINST US

And God said: Let there be a firmament made amidst the waters: and let it divide the waters from the waters. And God made a firmament, and divided the waters that were under the firmament, from those that were above the firmament. And it was so. And God called the firmament Heaven. And the evening and the morning were the second day.

GIVE US THIS DAY
OUR DAILY BREAD

God also said: Let the waters that are under the heaven, be gathered together in one place, and let the dry land appear. And it was so done. And God called the dry land Earth; and the gathering together of the waters, he called Seas. And God saw that it was good. And he said: Let the earth bring forth the green herb, and such as may seed, and the fruit tree yielding fruit after its kind, which may have seed in itself upon the earth. And it was so done… And God saw that it was good. And the evening and the morning were the third day.

THY WILL BE DONE…
IN HEAVEN

And God said: Let there be lights made in the firmament of heaven, to divide the day and the night, and let them be for signs, and for seasons, and for days and years: to shine in the firmament of heaven, and to give light upon the earth. And God made two great lights: a greater light to rule the day; and a lesser light to rule the night: and the stars. And he set them in the firmament of heaven to shine upon the earth… and to divide the light and the darkness. And God saw that it was good. And the evening and morning were the fourth day.

THY WILL BE DONE
ON EARTH AS IT IS
IN HEAVEN

God also said: Let the waters bring forth the creeping creature having life, and the fowl that may fly over the earth under the firmament of heaven. And God created the great whales, and every living and moving creature, which the waters brought forth, according to their kinds, and every winged fowl according to its kind. And God saw that it was good… And the evening and the morning were the fifth day.

THY KINGDOM COME

And God said: Let the earth bring forth the living creature in its kind, cattle and creeping things, and beasts of the earth… and God saw that it was good. And he said: Let us make man to our image and likeness; and let him have dominion over the fishes of the sea, and the fowls of the air, and the beasts, and the whole earth, and every creeping creature that moveth upon the face of the earth… And God saw all the things that he had made, and they were very good. And the evening and morning were the sixth day.

OUR FATHER WHO ART IN HEAVEN HALLOWED BE THY NAME	And on the seventh day God ended his work which he had made: and he rested on the seventh day from all his work which he had done. And he blessed the seventh day and sanctified it: because in it he had rested from all his work which God created and made.

ADAM, FIRST AND FALLEN

OUR FATHER WHO ART IN HEAVEN	And the Lord God formed man of the slime of the earth…
HALLOWED BE THY NAME	…and breathed into his face the breath of life, and man became a living soul. Gen. 2:7
THY KINGDOM COME	And the Lord God had planted a paradise of pleasure from the beginning: wherein he placed man whom he had formed. Gen. 2:8 And the Lord God said: It is not good for man to be alone: let us make him a help like unto himself. And the Lord God having formed out of the ground all the beasts of the earth, and all the fowls of the air, brought them to Adam to see what he would call them: for whatsoever Adam called any living creature the same is its name. And Adam called all the beasts by their names, and all the fowls of the air, and all the cattle of the field: but for Adam there was not found a helper like himself. Then the Lord God cast a deep sleep upon Adam: and when he was fast asleep, he took one of his ribs, and filled up flesh for it. And the Lord God built the rib which he took from Adam into a woman: and brought her to Adam. And Adam said: This now is bone of my bones, and flesh of my flesh; she shall be called woman, because she was taken out of man. Wherefore a man shall leave father and mother, and shall cleave to his wife: and they shall be two in one flesh. Gen. 2:18–24
THY WILL BE DONE ON EARTH AS IT IS IN HEAVEN	And the Lord God took man, and put him into the paradise of pleasure, to dress it, and to keep it. And he commanded him, saying: Of every tree of paradise thou shalt eat: but of the tree of knowledge of good and evil, thou shalt not eat. For in what day soever thou shalt eat of it, thou shalt die the death. Gen. 2:15–17
GIVE US THIS DAY OUR DAILY BREAD	And the Lord God brought forth of the ground all manner of trees, fair to behold, and pleasant to eat of: the tree of life also in the midst of paradise: and the tree of knowledge of good and evil. Gen. 2:9
AND FORGIVE US OUR TRESPASSES AS WE FORGIVE THOSE WHO TRESPASS AGAINST US	And the Lord God called Adam, and said to him: Where art thou? And he said: I heard thy voice in paradise; and I was afraid, because I was naked, and I hid myself. And he said to him: And who hath told thee that thou wast naked, but that thou hast eaten of the tree whereof I commanded thee that thou shouldst not eat? And Adam said: The woman, whom thou gavest me to be my companion, gave me of the tree, and I did eat. And the Lord God said to the woman: Why hast thou done this? And she answered: The serpent deceived me, and I did eat. Gen. 3:9–13

Now the serpent was more subtle than any of the beasts of the earth which the Lord God had made. And he said to the woman: Why hath God commanded you, that you should not eat of every tree of paradise? And the woman answered him, saying: Of the fruit of the trees that are in paradise we do eat: but of the fruit of the tree which is in the midst of paradise, God hath commanded us that we should not eat; and that we should not touch it, lest perhaps we die. And the serpent said to the woman: No, you shall not die the death. For God doth know that in what day soever you shall eat thereof, your eyes shall be opened: and you shall be as Gods, knowing good and evil. And the woman saw that the tree was good to eat, and fair to the eyes, and delightful to behold: and she took of the fruit thereof, and did eat, and gave to her husband, who did eat. And the eyes of them both were opened: and when they perceived themselves to be naked, they sewed together fig leaves, and made themselves aprons. Gen. 3:1–7

And the Lord God said to the serpent: Because thou hast done this thing, thou art cursed among all cattle, and beasts of the earth: upon thy breast shalt thou go, and earth shalt thou eat all the days of thy life. I will put enmities between thee and the woman, and thy seed and her seed: she shall cursh thy head, and thou shalt lie in wait for her heel. To the woman also he said: I will multiply thy sorrows, and thy conceptions: in sorrow shalt thou bring forth children, and thou shalt be under thy husband's power, and he shall have dominion over thee. And to Adam he said: Because thou hast hearkened to the voice of thy wife, and hast eaten of the tree, whereof I commanded thee, that thou shouldst not eat, cursed is the earth in thy work: with labour and toil shalt thou eat thereof all the days of thy life. Thorns and thistles shall it bring forth to thee, and thou shalt eat the herbs of the earth. In the sweat of thy face shalt thou eat bread till thou return to the earth out of which thou wast taken: for dust thou art, and into dust thou shalt return. Gen. 3:14–10
And he said: Behold Adam is become as one of us, knowing good and evil: now therefore lest perhaps he put forth his hand and take also of the tree of life, and eat, and live for ever. And the Lord God sent him out of the paradise of pleasure, to till the earth from which he was taken. And he cast out Adam: and placed before the paradise of pleasure Cherubims, and a flaming sword, turning every way, to keep the way of the tree of life. Gen. 3:22–24

ABRAHAM AND ISAAC,
THE HOLOCAUST OF THE ONLY-BEGOTTEN

GENESIS 22:1–18

AND LEAD US NOT
INTO TEMPTATION
BUT DELIVER
US FROM EVIL

After these things, God tempted Abraham, and said to him: Abraham, Abraham. And he answered: Here I am. He said to him: Take thy only begotten son Isaac, whom thou lovest, and go into the land of vision: and there thou shalt offer him for a holocaust upon one of the mountains which I will show thee. So Abraham rising up in the night, saddled his ass: and took with him two young men, and Isaac his son: and when he had cut wood for the holocaust he went his way to the place which God had commanded him. And on the third day, lifting up his eyes, he saw the place afar off. And he said to his young men: Stay you here with the ass: I and the boy will go with speed as far as yonder, and after we have worshipped, will return to you. And he took the wood for the holocaust, and laid it upon Isaac his son: and he himself carried in his hands fire and a sword.

AND FORGIVE US OUR
TRESPASSES AS WE
FORGIVE THOSE
WHO TRESPASS
AGAINST US

And as they two went on together, Isaac said to his father: My father. And he answered: What wilt thou, son? Behold, saith he, fire and wood: where is the victim for the holocaust? And Abraham said: God will provide himself a victim for an holocaust, my son. So they went on together.

GIVE US THIS DAY
OUR DAILY BREAD

And they came to the place which God had shown him, where he built an altar, and laid the wood in order upon it: and when he had bound Isaac his son, he laid him on the altar upon the pile of wood. And he put forth his hand and took the sword, to sacrifice his son. And behold an angel of the Lord from heaven called to him, saying: Abraham, Abraham. And he answered: Here I am. And he said to him: Lay not thy hand upon the boy, neither do thou any thing to him: now I know that thou fearest God, and hast not spared thy only begotten son for my sake. Abraham lifted up his eyes, and saw behind his back a ram amongst the briers sticking fast by the horns, which he took and offered for a holocaust instead of his son. And he called the name of that place, The Lord seeth. Whereupon even to this day it is said: In the mountain the Lord will see.

THY WILL BE DONE
ON EARTH AS IT IS
IN HEAVEN

And the angel of the Lord called to Abraham a second time from heaven, saying: By my own self have I sworn, saith the Lord: because thou hast done this thing, and hast not spared thy only begotten son for my sake: I will bless thee, and I will multiply thy seed as the stars of heaven, and as the sand that is by the seashore: thy seed shall possess the gates of their enemies.

OUR FATHER WHO
ART IN HEAVEN
HALLOWED BE
THY NAME
THY KINGDOM COME

And in thy seed shall all the nations of the earth be blessed, because thou hast obeyed my voice.

JACOB'S DREAM

GENESIS 28:12–17

OUR FATHER WHO ART IN HEAVEN HALLOWED BE THY NAME
And he saw in his sleep a ladder standing upon the earth, and the top thereof touching heaven; the angels also of God ascending and descending by it; and the Lord, leaning upon the ladder, saying to him: I am the Lord God of Abraham thy father and the God of Isaac.

THY KINGDOM COME
The land, wherein thou sleepest, I will give to thee and to thy seed.

THY WILL BE DONE ON EARTH AS IT IS IN HEAVEN
And thy seed shall be as the dust of the earth: Thou shalt spread abroad to the west, and to the east, and to the north, and to the south.

GIVE US THIS DAY OUR DAILY BREAD
And in thee all the tribes of the earth shall be blessed.[1]

AND FORGIVE US OUR TRESPASSES AS WE FORGIVE THOSE WHO TRESPASS AGAINST US
And I will be thy keeper whithersoever thou goest, and will bring thee back into this land: neither will I leave thee, till I shall have accomplished all that I have said.

AND LEAD US NOT INTO TEMPTATION
And when Jacob awaked out of sleep, he said: Indeed the Lord is in this place, and I knew it not.

BUT DELIVER US FROM EVIL
And trembling he said: How terrible is this place! This is no other but the house of God, and the gate of heaven.

---

1. In Jacob's vision of the ladder we see the anticipation of Christ Himself and his rigorous theorem: "I am the way, and the truth and the life. No one cometh to the Father, but by me" (John 14:6). Christ is 'the Life', the God who breathed life into the first Adam and is the last Adam, the 'begetter' of all the saved, the living stone upon which Jacob slept and which he named Bethel, the 'house of God', symbol of the Incarnation, God's dwelling among us in the flesh. Christ is 'the Way', the ladder reaching between heaven and earth by which, by Whom we approach the Father: "You shall see the heaven opened and the angels of God ascending and descending upon the Son of man" (John 1:51). Christ is 'the Truth', the express image of the Father's subtance (Heb. 1:3), only one with the Father leaning on the top of the ladder, or, more truly, the One upon Whom the ladder and all things 'lean'.

2. This is the final ratification of the Covenant of the Patriarchs. With Abraham and Isaac, Jacob forms a patriarchal trinity of witnesses: Abraham, from whom has sprung all the children of Israel (not only Jews, but also Christians and Muslims claim him as their 'father among the living') and to whose bosom the blessed of Israel return; Isaac, the only free-born son, committed to be sacrificed but spared at the point of sacrifice; and Jacob/Israel, who wrestled with an angel and overcame him, who in spirit dreamed of the angelic ladder between heaven and earth, and from whom sprang the twelve tribes, just as there are many gifts but only one Spirit.

THE BURNING BUSH

EXODUS 3:1–15

For just as it is ignorance which scatters those in error, so it is the presence of the light of the mind which gathers and unites together those receiving illumination. It perfects them. It returns them toward the truly real. It returns them from their numerous false notions and, filling them with one unifying light, it gathers their clashing fancies into a single, pure, coherent, and true knowledge. — Dionysius the Areopagite, *The Divine Names*, IV, 701b

BUT DELIVER US FROM EVIL

Now Moses fed the sheep of Jethro his father-in-law, the priest of Madian: and he drove the flock to the inner part of the desert, and came to the mountain of God, Horeb. And the Lord appeared to him in a flame of fire out of the midst of a bush: and he saw that the bush was on fire and was not burnt. And Moses said: I will go and see this great sight, why the bush is not burnt. And when the Lord saw that he went forward to see, he called to him out of the midst of the bush, and said: Moses, Moses. And he answered: Here I am.[1]

AND LEAD US NOT INTO TEMPTATION

And he said: Come not nigh hither. Put off the shoes from thy feet: for the place whereon thou standest is holy ground. And he said: I am the God of thy father, the God of Abraham, the God of Isaac, and the God of Jacob. Moses hid his face: for he durst not look at God.

AND FORGIVE US OUR TRESPASSES AS WE FORGIVE THOSE WHO TRESPASS AGAINST US

And the Lord said to him: I have seen the affliction of my people in Egypt, and I have heard their cry; because of the rigor of them that are over the works.

GIVE US THIS DAY OUR DAILY BREAD

And knowing their sorrow, I am come down to deliver them out of the hands of the Egyptians; and to bring them out of that land into a good and spacious land, into a land that floweth with milk and honey, to the places of the Chanaanite, and Hethite, and Amorrhite, and Pherezite, and Hevite, and Jebusite.

THY WILL BE DONE ON EARTH AS IT IS IN HEAVEN

For the cry of the children of Israel is come unto me: and I have seen their affliction, wherewith they are oppressed by the Egyptians. But come, and I will send thee to Pharao, that thou mayest bring forth my people, the children of Israel out of Egypt.

---

1. This 'Here I am', the response of Moses to God's calling him by name, is to be found in the Old Testament both before and after Moses. Now the circumstances surrounding these 'Here I ams', when brought together, form a contemplation on the Lord's Prayer in their own right, as if each petition were another way to say 'Here I am' to God for His calling each of us by name: *Our Father who art in heaven, hallowed by thy name* & *Deliver us from evil*—Exodus 3:4 (God reveals His name to Moses and promises to deliver the Hebrews out of Egypt); *Thy kingdom come*—Genesis 46:2 (God promises to make of Jacob a great nation); *Thy will be done on earth as it is in heaven*—Genesis 7:11 (an angel of the Lord conveys to Abraham that it is God's will to spare Isaac's life); *Give us this day our daily bread*—Genesis 31:11 (an angel of the Lord assures Jacob that God will provide his 'wages'); *And forgive us our trespasses as we forgive those who trespass against us*—Isaiah 6:8 (Isaiah's sin is forgiven by the touch of a burning coal and he in turn agrees to be a 'sign of contradiction to a trespassing generation); *And lead us not into temptation*—Genesis 22:1 (the testing of Abraham over the slaying of his only son); *But deliver us from evil*—1 Kings 3:2–15 (God fortells to Samuel the tragic consequences of blasphemy for Eli and his family).

THY KINGDOM COME

And Moses said to God: Who am I that I should go to Pharao, and should bring forth the children of Israel out of Egypt? And he said to him: I will be with thee. And this thou shalt have for a sign, that I have sent thee: When thou shalt have brought my people out of Egypt, thou shalt offer sacrifice to God upon this mountain.

OUR FATHER WHO
ART IN HEAVEN
HALLOWED BE
THY NAME

Moses said to God: Lo, I shall go to the children of Israel, and say to them: The God of your fathers has sent me to you. If they should say to me: What is his name? What shall I say to them? God said to Moses: I AM WHO AM. He said: Thus shalt thou say to the children of Israel: HE WHO IS hath sent me to you. And God said again to Moses:: Thus shalt thou say to the children of Israel: The Lord God of your fathers, the God of Abraham, the God of Isaac, and the God of Jacob, hath sent me to you. This is my name for ever, and this is my memorial unto all generations.

EXODUS

OUR FATHER WHO
ART IN HEAVEN
HALLOWED BE
THY NAME

And the Lord spoke to Moses face to face, as a man is wont to speak to his friend... For how shall we be able to know, I and thy people, that we have found grace in thy sight, unless thou walk with us: that we may be glorified by all people that dwell upon the earth? And the Lord said to Moses: This word also, which thou hast spoken, will I do. For thou hast found grace before me: and thee have I known by name. And he said: Shew me thy glory. He answered: I will shew thee all good, and I will proclaim in the name of the Lord before thee: And I will have mercy on whom I will: and I will be merciful to whom it shall please me. And again he said: Thou canst not see my face: for man shall not see my face and live. And again he said: Behold, there is a place with me, and thou shalt stand upon the rock. And when my glory shall pass, I will set thee in a hole of the rock, and protect thee with my right hand, till I pass. And I will take away my hand, and thou shalt see my back parts: but my face thou canst not see. Exod. 33:11, 16–23

THY KINGDOM COME

And the Lord said to him: I have seen the affliction of my people in Egypt, and I have heard their cry; because of the rigor of them that are over the works. And knowing their sorrow, I am come down to deliver them out of the hands of the Egyptians; and to bring them out of that land into a good and spacious land, into a land that floweth with milk and honey. Exod. 3:7–8

THY WILL BE DONE
ON EARTH AS IT IS
IN HEAVEN

Let the children of Israel keep the sabbath, and celebrate it in their generations. It is an everlasting covenant between me and the children of Israel, and a perpetual sign. For in six days the Lord made heaven and earth: and in the seventh he ceased from work. And the Lord, when he had ended these words in mount Sinai, gave to Moses two stone tables of testimony, written with the finger of God... And Moses returned from the mount, carrying the two tables of the testimony in his hand, written on both sides, and made by the work of God. The writing also of God was graven in the tables... And when he came nigh to the camp, he saw the calf, and the dances: and being very angry, he threw the tables out of his hand, and broke them at the foot of the mount... And after this he said: Hew thee two tables of stone like unto the former: and I will write upon

them the words which were in the tables, which thou brokest… I will make a covenant in the sight of all. I will do signs such as were never seen upon the earth, nor in any nations: that this people, in the midst of whom thou art, may see the terrible work of the Lord which I will do.
Exod. 31:16–18; 32:15–16, 19; 34:1, 10

GIVE US THIS DAY
OUR DAILY BREAD

And all the congregation of the children of Israel murmured against Moses and Aaron in the wilderness. And the children of Israel said to them: Would to God we had died by the hand of the Lord in the land of Egypt, when we sat over the flesh pots, and ate bread to the full. Why have you brought us into this desert, that you might destroy all the multitude with famine? And the Lord said to Moses: Behold I will rain bread from heaven for you. Let the people go forth, and gather what is sufficient for every day: that I may prove them whether they will walk in my law, or not. Exod. 16:2–4

AND FORGIVE US OUR
TRESPASSES AS WE
FORGIVE THOSE
WHO TRESPASS
AGAINST US

I beseech thee: this people hath sinned a heinous sin, and they have made to themselves gods of gold. Either forgive them this trespass, or if thou do not, strike me out of the book that thou hast written. Exod. 32:31–32

AND LEAD US NOT
INTO TEMPTATION

And the Lord said to Moses: Go before the people, and take with thee of the ancients of Israel. And take in thy hand the rod wherewith thou didst strike the river, and go. Behold, I will stand there before thee, upon the rock Horeb: and thou shalt strike the rock, and water shall come out of it that the people may drink. Moses did so before the ancients of Israel: and he called the name of the place Temptation, because of the chiding of the children of Israel; and for that they tempted the Lord, saying: Is the Lord amongst us or not? Exod. 17:5–7

BUT DELIVER
US FROM EVIL

And when Moses had stretched forth his hand towards the sea, it returned at the first break of day to the former place: and as the Egyptians were fleeing away, the waters came upon them, and the Lord shut them up in the middle of the waves… But the children of Israel marched through the midst of the sea upon dry land: and the waters were to them as a wall on the right hand and on the left. And the Lord delivered Israel on that day out of the hands of the Egyptians. Exod. 14:27, 29–30

THE TEN COMMANDMENTS

EXODUS 20:1–19

OUR FATHER WHO
ART IN HEAVEN

And the Lord spoke all these words: I am the Lord thy God, who brought thee out of the land of Egypt, out of the house of bondage. Thou shalt not have strange gods before me. Thou shalt not make to thyself a graven thing, nor the likeness of any thing that is in heaven above, or in the earth beneath, nor of those things that are in the waters under the earth. Thou shalt not adore them, nor serve them: I am the Lord thy God, mighty, jealous, visiting the iniquity of the fathers upon the children, unto the third and fourth generation of them that hate me: And shewing mercy unto thousands to them that love me, and keep my commandments.

HALLOWED BE
THY NAME

Thou shalt not take the name of the Lord thy God in vain: for the Lord will not hold him guiltless that shall take the name of the Lord his God in vain.

THY KINGDOM COME

Remember that thou keep holy the sabbath day. Six days shalt thou labor, and shalt do all thy works. But on the seventh day is the sabbath of the Lord thy God: thou shalt do no work on it, thou nor thy son, nor thy daughter, nor thy manservant, nor thy maidservant, nor thy beast, nor the stranger that is within thy gates. For in six days the Lord made heaven and earth, and the sea, and all things that are in them, and rested on the seventh day: therefore the Lord blessed the seventh day, and sanctified it.

THY WILL BE DONE
ON EARTH AS IT IS
IN HEAVEN
GIVE US THIS DAY
OUR DAILY BREAD

Honor thy father and thy mother, that thou mayest be longlived upon the land which the Lord thy God will give thee.

AND FORGIVE US OUR
TRESPASSES AS WE
FORGIVE THOSE
WHO TRESPASS
AGAINST US
AND LEAD US NOT
INTO TEMPTATION

Thou shalt not kill. Thou shalt not commit adultery. Thou shalt not steal. Thou shalt not bear false witness against thy neighbor. Thou shalt not covet thy neighbor's house: neither shalt thou desire his wife, nor his servant, nor his handmaid, nor his ox, nor his ass, nor any thing that is his.

BUT DELIVER
US FROM EVIL

And all the people saw the voices and the flames, and the sound of the trumpet, and the mount smoking: and being terrified and struck with fear, they stood afar off, saying to Moses: Speak thou to us, and we will hear: let not the Lord speak to us, lest we die.

ON SINAI'S HEIGHT, THE LORD GOD

EXODUS 34:4–8

Rising very early he went up into the Mount Sinai, as the Lord had commanded him, carrying with him the tables. And when the Lord was come down in a cloud, Moses stood with him, calling upon the name of the Lord. And when he passed before him, he said:

OUR FATHER WHO ART IN HEAVEN HALLOWED BE THY NAME	O the Lord, the Lord God,
THY KINGDOM COME	merciful and gracious,
THY WILL BE DONE ON EARTH AS IT IS IN HEAVEN	patient and of much compassion, and true,
GIVE US THIS DAY OUR DAILY BREAD	Who keepest mercy unto thousands:
AND FORGIVE US OUR TRESPASSES AS WE FORGIVE THOSE WHO TRESPASS AGAINST US	who takest away iniquity, and wickedness, and sin,
AND LEAD US NOT INTO TEMPTATION	and no man of himself is innocent before thee.
BUT DELIVER US FROM EVIL	Who renderest the iniquity of the fathers to the children, and to the grand-children unto the third and fourth generation.

And Moses making haste, bowed down prostrate unto the earth, and adoring.

COMMENTARY

This passage from Exodus is one of the central texts of the Israel of God, what Rabbinic tradition has named the 'Thirteen Attributes of Mercy', as well as the 'Thirteen Attributes of Love,' with commentators undecided as to the exact division of the text to make up the thirteen. Standing aright in fear and love, what exceedingly great knowledge does the God who would not show His face to Moses (Exod. 34:20) reveal to him and to us! Only for a moment speak not as yet of Christ, and then speak of Him… all the attributes follow Him then, now and unto the ages of ages.

THE EXPOITS OF ELIJAH, THE POWER OF GOD'S HOLY NAME

Elijah means 'Yahweh is God', each episode of his life reveals the power of this meaning. — GJC

	THE EXPOITS OF ELIJAH	THE POWER OF GOD'S HOLY NAME
OUR FATHER WHO ART IN HEAVEN HALLOWED BE THY NAME THY KINGDOM COME	Theophany on Horeb	His name shall be blessed unto the ages, before the sun doth His name continue. And in Him shall be blessed all the tribes of the earth, all the nations shall call Him blessed. Blessed is the Lord, the God of Israel, who alone doeth wonders. And blessed is the name of His glory for ever, and unto the ages of ages. And all the earth shall be filled with His glory. So be it. So be it. Psalm 71:17–19
THY WILL BE DONE ON EARTH AS IT IS IN HEAVEN	The shutting up of the rain for three years and its release	God of hosts, return again; and look down from heaven and behold, and visit this vine, and perfect that which Thy right hand hath planted, and look upon the son of man whom Thou madest strong for Thyself. It is burned with fire and is dug up; at the rebuke of Thy face they shall perish. Let Thy hand be upon the man of Thy right hand, and upon the son of man whom Thou madest strong for Thyself. And we will not depart from Thee; Thou shalt quicken us, and we will call upon Thy name. O Lord God of hosts, make us to return and cause Thy face to shine, and we shall be saved. Psalm 79:15–20
GIVE US THIS DAY OUR DAILY BREAD	The miraculous provision of meal and oil for the widow and the raising of her son from the dead	God, my God, unto Thee I rise early at dawn. My soul hath thirsted for Thee; how often hath my flesh longed after Thee in a land barren and untrodden and unwatered. So in the sanctuary have I appeared before Thee to see Thy power and Thy glory, For Thy mercy is better than lives; my lips shall praise Thee. So shall I bless Thee in my life, and in Thy name will I lift up my hands. As with marrow and fatness let my soul be filled, and with lips rejoicing shall my mouth praise Thee. Psalm 62:1–6

	THE EXPOITS OF ELIJAH	THE POWER OF GOD'S HOLY NAME
AND FORGIVE US OUR TRESPASSES AS WE FORGIVE THOSE WHO TRESPASS AGAINST US	Fire called down upon the first two captains and their twice-fifty men sent to retrieve Elijah from the hilltop,	The Lord is king, let the peoples rage; He sitteth on the cherubim, let the earth be shaken. The Lord is great in Sion, and He is high above all peoples. Let them confess Thy great name, for it is terrible and holy; and the king's honor loveth judgment. Thou hast prepared uprightness; judgment and righteousness in Jacob hast Thou wrought. Psalm 98:1–3
AND LEAD US NOT INTO TEMPTATION	The sparing of the third fifty and their captain who humbled himself	For Thou hast humbled us in a place of affliction, and the shadow of death hath covered us. If we have forgotten the name of our God, and if we have stretched out our hands to a strange god, shall not God search out these things? For He knoweth the secrets of the heart. Psalm 43:20–22
BUT DELIVER US FROM EVIL	Contest with the prophets of Baal	God, in Thy name save me, and in Thy strength do Thou judge me. O God, hearken unto my prayer, give ear unto the words of my mouth. For strangers are risen up against me, and mighty men have sought after my soul and have not set God before themselves. For behold, God helpeth me, and the Lord is the protector of my soul. He will bring evils upon mine enemies. Utterly destroy them by Thy truth. Willingly shall I sacrifice unto Thee; I will confess Thy name, O Lord, for it is good. For out of every affliction hast Thou delivered me, and mine eye hath looked down upon mine enemies. Psalm 53

COMMENTARY

CAPTAINS AND THEIR MEN A striking parallel to this episode is to be found in the Gospel of John, where the crowd sent to apprehend Jesus of Nazareth "went backward and fell to the ground" when Jesus replied: "I am he." (John 18:6). By this is signified the voluntary nature of Christ's sacrifice as well as the meek and victorious power of his name, foreshadowed in the "whistling of a gentle air" (3 Kings 19:12) after the great and strong wind, the earthquake and the fire.

SCRUTINY BY THE DEEP THINGS OF GOD

JOB 38:1–17, 42:1–16

Eye hath not seen, nor ear heard, neither hath it entered into the heart of man, what things God hath pre-pared for them that love him. But to us, God hath revealed them, by his Spirit. For the Spirit searcheth all things, yea, the deep things of God. 1 Corinthians 2:9–10

OUR FATHER WHO
ART IN HEAVEN
HALLOWED BE
THY NAME

Then the Lord answered Job out of a whirlwind, and said: Who is this that wrappeth up sentences in unskillful words? Gird up thy loins like a man. I will ask thee, and answer thou me.

THY KINGDOM COME

Where wast thou when I laid the foundations of the earth? Tell me if thou hast understanding. Who hath laid the measures thereof, if thou knowest? Or who hath stretched the line upon it? Upon what are its bases grounded? Or who laid the corner stone thereof, when the morning stars praised me together, and all the sons of God made a joyful melody?

THY WILL BE DONE
ON EARTH AS IT IS
IN HEAVEN

Who shut up the sea with doors, when it broke forth as issuing out of the womb; when I made a cloud the garment thereof, and wrapped it in a mist as in swaddling bands? I set my bounds around it, and made it bars and doors; and I said: Hitherto thou shalt come, and shalt go no further. And here thou shalt break thy swelling waves. Didst thou since thy birth command the morning, and shew the dawning of the day its place? And didst thou hold the extremities of the earth shaking them? And has thou shaken the ungodly out of it?

GIVE US THIS DAY
OUR DAILY BREAD

The seal shall be restored as clay, and shall stand as a garment.

AND FORGIVE US OUR
TRESPASSES AS WE
FORGIVE THOSE
WHO TRESPASS
AGAINST US

From the wicked their light shall be taken away; and the high arm shall be broken.

AND LEAD US NOT
INTO TEMPTATION

Hast thou entered into the depths of the sea, and walked in the lowest parts of the deep?

BUT DELIVER
US FROM EVIL

Have the gates of death been opened to thee, and hast thou seen the darksome doors?

OUR FATHER WHO
ART IN HEAVEN
HALLOWED BE
THY NAME

Then Job answered the Lord, and said: I know that thou canst do all things, and no thought is hid from thee.

THE DIVIDING OF THE WATERS
A VISTA ON THE OLD TESTAMENT

And God said: Let there be a firmament made amidst the waters:
and let it divide the waters from the waters. Genesis 1:6

And forgive us our trespasses as we forgive those who trespass against us
And lead us not into temptation
But deliver us from evil

UPON DRY LAND IN THE MIDST OF THE SEA

OUR FATHER WHO
ART IN HEAVEN
HALLOWED BE
THY NAME

And Moses said to the people: Fear not: stand and see the great wonders of the Lord, which he will do this day: for the Egyptians, whom you see now, you shall see no more for ever. The Lord will fight for you, and you shall hold your peace.

THY KINGDOM COME

And the Lord said to Moses: Why criest thou to me? Speak to the children of Israel to go forward.

THY WILL BE DONE
ON EARTH AS IT IS
IN HEAVEN

But lift thou up thy rod, and stretch forth thy hand over the sea, and in heaven divide it: that the children of Israel may go through the midst of the sea on dry ground. And I will harden the heart of the Egyptians to pursue you: and I will be glorified in Pharao, and in all his host, and in his chariots, and in his horsemen. And the Egyptians shall know that I am the Lord, when I shall be glorified in Pharao, and in his chariots and in his horsemen. And the angel of God, who went before the camp of Israel, removing, went behind them: and together with him the pillar of the cloud, leaving the forepart, stood behind, between the Egyptians' camp and the camp of Israel: and it was a dark cloud, and enlightening the night, so that they could not come at one another all the night.

GIVE US THIS DAY
OUR DAILY BREAD

And when Moses had stretched forth his hand over the sea, the Lord took it away by a strong and burning wind blowing all the night, and turned it into dry ground: and the water was divided. And the children of Israel went in through the midst of the sea dried up: for the water was as a wall on their right hand and on their left.

AND FORGIVE US OUR
TRESPASSES AS WE
FORGIVE THOSE
WHO TRESPASS
AGAINST US

And the Egyptians pursuing went in after them, and all Pharao's horses, his chariots and horsemen through the midst of the sea, and now the morning watch was come, and behold the Lord looking upon the Egyptian army through the pillar of fire and of the cloud, slew their host. And overthrew the wheels of the chariots, and they were carried into the deep. And the Egyptians said: Let us flee from Israel: for the Lord fighteth for them against us.

AND LEAD US NOT
INTO TEMPTATION

And the Lord said to Moses: Stretch forth they hand over the sea, that the waters may come again upon the Egyptians, upon their chariots and horsemen. And when Moses had stretched forth his hand towards the sea, it returned at the first break of day to the former place: and as the Egyptians were fleeing away, the waters came upon them, and the Lord shut them up in the middle of the waves. And the waters returned, and covered the chariots and the horsemen of all the army of Pharao, who had come into the sea after them, neither did there so much as one of them remain.

BUT DELIVER
US FROM EVIL

But the children of Israel marched through the midst of the sea upon dry land, and the waters were to them as a wall on the right hand and on the left: and the Lord delivered Israel on that day out of the hands of the Egyptians.
Exod. 14:13–30

Give us this day our daily bread

INTO A LAND FLOWING WITH MILK AND HONEY

OUR FATHER WHO
ART IN HEAVEN
HALLOWED BE
THY NAME

And Josue said to the people: Be ye sanctified: for to morrow the Lord will do wonders among you.

THY KINGDOM COME

And he said to the priests: Take up the ark of the covenant, and go before the people. And they obeyed his commands, and took it up and walked before them.

THY WILL BE DONE
ON EARTH AS IT IS
IN HEAVEN

And the Lord said to Josue: This day will I begin to exalt thee before Israel: that they may know that as I was with Moses, so I am with thee also. And do thou command the priests that carry the ark of the covenant, and say to them: When you shall have entered into part of the water of the Jordan, stand in it.

GIVE US THIS DAY
OUR DAILY BREAD

And Josue said to the children of Israel: Come hither and hear the word of the Lord your God. And again he said: By this you shall know that the Lord the living God is in the midst of you,

AND FORGIVE US OUR
TRESPASSES AS WE
FORGIVE THOSE
WHO TRESPASS
AGAINST US

and that he shall destroy before your sight the Chanaanite and the Hethite, the Hevite and the Pherezite, the Gergesite also and the Jebusite, and the Amor-rhite. Behold the ark of the covenant of the Lord of all the earth shall go before you into the Jordan. Prepare ye twelve men of the tribes of Israel, one of every tribe.

AND LEAD US NOT
INTO TEMPTATION

And when the priests, that carry the ark of the Lord the God of the whole earth, shall set the soles of their feet in the waters of the Jordan, the waters that are beneath shall run down and go off: and those that come from above, shall stand together upon a heap. So the people went out of their tents, to pass over the Jordan: and the priests that carried the ark of the covenant. went on before them. And as soon as they came into the Jordan, and their feet were dipped in part of the water, (now the Jordan, it being harvest time, had filled the banks of its channel) the waters that came down from above stood in one place, and swelling up like a mountain, were seen afar off from the city that is called Adom, to the place of Sarthan: but those that were beneath, ran down into the sea of the wilderness (which now is called the Dead Sea) until they wholly failed.

BUT DELIVER
US FROM EVIL

And the people marched over against Jericho: and the priests that carried the ark of the covenant of the Lord, stood girded upon the dry ground in the midst of the Jordan, and all the people passed over through the channel that was dried up. Joshua 3:5–17

Thy will be done on earth as it is in heaven

'MY FATHER, MY FATHER, THE CHARIOT OF ISRAEL, AND THE DRIVER THEREOF'

BUT DELIVER
US FROM EVIL

And it came to pass, when the Lord would take up Elias into heaven by a whirl-wind, that Elias and Eliseus were going from Gilgal. And Elias said to Eliseus: Stay thou here, because the Lord hath sent me as far as Bethel. And Eliseus said to him: As the Lord liveth, and as thy soul liveth, I will not leave thee.

AND LEAD US NOT
INTO TEMPTATION

And when they were come down to Bethel, the sons of the prophets, that were at Bethel, came forth to Eliseus, and said to him: Dost thou know that this day the Lord will take away thy master from thee? And he answered: I also know it: hold your peace. And Elias said to Eliseus: Stay here because the Lord hath sent me to Jericho. And he said: As the Lord liveth, and as thy soul liveth, I will not leave thee. And when they were come to Jericho, the sons of the prophets that were at Jericho, came to Eliseus, and said to him: Dost thou know that this day the Lord will take away thy master from thee? And he said: I also know it: hold your peace. And Elias said to him: Stay here, because the Lord hath sent me as far as the Jordan. And he said: As the Lord liveth, and as thy soul liveth, I will not leave thee; and they two went on together, and fifty men of the sons of the prophets followed them, and stood in sight at a distance: but they two stood by the Jordan.

AND FORGIVE US OUR
TRESPASSES AS WE
FORGIVE THOSE
WHO TRESPASS
AGAINST US

And Elias took his mantle and folded it together, and struck the waters, and they were divided hither and thither, and they both passed over on dry ground.

GIVE US THIS DAY
OUR DAILY BREAD

And when they were gone over, Elias said to Eliseus: Ask what thou wilt have me to do for thee, before I be taken away from thee. And Eliseus said: I beseech thee that in me may be thy double spirit.

THY WILL BE DONE
ON EARTH AS IT IS
IN HEAVEN

And he answered: Thou hast asked a hard thing: nevertheless if thou see me when I am taken from thee, thou shalt have what thou hast asked: but if thou see me not, thou shalt not have it.

THY KINGDOM COME

And as they went on, walking and talking together, behold a fiery chariot, and fiery horses parted them both asunder: and Elias went up by a whirlwind into heaven.

OUR FATHER WHO ART IN HEAVEN HALLOWED BE THY NAME	And Eliseus saw him, and cried: My father, my father, the chariot of Israel, and the driver thereof.
THY KINGDOM COME	And he saw him no more: and he took hold of his own garments, and rent them in two pieces. And he took up the mantle of Elias, that fell from him: and going back, he stood upon the bank of the Jordan, and he struck the waters with the mantle of Elias, that had fallen from him, and they were not divided.
THY WILL BE DONE ON EARTH AS IT IS IN HEAVEN	And he said: Where is now the God of Elias? And he struck the waters, and they were divided, hither and thither, and Eliseus passed over.
GIVE US THIS DAY OUR DAILY BREAD	And the sons of the prophets at Jericho, who were over against him, seeing it said: The spirit of Elias hath rested upon Eliseus. And coming to meet him, they worshipped him, falling to the ground,
AND FORGIVE US OUR TRESPASSES AS WE FORGIVE THOSE WHO TRESPASS AGAINST US	and they said to him: Behold, there are with thy servants fifty strong men, that can go, and seek thy master, lest perhaps the spirit of the Lord hath taken him up and cast him upon some mountain or into some valley. And he said: Do not send.
AND LEAD US NOT INTO TEMPTATION	But they pressed him, till he consented, and said: Send. And they sent fifty men: and they sought three days but found him not. And they came back to him: for he abode at Jericho, and he said to them: Did I not say to you: Do not send?
BUT DELIVER US FROM EVIL	And the men of the city said to Eliseus: Behold the situation of this city is very good, as thou, my lord, seest: but the waters are very bad, and the ground barren. And he said: Bring me a new vessel, and put salt into it. And when they had brought it, he went out to the spring of the waters, and cast the salt into it, and said: Thus saith the Lord: I have healed these waters, and there shall be no more in them death or barrenness. And the waters were healed unto this day, according to the word of Eliseus, which he spoke. And he went up from thence to Bethel: and as he was going up by the way, little boys came out of the city and mocked him, saying: Go up, thou bald head; go up, thou bald head. And looking back, he saw them, and cursed them in the name of the Lord: and there came forth two bears out of the forest, and tore of them two and forty boys. 4 Kings 2:1-24

Our Father who art in heaven
Hallowed be thy name
Thy kingdom come

A SAPPHIRE THRONE AND THE LIKENESS OF THE GLORY OF THE LORD

OUR FATHER WHO ART IN HEAVEN

Now it came to pass in the thirtieth year, in the fourth month, on the fifth day of the month, when I was in the midst of the captives by the river Chobar, the heavens were opened, and I saw the visions of God.

HALLOWED BE THY NAME

On the fifth day of the month, the same was the fifth year of the captivity of king Joachin, the word of the Lord came to Ezechiel the priest the son of Bud in the land of the Chaldeans, by the river Chobar: and the hand of the Lord was there upon him.

THY KINGDOM COME

And I saw, and behold a whirlwind came out of the north: and a great cloud, and a fire infolding it, and brightness was about it: and out of the midst thereof, that is, out of the midst of the fire, as it were the resemblance of amber:

THY WILL BE DONE ... AS IT IS IN HEAVEN

And in the midst thereof the likeness of four living creatures: and this was their appearance: there was the likeness of a man in them. Every one had four faces, and every one four wings. Their feet were straight feet, and the sole of their foot was like the sole of a calf's foot, and they sparkled like the appearance of glowing brass. And they had the hands of a man under their wings on their four sides: and they bad faces, and wings on the four sides, and the wings of one were joined to the wings of another. They turned not when they went: but every one went straight forward. And as for the likeness of their faces: there was the face of a man, and the face of a lion on the right side of all the four: and the face of an ox, on the left side of all the four: and the face of an eagle over all the four. And their faces, and their wings were stretched upward: two wings of every one were joined, and two covered their bodies: And every one of them went straight forward: whither the impulse of the spirit was to go, thither they went: and they turned not when they went. And as for the likeness of the living creatures, their appearance was like that of burning coals of fire, and like the appearance of lamps. This was the vision running to and fro in the midst of the living creatures, a bright fire, and lightning going forth from the fire. And the living creatures ran and returned like flashes of lightning.

...ON EARTH

Now as I beheld the living creatures, there appeared upon the earth by the living creatures one wheel with four faces. And the appearance of the wheels, and the work of them was like the appearance of the sea: and the four had all one likeness: and their appearance and their work was as it were a wheel in the midst of a wheel. When they went, they went by their four parts: and they turned not when they went. The wheels had also a size, and a height, and a dreadful appearance: and the whole body was full of eyes round about all the four. And when the living creatures went, the wheels also went together by them: and when the living creatures were lifted up from the earth, the wheels also were lifted up with them. Whithersoever the spirit went, thither as the spirit went the wheels also were lifted up withal, and followed it: for the spirit of life was in the wheels. When those went these went, and when those stood these stood, and when those were lifted up from the earth, the wheels also were lifted up together, and followed them: for the spirit of life was in the wheels. And over the heads of the living creatures was the likeness of the firmament, as the appearance of crystal terrible to behold, and stretched out over their heads above. And under the firmament were their wings straight, the one toward the other, every one with two wings covered his body, and the other was covered in like manner. And I heard the noise of their wings, like the noise of many waters, as it were the voice of the most high God: when they walked, it was like the voice of a multitude, like the noise of an army, and when they stood, their wings were let down. For when a voice came from above the firmament, that was over their heads, they stood, and let down their wings.

GIVE US THIS DAY OUR
SUPERSUBSTANTIAL
BREAD And above the firmament that was over their heads, was the likeness of a throne, as the appearance of the sapphire stone, and upon the likeness of the throne, was a likeness as of the appearance of a man above upon it. And I saw as it were the resemblance of amber as the appearance of fire within it round about: from his loins and upward, and from his loins downward, I saw as it were the resemblance of fire shining round about. As the appearance of the rainbow when it is in a cloud on a rainy day: this was the appearance of the brightness round about. This was the vision of the likeness of the glory of the Lord. And I saw, and I fell upon my face, and I heard the voice of one that spoke. And he said to me: Son of man, stand upon thy feet, and I will speak to thee. And the spirit entered into me after that he spoke to me, and he set me upon my feet:

AND FORGIVE US OUR
TRESPASSES AS WE
FORGIVE THOSE
WHO TRESPASS
AGAINST US and I heard him speaking to me, and saying: Son of man, I send thee to the children of Israel, to a rebellious people, that hath revolted from me, they, and their fathers, have transgressed my covenant even unto this day.

AND LEAD US NOT
INTO TEMPTATION
BUT DELIVER
US FROM EVIL And they to whom I send thee are children of a hard face, and of an But obstinate heart: and thou shalt say to them: Thus saith the Lord God: If so be they at least will hear, and if so be they will forbear, for they are a provoking house: and they shall know that there hath been a prophet in the midst of them. And thou, O son of man, fear not, neither be thou afraid of their words: for thou art among unbelievers and destroyers, and thou dwellest with scorpions. Fear not their words, neither be thou dismayed at their looks: for they are a provoking house. And thou shalt speak my words to them, if perhaps they will hear, and forbear: for they provoke me to anger.

AND FORGIVE US OUR
TRESPASSES AS WE
FORGIVE THOSE
WHO TRESPASS
AGAINST US But thou, O son of man, hear all that I say to thee: and do not thou provoke me, as that house provoketh me:

GIVE US THIS DAY
OUR DAILY BREAD

open thy mouth, and eat what I give thee. And I looked, and behold, a hand was sent to me, wherein was a book rolled up: and he spread it before me, and it was written within and without: and there were written in it lamentations, and canticles, and woe. And he said to me: Son of man, eat all that thou shalt find: eat this book, and go speak to the children of Israel. And I opened my mouth, and he caused me to eat that book: And he said to me: Son of man, thy belly shall eat, and thy bowels shall be filled with this book, which I give thee. And I did eat it: and it was sweet as honey in my mouth.

THY WILL BE DONE
ON EARTH AS IT IS
IN HEAVEN

And he said to me: Son of man, go to the house of Israel, and thou shalt speak my words to them. For thou art not sent to a people of a profound speech, and of an unknown tongue, but to the house of Israel: Nor to many nations of a strange speech, and of an unknown tongue, whose words thou canst not understand: and if thou wert sent to them, they would hearken to thee. But the house of Israel will not hearken to thee: because they will not hearken to me: for all the house of Israel are of a hard forehead and an obstinate heart. Behold I have made thy face stronger than their faces: and thy forehead harder than their foreheads. I have made thy face like an adamant and like flint: fear them not, neither be thou dismayed at their presence: for they are a provoking house.

THY KINGDOM COME

And he said to me: Son of man, receive in thy heart, and hear with thy ears, all the words that I speak to thee: And go get thee in to them of the captivity, to the children of thy people, and thou shalt speak to them, and shalt say to them: Thus saith the Lord: If so be they will hear and will forbear.

OUR FATHER WHO
ART IN HEAVEN
HALLOWED BE
THY NAME

And the spirit took me up, and I heard behind me the voice of a great commotion, saying: Blessed be the glory of the Lord, from his place. And the noise of the wings of the living creatures striking one against another, and the noise of the wheels following the living creatures, and the noise of a great commotion. The spirit also lifted me, and took me up: and I went away in bitterness in the indignation of my spirit: for the hand of the Lord was with me, strengthening me.

THY KINGDOM COME

And I came to them of the captivity, to the heap of new corn, to them that dwelt by the river Chobar, and I sat where they sat: and I remained there seven days mourning in the midst of them.

THY WILL BE DONE
ON EARTH AS IT IS
IN HEAVEN

And at the end of seven days the word of the Lord came to me, saying: Son of man, I have made thee a watchman to the house of Israel:

GIVE US THIS DAY
OUR DAILY BREAD

and thou shalt hear the word out of my mouth, and shalt tell it them from me.

AND FORGIVE US OUR TRESPASSES AS WE FORGIVE THOSE WHO TRESPASS AGAINST US	If, when I say to the wicked, Thou shalt surely die: thou declare it not to him, nor speak to him, that he may be converted from his wicked way, and live: the same wicked man shall die in his iniquity, but I will require his blood at thy hand. But if thou give warning to the wicked, and he be not converted from his wickedness, and from his evil way: he indeed shall die in his iniquity, but thou hast delivered thy soul.
AND LEAD US NOT INTO TEMPTATION	Moreover if the just man shall turn away from his justice, and shall commit iniquity: I will lay a stumblingblock before him, he shall die, because thou hast not given him warning: he shall die in his sin, and his justices which he hath done, shall not be remembered: but I will require his blood at thy hand.
BUT DELIVER US FROM EVIL	But if thou warn the just man, that the just may not sin, and he doth not sin: living he shall live, because thou hast warned him, and thou hast delivered thy soul. Ezech. 1:1-3:21

MESSIANIC PROPHECY FULFILLED IN THE LORD'S PRAYER

OUR FATHER WHO ART IN HEAVEN HALLOWED BE THY NAME	For a child is born to us, and a son is given to us, and the government is upon his shoulder: and Thy kingdom come his name shall be called, Wonderful, Counsellor, God the Mighty, the Father of the world to come, the Prince of peace. His empire shall be multiplied, and there shall be no end of peace. He shall sit upon the throne of David, and upon his kingdom: to establish it and strengthen it with judgment and with justice, from henceforth and for ever. The zeal of the Lord of hosts will perform this. Isa. 9:6–7
HALLOWED BE THY NAME THY KINGDOM COME	And thou shalt take gold and silver and shalt make crowns: and thou shalt set them on the head of Jesus the son of Josedec, the high priest. And thou shalt speak to him, saying: Behold a man, the Orient is his name. And under him shall he spring up and shall build a temple to the Lord. Yea, he shall build a temple to the Lord: and he shall bear the glory and shall sit and rule upon his throne: and he shall be a priest upon his throne: and the counsel of peace shall be between them both. Zech. 6:11–13
THY KINGDOM COME THY WILL BE DONE ON EARTH AS IT IS IN HEAVEN	And there shall come forth a rod out of the root of Jesse: and a flower shall rise up out of his root. And the spirit of the Lord shall rest upon him: the spirit of wisdom and of understanding, the spirit of counsel and of fortitude, the spirit of knowledge and of godliness. And he shall be filled with the spirit of the fear of the Lord. He shall not judge according to the sight of the eyes, nor reprove according to the hearing of the ears. But he shall judge the poor with justice, and shall reprove with equity for the meek of the earth. And he shall strike the earth with the rod of his mouth: and with the breath of his lips he will slay the wicked. And justice shall be the girdle of his loins: and faith the girdle of his reins. The wolf shall dwell with the lamb: the leopard shall lie down with the kid. The calf and the lion and the sheep shall abide together: and a little child shall lead them. The calf and the bear shall feed, their young ones shall rest, together: and the lion shall eat straw like the ox. And the sucking child shall play on the hole of the asp: and the weaned child shall thrust his hand into the den

of the basilisk. They shall not hurt, nor shall they kill in all my holy mountain: for the earth is filled with the knowledge of the Lord, as the covering waters of the sea. In that day, the root of Jesse, who standeth for an ensign of the people, him the Gentiles shall beseech: and his sepulcher shall be glorious. Isa. 11:1–10

GIVE US THIS DAY OUR DAILY BREAD

For thy servant David's sake, turn not away the face of thy anointed. The Lord hath sworn truth to David, and he will not make it void: Of the fruit of thy womb I will set upon thy throne, if thy children will keep my covenant, and these my testimonies which I shall teach them: their children also for evermore shall sit upon thy throne. For the Lord hath chosen Sion: he hath chosen it for his dwelling. This is my rest for ever and ever: here will I dwell, for I have chosen it. Blessing I will bless her widow: I will satisfy her poor with bread. I will clothe her priests with salvation: and her saints shall rejoice with exceeding great joy. There will I bring forth a horn to David: I have prepared a lamp for my anointed. His enemies I will clothe with confusion: but upon him shall my sanctification flourish. Psalm 131:10–18

AND FORGIVE US OUR TRESPASSES AS WE FORGIVE THOSE WHO TRESPASS AGAINST US

Be comforted, be comforted, my people, saith your God. Speak ye to the heart of Jerusalem, and call to her: for her evil is come to an end, iniquity is forgiven. She hath received of the hand of the Lord her double for all her sins. The voice of one crying in the desert: Prepare ye the way of the Lord, make straight in the wilderness the paths of our God. Every valley shall be exalted and every mountain and hill shall be made low: and the crooked shall become straight, and the rough ways plain. And the glory of the Lord shall be revealed: and all flesh together shall see, that the mouth of the Lord has spoken. Isa. 40:1–5

AND LEAD US NOT INTO TEMPTATION

Sanctify the Lord of hosts himself: and let him be your fear, and let him be your dread. And he shall be a sanctification to you. But for a stone of stumbling, and for a rock of offence to the two houses of Israel, for a snare and a ruin to the inhabitants of Jerusalem. And very many of them shall stumble and fall, and shall be broken in pieces, and shall be snared, and taken. Bind up the testimony, seal the law among my disciples. And I will wait for the Lord, who hath hid his face from the house of Jacob, and I will look for him. Behold I and my children, whom the Lord hath given me for a sign, and for a wonder in Israel from the Lord of hosts, who dwelleth in mount Sion. And when they shall say to you: Seek of pythons, and of diviners, who mutter in their enchantments: should not the people seek of their God, for the living of the dead? To the law rather, and to the testimony. And if they speak not according to this word, they shall not have the morning light. Isa. 8:13–20

BUT DELIVER US FROM EVIL

Now the Lord prepared a great fish to swallow up Jonas: and Jonas was in the belly of the fish three days and three nights. And Jonas prayed to the Lord his God out of the belly of the fish. And he said: I cried out of my affliction to the Lord: and he heard me. I cried out of the belly of hell: and thou hast heard my voice. And thou hast cast me forth into the deep in the heart of the sea, and a flood hath compassed me: all thy billows and thy waves have passed over me. And I said: I am cast away out of the sight of thy eyes: but yet I shall see the holy temple again. The waters compassed me about even to the soul: the deep hath closed me round about: the sea hath covered my head. I went down to the lowest parts of the mountains: the bars of the earth have shut me up for ever: and thou wilt bring up my life from corruption, O Lord my God. When my soul was in distress within me, I remembered the Lord: that my prayer may come to thee, unto thy holy temple. They that are vain and observe vanities forsake their own mercy. But I with the voice of praise will sacrifice to thee: I will pay whatsoever I have vowed for my salvation to the Lord. And the Lord spoke to the fish: and it vomited out Jonas upon dry land. Jon. 2:1–11

PURIFYING THE DEEP FONT OF THE WORLD

OUR FATHER WHO ART IN HEAVEN, HALLOWED BE THY NAME—*ICHTHUS*
THY KINGDOM COME—*A Midnight Song to the Most Holy Theotokos,*
A Prayer of St. Basil the Great
THY WILL BE DONE ON EARTH AS IT IS IN HEAVEN—*The Saving Dimensions of the*
Lord's Prayer
GIVE US THIS DAY OUR DAILY BREAD—*The Gift of Tears*
AND FORGIVE US OUR TRESPASSES AS WE FORGIVE THOSE WHO TREPASS AGAINST US—
Forgiveness, Seventy Times Seven Times, Repentance
AND LEAD US NOT INTO TEMPTATION—*Temptation, Temptation in the Wilderness*
BUT DELIVER US FROM EVIL—*Sin, Hyprocrisy, Rejected of Men, Exorcism*
AMEN—*A Sign Which Shall Be Contradicted, John the Baptist,*
Paradoxes of the Ascetic Way

A SIGN WHICH SHALL BE CONTRADICTED

OUR FATHER WHO
ART IN HEAVEN
HALLOWED BE
THY NAME

They answered, and said to him: Abraham is our father. Jesus saith to them: If you be the children of Abraham, do the works of Abraham. But now you seek to kill me, a man who have spoken the truth to you, which I have heard of God. This Abraham did not. You do the works of your father. They said therefore to him: We are not born of fornication: we have one Father, even God. Jesus therefore said to them: If God were your Father, you would indeed love me. For from God I proceeded, and came; for I came not of myself, but he sent me: Why do you not know my speech? Because you cannot hear my word. You are of your father the devil, and the desires of your father you will do. He was a murderer from the beginning, and he stood not in the truth; because truth is not in him. When he speaketh a lie, he speaketh of his own: for he is a liar, and the father thereof. But if I say the truth, you believe me not. Which of you shall convince me of sin? if I say the truth to you, why do you not believe me? He that is of God, heareth the words of God. Therefore you hear them not, because you are not of God. The Jews therefore answered, and said to him: Do not we say well that thou art a Samaritan, and hast a devil? Jesus answered: I have not a devil: but I honor my Father, and you have dishonored me. But I seek not my own glory: there is one that seeketh and judgeth. Amen, amen I say to you: If any man keep my word, he shall not see death for ever. The Jews therefore said: Now we know that thou hast a devil. Abraham is dead, and the prophets; and thou sayest: If any man keep my word, he shall not taste death for over. Art thou greater than our father Abraham, who is dead? and the prophets are dead. Whom dost thou make thyself? Jesus answered: If I glorify myself, my glory is nothing. It is my Father that glorifieth me, of whom you say that he is your God. And you have not known him, but I know him. And if I shall say that I know him not, I shall be like to you, a liar. But I do know him, and do keep his word. Abraham your father rejoiced that he might see my day: he saw it, and was glad. The Jews therefore said to him: Thou art not yet fifty years old, and hast thou seen Abraham? Jesus said to them: Amen, amen I say to you, before Abraham was made, I am. John 8:39–58

THY KINGDOM COME

Pilate therefore saith to him: Speakest thou not to me,? Knowest thou not that I have power to crucify thee, and I have power to release thee Jesus answered: Thou shouldst not have any power against me, unless it were given thee from above. Therefore, he that hath delivered me to thee, hath the greater sin. And from henceforth Pilate sought to release him. But the Jews cried out, saying: If thou release this man, thou art not Caesar's friend. For whosoever maketh himself a king, speaketh against Caesar. Now when Pilate had heard these words, he brought Jesus forth, and sat down in the judgment seat... and he saith to the Jews: Behold your king. But they cried out: Away with him; away with him; crucify him. Pilate saith to them: Shall I crucify your king? The chief priests answered: We have no king but Caesar. Then therefore he delivered him to them to be crucified. And they took Jesus, and led him forth. And bearing his own cross, he went forth to that place which is called Calvary, but in Hebrew Golgotha. Where they crucified him, and with him two others, one on each side, and Jesus in the midst. And Pilate wrote a title also, and he put it upon the cross. And the writing was: Jesus Of Nazareth, The King Of The Jews. This title therefore many of the Jews did read: because the place where Jesus was crucified was nigh to the city: and it was written in Hebrew, in Greek, and in Latin. Then the chief priests of the Jews said to Pilate: Write not, The King of the Jews; but that he said, I am the King of the Jews. Pilate answered: What I have written, I have written. John 19:10–22

THY WILL BE DONE
ON EARTH AS IT IS
IN HEAVEN

And Pilate again spoke to them, desiring to release Jesus. But they cried again, saying: Crucify him, crucify him. And he said to them the third time: Why, what evil hath this man done? I find no cause of death in him. I will chastise him therefore, and let him go. But they were instant with loud voices, requiring that he might be crucified; and their voices prevailed. And Pilate gave sentence that it should be as they required. And he released unto them him who for murder and sedition, had been cast into prison, whom they had desired; but Jesus he delivered up to their will. Luke 23:20–25

GIVE US THIS DAY
OUR DAILY BREAD

When Jesus had said these things, he was troubled in spirit; and he testified, and said: Amen, amen I say to you, one of you shall betray me. The disciples therefore looked one upon another, doubting of whom he spoke. Now there was leaning on Jesus' bosom one of his disciples, whom Jesus loved. Simon Peter therefore beckoned to him, and said to him: Who is it of whom he speaketh? He therefore, leaning on the breast of Jesus, saith to him: Lord, who is it? Jesus answered: He it is to whom I shall reach bread dipped. And when he had dipped the bread, he gave it to Judas Iscariot, the son of Simon. And after the morsel, Satan entered into him. And Jesus said to him: That which thou dost, do quickly… He therefore having received the morsel, went out immediately. And it was night. John 13:21–27, 30

Contradiction of the Contradiction

AND FORGIVE US OUR
TRESPASSES AS WE
FORGIVE THOSE
WHO TRESPASS
AGAINST US

And the scribes who were come down from Jerusalem, said: He hath Beelzebub, and by the prince of devils he casteth out devils. And after he had called them together, he said to them in parables: How can Satan cast out Satan? And if a kingdom be divided against itself, that kingdom cannot stand. And if a house be divided against itself, that house cannot stand. And if Satan be risen up against himself, he is divided, and cannot stand, but hath an end. Mark 3:22–26

AND LEAD US NOT
INTO TEMPTATION

And when he was come forth to the land, there met him a certain man who had a devil now a very long time… And when he saw Jesus, he fell down before him; and crying out with a loud voice, he said: What have I to do with thee, Jesus, Son of the most high God? I beseech thee, do not torment me. For he commanded the unclean spirit to go out of the man… And Jesus asked him, saying: What is thy name? But he said: Legion; because many devils were entered into him. And they besought him that he would not command them to go into the abyss. And there was there a herd of many swine feeding on the mountain; and they besought him that he would suffer them to enter into them. And he suffered them. The devils therefore went out of the man, and entered into the swine; and the herd ran violently down a steep place into the lake, and were stifled. Luke 8:27–33

And there came down fire from God out of heaven, and devoured them; and the devil, who seduced them, was cast into the pool of fire and brimstone, where both the beast and the false prophet shall be tormented day and night for ever and ever. And I saw a great white throne, and one sitting upon it, from whose face the earth and heaven fled away, and there was no place found for them. And I saw the dead, great and small, standing in the presence of the throne, and the books were opened; and another book was opened, which is the book of life; and the dead were judged by those things which were written in the books, according to their works. And the sea gave up the dead that were in it, and death and hell gave up their dead that were in them; and they were judged every one according to their works. And hell and death were cast into the pool of fire. This is the second death. And whosoever was not found written in the book of life, was cast into the pool of fire. Apoc. 20:9–15

REJECTED OF MEN

REJECTED BY HIS OWN

OUR FATHER WHO
ART IN HEAVEN
HALLOWED BE
THY NAME
Rise up, let us go. Behold, he that will betray me is at hand. And while he was yet speaking, cometh Judas Iscariot, one of the twelve: and with him a great multitude with swords and staves, from the chief priests and the scribes and the ancients. And he that betrayed him, had given them a sign, saying: Whomsoever I shall kiss, that is he; lay hold on him, and lead him away carefully. And when he was come, immediately going up to him, he saith: Hail, Rabbi; and he kissed him. But they laid hands on him, and held him. Mark 14:42–46

REJECTED BY THE RULERS OF THE PEOPLE

THY KINGDOM COME
They cried out: Away with him; away with him; crucify him. Pilate saith to them: Shall I crucify your king? The chief priests answered: We have no king but Caesar. John 19: 15

REJECTED BY THE WELL-INTENTIONED

THY WILL BE DONE
ON EARTH AS IT IS
IN HEAVEN
Master, all these things I have observed from my youth. And Jesus looking on him, loved him, and said to him: One thing is wanting unto thee: go, sell whatsoever thou hast, and give to the poor, and thou shalt have treasure in heaven; and come, follow me. Who being struck sad at that saying, went away sorrowful: for he had great possessions. Mark 10:20–22

REJECTED BY THE BUYERS AND SELLERS

GIVE US THIS DAY
OUR DAILY BREAD
And they that fed them fled, and told it in the city and in the fields. And they went out to see what was done: And they came to Jesus, and they see him that was troubled with the devil, sitting, clothed, and well in his wits, and they were afraid. And they that had seen it, told them, in what manner he had been dealt with who had the devil; and concerning the swine. And they began to pray him that he would depart from their coasts. Mark 5:14–16

AND FORGIVE US OUR
TRESPASSES AS WE
FORGIVE THOSE
WHO TRESPASS
AGAINST US

REJECTED BY THE EVIL-DOER

And one of those robbers who were hanged, blasphemed him, saying: If thou be Christ, save thyself and us. But the other answering, rebuked him, saying: Neither dost thou fear God, seeing thou art condemned under the same condemnation? And we indeed justly, for we receive the due reward of our deeds; but this man hath done no evil. Luke 23:39–41

AND LEAD US NOT
INTO TEMPTATION
BUT DELIVER
US FROM EVIL

REJECTED UNTO CHRIST

These things I command you, that you love one another. If the world hate you, know ye, that it hath hated me before you. If you had been of the world, the world would love its own: but because you are not of the world, but I have chosen you out of the world, therefore the world hateth you. John 15:17–19

JOHN THE BAPTIST, PARADOXES OF THE ASCETIC WAY

All subsequent desert-dwellers followed in his footsteps, inspiring themselves with his example and emulating his rule of life. That's why all who abandon the world must delve into the elements of the life of the Lord's Forerunner John, in order to direct their life's course according to these elements. — Theophan the Recluse, *Kindling the Divine Spark,* Homily 2

OUR FATHER WHO
ART IN HEAVEN

There was a man sent from God, whose name was John…

HALLOWED BE
THY NAME

…This man came for a witness, to give testimony of the light, that all men might believe through him. He was not the light, but was to give testimony of the light… John beareth witness to him and cryeth out, saying: This was he of whom I spoke: He that shall come after me is preferred before me; because he was before me. And of his fulness we all have received; and grace for grace. For the law was given by Moses; grace and truth came by Jesus Christ. John 1:6–8, 15–17

THY KINGDOM COME

This is he of whom it is written: Behold, I send my angel before thy face, who shall prepare thy way before thee. Amen, I say to you, there has not risen among them that are born of women a greater [prophet] than John the Baptist; yet he that is the lesser in the kingdom of heaven is greater than he. And from the days of John the Baptist until now, the kingdom of heaven suffereth violence and the violent bear it away. For all the prophets and the law prophesied until John; and if you will receive it he is Elias that is to come. He that hath ears to hear, let him hear. Matt. 11:10–14

Do penance; for the kingdom of heaven is at hand. Matt. 3:2

THY WILL BE DONE
ON EARTH AS IT IS
IN HEAVEN

I am not the Christ. And they asked him: What then? Art thou Elias? And he said: I am not. Art thou the prophet? And he answered: No… I am the voice of one crying in the wilderness, Make straight the way of the Lord. John 1:20–21, 23

A man cannot receive any thing, unless it be given him from heaven. You yourselves do bear me witness that I said that I am not Christ, but that I am sent before him. He that hath the bride is the bridegroom; but the friend of the bridegroom, who standeth and heareth him, rejoiceth with joy because of the bridegroom's voice. This my joy is fulfilled. He must increase; but I must decrease. He that cometh from above is above all. He that is of the earth, of the earth he is, and of the earth he speaketh. He that cometh from heaven is above all. And what he hath seen and heard, that he testifieth; and no man receiveth his testimony. He that hath received his testimony hath set to his seal that God is true. For he whom God hath sent speaketh the words of God; for God doth not give the Spirit by measure. John 3:27–34

GIVE US THIS DAY OUR DAILY BREAD

For John the Baptist came neither eating bread nor drinking wine. And you say: He hath a devil. The Son of man is come eating and drinking. And you say: Behold, a man that is a glutton and a drinker of wine. Luke 7:33–34
Can you make the children of the bridegroom fast whilst the bridegroom is with them? But the days will come when the bridegroom shall be taken away from them; then they shall fast in those days. Luke 5:34–35

AND FORGIVE US OUR TRESPASSES AS WE FORGIVE THOSE WHO TRESPASS AGAINST US

He shall convert many of the children of Israel to the Lord their God. and he shall go before him in the spirit and power of Elias; that he may turn the hearts of the fathers unto the children and the incredulous to the wisdom of the just, to prepare unto the Lord a perfect people. Luke 1:16–17

AND LEAD US NOT INTO TEMPTATION

Now, when John had heard in prison the works of Christ, sending two of his disciples, he said to him: Art thou he that is to come, or look we for another? And Jesus, making answer, said to them: Go and relate to John what you have heard and seen. The blind see, the lame walk, the lepers are cleansed, the deaf hear, the dead rise again, the poor have the gospel preached to them. And blessed is he that shall not be scandalized in me. Matt. 11:2–6

BUT DELIVER US FROM EVIL

And thou, child, shalt be called the prophet of the Highest; for thou shalt go before the face of the Lord to prepare his ways; to give knowledge of salvation to his people unto the remission of their sins; through the bowels of the mercy of our God in which the Orient from on high hath visited us; to enlighten them that sit in darkness and in the shadow of death; to direct our feet into the way of peace. Luke 1:76–79

SIN

If we say that we have no sin, we deceive ourselves and the truth is not in us. 1 John 1:8

OUR FATHER WHO
ART IN HEAVEN
HALLOWED BE
THY NAME

He that commmitteth sin is of the devil: for the devil sinneth from the beginning. For this purpose, the Son of God appeared, that he might destroy the works of the devil. Whosoever is born of God, commmitteth not sin: for his seed abideth in him, and he can not sin, because he is born of God. In this the children of God are manifest, and the children of the devil. Whosoever is not just, is not of God, nor he that loveth not his brother. 1 John 3:8–10
Lord Jesus Christ, Son of God, have mercy on me a sinner.

THY KINGDOM COME

For if by one man's offence death reigned through one; much more they who receive abundance of grace, and of the gift, and of justice, shall reign in life through one, Jesus Christ. Therefore, as by the offence of one, unto all men to condemnation; so also by the justice of one, unto all men to justification of life. For as by the disobedience of one man, many were made sinners; so also by the obedience of one, many shall be made just. Rom. 5:17–19
Lord Jesus Christ, Son of God, have mercy on me a sinner.

THY WILL BE DONE
ON EARTH AS IT IS
IN HEAVEN

For if we sin wilfully after having the knowledge of the truth, there is now left no sacrifice for sins, but a certain dreadful expectation of judgment, and the rage of a fire which shall consume the adversaries. Heb. 10:26–27
Lord Jesus Christ, Son of God, have mercy on me a sinner.

GIVE US THIS DAY
OUR DAILY BREAD

For if a man see him that hath knowledge sit at meat in the idol's temple, shall not his conscience, being weak, be emboldened to eat those things which are sacrificed to idols ? And through thy knowledge shall the weak brother perish, for whom Christ hath died ? Now when you sin thus against the brethren, and wound their weak conscience, you sin against Christ. 1 Cor. 8:10–12
Lord Jesus Christ, Son of God, have mercy on me a sinner.

AND FORGIVE US OUR
TRESPASSES AS WE
FORGIVE THOSE
WHO TRESPASS
AGAINST US

Then his lord called him; and said to him: Thou wicked servant, I forgave thee all the debt, because thou besoughtest me: shouldst not thou then have had compassion also on thy fellow servant, even as I had compassion on thee? And his lord being angry, delivered him to the torturers until he paid all the debt. So also shall my heavenly Father do to you, if you forgive not every one his brother from your hearts. Matt. 18:32–35
Lord Jesus Christ, Son of God, have mercy on me a sinner.

AND LEAD US NOT
INTO TEMPTATION

And where sin abounded, grace did more abound. That as sin hath reigned to death; so also grace might reign by justice unto life everlasting, through Jesus Christ our Lord. What shall we say, then? shall we continue in sin, that grace may abound? God forbid. For we that are dead to sin, how shall we live any longer therein? Rom. 5:20–6:2
Lord Jesus Christ, Son of God, have mercy on me a sinner.

BUT DELIVER US FROM EVIL	Pilate therefore saith to him: Speakest thou not to me? knowest thou not that I have power to crucify thee, and I have power to release thee? Jesus answered: Thou shouldst not have any power against me, unless it were given thee from above. Therefore, he that hath delivered me to thee, hath the greater sin. John 19:10–11 Whosoever committeth sin commmitteth also iniquity; and sin is iniquity. And you know that he appeared to take away our sins, and in him there is no sin. Whosoever abideth in him, sinneth not; and whosoever sinneth, hath not seen him, nor known him. Little children, let no man deceive you. He that doth justice is just, even as he is just. He that commmitteth sin is of the devil: for the devil sinneth from the beginning. For this purpose, the Son of God appeared, that he might destroy the works of the devil. 1 John 3:4–8 *Lord Jesus Christ, Son of God, have mercy on me a sinner.*

HYPOCRISY, AN EXAMINATION OF CONSCIENCE

Woe to you, scribes and Pharisees, hypocrites; because you are like to whited sepulchers, which outwardly appear to men beautiful, but within are full of dead men's bones and of all filthiness. So you also outwardly indeed appear to men just; but inwardly you are full of hypocrisy and iniquity. Matthew 23:27–28

OUR FATHER WHO ART IN HEAVEN	And you have made void the commandment of God for your tradition. Hypocrites, well hath Isaias prophesied of you saying: This people honoreth me with their lips; but their heart is far from me; and in vain do they worship me, teaching doctrines and commandments of men.[1] Matt. 15:6–9
HALLOWED BE THY NAME	And when ye pray ye shall not be as the hypocrites that love to stand and pray in the synagogues and corners of the streets, that they may be seen by men: Amen, I say to you, they have received their reward. Matt. 6:5
THY KINGDOM COME	But woe to you, scribes and Pharisees, hypocrites, because you shut the kingdom of heaven against men; for you yourselves do not enter in and those that are going in you suffer not to enter. Matt. 23:13
THY WILL BE DONE ON EARTH AS IT IS IN HEAVEN	And there came to him the Pharisees and the Sadducees tempting; and they asked him to shew them a sign from heaven. And he answered and said to them: When it is evening, you say: It will be fair weather, for the sky is red. And in the morning: Today there will be a storm, for the sky is red and lowering. Hypocrites! You know then how to discern the face of the sky; and can you not know the signs of the times? A wicked and adulterous generation seeketh after a sign; and a sign shall not be given it, but the sign of Jonas the prophet. And he left them and went away. Matt. 16:1–4

---

1. Every time we 'innovate' we make a double confession, both to some inadequacy in our own faith and to our despair over God's ever-presence within it. There is only one innovation: the putting on of the new man in Christ, and all else follows from this. Likewise, every time we 'mitigate' our faith, every time we 'relativize' it— at the present time our multi-cultural awareness makes us especially prone to this —, we fall into presumption and, because of it, ours is a superficial faith. The mystery of other faiths is in God's hands not ours; say peace to them, presume nothing, and plunge ever deeper into the great mystery of Christ. To be anything less than whole-hearted in our faith is hypocrisy.

And when great multitudes stood about him, so that they trod one upon the other, he began to say to his disciples: Beware ye the leaven of the Pharisees, which is hypocrisy. For there is nothing covered which shall not be revealed; nor hidden that shall not be known. For what soever things you have spoken in darkness shall be published in the light; and that which you have spoken in the ear in the chambers shall be preached on the housetops. And I say to you, my friends: Be not afraid of them that kill the body and after that have no more that they can do. But I will shew you whom you shall fear; fear ye him who, after he hath killed, hath power to cast into hell. Yea, I say to you: Fear him. Luke 12:1–5

AND FORGIVE US OUR
TRESPASSES AS WE
FORGIVE THOSE
WHO TRESPASS
AGAINST US
Judge not that you may not be judged. For, with what judgment you judge, you shall be judged; and, with what measure you mete, it shall be measured to you again. And why seest thou the mote that is in thy brother's eye; and seest not the beam that is in thy own eye? Or, how sayest thou to thy brother: Let me cast the mote out of thy eye; and, behold, a beam is in thy own eye? Thou hypocrite, cast out first the beam out of thy own eye; and then thou shalt see to cast out the mote out of thy brother's eye. Matt. 7:1–5

AND LEAD US NOT
INTO TEMPTATION
Is it lawful to give tribute to Caesar or not? But Jesus, knowing their wickedness, said: Why do you tempt me, ye hypocrites? Shew me the coin of the tribute. And they offered him a penny. And Jesus saith to them: Whose image and inscription is this? They say to him: Caesar's. Then he saith to them: Render therefore to Caesar the things that are Caesar's; and to God, the things that are God's. Matt. 22:17–21

BUT DELIVER
US FROM EVIL
And he was teaching in their synagogue on their sabbath. And, behold, there was a woman who had a spirit of infirmity eighteen years. And she was bowed together; neither could she look upwards at all. Whom when Jesus saw, he called her unto him and said to her: Woman, thou art delivered from thy infirmity. And he laid hands upon her; and immediately she was made straight and glorified God. And the ruler of the synagogue (being angry that Jesus had healed on the sabbath) answering, said to the multitude: Six days there are wherein you ought to work. In them therefore come and be healed; and not on the sabbath day. And the Lord, answering him, said: Ye hypocrites, doth not every one of you, on the sabbath day, loose his ox or his ass from the manger and lead them to water? And ought not this daughter of Abraham, whom Satan hath bound, lo, these eighteen years, be loosed from this bond on the sabbath day?[1] And, when he said these things, all his adversaries were ashamed; and all the people rejoiced for all the things that were gloriously done by him. Luke 13:10–17

---

1. We are hypocrites whenever we see another's 'deliverance from evil' as untimely, as frustrating to our own plans. But we are also hypocrites each time we rejoice in another's 'subjection to evil', whether it is advantageous to our own plans, merely titillates our own evil-mindedness, or causes us to take comfort in another's suffering, relying on another's suffering to make our own seem not so unbearable, for in this we have turned away from the very source of deliverance in the providence of our compassionate God, relying on our own wisdom to make of our neighbor's wretchedness an acceptable crutch for our own infirmities.

EXORCISM

OUR FATHER WHO ART IN HEAVEN

All these things will I give thee, if falling down thou wilt adore me. Then Jesus saith to him: Begone, Satan! For it is written: The Lord thy God thou shalt adore, and him only shalt thou serve. Then the devil left him. And, behold, angels came and ministered to him. Matt. 4:9–11

HALLOWED BE THY NAME

And there was in their synagogue a man with an unclean spirit; and he cried out, saying: What have we to do with thee, Jesus of Nazareth? Art thou come to destroy us? I know who thou art, the Holy One of God. And Jesus threatened him, saying: Speak no more, and go out of the man. And the unclean spirit, tearing him and crying out with a loud voice, went out of him. And they were all amazed, insomuch that they questioned among themselves, saying: What thing is this? What is this new doctrine? For with power he commandeth even the unclean spirits; and they obey him. Mark 1:23–27

And the seventy-two returned with joy, saying: Lord, the devils also are subject to us in thy name. And he said to them: I saw Satan like lightning falling from heaven. Luke 10:17–18

THY KINGDOM COME

Then was offered to him one possessed with a devil, blind and dumb; and he healed him, so that he spoke and saw. And all the multitudes were amazed and said: Is not this the Son of David? But the Pharisees, hearing it, said: This man casteth not out devils but by Beelzebub the prince of the devils. And Jesus, knowing their thoughts, said to them: Every kingdom divided against itself shall be made desolate; and every city or house divided against itself shall not stand. And, if Satan cast out Satan, he is divided against himself; how then shall his kingdom stand? And, if I by Beelzebub cast out devils, by whom do your children cast them out? Therefore they shall be your judges. But, if I by the Spirit of God cast out devils, then is the kingdom of God come upon you. Matt. 12:22–28

THY WILL BE DONE ON EARTH AS IT IS IN HEAVEN

Master, I have brought my son to thee, having a dumb spirit. Who, wheresoever he taketh him, dasheth him, and he foameth, and gnasheth with the teeth, and pineth away; and I spoke to thy disciples to cast him out, and they could not. Who answering them, said: O incredulous generation, how long shall I be with you? how long shall I suffer you? bring him unto me. And they brought him. And when he had seen him, immediately the spirit troubled him; and being thrown down upon the ground, he rolled about foaming. And he asked his father: How long time is it since this hath happened unto him? But he said: From his infancy: and oftentimes hath he cast him into the fire and into waters to destroy him. But if thou canst do any thing, help us, having compassion on us. And Jesus saith to him: If thou canst believe, all things arepossible to him that believeth. And immediately the father of the boy crying out, with tears said: I do believe, Lord: help my unbelief. And when Jesus saw the multitude running together, he threatened the unclean spirit, saying to him: Deaf and dumb spirit, I command thee, go out of him; and enter not anymore into him. And crying out, and greatly tearing him, he went out of him, and he became as dead, so that many said: He is dead. But Jesus taking him by the hand, lifted him up; and he arose.

And when he was come into the house, his disciples secretly asked him: Why could not we cast him out? And he said to them: This kind can go out by nothing, but by prayer and fasting. Mark 9:16–28

And behold a woman that was in the city, a sinner (Mary, who is called Magdalen, out of whom seven devils were gone forth), when she knew that he sat at meat in the Pharisee's house, brought an alabaster box of ointment; and standing behind at his feet, she began to wash his feet, with tears, and wiped them with the hairs of her head, and kissed his feet, and anointed them with the ointment. And the Pharisee, who had invited him, seeing it, spoke within himself, saying: This man, if he were a prophet, would know surely who and what manner of woman this is that toucheth him, that she is a sinner. And Jesus answering, said to him: Simon, I have somewhat to say to thee. But he said: Master, say it. A certain creditor had two debtors, the one who owed five hundred pence, and the other fifty. And whereas they had not wherewith to pay, he forgave them both. Which therefore of the two loveth him most? Simon answering, said: I suppose that he to whom he forgave most. And he said to him: Thou hast judged rightly. And turning to the woman, he said unto Simon: Dost thou see this woman? I entered into thy house, thou gavest me no water for my feet; but she with tears hath washed my feet, and with her hairs hath wiped them. Thou gavest me no kiss; but she, since she came in, hath not ceased to kiss my feet. My head with oil thou didst not anoint; but she with ointment hath anointed my feet. Wherefore I say to thee: Many sins are forgiven her, because she hath loved much. But to whom less is forgiven, he loveth less. And he said to her: Thy sins are forgiven thee. And they that sat at meat with him began to say within themselves: Who is this that forgiveth sins also? And he said to the woman: Thy faith hath made thee safe, go in peace. Luke 7:37–50

And the Lord said: Simon, Simon, behold, Satan hath desired to have you, that he may sift you as wheat. But I have prayed for thee that thy faith fail not; and thou, being once converted, confirm thy brethren. Who said to him: Lord, I am ready to go with thee, both into prison and to death. And he said: I say to thee, Peter, the cock shall not crow this day, till thou thrice deniest that thou knowest me. Luke 22:31–34

And when he was come on the other side of the water, into the country of the Gerasens, there met him two that were possessed with devils, coming out of the sepulchers, exceeding fierce, so that none could pass by that way. And behold they cried out, saying: What have we to do with thee, Jesus Son of God? art thou come hither to torment us before the time? And there was, not far from them, an herd of many swine feeding. And the devils besought him, saying: If thou cast us out hence, send us into the herd of swine. And he said to them: Go. But they going out went into the swine, and behold the whole herd ran violently down a steep place into the sea: and they perished in the waters. And they that kept them fled: and coming into the city, told every thing, and concerning them that had been possessed by the devils. And behold the whole city went out to meet Jesus, and when they saw him, they besought him that he would depart from their coasts. Matt. 8:28–34

TEMPTATION

OUR FATHER WHO
ART IN HEAVEN
HALLOWED BE
THY NAME
THY KINGDOM COME

Blessed be the God and Father of our Lord Jesus Christ, who according to his great mercy hath regenerated us unto a lively hope, by the resurrection of Jesus Christ from the dead, unto an inheritance incorruptible, and undefiled, and that can not fade, reserved in heaven for you, who, by the power of God, are kept by faith unto salvation, ready to be revealed in the last time. Wherein you shall greatly rejoice, if now you must be for a little time made sorrowful in divers temptations: That the trial of your faith (much more precious than gold which is tried by the fire) may be found unto praise and glory and honor at the appearing of Jesus Christ. 1 Pet. 1:3–7

THY KINGDOM COME
THY WILL BE DONE
ON EARTH AS IT IS
IN HEAVEN

Because thou hast kept the word of my patience, I will also keep thee from the hour of the temptation, which shall come upon the whole world to try them that dwell upon the earth. Behold, I come quickly: hold fast that which thou hast, that no man take thy crown. Apoc. 3:10–11

THY WILL BE DONE
ON EARTH AS IT IS
IN HEAVEN
GIVE US THIS DAY
OUR DAILY BREAD

Then Jesus was led by the spirit into the desert, to be tempted by the devil. And when he had fasted forty days and forty nights, afterwards he was hungry. And the tempter coming said to him: If thou be the Son of God, command that these stones be made bread. Who answered and said: It is written, Not in bread alone doth man live, but in every word that proceedeth from the mouth of God. Matt. 4:1–4

GIVE US THIS DAY
OUR DAILY BREAD
AND FORGIVE US OUR
TRESPASSES AS WE
FORGIVE THOSE
WHO TRESPASS
AGAINST US

And he said to them: The kings of the Gentiles lord it over them; and they that have power over them, are called beneficent. But you not so: but he that is the greater among you, let him become as the younger; and he that is the leader, as he that serveth. For which is greater, he that sitteth at table, or he that serveth? Is it not he that sitteth at table? but I am in the midst of you, as he that serveth: and you are they who have continued with me in my temptations: and I dispose to you, as my Father hath disposed to me, a kingdom; that you may eat and drink at my table, in my kingdom: and may sit upon thrones, judging the twelve tribes of Israel. Luke 22:25–30

AND FORGIVE US OUR
TRESPASSES AS WE
FORGIVE THOSE
WHO TRESPASS
AGAINST US
AND LEAD US NOT
INTO TEMPTATION

My brethren, count it all joy, when you shall fall into diverse temptations; knowing that the trying of your faith worketh patience. And patience hath a perfect work; that you may be perfect and entire, failing in nothing. James 1:2–4 Wherefore he that thinketh himself to stand, let him take heed lest he fall. Let no temptation take hold on you, but such as is human. And God is faithful, who will not suffer you to be tempted above that which you are able: but will make also with temptation issue, that you may be able to bear it. 1 Cor. 10:12–13

AND LEAD US NOT
INTO TEMPTATION
BUT DELIVER
US FROM EVIL

The Lord knoweth how to deliver the godly from temptation, but to reserve the unjust unto the day of judgment to be tormented. 2 Pet. 2:9
Neither let us tempt Christ: as some of them tempted, and perished by the serpents. 1 Cor. 10:9

TEMPTATION IN THE WILDERNESS

MATTHEW 4:1–11

If we observe the successive steps of the temptation, we shall be able to estimate by how much we are freed from temptation. The old enemy tempted the first man through his belly, when he persuaded him to eat of the forbidden fruit; through ambition when he said, "Ye shall be as gods;" through covetousness when he said, "Knowing good and evil;" for there is a covetousness not only of money, but of greatness, when a high estate above our measure is sought. By the same method in which he had overcome the first Adam, in that same was he overcome when he tempted the second Adam. He tempted through the belly when he said, "Command that these stones become loaves;" through ambition when he said, "If thou be the Son of God, cast thyself down from hence;" through covetousness of lofty condition in the words, "All these things will I give thee." Gregory the Great, *Gospel Homilies*, 14

Then Jesus was led by the spirit
into the desert, to be tempted by the devil.

And when he had fasted forty days and forty nights, afterwards he was hungry. And the tempter coming said to him: If thou be the Son of God, command that these stones be made bread.[1] Who answered and said: It is written, Not in bread alone doth man live, but in every word that proceedeth from the mouth of God.

Then the devil took him up into the holy city, and set him upon the pinnacle of the temple,[2] and said to him: If thou be the Son of God, cast thyself down, for it is written: That he hath given his angels charge over thee, and in their hands shall they bear thee up, lest perhaps thou dash thy foot against a stone. Jesus said to him: It is written again: Thou shalt not tempt the Lord thy God.

Again the devil took him up into a very high mountain, and shewed him all the kingdoms of the world, and the glory of them, and said to him: All these will I give thee, if falling down thou wilt adore me.[3] Then Jesus saith to him: Begone, Satan: for it is written: The Lord thy God shalt thou adore, and him only shalt thou serve.

Then the devil left him; and behold
angels came and ministered to him.

---

1. Israel murmered for bread in the wilderness of Sin and God rained down manna (Exod. 16).

2. Israel murmured at Rephidim for lack of water. Moses ascended Horeb, struck the rock shown him by the Lord, and water gushed forth (Exod. 17).

3. Moses came down from Mount Sinai to find Israel worshiping a golden calf (Exod. 32).

THE THREE EXEMPLARY TEMPTATIONS OF CHRIST

THE THREE TEMPTATIONS	THREE SUPREME FUNCTIONS OF CHRIST	THREE ASCETIC VOWS
Changing stones into bread	Prophet and fulfillment of prophecy, Thaumaturge	Poverty

Thy will be done on earth as it is in heaven
Give us this day our daily bread

Not by bread alone doth man live, but in
every word that proceedeth from the mouth of God. Deut. 8:3

A high mountain, Rulership of nations	King	Chastity

Thy kingdom come

The Lord thy God shalt thou adore, and him only shalt thou serve. Deut. 10:20

A pinnacle of the Temple, Tempting God	Priest	Obedience

Our Father who art in heaven hallowed be thy name

Thou shalt not tempt the Lord
thy God. Deut. 6:16

Although Christ initially refutes each temptation by quoting Deuteronomy, we see Him then, in the course of His three-year ministry, refute them in a more mysterious way: Christ, the 'spiritual rock' (1 Cor. 10:4), becomes himself a 'living bread' in the Eucharist; Christ comes to rule the world from the humiliating throne of the Cross, and, ascending into heaven, he casts Himself far beyond the pinnacles of any earthly temple. Also Satan, in tempting Christ to exercise the three functions[1] that are His alone to exercise, inadvertently divulges the chief 'duties' of every Christian and how they are to be carried out. With 1 Peter 2:9, we find that we are all called to share in these supreme functions of Christ: "But you are a chosen generation... a holy nation... that you may declare his virtues who hath called you out of darkness into his marvelous light" = prophet, "a kingly priesthood" = king and priest. And, with the three ascetic vows, we see in what manner we are called to exercise these functions:

Poverty, antidote to the concupiscible power. The renunciation of power for one's own sake, of the desire to immerse oneself in a 'bath' of instant or immoderate gratifications; accomplished by the ascetic exploit of fasting and abstinence: "Give us this day our daily bread... and lead us not into temptation, but deliver us from evil."

Chastity, antidote to the irascible or desiring power. The renunciation of power over others; accomplished by the ascetic exploit of almsgiving: "Thy will be done on earth as it is in heaven...and forgive us our trespasses as we forgive those who trespass against us, and lead us not into temptation, but deliver us from evil."

Obedience, antidote to the rational power. The renunciation of spiritual power, 'mental' power, the casting down of God's commandments and the raising up of a 'little god'; accomplished by the ascetic exploit of self-abasement, humble mindedness, foolishness for the sake of Christ: "Our Father who art in heaven, hallowed be thy name, thy kingdom come... and lead us not into temptation, but deliver us from evil."

Surely no one is beyond being tempted, but the means of thwarting it are quick to hand and have been recommended by Jesus himself to his disciples from the garden of Gethsemane: Watch ye; and pray that ye enter not into temptation (Matt. 26:41 and Mark 14:38).

---

1. Father Dumitru Staniloae has given an extensive and illuminating treatment of these three functions in *The Experience of God, Orthodox Dogmatic Theology*, vol. 3, pp. 85–155. They were first attributed to Christ by Irenaeus of Lyons in *Against the Heresies* (III, 11, 8).

THE GUARDING OF THE HEART

OUR FATHER WHO ART IN HEAVEN HALLOWED BE THY NAME	Prayer: Lord Jesus Christ, Son of God, have mercy on me a sinner. [1]

THY KINGDOM COME	Watchfulness (*nepsis*): Then shall the kingdom of heaven be like to ten virgins, who taking their lamps, went out to meet the bridegroom and the bride… At midnight there was a cry made: Behold the bridegroom cometh. Go ye forth to meet him… Now whilst (the five foolish virgins) went to buy (oil for their lamps) the bridegroom came; and they that were ready went in with him to the marriage. And the door was shut. But at last came also the other virgins, saying: Lord, Lord, open to us. But he answering said: Amen, I say to you, I know you not. Watch ye, therefore, because you know not the day nor the hour." Matt. 25:1–13

FIVE STAGES OF TEMPTATION AND RESCUE OF THE UNGUARDED HEART

THY WILL BE DONE ON EARTH AS IT IS IN HEAVEN	Provocation (*prosbole*) A transgressive thought arises and, without a response, may pass away unremarked, although, if repeated, may become increasingly familiar. *I am falling into the pit. Rescue me, O Christ.*

GIVE US THIS DAY OUR DAILY BREAD	Momentary disturbance (*pararripismos*) The troubling of the heart. Thought becomes theme. *I am falling into the pit. Rescue me, O Christ.*

AND FORGIVE US OUR TRESPASSES AS WE FORGIVE THOSE WHO TRESPASS AGAINST US	Communion/Coupling (*homilia/syndyasmos*) Inner debate with and then a yielding to the thought. *I am falling into the pit. Rescue me, O Christ.*

AND LEAD US NOT INTO TEMPTATION	Assent (*synkatathesis*) The thought is ratified. The heart enters the captivity of sin. *I have fallen into the pit. Rescue me, O Christ.*

BUT DELIVER US FROM EVIL	Prepossession (*prolipsis*) Thought is accomplished, deeds are done. *Even now rescue me, O Christ.* Passion (*pathos*) Deeds are repeated and become habitual. Hatred and a kind of love war in the heart, sometimes just below a seemingly complacent surface. *Especially now rescue me, O Christ.*

---

1. Originally lists of scriptural quotes were compiled to 'answer' and refute demonic promptings as did Christ (see the *Antirrhetikos* of Evagrius), but with time it was realized that the name of Christ was enough and "the Jesus Prayer replaced the complicated catalogues" (Spidlik, *The Spirituality of the Christian East*, p. 244).

SEVENTY TIMES SEVEN TIMES

MATTHEW 18:21–35

THY KINGDOM COME

Then came Peter unto him and said: Lord, how often shall my brother offend against me, and I forgive him? till seven times? Jesus saith to him: I say not to thee, till seven times; but till seventy times seven times Therefore is the kingdom of heaven likened to a king, who would take an account of his servants. And when he had begun to take the account, one was brought to him, that owed him ten thousand talents.

THY WILL BE DONE
ON EARTH AS IT IS
IN HEAVEN

And as he had not wherewith to pay it, his lord commanded that he should be sold, and his wife and children and all that he had, and payment to be made.

GIVE US THIS DAY
OUR DAILY BREAD

But that servant falling down, besought him, saying: Have patience with me, and I will pay thee all.

AND FORGIVE US OUR
TRESPASSES AS WE
FORGIVE THOSE
WHO TRESPASS
AGAINST US

And the lord of that servant being moved with pity, let him go and forgave him the debt.

AND LEAD US NOT
INTO TEMPTATION

But when that servant was gone out, he found one of his fellow servants that owed him an hundred pence: and laying hold of him, throttled him, saying: Pay what thou owest. And his fellow servant falling down, besought him, saying: Have patience with me, and I will pay thee all. And he would not: but went and cast him into prison, till he paid the debt. Now his fellow servants seeing what was done, were very much grieved, and they came and told their lord all that was done.

BUT DELIVER
US FROM EVIL

Then his lord called him; and said to him: Thou wicked servant, I forgave thee all the debt, because thou besoughtest me: Shouldst not thou then have had compassion also on thy fellow servant, even as I had compassion on thee? And his lord being angry, delivered him to the torturers until he paid all the debt.

OUR FATHER WHO
ART IN HEAVEN
HALLOWED BE
THY NAME

So also shall my heavenly Father do to you, if you forgive not every one his brother from your hearts.

REPENTANCE

Now I am glad: not because you were made sorrowful; but because you were made sorrowful unto penance. For you were made sorrowful according to God, that you might suffer damage by us in nothing. For the sorrow that is according to God worketh penance, steadfast unto salvation; but the sorrow of the world worketh death. 2 Corinthians 7:9–10

OUR FATHER WHO
ART IN HEAVEN

Then began he to upbraid the cities wherein were done the most of his miracles, for that they had not done penance. Woe to thee, Corozain, woe to thee, Bethsaida: for if in Tyre and Sidon had been wrought the miracles that have been wrought in you, they had long ago done penance in sackcloth and ashes. But I say unto you, it shall be more tolerable for Tyre and Sidon in the day of judgment, than for you. and thou Capharnaum, shalt thou be exalted up to heaven? thou shalt go down even unto hell. For if in Sodom had been wrought the miracles that have been wrought in thee, perhaps it had remained into this day. But I say unto you, that it shall be more tolerable for the land of Sodom in the day of judgment, than for thee. At that time Jesus answered and said: I confess to thee, O Father, Lord of heaven and earth, because thou hast hid these things from the wise and prudent, and hast revealed them to the little ones. Yea, Father; for so hath it seemed good in thy sight. Matt. 11:20–26

HALLOWED BE
THY NAME

Thus it is written, and thus it behooved Christ to suffer, and to rise again from the dead, the third day: And that penance and remission of sins should be preached in his name, unto all nations, beginning at Jerusalem. Luke 24:46–47
And to the angel of the church of Sardis, write: These things saith he, that hath the seven spirits of God, and the seven stars: I know thy works, that thou hast the name of being alive: and thou art dead. Be watchful and strengthen the things that remain, which are ready to die. For I find not thy works full before my God. Have in mind therefore in what manner thou hast received and heard: and observe, and do penance. If then thou shalt not watch, I will come to thee as a thief, and thou shalt not know at what hour I will come to thee. But thou hast a few names in Sardis, which have not defiled their garments: and they shall walk with me in white, because they are worthy. He that shall overcome, shall thus be clothed in white garments, and I will not blot out his name out of the book of life, and I will confess his name before my Father, and before his angels. Apoc. 3:1–5

THY KINGDOM COME

And Jesus answering, said to them: They that are whole, need not the physician: but they that are sick. I came not to call the just, but sinners to penance. Luke 5 :31–32
The Lord delayeth not his promise, as some imagine, but dealeth patiently for your sake, not willing that any should perish, but that all should return to penance. 2 Pet. 3:9
Be penitent, therefore, and be converted, that your sins may be blotted out. That when the times of refreshment shall come from the presence of the Lord, and he shall send him who hath been preached unto you, Jesus Christ, whom heaven indeed must receive, until the times of the restitution of all things, which God hath spoken by the mouth of his holy prophets, from the beginning of the world. Acts 3:19–21

What man of you that hath an hundred sheep: and if he shall lose one of them, doth he not leave the ninety-nine in the desert, and go after that which was lost, until he find it? And when he hath found it, say it upon his shoulders, rejoicing: And coming home, call together his friends and neighbors, saying to them: Rejoice with me, because I have found my sheep that was lost? I say to you, that even so there shall be joy in heaven upon one sinner that doth penance, more than upon ninety-nine just who need not penance. Luke 15:4–7

GIVE US THIS DAY
OUR DAILY BREAD

I indeed baptize you in the water unto penance, but he that shall come after me, is mightier than I, whose shoes I am not worthy to bear; he shall baptize you in the Holy Spirit and fire. Whose fan is in his hand, and he will thoroughly cleanse his floor and gather his wheat into the barn; but the chaff he will burn with unquenchable fire. Matt. 3:11–2

AND FORGIVE US OUR
TRESPASSES AS WE
FORGIVE THOSE
WHO TRESPASS
AGAINST US

Wherefore thou art inexcusable, O man, whosoever thou art that judgest. For wherein thou judgest another, thou condemnest thyself. For thou dost the same things which thou judgest. For we know that the judgment of God is, according to truth, against them that do such things. And thinkest thou this, O man, that judgest them who do such things, and dost the same, that thou shalt escape the judgment of God? Or despisest thou the riches of his goodness, and patience, and longsuffering? Knowest thou not, that the benignity of God leadeth thee to penance? But according to thy hardness and impenitent heart, thou treasurest up to thyself wrath, against the day of wrath, and revelation of the just judgment of God. Who will render to every man according to his works. Rom. 2:1–6

AND LEAD US NOT
INTO TEMPTATION
BUT DELIVER
US FROM EVIL

And there were present, at that very time, some that told him of the Galileans, whose blood Pilate had mingled with their sacrifices. And he answering, said to them: Think you that these Galileans were sinners above all the men of Galilee, because they suffered such things? No, I say to you: but unless you shall do penance, you shall all likewise perish. Or those eighteen upon whom the tower fell in Siloe, and slew them: think you, that they also were debtors above all the men that dwelt in Jerusalem? No, I say to you; but except you do penance, you shall all likewise perish. Luke 13:1–5

THE PRODIGAL SON— Luke 15:11–24

BUT DELIVER
US FROM EVIL

A certain man had two sons: And the younger of them said to his father: Father, give me the portion of substance that falleth to me. And he divided unto them his substance. And not many days after, the younger son, gathering all together, went abroad into a far country: and there wasted his substance, living riotously.

AND LEAD US NOT
INTO TEMPTATION

And after he had spent all, there came a mighty famine in that country; and he began to be in want.

AND FORGIVE US OUR
TRESPASSES AS WE
FORGIVE THOSE
WHO TRESPASS
AGAINST US

And he went and cleaved to one of the citizens of that country. And he sent him into his farm to feed swine. And he would fain have filled his belly with the husks the swine did eat; and no man gave unto him. And returning to himself, he said:

<table>
<tr><td>GIVE US THIS DAY
OUR DAILY BREAD</td><td>How many hired servants in my father's house abound with bread, and I here perish with hunger?</td></tr>
<tr><td>THY WILL BE DONE
ON EARTH AS IT
IS IN HEAVEN</td><td>I will arise, and will go to my father, and say to him: Father, I have sinned against heaven, and before thee: I am not worthy to be called thy son: make me as one of thy hired servants. And rising up he came to his father. And when he was yet a great way off, his father saw him, and was moved with compassion, and running to him fell upon his neck, and kissed him. And the son said to him: Father, I have sinned against heaven, and before thee, I am not now worthy to be called thy son.</td></tr>
<tr><td>THY KINGDOM COME</td><td>And the father said to his servants: Bring forth quickly the first robe, and put it on him, and put a ring on his hand, and shoes on his feet: And bring hither the fatted calf, and kill it, and let us eat and make merry:</td></tr>
<tr><td>OUR FATHER WHO
ART IN HEAVEN
HALLOWED BE
THY NAME</td><td>Because this my son was dead, and is come to life again: was lost, and is found.</td></tr>
</table>

FORGIVENESS

<table>
<tr><td>OUR FATHER WHO
ART IN HEAVEN</td><td>But all things are of God, who hath reconciled us to himself by Christ and hath given to us the ministry of reconciliation. For God indeed was in Christ, reconciling the world to himself, not imputing to them their sins. And he hath placed in us the word of reconciliation. 2 Cor. 5:18–19</td></tr>
<tr><td>HALLOWED BE
THY NAME</td><td>And he commanded us to preach to the people and to testify that it is he who was appointed by God to be judge of the living and the dead. To him all the prophets give testimony, that by his name all receive remission of sins, who believe in him. Acts 10:42–43</td></tr>
<tr><td>THY KINGDOM COME</td><td>And you, when you were dead in your sins and the uncircumcision of your flesh, he hath quickened together with him, forgiving you all offenses; blotting out the handwriting of the decree that was against us. And he hath taken the same out of the way, fastening it to the cross. And, despoiling the principalities and powers, he hath exposed them confidently in open shew, triumphing over them in himself. Col. 2:13–15</td></tr>
<tr><td>THY WILL BE DONE
ON EARTH AS IT IS
IN HEAVEN</td><td>And when you shall stand to pray, forgive, if you have aught against any man; that your Father also, who is in heaven, may forgive you your sins. But if you will not forgive, neither will your Father that is in heaven forgive you your sins. Mark 11:25–26
Even so it is not the will of your Father who is in heaven that one of these little ones should perish. Matt. 18:14
Amen, I say to you, whatsoever you shall bind upon earth shall be bound also in heaven; and whatsoever you shall loose upon earth shall be loosed also in heaven. Matt. 18:18</td></tr>
</table>

GIVE US THIS DAY
OUR DAILY BREAD

And, whilst they were at supper, Jesus took bread and blessed and broke and gave to his disciples and said: This is my body. And, taking the chalice, he gave thanks and gave to them, saying: Drink ye all of this. for this is my blood of the new testament, which shall be shed for many unto remission of sins. Matt. 26:26–28

AND FORGIVE US OUR
TRESPASSES AS WE
FORGIVE THOSE
WHO TRESPASS
AGAINST US

Take heed to yourselves. If thy brother sin against thee, reprove him: and if he do penance, forgive him. And if he sin against thee seven times in a day, and seven times in a day be converted unto thee, saying, I repent; forgive him. Luke 17:3–4

But, before all things, have a constant mutual charity among ourselves; for charity covereth a multitude of sins. 1 Pet. 4:8

My brethren, if any of you err from the truth and one convert him; he must know that he who causeth a sinner to be converted from the error of his way shall save his soul from death and shall cover a multitude of sins. James 5:19–20

AND LEAD US NOT
INTO TEMPTATION

If we say that we have fellowship with him and walk in darkness, we lie and do not the truth. But if we walk in the light, as he also is in the light, we have fellowship with one another; and the blood of Jesus Christ his Son cleanseth us from sin. If we say that we have no sin, we deceive ourselves and the truth is not in us. If we confess our sins, he is faithful and just, to forgive us our sins and to cleanse us from all iniquity. If we say that we have not sinned, we make him a liar; and his word is not in us. 1 John 1:6–10

BUT DELIVER
US FROM EVIL

And the scribes and the Pharisees bring unto him a woman taken in adultery: and they set her in the midst, and said to him: Master, this woman was even now taken in adultery. Now Moses in the law commanded us to stone such a one. But what sayest thou? And this they said tempting him, that they might accuse him. But Jesus bowing himself down, wrote with his finger on the ground. When therefore they continued asking him, he lifted up himself, and said to them: He that is without sin among you, let him first cast a stone at her. And again stooping down, he wrote on the ground. But they hearing this, went out one by one, beginning at the eldest. And Jesus alone remained, and the woman standing in the midst. Then Jesus lifting up himself, said to her: Woman, where are they that accused thee? Hath no man condemned thee? Who said: No man, Lord. And Jesus said: Neither will I condemn thee. Go, and now sin no more. John 8:3–11

THE GIFT OF TEARS

OUR FATHER WHO
ART IN HEAVEN
HALLOWED BE
THY NAME

Jesus saith to her: Woman, why weepest thou? whom seekest thou? She, thinking it was the gardener, saith to him: Sir, if thou hast taken him hence, tell me where thou hast laid him, and I will take him away. Jesus saith to her: Mary. She turning, saith to him: Rabboni (which is to say, Master). Jesus saith to her: Do not touch me, for I am not yet ascended to my Father. But go to my brethren, and say to them: I ascend to my Father and to your Father, to my God and your God. John 20:15–17

THY KINGDOM COME

Amen, amen I say to you, that you shall lament and weep, but the world shall rejoice; and you shall be made sorrowful, but your sorrow shall be turned into joy. A woman, when she is in labor, hath sorrow, because her hour is come; but when she hath brought forth the child, she remembereth no more the anguish, for joy that a man is born into the world. So also you now indeed have sorrow; but I will see you again, and your heart shall rejoice; and your joy no man shall take from you. John 16:20–22

THY WILL BE DONE
ON EARTH AS IT IS
IN HEAVEN

And I heard a loud voice in heaven, saying: Now is come salvation, and strength, and the kingdom of our God, and the power of his Christ: because the accuser of our brethren is cast forth, who accused them before our God day and night. And they overcame him by the blood of the Lamb, and by the word of the testimony, and they loved not their lives unto death. Therefore rejoice, O heavens, and you that dwell therein. Woe to the earth, and to the sea, because the devil is come down unto you, having great wrath, knowing that he hath but a short time. Apoc. 12:10–12

GIVE US THIS DAY
OUR DAILY BREAD

But woe to you that are rich: for you have your consolation. Woe to you that are filled: for you shall hunger. Woe to you that now laugh: for you shall mourn and weep. Luke 6:24–25

AND FORGIVE US OUR
TRESPASSES AS WE
FORGIVE THOSE
WHO TRESPASS
AGAINST US

Now I am glad: not because you were made sorrowful; but because you were made sorrowful unto penance. For you were made sorrowful according to God, that you might suffer damage by us in nothing. For the sorrow that is according to God worketh penance, steadfast unto salvation; but the sorrow of the world worketh death. For behold this selfsame thing, that you were made sorrowful according to God, how great carefulness it worketh in you; yea defence, yea indignation, yea fear, yea desire, yea zeal, yea revenge: in all things you have shewed yourselves to be undefiled in the matter. 2 Cor. 7:9–11

AND LEAD US NOT
INTO TEMPTATION

And there followed him a great multitude of people, and of women, who bewailed and lamented him. But Jesus turning to them, said: Daughters of Jerusalem, weep not over me; but weep for yourselves, and for your children. For behold, the days shall come, wherein they will say: Blessed are the barren, and the wombs that have not borne, and the paps that have not given suck. Then shall they begin to say to the mountains: Fall upon us; and to the hills: Cover us. For if in the green wood they do these things, what shall be done in the dry? Luke 23:27–31

Now when Peter was in the court below, there cometh one of the maidservants of the high priest. And when she had seen Peter warming himself, looking on him she saith: Thou also wast with Jesus of Nazareth. But he denied, saying: I neither know nor understand what thou sayest. And he went forth before the court; and the cock crew. And again a maidservant seeing him, began to say to the standers by: This is one of them. But he denied again. And after a while they that stood by said again to Peter: Surely thou art one of them; for thou art also a Galilean. But he began to curse and to swear, saying; I know not this man of whom you speak.[2] And immediately the cock crew again. And Peter remembered the word that Jesus had said unto him: Before the cock crow twice, thou shalt thrice deny me. And he began to weep. Mark 14:66–72

THE SAVING DIMENSIONS OF THE LORD'S PRAYER

I confess to thee, O Father, Lord of heaven and earth, because thou hast hid these things from the wise and the prudent and hast revealed them to little ones. Yea Father; for so hath it seemed good in thy sight. All things are delivered[2] to me by my Father. And no one knoweth the Son but the Father; neither doth any one know the Father, but the Son and he to whom it shall please the Son to reveal him. Matthew 11:25–27

OUR FATHER WHO
ART IN HEAVEN

And we have seen and do testify that the Father hath sent his Son to be the Savior of the world. Whosoever shall confess that Jesus is the Son of God, God abideth in him, and he in God. 1 John 4:14–15

HALLOWED BE
THY NAME

Be it known to you all and to all the people of Israel, that by the name of our Lord Jesus Christ of Nazareth, whom you crucified, whom God hath raised from the dead, even by him, this man standeth before you, whole… Neither is there salvation in any other. For there is no other name under heaven given to men, whereby we must be saved. Acts 4:10, 12

THY KINGDOM COME

After this, I saw a great multitude, which no man could number, of all nations and tribes and peoples and tongues, standing before the throne and in sight of the Lamb, clothed with white robes and palms in their hands. And they cried with a loud voice saying: Salvation to our God, who sitteth upon the throne and to the Lamb. Apoc. 7:9–10

THY WILL BE DONE
ON EARTH AS IT IS
IN HEAVEN

Grace be to you, and peace from God the Father and from our Lord Jesus Christ, who gave himself for our sins, that he might deliver us from this present wicked world, according to the will of God and our Father. Gal. 1:3–4

GIVE US THIS DAY
OUR DAILY BREAD

I have meat to eat which you know not. The disciples therefore said one to another: Hath any man brought him to eat? Jesus saith to them: My meat is to do the will of him that sent me, that I may perfect his work. Do not you say: There

---

1. How much more numerous than these three are our own denials and even betrayals? And yet if we, like Peter, unite the memory of these with his (and our) three-fold and steadfast pledge of love for the Savior (John 21:15–17), there will spring up an inexhaustible font of tears, a 'tender weeping' will overcome us, and it is through exactly these tears of sorrow and love combined that the 'eye of the heart' will first open and cast its gaze upon the world. O Lord, upon that day do thou remember me!

2. As all things are 'delivered to' (bestowed on) the Son, so does the Son have the power to 'deliver' (save) all things from the world, the flesh and the Devil.

are yet four months, and then the harvest cometh? Behold, I say to you, lift up your eyes, and see the countries; for they are white already to harvest. And he that reapeth receiveth wages and gathereth fruit unto life everlasting; that both he that soweth and he that reapeth may rejoice together. John 4:32–36

AND FORGIVE US OUR TRESPASSES AS WE FORGIVE THOSE WHO TRESPASS AGAINST US

What I have pardoned, if I have pardoned any thing, for your sakes have I done it in the person of Christ; that we be not overreached by Satan. For we are not ignorant of his devices. 2 Cor. 2:10–11

AND LEAD US NOT INTO TEMPTATION

Blessed is the man that endureth temptation; for, when he hath been proved, he shall receive the crown of life which God hath promised to them that love him. James 1:12

BUT DELIVER US FROM EVIL

He saved others; himself he cannot save. If he be the king of Israel, let him come down from the cross… He trusted in God: let him now deliver him if he will have him. For he said: I am the Son of God. Matt. 27:42–43
Jesus of Nazareth, a man approved of God among you by miracles and wonders and signs, which God did by him, in the midst of you…this same being delivered up…crucified and slain… God hath raised up, having loosed the sorrows of hell, as it was impossible that he should be holden by it. Acts 2:22–24

A PRAYER OF ST. BASIL THE GREAT

(from *Orthodox Daily Prayers*)

BUT DELIVER US FROM EVIL

Almighty Lord, the God of hosts and of all flesh, thou livest in the heights, yet lookest down on the humble, proving the hearts and emotions, clearly foreknowing the secrets of men. Thou art the Light without beginning, in whom there is no variation nor shadow of change. O Immortal King, accept the prayers which we now offer thee from defiled lips. Free us from the sins we have committed in deed, word or thought, knowingly and unknowingly.

AND LEAD US NOT INTO TEMPTATION

Cleanse us from all defilement of flesh and spirit.

AND FORGIVE US OUR TRESPASSES AS WE FORGIVE THOSE WHO TRESPASS AGAINST US

Grant us to pass through the entire night of this present life with a watchful heart and a sober mind, awaiting the coming of the bright and manifest day of thine only-begotten Son, our Lord, God and Savior Jesus Christ, when the Judge of all will come with glory to reward each according to his deeds.

THY WILL BE DONE ON EARTH AS IT IS IN HEAVEN GIVE US THIS DAY OUR DAILY BREAD

May we not be found fallen and lazy, but alert and roused to action, prepared to enter into his joy and the divine chamber of his glory, where the voice of those who feast is unceasing…

THY KINGDOM COME	…and indescribable is the delight of those who behold the inexpressible beauty of thy countenance.
OUR FATHER WHO ART IN HEAVEN HALLOWED BE THY NAME	For thou art the true light which enlightens and sanctifies all, and all creation hymns thee unto ages of ages.

A MIDNIGHT SONG TO THE MOST HOLY THEOTOKOS

(from *Orthodox Daily Prayers*)

OUR FATHER WHO ART IN HEAVEN HALLOWED BE THY NAME THY KINGDOM COME THY WILL BE DONE ON EARTH AS IT IS IN HEAVEN	I Hymn your Grace, O Lady, and pray that you grace my mind. Teach me to walk correctly in heaven on the path of Christ's commandments. Strengthen me to watch in song dispelling the despair of sleep. I am bound by fetters of sin, free me by your prayers, O Bride of God! Keep me in the night and in the day delivering me from warring enemies.
GIVE US THIS DAY OUR DAILY BREAD	As you bore the life-giving God, give life to me who am wounded by passions. As you bore the unsetting Light, enlighten my blinded soul. O wondrous palace of the Master, make me a home of the divine Spirit.
AND FORGIVE US OUR TRESPASSES AS WE FORGIVE THOSE WHO TRESPASS AGAINST US	As you bore the Physician, heal my soul of its passion-filled years. I am tossed in the tempest of life: direct me to the path of repentance.
AND LEAD US NOT INTO TEMPTATION BUT DELIVER US FROM EVIL	Deliver me from the eternal flame, from the evil worm, and from hell. Make me not a joy for demons though I am guilty of many sins.
AND FORGIVE US OUR TRESPASSES AS WE FORGIVE THOSE WHO TRESPASS AGAINST US	Make me new, most undefiled one, for I am aged by senseless sins. Estrange me from all torments, and pray for me to the Master of all. Grant that, with all the saints, I may inherit the joys of heaven. Hear, most holy Virgin, the voice of your useless servant. Grant me a torrent of tears, most pure one, to wash the filth of my soul.
GIVE US THIS DAY OUR DAILY BREAD	The groans of my heart I bring you unceasingly: open your heart, O Lady!
THY WILL BE DONE ON EARTH AS IT IS IN HEAVEN	Accept my prayerful service, and take it to the compassionate God. You who are far higher than the angels, raise me above this world's confusion.

THY KINGDOM COME	O light-bearing heavenly cloud, direct spiritual grace into me.
OUR FATHER WHO ART IN HEAVEN HALLOWED BE THY NAME	I raise in praise, all-undefiled one, hands and lips defiled by sin. Deliver me from soul-corrupting harm, praying fervently to Christ, To whom glory and worship are due, now and ever and unto ages of ages. Amen.

ICHTHUS

The Inscription of Pectorius

OUR FATHER WHO ART IN HEAVEN	I	Thou, the divine child of the heavenly Fish
HALLOWED BE THY NAME	X	Keep pure thy heart among the mortals
THY KINGDOM COME	Θ	Once thou hast been washed in the fountain of divine waters. Refresh thy soul, friend,
	Y	With the ever flowing waters of wealth-giving wisdom.
THY WILL BE DONE ON EARTH AS IT IS IN HEAVEN	Σ	Take from the Redeemer of saints the honey-sweet food;
GIVE US THIS DAY OUR DAILY BREAD		I pray thee, Lord Savior, satisfy his hunger with the Fish.
AND FORGIVE US OUR TRESPASSES AS WE FORGIVE THOSE WHO TRESPASS AGAINST US AND LEAD US NOT INTO TEMPTATION BUT DELIVER US FROM EVIL		May my mother rest peacefully, I beseech thee, Light of the dead, Aschandius, father, my heart's beloved With my dearest mother and my brother In the peace of the Fish remember thy Pectorius.

ICHTHUS, the Greek word for 'fish' (ΙΧΘΥΣ), was a cryptogram used in early Christian times, each letter being an initial letter in the formula Jesus Christ, Son of God, Savior (Ἰησοῦς Χριστὸς Θεοῦ Υἱός Σῶτερ). It is possibly an early form of the 'Jesus Prayer', where Savior is, as I. Hausherr points out, equivalent to *Have mercy on me a sinner*.[1] The ICHTHUS is at once a symbol of Christ, the Eucharist, and the Christian faithful—as a fish in water, the Christian should be continually (cf. 1 Thessalonians 5:17) immersed in and cleansed with prayer, immersed in Christ and the Eucharist. We see this wondrously confirmed in the 'Inscription of Pectorius' (Autun, late second-early third century AD) where the initial letters of the of the first five verses spell out: ΙΧΘΥΣ, while the entire inscription can be seen as a ciphering forth of the Lord's Prayer.

---

1. *The Name of Jesus*, p. 69.

A LAMP ON THE FURTHER SHORE

OUR FATHER WHO ART IN HEAVEN,
HALLOWED BE THY NAME—*Betrothed to the Holy One*
THY KINGDOM COME—*Perfected in Charity*
THY WILL BE DONE ON EARTH AS IT IS IN HEAVEN—*The Truth of Charity*
GIVE US THIS DAY OUR DAILY BREAD—*Agape*
AND FORGIVE US OUR TRESPASSES
AS WE FORGIVE THOSE WHO TRESPASS AGAINST US—*Charity*
AND LEAD US NOT INTO TEMPTATION—*Psalm 118, The Letter* He
BUT DELIVER US FROM EVIL—*Love, the Fulfillment of the Law in Faith*

LOVE, THE FULFILLMENT OF THE LAW IN FAITH

FROM THE EPISTLE TO THE ROMANS

OUR FATHER WHO ART IN HEAVEN HALLOWED BE THY NAME

For if they who are of the law be heirs, faith is made void: the promise is made of no effect. For the law worketh wrath. For where there is no law, neither is there transgression. Therefore is it of faith, that according to grace the promise might be firm to all the seed: not to that only which is of the law, but to that also which is of the faith of Abraham, who is the father of us all. Rom. 4:14–16

THY KINGDOM COME

LOVE OF GOD — For they, not knowing the justice of God and seeking to establish their own, have not submitted themselves to the justice of God. For the end of the law is Christ: unto justice to everyone that believeth. For Moses wrote that the justice which is of the law: The man that shall do it shall live by it. But the justice which is of faith, speaketh thus: Say not in thy heart: Who shall ascend into heaven? That is to bring Christ down; or who shall descend into the deep? That is, to bring up Christ again from the dead. But what saith the scripture? The word is nigh thee; even in thy mouth and in thy heart. This is the word of faith, which we preach. For if thou confess with thy mouth the Lord Jesus and believe in thy heart that God hath raised him up from the dead, thou shalt be saved. Rom. 10:3–9

LOVE OF NEIGHBOR — For: Thou shalt not commit adultery: Thou shalt not kill: Thou shalt not steal: Thou shalt not bear false witness: Thou shalt not covet. And if there be any other commandment, it is comprised in this word: Thou shalt love thy neighbor as thyself. The love of our neighbor worketh no evil. Love therefore is the fulfilling of the law. Rom. 13:9–10

THY WILL BE DONE ON EARTH AS IT IS IN HEAVEN

For we account a man to be justified by faith, without the works of the law. Is he the God of the Jews only? Is he not also of the Gentiles? yes, of the Gentiles also. For it is one God that justifieth circumcision by faith and uncircumcision through faith. Do we then, destroy the law through faith? God forbid! But we establish the law. Rom. 3:28–31

GIVE US THIS DAY OUR DAILY BREAD

For as by the disobedience of one man, many were made sinners: so also by the obedience of one, many shall be made just. Now the law entered in that sin might abound. And where sin abounded, grace did more abound. That as sin hath reigned to death: so also grace might reign by justice unto life everlasting, through Jesus Christ our Lord. Rom. 5:19–21

AND FORGIVE US OUR TRESPASSES AS WE FORGIVE THOSE WHO TRESPASS AGAINST US

For whosoever have sinned without the law shall perish without the law: and whosoever have sinned in the law shall be judged by the law. For not the hearers of the law are just before God: but the doers of the law shall be justified. Rom. 2:12–13

AND LEAD US NOT INTO TEMPTATION

But I see another law in my members, fighting against the law of my mind and captivating me in the law of sin that is in my members. Rom. 7:23

| BUT DELIVER US FROM EVIL | Unhappy man that I am, who shall deliver me from the body of this death? The grace of God, by Jesus Christ our Lord. Therefore, I myself, with the mind serve the law of God: but with the flesh, the law of sin. Rom. 7:24–25 |

PSALM 118~THE LETTER *HE*

PSALM 118:33–48

OUR FATHER WHO ART IN HEAVEN HALLOWED BE THY NAME	Set before me for a law the way of thy justifications, O Lord: and I will always seek after it.
THY KINGDOM COME	Give me understanding, and I will search thy law: and I will keep it with my whole heart.
THY WILL BE DONE ON EARTH AS IT IS IN HEAVEN	Lead me into the path of thy commandments: for this same I have desired.
GIVE US THIS DAY OUR DAILY BREAD	Incline my heart into thy testimonies and not to covetousness.
AND FORGIVE US OUR TRESPASSES AS WE FORGIVE THOSE WHO TRESPASS AGAINST US	Turn away my eyes that they may not behold vanity: quicken me in thy way.
AND LEAD US NOT INTO TEMPTATION	Establish thy word to thy servant, in thy fear.
BUT DELIVER US FROM EVIL	Turn away my reproach which I have apprehended: for thy judgments are delightful. Behold, I have longed after thy precepts: quicken me in thy justice.

CHARITY

OUR FATHER WHO ART IN HEAVEN	God is charity 1 John 4:8
HALLOWED BE THY NAME (*the Son*)	In this is charity; not as though we had loved God, but because he hath first loved us, and sent his Son to be a propitiation for our sins. 1 John 4:10 Thou shalt love the Lord thy God with thy whole heart…
THY KINGDOM COME (*the Holy Spirit*)1	…and with thy whole soul…
THY WILL BE DONE ON EARTH AS IT IS IN HEAVEN (*the angels*)	…and with thy whole mind…
GIVE US THIS DAY OUR DAILY BREAD (*mankind and the cosmos*)	…and with thy whole strength.
AND FORGIVE US OUR TRESPASSES AS WE FORGIVE THOSE WHO TRESPASS AGAINST US	…Thou shalt love thy neighbor as thyself. Mark 12:30–31 God hath so loved us, we also ought to love one another. 1 John 4:11
AND LEAD US NOT INTO TEMPTATION BUT DELIVER US FROM EVIL	Love your enemies; do good to them that hate you; and pray for them that persecute and calumniate you. Matt. 6:44

---

1. "The words of the prayer point out the Father, the Father's name, and the Father's kingdom to help us learn from the source himself to honor, to invoke and to adore the one Trinity. For the name of God the Father who subsists essentially is the only-begotten Son, and the kingdom of God the Father who subsists essentially is the Holy Spirit."— Maximus the Confessor, *On the Lord's Prayer.*

AGAPE

THE SACRED SEVENFOLD LOVE OF GOD AND NEIGHBOR

The word 'love' (ἀγάπη/ἀγάπην) occurs seven times in John's Gospel. In the early Church it became the term used to designate a communal feast that accompanied the celebration of the liturgy. —GJC

OUR FATHER WHO ART IN HEAVEN HALLOWED BE THY NAME

Father, I will that where I am, they also whom thou hast given me may be with me; that they may see my glory which thou hast given me, because thou hast loved me before the creation of the world. Just Father, the world hath not known thee; but I have known thee: and these have known that thou hast sent me. And I have made known thy name to them, and will make it known; that the love [ἀγάπη] wherewith thou hast loved me, may be in them, and I in them. John 17:24–26

THY KINGDOM COME

As the Father hath loved me, I also have loved you. Abide in my love [ἀγάπη]. John 15:9

THY WILL BE DONE ON EARTH AS IT IS IN HEAVEN

If you keep my commandments, you shall abide in my love [ἀγαπη]; as I also have kept my Father's commandments, and do abide in his love [ἀγάπη]. These things I have spoken to you, that my joy may be in you, and your joy may be filled. John 15:10–11

GIVE US THIS DAY OUR DAILY BREAD

This is my commandment, that you love one another, as I have loved you. Greater love [ἀγάπην] than this no man hath, that a man lay down his life for his friends. John 15:12–13

AND FORGIVE US OUR TRESPASSES AS WE FORGIVE THOSE WHO TRESPASS AGAINST US

A new commandment I give unto you: That you love one another, as I have loved you, that you also love one another. By this shall all men know that you are my disciples, if you have love [ἀγάπην] one for another. John 13:34–35

AND LEAD US NOT INTO TEMPTATION BUT DELIVER US FROM EVIL

Search the scriptures, for you think in them to have life everlasting; and the same are they that give testimony of me. And you will not come to me that you may have life. I receive glory not from men. But I know you, that you have not the love [ἀγάπην] of God in you. I am come in the name of my Father, and you receive me not: if another shall come in his own name, him you will receive. How can you believe, who receive glory one from another: and the glory which is from God alone, you do not seek? John 5 :39–44

THE TRUTH OF CHARITY

1 CORINTHIANS 13:1–12

OUR FATHER WHO ART IN HEAVEN HALLOWED BE THY NAME — If I speak with the tongues of men, and of angels, and have not charity, I am become as sounding brass, or a tinkling cymbal.

THY KINGDOM COME — And if I should have prophecy and should know all mysteries, and all knowledge,

THY WILL BE DONE ON EARTH AS IT IS IN HEAVEN — and if I should have all faith, so that I could remove mountains, and have not charity, I am nothing.

GIVE US THIS DAY OUR DAILY BREAD — And if I should distribute all my goods to feed the poor, and if I should deliver my body to be burned, and have not charity, it profiteth me nothing.

AND FORGIVE US OUR TRESPASSES AS WE FORGIVE THOSE WHO TRESPASS AGAINST US — Charity is patient, is kind: charity envieth not, dealeth not perversely; is not puffed up; is not ambitious, seeketh not her own, is not provoked to anger,

AND LEAD US NOT INTO TEMPTATION — thinketh no evil;

BUT DELIVER US FROM EVIL — rejoiceth not in iniquity, but rejoiceth with the truth;

AND LEAD US NOT INTO TEMPTATION — beareth all things,

AND FORGIVE US OUR TRESPASSES AS WE FORGIVE THOSE WHO TRESPASS AGAINST US — believeth all things, hopeth all things, endureth all things.

GIVE US THIS DAY OUR DAILY BREAD — Charity never falleth away: whether prophecies shall be made void, or tongues shall cease, or knowledge shall be destroyed.

THY WILL BE DONE ON EARTH AS IT IS IN HEAVEN — For we know in part, and we prophesy in part. But when that which is perfect is come, that which is in part shall be done away.

THY KINGDOM COME	When I was a child, I spoke as a child, I understood as a child, I thought as a child. But, when I became a man, I put away the things of a child. We see now through a glass in a dark manner; but then face to face.
OUR FATHER WHO ART IN HEAVEN HALLOWED BE THY NAME	Now I know I part; but then I shall know even as I am known.

PERFECTED IN CHARITY

1 JOHN 4:11–18

He who has attained perfect love, and has ordered his whole life in accordance with it, is the person who says 'Lord Jesus' in the Holy Spirit. — Maximus the Confessor, *Texts on Love*, IV, 39

OUR FATHER WHO ART IN HEAVEN HALLOWED BE THY NAME	My dearest, if God hath so loved us; we also ought to love one another. No man hath seen God at any time. If we love one another, God abideth in us, and his charity is perfected in us.
THY KINGDOM COME	In this we know that we abide in him, and he in us: because he hath given us of his spirit.
THY WILL BE DONE ON EARTH AS IT IS IN HEAVEN	And we have seen, and do testify, that the Father hath sent his Son to be the Savior of the world. Whosoever shall confess that Jesus is the Son of God, God abideth in him, and he in God.
GIVE US THIS DAY OUR DAILY BREAD	And we have known, and have believed the charity, which God hath to us. God is charity: and he that abideth in charity, abideth in God, and God in him.
AND FORGIVE US OUR TRESPASSES AS WE FORGIVE THOSE WHO TRESPASS AGAINST US	In this is the charity of God perfected with us, that we may have confidence in the day of judgment: because as he is, we also are in this world.
AND LEAD US NOT INTO TEMPTATION	Fear is not in charity: but perfect charity casteth out fear, because fear hath pain.
BUT DELIVER US FROM EVIL	And he that feareth, is not perfected in charity.

BETROTHED TO THE HOLY ONE

And the bridegroom shall rejoice over the bride, and thy God shall rejoice over thee. Upon thy walls, O Jerusalem, I have appointed watchmen all the day, and all the night, they shall never hold their peace. You that are mindful of the Lord, hold not your peace, and give him no silence till he establish, and till he make Jerusalem a praise in the earth.

Isaiah 62:5–7

OUR FATHER WHO ART IN HEAVEN HALLOWED BE THY NAME
Thy name is as oil poured out: therefore young maidens have loved thee. Song of Songs 1:2

THY KINGDOM COME
Draw me: we will run after thee to the odour of thy ointments. The king hath brought me into his storerooms: we will be glad and rejoice in thee. Song of Songs 1:3
I sleep, and my heart watcheth: the voice of my beloved knocking: Open to me, my sister, my love, my dove, my undefiled. Song of Songs 5:2

THY WILL BE DONE ON EARTH AS IT IS IN HEAVEN
Behold my beloved speaketh to me: Arise, make haste, my love, my dove, my beautiful one, and come. For winter is now past, the rain is over and gone. The flowers have appeared in our land, the time of pruning is come: the voice of the turtle is heard in our land: the fig tree hath put forth her green figs: the vines in flower yield their sweet smell. Arise, my love, my beautiful one, and come. Song of Songs 2:10–13

GIVE US THIS DAY OUR DAILY BREAD
As the apple tree among the trees of the woods, so is my beloved among the sons. I sat down under his shadow, whom I desired: and his fruit was sweet to my palate. He brought me into the cellar of wine, he set in order charity in me. Stay me up with flowers, compass me about with apples: because I languish with love. Song of Songs 2:3–5

AND FORGIVE US OUR TRESPASSES AS WE FORGIVE THOSE WHO TRESPASS AGAINST US
I opened the bolt of my door to my beloved: but he had turned aside, and was gone. My soul melted when he spoke: I sought him, and found him not: I called, and he did not answer me. The keepers that go about the city found me: they struck me: and wounded me: the keepers of the walls took away my veil from me. I adjure you, O daughters of Jerusalem, if you find my beloved, that you tell him that I languish with love. Song of Songs 5:6–8

AND LEAD US NOT INTO TEMPTATION
My dove in the clefts of the rock, in the hollow places of the wall, shew me thy face, let thy voice sound in my ears: for thy voice is sweet, and thy face comely. Catch us the little foxes that destroy the vines: for our vineyard hath flourished. My beloved to me, and I to him who feedeth among the lilies, till the day break, and the shadows retire. Song of Songs 2:14–17

BUT DELIVER US FROM EVIL
Put me as a seal upon thy heart, as a seal upon thy arm, for love is strong as death, jealousy as hard as hell, the lamps thereof are fire and flames. Many waters cannot quench charity, neither can the floods drown it: if a man should give all the substance of his house for love, he shall despise it as nothing. Song of Songs 8:6–7

II

THE SACRAMENTS

GIVE US THIS DAY OUR DAILY BREAD

INTRODUCTION

And behold a certain lawyer stood up, tempting him, and saying, Master, what must I do to possess eternal life? But he said to him: What is written in the law? how readest thou? He answering, said: Thou shalt love the Lord thy God with thy whole heart, and with thy whole soul, and with all thy strength, and with all thy mind: and thy neighbor as thyself. And he said to him: Thou hast answered right: this do, and thou shalt live. But he willing to justify himself, said to Jesus: And who is my neighbor? And Jesus answering, said: A certain man went down from Jerusalem to Jericho, and fell among robbers, who also stripped him, and having wounded him went away, leaving him half dead. And it chanced, that a certain priest went down the same way: and seeing him, passed by. In like manner also a Levite, when he was near the place and saw him, passed by. But a certain Samaritan being on his journey, came near him; and seeing him, was moved with compassion. And going up to him, bound up his wounds, pouring in oil and wine: and setting him upon his own beast, brought him to an inn, and took care of him. And the next day he took out two pence, and gave to the host, and said: Take care of him; and whatsoever thou shalt spend over and above, I, at my return, will repay thee. Which of these three, in thy opinion, was neighbor to him that fell among the robbers? But he said: He that shewed mercy to him. And Jesus said to him: Go, and do thou in like manner. Luke 10:25–37

With the sacraments are to be found both the communication of Grace, the life of the one God, and the grace of neighborliness, the consequence of life in the triune God. When Christ, through the parable of the Good Samaritan, identified the 'neighbor' as the one who showed mercy to another and advised the lawyer who questioned Him to do likewise, He joined the first part of the greatest Commandment, the love of God, indivisibly to the second, for who is more merciful to us than God, and who but God is the greatest but least understood of neighbors, being not only the 'good Samaritan', but also the 'great Samaritan', the one who provides for our complete healing even when seemingly absent? With the hastily administered wayside 'first aid' and with the more leisurely and provided for recuperative stay at the inn, we find evidence of both the sacraments themselves and the 'sacrament' of the Church (marriage in the all-inclusive sense). With the 'binding up of the wounds', the 'pouring in of oil and wine' and the 'care-taking'—both personal and delegated—at the inn, we have a parable of the sacramental mysteries: in the 'binding up of the wounds' can be seen the sacraments of Bapstism and Repentance (covered in the first chapter); with the 'pouring in of oil and wine' can be seen the two anointings of Chrismation and Unction—both using holy oils—and the Priesthood, that means by which all the sacramental mysteries, but especially the outpouring of the Holy Mysteries in the Eucharist, are assured; while through the door of the inn thrown wide can be seen that abiding together with our Savior Christ, both for 'awhile' in the Eucharist, and when He 'returns to repay' in the awesome gladness of His Second Coming. With such mysteries as these, what remains of 'ordinary life', what remains of 'tragedy'? With eyes closed against the pain, we lie there on the ground as a numbness begins to consume our body; only our ears are attentive to the footsteps drawing nigh…

THE SEVEN SACRAMENTS

OUR FATHER WHO ART IN HEAVEN HALLOWED BE THY NAME — Holy Orders

THY KINGDOM COME — Chrismation

THY WILL BE DONE ON EARTH AS IT IS IN HEAVEN — Marriage

GIVE US THIS DAY OUR DAILY BREAD — Eucharist

AND FORGIVE US OUR TRESPASSES AS WE FORGIVE THOSE WHO TRESPASS AGAINST US — Confession

AND LEAD US NOT INTO TEMPTATION — Unction

BUT DELIVER US FROM EVIL — Baptism

HOLY ORDERS

THE LAYING ON AND THE LIFTING UP OF HANDS

We see our human hierarchy… as our nature allows, pluralized in a great variety of perceptible symbols lifting us upward hierarchically until we are brought as far as we can be into the unity of divinization. — Dionysius the Areopagite, *The Ecclesiastical Hierarchy,* 373a.

OUR FATHER WHO
ART IN HEAVEN
HALLOWED BE
THY NAME

Our Father who art in heaven, hallowed be thy name
Thy kingdom come
Lord, I have cried unto Thee, hearken unto me; attend to the voice of my supplication when I cry unto Thee.

Thy will be done on earth as it is in heaven
Let my prayer be set forth as incense before Thee, the lifting up of my hands as an evening sacrifice.

Give us this day our daily bread
Set, O Lord, a watch before my mouth, and a door of enclosure round about my lips.

And forgive us our trespasses as we forgive those who trespass against us
and lead us not into temptation
Incline not my heart unto words of evil, to make excuse with excuses in sins, with men that work iniquity; and I will not join with their chosen.

But deliver us from evil
The righteous man will chasten me with mercy and reprove me; as for the oil of the sinner, let it not anoint my head. Psalm 140:1–6

THY KINGDOM COME

Bishop: Till I come, attend unto reading, to exhortation, and to doctrine. Neglect not the grace that is in thee, which was given thee by prophesy, with imposition of the hands of the priesthood. Meditate upon these things, be wholly in these things: that thy profiting may be manifest to all. Take heed to thyself and to doctrine: be earnest in them. For in doing this thou shalt both save thyself and them that hear thee. 1 Tim. 4:13–16

THY WILL BE DONE
ON EARTH AS IT IS
IN HEAVEN

Priest: And when they had ordained to them priests in every church, and had prayed with fasting, they commended them to the Lord, in whom they believed. Acts 14:22
I desire therefore, first of all, that supplications, prayers, intercessions, and thanksgivings be made for all men: for kings, and for all that are in high station: that we may lead a quiet and a peaceable life in all piety and chastity. For this is good and acceptable in the sight of God our Savior, who will have all men to be saved, and to come to the knowledge of the truth. For there is one God, and one mediator of God and men, the man Christ Jesus: who gave himself a redemption for all, a testimony in due times. Whereunto I am appointed a preacher and an apostle, (I say the truth, I lie not,) a doctor of the Gentiles in faith and truth. I will therefore that men pray in every place, lifting up pure hands, without anger and contention. 1 Tim. 2:1–9

Deacon: Then the twelve calling together the multitude of the disciples, said: It is not reason that we should leave the word of God, and serve tables. Wherefore, brethren, look ye out among you seven men of good reputation, full of the Holy Spirit and wisdom, whom we may appoint over this business. But we will give ourselves continually to prayer, and to the ministry of the word. And the saying was liked by all the multitude. And they chose Stephen, a man full of faith, and of the Holy Spirit, and Philip, and Prochorus, and Nicanor, and Timon, and Parmenas, and Nicolas, a proselyte of Antioch. These they set before the apostles; and they praying, imposed hands upon them. Acts 6:2–6

And when Simon saw, that by the imposition of the hands of the apostles, the Holy Spirit was given, he offered them money, saying: Give me also this power, that on whomsoever I shall lay my hands, He may receive the Holy Spirit. But Peter said to him: Keep thy money to thyself, to perish with thee, because thou hast thought that the gift of God may be purchased with money. Thou hast no part nor lot in this matter. For thy heart is not right in the sight of God. Do penance therefore for this thy wickedness; and pray to God, that perhaps this thought of thy heart may be forgiven thee. For I see thou art in the gall of bitterness, and in the bonds of iniquity. Then Simon answering, said: Pray you for me to the Lord, that none of these things which you have spoken may come upon me. Acts 8:18–24

THE PRIESTHOOD

Our Father who art in heaven
Hallowed be thy name
Thy kingdom come

A HIGH PRIEST FOREVER ACCORDING TO THE ORDER OF MELCHISEDECH

So Christ also did not glorify himself, that he might be made a high priest; but he that said unto him: Thou art my Son; this day have I begotten thee. And, whereas indeed he was the Son of God, he learned of obedience by the things which he suffered. And, being consummated, he became, to all that obey him, the cause of eternal salvation; called by God a high priest according to the order of Melchisedech… For this Melchisedech was king of Salem, priest of the most high God… Without father, without mother, without genealogy, having neither beginning of days nor end of life, but likened unto the Son of God, continueth a priest forever. Heb. 5:5, 8–10, 7:1, 3

Wherefore, when he cometh into the world he saith: Sacrifice and oblation thou wouldst not; but a body thou hast fitted to me… Then said I: Behold, I come to do thy will, O God… in the which will, we are sanctified by the oblation of the body of Jesus Christ once. And every priest indeed standeth daily ministering, and often offering the same sacrifices, which can never take away sins. But this man, offering one sacrifice for sins, forever sitteth on the right hand of God. Heb. 10:5, 9–12

For I have received of the Lord that which also I delivered unto you, that the Lord Jesus, the same night in which he was betrayed, took bread, and, giving thanks, broke, and said: Take ye and eat: This is my body, which shall be delivered for you. This do for the commemoration of me. 1 Cor. 11:23–24

AND FORGIVE US OUR TRESPASSES AS WE FORGIVE THOSE WHO TRESPASS AGAINST US

Having therefore, brethren, a confidence in the entering into the Holies by the blood of Christ; a new and living way which he hath dedicated for us through the veil, that is to say, his flesh; and a high priest over the house of God; let us draw near with a true heart, in fulness of faith, having our hearts sprinkled from an evil conscience, and our bodies washed with clean water... And let us consider one another, to provoke unto charity and to good works; not forsaking our assembly, as some are accustomed; but comforting one another, and so much the more as we see the day approaching. Heb. 10:19–22, 24–25

AND LEAD US NOT INTO TEMPTATION

Having, therefore, a great high priest who hath passed into the heavens, Jesus the Son of God; let us hold fast our confession. For we have not a priest who cannot have compassion on our infirmities; but one tempted in all things like as we are, without sin. Let us go, therefore, with confidence to the throne of grace; that we may obtain mercy and find grace in seasonable aid. Heb. 4:14–16

BUT DELIVER US FROM EVIL

For Jesus is not entered into the Holies made with hands, the patterns of the true; but into Heaven itself, that he may appear now in the presence of God for us. Nor yet that he should offer himself often, as the high priest entereth into the Holies every year with the blood of others; for then he ought to have suffered from the beginning of the world. But now once, at the end of ages, he hath appeared for the destruction of sin by the sacrifice of himself. And as it is appointed unto men once to die, and after this the judgment; so also Christ was offered once to exhaust the sins of many. The second time he shall appear without sin to them that expect him unto salvation. Heb. 9:24–28

Thy will be done on earth as it is in heaven
Give us this day our daily bread

JESUS CHRIST: HIGH PRIEST, SACRIFICE AND VICTIM

A VERBAL ICON OF THE JESUS PRAYER

LORD JESUS CHRIST SON OF GOD

High Priest: Having therefore, brethren, a confidence in the entering into the Holies by the blood of Christ; a new and living way which he hath dedicated for us through the veil, that is to say, his flesh; and a high priest over the house of God; let us draw near with a true heart, in fulness of faith, having our hearts sprinkled from an evil conscience, and our bodies washed with clean water. Heb. 10:19–22

HAVE MERCY ON ME

Sacrifice: Wherefore, when he cometh into the world he saith: Sacrifice and oblation thou wouldest not; but a body thou hast fitted to me. Holocausts for sin did not please thee. Then said I: Behold, I come. In the head of the book it is written of me that I should do thy will, O God. In saying before: Sacrifices and oblations and holocausts for sin thou wouldest not; neither are they pleasing to thee, which are offered according to the law; then said I: Behold, I come to do thy will, O God; he taketh away the first, that he may establish that which followeth. In the which will, we are sanctified by the oblation of `the body of Jesus Christ once. Heb. 10:5–10

Therefore doth the Father love me; because I lay down my life, that I may take it up again. No man taketh it away from me; but I lay it down of myself. And I have power to lay it down; and I have power to take it up again. This commandment have I received of my Father. John 10:17–18

A SINNER *Victim*: Him, who knew no sin, he hath made sin for us; that we might be made the justice of God in him. 2 Cor. 5:21

And forgive us our trespasses as we
forgive those who trespass against us

APOSTLESHIP

OUR FATHER WHO ART IN HEAVEN HALLOWED BE THY NAME Father… Sanctify them in truth. Thy word is truth. As thou hast sent me into the world, I also have sent them into the world. And for them do I sanctify myself, that they also may be sanctified in truth. And not for them only do I pray, but for them also who through their word shall believe in me. John 17:1, 17–20

THY KINGDOM COME They therefore who were come together asked him, saying: Lord, wilt thou at this time restore again the kingdom of Israel? But he said to them: It is not for your to know the times or moments, which the Father has put in his own power; but you shall receive the power of the Holy Spirit coming upon you, and you shall be witnesses unto me in Jerusalem, and in all Judea and Samaria, and even to the uttermost part of the earth. Acts 1:6–8

THY WILL BE DONE ON EARTH AS IT IS IN HEAVEN Be ye subject therefore to every human creature for God's sake; whether it be to the king as excelling, or to governors as sent by him for the punishment of evil-doers, and for the praise of the good. For so is the will of God, that by doing well you may put to silence the ignorance of foolish men; as free and not as making liberty a cloak for malice but as the servants of God. 1 Pet. 2:13–16

GIVE US THIS DAY OUR DAILY BREAD He that is greater among you, let him become as the younger; and he that is the leader, as he that serveth. For which is greater, he that sitteth at table or he that serveth? Is not he that sitteth at table? But I am in the midst of you, as he that serveth… And I dispose to you, as my Father hath disposed to me, a kingdom; that you may eat and drink at my table, in my kingdom; and may sit upon thrones, judging the twelve tribes of Israel. Luke 22:26–27, 29–30

AND FORGIVE US OUR TRESPASSES AS WE FORGIVE THOSE WHO TRESPASS AGAINST US Peace be to you. As the Father hath sent me, I also send you. When he had said this, he breathed on them; and he said to them: Receive ye the Holy Spirit; whose sins you shall forgive, they are forgiven them; and whose sins you shall retain, they are retained. John 20:21–23

Peter came unto him and said: Lord, how often shall my brother offend against me, and I forgive him? Till seven times? Jesus saith to him: I say not to thee, till seven times, but till seventy times seven times. Matt. 18:21–22

AND LEAD US NOT INTO TEMPTATION Behold, the hour cometh, and it is now come, that you shall be scattered every man to his own and shall leave me alone. And yet I am not alone, because the

Father is with me. These things I have spoken to you, that in me you may have peace. In the world you shall have distress. But have confidence. I have overcome the world. John 16:32–33

BUT DELIVER
US FROM EVIL

And when he was come into the house his disciples secretly asked him: Why could not we cast him [the deaf and dumb spirit] out? And he said to them: This kind can go out by nothing but by prayer and fasting. Mark 9:27–28

And lead us not into temptation

THE APOSTLES

OUR FATHER WHO
ART IN HEAVEN
HALLOWED BE
THY NAME

Philip:
Philip saith to him: Lord, shew us the Father and it is enough for us. Jesus saith to him: Have I been so long a time with you and have you not known me? Philip, he that seeth me seeth the Father also... The words that I speak to you, I speak not of myself. But the Father who abideth in me, he doth the works... Amen, Amen, I say to you, he that believeth in me, the works that I do he also shall do... because I go the Father; and whatsoever you shall ask the Father in my name, that will I do; that the Father may be glorified in the Son. John 14:8–10, 12–13

THY KINGDOM COME

Andrew, the First-Called:
And Andrew, the brother of Simon Peter... findeth first his brother Simon and saith to him: We have found the Messias, which is, being interpreted, the Christ. John 1:40–41
Nathanael, the Israelite without guile:
Rabbi, thou art the Son of God; thou art the king of Israel. Jesus answered and said to him: Because I said unto thee, I saw thee under the fig-tree, thou believest; greater things than these shalt thou see. and he saith to him: Amen, amen, I say to you, you shall see the heaven opened and the angels of God ascending and descending upon the Son of man. John 1:49–51

THY WILL BE DONE
ON EARTH AS IT IS
IN HEAVEN

James and John, the Sons of Thunder:
(I am come to cast fire on the earth. And what will I, but that it be kindled? And I have a baptism wherewith I am to be baptized. And how am I straitened until it be accomplished. Luke 12:49–50)
And when his disciples, James and John, had seen [that the Samaritans received him not] they said: Lord, wilt thou that we command fire to come down from heaven and consume them? And turning he rebuked them, saying: You know not of what spirit you are. The Son of man came not to destroys souls, but to save. Luke 9:54–56
Grant to us that we may sit, one on thy right hand and the other on thy left hand in thy glory. And Jesus said to them: You know not what you ask. Can you drink of the chalice that I drink of or be baptized with the baptism wherewith I am baptized? But they said to him: We can. And Jesus saith to them: You shall indeed drink of the chalice that I drink of; and with the baptism wherewith I am baptized you shall be baptized. But to sit on my right hand or on my left is not is not mine to give to you, but to them for whom it is prepared... Who-

soever will be first among you shall be the servant of all. For the Son of man also is not come to be ministered unto; but to minister and to give his life as a redemption for many. Mark 10:37–40, 44–45

GIVE US THIS DAY
OUR DAILY BREAD

Simon Peter:
As the living Father hath sent me and I live by the Father; so he that eateth me, the same also shall live by me… Many therefore of his disciples, hearing it, said: This saying is hard; and who can hear it? (…) After this, many of his disciples went back and walked no more with him. Then Jesus said to the twelve: Will you also go away? And Simon Peter answered him: Lord, to whom shall we go? Thou hast the words of eternal life. And we have believed and have known that thou art the Christ, the Son of God. John 6:58, 61, 67–70
When therefore they had dined, Jesus saith to Simon Peter: Simon, son of John, lovest thou me more than these? He saith to him: Yea, Lord, thou knowest that I love thee. He saith to him: Feed my lambs. He saith to him again: Simon, son of John, lovest thou me? He saith to him: Yea, Lord, thou knowest that I love thee. He saith to him: Feed my lambs. He said to him the third time: Simon, son of John, lovest thou me? Peter was grieved because he had said to him the third time: lovest thou me? And he said to him: Lord, thou knowest all things; thou knowest that I love thee. He said to him: Feed my sheep. John 21:15–17

AND FORGIVE US OUR
TRESPASSES AS WE
FORGIVE THOSE
WHO TRESPASS
AGAINST US

Paul, first persecutor and then apostle:
And last of all, he was seen also by me, as by one born out of due time. For I am the least of the apostles, who am not worthy to be called an apostle, because I persecuted the church of God. But, by the grace of God, I am what I am. And his grace in me hath not been void; but I have labored more abundantly than all they. Yet not I, but the grace of God with me. 1 Cor. 15:8–10

AND LEAD US NOT
INTO TEMPTATION

Thomas, the twin:
Except I shall see in his hands the print of the nails and put my finger into the place of the nails and put my hand into his side, I will not believe… Jesus cometh, the doors being shut, and stood in the midst and said: Peace be to you. Then he saith to Thomas: Put in thy finger hither and see my hands; and bring hither thy hand and put it into my side; and be not faithless, but believing. Thomas answered and said to him: My Lord and my God. Jesus saith to him: Because thou hast seen me, Thomas, thou hast believed; blessed are they that have not seen and have believed. John 20:25–29

BUT DELIVER
US FROM EVIL

Judas Iscariot:
Those whom thou gavest me have I kept; and none of them is lost, but the son of perdition, that the scripture may be fulfilled. John 17:12

But deliver us from evil

THE WASHING OF FEET

JOHN 13:3–19

OUR FATHER WHO
ART IN HEAVEN
HALLOWED BE
THY NAME
Knowing that the Father had given him all things into his hands and that he came from God, and goeth to God;

OUR FATHER WHO ART IN HEAVEN HALLOWED BE THY NAME

Knowing that the Father had given him all things into his hands and that he came from God, and goeth to God;

THY KINGDOM COME

He riseth from supper, and layeth aside his garments, and having taken a towel, girded himself. After that, he putteth water into a basin, and began to wash the feet of the disciples, and to wipe them with the towel wherewith he was girded. He cometh therefore to Simon Peter. And Peter saith to him: Lord, dost thou wash my feet? Jesus answered, and said to him: What I do thou knowest not now; but thou shalt know hereafter.

THY WILL BE DONE ON EARTH AS IT IS IN HEAVEN

Peter saith to him: Thou shalt never wash my feet. Jesus answered him: If I wash thee not, thou shalt have no part with me. Simon Peter saith to him: Lord, not only my feet, but also my hands and my head.

GIVE US THIS DAY OUR DAILY BREAD

Jesus saith to him: He that is washed, needeth not but to wash his feet, but is clean wholly.[1]

AND FORGIVE US OUR TRESPASSES AS WE FORGIVE THOSE WHO TRESPASS AGAINST US

And you are clean, but not all. For he knew who he was that would betray him; therefore he said: You are not all clean. Then after he had washed their feet, and taken his garments, being set down again, he said to them: Know you what I have done to you? You call me Master, and Lord; and you say well, for so I am. If then I being your Lord and Master, have washed your feet; you also ought to wash one another's feet. For I have given you an example, that as I have done to you, so you do also.

AND LEAD US NOT INTO TEMPTATION

Amen, amen I say to you: The servant is not greater than his lord; neither is the apostle greater than he that sent him. If you know these things, you shall be blessed if you do them.

BUT DELIVER US FROM EVIL

I speak not of you all: I know whom I have chosen. But that the scripture may be fulfilled: He that eateth bread with me, shall lift up his heel against me. At present I tell you, before it come to pass: that when it shall come to pass, you may believe that I am he.

---

1. See how, in lowliness, truest needs are met.

THE DIVINE MYSTERIES

WORDS OF THY PRIEST, THE RIGHTLY DIVIDED WORD OF THY TRUTH

DIVINE LITURGY

It is proper and right to sing to You, bless You, praise You, thank You and worship You in all places of Your dominion; for You are God ineffable, beyond comprehension, invisible, beyond understanding, existing forever and always the same; You and Your only begotten Son and Your Holy Spirit. You brought us into being out of nothing, and when we fell, You raised us up again. You did not cease doing everything until You led us to heaven and granted us Your kingdom to come. For all these things we thank You and Your only begotten Son and Your Holy Spirit; for all things that we know and do not know, for blessings seen andunseen that have been bestowed upon us. We also thank You for this liturgy which You are pleased to accept from our hands, even though You are surrounded by thousands of Archangels and tens of thousands of Angels, by the Cherubim and Seraphim, six-winged, many-eyed, soaring with their wings, singing the victory hymn, proclaiming, crying out, and saying: Holy, holy, holy, Lord Sabaoth, heaven and earth are filled with Your glory. Hosanna in the highest. Blessed is He who comes in the name of the Lord. Hosanna to God in the highest. Together with these blessed powers, merciful Master, we also proclaim and say: You are holy and most holy, You and Your only begotten Son and Your Holy Spirit. You are holy and most holy, and sublime is Your glory. You so loved Your world that You gave Your only begotten Son so that whoever believes in Him should not perish, but have eternal life.
(From the *Liturgy of St John Chrysostom*)

CHRISMATION

Blessed are You, Lord, God, Ruler of all, Source of all good things, Sun of Righteousness. You have raised up a light of salvation for those in darkness, through the manifestation of Your only-begotten Son and our God. Though we are unworthy, You have given us a blessed cleansing in holy water and a divine sanctification through holy anointing. Now, to Your newly enlightened servant, You have been pleased to give new birth by water and the Spirit, for the forgiveness of his (her) sins, whether committed willingly or unwillingly. Therefore, O Master and gracious King of all, grant him (her) also the seal of the gift of Your holy, almighty and adorable Spirit and the communion of the holy Body and precious Blood of Your Christ. Keep him (her) in Your holiness, strengthen him (her) in the true faith, and deliver him (her) from the evil one and all his deceitful ways. Keep him (her) in purity and righteousness by a fear of You that brings salvation, that he (she) may please You in his (her) every word and deed and become a son (daughter) and an heir of Your heavenly kingdom. For You are our God, a God of mercy and salvation, and we give glory to You, Father, Son and Holy Spirit, now and ever and forever. Amen. *After this prayer, the priest anoints the baptized person with holy chrism, making the sign of the cross on the forehead, eyes, nostrils, mouth, ears, breast hands and feet saying:* The seal of the gift of the Holy Spirit. Amen.

GIVE US THIS DAY
OUR DAILY BREAD
AND FORGIVE US OUR
TRESPASSES AS WE
FORGIVE THOSE
WHO TRESPASS
AGAINST US

BAPTISM

Blessed is God who enlightens and sanctifies everyone coming into the world, now and ever and forever. Amen. *The priest then takes some of the oil and makes the sign of the cross with it on the forehead, breast ears, shoulders, hands and feet of the candidate, saying: Forehead:* The servant of God (Name) is anointed with the oil of gladness in the Name of the Father, and of the Son and of the Holy Spirit. That his (her) mind may be opened to the understanding and acceptance of the mysteries of the faith of Christ, and to the knowledge of His truth, now and ever, and forever, amen. *Breast:* For the healing of soul and body, and that he (she) may love the Lord God with all his (her) heart, with all his (her) soul, and with all his (her) mind, and that he (she) may love his (her) neighbor as himself (herself). *Ears:* That his (her) ears may be ready to listen to the teachings of faith, and accept the words of the divine gospel. *Shoulders:* That he (she) may willingly take upon himself (herself) the easy yoke of Christ and gladly carry His light burden and that he (she) may shun all craving of sensuality. *Hands:* That he (she) may innocently raise his (her) hands to heaven and do the right thing at all times and bless the Lord. *Feet:* That he (she) may walk in the path of the commandments of Christ.

THE EXORCISMS

Drive out from him (her), O Lord, every evil and unclean spirit hiding and lurking in his (her) heart: the spirit of deceit, the spirit of wickedness, the spirit of idolatry and all greed, the spirit of untruth and every impurity brought about by the prompting of the devil. Make him (her) a spiritual lamb of the holy flock of Your Christ, a worthy member of Your Church, a son (daughter) and an heir to Your kingdom; that living according to Your commandments, preserving the seal unbroken and keeping his (her) baptismal robe undefiled, he (she) may obtain the happiness of the saints in Your kingdom. Through the grace, the mercies and the love of mankind of Your only-begotten Son, with whom You are blessed, together with Your All-holy, good and life-creating Spirit, now and ever and forever. Amen.

THE EXORCISMS (*continued*)

The Lord rebukes you, Satan: the Lord who came into the world and dwelt among us to destroy your tyranny and to deliver humanity; The Lord, who upon the tree triumphed over hostile powers, when the sun was darkened and the earth quaked, when the graves were opened and the bodies of the saints arose; the Lord, who by death destroyed death, and left powerless him who had the power of death, that is you, Satan. I adjure you by God who has shown us the tree of life and placed the Cherubim and the flaming sword every way to guard it. Be rebuked! I rebuke you by him who walked upon the surface of the sea as on dry land and rebuked the stormy winds, whose frown dries up the sea and whose rebuke melts away the mountains, for He himself now commands you through us! Be afraid, depart and keep away from this creature and never dare to return or hide yourself within him (her); lie not in wait for him (her) nor scheme against him (her) neither during the night nor during the day, neither in the morning nor at the noonday, but depart into your own dark abyss until the great day of judgment prepared for you! Fear God who is seated upon the Cherubim and looks upon the depths, fear him before whom the angels, archangels, thrones, dominations, principalities, powers, virtues, the many-eyed cherubim and the six-winged seraphim tremble, before whom tremble heaven and earth, the sea and all they contain. Begone and depart from the sealed and newly enlisted warrior of Christ our God; for I rebuke you by Him who walks on the wings of the wind and who makes the winds His messengers and flaming fire His servants. Begone and depart from this creature together with all your power and your angels. For glorified is the Name of the Father, and of the Son and of the Holy Spirit now and ever and forever.

BAPTISM

BAPTISM

OUR FATHER WHO ART IN HEAVEN HALLOWED BE THY NAME

I therefore, a prisoner in the Lord, beseech you that you walk worthy of the vocation in which you are called: With all humility and mildness, with patience, supporting one another in charity. Careful to keep the unity of the Spirit in the bond of peace. One body and one Spirit: as you are called in one hope of your calling. One Lord, one faith, one baptism. One God and Father of all, who is above all, and through all, and in us all. Eph. 4:1–6

THY KINGDOM COME

But after the faith is come, we are no longer under a pedagogue. For you are all the children of God by faith, in Christ Jesus. For as many of you as have been baptized in Christ, have put on Christ. There is neither Jew nor Greek: there is neither bond nor free: there is neither male nor female. For you are all one in Christ Jesus. And if you be Christ's, then are you the seed of Abraham, heirs according to the promise. Gal. 3:25–29

THY WILL BE DONE ON EARTH AS IT IS IN HEAVEN

Know you not that all we, who are baptized in Christ Jesus, are baptized in his death? For we are buried together with him by baptism into death; that as Christ is risen from the dead by the glory of the Father, so we also may walk in newness of life. Rom. 6:3–4

And Jesus coming, spoke to them, saying: All power is given to me in heaven and in earth. Going therefore, teach ye all nations: baptizing them in the name of the Father and of the Son and of the Holy Spirit. Teaching them to observe all things whatsoever I have commanded you. And behold I am with you all days, even to the consummation of the world. Matt. 28:18–20

GIVE US THIS DAY OUR DAILY BREAD

For in one Spirit were we all baptized into one body, whether Jews or Gentiles, whether bond or free; and in one Spirit we have all been made to drink. 1 Cor. 12:13

AND FORGIVE US OUR TRESPASSES AS WE FORGIVE THOSE WHO TRESPASS AGAINST US

Buried with him in baptism: in whom also you are risen again by the faith of the operation of God who hath raised him up from the dead. And you, when you were dead in your sins and the uncircumcision of your flesh, he hath quickened together with him, forgiving you all offences: blotting out the handwriting of the decree that was against us, which was contrary to us. And he hath taken the same out of the way, fastening it to the cross. Col. 2:12–14

AND LEAD US NOT INTO TEMPTATION

Now this I say, that every one of you saith: I indeed am of Paul; and I am of Apollo; and I am of Cephas; and I of Christ. Is Christ divided? Was Paul then crucified for you? or were you baptized in the name of Paul? I give God thanks, that I baptized none of you but Crispus and Caius; lest any should say that you were baptized in my name. 1 Cor. 1:12–15

BUT DELIVER US FROM EVIL

Because Christ also died once for our sins, the just for the unjust: that he might offer us to God, being put to death indeed in the flesh, but enlivened in the spirit, in which also coming he preached to those spirits that were in prison: which had been some time incredulous, when they waited for the patience of God in the days of Noe, when the ark was a building: wherein a few, that is, eight souls, were saved by water. Whereunto baptism being of the like form, now saveth you also: not the putting away of the filth of the flesh, but the examination of a good conscience towards God by the resurrection of Jesus Christ. 1 Pet. 3:18–21 He that believeth and is baptized, shall be saved: but he that believeth not shall be condemned. Mark 16:16

BAPTIZED IN THE NAME OF THE LORD

FROM *THE ACTS OF THE APOSTLES*

OUR FATHER WHO ART IN HEAVEN HALLOWED BE THY NAME

Then Paul said: John baptized the people with the baptism of penance saying: That they should believe in him, who was to come after him, that is to say, in Jesus. Having heard these things, they were baptized in the name of the Lord Jesus. And when Paul had imposed his hands on them, the Holy Spirit came upon them: and they spoke with tongues and prophesied. Acts 19:4–6

THY KINGDOM COME

But when they had believed Philip preaching of the kingdom of God, in the name of Jesus Christ, they were baptized, both men and women. Acts 8:12

THY WILL BE DONE ON EARTH AS IT IS IN HEAVEN

But he said: The God of our fathers hath preordained thee that thou shouldst know his will and see the Just One and shouldst hear the voice from his mouth. For thou shalt be his witness to all men of those things which thou hast seen and heard. And now why tarriest thou? Rise up and be baptized and wash away thy sins, invoking his name. Acts 22:14–16

GIVE US THIS DAY OUR DAILY BREAD

And bringing them out, he [the keeper of the prison] said: Masters, what must I do, that I may be saved? But they said: believe in the Lord Jesus: and thou shalt be saved, and thy house. And they preached the word of the Lord to him and to all that were in his house. And he, taking them the same hour of the night, washed their stripes: and himself was baptized, and all his house immediately. And when he had brought them into his own house, he laid the table for them: and rejoiced with all his house, believing God. Acts 16:30–34

AND FORGIVE US OUR TRESPASSES AS WE FORGIVE THOSE WHO TRESPASS AGAINST US

And when I had begun to speak, the Holy Spirit fell upon them, as upon us also in the beginning. And I remembered the word of the Lord, how that he said: John indeed baptized with water but you shall be baptized with the Holy Spirit. If then God gave them the same grace as to us also who believed in the Lord Jesus Christ: who was I, that could withstand God? Having heard these things, they held their peace and glorified God, saying: God then hath also to the Gentiles given repentance, unto life. Acts 11:15–18

AND LEAD US NOT INTO TEMPTATION

And the faithful of the circumcision, who came with Peter, were astonished for that the grace of the Holy Spirit was poured out upon the Gentiles also. For they heard them speaking with tongues and magnifying God. Then Peter answered: Can any man forbid water, that these should not be baptized, who have received the Holy Spirit, as well as we? And he commanded them to be baptized in the name of the Lord Jesus Christ. Acts 10:45–48

But Peter said to them: Do penance: and be baptized every one of you in the name of Jesus Christ, for the remission of your sins. And you shall receive the gift of the Holy Spirit. For the promise is to you and to your children and to all that are far off, whomsoever the Lord our God shall call. And with very many other words did he testify and exhort them, saying: Save yourselves from this perverse generation. They therefore that received his word were baptized: and there were added in that day about three thousand souls. Acts 2:38–41

CONFESSION

CONFESSION, A WAY TO THE ONE HEART

Confession... is a second baptism for penitents, more laborious than the first baptism, and just as necessary for salvation as the first baptism, — Nikodemos the Hagiorite, *The Exomologetarion*

And I will give them one heart, and will put a new spirit in their bowels: and I will take away the stony heart out of their flesh, and will give them a heart of flesh: that they may walk in my commandments, and keep my judgments, and do them: and that they may be my people, and I may be their God. Ezechiel 11:19–20

FREEDOM FROM THE BONDS OF SIN~ONE HEART

OUR FATHER WHO
ART IN HEAVEN
HALLOWED BE
THY NAME

For the creature was made subject to vanity: not willingly, but by reason of him that made it subject, in hope. Because the creature also itself shall be delivered from the servitude of corruption, into the liberty of the glory of the children of God. For we know that every creature groaneth and travaileth in pain, even till now. And not only it, but ourselves also, who have the firstfruits of the Spirit: even we ourselves groan within ourselves, waiting for the adoption of the sons of God, the redemption of our body. Rom. 8:20–23

SPIRITUAL COUNSEL~THE INSTRUCTED HEART OF PROVERBS 20:5

THY KINGDOM COME

But the sensual man perceiveth not these things that are of the Spirit of God. For it is foolishness to him: and he cannot understand, because it is spiritually examined. But the spiritual man judgeth all things: and he himself is judged of no man. For who hath known the mind of the Lord, that he may instruct him? But we have the mind of Christ. 1 Cor. 2:14–16

CONFESSION AND FORGIVENESS OF SIN~THE HEART OF FLESH

THY WILL BE DONE
ON EARTH AS IT IS
IN HEAVEN

Confess therefore your sins one to another: and pray one for another, that you may be saved. For the continual prayer of a just man availeth much. James 5:16

THE DECISIVE MOMENT~THE CONTRITE HEART OF PSALM 50:19

GIVE US THIS DAY
OUR DAILY BREAD

And returning to himself, he said: How many hired servants in my father's house abound with bread, and I here perish with hunger! I will arise and will go to my father and say to him: Father, I have sinned against heaven and before thee. Luke 15:17–18

EXAMINATION OF CONSCIENCE~THE STONY HEART

AND FORGIVE US OUR
TRESPASSES AS WE
FORGIVE THOSE
WHO TRESPASS
AGAINST US
AND LEAD US NOT
INTO TEMPTATION

Brethren, and if a man be overtaken in any fault, you, who are spiritual, instruct such a one in the spirit of meekness, considering thyself, lest thou also be tempted. Bear ye one another's burdens: and so you shall fulfil the law of Christ. Gal. 6:1–2

BUT DELIVER
US FROM EVIL

If we say that we have no sin, we deceive ourselves and the truth is not in us. If we confess our sins, he is faithful and just, to forgive us our sins and to cleanse us from all iniquity. 1 John 1:8–9

BETWEEN DELIVERANCE AND DEIFICATION
THE SIGNS OF FORGIVENESS OF SINS FROM GOD

ACCORDING TO NIKODEMUS THE HAGIORITE

OUR FATHER WHO
ART IN HEAVEN
HALLOWED BE
THY NAME

DEIFICATION

THY KINGDOM COME

4th sign: "when a person removes all of the passionate effects of sin from his heart, and forgets them to such an extent that they no longer assault him"[1]

THY WILL BE DONE
ON EARTH AS IT IS
IN HEAVEN

3rd sign: "when someone remembers his sins and rejoices and glorifies God on account of the many virtues he acquired on account of his sins through divine grace and repentance"

GIVE US THIS DAY
OUR DAILY BREAD

FRERQUENT COMMUNION OF THE
IMMACULATE MYSTERIES OF CHRIST[2]

AND FORGIVE US OUR
TRESPASSES AS WE
FORGIVE THOSE
WHO TRESPASS
AGAINST US

2nd sign: "when a person remembers his sins dispassionately, that is, without pleasure or grief and hate"

AND LEAD US NOT
INTO TEMPTATION

1st sign: "a person hates sin from the bottom of his heart whenever it is recollected, being afraid that he might again fall into sin"

BUT DELIVER
US FROM EVIL

DELIVERANCE

---

1. All quoted passages from Nikodemus the Hagiorite's *Exomologetarion*, p. 433.

2. Frequent communion is 'in the midst' of these four signs, not as one of them, but as one with 'deliverance' and 'deification'. And yet it too is a sign in how many ways of God's forgiveness of sins *in* the sacrament of Confession. See Nikodemus the Hagiorite, *Concerning Frequent Communion of the Immaculate Mysteries of Christ*, pp. 72–73 (this work includes a commentary on the Lord's Prayer).

ANOINTINGS

THE SACRAMENT OF HEALING

Is any man sick among you? Let him bring in the priests of the church and let them pray over him, anointing him with oil in the name of the Lord. And the prayer of faith shall save the sick man. And the Lord shall raise him up; and if he be in sins, they shall be forgiven him. James 5:14–15

OUR FATHER WHO ART IN HEAVEN

Jesus saith: Take away the stone. Martha, the sister of him that was dead, saith to him: Lord, by this time he stinketh, for he is now of four days. Jesus saith to her: Did not I say to thee that if thou believe, thou shalt see the glory of God? They took therefore the stone away. And Jesus, lifting up his eyes, said: Father, I give thee thanks that thou hast heard me. And I knew that thou hearest me always; but because of the people who stand about have I said it, that they may believe that thou hast sent me. When he had said these things, he cried with a loud voice: Lazarus, come forth. And presently he that had been dead came forth. John 11:39–44

HALLOWED BE THY NAME

And in the synagogue there was a man who had an unclean devil; and he cried out with a loud voice, saying: Let us alone. What have we to do with thee, Jesus of Nazareth? Art thou come to destroy us? I know thee who thou art, the holy one of God. And Jesus rebuked him, saying: Hold thy peace and go out of him. And, when the devil had thrown him into the midst, he went out of him and hurt him not at all. Luke 4:33–35

THY KINGDOM COME

And, behold, two blind men then sitting by the way-side heard that Jesus passed by. And they cried out, saying: O Lord, thou son of David, have mercy on us.[1] And the multitude rebuked them that they should hold their peace. But they cried out the more, saying: O Lord, thou son of David, have mercy on us. And Jesus stood and called them and said: What will ye that I do to you? They say to him: Lord, that our eyes be opened. And Jesus, having compassion on them, touched their eyes; and immediately they saw and followed him. Matt. 20:30–34

THY WILL BE DONE ON EARTH AS IT IS IN HEAVEN

And Jesus, passing by, saw a man who was blind from his birth. And is disciples asked him: Rabbi, who hath sinned, this man or his parents, that he should be born blind? Jesus answered: Neither hath this man sinned, nor his parents; but that the works of God should be made manifest in him,[2] I must work the works of him that sent me, whilst it is day; the night cometh, when no man can work. As long as I am in the world, I am the light of the world. When he had said these things, he spat on the ground and made clay of the spittle and spread

---

1. This is the first utterance of the 'Jesus Prayer'. As it brought healing to the eyes of the blind, may it also heal the blindness of our hearts so that we might see God and live.

2. Is Christ speaking about just this individual, or is he speaking about all who suffer, even those who have sinned? In the Old Testament (Exod. 20:5) we hear God say to the idolaters: "I am the Lord thy God, mighty, jealous, visiting the iniquity of the fathers upon the children, unto the third and fourth generation of them that hate me..." But Christ has come not to abolish the Law but to fulfill it, a fulfillment declared in the very next verse: "...and shewing mercy unto thousands [of generations] to them that love me, and keep my commandments." What is abolished by Mercy and Love incarnate is the power of suffering, sin and death over us, the power of anything that might 'determine' our lives, for with God—and with the love of God—all things are possible. Whenever the 'daystar' of Christ—the love of Christ and Christ himself—rises in our hearts, then light breaks across the world, and the world, even in its compulsive rush to extinction, is "delivered from the servitude of corruption, into the liberty of the glory of the children of God" (Rom. 8:21).

the clay upon the eyes, and said to him: Go, wash in the pool of Siloe, which is interpreted Sent. He went therefore and washed; and he came seeing. John 9:1–7

GIVE US THIS DAY OUR DAILY BREAD

And, behold, a woman of Canaan, who came out of those coasts, crying out, said to him: Have mercy on me, O Lord, thou son of David; my daughter is grievously troubled by a devil. Who answered her not a word. And his disciples came and besought him, saying: Send her away, for she crieth after us. And he, answering, said: I was not sent but to the sheep that are lost of the house of Israel. But she came and adored him, saying: Lord, help me. Who answering said: It is not good to take the bread of the children and cast it to the dogs. But she said: Yea, Lord; for the whelps also eat of the crumbs that fall from the table of their masters. Then Jesus, answering, said to her: O woman, great is thy faith. Be it done to thee as thou wilt. And her daughter was cured from that hour. Matt. 15:22–28

AND FORGIVE US OUR TRESPASSES AS WE FORGIVE THOSE WHO TRESPASS AGAINST US

Master, I have brought my son to thee, having a dumb spirit. Who, wheresoever he taketh him, dasheth him; and he foameth and gnasheth with the teeth and pineth away. And I spoke to thy disciples to cast him out; and they could not. Who, answering him said: O incredulous generation, how long shall I be with you? How long shall I suffer you? Bring him unto me. And they brought him. And, when he had seen him, immediately the spirit troubled him; and being thrown down upon the ground he rolled about foaming. And he asked his father: How long time is it since this hath happened unto him? But he said: From his infancy. And oftentimes hath he cast him into the fire and into the waters to destroy him. But, if thou canst do anything, help us, having compassion on us. And Jesus saith to him: If thou canst believe, all things are possible to him that believeth. And immediately the father of the boy, crying out, with tears said: I do believe, Lord. Help my unbelief.1 And when Jesus saw the multitude running together, he threatened the unclean spirit, saying to him: Deaf and dumb spirit, I command thee, go out of him and enter not any more into him. And crying out and greatly tearing him he went out of him. And he became as dead, so that many said: He is dead. But Jesus, taking him by the hand, lifted him up. And he arose. And when he was come into the house his disciples secretly asked him: Why could not we cast him out? And he said to them: This kind can go out by nothing but by prayer and fasting. Mark 9:16–28

AND LEAD US NOT INTO TEMPTATION

And there was a certain man there [at the pond of Bethsaida] that had been eight and thirty years under his infirmity. Him when Jesus had seen lying, and knew that he had been now a long time, he saith to him: Wilt thou be made whole? The infirm man answered him: Sir, I have no man, when the water is troubled, to put me into the pond. For, whilst I am coming, another goeth down before me. Jesus saith to him: Arise, take up thy bed and walk. And immediately the man was made whole; and he took up his bed and walked…

---

1. In these very words are to be found the 'forgiveness' for the 'trespass' of every 'incredulous generation': "I do believe, Lord. Help my unbelief." If the Lord is master over the healing of our bodies, even more so is He master over the healing of our souls. And, in the greatest of difficulties—both our own and that of others —, what does He ask? Prayer and fasting—the very thing asked of us when we prepare to receive our Lord in the Communion of his Body and Blood.

Afterwards, Jesus findeth him in the temple and saith to him: Behold, thou art made whole; sin no more, lest some worse thing happen to thee. John 5:5–9, 14

BUT DELIVER
US FROM EVIL

And, behold, they brought to him one sick of the palsy lying in a bed. And Jesus, seeing their faith, said to the man sick of the palsy: Be of good heart, son. Thy sins are forgiven thee. And, behold, some of the scribes said within themselves: He blasphemeth. And Jesus, seeing their thoughts, said: Why do you think evil in your hearts? Which is easier, to say, Thy sins are forgiven thee; or to say, Arise, and walk? But that you may know that the Son of man hath power on earth to forgive sins, (then said he to the man sick of the palsy): Arise, take up thy bed and go into thy house. And he arose and went into his house. Matt. 9:2–7

THE MYSTERIES OF THE LORD'S ANOINTED

And as for you, let the unction, which you have received from him, abide in you, and you have no need that any man teach you; but as his unction teacheth you of all things, and is truth and is no lie. And as it hath taught you, abide in him. 1 John 2:27

OUR FATHER WHO
ART IN HEAVEN
HALLOWED BE
THY NAME
THY KINGDOM COME

And Jesus, being baptized, forthwith came out of the water; and lo, the heavens were opened to him, and he saw the Spirit of God descending as a dove and coming upon him. And behold, a voice from heaven, saying: This is my beloved Son, in whom I am well pleased. Matt. 3:16–17

THY KINGDOM COME
THY WILL BE DONE
ON EARTH AS IT IS
IN HEAVEN

Jesse therefore brought his seven sons before Samuel. And Samuel said to Jesse: The Lord hath not chosen any one of these. And Samuel said to Jesse: Are here all thy sons? He answered: There remaineth yet a young one, who keepeth the sheep. And Samuel said to Jesse: Send, and fetch him, for we will not sit down till he come hither. He sent therefore and brought him. Now, he was ruddy and beautiful to behold, and of a comely face. And the Lord said: Arise, and anoint him, for this is he. Then Samuel took the horn of oil, and anointed him in the midst of his brethren. And the spirit of the Lord came upon David from that day forward. 1 Kings 16:10–13

GIVE US THIS DAY
OUR DAILY BREAD

And when Jacob awaked out of sleep, he said: Indeed the Lord is in this place, and I knew it not. And trembling he said: How terrible is this place! This is no other but the house of God, and the gate of heaven. And Jacob, arising in the morning, took the stone, which he had laid under his head, and set it up for a title, pouring oil upon the top of it. And he called the name of the city Bethel, which before was called Luza. And he made a vow, saying: If God shall be with me, and shall keep me in the way by which I walk, and shall give me bread to eat, and raiment to put on, and I shall return prosperously to my father's house: the Lord shall be my God; and this stone, which I have set up for a title, shall be called the house of God; and of all things that thou shalt give to me, I will offer tithes to thee. Gen. 28:16–22

AND FORGIVE US OUR TRESPASSES AS WE FORGIVE THOSE WHO TRESPASS AGAINST US AND LEAD US NOT INTO TEMPTATION BUT DELIVER US FROM EVIL

Jesus, therefore, six days before the pasch, came to Bethany, where Lazarus had been dead, whom Jesus raised to life. And they made him supper there; and Martha served. But Lazarus was one of them that were at table with him. Mary therefore took a pound of ointment of right spikenard, of great price, and anointed the feet of Jesus and wiped his feet with her hair. And the house was filled with the odor of the ointment. Then one of his disciples, Judas Iscariot, he that was about to betray him, said: Why was not this ointment sold for three hundred pence and given to the poor? Now he said this not because he cared for the poor, but because he was a thief and, having the purse, carried the things that were put therein. Jesus therefore said: Let her alone, that she may keep it against the day of my burial. For the poor you have always with you; but me you have not always. John 12:1–8

COMMENTARY

BAPTISM OF CHRIST IN THE JORDAN This 'cascade' of the Holy Spirit upon Christ, who stands upright in the swirling depths of the Jordan, is that heavenly 'response' to the fulfilling of "all justice" (Matt. 3:15). It is the outward sign of that anointing by the Holy Spirit and fire (Matt. 3:11)—the most penetrating of all chrisms—transmitted from On High, to be poured out first on the Apostles and then on the entire Church. And, in 'all justice', Paul has captured our own 'moment of participation' in this baptismal scene:

Being justified, therefore, by faith, let us have peace with God, through our Lord Jesus Christ; by whom also we have access through faith into this grace wherein we stand; and glory in the hope of the glory of the sons of God (*Our Father who art in heaven, hallowed be thy name*). And not only so; but we glory also in tribulations (*But deliver us from evil*), knowing that tribulation worketh patience (*And lead us not into temptation, but deliver us from evil*); and patience trial (*And forgive us our trespasses as we forgive those who trespass against us, and lead us not into temptation*); and trail hope (*Give us this day our daily bread, and forgive us our trespasses as we forgive those who trespass against us*); and hope confoundeth not (*Give us this day our daily bread*); because the charity of God is poured forth into our hearts (*Thy will be done on earth as it is in heaven*), by the Holy Spirit who is given to us (*Thy kingdom come*). Rom. 5:1–5

THE ANOINTING OF SAMUEL KING The royal psalmist has written: "Unless the Lord build the house, they labor in vain that build it" (Psalm 126:1). In the prophet Samuel's anointing of David we see the true 'wealth' of the Christian kings and emperors; in the demise of Saul we see the spiritual bankruptcy of the Christian kings and emperors. Only in the enduring royalty of the Anointed One, the Messiah, our Christ, is our hope in a Christendom justified and, yes, fulfilled even now.

THE ANOINTING OF THE BETHEL STONE Here we glimpse a prefiguration of that anointing of all creation, which begins with those vessels set aside for hallowed use : chalices and bells, churches and altars, while the gospel is being preached to every creature (Mark 16:15), and ends in the anointing of all life by the new heaven and the new earth at last poured forth.

THE ANOINTING OF CHRIST BY MARY Indeed, Mary has not poured out all of the precious ointment. Some must be retained for his burial. If we can see in Mary's anointing of the Lord a prefiguration of the sacrament of Unction, then we must be ready to share in her joy when she is unable to 'complete' this anointing at the empty tomb where, surprised by the Resurrection, "death is swallowed up in victory" (1 Cor. 15:54). This wonderful viaticum brought by the Church penetrates us through and through all the way to Christ!

CHRISMATION, THE SEAL OF THE GIFT OF THE HOLY SPIRIT

While thy body is anointed with the visible ointment, thy soul is sanctified by the Holy and life-giving Spirit. — Cyril of Jerusalem, *On the Mysteries* III, 3.

In truth, we have here a totally charismatic being. Far from a simple confirmation of baptismal promises, unction is the setting in motion of all the charismatic powers. Chrismation is inspired by the sacrings of the Old Testament, and cheirotony, χειροτονία, the laying on of hands, has been embedded in the chrismal signings. — Paul Evdokimov, *Orthodoxy*

OUR FATHER WHO
ART IN HEAVEN
HALLOWED BE
THY NAME

1) But you have the unction from the Holy One and know all things.

2) I have not written to you as to them that know not the truth, but as to them that know it: and that no lie is of the truth.

3) Who is a liar, but he who denieth that Jesus is the Christ? This is Antichrist, who denieth the Father and the Son. Whosoever denieth the Son, the same hath not the Father.

4) He that confesseth the Son hath the Father also. As for you, let that which you have heard from the beginning abide in you. If that abide in you, which you have heard from the beginning, you also shall abide in the Son and in the Father.

3') And this is the promise which he hath promised us, life everlasting.

2') These things have I written to you concerning them that seduce you.

1') And as for you, let the unction, which you have received from him abide in you. And you have no need that any man teach you: but as his unction teacheth you of all things and is truth and is no lie. And as it hath taught you, abide in him.[1] 1 John 2:20–27

THY KINGDOM COME

Now he that confirmeth us with you in Christ and that hath anointed us, is God: who also hath sealed us and given the pledge of the Spirit in our hearts. 2 Cor. 1:21–22

And I saw another angel ascending from the rising of the sun, having the sign of the living God. And he cried with a loud voice to the four angels to whom it was given to hurt the earth and the sea, saying: Hurt not the earth nor the sea nor the trees, till we sign the servants of our God in their foreheads. And I heard the number of them that were signed. An hundred forty- four thousand were signed, of every tribe of the children of Israel. Apoc. 7:2–4

THY WILL BE DONE
ON EARTH AS IT IS
IN HEAVEN

In whom we also are called by lot, being predestinated according to the purpose of him who worketh all things according to the counsel of his will. That we may be unto the praise of his glory: we who before hoped in Christ: in whom you also, after you had heard the word of truth (the gospel of your salvation), in whom also believing, you were signed with the holy Spirit of promise. Who is the pledge of our inheritance, unto the redemption of acquisition, unto the praise of his glory. Eph. 1:11–14

---

1. In this chiasmus (cf. John Breck, *The Shape of Biblical Language*, p. 347), both periphery and center are joined in the Christian's dual 'having God' and 'abiding in God', the essence of Chrismation. And so it may be said that, just as Confession restores the initiating grace of Baptism, the Eucharist restores the perfecting grace of Chrismation.

Now, when the apostles, who were in Jerusalem, had heard that Samaria had received the word of God, they sent unto them Peter and John. Who, when they were come, prayed for them that they might receive the Holy Spirit. For he was not as yet come upon any of them: but they were only baptized in the name of the Lord Jesus. Then they laid their hands upon them: and they received the Holy Spirit. Acts 8:14–17

AND FORGIVE US OUR
TRESPASSES AS WE
FORGIVE THOSE
WHO TRESPASS
AGAINST US
AND LEAD US NOT
INTO TEMPTATION
BUT DELIVER
US FROM EVIL

And grieve not the holy Spirit of God: whereby you are sealed unto the day of redemption. Let all bitterness and anger and indignation and clamor and blasphemy be put away from you, with all malice. And be ye kind one to another: merciful, forgiving one another, even as God hath forgiven you in Christ. Eph. 4:30–32

AMEN

But the sure foundation of God
standeth firm, having this seal:

the Lord
knoweth who are his;
and let every one depart from iniquity
who nameth the name of
the Lord.[1]

−2 Tim. 2:19

---

1. Setting this passage in chiastic parallel to the Jesus Prayer, fosters an ever-saying of the blessed prayer:

Lord
Jesus Christ Son of God
have mercy on me a sinner
Lord Jesus Christ Son of
God

THE MYSTICAL BODY OF CHRIST~MARRIAGE

PATRON SAINTS OF THE LORD'S PRAYER

But you are come to mount Sion, and to the city of the living God, the heavenly Jerusalem, and to the company of many thousands of angels, and to the church of the firstborn, who are written in the heavens, and to God the judge of all, and to the spirits of the just made perfect, and to Jesus the mediator of the new testament, and to the sprinkling of blood which speaketh better than that of Abel. Hebrews 12:22–24

OUR FATHER WHO ART IN HEAVEN HALLOWED BE THY NAME	Seraphim of Sarov Symeon the New Theologian
THY KINGDOM COME	Paissy Velichkovsky Cyril and Methodius Gregory the Great[1]
THY WILL BE DONE ON EARTH AS IT IS IN HEAVEN	Vladimir and Olga Maximus the Confessor
GIVE US THIS DAY OUR DAILY BREAD	John Chrysostom Basil the Great Ignatius of Antioch[2]
AND FORGIVE US OUR TRESPASSES AS WE FORGIVE THOSE WHO TRESPASS AGAINST US	Protomartyr Stephen[3] Boris and Gleb
AND LEAD US NOT INTO TEMPTATION	Andrew of Crete Mary of Egypt
BUT DELIVER US FROM EVIL	Felicity and Perpetua Martyrs of the Russian Revolution

---

1. "Servant of the servants of God"

2. Hearing the lions roar before his martyrdom at the Coliseum in Rome, he cried out: "I am the wheat of of the Lord; I must be ground by the teeth of these beasts to be made the pure bread of Christ."

3. Where Stephen gazed upon the glory of God, Saul was blinded by it; where Stephen fell to earth the first martyr, Paul arose from it reconciled, the firstfruits of Stephen's blood.

FRIEND

OUR FATHER WHO
ART IN HEAVEN
HALLOWED BE
THY NAME

You are my friends, if you do the things that I command you. I will not now call you servants: for the servant knoweth not what his lord doth. But I have called you friends: because all things whatsoever I have heard of my Father, I have made known to you. John 15:14–15

THY KINGDOM COME

Hear, O Jesus thou high priest, thou and thy friends that dwell before thee, for they are portending men: for behold, I will bring my servant the Orient. For behold the stone that I have laid before Jesus: upon one stone there are seven eyes: behold I will grave the graving thereof, saith the Lord of hosts: and I will take away the iniquity of that land in one day. In that day, saith the Lord of hosts, every man shall call his friend under the vine and under the fig tree. Zech. 3:8–10

Philip findeth Nathanael, and saith to him: We have found him of whom Moses in the law, and the prophets did write, Jesus the son of Joseph of Nazareth. And Nathanael said to him: Can any thing of good come from Nazareth? Philip saith to him: Come and see. Jesus saw Nathanael coming to him: and he saith of him: Behold an Israelite indeed, in whom there is no guile. Nathanael saith to him: Whence knowest thou me? Jesus answered, and said to him: Before that Philip called thee, when thou wast under the fig tree, I saw thee. Nathanael answered him, and said: Rabbi, thou art the Son of God, thou art the King of Israel. John 1:45–49

THY WILL BE DONE
ON EARTH AS IT IS
IN HEAVEN

If you keep my commandments, you shall abide in my love; as I also have kept my Father's commandments, and do abide in his love. These things I have spoken to you, that my joy may be in you, and your joy may be filled. This is my commandment, that you love one another, as I have loved you. Greater love than this no man hath, that a man lay down his life for his friends. John 15:10–13

GIVE US THIS DAY
OUR DAILY BREAD

And he said to them: Which of you shall have a friend, and shall go to him at midnight, and shall say to him: Friend, lend me three loaves, because a friend of mine is come off his journey to me, and I have not what to set before him. And he from within should answer, and say: Trouble me not, the door is now shut, and my children are with me in bed; I cannot rise and give thee. Yet if he shall continue knocking, I say to you, although he will not rise and give him, because he is his friend; yet, because of his importunity, he will rise, and give him as many as he needeth. And I say to you, Ask, and it shall be given you: seek, and you shall find: knock, and it shall be opened to you. Luke 11:5–9

AND FORGIVE US OUR
TRESPASSES AS WE
FORGIVE THOSE
WHO TRESPASS
AGAINST US

For John came neither eating nor drinking; and they say: He hath a devil. The Son of man came eating and drinking, and they say: Behold a man that is a glutton and a wine drinker, a friend of publicans and sinners. And wisdom is justified by her children. Then began he to upbraid the cities wherein were done the most of his miracles, for that they had not done penance. Woe to thee, Corozain, woe to thee, Bethsaida: for if in Tyre and Sidon had been wrought the miracles that have been wrought in you, they had long ago done penance in sackcloth and ashes. Matt. 11:18–21

AND LEAD US NOT INTO TEMPTATION	And I say to you, my friends: Be not afraid of them who kill the body, and after that have no more that they can do. But I will shew you whom you shall fear: fear ye him, who after he hath killed, hath power to cast into hell. Yea, I say to you, fear him. Are not five sparrows sold for two farthings, and not one of them is forgotten before God? Yea, the very hairs of your head are all numbered. Fear not therefore: you are of more value than many sparrows. Luke 12:4–7
BUT DELIVER US FROM EVIL	And he that betrayed him, gave him a sign, saying: Whomsoever I shall kiss, that is he, hold him fast. And forthwith coming to Jesus, he said: Hail, Rabbi. And he kissed him. And Jesus said to him: Friend, whereto art thou come? Then they came up, and laid hands on Jesus, and held him. Matt. 26:48–50

THE MYSTICAL BODY OF CHRIST ACCORDING TO PAUL

But we all, beholding the glory of the Lord with open face, are transformed into the same image from glory to glory, as by the Spirit of the Lord. 2 Corinthians 3:18

OUR FATHER WHO ART IN HEAVEN HALLOWED BE THY NAME	He [Christ] is the image of the invisible God, the first-born of all creation; for in him all things were created, in heaven and on earth, visible and invisible… all things were created through him and for him. He is before all things, and in him all things hold together. He is the head of the body, the church; he is the beginning, the first-born from the dead, that in everything he might be pre-eminent. For in him all the fulness of God was pleased to dwell. Col. 1:15–19
THY KINGDOM COME	If then you have been raised with Christ, seek the things that are above, where Christ is, seated at the right hand of God. Set your minds on the things that are above, not on the things that are on earth. For you have died, and your life is hid with Christ in God. When Christ who is our life appears, then you also will appear with him in glory. Col. 3:1–4
THY WILL BE DONE ON EARTH AS IT IS IN HEAVEN	Now there are varieties of gifts, but the same Spirit; and there are varieties of service, but the same Lord; and there are varieties of workings, but it is the same God who inspires them all in every one. To each is given the manifestation of the Spirit for the common good… All these are inspired by one and the same Spirit, who apportions to each one individually as he wills. For just as the body is one and has many members, and the members of the body, though many, are one body, so it is with Christ. For by one Spirit we were all baptized into one body — Jews or Greeks, slaves or free — and all were made to drink of one Spirit… Now you are the body of Christ and individually members of it. 1 Cor. 12:4–7, 11–13, 27
GIVE US THIS DAY OUR DAILY BREAD	The cup of blessing which we bless, is it not a participation in the blood of Christ? The bread which we break, is it not a participation in the body of Christ? Because there is one bread, we who are many are one body, for we all partake of the one bread. 1 Cor. 10:16–17
AND FORGIVE US OUR TRESPASSES AS WE FORGIVE THOSE WHO TRESPASS AGAINST US	For the body does not consist of one member but of many. If the… ear should say, "Because I am not an eye, I do not belong to the body," that would not make it any less a part of the body. If the whole body were an eye, where would be the hearing? … But as it is, God arranged the organs in the body, each one of them, as he chose. If all were a single organ, where would the body be? As it

is, there are many parts, yet one body. The eye cannot say to the hand, "I have no need of you," nor again the head to the feet, "I have no need of you." On the contrary, the parts of the body which seem to be weaker are indispensable, and those parts of the body we think less honorable we invest with the greater honor, and our unpresentable parts are treated with greater modesty, which our more presentable parts do not require. But God has so adjusted the body, giving the greater honor to the inferior part, that there may be no discord in the body, but that the members may have the same care for one another. If one member suffers, all suffer together; if one member is honored, al rejoice together. 1 Cor. 12:14, 16–26

AND LEAD US NOT INTO TEMPTATION BUT DELIVER US FROM EVIL

For I delight in the law of God in my inmost self, but I see in my members another law at war with the law of my mind and making me captive to the law of sin which dwells in my members. Wretched man that I am! Who will deliver me from the body of this death? Thanks be to God through Jesus Christ our Lord! So then, I of myself serve the law of God with my mind, but with my flesh I serve the law of sin. There is therefore now no condemnation for those who are in Christ Jesus. For the law of the Spirit of life in Christ Jesus has set me free from the law of sin and death. Rom. 7:22–8:2

THE MYSTICAL BODY OF CHRIST ACCORDING TO JOHN

But as many as received him, he gave them power to be made the sons of God, to them that believe in his name; who are born not of blood, nor of the will of the flesh, nor of the will of man, but of God. John 1:12–13

OUR FATHER WHO ART IN HEAVEN

That they all may be one, as thou, Father, in me, and I in thee; that they also may be one in us; that the world may believe that thou hast sent me… I in them, and thou in me; that they may be made perfect in one; and the world may know that thou hast sent me and hast loved them, as thou hast also loved me. John 17:21, 23

HALLOWED BE THY NAME

And I have made known thy name to them and will make it know; that the love wherewith thou hast loved me may be in them, and I in them. John 17:26

THY KINGDOM COME

Behold what manner of charity the Father hath bestowed upon us, that we should be called and should be the sons of God… Dearly beloved, we are now the sons of God; and it hath not yet appeared what we shall be. We know that when he shall appear we shall be like to him; because we shall see him as he is. 1 John 3:1–2

THY WILL BE DONE ON EARTH AS IT IS IN HEAVEN

By this hath the charity of God appeared towards us, because God hath sent his only begotten Son into the world, that we may live by him. In this is charity; not as though we had loved God, but because he hath loved us first, and sent his Son to be a propitiation for our sins. My dearest, if God hath so loved us, we also ought to love one another. 1 John 4:9–11

GIVE US THIS DAY OUR DAILY BREAD

For my flesh is meat indeed; and my blood is drink indeed. He that eateth my flesh and drinketh my blood abideth in me and I in him. As the living Father hath sent me and I live by the Father; so he that eateth me, the same also shall live by me. John 6:56–58

AND FORGIVE US OUR TRESPASSES AS WE FORGIVE THOSE WHO TRESPASS AGAINST US	My dearest, if God hath so loved us, we also ought to love one another. No man hath seen God at any time. If we love one another, God abideth in us; and his charity is perfected in us. 1 John 4:11–12
AND LEAD US NOT INTO TEMPTATION	By this we may be sure that we are in him: he who says he abides in him ought to walk in the same way in which he walked. 1 John 2:5–6
BUT DELIVER US FROM EVIL	Whosoever is born of God committeth not sin; for his seed abideth in him. And he cannot sin, because he is born of God. In this the children of God are manifest, and the children of the devil. Whosoever is not just is not of God, nor he that loveth not his brother. 1 John 3:9–10

And the Word was made flesh, and dwelt among us; and we saw his glory, the glory as it were of the only begotten of the Father, full of grace and truth.[1] John 1:14

THE WEDDING FEAST OF THE MYSTICAL BODY OF CHRIST

OUR FATHER WHO ART IN HEAVEN HALLOWED BE THY NAME THY KINGDOM COME	*The Lord of the Feast* Then I heard what seemed to be the voice of a great multitude, like the sound of many waters and like the sound of mighty thunderpeals, crying, "Hallelujah! For the Lord our God the Almighty reigns. Let us rejoice and exalt and give him glory, for the marriage of the Lamb has come, and his Bride has made herself ready; it was granted her to be clothed in white linen, bright and pure"—for the linen is the righteous deeds of the saints. And the angel said to me. "Write this: Blessed are those who are invited to the marriage supper of the Lamb." And he said to me, "These are true words of God." Apoc. 19:6–9
THY WILL BE DONE ON EARTH AS IT IS IN HEAVEN	*The Lady of the Feast* And I saw the holy city, New Jerusalem, coming down out of heaven from God, prepared as a bride adorned for her husband; and I heard a great voice from the throne saying, "Behold, the dwelling of God is with men. He will dwell with them, and they shall be his people, and God himself will be with them." Apoc. 21:2–3
GIVE US THIS DAY OUR DAILY BREAD	*The Feast* The cup of blessing which we bless, is it not a participation in the blood of Christ? The bread which we break, is it not a participation in the body of Christ? Because there is one bread, we who are many are one body, for we all partake of the one bread. 1 Cor. 10:16–17

---

1. Once the parallel between the first chapter of Genesis and John's Prologue is accepted, this passage can be seen in the light of Genesis 1:26 —"And the Word was made flesh, and dwelt among us; and he saw his image, the image as it were of the only begotten of the Father, full of likeness." Paul's passage in 2 Corinthians 3:18 can also be viewed in a similar way — "But we all, beholding the glory/image of the Lord with open face, are transformed into the same image from glory to glory, as by the Spirit/likeness of the Lord."

The Courtesy and Hospitality of the Table

Let the charity of the brotherhood abide in you. And hospitality do not forget: for by this some, being not aware of it, have entertained angels. Remember them that are in bands, as if you were bound with them: and them that labor, as being yourselves also in the body. Marriage honorable in all, and the bed undefiled. For fornicators and adulterers God will judge. Let your manners be without covetousness, contented with such things as you have. For he hath said: I will not leave thee: neither will I forsake thee. So that we may confidently say: The Lord is my helper: I will not fear what man shall do to me. Heb. 13:1–6

The Invitation to the Feast

Then he saith to his servants: The marriage indeed is ready; but they that were invited were not worthy. Go ye therefore into the highways; and as many as you shall find, call to the marriage. And his servants going forth into the ways, gathered together all that they found, both bad and good: and the marriage was filled with guests. And the king went in to see the guests: and he saw there a man who had not on a wedding garment. And he saith to him: Friend, how camest thou in hither not having on a wedding garment? But he was silent. Then the king said to the waiters: Bind his hands and feet, and cast him into the exterior darkness. There shall be weeping and gnashing of teeth. For many are called, but few are chosen. Matt. 22:8–14

The Joy of the Feast~The Now *of the Resurrection*

And there came to him some of the Sadducees, who deny that there is any resurrection: and they asked him, saying: Master, Moses wrote unto us: If any man's brother die, having a wife, and he leave no children, that his brother should take her to wife and raise up seed unto his brother. There were therefore seven brethren: and the first took a wife and died without children. And the next took her to wife: and he also died childless. And the third took her. And in like manner, all the seven: and they left no children and died. Last of all the woman died also. In the resurrection therefore, whose wife of them shall she be? For all the seven had her to wife. And Jesus said to them: The children of this world marry and are given in marriage: but they that shall be accounted worthy of that world and of the resurrection from the dead shall neither be married nor take wives. Neither can they die any more for they are equal to the angels and are the children of God, being the children of the resurrection. Now that the dead rise again, Moses also shewed at the bush, when he called the Lord: The God of Abraham and the God of Isaac and the God of Jacob. For he is not the God of the dead, but of the living: for all live to him. Luke 20:27–38

A Pascha of delight, Pascha, the Lord's Pascha, an all-venerable Pascha has dawned for us, Pascha. Let us embrace one another with joy. O Pascha, ransom from sorrow! Today Christ shone forth from a tomb as from a bridal chamber, and filled the women with joy, saying, 'Proclaim it to the Apostles'.

It is the day of Resurrection. Let us be radiant for the feast, and let us embrace one another. Let us say, Brethren, even to those that hate us. Let us forgive all things on the Resurrection, and so let us cry aloud, 'Christ is risen from the dead, trampling down death by death, and on those in the tombs bestowing life.'[1]

---

1. These are the final stichera of Paschal matins sung immediately before the Paschal Kiss is exchanged.

THE TRUE VINE

JOHN 15:1–11

OUR FATHER WHO ART IN HEAVEN HALLOWED BE THY NAME

I am the true vine; and my Father is the husbandman.

THY KINGDOM COME

These things I have spoken to you, that my joy may be in you, and your joy may be filled.

THY WILL BE DONE ON EARTH AS IT IS IN HEAVEN

In this is my Father glorified; that you bring forth very much fruit, and become my disciples. As the Father hath loved me, I also have loved you. Abide in my love. If you keep my commandments, you shall abide in my love; as I also have kept my Father's commandments, and do abide in his love.

GIVE US THIS DAY OUR DAILY BREAD

If you abide in me, and my words abide in you, you shall ask whatever you will, and it shall be done unto you.

AND FORGIVE US OUR TRESPASSES AS WE FORGIVE THOSE WHO TRESPASS AGAINST US

Abide in me, and I in you. As the branch cannot bear fruit of itself, unless it abide in the vine, so neither can you, unless you abide in me. I am the vine; you the branches: he that abideth in me, and I in him, the same beareth much fruit: for without me you can do nothing. If any one abide not in me, he shall be cast forth as a branch, and shall wither, and they shall gather him up, and cast him into the fire, and he burneth.

AND LEAD US NOT INTO TEMPTATION

…and every one that beareth fruit, he will purge it, that it may bring forth more fruit. Now you are clean by reason of the word, which I have spoken to you.

BUT DELIVER US FROM EVIL

I am the true vine; and my Father is the husbandman. Every branch in me, that beareth not fruit, he will take away…

THE EUCHARISTIC BODY OF CHRIST

LITURGICAL TIME, PLACE, AND CIRCUMSTANCE

THE LITURGICAL YEAR

The time is accomplished and the kingdom of God is at hand. Repent and believe the gosptel. Mark 1:15

OUR FATHER WHO ART IN HEAVEN HALLOWED BE THY NAME	Transfiguration[1] / Dormition of Mary[2]
THY KINGDOM COME	Pentecost
THY WILL BE DONE ON EARTH AS IT IS IN HEAVEN	Ascension
GIVE US THIS DAY OUR DAILY BREAD	Great Thursday / Pascha
AND FORGIVE US OUR TRESPASSES AS WE FORGIVE THOSE WHO TRESPASS AGAINST US	Great Friday
AND LEAD US NOT INTO TEMPTATION	The Great Fast
BUT DELIVER US FROM EVIL	The Nativity of Our Lord / Theophany

---

1. The apotheosis of God in man. (God became man…)
2. The apotheosis of man in God. (…so that man might become God.)

THE COMING TO BIRTH OF TRUE CHRISTIANS

The icon of the *Deisis*[1] is a 'family' portrait. We have a mother, the Holy Virgin, her son, Christ the Savior, and his cousin, her nephew, John the Forerunner. The Holy Virgin and John stand in attitudes of earnest prayer or supplication, hence the icon's name (*Deisis* = supplication). But what does this icon have to do with the Christian year? Of all the 'cloud of witnesses' celebrated in the course of the year, only these three are honored, not only in their births, but also in their conceptions. And, to repeat, all three are blood relatives, as if to say: if we would come to birth in the course of the year as true Christians, we too, as 'blood' relatives, as adopted in the blood of the Lamb, must attend to a world in gestation. To do this, our life must enter three increasingly narrow sweeps of time: first, the life of the Holy Virgin, basically the entire Church year; next, the three individual spans of gestation representing the three overlapping stages of the Christian way, with the addition of a mysterious fourth; and finally, with Christ's nine-month gestation as background, we turn to the 'empty quarter' of *His* year: *our* passage from image to likeness, *our* entry into the fullness of Christian life—life eternal.

Just as Christ dwelt for nine months in the womb of the Holy Virgin, so, in her own earthly life, she beheld the earthly life of her son the Son from birth to His going up to heaven. To this the Church's liturgical year bears witness, with the celebration of her birth on September 8th the first major feast of the year (which begins on Sept. 1st), and the celebration of her 'falling asleep' on August 15th the last major feast of the year. She who kept all the things of the Son in her heart (Luke 2:51), who sang to the evangelists the unknown parts of the their Gospels, 'keeps' the entirety of the liturgical year for us as well, and we too are gathered to her motherly embrace.

What is, then, this life in her family? As foretold by the *Deisis*, we come into our inheritance by the three sometimes concurrent stages of life in Christ. With John the Forerunner we see the embodiment of ascetic struggle: withdrawal to the desert (Luke 1:80), the wearing of simple clothing—camel's hair and a leather belt—and the eating of an even simpler diet—locusts and wild honey (Mark 1:6). Here is *catharsis*, repentance preached and lived. With the Holy Theotokos we see an astonishing sobriety—her matter of fact replies to the angel Gabriel at the Annunciation, and to Christ at the wedding feast at Cana, sobriety in the midst of signs and wonders; to keep vigil with her while we are 'expectant' of the Son is to be anointed with light. Here is illumination, *theoria* at its most intense: daily witness to and remembrance of Christ's

---

1. Father Sergius Bulgakov makes this illuminating observation about the icon in *The Friend of the Bridegroom*, trans. B. Jakim, p. 143): "The *Deisis* implies something even more significant. Here it is a question not of a prayer among the prayers of other saints and with them, but of a certain primacy of presence, a leading of the entire Church in prayer. And this concerns not only the presence of the Mother of God and not only of the Forerunner but of the two together. This is not only a presence *together* in prayer but a *union* in Christ and through Christ in the fullness of the *whole* prayer of the Church. It is a kind of high-priesthood in the Church, a presence before Christ's throne in prayer, a liturgy celebrated in the name of the whole Church."

saving words and deeds to the very least detail. With Christ all promises are fulfilled in *His* coming to birth. Here is perfection, *theosis*, where being and worship achieve their mysterious unison in Christ—deified life in the Holy Spirit. "That they all may be one, as thou, Father, in me, and I in thee… I in them, and thou in me: that they may be made perfect in one" (John 17:21, 23).

But there is a fourth gestational set of feasts: nine months fall between the feast of the Holy Virgin's entry into the Temple (Nov. 21st) and the feast of Dormition, of her falling asleep, the completion of earthly life and the 'seamless' beginning of her heavenly life. With the exemplar feasts of the Forerunner, the Theotokos and Christ, the Christian way stretches from here to beyond the horizon. With these two 'temple' feasts we are reminded of the torches[1]—prayer and worship, the love of God—that must accompany the Christian way until our own 'falling asleep' and entry into the Temple that is to come[2] and, even now, is[3]: the immaculate fading of time into eternity.

Passing from this mysterious foretaste of the world to come, we enter upon the real work of the Christian year, mindful of all that precedes it.

The 'empty quarter' marked out between Christ's nativity (Dec. 25th) and the Annunciation (March 25th), is a time for heightened, even extreme contemplation and ascetic effort. At the beginning of this span fall the feasts of the Nativity and Theophany, pre-eminent feasts of the image, where the new-born and the mature Christ stand side by side so to speak for our contemplation; at the end fall the 'feasts' of Holy Week and the Feast of Feasts,[4] Pascha, pre-eminent feasts of the likeness, where all the commandments of Christ's public life are set in motion and converge at the blinding focus of the Cross, only to be 'unblinded' in the light of the Resurrection. And in the middle falls the Great Fast, that workshop of the soul that tempers and readies our image for likeness. Where else in the course of the year are we offered such a clear view of the very image of God incarnate than at the birth of Our Lord and at His baptism? where else such a clear view of the very likeness of those things suffered for our salvation, those things that strip us of every rationale to remain as mere bystanders, those things "that are wanting of the sufferings of Christ, in my flesh, for his body, which is the church" (Col. 1:24)? Out of this narrow cluster of feasts that has exploded into the entire calendar of the Church's year comes the genesis of our image into our likeness, the travail of our birth as true Christians… and the joy that Christ is born into the world anew in us.

---

1. "The young girls rejoice today, and with their lamps in hand they go in reverence before the spiritual Lamp, as she enters into the Holy of Holies. They foreshadow the brightness past speech that is to shine forth from her and to give light by the Spirit to those that sit in the darkness of ignorance." *Entry of the Most Holy Theotokos*, tone four, great vespers (*The Festal Menaion*, p. 167).

2. "And I saw no temple therein. For the Lord God Almighty is the temple thereof, and the Lamb. And the city hath no need of the sun, nor of the moon, to shine in it. For the glory of God hath enlightened it: and the Lamb is the lamp thereof" (Apoc. 21:22–23).

3. In the gentle twilight past understanding that illumines these two feasts all the apostolic teachings on the temple are knit together (1 Cor. 3:10–16, 6:19–20, 1 Pet. 2:4–5, etc.): "As the effects of the sun upon us disappear, we need it to continue revolving around us time and time again. Since, however, the gifts bestowed by the Ever-Virgin are incorruptible, she only had to complete one circuit and by so doing has brought neverending illumination to all, causing to rise upon us, in a manner defying description, that Sun, 'with whom is no variableness, neither shadow of turning' (James 1:17)." —Gregory Palamas, *On the Entry of the Mother of God into the Holy of Holies II*, trans. C. Veniamin, in *Mary the Mother of God. Sermons by Saint Gregory Palamas*, p. 33.

4. Pascha, being a *movable* feast, varies from year to year and seldom falls on March 25th.

PILGRIMAGE TO PASCHA

THE FIVE SUNDAYS OF LENT AND LAZARUS SATURDAY

Θ[1]

OUR FATHER WHO ART IN HEAVEN HALLOWED BE THY NAME THY KINGDOM COME	First Sunday: The Sunday of Orthodoxy (Image—in theory; the restoration of the holy icons, the defense of the image)
THY WILL BE DONE ON EARTH AS IT IS IN HEAVEN	Second Sunday: Gregory Palamas (Likeness/Deification—in theory; the defense of the holy Hesychasts, those who strive for likeness)
GIVE US THIS DAY OUR DAILY BREAD	Third Sunday: The Adoration of the Cross (The reuniting of Image and Likeness; a taste for the Cross brings image ever closer to likeness)
AND FORGIVE US OUR TRESPASSES AS WE FORGIVE THOSE WHO TRESPASS AGAINST US	Fourth Sunday: John of the Ladder (Image—in practice)
AND LEAD US NOT INTO TEMPTATION	Fifth Sunday: Mary of Egypt (Likeness—in practice)
BUT DELIVER US FROM EVIL	Saturday before Palm Sunday: Lazarus Saturday (Image and Likeness completely united in the resurrection of the blessed)

Π[2]

COMMENTARY

Our passage through Lent can be seen as a living exegesis of Jacob's ladder, where our 'ascents' are fixed in a worshiping contemplation of God, and our 'descents' fixed in the ascetic practice of the virtues. Like a golden thread, this symbolism of the ladder weaves in and out through Lent: in the Gospel reading for the first Sunday we hear Christ declare that we shall "see Heaven open and the angels ascending and descending upon the Son of Man"; the fourth Sunday celebrates John of the Ladder (John Climacus),

---

1. Θ (*theta*) is the first letter in *Theoria* = contemplation, the 'theoretical'.
2. Π (*pi*) is the first letter in *Practica* = activity, the practical.

whose book, *The Ladder of Divine Ascent,* stands in the forefront of Lenten literature, and finally, midmost and at the very heart of Lent, the third Sunday celebrates the ultimate ladder, the life-giving Cross of Christ.

Another ladder is to be found on the garment of Lady Philosophy in Boethius' *Consolation of Philosophy* (Bk.1,Pr.1). Instead of Philosophy, though, this woman should be seen as a personification of Lent:

> There appeared standing above me a woman of majestic countenance whose flashing eyes seemed wise beyond the ordinary wisdom of men. Her color was bright, suggesting boundless vigor, and yet she seemed so old that she could not be thought of as belonging to our age. Her height seemed to vary: sometimes she seemed of ordinary human stature, then again her head seemed to touch the top of the heavens. And when she raised herself to her full height she penetrated heaven itself, beyond the vision of human eyes. Her clothing was made of the most delicate threads, and by the most exquisite workmanship... At the lower edge of her robe was woven the Greek Π, at the top the letter Θ, and between them were seen clearly marked stages, like stairs, ascending from the lowest level to the highest.

Here in this personification is at once the unriddling of philosophy and the 'becoming' of Christians. Forty days—no more is needed.

THE HALLOWING OF THE LORD'S DAY

OUR FATHER WHO ART IN HEAVEN HALLOWED BE THY NAME

A LORD'S DAY THEOPHANY

Our Father who art in heaven hallowed be thy name
And I turned to see the voice that spoke with me. And being turned, I saw seven golden candlesticks:. And in the midst of the seven golden candlesticks, one like to the Son of man, clothed with a garment down to the feet, and girt about the paps with a golden girdle. And his head and his hairs were white, as white wool, and as snow, and his eyes were as a flame of fire, And his feet like unto fine brass, as in a burning furnace. And his voice as the sound of many waters.

Thy kingdom come
And he had in his right hand seven stars. And from his mouth came out a sharp two edged sword: and his face was as the sun shineth in his power.

Thy will be done on earth as it is in heaven
And when I had seen him, I fell at his feet as dead. And he laid his right hand upon me, saying: Fear not. I am the First and the Last,

Give us this day our daily bread
And alive, and was dead, and behold I am living for ever and ever,

And forgive us our trespasses as we forgive those who trespass against us
and lead us not into temptation but deliver us from evil
and have the keys of death and of hell. Apoc. 1:12–18

THY KINGDOM COME

I John, your brother and your partner in tribulation, and in the kingdom, and patience in Christ Jesus, was in the island, which is called Patmos, for the word of God, and for the testimony of Jesus. I was in the spirit on the Lord's day, and heard behind me a great voice, as of a trumpet, Saying: What thou seest, write in a book, and send to the seven churches which are in Asia, to Ephesus, and to Smyrna, and to Pergamus, and to Thyatira, and to Sardis, and to Philadelphia, and to Laodicea. Apoc. 1:9–11

Thy will be done on earth as it is in heaven	Afterwards, Jesus findeth him in the temple, and saith to him: Behold thou art made whole: sin no more, lest some worse thing happen to thee. The man went his way, and told the Jews, that it was Jesus who had made him whole. Therefore did the Jews persecute Jesus, because he did these things on the sabbath. But Jesus answered them: My Father worketh until now; and I work. Hereupon therefore the Jews sought the more to kill him, because he did not only break the sabbath, but also said God was his Father, making himself equal to God. Then Jesus answered, and said to them: Amen, amen, I say unto you, the Son cannot do any thing of himself, but what he seeth the Father doing: for what things soever he doth, these the Son also doth in like manner. For the Father loveth the Son, and sheweth him all things which himself doth: and greater works than these will he shew him, that you may wonder. John 5:14–20
Give us this day our daily bread	And it came to pass again, as the Lord walked through the corn fields on the sabbath, that his disciples began to go forward, and to pluck the ears of corn. And the Pharisees said to him: Behold, why do they on the sabbath day that which is not lawful? And he said to them: Have you never read what David did when he had need, and was hungry himself, and they that were with him? How he went into the house of God, under Abiathar the high priest, and did eat the loaves of proposition, which was not lawful to eat but for the priests, and gave to them who were with him? And he said to them: The sabbath was made for man, and not man for the sabbath. Therefore the Son of man is Lord of the sabbath also. Mark 2:23–28
And forgive us our trespasses as we forgive those who trespass against us	And the ruler of the synagogue (being angry that Jesus had healed on the sabbath) answering, said to the multitude: Six days there are wherein you ought to work. In them therefore come, and be healed; and not on the sabbath day. And the Lord answering him, said: Ye hypocrites, doth not every one of you, on the sabbath day, loose his ox or his ass from the manger, and lead them to water? And ought not this daughter of Abraham, whom Satan hath bound, lo, these eighteen years, be loosed from this bond on the sabbath day? And when he said these things, all his adversaries were ashamed: and all the people rejoiced for all the things that were gloriously done by him. Luke 13:14–17
And lead us not into temptation	For in a certain place he spoke of the seventh day thus: And God rested the seventh day from all his works. And in this place again: If they shall enter into my rest. Seeing then it remaineth that some are to enter into it, and they, to whom it was first preached, did not enter because of unbelief: Again he limiteth a certain day, saying in David, To day, after so long a time, as it is above said: To day if you shall hear his voice, harden not your hearts. For if Jesus had given them rest, he would never have afterwards spoken of another day. There remaineth therefore a day of rest for the people of God. For he that is entered into his rest, the same also hath rested from his works, as God did from his. Let us hasten therefore to enter into that rest; lest any man fall into the same example of unbelief. Heb. 4:4–11
But deliver us from evil	And you, when you were dead in your sins, and the uncircumcision of your flesh; he hath quickened together with him, forgiving you all offences: Blotting out the handwriting of the decree that was against us, which was contrary to

us. And he hath taken the same out of the way, fastening it to the cross: and despoiling the principalities and powers, he hath exposed them confidently in open shew, triumphing over them in himself. Let no man therefore judge you in meat or in drink, or in respect of a festival day, or of the new moon, or of the sabbaths, which are a shadow of things to come, but the body is of Christ. Let no man seduce you, willing in humility, and religion of angels, walking in the things which he hath not seen, in vain puffed up by the sense of his flesh, And not holding the head, from which the whole body, by joints and bands, being supplied with nourishment and compacted, groweth unto the increase of God. Col. 2:13–19

THE MYSTERIES OF THE TEMPLE

But I cannot refrain from reminding you that it is not enough for you to appear before the face of the Lord in the temple which is outside of you. You must also erect a temple of the Lord within yourselves so as to always have Him in you and by you. Theophan the Recluse, *Kindling the Divine Spark*

OUR FATHER WHO ART IN HEAVEN

And there came one of the seven angels… and spoke with me saying: Come and I will shew thee the bride, the wife of the Lamb. And he took me up in spirit to a great and high mountain; and he shewed me the holy city Jerusalem, coming down out of heaven from God, having the glory of God… And I saw no temple therein; for the Lord God Almighty is the temple thereof, and the Lamb. Apoc. 21:9–11, 22

HALLOWED BE THY NAME

The woman saith to him: Sir, I perceive that thou art a prophet. Our fathers adored on this mountain; and you say that at Jerusalem is the place where men must adore. Jesus saith to her: Woman, believe me that the hour cometh, when you shall neither on this mountain, nor in Jerusalem, adore the Father. You adore that which you know not; we adore that which we know. For salvation is of the Jews. But the hour cometh, and now is, when the true adorers shall adore the Father in spirit and in truth. For the Father also seeketh such to adore him. God is spirit; and they that adore him must adore him in spirit and in truth. John 4:19–24

THY KINGDOM COME THY WILL BE DONE ON EARTH AS IT IS IN HEAVEN

Be you also as living stones built up, a spiritual house, a holy priesthood, to offer up spiritual sacrifices, acceptable to God by Jesus Christ. Wherefore it is said in the scripture: Behold, I lay in Sion a chief corner-stone, elect, precious; and he that shall believe in him shall not be confounded. To you therefore that believe, he is honor; but to them that believe not, the stone which the builders rejected, the same is made the head of the corner; and a stone of stumbling and a rock of scandal, to them who stumble at the word, neither do believe, whereunto also they are set. But you are a chosen generation, a kingly priesthood, a holy nation, a purchased people; that you may declare his virtues, who hath called you out of darkness into his marvelous light; who in time past were not a people; but are now the people of God. Who had not obtained mercy; but now have obtained mercy. 1 Pet. 2:5–10

GIVE US THIS DAY OUR DAILY BREAD

And Jesus went up to Jerusalem. And he found in the temple them that sold oxen and sheep and doves, and the changers of money, sitting. And when he had made, as it were, a scourge of little cords, he drove them all out of the temple, the sheep also and the oxen; and the money of the changers he poured out, and the tables he overthrew. And to them that sold doves he said: Take these things hence, and make not the house of my Father a house of traffic. And his disciples remembered, that it was written: The zeal of my house has eaten me up. The Jews, therefore, answered and said to him: What sign dost thou shew unto us, seeing thou dost these things? Jesus answered and said to them: Destroy this temple; and in three days I will raise it up. The Jews then said: Six and forty years was this temple in building; and wilt thou raise it up in three days? But he spoke of the temple of his body. When therefore he was risen again from the dead, his disciples remembered that he had said this; and they believed the scripture and the word that Jesus had said. John 2:13–22

AND FORGIVE US OUR TRESPASSES AS WE FORGIVE THOSE WHO TRESPASS AGAINST US

But Christ, being come a high priest of the good things to come, by a greater and more perfect tabernacle, not made with hands, that is, not of this creation; neither by the blood of goats or of calves, but by his own blood, entered once into the Holies, having obtained eternal redemption. For if the blood of goats and of oxen and the ashes of an heifer, being sprinkled, sanctify such as are defiled, to the cleansing of the flesh; how much more shall the blood of Christ, who by the Holy Spirit offered himself unspotted unto God, cleanse our conscience from dead works, to serve the living God? Heb. 9:11–14

AND LEAD US NOT INTO TEMPTATION BUT DELIVER US FROM EVIL

Jesus saith to them: Have you never read in the Scriptures: The stone which the builders rejected, the same is become the head of the corner? By the Lord this has been done; and it is wonderful in our eyes. Therefore I say to you that the kingdom of God shall be taken from you and shall be given to a nation yielding the fruits thereof. And whosoever shall fall on this stone shall be broken; but on whomsoever it shall fall, it shall grind him to powder. Matt. 21:42–44

SEPARATE YET ALL-ENCOMPASSING, THE TEMPLE OF THE LIVING GOD

Our mouth is open to you, O ye Corinthians; our heart is enlarged… be you also enlarged. 2 Corinthians 6:11, 13

OUR FATHER WHO ART IN HEAVEN HALLOWED BE THY NAME

And I will be their God, and they shall be my people.

THY KINGDOM COME

For you are the temple of the living God; as God saith: I will dwell in them, and walk among them;

THY WILL BE DONE ON EARTH AS IT IS IN HEAVEN

And what agreement hath the temple of God with idols?

GIVE US THIS DAY OUR DAILY BREAD

Or what part hath the faithful with the unbeliever?

AND FORGIVE US OUR TRESPASSES AS WE FORGIVE THOSE WHO TRESPASS AGAINST US	And what concord hath Christ with Belial?
AND LEAD US NOT INTO TEMPTATION	Or what fellowship hath light with darkness?
BUT DELIVER US FROM EVIL	Bear not the yoke with unbelievers. For what participation hath justice with injustice? 2 Cor. 6:14–16

SOLOMON'S TEMPLE

APPROACH TO THE TEMPLE

BUT DELIVER US FROM EVIL	The Sea of Brass
AND LEAD US NOT INTO TEMPTATION	Altar of Burnt-Offerings

PORCH OF THE TEMPLE

AND FORGIVE US OUR TRESPASSES AS WE FORGIVE THOSE WHO TRESPASS AGAINST US	The Pillars of the Temple

HOLY PLACE

GIVE US THIS DAY OUR DAILY BREAD	The Table of the Show-Bread or Bread of the Presence
THY WILL BE DONE ON EARTH AS IT IS IN HEAVEN	The Ten Golden Candlesticks

HOLY OF HOLIES

THY KINGDOM COME	The Temple Veil
OUR FATHER WHO ART IN HEAVEN HALLOWED BE THY NAME	The Ark of the Covenant

SOLOMON'S PRAYER

2 CHRONICLES 6:13–42

OUR FATHER WHO ART IN HEAVEN HALLOWED BE THY NAME

Kneeling down in the presence of all the multitude of Israel, and lifting up his hands towards heaven, he said: O Lord God of Israel, there is no God like thee in heaven nor in earth: who keepest covenant and mercy with thy servants, that walk before thee with all their hearts: Who hast performed to thy servant David my father all that thou hast promised him: and hast accomplished in fact, what thou hast spoken with thy mouth, as also the present time proveth.

THY KINGDOM COME

Now then, O Lord God of Israel, fulfil to thy servant David my father, whatsoever thou hast promised him, saying: There shall not fail thee a man in my sight, to sit upon the throne of Israel: yet so that thy children take heed to their ways, and walk in my law, as thou hast walked before me. And now, Lord God of Israel, let thy word be established which thou hast spoken to thy servant David.

THY WILL BE DONE ON EARTH AS IT IS IN HEAVEN

Is it credible then that God should dwell with men on the earth? If heaven and the heavens of heavens do not contain thee, how much less this house, which I have built? But to this end only it is made, that thou mayest regard the prayer of thy servant and his supplication, O Lord my God: and mayest hear the prayers which thy servant poureth out before thee.

GIVE US THIS DAY OUR DAILY BREAD

That thou mayest open thy eyes upon this house day and night, upon the place wherein thou hast promised that thy name should be called upon, and that thou wouldst hear the prayer which thy servant prayeth in it: hearken then to the prayers of thy servant, and of thy people Israel. Whosoever shall pray in its place, hear thou from thy dwelling place, that is, from heaven, and shew mercy.

AND FORGIVE US OUR TRESPASSES AS WE FORGIVE THOSE WHO TRESPASS AGAINST US

If any man sin against his neighbor, and come to swear against him, and bind himself with a curse before the altar in this house: then hear thou from heaven, and do justice to thy servants, so to requite the wicked by making his wickedness fall upon his own head, and to revenge the just, rewarding him according to his justice. If thy people Israel be overcome by their enemies, (for they will sin against thee,) and being converted shall do penance, and call upon thy name, and pray to thee in this place, then hear thou from heaven, and forgive the sin of thy people Israel and bring them back into the land which thou gavest to them, and their fathers.

AND LEAD US NOT INTO TEMPTATION

If the heavens be shut up, and there fall no rain by reason of the sin of the people, and they shall pray to thee in this place, and confess to thy name, and be converted from their sins, where thou dost afflict them, then hear thou from heaven, O Lord, and forgive the sins of thy servants and of thy people Israel and teach them the good way in which they may walk: and give rain to thy land which thou hast given to thy people to possess. If a famine arise in the land, or a pestilence or blasting, or mildew, or locusts, or caterpillars: or if their enemies waste the country, and besiege the cities, whatsoever scourge or infirmity shall be upon them: then if any of thy people Israel, knowing his own scourge and infirmity shall pray, and shall spread forth his hands in this house, hear thou from heaven, from thy high dwelling place, and forgive, and render to every one according to his ways, which thou knowest him to have in his heart: for thou only knowest the hearts of the children of men: that they may fear thee, and walk in thy ways all the days that they live upon the face of the land, which thou hast given to our fathers. If the stranger also, who is not of thy people Israel, come from a far country, for the sake of thy great name, and thy strong hand, and thy stretched out arm, and adore in this place: hear thou from heaven thy firm dwelling place, and do all that which that stranger shall call upon thee for: that all the people of the earth may know thy name, and may fear thee, as thy people Israel, and may know, that thy name is invoked upon this house, which I have built. If thy people go out to war against their enemies, by the way that thou shalt send them, and adore thee towards the way of this city, which thou hast chosen, and the house which I have built to thy name: then hear thou from heaven their prayers, and their supplications, and revenge them.

BUT DELIVER US FROM EVIL

And if they sin against thee (for there is no man that sinneth not) and thou be angry with them, and deliver them up to their enemies, and they lead them away captive to a land either afar off, or near at hand, and if they be converted in their heart in the land to which they were led captive, and do penance, and pray to thee in the land of their captivity saying: we have sinned, we have done wickedly, we have dealt unjustly: and return to thee with all their heart, and with all their soul, in the land of their captivity, to which they were led away, and adore thee towards the way of their own land which thou gavest their fathers, and of the city, which thou hast chosen, and the house which I have built to thy name: then hear thou from heaven, that is, from thy firm dwelling place, their prayers, and do judgment, and forgive thy people, although they have sinned: for thou art my God: let thy eyes, I beseech thee, be open, and let thy ears be attentive to the prayer, that is made in this place. Now therefore arise, O Lord God, into thy resting place, thou and the ark of thy strength: let thy priests, O Lord God, put on salvation, and thy saints rejoice in good things. O Lord God, turn not away the face of thy anointed: remember the mercies of David thy servant.

THE ARK OF THE COVENANT

As it was answered to Moses, when he was to finish the tabernacle: See (saith he) that thou make all things according to the pattern which was shewn thee on the mount. But now he hath obtained a better ministry, by how much also he is a mediator of a better testament, which is established on better promises. Hebrews 8:5–6

OUR FATHER WHO ART IN HEAVEN HALLOWED BE THY NAME

After all things were perfected, the cloud covered the tabernacle of the testimony, and the glory of the Lord filled it. Neither could Moses go into the tabernacle of the covenant, the cloud covering all things and the majesty of the Lord shining, for the cloud had covered all. Exod. 40:31–33

THY KINGDOM COME

And they shall make me a sanctuary, and I will dwell in the midst of them: According to all the likeness of the tabernacle which I will shew thee, and of all the vessels for the service thereof: and thus you shall make it: Frame an ark of setim wood, the length whereof shall be of two cubits and a half: the breadth, a cubit and a half: the height, likewise, a cubit and a half. And thou shalt overlay it with the purest gold within and without: and over it thou shalt make a golden crown round about... And thou shalt put in the ark the testimony which I will give thee. Thou shalt make also a propitiatory of the purest gold: the length thereof shall be two cubits and a half, and the breadth a cubit and a half. Thou shalt make also two cherubims of beaten gold, on the two sides of the oracle. Let one cherub be on the one side, and the other on the other. Let them cover both sides of the propitiatory, spreading their wings, and covering the oracle, and let them look one towards the other, their faces being turned towards the propitiatory wherewith the ark is to be covered. In which thou shalt put the testimony that I will give thee...

THY WILL BE DONE ON EARTH AS IT IS IN HEAVEN

Thence will I give orders, and will speak to thee over the propitiatory, and from the midst of the two cherubims, which shall be upon the ark of the testimony, all things which I will command the children of Israel by thee. Exod. 25:8–11, 16–22

GIVE US THIS DAY OUR DAILY BREAD

And the house of Israel called the name thereof Manna: and it was like coriander seed white, and the taste thereof like to flour with honey. And Moses said: This is the word which the Lord hath commanded: Fill a gomor of it, and let it be kept unto generations to come hereafter, that they may know the bread wherewith I fed you in the wilderness, when you were brought forth out of the land of Egypt. And Moses said to Aaron: Take a vessel, and put manna into it, as much as a gomor can hold: and lay it up before the Lord to keep unto your generations, as the Lord commanded Moses. And Aaron put it in the tabernacle to be kept. Exod. 16:31–34

AND FORGIVE US OUR TRESPASSES AS WE FORGIVE THOSE WHO TRESPASS AGAINST US

Whomsoever of these I shall choose, his rod shall blossom: and I will make to cease from me the murmurings of the children of Israel, wherewith they murmur against you. And Moses spoke to the children of Israel: and all the princes gave him rods one for every tribe: and there were twelve rods besides the rod of Aaron. And when Moses had laid them up before the Lord in the tabernacle of the testimony: He returned on the following day, and found that the rod of

Aaron[1] for the house of Levi, was budded: and that the buds swelling it had bloomed blossoms, which spreading the leaves, were formed into almonds. Moses therefore brought out all the rods from before the Lord to all the children of Israel: and they saw, and every one received their rods. And the Lord said to Moses: Carry back the rod of Aaron into the tabernacle of the testimony, that it may be kept there for a token of the rebellious children of Israel, and that their complaints may cease from me lest they die. And Moses did as the Lord had commanded. Num. 17:5–11

AND LEAD US NOT
INTO TEMPTATION
BUT DELIVER
US FROM EVIL Therefore after Moses had wrote the words of this law in a volume, and finished it: He commanded the Levites, who carried the ark of the covenant of the Lord. saying: Take this book, and put it in the side of the ark of the covenant of the Lord your God: that it may be there for a testimony against thee. For I know thy obstinacy, and thy most stiff neck, While I am yet living, and going in with you, you have always been rebellious against the Lord: how much more when I shall be dead? Gather unto me all the ancients of your tribes, and your doctors, and I will speak these words in their hearing, and will call heaven and earth to witness against them. For I know that, after my death, you will do wickedly, and will quickly turn aside from the way that I have commanded you: and evils shall come upon you in the latter times, when you shall do evil in the sight of the Lord, to provoke him by the works of your hands. Moses therefore spoke, in the hearing of the whole assembly of Israel, the words of this canticle, and finished it even to the end,

THE CANTICLE OF MOSES

OUR FATHER WHO ART IN HEAVEN HALLOWED BE THY NAME
Hear, O ye heavens, the things I speak, let the earth give ear to the words of my mouth. Let my doctrine gather as the rain, let my speech distil as the dew, as a shower upon the herb, and as drops upon the grass. Because I will invoke the name of the Lord: give ye magnificence to our God.

THY KINGDOM COME
The works of God are perfect, and all his ways are judgments.

THY WILL BE DONE ON EARTH AS IT IS IN HEAVEN
God is faithful and without any iniquity, he is just and right. They have sinned against him, and are none of his children in their filth: they are a wicked and perverse generation. Is this the return thou makest to the Lord, O foolish and senseless people? Is not he thy father, that hath possessed thee, and made thee, and created thee? Remember the days of old, think upon every generation: ask thy father, and he will declare to thee: thy elders and they will tell thee. When the Most High divided the nations: when he separated the sons of Adam, he appointed the bounds of people according to the number of the children of Israel. But the Lord's portion is his people: Jacob the lot of his inheritance. He found him in a desert land, in a place of horror, and of vast wilderness: he led him about, and taught him: and he kept him as the apple of his eye. As the eagle enticing her young to fly, and hovering over them, he spread his wings, and hath taken him and carried him on his shoulders. The Lord alone was his leader: and there was no strange god with him.

---

1. The same Aaron, who was swayed by the people to fashion an idol and proclaim a festival in its honor, is now, along with his kindred, miraculously confirmed to the priesthood.

He set him upon high land: that he might eat the fruits of the fields, that he might suck honey out of the rock, and oil out of the hardest stone, Butter of the herd, and milk of the sheep with the fat of lambs, and of the rams of the breed of Basan: and goats with the marrow of wheat, and might drink the purest blood of the grape.

AND FORGIVE US OUR
TRESPASSES AS WE
FORGIVE THOSE
WHO TRESPASS
AGAINST US

The beloved grew fat, and kicked: he grew fat, and thick and gross, he forsook God who made him, and departed from God his Savior. They provoked him by strange gods, and stirred him up to anger, with their abominations. They sacrificed to devils and not to God: to gods whom they knew not: that were newly come up, whom their fathers worshipped not. Thou hast forsaken the God that begot thee, and hast forgotten the Lord that created thee. The Lord saw, and was moved to wrath: because his own sons and daughters provoked him. And he said: I will hide my face from them, and will consider what their last end shall be: for it is a perverse generation, and unfaithful children. They have provoked me with that which was no god, and have angered me with their vanities: and I will provoke them with that which is no people, and will vex them with a foolish nation. A fire is kindled in my wrath, and shall burn even to the lowest hell: and shall devour the earth with her increase, and shall burn the foundations of the mountains.

AND LEAD US NOT
INTO TEMPTATION

I will heap evils upon them, and will spend my arrows among them. They shall be consumed with famine, and birds shall devour them with a most bitter bite: I will send the teeth of beasts upon them, with the fury of creatures that trail upon the ground, and of serpents. Without, the sword shall lay them waste, and terror within, both the young man and the virgin, the sucking child with the man in years. I said: Where are they? I will make the memory of them to cease from among men. But for the wrath of the enemies I have deferred it: lest perhaps their enemies might be proud, and should say: Our mighty hand, and not the Lord, hath done all these things. They are a nation without counsel, and without wisdom. O that they would be wise and would understand, and would provide for their last end. How should one pursue after a thousand, and two chase ten thousand? Was it not, because their God had sold them, and the Lord had shut them up? For our God is not as their gods: our enemies themselves are judges. Their vines are of the vineyard of Sodom, and of the suburbs of Gomorrha: their grapes are grapes of gall, and their clusters most bitter. Their wine is the gall of dragons, and the venom of asps, which is incurable. Are not these things stored up with me, and sealed up in my treasures?

BUT DELIVER
US FROM EVIL

Revenge is mine, and I will repay them in due time, that their foot may slide: the day of destruction is at hand, and the time makes haste to come. The Lord will judge his people, and will have mercy on his servants : he shall see that their hand is weakened, and that they who were shut up have also failed, and they that remained are consumed. And he shall say: Where are their gods, in whom they trusted? Of whose victims they ate the fat, and drank the wine of their drink offerings: let them arise and help you, and protect you in your distress. See ye that I alone am, and there is no other God besides me: I will kill and I will make to live: I will strike, and I will heal, and there is none that can deliver out of my hand. I will lift up my hand to heaven, and I will say: I live for ever. If

I shall whet my sword as the lightning, and my hand take hold on judgment: I will render vengeance to my enemies, and repay them that hate me. I will make my arrows drunk with blood, and my sword shall devour flesh, of the blood of the slain and of the captivity, of the bare head of the enemies. Praise his people, ye nations, for he will revenge the blood of his servants: and will render vengeance to their enemies, and he will be merciful to the land of his people." Deut. 31:24–32:43

THE CHURCH OF GOD

Whoever has been fortunate enough to have been spiritually and wisely initiated into what is accomplished in church has rendered his soul divine and a veritable church of God. It is perhaps for this reason that the church made by human hands which is its symbolic copy because of the variety of divine things which are in it has been given to us for our guidance toward the highest good. Maximus the Confessor, *The Church's Mystagogy*, Chapter 5

OUR FATHER WHO ART IN HEAVEN HALLOWED BE THY NAME	The sanctuary within which and the altar upon which the sacred mystery of the Eucharist is enacted, and from which flows the deifying life of the sacraments.
THY KINGDOM COME	The royal doors, upon which is seen the Annunciation (i.e. the Incarnation, the coming of the King) and the Evangelists (the heralds of the King).
THY WILL BE DONE ON EARTH AS IT IS IN HEAVEN	The icon screen, upon which is figured the coming of the Kingdom in the economy of our salvation. Icons bring before us those events in which and people in whom heaven has touched earth.
GIVE US THIS DAY OUR DAILY BREAD	The ambon or pulpit, where the Gospel is proclaimed,[1] and the easternmost part of the nave, where the Holy Mysteries are distributed to the faithful. Here also is the tetrapod upon which various objects, such as the icon of the feast being celebrated, are placed for a blessing.
AND FORGIVE US OUR TRESPASSES AS WE FORGIVE THOSE WHO TRESPASS AGAINST US	The nave or *naos*, in which prevails that peace of God which must be shared among all who worship.[2]
AND LEAD US NOT INTO TEMPTATION BUT DELIVER US FROM EVIL	The vestibule or narthex, where preparatory prayers are offered to insure an undistracted spirit of zeal for worship in the Father's house,[3] and where the exorcisms are read at Baptism, where Satan is renounced.

---

1. "Not in bread alone doth man live, but in every word that proceedeth from the mouth of God" (Matt. 4:4).

2. "If therefore thou offer thy gift at the altar, and there thou remember that thy brother hath any thing against thee; leave there thy offering before the altar and go first to be reconciled to thy brother; and then coming thou shalt offer thy gift" (Matt. 5:23–24).

3. Cf. the cleansing of the Temple (Matt. 21:12–13, Mark 11:15–17, John 2:14–17).

PRESENTATION IN THE TEMPLE

THE CHURCHING OF AN INFANT

	THE THREE AGES OF MAN	THE THREE MYSTICAL AGES
Entry & Vestibule AND FORGIVE US OUR TRESPASSES AS WE FORGIVE THOSE WHO TRESPASS AGAINST US AND LEAD US NOT INTO TEMPTATION BUT DELIVER US FROM EVIL	Infancy & childhood: "I will go into Your House, I will worship toward Your Holy Temple in fear of You." (Psalm 5:8)	Origins: Eden, Paradise lost, the past
Nave THY WILL BE DONE ON EARTH AS IT IS IN HEAVEN GIVE US THIS DAY OUR DAILY BREAD	Maturity: "In the midst of the congregation I will sing praises to You." (Psalm 25:12)	The Kairos: the auspicious time, the present
Sanctuary & Altar OUR FATHER WHO ART IN HEAVEN HALLOWED BE THY NAME THY KINGDOM COME	Old age, death, the resurrection of the body & life everlasting: "Lord, now let Your servant depart in peace, according to Your word; for my eyes have seen Your salvation, which You have prepared before the face of all people, a Light to enlighten the Gentiles, and the Glory of Your people in Israel." (Luke 2:29–32)	The Eschaton: Paradise regained, the New Jerusalem, the future, the Ever-Present

COMMENTARY

Forty days after His birth Mary and Joseph brought Christ, in fulfillment of the precepts of Mosaic law, to the Temple where they heard the prophetic words of Simeon and Anna. This event is celebrated as a feast on February 2, but it is also celebrated in the 'churching' of an infant, customarily performed forty days after birth and prior to Baptism. As reflected through its ritual, in which the priest carries the infant by stages from vestibule to sanctuary, churching represents both an introduction to Church life, a catechumenate for infants so to speak, and a forecast of one's entire life in the Church. The words quoted above, successively uttered by the priest at each pause in his progress through the length of the church, are verbal icons of our passage through life on the way to becoming true Christians, true Christs, for Simeon's words bear the same import as those of John the Baptist: "He must increase; but I must decrease" (John 3:30).

AN ICONOSTASIS OF THE LORD'S PRAYER

Our Father who art in heaven Hallowed be thy name

THE THEOPHANIC ICON OF THE LORD

OUR FATHER WHO ART IN HEAVEN	Icon of the Pantocrater
HALLOWED BE THY NAME	"He that seeth me seeth the Father also" (John 14:9).

COMMENTARY

Christ blesses us with his right hand, while, with his left, he offers the book of Gospels. His hands indicate how we should worship the Father: the blessing hand = 'in spirit', the hand holding the testimony of the Gospels = 'in truth'. From his right hand streams the grace of charity from the very heart of Christ; while his left hand steadies us with his Gospel until we have become steadfast in it, until we have truly learned it 'by heart'. Christ and the Holy Spirit have been called 'the two hands of the Father': here, in this icon, Christ's two hands—indicating worship of the Father—take their source in and convey us back to his hidden heart, which is only one with the Father. How else will Christ take us to his heart if not by his two hands? Keeping in mind that Christ came the first time, not to judge the world (John 3:17), but to show it great mercy; we must remember that, with his Second Coming, his hands will assume a different meaning: then his left hand will hold the Lamb's book of life wherein all who are saved will find their names, while his right hand will separate the sheep from the goats according to their recognition or non-recognition of Christ in the poor and the needy (Matt. 25:31–46), according to whether or not their own hands have been busy with the promptings of their inmost hearts.

Thy kingdom come

THEOPHANIC ICONS OF THE LIKENESS

THY KINGDOM COME	Icon of Pentecost
THY WILL BE DONE ON EARTH AS IT IS IN HEAVEN	Icon of the Descent into Hell

THEOPHANIC ICONS OF THE IMAGE

GIVE US THIS DAY OUR DAILY BREAD	Icon of the Transfiguration
AND FORGIVE US OUR TRESPASSES AS WE FORGIVE THOSE WHO TRESPASSES AGAINST US AND LEAD US NOT INTO TEMPTATION BUT DELIVER US FROM EVIL	Icon of the Baptism in the Jordan

Of all the icons on the iconostasis, four are termed 'theophanic', each in different ways revealing and conveying the single divinity of the Father, Son and Holy Spirit according to the 'economy' of Persons within the created universe. These icons are also those richest in teaching about what an icon is.

The feast of Christ's baptism in the Jordan is itself called 'Theophany' and is thus a most fitting place to start. Central to this icon-scene is Christ, the Son of God, the dove of the Holy Spirit of God and the voice of God the Father. But these 'presences' alone do not make of this scene a theophany; what makes it such is the presence of three types of witnesses: John the Baptist, the most significant for the human world; the angels, who represent the bodiless powers, and the figure or figures put to flight in the depths of the Jordan, representing the 'ancient serpent' or the elements of the world subjected to corruption by the sin of Adam. But, in the very beholding of this scene, thanks to that inverse perspective common to icons, we too become fellow witnesses and contemporaries of the Baptist; it is not we who have approached the scene, it is the scene that first approaches us (cf. 1 John 4:19). This is the very 'shore' where we ourselves stand to recognize the image, an image newly emerged, washed and sparkling with the waters of the Jordan, an image steadfast amidst the flux of things, an image of origins native to our sight.

With the icon for the feast of the Transfiguration the 'image beheld' is no longer static but radiant, and threatens to consume the flux of life with its dominion. Here there are no common boundaries: seized by this light, the prophets of bygone times draw near and the disciples fall back dazzled. The image no longer keeps to a given position in time or space; it is conveyed by some entirely different light, a light shining both hiddenly here within us, as well as overtly and so long ago upon the holy mount, a nourishing and strengthening light which enables us to see the image in a different way, the way of likeness.

With the icons of Christ's Baptism and Transfiguration the image remains, as it were, alone. But, with the icon of Christ's descent into Hell, we behold a startling change: the image of Christ the New Adam, having already trampled down the gates of Hell, reaches into the greatest depth of human loss (for us the only truly meaningful place), grasps the hands of the Old Adam and Eve in a deathless grip, and our image is touched by likeness, the Old Adam and Eve are betrothed to their prototype in Christ.

If the icon of the Descent represents a betrothal, the icon of Pentecost represents a wedding feast. The fire that generated the light by which we originally saw the image descends from on high. What began as a baptism by water in the virtuality of the image, in the life of Christ, becomes a baptism by fire in the actuality of the likeness, in the living Spirit. And so, confronted by this reunion of image and likeness portrayed by the holy icons, we come forward to receive the Eucharist, to be gripped by the hand (Or is it the heart?) of Christ and be filled with all the fulness of the Spirit.

But what is an icon? A feast for the eyes, a foretaste of the heart's own banquet, and even a seeing with the eye (image) of the heart (likeness).[1]

---

1. Cf. Eph. 1:18.

Thy will be done on earth as it is in heaven
Give us this day our daily bread

ICONS OF THE THEOTOKOS

OUR FATHER WHO ART IN HEAVEN	Christ the Pantocrater[1]
HALLOWED BE THY NAME	Virgin of the Sign
THY KINGDOM COME	Virgin of Tenderness
THY WILL BE DONE ON EARTH AS IT IS IN HEAVEN	Virgin Showing the Way
GIVE US THIS DAY OUR DAILY BREAD	Nativity of Christ
AND FORGIVE US OUR TRESPASSES AS WE FORGIVE THOSE WHO TRESPASS AGAINST US	In Thee, All Creatures Rejoice
AND LEAD US NOT INTO TEMPTATION	Protection of the Mother of God
BUT DELIVER US FROM EVIL	Dormition of the Mother of God

And forgive us our trespasses as we forgive those who trespass against us
And lead us not into temptation, but deliver us from evil

OLD TESTAMENT ICONS

OUR FATHER WHO ART IN HEAVEN HALLOWED BE THY NAME	Old Testament Trinity
THY KINGDOM COME	Divine Wisdom
THY WILL BE DONE ON EARTH AS IT IS IN HEAVEN	Elijah taken up in the fiery chariot
GIVE US THIS DAY OUR DAILY BREAD	Elijah fed by a raven in the desert
AND FORGIVE US OUR TRESPASSES AS WE FORGIVE THOSE WHO TRESPASS AGAINST US AND LEAD US NOT INTO TEMPTATION BUT DELIVER US FROM EVIL	Mother of God 'The Unburnt Bush'

---

1. Depicted as a child at the heart of the Virgin of the Sign

ICONOGRAPHY

(Analogous to the cosmogonic process[1])

OUR FATHER WHO ART IN HEAVEN HALLOWED BE THY NAME	Inscription and blessing of the icon
THY KINGDOM COME	Painting and gilding
THY WILL BE DONE ON EARTH AS IT IS IN HEAVEN	Etching
GIVE US THIS DAY OUR DAILY BREAD	Drawing
AND FORGIVE US OUR TRESPASSES AS WE FORGIVE THOSE WHO TRESPASS AGAINST US	Gessoing[2]
AND LEAD US NOT INTO TEMPTATION	Preparation of the board
BUT DELIVER US FROM EVIL	Selection of the board

---

1. See 'Creation', pp. 12–13.
2. The process of reconciling wood to icon.

VESPERS: THE LIGHTING OF THE LAMPS

OUR FATHER WHO
ART IN HEAVEN
HALLOWED BE
THY NAME

O Thou Who with never-silent hymns and unceasing doxologies art praised in song by the Holy Hosts, fill our mouth with Thy praise, that we may magnify Thy holy name. And grant unto us part and inheritance with all that truly fear Thee and keep Thy commandments, through the intercessions of the holy Theotokos and of all Thy saints. For unto Thee is due all glory, honor and worship: to the Father, and to the Son, and to the Holy Spirit, now and ever and unto the ages of ages. Amen. *Fourth Prayer*

For Sion's sake I will not hold my peace, and for the sake of Jerusalem, I will not rest till her just one come forth as brightness, and her savior be lighted as a lamp. And the Gentiles shall see thy just one, and all kings thy glorious one: and thou shalt be called by a new name, which the mouth of the Lord shall name. Isa. 62:1–2

THY KINGDOM COME

O God, great and wondrous, Who with goodness unsearchable and abundant providence orderest all things, and grantest unto us earthly good things; Who hast given us a pledge of the promised kingdom through the good things already bestowed upon us; and hast made us to shun all evil during that part of the day which is past: Grant us also to fulfill the remainder of this day blamelessly before Thy holy glory; to hymn Thee, the only Good One, our God, Who lovest mankind. For Thou art our God, and unto Thee do we send up glory: to the Father, and to the Son, and to the Holy Spirit, now and ever, and unto the ages of ages. Amen. *Sixth Prayer*

And he said to them: Doth a candle come in to be put under a bushel, or under a bed? and not to be set on a candlestick? For there is nothing hid, which shall not be made manifest: neither was it made secret, but that it may come abroad. If any man have ears to hear, let him hear. Mark 4:21–23

THY WILL BE DONE
ON EARTH AS IT IS
IN HEAVEN

O Lord, compassionate and merciful, long-suffering and plenteous in mercy, give ear unto our prayer and attend to the voice of our supplication; work in us a sign unto good; guide us in Thy way, that we may walk in Thy truth; make glad our hearts, that we may fear Thy holy name; for Thou art great and workest wonders, Thou alone art God, and there is none like unto Thee among the gods, O Lord strong in mercy and good in might, to help and comfort, and to save all that hope in Thy holy name. For unto Thee is due all glory, honor and worship: to the Father, and to the Son, and to the Holy Spirit, now and ever, and unto the ages of ages. Amen. *First Prayer*

The spirit of a man is the lamp of the Lord, which searcheth all the hidden things of the bowels. Prov. 20:27

GIVE US THIS DAY
OUR DAILY BREAD

O Lord our God, remember us, Thy sinful and unprofitable servants, when we call upon Thy holy, venerable name, and turn us not away in shame from the expectation of Thy mercy; but grant us, O Lord, all our requests which are unto salvation, and vouchsafe us to love and to fear Thee with our whole heart, and to do Thy will in all things. For a good God art Thou, and the Lover of mankind, and unto Thee do we send up glory, to the Father, and to the Son, and tothe Holy Spirit, now and ever, and unto the ages of ages. Amen. *Third Prayer*

Thy word is a lamp to my feet, and a light to my paths.
I have sworn and am determined to keep the judgments of thy justice.
I have been humbled, O Lord, exceedingly:
quicken thou me according to thy word. Psalm 118:105–107

AND FORGIVE US OUR TRESPASSES AS WE FORGIVE THOSE WHO TRESPASS AGAINST US

O Lord, O Lord, Who upholds all things in the most pure hollow of Thy hand, Who art long-suffering toward us all and repentest Thee at our wickedness, remember Thy compassion and Thy mercy. Visit us with Thy goodness, and grant unto us during the remainder of the present day, by Thy grace, to flee the divers subtle snares of the Evil One, and to keep our life unassailed through the grace of Thine all-holy Spirit, through the mercy and love for mankind of Thine only-begotten son, with Whom Thou art blessed, together with Thine all-holy and good, and life-creating Spirit, now and ever, and unto the ages of ages. Amen. *Fifth Prayer*

Or what woman having ten groats, if she lose one groat, doth not light a candle and sweep the house and seek diligently until she find it? And when she hath found it, call together her friends and neighbors, saying: Rejoice with me, because I have found the groat which I had lost. So I say to you, there shall be joy before the angels of God upon one sinner doing penance. Luke 15:8–10

AND LEAD US NOT INTO TEMPTATION

O Lord, rebuke us not in Thine anger, nor chasten us in Thy wrath, but deal with us according to Thy mercy, O Physician and Healer of our souls. Guide us unto the haven of Thy will; enlighten the eyes of our hearts to the knowledge of Thy truth; and grant unto us that the remainder of the present day and the whole time of our life may be peaceful and sinless, through the intercessions of the holy Theotokos and of all the saints. For Thine is the dominion, and Thine is the kingdom, and the power, and the glory: of the Father, and of the Son, and of the Holy Spirit, now and ever, and unto the ages of ages. Amen. *Second Prayer*

For thou lightest my lamp, O Lord: O my God, enlighten my darkness.
For by thee I shall be delivered from temptation;
and through my God I shall go over a wall. Psalm 17:29–30

BUT DELIVER US FROM EVIL

Our Father who art in heaven
Hallowed be thy name

O God, great and most high, Who alone hast immortality, and dwellest in light unapproachable;

Thy kingdom come

Who hast fashioned all creation in wisdom; Who hast divided the light from the darkness, and hast set the sun for dominion of the day, the moon the stars for dominion of the night; Who hast vouchsafed unto us sinners at this present hour to come before Thy presence with thanksgiving and to offer thee evening doxology;

Thy will be done on earth as it is in heaven

Do thyself direct our prayer as incense before Thee and accept it for a sweet smelling savor;

Give us this day our daily bread

grant unto us that the present evening and the coming night be peaceful. Cloth us with the armor of light.

And forgive us our trepasses as we
forgive those who trespass against
And lead us not into temptation

Deliver us from the terror by night and from everything that walketh in darkness. And grant that the sleep which Thou hast given for the repose of our infirmity may be free from all fantasies of the Devil.

But deliver us from evil

Yea, O Master, Giver of good things, may we, being moved to compunction upon our beds, remember Thy name in the night, and, enlightened by meditation on Thy commandments, rise up in joyfulness of soul to the glorification of Thy goodness, offering prayers and supplications to Thy lovingkindness for our own sins and for those of all Thy people, whom do Thou visit in mercy, through the intercessions of the Holy Theotokos. For a good God art Thou, and unto Thee do we send up glory: to the Father and to the Son, and to the Holy Spirit, now and ever, and unto the ages of ages. Amen. *Seventh Prayer*[1]

And the poor people thou wilt save: and with thy eyes thou shalt humble the haughty. For thou art my lamp O Lord: and thou, O Lord, wilt enlighten my darkness. 2 Kings 22:28–29

---

1. Lamplighting prayers are from the priest's *Sluzebnic* (www.orthodox.net/services/sluzebnic-vespers-lamp-lighting-prayers.html).

SUN AT MIDNIGHT

FROM THE *CANONS TO THE HOLY TRINITY* BY METROPHANES[1]
SUNG AT SUNDAY'S MIDNIGHT OFFICE

And the light shineth in darkness: and the darkness did not comprehend it. John 1:5

OUR FATHER WHO ART IN HEAVEN HALLOWED BE THY NAME

Born from you, Father, as befitted God, without change, the Son shone forth, light from light, in no way different, and the divine Spirit as light proceeded. And we faithfully worship and glorify the three-personned radiance of one Godhead. *Tone 1 Ode 3*

THY KINGDOM COME

O Sun of glory who train me with your divinely working radiance and ever guide me to be well-pleasing to your three-personned Godhead, make me a partaker of your divine Kingdom. *Tone 6 Ode 5*

THY WILL BE DONE ON EARTH AS IT IS IN HEAVEN

The spiritual beings you conceived and caused them to subsist to hymn your Godhead unceasingly, O God, triple light and maker of all; but accept too the supplication of creatures of clay and earth, and their entreaty, as you are compassionate. *Tone 5 Ode 3*

GIVE US THIS DAY OUR DAILY BREAD

Make me a temple of your radiance with triple light, of communion and participation, O Lover of humankind, source of good; show me, Master, sole Ruler, my God and Lord of glory, to be unapproachable by invisible foes and passions of the flesh, that I may sing your praise to all the ages. *Tone 7 Ode 8*

AND FORGIVE US OUR TRESPASSES AS WE FORGIVE THOSE WHO TRESPASS AGAINST US

O Sun who never set, grant your radiance to the hearts of your servants, enlighten their souls and ransom them from many offences, O only all-merciful and Three-personned, and count us worthy of your unsullied life. *Tone 6 Ode 9*

AND LEAD US NOT INTO TEMPTATION

Now I direct my whole heart and mind, and all the inclinations of my soul and body to you, my fashioner and deliverer, sole Sovereign of triple light, and I cry out to you: Save me your servant from temptations and afflictions of every kind. *Tone 4 Ode 9*

BUT DELIVER US FROM EVIL

O Godhead, who are light of equal honour and of triple sun and which gives light, illumine those who sing you with faith and deliver them from gloomy evil doing, and count them worthy of your shining tabernacles, O supremely good. *Tone 6 Ode 9*

---

1. Trans. Archimandrite Ephrem, www.anastasis.org.uk.

HYMNS OF ASCENT

FROM THE *ANAVATHMOI*[1] OF THE SUNDAY *ORTHOS* SERVICE

OUR FATHER WHO
ART IN HEAVEN
HALLOWED BE
THY NAME

O Christ the Fruit of the womb, by the Spirit are the saints forever as adopted sons to You as to a father. *Mode 3 Antiphon 2*

THY KINGDOM COME

In the Holy Spirit is universal dominion, which the armies above worship, as does everything that has breath below. *Plagal of the Second Antiphon 3*

THY WILL BE DONE
ON EARTH AS IT IS
IN HEAVEN

In the Holy Spirit is the cause of universal salvation. When He blows on someone as befits His nature, He quickly uplifts him from the mundane, gives him wings, augments him, ranges him on high. *Plagal of the Second Antiphon 1*

GIVE US THIS DAY
OUR DAILY BREAD

Those who sow shedding godly tears when the south wind is blowing, joyously will harvest ears of life everlasting. *Mode 3 Antiphon 1*

AND FORGIVE US OUR
TRESPASSES AS WE
FORGIVE THOSE
WHO TRESPASS
AGAINST US

Have mercy, O my Christ, on us who hourly commit sin against You manifoldly; and give us means before the end to turn to You in repentance. *Mode 2 Antiphon 1*

AND LEAD US NOT
INTO TEMPTATION

From my youth does the enemy tempt me, and with the pleasures he scorches me. But trusting You, O Lord, monumentally do I defeat him. *Plagal of the Fourth Antiphon 1*

BUT DELIVER
US FROM EVIL

Let not my soul be caught like a sparrow in their teeth, O Logos. Woe is me! How shall I be delivered from the enemy, enamored with sin as I am? *Plagal of the Second Antiphon 2*

---

1. See www.goarch.org/chapel/liturgical_texts/sundayorthros. In his *Nea Klimax* (*New Ladder*) St. Nicodemos of the Holy Mountain takes the 75 Hymns of Degrees or Ascent sung on Sunday morning and brings them into harmony and analogy with *The Ladder of Divine Ascent* by St. John Climacus (see *infra* p. 254).

THE LITURGY

A LITURGICAL PREFACE

But thou, when thou shalt pray, enter into thy chamber and, having shut the door, pray to thy Father in secret, and thy Father who seeth in secret will repay thee. Matthew 6:6

STAGES OF PRAYER	STAGES OF THE LITURGY[1]
WHEN THOU SHALT PRAY, ENTER INTO THY CHAMBER	From the beginning of the Liturgy to the Gospel
AND, HAVING SHUT THE DOOR,	Dismissal of the catechumens, the Creed,[2] the Cherubic Hymn[3]
PRAY TO THY FATHER IN SECRET[4]	Consecration and Epiclesis
AND THY FATHER WHO SEETH IN SECRET WILL REPAY THEE.[5]	Communion

1. In liturgical prayer private prayer comes face to face with its greatest exemplar, and, as we grow into the likeness of Christ, private prayer becomes itself a liturgy, just as in the Liturgy we find ourselves 'alone together' in Christ's Mystical Body—yet another paradox of the Christian way.

2. A 'horizontal' shutting-of-the-door, a shutting out of the disbelief of the profane mind. The acclamation which precedes the Creed declares: "The doors, the doors! In wisdom let us be attentive."

3. A 'vertical' shutting-of-the-door, its inward effect an opening upwards into celestial realities.

4. In both Eastern and Western liturgies the Consecration/Epiclesis has traditionally been said 'secretly' by the priest.

5. In light of this correspondence, our reward is nothing less than the Son of God Himself, nothing less than everything, for Christ "is all and in all" (Col. 3:11).

PROSKOMIDE AND LITURGY OF THE CATECHUMENS

PRAYER TO THE HOLY SPIRIT

The true aim of our Christian life consists in the acquisition of the Holy Spirit of God. —Seraphim of Sarov

OUR FATHER WHO ART IN HEAVEN	In the name of the Father
HALLOWED BE THY NAME	and of the Son
THY KINGDOM COME	and of the Holy Spirit:, now and ever and unto ages of ages. Amen.
	O heavenly king, comforter, spirit of truth,
THY WILL BE DONE ON EARTH AS IT IS IN HEAVEN	who art everywhere present and fill all things,
GIVE US THIS DAY OUR DAILY BREAD	treasury of blessings and giver of life, come and abide in us,
AND FORGIVE US OUR TRESPASSES AS WE FORGIVE THOSE WHO TRESPASS AGAINST US	cleanse us of all stain
AND LEAD US NOT INTO TEMPTATION BUT DELIVER US FROM EVIL	and save our souls, O gracious one.

CALLED TO THE LORD'S TABLE

OUR FATHER WHO
ART IN HEAVEN
HALLOWED BE
THY NAME

And there came to him great multitudes, having with them the dumb, the blind, the lame, the maimed, and many others: and they cast them down at his feet, and he healed them: so that the multitudes marvelled seeing the dumb speak, the lame walk, and the blind see: and they glorified the God of Israel…

THY KINGDOM COME

And Jesus called together his disciples, and said: I have compassion on the multitudes, because they continue with me now three days, and have not what to eat, and I will not send them away fasting, lest they faint in the way. And the disciples say unto him: Whence then should we have so many loaves in the desert, as to fill so great a multitude? And Jesus said to them: How many loaves have you? But they said: Seven, and a few little fishes…

THY WILL BE DONE
ON EARTH AS IT IS
IN HEAVEN

And he commanded the multitude to sit down upon the ground. And taking the seven loaves and the fishes, and giving thanks, he brake, and gave to his disciples, and the disciples to the people…

GIVE US THIS DAY
OUR DAILY BREAD

And they did all eat, and had their fill. And they took up seven baskets full, of what remained of the fragments. And they that did eat, were four thousand men, beside children and women. Matt. 15:30–38

AND FORGIVE US OUR
TRESPASSES AS WE
FORGIVE THOSE
WHO TRESPASS
AGAINST US

Behold Israel according to the flesh. Are not they that eat of the sacrifices partakers of the altar? What then? Do I say that what is offered in sacrifice to idols is any thing? Or that the idol is any thing? But the things which the heathens sacrifice, they sacrifice to devils and not to God. And I would not that you should be made partakers with devils. You cannot drink the chalice of the Lord and the chalice of devils: you cannot be partakers of the table of the Lord and of the table of devils. 1 Cor. 10:18–21

AND LEAD US NOT
INTO TEMPTATION

And Levi made him a great feast in his own house; and there was a great company of publicans, and of others, that were at table with them. But the Pharisees and scribes murmured, saying to his disciples: Why do you eat and drink with publicans and sinners? And Jesus answering, said to them: They that are whole, need not the physician: but they that are sick. I came not to call the just, but sinners to penance. Luke 5:29–32

BUT DELIVER
US FROM EVIL

And behold, there was a man named Zacheus, who was the chief of the publicans, and he was rich. And he sought to see Jesus who he was, and he could not for the crowd, because he was low of stature. And running before, he climbed up into a sycamore tree, that he might see him; for he was to pass that way. And when Jesus was come to the place, looking up, he saw him, and said to him: Zacheus, make haste and come down; for this day I must abide in thy house. And he made haste and came down; and received him with joy. And when all saw it, they murmured, saying, that he was gone to be a guest with a man that was a sinner. But Zacheus standing, said to the Lord: Behold, Lord, the half of my goods I give to the poor; and if I have wronged any man of any thing, I restore him fourfold. Jesus said to him: This day is salvation come to this house, because he also is a son of Abraham. Luke 19:2–5

BREAD FROM THE HAND OF GOD

MATTHEW 6:25–34

On account of life in the Spirit we are content to use the present life in such a way as not to refrain from sustaining it by bread alone or from keeping up its good physical health; as far as this is permitted us, not in order to live but rather to live for God. We thus make of the body rendered spiritual by its virtues a messenger of the soul, and by its steadfastness in the good we make the soul a herald of God. We naturally limit the bread to but one day without daring to extend the request to a second one after this because of the giver of the prayer. — Maximus the Confessor, *On the Lord's Prayer*

OUR FATHER WHO
ART IN HEAVEN
HALLOWED BE
THY NAME

Therefore I say to you, be not solicitous for your life, what you shall eat, nor for your body, what you shall put on. Is not the life more than the meat: and the body more than the raiment? Behold the birds of the air, for they neither sow, nor do they reap, nor gather into barns: and your heavenly Father feedeth them. Are not you of much more value than they?

THY KINGDOM COME

And which of you by taking thought, can add to his stature by one cubit? And for raiment why are you solicitous? Consider the lilies of the field, how they grow: they labor not, neither do they spin. But I say to you, that not even Solomon in all his glory was arrayed as one of these.

THY WILL BE DONE
ON EARTH AS IT IS
IN HEAVEN

And if the grass of the field, which is today, and tomorrow is cast into the oven, God doth so clothe: how much more you, O ye of little faith?

GIVE US THIS DAY
OUR DAILY BREAD

Be not solicitous therefore, saying, What shall we eat: or what shall we drink, or wherewith shall we be clothed? For after all these things do the heathens seek. For your Father knoweth that you have need of all these things.

AND FORGIVE US OUR
TRESPASSES AS WE
FORGIVE THOSE
WHO TRESPASS
AGAINST US

Seek ye therefore first the kingdom of God, and his justice, and all these things shall be added unto you.

AND LEAD US NOT
INTO TEMPTATION

Be not therefore solicitous for tomorrow; for the morrow will be solicitous for itself.

BUT DELIVER
US FROM EVIL

Sufficient for the day is the evil thereof.

BLESSED

The universe of the liturgy begins in: "Blessed is the kingdom of the Father, and of the Son, and of the Holy Spirit, now and ever, and unto ages of ages", and ends in the thrice-repeated: "Blessed be the name of the Lord, now and forever." Let it be said, then, that the liturgy actually transpires in that 'blessed' interval between the "Hallowed be thy name" and the "Thy kingdom come" of the Lord's Prayer, where His kingdom has come and His name is hallowed. — GJC

OUR FATHER WHO ART IN HEAVEN HALLOWED BE THY NAME — Blessed by the God and Father of our Lord Jesus Christ, who hath blessed us with spiritual blessings in heavenly places, in Christ: As he chose us in him before the foundation of the world, that we should be holy and unspotted in his sight in charity. Eph. 1:3–4

THY KINGDOM COME — Blessed are those servants, whom the Lord when he cometh, shall find watching. Amen I say to you, that he will gird himself, and make them sit down to meat, and passing will minister unto them. And if he shall come in the second watch, or come in the third watch, and find them so, blessed are those servants. Luke 12:37–38

THY WILL BE DONE ON EARTH AS IT IS IN HEAVEN — And it came to pass, as he spoke these things, a certain woman from the crowd, lifting up her voice, said to him: Blessed is the womb that bore thee, and the paps that gave thee suck. But he said: Yea rather, blessed are they who hear the word of God, and keep it. Luke 11:27–28

GIVE US THIS DAY OUR DAILY BREAD — And thou shalt be blessed, because they have not wherewith to make thee recompense: for recompense shall be made thee at the resurrection of the just. When one of them that sat at table with him, had heard these things, he said to him: Blessed is he that shall eat bread in the kingdom of God. Luke 14:15–16

AND FORGIVE US OUR TRESPASSES AS WE FORGIVE THOSE WHO TRESPASS AGAINST US — But to him that worketh not, yet believeth in him that justifieth the ungodly, his faith is reputed to justice, according to the purpose of the grace of God. As David also termeth the blessedness of a man, to whom God reputeth justice without works: Blessed are they whose iniquities are forgiven, and whose sins are covered. Blessed is the man to whom the Lord hath not imputed sin. Rom. 4:5–8

AND LEAD US NOT INTO TEMPTATION — Blessed is the man that endureth temptation; for when he hath been proved, he shall receive a crown of life, which God hath promised to them that love him. James 1:12

BUT DELIVER US FROM EVIL — And in fine, be ye all of one mind, having compassion one of another, being lovers of the brotherhood, merciful, modest, humble: not rendering evil for evil, nor railing for railing, but contrariwise, blessing: for unto this are you called, that you may inherit a blessing. 1 Pet. 3:8–9

WRITTEN IN THE HEART: THE BEATITUDES

Every scribe instructed in the kingdom of heaven is like to a man that is a householder, who bringeth forth out of his treasure things both old and new. Matthew 13:52

And the Lord said to Moses: come up to me into the mount,	You are the epistle of Christ, ministered by us, and written:
and be there.	not with ink
And I will give thee tables of stone, and the commandments	but with the Spirit of the living God; not in tables of stone
which I have written that thou mayest teach them. Exod. 24:12	but in the fleshly tables of the heart. 2 Cor. 3:3

THE TEN COMMANDMENTS

I am the lord thy God,
thou shalt not have strange gods before me.
Thou shalt not take
the name of the lord thy god in vain.
Remember that thou keep holy the sabbath day.

Honor thy father and thy mother.
Thou shalt not kill.
Thou shalt not commit adultery.
Thou shalt not steal.
Thou shalt not bear false witness
against thy neighbor.
Thou shalt not covet thy neighbor's wife.
Thou shalt not covet thy neighbor's goods

THE TWO GREATEST COMMANDMENTS

The first commandment of all is,
'Hear, O Israel; the Lord thy God is one God.
And thou shalt love the Lord thy God
with thy whole heart,
and with thy whole soul,
and with thy whole mind,
and with thy whole strength' …

And the second is like to it:
Thou shalt love thy neighbor as thyself.
There is no other commandment
greater than these.
Mark 12:29–31

THE EIGHT BEATITUDES

MATTHEW 5:3–10

OUR FATHER WHO ART IN HEAVEN
HALLOWED BE THY NAME

Blessed are the poor in spirit: for theirs is the kingdom of heaven.

Hearken, my dearest brethren: hath not God chosen the poor in this world, rich in faith, and heirs of the kingdom which God hath promised to them that love him? James 2:5

THY KINGDOM COME

Blessed are they that mourn: for they shall be comforted.

For we know that every creature groaneth and travaileth in pain, even till now. And not only it, but ourselves also, who have the firstfruits of the Spirit, even we ourselves groan within ourselves, waiting for the adoption of the sons of God, the redemption of our body. Rom. 8:22–23

THY WILL BE DONE ON EARTH
AS IT IS IN HEAVEN

Blessed are the meek: for they shall possess the land.

Brethren, and if a man be overtaken in any fault, you, who are spiritual, instruct such a one in the spirit of meekness, considering thyself, lest thou also be tempted. Bear ye one another's burdens; and so you shall fulfil the law of Christ. For if any man think himself to be some thing, whereas he is nothing, he deceiveth himself. But let every one prove his own work, and so he shall have glory in himself only, and not in another. For every one shall bear his own burden. And let him that is instructed in the word, communicate to him that instructeth him, in all good things. Be not deceived, God is not mocked. For what things a man shall sow, those also shall he reap. For he that soweth in his flesh, of the flesh also shall reap corruption. But he that soweth in the spirit, of the spirit shall reap life everlasting. Gal. 6:1–8

GIVE US THIS DAY
OUR DAILY BREAD

Blessed are they that hunger and thirst after justice for they shall have their fill.

For the kingdom of God is not meat and drink; but justice, and peace, and joy in the Holy Spirit. Rom. 14:17
That you may approve the better things, that you may be sincere and without offence unto the day of Christ, filled with the fruit of justice, through Jesus Christ, unto the glory and praise of God. Phil. 1:10–11

AND FORGIVE US OUR TRESPASSES
AS WE FORGIVE THOSE WHO
TRESPASS AGAINST US

Blessed are the merciful: for they shall obtain mercy.

Be ye therefore merciful, as your Father also is merciful. Judge not: and you shall not be judged. Condemn not: and you shall not be condemned. Forgive: and you shall be forgiven. Give: and it shall be given to you: good measure and pressed down and shaken together and running over shall they give into your bosom. For with the same measure that you shall mete withal, it shall be measured to you again. Luke 6:36–38

AND LEAD US NOT   *Blessed are the clean of heart: for they*
INTO TEMPTATION   *shall see God.*

Blessed is the man that endureth temptation; for when he hath been proved, he shall receive a crown of life, which God hath promised to them that love him. James 1:12

BUT DELIVER   *Blessed are the peacemakers: for they shall*
US FROM EVIL   *be called children of God. Blessed are they*
that suffer persecution for justice' sake: for theirs is
the kingdom of heaven.

Because in him, it hath well pleased the Father, that all fullness should dwell; and through him to reconcile all things unto himself, making peace through the blood of his cross, both as to the things that are on earth, and the things that are in heaven. Col. 1:19–20

What shall we then say to these things? If God be for us, who is against us? He that spared not even his own Son, but delivered him up for us all, how hath he not also, with him, given us all things? Who shall accuse against the elect of God? God that justifieth. Who is he that shall condemn? Christ Jesus that died, yea that is risen also again; who is at the right hand of God, who also maketh intercession for us. Who then shall separate us from the love of Christ? Shall tribulation? or distress? or famine? or nakedness? or danger? or persecution? or the sword? (As it is written: For thy sake we are put to death all the day long. We are accounted as sheep for the slaughter.) But in all these things we overcome, because of him that hath loved us. For I am sure that neither death, nor life, nor angels, nor principalities, nor powers, nor things present, nor things to come, nor might, nor height, nor depth, nor any other creature, shall be able to separate us from the love of God, which is in Christ Jesus our Lord. Rom. 8:31–39

COMMENTARY

Entry into the Beatitudes is gained through the Commandments, both the ten and the two. If Christ's extolling of the two greatest commandments, as related in Matthew (22:34–40), Mark (12:29–31), and Luke (10:25–28), can be seen as a call to interiorize and make perfect the ten commandments—illustrated in the parallel passages above—, then the eight Beatitudes can be seen as a direct, spiritual reverberation of this love of God and neighbor. By itself alone the first Beatitude of the 'poor in spirit' represents our true state once the entirety of our being has been swept by the love of God: we were nothing before the touch of the Creator's hand, and now once again we are as nothing and know it. Such is the promise of the Father invoked by James over the poor. This is not a sterile, obliterating poverty, but a fertile poverty watered by the 'tears' of the second beatitude. Here, in second place, we are reminded and re-reminded—tears are seldom solitary except for the dying—of all the distances between ourselves and God's Kingdom: sins, confusions, and all those other un-named spurious 'goods' that pour into and out of the emptiness of the creature. Whoever truly recognizes this distance receives the gift of tears, of true lamentation. But here—and this is the miraculous, unprecedented import of the Beatitude—we find the full 'rounding out' of the first Beatitude: we are comforted! But "how shall this be done?...The Holy Spirit shall come upon thee, and the power of the most High shall overshadow thee" (Luke 1:34–35). As with Mary it is the only Paraclete, the sole Comforter who will do this thing, and wipe away all tears (Apoc. 7:17). With the first Beatitude we share in the self-emptying incarnation and death of Christ, with the second we share in all the fullness of the Holy Spirit: we have crossed the great divide between humanity and Trinity.

Taken together, the next three beatitudes represent the original charter of a truly Christian society: even now the meek have brought heaven to earth and humbled every utopia, even now justice and mercy have met and kissed (Psalm 84:11), despite the darkness of every age and the lateness of every hour. This is true hospitality, the love of neighbor.

Love of self is reserved for the last three Beatitudes, for only this self can place a watch and guard over its heart while awaiting the revelation of its God, only this self can give its full allegiance to the commonwealth of the blessed and act accordingly, only this self can endure until the end because so wondrously imbued with the grace of God.

Lastly, Christ has given us a foretaste of the Trinity in the Beatitudes as a whole:

At the center of each Beatitude sparkles a facet of the 'characterology' of Jesus Christ, one of the 'names' of the God-Man, one of the virtues by which we might glimpse His psychology, and each one of which we too must embody if we are to attain that God-likeness to which we are called: The Poor in Spirit, The Meek One (cf. Matt. 11:29), The One Who Mourns for Sin and its Consequences (as at the death of Lazarus, and in the Garden of Gethsemane), The One Who Hungers and Thirsts after Justice, The Merciful Lord, The All-Pure of Heart, The Prince of Peace (cf. Eph. 2:13–18), The Persecuted One. This last of 'titles' can be seen as summarizing all the rest. For what is persecution if not that 'furnace of affliction' which consumes the separateness of the virtues and unifies our being in the love of God?

Once we recognize Christ the Son of God at the center of each Beatitude, we can go further and see the Holy Spirit in the initial 'Blessed', for it is the Holy Spirit who bestows the initial blessing: it is He who broods over the face of the Deep and overshadows the Holy Virgin so that all generations might call her 'blessed'. Nor is the presence of the Father lacking, for, with the last part of each beatitude, we come to the 'ontologies', to those superabundant states of being contained in the kingdom of heaven (just as the Beatitudes are 'contained' by the repeated phrase: "theirs is the kingdom of heaven"), where Christ will hand over the kingdom to the Father and God will be all in all (1 Cor. 15:28).

THE BEATITUDES AND THE GIFTS OF THE HOLY SPIRIT

And there shall come forth a rod out of the root of Jesse, and a flower shall rise up out of his root. And the spirit of the Lord shall rest upon him: the spirit of wisdom, and of understanding, the spirit of counsel, and of fortitude, the spirit of knowledge, and of godliness. And he shall be filled with the spirit of the fear of the Lord. Isaiah 11:1–3

The gifts of the Holy Spirit can be fitted to these petitions [of the Lord's Prayer] in different ways, either ascending or descending. Ascending we can attach the first petition to fear, inasmuch as fear produces poverty of spirit and makes us seek God's honor, so that we say, 'Hallowed be thy name.' Descending, we can say that the final gift, that of wisdom, which makes people into God's children, goes with this petition. — Thomas Aquinas, *Lectures on St Matthew.*

ACCORDING TO AUGUSTINE

	THE BEATITUDES	THE GIFTS
OUR FATHER WHO ART IN HEAVEN HALLOWED BE THY NAME	The Poor in Spirit	Fear of the Lord
THY KINGDOM COME	The Meek	Piety
THY WILL BE DONE ON EARTH AS IT IS IN HEAVEN	The Mournful	Knowledge
GIVE US THIS DAY OUR DAILY BREAD	Those who Hunger and Thirst after Justice	Fortitude
AND FORGIVE US OUR TRESPASSES AS WE FORGIVE THOSE WHO TRESPASS AGAINST US	The Merciful	Counsel
AND LEAD US NOT INTO TEMPTATION	The Clean of Heart	Understanding
BUT DELIVER US FROM EVIL	The Peacemakers	Wisdom

ACCORDING TO INVERSE PERSPECTIVE

	THE BEATITUDES	THE GIFTS
OUR FATHER WHO ART IN HEAVEN HALLOWED BE THY NAME	The Peacemakers	Wisdom
THY KINGDOM COME	The Clean of Heart	Understanding
THY WILL BE DONE ON EARTH AS IT IS IN HEAVEN	The Merciful	Counsel
GIVE US THIS DAY OUR DAILY BREAD	Remains the same and betokens Christ the Mediator, our immutable Pivot and Center in the Eucharist.	
AND FORGIVE US OUR TRESPASSES AS WE FORGIVE THOSE WHO TRESPASS AGAINST US	The Mournful	Knowledge
AND LEAD US NOT INTO TEMPTATION	The Meek	Piety
BUT DELIVER US FROM EVIL	The Poor in Spirit	Fear of the Lord

THE GREAT LITANY

To beg God's mercy is to ask for his kingdom, that kingdom which Christ promised to give to those who seek for it, assuring them that all things else of which they have need will be added unto them.
—Nicholas Cabasilas, *Commentary on the Divine Liturgy*, 11,13.

OUR FATHER WHO ART IN HEAVEN HALLOWED BE THY NAME	In peace let us pray to the Lord. *Lord, have mercy.* For the peace of God and the salvation of our souls, let us pray to the Lord. *Lord, have mercy.*
THY KINGDOM COME	For peace of the whole world, for the stability of the holy churches of God, and for the unity of all, let us pray to the Lord. *Lord, have mercy.* For this holy house and for those who enter it with faith, reverence, and the fear of God, let us pray to the Lord. *Lord, have mercy.* For our Archbishop, our Bishop, the honorable presbyters, the deacons in the service of Christ, and all the clergy and laity, let us pray to the Lord. *Lord, have mercy.*
THY WILL BE DONE ON EARTH AS IT IS IN HEAVEN	For our country, the president, and all those in public service, let us pray to the Lord. *Lord, have mercy.* For this parish and city, for every city and country, and for the faithful who live in them, let us pray to the Lord. *Lord, have mercy.*
GIVE US THIS DAY OUR DAILY BREAD	For favorable weather, an abundance of the fruits of the earth, and temperate seasons, let us pray to the Lord. *Lord, have mercy.* For travelers by land, sea, and air, for the sick, the suffering, the captives, and for their salvation, let us pray to the Lord. *Lord, have mercy.*
AND FORGIVE US OUR TRESPASSES AS WE FORGIVE THOSE WHO TRESPASS AGAINST US AND LEAD US NOT INTO TEMPTATION	For our deliverance from all affliction, wrath, danger, and distress, let us pray to the Lord. *Lord, have mercy.*
BUT DELIVER US FROM EVIL	Help us, save us, have mercy upon us, and protect us, O God, by Your grace. *Lord, have mercy.*

THE WORD OF GOD

Be ye doers of the word and not hearers only. James 1:22

OUR FATHER WHO
ART IN HEAVEN
HALLOWED BE
THY NAME

In the beginning was the Word, and the Word was with God, and the Word was God... But as many as received him, he gave them the power to be made the sons of God, to them that believe in his name. John 1:1, 12
And the word which you have heard is not mine; but the Father's who sent me. John 14:24

THY KINGDOM COME

That which was from the beginning, which we have heard, which we have seen with our eyes, which we have looked upon and our hands have handled, of the word of life; for the life was manifested; and we have seen and do bear witness and declare unto you the life eternal, which was with the Father and hath appeared to us. 1 John 1:1–2

THY WILL BE DONE
ON EARTH AS IT IS
IN HEAVEN

Heaven and earth shall pass away; but my word shall not pass away. Mark 13:31
For we know that every creature groaneth and travaileth in pain, even till now. And not only it, but ourselves also, who have the first-fruits of the Spirit; even we ourselves groan within ourselves, waiting for the adoption of the sons of God, the redemption of our body... Likewise, the Spirit also helpeth our infirmity. For we know not what we should pray for as we ought; but the Spirit himself asketh for us with unspeakable groanings. Rom. 8:22–23, 26

GIVE US THIS DAY
OUR DAILY BREAD

Man liveth not by bread alone, but by every word of God. Luke 4:4

AND FORGIVE US OUR
TRESPASSES AS WE
FORGIVE THOSE
WHO TRESPASS
AGAINST US

Purifying your souls in the obedience of charity, with a brotherly love, from a sincere heart love one another earnestly; being born again not of corruptible seed, but of incorruptible, by the word of God who liveth and remaineth for ever. 1Pet. 1:22–23

AND LEAD US NOT
INTO TEMPTATION

For the word of God is living and effectual and more piercing than any two-edged sword and reaching unto the division of the soul and the spirit, of the joints also and the marrow; and is a discerner of the thoughts and intents of the heart. Heb. 4:12
Be strengthened in the Lord, and in the might of his power, that you may be able to stand against the deceits of the devil... Therefore, take unto you the armor of God, that you may be able to resist in the evil day and to stand in all things perfect. Stand, therefore, having your loins girt about with truth and having on the breastplate of justice; and your feet shod with the preparation of the gospel of peace; in all things taking the shield of faith, wherewith you may be able to extinguish all the fiery darts of the most wicked one. And take unto you the helmet of salvation and the sword of the Spirit (which is the word of God). Eph. 6:10–17

BUT DELIVER
US FROM EVIL

When any one heareth the word of the kingdom, and understandeth it not, there cometh the wicked one and catcheth away that which was sown in his heart, and this is he that received the seed by the way-side. Matt. 13:19

THE LORD'S PRAYER OF THE MYSTERIES

Our Father who art in heaven
Hallowed be thy name

Paul, an apostle of Jesus Christ, by the will of God, to all the saints who are at Ephesus and to the faithful in Christ Jesus. Grace be to you and peace, from God the Father and from the Lord Jesus Christ.

Blessed be the God and Father of our Lord Jesus Christ, who hath blessed us with spiritual blessings in heavenly places, in Christ: as he chose us in him before the foundation of the world, that we should be holy and unspotted in his sight in charity. Who hath predestinated us unto the adoption of children through Jesus Christ unto himself: according to the purpose of his will: unto the praise of the glory of his grace, in which he hath graced us, in his beloved son. In whom we have redemption through his blood, the remission of sins, according to the riches of his, grace, which hath superabounded in us, in all wisdom and prudence, that he might make known unto us the mystery of his will, according to his good pleasure, which he hath purposed in him, in the dispensation of the fulness of times, to re-establish all things in Christ, that are in heaven and on earth, in him. In whom we also are called by lot, being predestinated according to the purpose of him who worketh all things according to the counsel of his will. That we may be unto the praise of his glory: we who before hoped in Christ: in whom you also, after you had heard the word of truth (the gospel of your salvation), in whom also believing, you were signed with the holy Spirit of promise. Who is the pledge of our inheritance, unto the redemption of acquisition, unto the praise of his glory.

Wherefore, I also, hearing of your faith that is in the Lord Jesus and of your love towards all the saints, cease not to give thanks for you, making commemoration of you in my prayers, that the God of our Lord Jesus Christ, the Father of glory, may give unto you the spirit of wisdom and of revelation, in the knowledge of him: the eyes of your heart enlightened that you may know what the hope is of his calling and what are the riches of the glory of his inheritance in the saints. And what is the exceeding greatness of his power towards us, who believe according to the operation of the might of his power, which he wrought in Christ, raising him up from the dead and setting him on his right hand in the heavenly places. Above all principality and power and virtue and dominion and every name that is named, not only in this world, but also in that which is to come. And he hath subjected all things under his feet and hath made him head over all the church, which is his body and the fulness of him who is filled all in all. (1:1–23)

Thy kingdom come

And you, when you were dead in your offences and sins, wherein in time past you walked according to the course of this world, according to the prince of the power of this air, of the spirit that now worketh on the children of unbelief: in which also we all conversed in time past, in the desires of our flesh, fulfilling the will of the flesh and of our thoughts, and were by nature children of wrath, even as the rest: but God (who is rich in mercy) for his exceeding charity wherewith he loved us even when we were dead in sins, hath quickened us together in Christ (by whose grace you are saved) and hath raised us up together and hath made us sit together in the heavenly places, through Christ Jesus. That he might shew in the ages to come the abundant riches of his grace, in his bounty towards us in Christ Jesus. For by grace you are saved through faith: and that not of yourselves, for it is the gift of God. Not of works, that no man may glory. For we are his workmanship, created in Christ Jesus in good works, which God hath prepared that we should walk in them.

For which cause be mindful that you, being heretofore gentiles in the flesh, who are called uncircumcision by that which is called circumcision in the flesh, made by hands: that you were at that time without Christ, being aliens from the conversation of Israel and strangers to the testament, having no hope of the promise and without God in this world. But now in Christ Jesus, you, who some time were afar off, are made nigh by the blood of Christ.

For he is our peace, who hath made both one, and breaking down the middle wall of partition, the enmities in his flesh: making void the law of commandments contained in decrees: that he might make the two in himself into one new man, making peace, and might reconcile both to God in one body by the cross, killing the enmities in himself. And coming, he preached peace to you that were afar off: and peace to them that were nigh. For by him we have access both in one Spirit to the Father.

Now therefore you are no more strangers and foreigners: but you are fellow citizens with the saints and the domestics of God, built upon the foundation of the apostles and prophets, Jesus Christ himself being the chief corner stone: in whom all the building, being framed together, groweth up into an holy temple in the Lord. In whom you also are built together into an habitation of God in the Spirit.

For this cause, I Paul, the prisoner of Jesus Christ, for you Gentiles: if yet you have heard of the dispensation of the grace of God which is given me towards you: how that, according to revelation, the mystery has been made known to me, as I have written above in a few words: as you reading, may understand my knowledge in the mystery of Christ, which in other generations was not known to the sons of men, as it is now revealed to his holy apostles and prophets in the Spirit: that the Gentiles should be fellow heirs and of the same body: and copartners of his promise in Christ Jesus, by the gospel of which I am made a minister, according to the gift of the grace of God, which is given to me according to the operation of his power. To me, the least of all the saints, is given this grace, to preach among the Gentiles the unsearchable riches of Christ: and to enlighten all men, that they may see what is the dispensation of the mystery which hath been hidden from eternity in God who created all things: that the manifold wisdom of God may be made known to the principalities and powers in heavenly places through the church, according to the eternal purpose which he made in Christ Jesus our Lord: in whom we have boldness and access with confidence by the faith of him. Wherefore I pray you not to faint at my tribulations for you, which is your glory.

For this cause I bow my knees to the Father of our Lord Jesus Christ, of whom all paternity in heaven and earth is named: that he would grant you, according to the riches of his glory, to be strengthened by his Spirit with might unto the inward man: that Christ may dwell by faith in your hearts: that, being rooted and founded in charity, you may be able to comprehend, with all the saints, what is the breadth and length and height and depth, to know also the charity of Christ, which surpasseth all knowledge: that you may be filled unto all the fulness of God.

Now to him who is able to do all things more abundantly than we desire or understand, according to the power that worketh in us: to him be glory in the church and in Christ Jesus, unto all generations, world without end. Amen. (2:1–3:21)

Thy will be done on earth as it is in heaven

I therefore, a prisoner in the Lord, beseech you that you walk worthy of the vocation in which you are called: with all humility and mildness, with patience, supporting one another in charity. Careful to keep the unity of the Spirit in the bond of peace. One body and one Spirit: as you are called in one hope of your calling. One Lord, one faith, one baptism. One God and Father of all, who is above all, and through all, and in us all. But to every one of us is given grace, according to the measure of the giving of Christ. Wherefore he saith: Ascending on high, he led captivity captive: he gave gifts to men. Now that he ascended, what is it, but because he also descended first into the lower parts of the earth? He that descended is the same also that ascended above all the heavens: that he might fill all things. And he gave some apostles, and some prophets, and other some evangelists, and other some pastors and doctors: for the perfecting of the saints, for the word of the ministry, for the edifying of the body of Christ: until we all meet into the unity of faith and of the knowledge of the Son of God, unto a perfect man, unto the measure of the age of the fulness of Christ: that henceforth we be no more children tossed to and fro and carried about with every wind of doctrine, by the wickedness of men, by cunning craftiness by which they lie in wait to deceive. But doing the truth in charity, we may in all things grow up in him who is the head, even Christ: from whom the whole body, being compacted and fitly joined together, by what every joint supplieth, according to the operation in the measure of every part, maketh increase of the body, unto the edifying of itself in charity.

This then I say and testify in the Lord: That henceforward you walk not as also the Gentiles walk in the vanity of their mind: having their understanding darkened: being alienated from the life of God through the ignorance that is in them, because of the blindness of their hearts. Who despairing have given themselves up to lascivi-ousness, unto the working of all uncleanness, unto covetousness. But you have not so learned Christ: if so be that you have heard him and have been taught in him, as the truth is in Jesus: to put off, according to former conversation, the old man, who is corrupted according to the desire of error. And be renewed in spirit of your mind: and put on the new man, who according to God is created in justice and holiness of truth.

Wherefore, putting away lying, speak ye the truth, every man with his neigh-bour. For we are members one of another. Be angry: and sin not. Let not the sun go down upon your anger. Give not place to the devil. He that stole, let him now steal no more: but rather let him labour, working with his hands the thing which is good, that he may have something to give to him that suffereth need. Let no evil speech proceed from your mouth: but that which is good, to the edification of faith: that it may administer grace to the hearers. And grieve not the holy Spirit of God: whereby you are sealed unto the day of redemption. Let all bitterness and anger and indignation and clamour and blasphemy be put away from you, with all malice. And be ye kind one to another: merciful, forgiving one another, even as God hath forgiven you in Christ.

Be ye therefore followers of God, as most dear children: and walk in love, as Christ also hath loved us and hath delivered himself for us, an oblation and a sacrifice to God for an odour of sweetness. But fornication and all uncleanness or covetousness, let it not so much as be named among you, as becometh saints: or obscenity or foolish talking or scurrility, which is to no purpose: but rather giving of thanks. For know you this and understand: That no fornicator or unclean or covetous person (which is a serving of idols) hath inheritance in the kingdom of Christ and of God. (4:1–5:5)

Give us this day our daily bread

Let no man deceive you with vain words. For because of these things cometh the anger of God upon the children of unbelief. Be ye not therefore partakers with them. For you were heretofore darkness, but now light in the Lord. Walk then as children of the light. For the fruit of the light is in all goodness and justice and truth: proving what is well pleasing to God. And have no fellowship with the unfruitful works of darkness: but rather reprove them. For the things that are done by them in secret, it is a shame even to speak of. But all things that are reproved are made manifest by the light: for all that is made manifest is light. Wherefore he saith: Rise, thou that sleepest, and arise from the dead: and Christ shall enlighten thee.

See therefore, brethren, how you walk circumspectly: not as unwise, but as wise: redeeming the time, because the days are evil. Wherefore, become not unwise: but understanding what is the will of God. And be not drunk with wine, wherein is luxury: but be ye filled with the Holy Spirit, speaking to yourselves in psalms and hymns and spiritual canticles, singing and making melody in your hearts to the Lord: giving thanks always for all things, in the name of our Lord Jesus Christ, to God and the Father: being subject one to another, in the fear of Christ. (5:6–5:21)

And forgive us our trespasses as we forgive those who trespass against us

Let women be subject to their husbands, as to the Lord: because the husband is the head of the wife, as Christ is the head of the church. He is the savior of his body. Therefore as the church is subject to Christ: so also let the wives be to their husbands in all things. Husbands, love your wives, as Christ also loved the church and delivered himself up for it: that he might sanctify it, cleansing it by the laver of water in the word of life: that he might present it to himself, a glorious church, not having spot or wrinkle or any such thing; but that it should be holy and without blemish. So also ought men to love their wives as their own bodies. He that loveth his wife loveth himself. For no man ever hated his own flesh, but nourisheth and cherisheth it, as also Christ doth the church: because we are members of him, body, of his flesh and of his bones. For this cause shall a man leave his father and mother: and shall cleave to his wife. And they shall be two in one flesh. This is a great sacrament: but I speak in Christ and in the church. Nevertheless, let every one of you in particular love for his wife as himself: And let the wife fear her husband.

Children, obey your parents in the Lord: for this is just. Honour thy father and thy mother, which is the first commandment with a promise: that it may be well with thee, and thou mayest be long lived upon earth. And you, fathers, provoke not your children to anger: but bring them up in the discipline and correction of the Lord.

Servants, be obedient to them that are your lords according to the flesh, with fear and trembling, in the simplicity of your heart, as to Christ. Not serving to the eye, as it were pleasing men: but, as the servants of Christ, doing the will of God from the heart. With a good will serving, as to the Lord, and not to men. Knowing that whatsoever good thing any man shall do, the same shall he receive from the Lord, whether he be bond or free. And you, masters, do the same things to them, forbearing threatenings: knowing that the Lord both of them and you is in heaven. And there is no respect of persons with him. (5:22–6:9)

And lead us not into temptation

Finally, brethren, be strengthened in the Lord and in the might of his power. Put you on the armour of God, that you may be able to stand against the deceits of the devil. For our wrestling is not against flesh and blood; but against principalities and powers, against the rulers of the world of this darkness, against the spirits of wickedness in the high places. Therefore, take unto you the armour of God, that you may be able to resist in the evil day and to stand in all things perfect. Stand therefore, having your loins girt about with truth and having on the breastplate of justice: and your feet shod with the preparation of the gospel of peace. In all things taking the shield of faith, wherewith you may be able to extinguish all the fiery darts of the most wicked one. And take unto you the helmet of salvation and the sword of the Spirit (which is the word of God). By all prayer and supplication praying at all times in the spirit: and in the same watching with all instance and supplication for all the saints: and for me, that speech may be given me, that I may open my mouth with confidence, to make known the mystery of the gospel, for which I am an ambassador in a chain: so that therein I may be bold to speak according as I ought.

But that you also may know the things that concern me and what I am doing, Tychicus, my dearest brother and faithful minister in the Lord, will make known to you all things: whom I have sent to you for this same purpose: that you may know the things concerning us, and that he may comfort your hearts. (6:10–22)

But deliver us from evil

Peace be to the brethren and charity with faith, from God the Father and the Lord Jesus Christ. Grace be with all them that love our Lord Jesus Christ in incor-ruption. Amen. (6:23–24)

THE FOUR SENSES OF SCRIPTURE

A person ought to describe threefold in his soul the meaning of the divine letters... just as a human being is said to be made up of body, soul, and spirit, so also is sacred Scripture, which has been granted by God's gracious dispensation for man's salvation. —Origen, *On First Principles*, II, 4.

So long as he cleaves to the letter, his inner hunger for spiritual knowledge will not be satisfied; for he has condemned himself like the wily serpent to feed on the earth—that is, on the outward or literal form—of Scripture, and does not, as a true disciple of Christ, feed on heaven—that is, on the spirit and soul of Scripture, in other words, on celestial and angelic bread. I mean that he does not feed through Christ on the spiritual contemplation and knowledge of the Scriptures, which God gives unstintingly to those who love him, in accordance with the text: 'He gave them the bread of heaven; man ate the food of angels' (Psalm 77:24–25). — Maximus the Confessor, *Various Texts*, Fifth Century, 35.

	THE FOUR SENSES OF SCRIPTURE	'IN THE BREAKING OF BREAD' SCRIPTURAL PARALLELS
OUR FATHER WHO ART IN HEAVEN HALLOWED BE THY NAME	The Anagogical: prefigurings of life in glory, the inexpressible expressed (Spirit)	Give us this day our supersubstantial bread. Matt. 6:11 To him that overcometh I will give the hidden manna and a white stone—a stone with a new name written on it which no one knows except the one receiving it. Apoc. 2:17
THY KINGDOM COME	The Tropological, The Moral: signposts for the living-out of scripture (Soul, as it verges on the Spirit)	Man liveth not by bread alone, but by every word of God. Luke 4:4
THY WILL BE DONE ON EARTH AS IT IS IN HEAVEN	The Allegorical: scripture fulfilled[1] (Soul, as it verges on the Body)	The bread of God is that which cometh down from heaven and giveth life to the world... I am the bread of life. John 6:33–35
GIVE US THIS DAY OUR DAILY BREAD	The Literal: facts, the anchor and support of the other senses (Body)	Give us this day our daily bread. Luke 11:4

---

1. Cf. Matt. 26:54, Mark 14:49, 15:28, Luke 4:21, Acts 1:16. The deeds and teachings of Christ are seen as cast backwards into, or anticipated in, the Old Testament, and as cast forward into the ecclesial life of sacrament and doctrine. This sense has little to do with the rhetorical device called 'allegory', but everything to do with seeing the prehistory and history of Christianity as framed by the life of Christ.

	THE FOUR SENSES OF SCRIPTURE	'IN THE BREAKING OF BREAD' SCRIPTURAL PARALLELS
AND FORGIVE US OUR TRESPASSES AS WE FORGIVE THOSE WHO TRESPASS AGAINST US AND LEAD US NOT INTO TEMPTATION BUT DELIVER US FROM EVIL	Unison of the Senses[1] (Body, Soul, Spirit)	And, taking bread, he gave thanks and brake, and gave to them saying: This is my body, which is given for you. Luke 22:19

EXEGESIS

Just as the understanding of the Law and the Prophets as precursors of the coming of the Word in the flesh instructed souls about Christ, so has this same glorified Word of God incarnate become a precursor of his spiritual coming and he instructs souls by his words about the acceptance of his visible divine coming. This coming he always effects by changing those who are worthy from the flesh to the spirit through the virtues. And he will do this also at the end of time, clearly revealing to all what is still secret. Maximus the Confessor, *Texts of Theology*, II, 29

OUR FATHER WHO ART IN HEAVEN

No one knoweth who the Son is, but the Father; and who the Father is, but the Son and to whom the Son will reveal him. And turning to his disciples he said: Blessed are the eyes that see the things which you see. For I say to you that many prophets and kings have desired to see the things that you see and have not seen them; and to hear the things that you hear and have not heard them. Luke 10:22–24

HALLOWED BE THY NAME

These things saith the Holy One and the True One, he that hath the key of David, he that openeth and no man shutteth, shutteth and no man openeth: I know thy works. Behold, I have given before thee a door opened, which no man can shut; because thou hast a little strength and hast kept my word and hast not denied my name… He that shall overcome, I will make him a pillar in the temple of my God; and he shall go out no more. And I will write upon him the name of my God, and the name of the city of my God, the New Jerusalem, which cometh down out of heaven from my God, and my new name. He that hath an ear, let him hear what the Spirit saith to the churches. Apoc. 3:7–8, 12–13

THY KINGDOM COME

After these things, I looked; and, behold, a door was opened in heaven. And the first voice which I heard, as it were of a trumpet speaking with me, said: Come up hither and I will shew thee the things which must be done hereafter. And immediately I was in the spirit. And, behold, there was a throne set in heaven, and upon the throne one sitting… And I saw, in the right hand of him that sat on the throne, a book, written within and without, sealed with seven seals. And I saw a strong angel, proclaiming with a loud voice: Who is worthy to open the

---

1. "For a Christian, Scripture… is a Word of life for everyone; its concrete, direct language can touch the simplest souls, sometimes the simplest especially. And the mystery of it all will always be beyond the most erudite." Olivier Clément, *The Roots of Christian Mysticism*, p. 102.

book and to loose the seals thereof? And no man was able, neither in heaven nor on earth nor under the earth, to open the book, nor to look on it. And I wept much, because no man was found worthy to open the book, nor to see it. And one of the ancients said to me: Weep not; behold, the lion of the tribe of Juda, the root of David, hath prevailed to open the book and to loose the seven seals thereof. And I saw; and, behold, in the midst of the throne and of the four living creatures, and in the midst of the ancients, a Lamb standing, as it were slain, having seven horns and seven eyes; which are the seven Spirits of God, sent forth into all the earth. And he came and took the book out of the right hand of him that sat on the throne. Apoc. 4:1–2, 5:1–7

THY WILL BE DONE ON EARTH AS IT IS IN HEAVEN

Heaven and earth shall pass away; but my word shall not pass away. Mark 13:31 Do not think that I am come to destroy the law or the prophets. I am not come to destroy, but to fulfill. For, amen, I say unto you, till heaven and earth pass, one jot or one tittle shall not pass of the law, till all be fulfilled. He therefore that shall break one of these least commandments and shall so teach men shall be called the least in the kingdom of heaven. But he that shall do and teach, he shall be called great in the kingdom of heaven. For I tell you, that unless your justice abound more than that of the scribes and Pharisees, you shall not enter into the kingdom of heaven. Matt. 5:17–20

GIVE US THIS DAY OUR DAILY BREAD

Then he said to them: O foolish and slow of heart to believe in all things which the prophets have spoken. Ought not Christ to have suffered these things and so to enter into his glory? And beginning at Moses and all the prophets, he expounded to them in all the scriptures the things that were concerning him. And they drew nigh to the town, whither they were going; and he made as though he would go farther. But they constrained him, saying: Stay with us, because it is towards evening and the day is now far spent. And he went in with them. And it came to pass, whilst he was at table with them, he took bread and blessed and brake and gave to them. And their eyes were opened; and they knew him. And he vanished out of their sight. And they said one to the other: Was not our heart burning within us whilst he spoke in the way and opened to us the scriptures? Luke 24:25–32

AND FORGIVE US OUR TRESPASSES AS WE FORGIVE THOSE WHO TRESPASS AGAINST US

And he said to them: These are the words which I spoke to you while I was yet with you, that all things must needs be fulfilled which are understanding, that they might understand the scriptures. And he said to them: Thus it is written, and thus it behooved Christ to suffer and to rise again from the dead, the third day; and that penance and remission of sins should be preached in his name, unto all nations, beginning at Jerusalem. And you are witnesses of these things. And I send the promise of my Father upon you. Luke 24:44–49

AND LEAD US NOT INTO TEMPTATION

And he said to them: To you it is given to know the mystery of the kingdom of God; but to them that are without, all things are done in parables; that seeing they may see and not perceive; and hearing they may hear and not understand;

lest at any time they should be converted and their sins should be forgiven them.[1] Mark 4:11–12

BUT DELIVER US FROM EVIL`
For this cause also the wisdom of God said: I will send to them prophets and apostles; and some of them they will kill and persecute; that the blood of all the prophets which was shed from the foundation of the world may be required of this generation, from the blood of Abel unto the blood of Zacharias, who was slain between the altar and the temple. Yea, I say to you: It shall be required of this generation. Woe to you lawyers, for you taken away the key of knowledge. You yourselves have not entered in; and those that were entering in, you have hindered. Luke 11:49–52

---

1. Why this reluctance of the Lord to pardon those 'without'? Paul comes to our assistance here, for his words about the Eucharist may just as well be applied to Scripture: "Whosoever shall eat this bread, or drink the chalice of the Lord unworthily, shall be guilty of the body and of the blood of the Lord... He that eateth and drinketh unworthily, eateth and drinketh judgment to himself, not discerning the body of the Lord" (1 Cor. 11:27, 29). To violate either the anaphora of the Liturgy or the anagogia of Scripture is a violation of the Lord's most intimate hospitality; we were strangers and he took us for his children and his friends, his very own. And yet there are some for whom this hospitality goes unrecognized, since hospitality is free from all coercion, and even God—especially God—will not remove the willful veil from our hearts once we have installed it there in our own reluctance. To those who are near the 'logic' of Scripture is luminous, to those afar it is an irritant: they recognize 'something', but they are always trying to explain it away or explain it 'differently'.

ON THE WAY TO EMMAUS: THE SEVENFOLD
INTERPRETIVE GIFT OF THE SCRIPTURES

	THE FOUR SENSES (THAT ARE ONLY ONE)	THE SEVEN GIFTS (THAT ARE ONLY ONE)	THE THREE WAYS (THAT ARE ONLY ONE)
		For the letter killeth...	
BUT FORGIVE US OUR TRESPASSES AS WE FORGIVE THOSE WHO TRESPASS AGAINST US AND LEAD US NOT INTO TEMPTATION BUT DELIVER US FROM EVIL	Literal	Piety Fear of the Lord	Purgative
		but the spirit quickeneth. 2 Cor. 3:6	
GIVE US THIS DAY OUR DAILY BREAD	Figurative	Knowledge Piety	Illuminative
THY WILL BE DONE ON EARTH AS IT IS IN HEAVEN	Moral	Counsel Fortitude	
OUR FATHER WHO ART IN HEAVEN HALLOWED BE THY NAME THY KINGDOM COME	Anagogic	Wisdom Understanding	Unitive

COMMENTARY

PAIRING OF GIFTS The gifts are paired here because of their bestowal upon the intellect and the will. On the literal level intellect and will are at their greatest distance from each other. But, from fear to wisdom, the gifts make out of the 'neighborliness' of the faculties a unison of prayer in the love of God. In the 'letter' we come talking and reasoning, like the two disciples, out of the Jerusalem of the Scriptures, but, in the 'spirit', it is Jesus who draws near and reveals himself to us in the gifts, casting the fire of the Scriptures into our hearts and bringing about our sudden return to Jerusalem.

THE LETTER KILLETH To concentrate solely on the letter of the Scriptures is an abuse of and, ultimately, lethal to the intellect; and yet 'the letter' has a positive side, it is also 'dangerous' because lethal to the passions, to all that defies the 'jot and tittle' of the commandments.

PIETY Piety is repeated because it represents a bridge between the letter and the spirit of Scripture. We do not 'reason' our way from the letter to the spirit; it is only by a 'gift' that we are able to enter into a knowledge of Scripture... and on and on into that 'burning of the heart' which has everything to do with that great mystery: the 'wisdom' of Scripture.

LITURGY OF THE FAITHFUL

LITURGY OF THE FAITHFUL

OUR FATHER WHO ART IN HEAVEN
HALLOWED BE THY NAME

The Cherubic Hymn
(The Anaphora begins)

THY KINGDOM COME
THY WILL BE DONE ON EARTH
AS IT IS IN HEAVEN

Consecration and Epiclesis
(Completion of the Anaphora)

(The line of demarcation
between the heavenly and earthly
petitions of the lord's prayer)

The Lord's Prayer
(Besides being mediatory in meaning
and the words of the Divine Mediator
Himself, the Lord's Prayer, as summary
and recapitulation of the Anaphora, and
as preparation for and anticipation of
Communion, holds a mediatory position
in the Liturgy, uniting *before* and *after*
into a seamless whole.)

GIVE US THIS DAY OUR DAILY BREAD
AND FORGIVE US OUR TRESPASSES
AS WE FORGIVE THOSE WHO
TRESPASS AGAINST US
AND LEAD US NOT
INTO TEMPTATION
BUT DELIVER
US FROM EVIL

Communion
(Both remedy and participation
in the Mystical Body
of Christ)

Are they [the angels] *not all ministering* [λειτουργικὰ, liturgical] *spirits, sent to minister for them who shall receive the inheritance of salvation?* Hebrews 1:14

We are an image of the cherubim, that is to say we are identified with them; we are cherubim 'in a mystery', that is to say inwardly and liturgically, and hence truly. — Archimandrite Vasileios, *Hymn of Entry*

OUR FATHER WHO ART IN HEAVEN HALLOWED BE THY NAME

Our Father who art in heaven hallowed be thy name
O holy God, who restest in thy Saints, who art hymned by the Seraphim with thrice-holy voice, and art glorified by the Cherubim, and worshipped by all the heavenly Powers,
Thy kingdom come
and who from non-being hast brought all things into being, who hast created man after thine image and likeness,
Thy will be done on earth as it is in heaven
and hast adorned him with thine every gift,
Give us this day our daily bread
who givest to him that asketh wisdom and understanding,
And forgive us our trespasses as we forgive those who trespass against us
and who despisest not him that sinneth, but hast set forth repentance unto salvation, who hast vouchsafed us, thy humble and unworthy servants, even at this hour, to stand before the glory of thy holy Altar, and to offer thee due worship and glorification, thyself, O Master, accept even from the mouths of us sinners the Thrice-holy Hymn and visit us in thy lovingkindness.
And lead us not into temptation, but deliver us from evil
Pardon us every offense, voluntary and involuntary, sanctify our souls and bodies, and grant us to serve thee in holiness all the days of our life, through the intercessions of the holy Theotokos, and all the Saints, who from everlasting have been well-pleasing unto thee. (*Prayer of the Trisagion Hymn*)

THY KINGDOM COME

Let us who in a mystery represent the Cherubim, and chant the thrice-holy hymn to the life-creating Trinity, now lay aside all earthly care, that we may receive the King of all, who cometh invisibly upborne by angelic hosts. Alleluia. Alleluia. Alleluia. (*The Cherubic Hymn*)

THY WILL BE DONE ON EARTH AS IT IS IN HEAVEN

Bless the Lord, O you His angels. You mighty ones who do His word, hearkening to the voice of His words. Bless the Lord, all His hosts, His ministers that do His will. (*First Antiphon*)

GIVE US THIS DAY OUR DAILY BREAD

An angel of peace, a faithful guide and guardian of our souls and bodies, let us ask of the Lord. (*Ectenia*)

AND FORGIVE US OUR TRESPASSES AS WE FORGIVE THOSE WHO TRESPASS AGAINST US AND LEAD US NOT INTO TEMPTATION BUT DELIVER US FROM EVIL

None is worthy among those that are bound with carnal desires and pleasures to approach or draw nigh or to minister to thee, O King of glory, for to serve thee is a great and fearful thing even unto the heavenly Powers. (*Priest during the Cherubic Hymn*)

THE APOSTLES' CREED

To today's confirmed esoterist it seems most unlikely that the Creed and the Lord's Prayer— so banal and anodyne have they become—were once the focus of a secret tradition. And yet… it is a well-proven fact whose traces have not entirely vanished. For my part, I attribute the greatest importance to this as a most irrefutable witness to what the Church saw as truly esoteric. —Jean Borella, *Guénonian Esoterism and Christian Mystery*

OUR FATHER WHO ART IN HEAVEN	I believe in God, the Father Almighty, Creator of heaven and earth;
HALLOWED BE THY NAME	and in Jesus Christ, His only Son, our Lord: who was conceived by the Holy Spirit, born of the Virgin Mary, suffered under Pontius Pilate, was crucified; died, and was buried. He descended into hell; the third day He arose again from the dead; He ascended into heaven, sitteth at the right hand of God the Father Almighty; from thence He shall come to judge the living and the dead.
THY KINGDOM COME	I believe in the Holy Spirit,
THY WILL BE DONE ON EARTH AS IT IS IN HEAVEN	the holy catholic Church,
GIVE US THIS DAY OUR DAILY BREAD	the communion of saints,
AND FORGIVE US OUR TRESPASSES AS WE FORGIVE THOSE WHO TRESPASS AGAINST US AND LEAD US NOT INTO TEMPTATION	the forgiveness of sins,
BUT DELIVER US FROM EVIL	the resurrection of the body, and life everlasting. Amen.

COMMENTARY

CREED AND LORD'S PRAYER When juxtaposed in this way, the Creed appears as the static portion of our earthly 'symbol of faith'—and yet inspired by the Holy Spirit "who will lead you into all truth", into the inner dynamism of Holy Tradition—, while the Lord's Prayer is its dynamic portion—and yet decreed by the Son and set inalterably in the 'stone tables' of Scripture—, with both portions, Tradition and Scripture, to be fully explained only in the Parousia of the Bridegroom and the Bride. But, for now, do our hearts not burn while He speaks to us in the Way (i.e. Tradition; cf. Acts 19:23 and 24:22) and opens to us the Scriptures (Luke 24:27)? And this is why, as preamble to the Creed, the Church exclaims: "Let us love one another that with one mind we may confess: Father, Son, and Holy Spirit, the Trinity one in essence and undivided." Doctrine is an affair of the heart; when head and heart are fully engaged, there is no incompatibility or indifference between them.

HOLY, CATHOLIC CHURCH   In the later Nicene Creed[1] the Church is qualified by four 'marks': the Church is *one*, *holy*, *catholic* and *apostolic*. With these four marks the Church bears the imprint of one God in three divine Persons: the Church is *one* because of her belief in one God, and she is *holy*, *catholic* and *apostolic* because of her belief in a Trinity of Persons. *Holy* by the Father ("Our Father who art in heaven, hallowed be thy name." Matt. 6:9). *Catholic* by the Son ("The Father loveth the Son; and he hath given all things into his hands." John 3:35). And *apostolic* (ἀπόστολος = one who is sent) by the Holy Spirit ("But when the Paraclete cometh, whom I will send you from the Father, the Spirit of Truth, who proceedeth from the Father, he shall give testimony of me." John 15:26).

COMMUNION OF SAINTS   By petitioning for 'our daily bread', we bring ourselves into agreement with and are conformed to the 'will of heaven'. These two central petitions thus represent the very ratification and seal of our covenant with the Father in the Son by the Holy Spirit; through the 'indwelling' of the Holy Trinity in the saints, the Church is God incarnate in the world, *is* the Mystical Body of Christ.

LIFE EVERLASTING   Christ reveals the import of eternal or everlasting life in a single trinitarian sentence: "Now this is eternal life: That they may know thee, the only true God [Father], and Jesus Christ [Son], whom thou hast sent [Holy Spirit]" (John 17:3). The Creed thus begins as it ends: with the Trinity. It begins with acknowledgement of God's mighty self-disclosure and ends with the creature's partaking of it for evermore: deification.[2]

---

1. The Nicene-Constantinopolitan Creed, the only one validated by an ecumenical council, is actually the Creed used in the liturgy. The Orthodox honor the Apostles' Creed "as an ancient statement of faith, and accept its teaching; but it is simply a local western Baptismal Creed" (Ware, *The Orthodox Church*, p. 202). The Apostles' Creed is offered here because better suited to the 'template' of the Lord's Prayer; cf., however, the Appendix for a presentation of the Nicene Creed.

2. See 'Eternal Life', p. 391.

LITURGY OF THE VIRTUES

OUR FATHER WHO
ART IN HEAVEN
HALLOWED BE
THY NAME

Priest: Let us love one another that with one accord we may confess:
Choir: Father, Son, and Holy Spirit, the Trinity, One in essence and undivided.
(Invocation prior to the Creed)

FAITH SUMMONED, HOPE REALIZED IN THE ANAPHORA

THY KINGDOM COME
THY WILL BE DONE
ON EARTH AS IT
IS IN HEAVEN

Priest: Let us lift up our hearts.
Choir: We lift them up unto the Lord.
Priest: Let us give thanks unto the Lord.
Choir: It is meet and right to worship Father, Son, and Holy Spirit, the Trinity one in essence and undivided. (Invocation prior to the Consecration)

Priest: Thine own of thine own we offer unto thee on behalf of all and for all.
Choir: We hymn thee, we bless thee, we give thanks unto thee, O Lord, and we pray unto thee, O our God.
Priest: Again we offer unto thee this rational and bloodless worship, and we call upon thee and pray thee, and supplicate thee: send down thy Holy Spirit upon us and upon these Gifts set forth. (Invocation prior to the Epiclesis)

HOPE SUMMONED, LOVE REALIZED IN COMMUNION

GIVE US THIS DAY
OUR DAILY BREAD
AND FORGIVE US OUR
TRESPASSES AS WE
FORGIVE THOSE
WHO TRESPASS
AGAINST US
AND LEAD US NOT
INTO TEMPTATION
BUT DELIVER
US FROM EVIL

Priest: The servant of God, [Name], partakes of the precious and holy Body and Blood of our Lord and God and Savior Jesus Christ unto forgiveness of his sins unto life eternal. (Prayer over the communicant)

A MERCY OF PEACE, A SACRIFICE OF PRAISE,
THE FOURFOLD SACRIFICE OF THE LITURGY

In the holy sacrifice we make supplication as well as thanksgiving; but the thanksgiving is God's work, the supplication is the result of our weakness. Thanksgiving is concerned with a far wider field than supplication is. It is concerned with absolutely everything; supplication with only a few things. — Nicholas Cabasilas, *A Commentary on the Divine Liturgy*, v, 52.

A SACRIFICE OF PRAISE AND THANKSGIVING

OUR FATHER WHO
ART IN HEAVEN
HALLOWED BE
THY NAME

For of him, and by him, and in him, are all things: to him be glory for ever. Amen. I beseech you therefore, brethren, by the mercy of God, that you present your bodies a living sacrifice, holy, pleasing unto God, your reasonable service. And be not conformed to this world; but be reformed in the newness of your mind, that you may prove what is the good, and the acceptable, and the perfect will of God. Rom. 11:36–12:1–2

A SACRIFICE UNITING ALL THE FAITHFUL

THY KINGDOM COME

For we have not here a lasting city, but we seek one that is to come. By him therefore let us offer the sacrifice of praise always to God, that is to say, the fruit of lips confessing to his name. Heb. 13:14–15

A SACRIFICE OF ENTREATY

THY WILL BE DONE
ON EARTH AS IT
IS IN HEAVEN

Be ye therefore followers of God, as most dear children; and walk in love, as Christ also hath loved us, and hath delivered himself for us, an oblation and a sacrifice to God for an odor of sweetness. Eph. 5:1–2

GIVE US THIS DAY
OUR DAILY BREAD

And do not forget to do good, and to impart; for by such sacrifices God's favor is obtained. Heb. 13:16

A PROPITIATORY SACRIFICE

AND FORGIVE US OUR
TRESPASSES AS WE
FORGIVE THOSE
WHO TRESPASS
AGAINST US
AND LEAD US NOT
INTO TEMPTATION
BUT DELIVER
US FROM EVIL

But this man offering one sacrifice for sins, for ever sitteth on the right hand of God, from henceforth expecting, until his enemies be made his footstool. For by one oblation he hath perfected for ever them that are sanctified. Heb. 12:12–14

THE MYSTICAL SUPPER

OUR FATHER WHO
ART IN HEAVEN
HALLOWED BE
THY NAME

CHRIST'S DISCOURSE FOLLOWING THE LAST SUPPER

Father, the hour is come. Glorify thy Son, that thy Son may glorify thee. John 17:1
Just Father, …I have made thy name known to them and will make it known;
that the love wherewith thou hast loved me may be in them, and I in them.
John 17:25–26

THY KINGDOM COME

CHRIST'S PROMISE OF THE FEAST TO COME

I will not drink from henceforth of this fruit of the vine until that day when I
shall drink it with you new in the kingdom of my Father. Matt. 26:29

THY WILL BE DONE
ON EARTH AS IT IS
IN HEAVEN

CHRIST'S OBSERVANCE OF THE PASCH
AS PRESCRIBED IN GOD'S COVENANT WITH MOSES

Do not think that I am come to destroy the law or the prophets. I am come not
to destroy, but to fulfill. Matt. 5:17
And the day of the unleavened bread came, on which it was necessary that the
pasch should be killed. And he sent Peter and John, saying: Go, and prepare for
us the pasch, that we may eat. Luke 22:7–8

GIVE US THIS DAY
OUR DAILY BREAD

CHRIST'S INSTITUTION OF THE EUCHARIST

And whilst they were at supper, Jesus took bread and blessed and broke and
gave to his disciples and said: Take ye and eat. This is my body. Matt. 26:26

AND FORGIVE US OUR
TRESPASSES AS WE
FORGIVE THOSE
WHO TRESPASS
AGAINST US

CHRIST'S WASHING OF THE APOSTLE'S FEET

If then I, being your Lord and Master, have washed your feet; you also ought to
wash one another's feet. For I have given you an example, that as I have done to
you, so you do also. John 13:14–15

AND LEAD US NOT
INTO TEMPTATION

CHRIST'S FORETELLING OF PETER'S DENIAL

Amen, I say to you that in this night, before the cock crow, thou wilt deny me
thrice. Peter saith to him: Yea, though I should die with thee, I will not deny
thee. And in like manner said all the apostles. Matt. 26:34–35

BUT DELIVER
US FROM EVIL

CHRIST'S BETRAYAL BY JUDAS

The Son of man indeed goeth, as it is written of him. But woe to that man by
whom the Son of man shall be betrayed. It were better for him if that man had
not been born. And Judas, that betrayed him, answering, said: Is it I, Rabbi? He
saith to him: Thou hast said it. Matt. 26:24–25

THE LIVING BREAD

JOHN 6:30–67

OUR FATHER WHO
ART IN HEAVEN
HALLOWED BE
THY NAME

They said therefore to him: What sign therefore dost thou shew, that we may see, and may believe thee? What dost thou work? Our fathers did eat manna in the desert, as it is written: He gave them bread from heaven to eat. Then Jesus said to them: Amen, amen I say to you; Moses gave you not bread from heaven, but my Father giveth you the true bread from heaven. For the bread of God is that which cometh down from heaven, and giveth life to the world.

THY KINGDOM COME

They said therefore unto him: Lord, give us always this bread. And Jesus said to them: I am the bread of life: he that cometh to me shall not hunger: and he that believeth in me shall never thirst. But I said unto you, that you also have seen me, and you believe not.

THY WILL BE DONE
ON EARTH AS IT IS
IN HEAVEN

All that the Father giveth to me shall come to me; and him that cometh to me, I will not cast out. Because I came down from heaven, not to do my own will, but the will of him that sent me. Now this is the will of the Father who sent me: that of all that he hath given me, I should lose nothing; but should raise it up again in the last day. And this is the will of my Father that sent me: that every one who seeth the son, and believeth in him, may have life everlasting, and I will raise him up in the last day. The Jews therefore murmured at him, because he had said: I am the living bread which came down from heaven. And they said: Is not this Jesus, the son of Joseph, whose father and mother we know? How then saith he, I came down from heaven? Jesus therefore answered, and said to them: Murmur not among yourselves. No man can come to me, except the Father, who hath sent me, draw him; and I will raise him up in the last day. It is written in the prophets: And they shall all be taught of God. Every one that hath heard of the Father, and hath learned, cometh to me. Not that any man hath seen the Father; but he who is of God, he hath seen the Father.

GIVE US THIS DAY
OUR DAILY BREAD

Amen, amen I say unto you: He that believeth in me, hath everlasting life. I am the bread of life. Your fathers did eat manna in the desert, and are dead. This is the bread which cometh down from heaven; that if any man eat of it, he may not die. I am the living bread which came down from heaven. If any man eat of this bread, he shall live for ever; and the bread that I will give, is my flesh, for the life of the world.

AND FORGIVE US OUR
TRESPASSES AS WE
FORGIVE THOSE
WHO TRESPASS
AGAINST US

The Jews therefore strove among themselves, saying: How can this man give us his flesh to eat? Then Jesus said to them: Amen, amen I say unto you: Except you eat the flesh of the Son of man, and drink his blood, you shall not have life in you. He that eateth my flesh, and drinketh my blood, hath everlasting life: and I will raise him up in the last day. For my flesh is meat indeed: and my blood is drink indeed. He that eateth my flesh, and drinketh my blood, abideth in me, and I in him. As the living Father hath sent me, and I live by the Father; so he that eateth me, the same also shall live by me. This is the bread that came down from heaven. Not as your fathers did eat manna, and are dead. He that eateth this bread, shall live for ever. These things he said, teaching in the synagogue, in Capharnaum.

AND LEAD US NOT INTO TEMPTATION	Many therefore of his disciples, hearing it, said: This saying is hard, and who can hear it? But Jesus, knowing in himself, that his disciples murmured at this, said to them: Doth this scandalize you? If then you shall see the Son of man ascend up where he was before? It is the spirit that quickeneth: the flesh profiteth nothing. The words that I have spoken to you, are spirit and life.

But deliver us from evil — But there are some of you that believe not. For Jesus knew from the beginning, who they were that did not believe, and who he was, that would betray him. And he said: Therefore did I say to you, that no man can come to me, unless it be given him by my Father. After this many of his disciples went back; and walked no more with him.

HIS BLOOD FOR THE LIFE OF THE WORLD

OUR FATHER WHO ART IN HEAVEN HALLOWED BE THY NAME — And this is the testimony that God hath given to us eternal life. And this life is in his Son. He that hath the Son hath life. He that hath not the Son hath not life. These things I write to you that you may know that you have eternal life: you who believe in the name of the Son of God. And this is the confidence which we have towards him: That, whatsoever we shall ask according to his will, he heareth us. 1 John 5:11–14

And may the God of peace, who brought again from the dead the great pastor of the sheep, our Lord Jesus Christ, in the blood of the everlasting testament, fit you in all goodness, that you may do his will; doing in you that which is well pleasing in his sight, through Jesus Christ, to whom is glory for ever and ever. Amen. Heb. 13:20–21

THY KINGDOM COME — Again therefore, Jesus spoke to: them, saying: I am the light of the world. He that followeth me walketh not in darkness, but shall have the light of life. The Pharisees therefore said to him: Thou givest testimony of thyself. Thy testimony is not true. Jesus answered and said to them: Although I give testimony of myself, my testimony is true: for I know whence I came and whither I go. John 8:12–14

Wherefore Jesus also, that he might sanctify the people by his own blood, suffered without the gate. Let us go forth therefore to him without the camp, bearing his reproach. For, we have not here a lasting city: but we seek one that is to come. Heb. 13:12–14

THY WILL BE DONE ON EARTH AS IT IS IN HEAVEN — And he said to me: It is done. I am Alpha and Omega: the Beginning and the End. To him that thirsteth, I will give of the fountain of the water of life, freely. Apoc. 21:6

For all have sinned and do need the glory of God. Being justified freely by his grace, through the redemption that is in Christ Jesus, whom God hath proposed to be a propitiation, through faith in his blood, to the shewing of his justice, for the remission of former sins, through the forbearance of God, for the shewing of his justice in this time: that he himself may be just and the justifier of him who is of the faith of Jesus Christ. Rom. 3:23–26

GIVE US THIS DAY
OUR DAILY BREAD

And he said to them: Take heed and beware of all covetousness: for a man's life doth not consist in the abundance of things which he possesseth. And he spoke a similitude to them, saying: The land of a certain rich man brought forth plenty of fruits. And he thought within himself, saying: What shall I do, because I have no room where to bestow my fruits? And he said: This will I do: I will pull down my barns and will build greater: and into them will I gather all things that are grown to me and my goods. And I will say to my soul: Soul, thou hast much goods laid up for many years. Take thy rest: eat, drink, make good cheer. But God said to him: Thou fool, this night do they require thy soul of thee. And whose shall those things be which thou hast provided? So is he that layeth up treasure for himself and is not rich towards God. And he said to his disciples: Therefore I say to you: Be not solicitous for your life, what you shall eat, nor for your body, what you shall put on. The life is more than the meat: and the body is more than the raiment. Luke 12:15–23

I speak as to wise men: judge ye yourselves what I say. The chalice of benediction which we bless, is it not the communion of the blood of Christ? And the bread which we break, is it not the partaking of the body of the Lord? 1 Cor. 10:15–16

AND FORGIVE US OUR
TRESPASSES AS WE
FORGIVE THOSE
WHO TRESPASS
AGAINST US

For if by one man's offence death reigned through one; much more they who receive abundance of grace and of the gift and of justice shall reign in life through one, Jesus Christ. Therefore, as by the offence of one, unto all men to condemnation: so also by the justice of one, unto all men to justification of life. Rom. 5:17–18

But God commendeth his charity towards us: because when as yet we were sinners according to the time. Christ died for us. Much more therefore, being now justified by his blood, shall we be saved from wrath through him. For if, when we were enemies, we were reconciled to God by the death of his Son: much more, being reconciled, shall we be saved by his life. And not only so: but also we glory in God, through our Lord Jesus Christ, by whom we have now received reconciliation. Rom. 5:8–11

AND LEAD US NOT
INTO TEMPTATION

In all things we suffer tribulation: but are not distressed. We are straitened: but are not destitute. We suffer persecution: but are not forsaken. We are cast down: but we perish not. Always bearing about in our body the mortification of Jesus, that the life also of Jesus may be made manifest in our bodies. For we who live are always delivered unto death for Jesus' sake: that the life also of Jesus may be made manifest in our mortal flesh. 2 Cor. 4:8–11

For if the blood of goats and of oxen, and the ashes of an heifer, being sprinkled, sanctify such as are defiled, to the cleansing of the flesh: how much more shall the blood of Christ, who by the Holy Spirit offered himself unspotted unto God, cleanse our conscience from dead works, to serve the living God? Heb. 9:13–14

BUT DELIVER
US FROM EVIL

Amen, amen, I say unto you that he who heareth my word and believeth him that sent me hath life everlasting: and cometh not into judgment, but is passed from death to life. John 5:24

Therefore, whosoever shall eat this bread, or drink the chalice of the Lord unworthily, shall be guilty of the body and of the blood of the Lord. But let a man prove himself: and so let him eat of that bread and drink of the chalice. For he that eateth and drinketh unworthily eateth and drinketh judgment to himself, not discerning the body of the Lord. 1 Cor. 11:27–29

Then Jesus said to them: Amen, amen, I say unto you: except you eat the flesh of the Son of man and drink his blood, you shall not have life in you. He that eateth my flesh and drinketh my blood hath everlasting life: and I will raise him up in the last day. John 6:54–55

EPICLESIS: BY THE POWER OF THE HOLY SPIRIT

On as many as the grace which flows from God has breathed,
Resplendent, dazzling, transformed,
With a strange, most glorious transformation,
We have come to know the Essence of equal might, indivisible,
Wise, of triple radiance; and we give glory. Pentecost, Matins Ode 9

OUR FATHER WHO ART IN HEAVEN HALLOWED BE THY NAME

In the beginning God created heaven, and earth. And the earth was void and empty, and darkness was upon the face of the deep; and the spirit of God moved over the waters. And God said: Be light made. And light was made. Exod. 1:1–3

THY KINGDOM COME

And when the days of the Pentecost were accomplished, they were all together in one place: and suddenly there came a sound from heaven, as of a mighty wind coming: and it filled the whole house where they were sitting. And there appeared to them parted tongues, as it were of fire: and it sat upon every one of them. And they were all filled with the Holy Spirit: and they began to speak with divers tongues, according as the Holy Spirit gave them to speak. Acts 2:1–4

THY WILL BE DONE ON EARTH AS IT IS IN HEAVEN

And the angel answering, said to her: The Holy Spirit shall come upon thee and the power of the Most High shall overshadow thee. And therefore also the Holy which shall be born of thee shall be called the Son of God. And behold thy cousin Elizabeth, she also hath conceived a son in her old age: and this is the sixth month with her that is called barren. Because no word shall be impossible with God. And Mary said: Behold the handmaid of the Lord: be it done to me accord-ing to thy word. And the angel departed from her. Luke 1:35–38

GIVE US THIS DAY OUR DAILY BREAD

Once again we offer to You this spiritual worship without the shedding of blood, and we ask, pray, and entreat You: send down Your Holy Spirit upon us and upon these gifts here presented. And make this bread the precious Body of Your Christ. (*He blesses the holy Bread.*)… And that which is in this cup the precious Blood of Your Christ. (*He blesses the holy Cup.*)… Changing them by Your Holy Spirit. (*He blesses them both.*)… So that they may be to those who partake of them for vigilance of soul, forgiveness of sins, communion of Your Holy Spirit, fulfillment of the kingdom of heaven, confidence before You, and not in judgment or condemnation. Again, we offer this spiritual worship for those who repose in the faith, forefathers, fathers, patriarchs, prophets, apostles, preachers, evangelists, martyrs, confessors, ascetics, and for every righteous spirit made perfect in faith. *Liturgy of St. John Chrysostom,* Epiclesis prayers.

AND FORGIVE US OUR TRESPASSES AS WE FORGIVE THOSE WHO TRESPASS AGAINST US

He said therefore to them again: Peace be to you. As the Father hath sent me, I also send you. When he had said this, he breathed on them; and he said to them: Receive ye the Holy Spirit. Whose sins you shall forgive, they are forgiven them: and whose sins you shall retain, they are retained. John 20:21–23

AND LEAD US NOT INTO TEMPTATION

And what shall I yet say? For the time would fail me to tell of Gedeon, Barac, Samson, Jephthe, David, Samuel, and the prophets: who by faith conquered kingdoms, wrought justice, obtained promises, stopped the mouths of lions, quenched the violence of fire, escaped the edge of the sword, recovered strength from weakness, became valiant in battle, put to flight the armies of foreigners. Women received their dead raised to life again. But others were racked, not accepting deliverance, that they might find a better resurrection. And others had trial of mockeries and stripes: moreover also of bands and prisons. They were stoned, they were cut asunder, they were tempted, they were put to death by the sword, they wandered about in sheepskins, in goatskins, being in want, distressed, afflicted: of whom the world was not worthy: wandering in deserts, in mountains and in dens and in caves of the earth. And all these, being approved by the testimony of faith, received not the promise: God providing some better thing for us, that they should not be perfected without us. Heb. 11:32–40

BUT DELIVER US FROM EVIL

And when Moses had stretched forth his hand over the sea, the Lord took it away by a strong and burning wind blowing all the night, and turned it into dry ground: and the water was divided. And the children of Israel went in through the midst of the sea dried up; for the water was as a wall on their right hand and on their left. And the Egyptians pursuing went in after them, and all Pharao's horses, his chariots and horsemen, through the midst of the sea. And now the morning watch was come, and behold the Lord looking upon the Egyptian army through the pillar of fire and of the cloud, slew their host. And overthrew the wheels of the chariots, and they were carried into the deep. And the Egyptians said: Let us flee from Israel; for the Lord fighteth for them against us. Exod. 14:21–25

HYMNS TO THE THEOTOKOS

OUR FATHER WHO
ART IN HEAVEN
HALLOWED BE
THY NAME

It is truly meet and right to bless you, O Theotokos,
Ever blessed and most pure, and the Mother of our God.
More honorable than the Cherubim,
and more glorious beyond compare than the Seraphim,
Without defilement you gave birth to God the Word.
True Theotokos, we magnify you!
—from the *Divine Liturgy of St. John Chrysostom*

THY KINGDOM COME

All of creation rejoices in you, O Full of Grace,
The assembly of Angels and the race of men.
O Sanctified Temple and Rational Paradise! O Glory of Virgins!
From you, God was incarnate and became a child, our God before the ages.
He made your body into a throne,
and your womb He made more spacious than the heavens.
All of creation rejoices in you, O Full of Grace! Glory to you!
—from the *Divine Liturgy of St. Basil the Great*

THY WILL BE DONE
ON EARTH AS IT IS
IN HEAVEN

Rejoice, initiate of God's ineffable will:
Rejoice, assurance of those who pray in silence!
Rejoice, beginning of Christ's miracles:
Rejoice, crown of His dogmas!
Rejoice, heavenly ladder by which God came down:
Rejoice, bridge that conveyest us from earth to Heaven! …
Rejoice, O Bride Unwedded!
—from the *Akathist to our Most Holy Lady the Theotokos*, Ekos 2

GIVE US THIS DAY
OUR DAILY BREAD

O Theotokos, thou art a mystical Paradise, who untilled hast brought forth
Christ. He has planted upon earth the life-giving Tree of the Cross: therefore
at its Exaltation on this day, we worship Him and thee do we magnify.
—from Matins, Feast of The Exaltation of the Precious and Life-Giving Cross,
The Festal Menaion

AND FORGIVE US OUR
TRESPASSES AS WE
FORGIVE THOSE
WHO TRESPASS
AGAINST US

Have mercy on me, O loving Mother of the merciful God. Grant me compunction and contrition of heart, humility in my thoughts, and a release from
the slavery of my own reasonings. And enable me, even to my last breath, to
receive the sanctification of the most pure Mysteries, for the healing of soul
and body. Grant me tears of repentance and confession, that I may glorify you
all the days of my life, for you are blessed and greatly glorified forever.
—from Prayers of Thanksgiving After Communion, *Orthodox Daily Prayers*

AND LEAD US NOT
INTO TEMPTATION
BUT DELIVER
US FROM EVIL

Thou art a haven of salvation, O Lady, a guide and protection unto me, thy
servant. With love I set all my hope in thee: through thine intercessions before
God, may I be delivered from all harsh trials and temptation, and from everything which makes me stumble, that I may magnify thee with faith.
—from Matins, Second Sunday in Lent, *The Lenten Triodion*

PRAYER BEFORE COMMUNION

Broken and divided is the Lamb of God, which is broken and not disunited, which is ever eaten and never consumed, but sanctifieth those that partake thereof. — Liturgy of St Basil

OUR FATHER WHO ART IN HEAVEN HALLOWED BE THY NAME THY KINGDOM COME	I believe, O Lord, and I confess that Thou art truly the Christ, the Son of the living God,
THY WILL BE DONE ON EARTH AS IT IS IN HEAVEN	who camest into the world to save sinners, of whom I am first.
GIVE US THIS DAY OUR DAILY BREAD	I believe also that this is truly Thine own most pure Body, and that this is truly Thine own precious Blood.
AND FORGIVE US OUR TRESPASSES AS WE FORGIVE THOSE WHO TRESPASS AGAINST US AND LEAD US NOT INTO TEMPTATION BUT DELIVER US FROM EVIL	Therefore, I pray Thee: have mercy upon me and forgive my transgressions both voluntary and involuntary, of word and of deed, committed in knowledge or in ignorance. And make me worthy to partake without condemnation of Thy most pure Mysteries, for the remission of my sins, and unto life everlasting. Amen.
GIVE US THIS DAY OUR DAILY BREAD	Of Thy Mystical Supper, O Son of God, accept me today as a communicant;
THY WILL BE DONE ON EARTH AS IT IS IN HEAVEN	for I will not speak of Thy Mystery to Thine enemies, neither like Judas will I give Thee a kiss; but like the thief will I confess Thee:
THY KINGDOM COME	Remember me, O Lord, in Thy Kingdom.

PRAYER AFTER COMMUNION

THE DIDACHE, CHAPTER NINE

Now concerning the Eucharist, give thanks this way. First, concerning the cup: We thank thee, our Father, for the holy vine of David Thy servant, which You madest known to us through Jesus Thy Servant; to Thee be the glory for ever.. And concerning the broken bread: We thank Thee, our Father, for the life and knowledge which You madest known to us through Jesus Thy Servant; to Thee be the glory for ever. Even as this broken bread was scattered over the hills, and was gathered together and became one, so let Thy Church be gathered together from the ends of the earth into Thy kingdom; for Thine is the glory and the power through Jesus Christ for ever. — The Didache, 10

But after you are filled, give thanks this way:

OUR FATHER WHO ART IN HEAVEN HALLOWED BE THY NAME	We thank Thee, holy Father, for Thy holy name which You didst cause to tabernacle in our hearts,
THY KINGDOM COME	And for the knowledge and faith and immortality, which You made known to us through Jesus Thy Servant; to Thee be the glory for ever.
THY WILL BE DONE ON EARTH AS IT IS IN HEAVEN	Thou, Master almighty, didst create all things for Thy name's sake;
GIVE US THIS DAY OUR DAILY BREAD	You gavest food and drink to men for enjoyment, that they might give thanks to Thee; but to us You didst freely give spiritual food and drink and life eternal through Thy Servant. Before all things we thank Thee that You are mighty; to Thee be the glory for ever.
AND FORGIVE US OUR TRESPASSES AS WE FORGIVE THOSE WHO TRESPASS AGAINST US AND LEAD US NOT INTO TEMPTATION BUT DELIVER US FROM EVIL	Remember, Lord, Thy Church, to deliver it from all evil and to make it perfect in Thy love,
GIVE US THIS DAY OUR DAILY BREAD	and gather it from the four winds,
THY WILL BE DONE ON EARTH AS IT IS IN HEAVEN	sanctified for Thy kingdom which Thou have prepared for it; for Thine is the power and the glory for ever.
THY KINGDOM COME	Let grace come, and let this world pass away. Hosanna to the God (Son) of David! If any one is holy, let him come; if any one is not so, let him repent. Maranatha. Amen.

EUCHARISTIC THANKSGIVING

*If the Lord's Prayer is uttered by the Word who is only one with the Father, then this prayer issues from the very ground of all being, and, like memory, is a foretaste of our permanence in God: the holy (*intellect*), mighty (*will*) and immortal (*memory*) thankfulness of life in Christ.* — GJC

THANKFULNESS OF THE INTELLECT	THANKFULNESS OF BEING, OF MEMORY	THANKFULNESS OF THE WILL
Giving thanks always for all things, in the name of our Lord Jesus Christ, to God and the Father	OUR FATHER WHO ART IN HEAVEN HALLOWED BE THY NAME	All whatsoever you do in word or in work, do all in the name of the Lord Jesus Christ, giving thanks to God and the Father by him.
Speaking to yourselves in psalms and hymns and spiritual canticles, singing and making melody in your hearts to the Lord	THY KINGDOM COME THY WILL BE DONE ON EARTH AS IT IS IN HEAVEN	Let the word of Christ dwell in you abundantly, in all wisdom; teaching and admonishing one another, in Lord; psalms, hymns and spiritual canticles, singing in grace in your hearts to God.
And be not drunk with wine, wherein is luxury; but be ye filled with the Holy Spirit	GIVE US THIS DAY OUR DAILY BREAD	And let the peace of Christ rejoice in your hearts, wherein also you are Spirit. called in one body. And be ye thankful. But above all these things have charity, which is the bond of perfection.
See therefore, brethren, how you walk wise; circumspectly; not as unwise, but as redeeming the time, because the days are evil. Wherefore, become not unwise; but understanding what is the will of God. Eph. 5:15–20	AND FORGIVE US OUR TRESPASSES AS WE FORGIVE THOSE WHO TRESPASS AGAINST US AND LEAD US NOT INTO TEMPTATION BUT DELIVER US FROM EVIL	Put ye on therefore, as the elect of God, holy and beloved, the bowels of mercy, benignity, humility, modesty, patience; bearing with one another and forgiving one another, if any have a complaint against another. Even as the Lord has forgiven you, so do you also. Col. 3:12–17

THE NAME OF GOD

THE NAME OF GOD, WELL-SPRING OF THE SACRAMENTS

This is the Lord's doing, and it is wonderful in our eyes. Psalm 117:23

But we, having learned from the holy voice of Christ that "except a man be born again of water and of the Spirit he shall not enter into the kingdom of God" and that "He that eats My flesh and drinks My blood, shall live for ever," are persuaded that the mystery of godliness is ratified by the confession of the Divine Names—the Names of the Father, the Son, and the Holy Spirit, and that our salvation is confirmed by participation in the sacramental customs and tokens.
—Gregory of Nyssa, *Against Eunomius*, XI, 4.

OUR FATHER WHO
ART IN HEAVEN
HALLOWED BE
THY NAME

HOLY ORDERS (Ordination of a Priest)

Bishop: O God, great in might and inscrutable in wisdom, marvelous in counsel above the sons of men: You the same Lord, fill with the gift of Your Holy Spirit this man whom it has pleased You to advance to the degree of Priest; that he may become worthy to stand in innocence before Your altar, to proclaim the Gospel of Your kingdom, to minister the word of Your truth, to offer to You spiritual gifts and sacrifices; to renew Your people through the font of regeneration, that when he shall go to meet You, at the second coming of our great God and Savior, Jesus Christ, Your only-begotten Son, he may receive the reward of good stewardship in the order given to him, through the plenitude of Your goodness. For blessed and glorified is Your all-holy and majestic name, of the Father and the Son and of the Holy Spirit, now, and ever and to the ages of ages.

THY KINGDOM COME

CHRISMATION

The Priest chrismates the baptized and he makes on the person the Sign of the Cross with the Holy Chrism, on the forehead, the eyes, the nostrils, the mouth, the ears, the breast, the hands, and the feet. At each anointing and sealing, he says: The seal of the gift of the Holy Spirit. Amen.

THY WILL BE DONE
ON EARTH AS IT IS
IN HEAVEN

MARRIAGE

The Blessing and Crowning of the Bride and Groom:
The priest, taking up the crowns, first crowns the groom, saying three times: The servant of God (*Name*) is crowned to the servant of God, (*Name*), in the Name of the Father, and of the Son, and of the Holy Spirit.
Chanter: Amen.
And he then crowns the bride, saying three times: The servant of God (*Name*) is crowned to the servant of God (*Name*), in the Name of the Father, and of the Son, and of the Holy Spirit.
Chanter: Amen.
Placing the crowns on the heads of the bride and groom the priest sings the following verse from the Book of Psalms three times: Priest: O Lord, our God, crown them with glory and honor (*Psalm 8:6*).
The sponsor then exchanges the crowns three times, in the Name of the Father and the Son and the Holy Spirit.

GIVE US THIS DAY
OUR DAILY BREAD

THE EUCHARIST

Priest (in a low voice): Once again we offer to You this spiritual worship without the shedding of blood, and we ask, pray, and entreat You: send down Your Holy Spirit upon us and upon these gifts here presented. And make this bread the precious Body of Your Christ. (*He blesses the holy Bread.*)
Deacon (in a low voice): Amen.

Priest (*in a low voice*): And that which is in this cup the precious Blood of Your Christ. (*He blesses the holy Cup.*)
Deacon (*in a low voice*): Amen.
Priest (*in a low voice*): Changing them by Your Holy Spirit. (*He blesses them both.*)
Deacon (*in a low voice*): Amen. Amen. Amen.

AND FORGIVE US OUR TRESPASSES AS WE FORGIVE THOSE WHO TRESPASS AGAINST US

CONFESSION

Priest: May our Lord and God, Jesus Christ, by the grace and compassion of His love for mankind, forgive you, child, (*Name*), all your transgressions; and I, an unworthy priest, through His power given unto me, forgive you and absolve you from all your sins, in the Name of the Father, and of the Son, and of the Holy Spirit. Amen.

AND LEAD US NOT INTO TEMPTATION

UNCTION

Prayer over the Oil: O Lord Who, through Thy mercies and compassions, healest the disorders of our souls and bodies. Do Thou Thyself, O Master, sanctify this Oil, that it may be effectual unto them that are anointed with it for healing, and for the relief of every passion, of defilement of flesh and spirit, and of every ill, and that thereby may be glorified Thy most holy Name: of the Father, and of the Son, and of the Holy Spirit, now and ever, and unto the ages of ages. Amen.
Prayer over the Sick: O Holy Father, Physician of souls and bodies, Who didst send Thine Only-begotten Son, our Lord Jesus Christ, Who healeth every infirmity and delivereth from death: Do Thou heal Thy servant, (Name), of the bodily and spiritual infirmities which possess him/her, and enliven him/her through the grace of Thy Christ.

BUT DELIVER US FROM EVIL

BAPTISM

Blessing of the Baptismal Water:
Priest: You hallowed the streams of Jordan, sending down from the Heavens Your Holy Spirit, and crushed the heads of dragons that lurked therein. Do you yourself, O loving king, be present now also through the descent of your Holy Spirit and hallow this water. And give to it the Grace of Redemption, the Blessing of Jordan. Make it a fountain of incorruption, a gift of sanctification, a loosing of sins, a healing of sicknesses, a destruction of demons, unapproachable by hostile powers, filled with angelic might; and let them that take counsel together against Your creature flee there from, for I have called upon Your Name, O Lord, which is wonderful, and glorious, and terrible unto adversaries.
The Baptism:
The Priest baptizes him or her, holding him or her erect, and looking towards the East, says: The servant of God (*Name*) is baptized in the Name of the Father. Amen. And of the Son, Amen. And of the Holy Spirit, Amen. *At each invocation the Priest immerses and raises him or her up again.*

III

THE VIRTUES

THY WILL BE DONE ON EARTH AS IT IS IN HEAVEN

OUR FATHER WHO ART IN HEAVEN HALLOWED BE THY NAME THY KINGDOM COME—
The Angelic Life
THY WILL BE DONE ON EARTH AS IT IS IN HEAVEN—
Between Heaven and Earth: Ways of the Way, The Heavenward and Heavenly Will
GIVE US THIS DAY OUR DAILY BREAD—
An Anthropology of the Virtues
AND FORGIVE US OUR TRESPASSES AS WE FORGIVE THOSE WHO TRESPASS AGAINST US AND
LEAD US NOT INTO TEMPTATION BUT DELIVER US FROM EVIL—
An Initiation to the Virtues

INTRODUCTION

With the virtues we come to a 'meeting of the ways'. Looking back, we see what symmetry there is between Commandments and Virtues, between a diagnosis of our spiritual illnesses and their healing therapies, between seeing what our passions do to us and seeing ourselves dispassionately. And, in the middle distance, compassed about by the Commandments and the Virtues, we see the Sacraments, a situation which, if fully understood, indicates how to approach the sacraments, and especially the Eucharist: with repentance going before and a deepening humility coming after.

AN INITIATION TO THE VIRTUES

Although forewarned by John Climacus that "humility is a spiritual teaching of Christ led spiritually like a bride into the inner chamber of the soul of those deemed worthy of it, and it somehow eludes all description,"[1] yet the reason for this elusiveness is well-known: humility is ever 'away' or 'within'; it is to the other virtues that we must go to learn just exactly who is their mother. Without a humble prudence, a humble temperance, a humble justice, and a humble fortitude, all inspired by a humble faith, a humble hope, and a humble charity, there is nothing genuine here and every virtuous work betrays a desperate zeal. Take to yourself, then, holy humility and await there the summons that surely comes from God in faith; for, with humility, you cannot get ahead of yourself or anyone else—you are in God's time and in God's place.

AN ANTHROPOLOGY OF THE VIRTUES

Self-knowledge by itself is a mortuarial science, a science of the Old Adam through whom sin and through sin death entered the world. When Adam lost the outer Paradise of Eden, he also lost the inner Paradise of the virtues, the virtues: at once God-given and native to man. An anthropology that avoids taking into account the virtues is a study of the half-dead. It is to the virtues that we must turn if any 'wholeness' in the understanding of human psychology is to be achieved.

But self-knowledge cannot be gained from any mere understanding 'about' the virtues; they must be lived in daily toil: the 'tilling of the ground', the 'sweat of one's brow', and the 'pangs of childbirth'(Gen. 3:17–19); they have to be acquired. Only then will we grasp that the virtues are truly the 'other half' of our inner life, that without them there can be no wholeness, for, without them, there is no unity of being, no 'recollection'[2] before God, no passage from image to likeness of God.

Modern psychology offers a wealth of models and therapies developed mainly in the course of the last hundred years. But what of the deep wisdom of Christian psychology developed in the course of two thousand years? Beneath the aegis of such words as 'confluence', 'synthesis', and 'fullness' here is a glimpse into an inner life in Christ remarkably consistent through the millennia.

---

1. *Ladder*, Step 25, 41 (Luibheid and Russell, p. 224).
2. Recollection, to give it its deepest meaning, is the gathering together of all the dispersed elements of our nature held together—and eventually unified—by a grace-endowed *remembrance* of God.

THE HEAVENWARD AND HEAVENLY WILL

What is the will of God for us? Who is the will of God in us?

The human will is a master of approximations: it is 'free' and yet 'bound' in numerous and unsuspected ways, it can even wield great power — ideas and armies are at its command — and yet remain paltry. The will can 'do' many things, but, unaided by conscience, it remains alienated from its true task. So what is conscience? Dorotheos of Gaza defines it in this way: "When God created man, he breathed into him something divine, as it were a hot and bright spark added to reason, which lit up the mind and showed him the difference between right and wrong. This is called the conscience, which is the law of his nature."[1] Dorotheos is alluding here to this passage from Genesis: "And the Lord God formed man of the slime of the earth: and breathed into his face the breath of life, and man became a living soul" (Gen. 2:7); by this he indicates that the 'law' of our nature is identical to that original, life-giving breath of God. His will for us to live, our will to live in Him. What a miraculous power there is in the conscience-inspired will, for out of its awakening springs, fully formed, Christ himself: the Will-to-do-the-Will-of-God!

BETWEEN HEAVEN AND EARTH: WAYS OF THE WAY

For those, the violent, who would take heaven by storm, here are so many siege-ladders. Not by one ladder alone, though, do we swarm this bastion. Each ladder is there to support the others, and no ladder is ever 'my own'.

THE ANGELIC LIFE

Before our eyes are struck at last and lastingly by the eternal sunlight of the Gospel, there are dim shapes all about us that must first become clear. Have we consorted willingly or unwillingly with devils or angels? Now is the time for struggle and friendship; now is the time to join with our fellow-citizens of the world-to-come, to stand however fleetingly among the hierarchies of the blessed during the descent of grace and the ascent of joy.

---

1. *Discourses and Sayings*, p. 104

AN INITIATION TO THE VIRTUES

OUR FATHER WHO ART IN HEAVEN, HALLOWED BE THY NAME—
Nicodemus, A Doer of the Infgrafted Word
THY KINGDOM COME—*Hope, Stillness*
THY WILL BE DONE ON EARTH AS IT IS IN HEAVEN —*Faith, Simon Peter*
GIVE US THIS DAY OUR DAILY BREAD—*Fortitude, Patience*
AND FORGIVE US OUR TRESPASSES AS WE FORGIVRE THOSE WHO TRESPASS AGAINST US—
Love Justice, The Proportionality of the Virtues
AND LEAD US NOT INTO TEMPTATION—*Obedience, The Poverty of the Rich*
and the Wealth of the Poor, Temperance the Many-Named
BUT DELIVER US FROM EVIL—*The Virtues, Ephpheta, the Opening of the Ears*

THE VIRTUES

THE THREE THEOLOGICAL VIRTUES

OUR FATHER WHO   Charity
ART IN HEAVEN
HALLOWED BE
THY NAME

THY KINGDOM COME   Hope

THY WILL BE DONE   Faith
ON EARTH AS IT IS
IN HEAVEN

THE FOUR CARDINAL VIRTUES

GIVE US THIS DAY   Fortitude or Courage
OUR DAILY BREAD

AND FORGIVE US OUR   Justice
TRESPASSES AS WE
FORGIVE THOSE
WHO TRESPASS
AGAINST US

AND LEAD US NOT   Temperance or Self-Restraint
INTO TEMPTATION

BUT DELIVER   Prudence or Moral Judgment
US FROM EVIL

COMMENTARY

FAITH, HOPE AND CHARITY   "And now there remain faith, hope and charity, these three; but the greatest of these is charity" (1 Cor. 13:13). These first three requests and the practice of these first three virtues are mysterious anticipations of the eschaton, the final state of man in God. The virtues begin with charity, just as the Lord's prayer begins with the God who 'is love', ἀγάπη, charity (1 John 4:8). "I came down from heaven, not to do my own will but the will of him that sent me... And this is the will of my Father that sent me: that everyone that seeth the Son and believeth in him [Faith] may have [Hope] life everlasting [Charity]" (John 6:38, 40). But "The Son of Man, when he cometh, shall he find, think you, faith on earth? (Luke 18:8). Faith is the first theological virtue to be approached from the human side, while, from the divine, charity is first... and all there is.

Faith can be seen as that intellective 'presence' in our souls which points like an unerring compass toward Charity, while Hope can be seen as that volitive 'presence', that "zeal for my Father's house" which consumes both self and distances (horizontal distances in the love of neighbor and vertical distances in the love of God) with the pursuit of Charity. With Faith as the receptive power of Charity, the receiving of the Will (Love/Mercy) of God, and with Hope as the active power of Charity, the striving toward the Kingdom, it follows that the nearer Faith and Hope come to their eternal goal, the more they become Charity. Thus "Thy will be done", "Thy kingdom come" and "Hallowed be thy name" form a continuum which depends upon the grace-given capacity of the creature. Already in the faith of "Thy will be done" the fire of Charity is cast more and more on earth, and in the hope of "Thy kingdom come" those tongues of fire that fell to earth on Pentecost blaze up, filling the whole distance between heaven and earth with glory.

The Catholic metaphysician, Jean Borella, illuminates the mysterious symbiosis of intellect and will, which we see at work in Faith and Hope, in this way:

> There is an obscure side to a mirror, otherwise there is no reflection. Likewise there is an obscure side to the intellect, and this is the will which is basically the desire for being, just as the intellect is a perception of it. The will then seems to be another mode of the spirit. Let me say this: the human being is polarized into two opposed but inseparable and complimentary modes: intellect and will, with the intellect being the spirit's cognitive pole and the will its ontological pole. And we realize that the will has a share in the transcendence of the spirit when we see that, not only does the source of the will evade us, but that there is something of the unintelligible in its very nature. To the intellect, the will is like a power rising from the depths of its being, and this being cannot be grasped by the intellect: it is its own 'other side,' the backing of the mirror thanks to which it is not simply transparent.[1]

But intellect and will are not destined to remain 'poles apart' forever. As faith and hope draw closer through mutual inspiration, intellect and will likewise discover a growing proximity, for they gaze upon and touch and are what has just been called, because so fathomless, the 'depths of being', the unmirrored 'inner man of the heart', the unstinting, inexhaustible, and utterly silent font of charity.[2]

FORTITUDE   "Whosoever shall eat this bread, or drink the chalice of the Lord unworthily, shall be guilty of the body and of the blood of the Lord" (1 Cor. 11:27); but also, "Except you eat the flesh of the Son of man and drink his blood, you shall not have life in you" (John 6:54). Once humility is rooted in the soul, every reception of Communion represents a supreme act of daring — "the kingdom of heaven suffereth violence and the violent bear it away" (Matt. 11:12). And yet each Communion paradoxically brings a 'heavenly increase' of that courage that emboldens a return to the Lord's table.

JUSTICE   Contained in the Lord's Prayer's petition for forgiveness is the image of the 'scales of justice', with the weigh-pan of *forgive us our trespasses* incommensurably balanced against the weigh-pan of *we forgive those who trespass against us*; while the mysterious 'as' is positioned at the balance-point, indicating not only the impossibility of any comparison between the two, but also the surprising fact that they are after all one and the same. But Luke best sums up—gives the verdict on—this petition and life's imbalances. First the necessary preamble: "Be ye therefore merciful, as your Father also is merciful. Judge not, and you shall not be judged. Condemn not, and you shall not be condemned. Forgive, and you shall be forgiven"; but then this unexpected and overwhelming disclosure: "Give, and it shall be given to you: good measure and pressed down and shaken together and running over shall they give into your bosom. For with the same measure that you use, it shall be measured back to you" (Luke 6:36–38). So there are two measures at once 'the same' and yet one of which seems to exceed all measure. And the one that exceeds is immaterial, given directly to the heart, the depths of our being. Such is the justice of Christ and His fullness.

TEMPERANCE   Peter of Damaskos asks: "Where is… the heart's freedom from evil thoughts, the all-embracing self-control that restrains each member of the body and every thought and desire that is not indispensable for the soul's salvation or for bodily life?"[3] The answer and the Greek word for this virtue is 'sophrosyne', which is sometimes translated as 'chastity', but denotes something more 'all-embracing' than sexual continence. It is the virtue that safeguards "the liberty of the glory of the children of God" (Rom. 8:21) by recognizing tempting thoughts for what they are, thoughts that, day and night, course

---

1. *Amour et Vérité*, p. 117.
2. For the contemplations on charity, see above: 'A Lamp on the Further Shore', pp. 64–70
3. *A Treasury of Divine Knowledge*, 'The Third Stage of Contemplation' (*The Philokalia*, vol. 3, p. 115).

through our minds and hearts. For every thought upon which our attention focuses, Temperance has a ready question: Where does it lead, to a prison with cruel fellow-inmates and crueler guards, or to the casting aside of shackles unrecognized until the very 'moment' of the question? "Put ye on the Lord Jesus Christ, and make not provision for the flesh in its concupiscences" (Rom. 13:14)—again and again we are being asked to rise up to meet Christ 'in the air' (1 Thess. 4:16), to take to ourselves the nature of the birds... or the angels.

PRUDENCE   Although the foremost of the cardinal virtues, prudence falls last, at the very beginning of the hierarchy of practice, since by it is effected *diakrisis*, the graced act of discrimination bringing *metanoia* (conversion) in its train, the divino-human act of deliverance which begins the changes of the 'uncircumcised heart' into the 'inner man of the heart'. Although *syneidesis*, the spark of conscience, is the highest summit of the soul with respect to contemplation, it is also the initial minimum or 'mustard seed' with respect to action—the first shall be last and the last first.

Seen on the moral level as the spark of conscience, on the anagogical level, the level of sacred ontology, it is the life-giving touch that startles us at last into true creaturehood and the fiery breath which maintains us there. Christ and the Holy Spirit in the soul; sacred continuity and sacred discontinuity. Christ and sacred continuity: "Behold, I am with you all days, even to the consummation of the world" (Matt. 28:20) and "Heaven and earth shall pass away; but my words" (my commandments... but also my noetic sheep) "shall not pass away" (Luke 21:33). The Holy Spirit and sacred discontinuity: "The Spirit breatheth where he will and thou hearest his voice; but thou knowest not whence he cometh and whither he goeth" (John 3:8)—the fiery tides of sainthood and inspiration which sweep at times the world and individuals.

At the beginning of the 'moral way' there are only two levels: the literal and the figurative, the latter of which is thought to include both moral and anagogical reflection. This is the perspective of the discursive intelligence. From the perspective of the contemplative intellect, the literal and the figurative are grouped together, are seen as illustrative, paradigmatic, as the promise of what will be in the fullness of the anagogical level. The moral level represents the 'ratio', the 'work', the sacred effort, the synergy (the state of being harnessed to God—"Take my yoke upon you and learn of me... for my yoke is sweet and my burden light." Matt. 11:29–30) which shifts us from the becoming of the literal and figurative, to the being of the anagogical.

Prudence also effects a diagnosis; it differentiates the vices into their own hierarchy of disorder and pinpoints the 'predominant fault' in our character, so that, with such grace-imbued knowledge, we are able to grasp that very specific 'clue' leading us out of the confining depths of our sins into the great liberating depth of God. Just as the virtues find their reflection in the Lord's Prayer, so too the vices, although, in keeping with their nature, in a perverse way. Thus we see that the 'lesser' sins, the sins of the flesh, are treated under "and lead us not into temptation, but deliver us from evil." Do not be deceived, they are placed here because they so often form the very root of an evil tree. The more subtle vices, and therefore the vices more difficult to diagnose, find their reflection—or rather cure—only in the loftiest regions of the Lord's Prayer. But, even here, we can see how all the vices are never far from their infested roots, for, as the holy ascetics teach, God especially allows the lowly temptations of the flesh to be visited upon those who pride themselves on being above 'all that' as well as everything else.[1]

---

1. For the contemplations on Prudence, see below: 'The Mustard-Seed of Conscience', p. 237; 'Discernment', p. 239; and 'The Sun of Righteousness', p. 242.

THE EIGHT VICES ACCORDING TO JOHN CASSIAN

	THE EIGHT VICES	THE SOUL'S THREE ASPECTS
OUR FATHER WHO ART IN HEAVEN HALLOWED BE THY NAME	Pride	Rational
THY KINGDOM COME	Self-esteem	
THY WILL BE DONE ON EARTH AS IT IS IN HEAVEN	Listlessness	Irascible
GIVE US THIS DAY OUR DAILY BREAD	Dejection	
AND FORGIVE US OUR TRESPASSES AS WE FORGIVE THOSE WHO TRESPASS AGAINST US	Anger	
AND LEAD US NOT INTO TEMPTATION BUT DELIVER US FROM EVIL	Avarice Unchastity Gluttony	Concupiscible

By "Our Father who art in heaven hallowed be thy name", we learn the holy humility and awe that dispels pride; by "Thy kingdom come", we learn the holy service to others that dispels self-esteem; by "Thy will be done on earth as it is in heaven", we learn the holy joy that dispels listlessness; by "Give us this day our daily bread", we learn the holy patience for needs both great and small that dispels dejection; by "Forgive us our trespasses as we forgive those who trespass against us", we learn the holy meekness that turns away wrath; by "Lead us not into temptation, but deliver us from evil", we learn that there is a holy alms constantly falling from the hand of God upon each one of us in the form of people and things, an alms that we should both receive and distribute in our turn with respect and thankfulness.

EPHEPHETA, THE OPENING OF THE EARS

And taking him from the multitude apart, he put his fingers into his ears... and looking up to heaven, he groaned, and said to him: Ephpheta, which is, Be thou opened. And immediately his ears were opened... And he charged them that they should tell no man. But the more he charged them, so much the more a great deal did they publish it. Mark 7:33–36

The 'opening of the ears' was one of the rites administered to catechumens in the early church. It represented an attunement of the hearing to the saving word of faith. —GJC

OUR FATHER WHO ART IN HEAVEN	This is my beloved Son, in whom I am well pleased: hear ye him. Matt. 17:5 As for you, let that which you have heard from the beginning, abide in you. If that abide in you, which you have heard from the beginning, you also shall abide in the Son, and in the Father. 1 John 2:24
HALLOWED BE THY NAME	He that hath the bride, is the bridegroom: but the friend of the bridegroom, who standeth and heareth him, rejoiceth with joy because of the bridegroom's voice. This my joy therefore is fulfilled. John 3:29
THY KINGDOM COME	But when he, the Spirit of truth, is come, he will teach you all truth. For he shall not speak of himself; but what things soever he shall hear, he shall speak; and the things that are to come, he shall shew you. He shall glorify me; because he shall receive of mine, and shall shew it to you. John 16:13–14
THY WILL BE DONE ON EARTH AS IT IS IN HEAVEN	Faith then cometh by hearing; and hearing by the word of Christ. But I say: Have they not heard? Yes, verily, their [the preachers'] sound hath gone forth into all the earth, and their words unto the ends of the whole world. Rom. 10:17–18
GIVE US THIS DAY OUR DAILY BREAD	He, that hath an ear, let him hear what the Spirit saith to the churches: To him that overcometh, I will give the hidden manna. Apoc. 2:17
AND FORGIVE US OUR TRESPASSES AS WE FORGIVE THOSE WHO TRESPASS AGAINST US	And if any man hear my words, and keep them not, I do not judge him: for I came not to judge the world, but to save the world. He that despiseth me, and receiveth not my words, hath one that judgeth him; the word that I have spoken, the same shall judge him in the last day. John 12:47–48
AND LEAD US NOT INTO TEMPTATION	If I say the truth to you, why do you not believe me? He that is of God, heareth the words of God. John 8:46–47
BUT DELIVER US FROM EVIL	Amen, amen I say unto you, that he who heareth my word, and believeth him that sent me, hath life everlasting; and cometh not into judgment, but is passed from death to life. Amen, amen I say unto you, that the hour cometh, and now is, when the dead shall hear the voice of the Son of God, and they that hear shall live. John 5:24–25

OBEDIENCE

OUR FATHER WHO ART IN HEAVEN HALLOWED BE THY NAME	And whereas indeed he was the Son of God, he learned obedience by the things which he suffered. And being consummated, he became, to all that obey him, the cause of eternal salvation. Heb. 5:8–9

THY KINGDOM COME

Now to him that is able to establish you, according to my gospel and the preaching of Jesus Christ, according to the revelation of the mystery which was kept secret from eternity; (which now is made manifest by the scriptures of the prophets, according to the precept of the eternal God, for the obedience of faith) known among all nations: to God, the only wise, through Jesus Christ, to whom be honor and glory for ever and ever. Amen. Rom. 16:25–27

THY WILL BE DONE ON EARTH AS IT IS IN HEAVEN

As children of obedience, not fashioned according to the former desires of your ignorance, but according to him that hath called you, who is holy, be you also in all manner of conversation holy: because it is written: You shall be holy, for I am holy. 1 Pet. 1:14–16

GIVE US THIS DAY OUR DAILY BREAD

The God of our fathers hath raised up Jesus, whom you put to death, hanging him upon a tree. Him hath God exalted with his right hand, to be Prince and Savior. to give repentance to Israel and remission of sins. And we are witnesses of these things: and the Holy Spirit, whom God hath given to all that obey him. Acts 5:30–32

AND FORGIVE US OUR TRESPASSES AS WE FORGIVE THOSE WHO TRESPASS AGAINST US

Purifying your souls in the obedience of charity, with a brotherly love, from a sincere heart love one another earnestly: Being born again, not of corruptible seed, but incorruptible, by the word of God who liveth and remaineth for ever. 1 Pet. 1:22–23

AND LEAD US NOT INTO TEMPTATION

For though we walk in the flesh, we do not war according to the flesh. For the weapons of our warfare are not carnal but mighty to God, unto the pulling down of fortifications, destroying counsels, and every height that exalteth itself against the knowledge of God: and bringing into captivity every understanding unto the obedience of Christ: and having in readiness to revenge all disobedience, when your obedience shall be fulfilled. 2 Cor. 10:3–6

BUT DELIVER US FROM EVIL

But thanks be to God, that you were the servants of sin but have obeyed from the heart unto that form of doctrine into which you have been delivered. Being then freed from sin, we have been made servants of justice. Rom. 6:17–18

THE POVERTY OF THE RICH, THE WEALTH OF THE POOR

OUR FATHER WHO
ART IN HEAVEN
HALLOWED BE
THY NAME

For you know the grace of our Lord Jesus Christ, that being rich he became poor for your sakes: that through his poverty you might be rich. 2 Cor. 8:9

THY KINGDOM COME

Hearken, my dearest brethren: Hath not God chosen the poor in this world, rich in faith and heirs of the kingdom which God hath promised to them that love him? But you have dishonoured the poor man. Do not the rich oppress you by might? And do not they draw you before the judgment seats? Do not they blaspheme the good name that is invoked upon you? If then you fulfil the royal law, according to the scriptures: Thou shalt love thy neighbour as thyself; you do well. But if you have respect to persons, you commit sin, being reproved by the law as transgressors. And whosoever shall keep the whole law, but offend in one point, is become guilty of all. James 2:5–10

THY WILL BE DONE
ON EARTH AS IT IS
IN HEAVEN

Yet one thing is wanting to thee. Sell all whatever thou hast and give to the poor: and thou shalt have treasure in heaven. And come, follow me. Luke 18:22

The Rich Man and Lazarus

GIVE US THIS DAY
OUR DAILY BREAD

And it came to pass that the beggar died and was carried by the angels into Abraham's bosom. And the rich man also died: and he was buried in hell. And lifting up his eyes when he was in torments, he saw Abraham afar off and Lazarus in his bosom: And he cried and said: Father Abraham, have mercy on me and send Lazarus, that he may dip the tip of his finger in water to cool my tongue: for I am tormented in this flame.

AND FORGIVE US OUR
TRESPASSES AS WE
FORGIVE THOSE
WHO TRESPASS
AGAINST US

And Abraham said to him: Son, remember that thou didst receive good things in thy lifetime, and likewise Lazarus evil things: but now he is comforted and thou art tormented. And besides all this, between us and you, there is fixed a great chaos: so that they who would pass from hence to you cannot, nor from thence come hither.

AND LEAD US NOT
INTO TEMPTATION

And he said: Then, father, I beseech thee that thou wouldst send him to my father's house, for I have five brethren, that he may testify unto them, lest they also come into this place of torments. And Abraham said to him: They have Moses and the prophets. Let them hear them.

BUT DELIVER
US FROM EVIL

But he said: No, father Abraham: but if one went to them from the dead, they will do penance. And he said to him: If they hear not Moses and the prophets, neither will they believe, if one rise again from the dead. Luke 16:22–31

TEMPERANCE THE MANY-NAMED

ABSTINENCE, RENUNCIATION, SOBRIETY, HEEDFULNESS, CHASTITY, PURITY, SELF-RESTRAINT, WHOLENESS, HEALTHINESS, INNER INTEGRITY, SINCERITY, SIMPLICITY...

Chastity [temperance] is the name which is common to all the virtues. — John Climacus, *The Ladder*, Step 15, 3

OUR FATHER WHO ART IN HEAVEN HALLOWED BE THY NAME

But he that hath looked into the perfect law of liberty, and hath continued therein, not becoming a forgetful hearer, but a doer of the work; this man shall be blessed in his deed. And if any man think himself to be religious, not bridling his tongue, but deceiving his own heart, this man's religion is vain. Religion clean and undefiled before God and the Father, is this: to visit the fatherless and widows in their tribulation: and to keep one's self unspotted from this world. James 1:25–27

THY KINGDOM COME

Know you not that they that run in the race, all run indeed, but one receiveth the prize? So run that you may obtain. And every one that striveth for the mastery, refraineth himself from all things: and they indeed that they may receive a corruptible crown; but we an incorruptible one. I therefore so run, not as at an uncertainty: I so fight, not as one beating the air: but I chastise my body, and bring it into subjection: lest perhaps, when I have preached to others, I myself should become a castaway. 1 Cor. 9:24–27

THY WILL BE DONE ON EARTH AS IT IS IN HEAVEN

Wherefore having the loins of your mind girt up, being sober, trust perfectly in the grace which is offered you in the revelation of Jesus Christ, as children of obedience, not fashioned according to the former desires of your ignorance: but according to him that hath called you, who is holy, be you also in all manner of conversation holy: Because it is written: You shall be holy, for I am holy. 1 Pet. 1:13–16

GIVE US THIS DAY OUR DAILY BREAD

And take heed to yourselves, lest perhaps your hearts be overcharged with surfeiting and drunkenness, and the cares of this life, and that day come upon you suddenly. For as a snare shall it come upon all that sit upon the face of the whole earth. Watch ye, therefore, praying at all times, that you may be accounted worthy to escape all these things that are to come, and to stand before the Son of man. Matt. 26:34–36

AND FORGIVE US OUR TRESPASSES AS WE FORGIVE THOSE WHO TRESPASS AGAINST US

Yea, much more those that seem to be the more feeble members of the body, are more necessary. And such as we think to be the less honorable members of the body, about these we put more abundant honor; and those that are our uncomely parts, have more abundant comeliness. But our comely parts have no need: but God hath tempered the body together, giving to that which wanted the more abundant honor, that there might be no schism in the body; but the members might be mutually careful one for another. And if one member suffer any thing, all the members suffer with it; or if one member glory, all the members rejoice with it. Now you are the body of Christ, and members of member. 1 Cor. 12:22–27

For you, brethren, have been called unto liberty: only make not liberty an occasion to the flesh, but by charity of the spirit serve one another. For all the law is fulfilled in one word: Thou shalt love thy neighbor as thyself. But if you bite and devour one another; take heed you be not consumed one of another. I say then, walk in the spirit, and you shall not fulfil the lusts of the flesh. Gal. 5:13–16

AND LEAD US NOT INTO TEMPTATION BUT DELIVER US FROM EVIL

Now I am glad: not because you were made sorrowful; but because you were made sorrowful unto penance. For you were made sorrowful according to God, that you might suffer damage by us in nothing. For the sorrow that is according to God worketh penance, steadfast unto salvation; but the sorrow of the world worketh death. For behold this selfsame thing, that you were made sorrowful according to God, how great carefulness it worketh in you; yea defence, yea indignation, yea fear, yea desire, yea zeal, yea revenge: in all things you have shewed yourselves to be undefiled in the matter. 2 Cor. 7:9–11

LOVE JUSTICE

OUR FATHER WHO ART IN HEAVEN

You have heard that it hath been said, Thou shalt love thy neighbor, and hate thy enemy. But I say to you, Love your enemies: do good to them that hate you: and pray for them that persecute and calumniate you: that you may be the children of your Father who is in heaven, who maketh his sun to rise upon the good, and bad, and raineth upon the just and the unjust. Matt. 5:43–45

HALLOWED BE THY NAME

Know you not that the unjust shall not possess the kingdom of God? Do not err: neither fornicators, nor idolaters, nor adulterers, nor the effeminate, nor liers with mankind, nor thieves, nor covetous, nor drunkards, nor railers, nor extortioners, shall possess the kingdom of God. And such some of you were; but you are washed, but you are sanctified, but you are justified in the name of our Lord Jesus Christ, and the Spirit of our God. 1 Cor. 6:9–11

THY KINGDOM COME

Be not solicitous therefore, saying, What shall we eat: or what shall we drink, or wherewith shall we be clothed? For after all these things do the heathens seek. For your Father knoweth that you have need of all these things. Seek ye therefore first the kingdom of God, and his justice, and all these things shall be added unto you. Matt. 6:31–33

THY WILL BE DONE ON EARTH AS IT IS IN HEAVEN

Was not Abraham our father justified by works, offering up Isaac his son upon the altar? Seest thou, that faith did cooperate with his works; and by works faith was made perfect? And the scripture was fulfilled, saying: Abraham believed God, and it was reputed to him to justice, and he was called the friend of God. Do you see that by works a man is justified; and not by faith only? James 2:21–24

GIVE US THIS DAY OUR DAILY BREAD

Blessed are they that hunger and thirst after justice: for they shall have their fill. Matt. 5:6

AND FORGIVE US OUR TRESPASSES AS WE FORGIVE THOSE WHO TRESPASS AGAINST US

If we confess our sins, he is faithful and just, to forgive us our sins, and to cleanse us from all iniquity. If we say that we have not sinned, we make him a liar, and his word is not in us. 1 John 1:9

AND LEAD US NOT
INTO TEMPTATION

For whereas for the time you ought to be masters, you have need to be taught again what are the first elements of the words of God: and you are become such as have need of milk, and not of strong meat. For every one that is a partaker of milk, is unskillful in the word of justice: for he is a little child. But strong meat is for the perfect; for them who by custom have their senses exercised to the discerning of good and evil. Heb. 5:12–14

BUT DELIVER
US FROM EVIL

For if, flying from the pollutions of the world, through the knowledge of our Lord and Savior Jesus Christ, they be again entangled in them and overcome: their latter state is become unto them worse than the former. For it had been better for them not to have known the way of justice, than after theym have known it, to turn back from that holy commandment which was delivered to them. 2 Pet. 2:20–21

WISDOM 1:1–5

OUR FATHER WHO
ART IN HEAVEN
HALLOWED BE
THY NAME

Love justice,

THY KINGDOM COME

you that are the judges

THY WILL BE DONE
ON EARTH AS IT IS
IN HEAVEN

of the earth. Think of the Lord in goodness,

GIVE US THIS DAY
OUR DAILY BREAD

and seek him in simplicity of heart.

AND FORGIVE US OUR
TRESPASSES AS WE
FORGIVE THOSE
WHO TRESPASS
AGAINST US

For he is found by them that tempt him not: and he sheweth himself to them that have faith in him.

AND LEAD US NOT
INTO TEMPTATION

For perverse thoughts seperate from God: and his power, when it is tried, reproveth the unwise: For wisdom will not enter into a malicious soul, nor dwell in a body subject to sins.

BUT DELIVER
US FROM EVIL

For the Holy Spirit of discipline will flee from the deceitful, and will withdraw himself from thoughts that are without understanding, and he shall not abide when iniquity cometh in.

THE PROPORTIONALITY OF THE VIRTUES

I speak not as it were for want. For I have learned, in whatsoever state I am, to be content therewith. I know both how to be brought low, and I know how to abound (everywhere and in all things I am instructed); both to be full and to be hungry; both to abound and to suffer need. I can do all things in him who strengtheneth me. Philippians 4:11–13

THE THREE THEOLOGICAL VIRTUES

OUR FATHER WHO ART IN HEAVEN
HALLOWED BE THY NAME   Charity
thy kingdom come
thy will be done on earth
as it is in heaven
give us this day
our daily bread
and forgive us our trespasses
as we forgive those who
trespass against us
and lead us not into temptation
but deliver us from evil

OUR FATHER WHO ART IN HEAVEN
HALLOWED BE THY NAME
THY KINGDOM COME   Hope
thy will be done on earth
as it is in heaven
give us this day
our daily bread
and forgive us our trespasses
as we forgive those who
trespass against us
and lead us not into temptation
but deliver us from evil

OUR FATHER WHO ART IN HEAVEN
HALLOWED BE THY NAME
THY KINGDOM COME
THY WILL BE DONE ON EARTH
AS IT IS IN HEAVEN   Faith
give us this day
our daily bread
and forgive us our trespasses
as we forgive those who
trespass against us
and lead us not into temptation
but deliver us from evil

THE FOUR CARDINAL VIRTUES

OUR FATHER WHO ART IN HEAVEN
HALLOWED BE THY NAME
THY KINGDOM COME
THY WILL BE DONE ON EARTH
AS IT IS IN HEAVEN
GIVE US THIS DAY
OUR DAILY BREAD   Fortitude
and forgive us our trespasses
as we forgive those who
trespass against us
and lead us not into temptation
but deliver us from evil

OUR FATHER WHO ART IN HEAVEN
HALLOWED BE THY NAME
THY KINGDOM COME
THY WILL BE DONE ON EARTH
AS IT IS IN HEAVEN
GIVE US THIS DAY
OUR DAILY BREAD
AND FORGIVE US OUR TRESPASSES
AS WE FORGIVE THOSE WHO
TRESPASS AGAINST US   Justice
and lead us not into temptation
but deliver us from evil

OUR FATHER WHO ART IN HEAVEN
HALLOWED BE THY NAME
THY KINGDOM COME
THY WILL BE DONE ON EARTH
AS IT IS IN HEAVEN
GIVE US THIS DAY
OUR DAILY BREAD
AND FORGIVE US OUR TRESPASSES
AS WE FORGIVE THOSE WHO
TRESPASS AGAINST US
AND LEAD US NOT INTO TEMPTATION   Temperance
but deliver us from evil

OUR FATHER WHO ART IN HEAVEN
HALLOWED BE THY NAME
THY KINGDOM COME
THY WILL BE DONE ON EARTH
AS IT IS IN HEAVEN
GIVE US THIS DAY
OUR DAILY BREAD
AND FORGIVE US OUR TRESPASSES
AS WE FORGIVE THOSE WHO
TRESPASS AGAINST US
AND LEAD US NOT INTO TEMPTATION
BUT DELIVER US FROM EVIL   Prudence

In the saying of the Lord's Prayer chains of emphasis are created, those 'bonds of perfection' which unite us ever more closely with our God and Father. However, we must not think of these 'chains' as linked together in the usual way, but, like Ezekiel's wheels, one in the midst of the other and encircled with eyes: the 'eyes' or separate powers by which our 'perception' is gradually strengthened so that we might 'see' God and live,[1] the interpenetrating 'wheels' or unifying power by which all virtues are simultaneously present in the gifts and the Gift of God.

The three heavenly and theologic virtues begin with charity, the foremost of those things that endure and it alone is enough for us; all other virtues are the luminous shadows of its glory. Hope includes both the future of glory and the presence of ourselves, while all else is only there to give to each a distinctive 'note' in the great victory hymn of God's circumincessive Kingdom. Faith is the mighty hand of revelation and invitation which signs God's thrice-holy Name within the confines of the world, the wise hand of the Carpenter-King who goes about fashioning a holy bower for his beloved, a place of sunlight and joy for the needy despite the cold looming shadows of Babel.

The four cardinal virtues culminate with fortitude, the balance-point between heavenward impulse and earthly struggle. Here God's thrice-holy Name, God's thrice-holy Kingdom and God's thrice-holy Will become a Living Bread and Wine for the vigor of all. Once we partake of this life-giving, daily and supersubstantial Bread and Wine, we realize that we ourselves have become a 'balance-point' between the mysteries of Christ's resurrection (*Our Father who art in heaven, hallowed be thy name, thy kingdom come, thy will be done on earth as it is in heaven.*) and the mysteries of His Cross and sacrificial death (*Forgive us our trespasses as we forgive those who trespass against us, and lead us not into temptation, but deliver us from evil.*), and act accordingly. With fortitude we begin to realize that the sanctifying power of the theological virtues cannot be confined to their own domain, but seize and transform in turn each of the cardinal virtues.

With our new-found strength we reach out and fashion, in justice, what comes to hand according to the mandate of the New Covenant: it is the beam in our own eye rather than the mote in our neighbor's (Matt. 7:1–5). But our grasp must not be too weak or unsteady, so that this holy work is in danger of slipping from our hand (*And lead us not into temptation*: temperance), or too strong, so that the work is marred or even destroyed (*But deliver us from evil*: prudence). Justice supernaturalized inspires us with a right balance between itself and Mercy.

And finally, although charity is ultimate and, both in principle and in reality, encompasses all else ("Seek ye first the kingdom of God and his justice, and all else will be added unto you"), prudence supernaturalized is both wisdom and 'all else'; it is the totality and particularity of truest love.

---

1. To 'see God and live' is only possible if we see him with the 'perception' of Christ, only when we are 'synoptic' with Christ.

FORTITUDE

The pursuit of the virtues through one's own efforts does not confer complete strength on the soul unless grace transforms them into an essential inner disposition. — Gregory of Sinai, *On Commandments and Doctrines*, 86.

OUR FATHER WHO
ART IN HEAVEN
HALLOWED BE
THY NAME

Thou therefore, my son, be strong in the grace which is in Christ Jesus: and the things which thou hast heard of me by many witnesses, the same commend to faithful men, who shall be fit to teach others also. Labor as a good soldier of Christ Jesus. 2 Tim. 2:1–3

THY KINGDOM COME

Now to him who is able to do all things more abundantly than we desire or understand, according to the power that worketh in us; to him be glory in the church, and in Christ Jesus unto all generations, world without end. Amen. Eph. 3:20–21

THY WILL BE DONE
ON EARTH AS IT IS
IN HEAVEN

Having therefore, brethren, a confidence in the entering into the holies by the blood of Christ; a new and living way which he hath dedicated for us through the veil, that is to say, his flesh, and a high priest over the house of God: Let us draw near with a true heart in fulness of faith, having our hearts sprinkled from an evil conscience, and our bodies washed with clean water. Let us hold fast the confession of our hope without wavering (for he is faithful that hath promised), and let us consider one another, to provoke unto charity and to good works. Heb. 10: 9–24
I can do all these things in him who strengtheneth me. Phil. 4:13

GIVE US THIS DAY
OUR DAILY BREAD

And this is the confidence which we have towards him: that, whatsoever we shall ask according to his will, he heareth us. 1 John 5:14
Let us go therefore with confidence to the throne of grace: that we may obtain mercy, and find grace in seasonable aid. Heb. 4:16

AND FORGIVE US OUR
TRESPASSES AS WE
FORGIVE THOSE
WHO TRESPASS
AGAINST US

In this is the charity of God perfected with us, that we may have confidence in the day of judgment: because as he is, we also are in this world. Fear is not in charity: but perfect charity casteth out fear, because fear hath pain. And he that feareth, is not perfected in charity. Let us therefore love God, because God first hath loved us. 1 John 4:17–19

AND LEAD US NOT
INTO TEMPTATION

And he said to me: My grace is sufficient for thee; for power is made perfect in infirmity. Gladly therefore will I glory in my infirmities, that the power of Christ may dwell in me. For which cause I please myself in my infirmities, in reproaches, in necessities, in persecutions, in distresses, for Christ. For when I am weak, then am I powerful. 2 Cor. 12:9–10

BUT DELIVER
US FROM EVIL

And what shall I yet say? For the time would fail me to tell of Gedeon, Barac, Samson, Jephthe, David, Samuel, and the prophets: who by faith conquered kingdoms, wrought justice, obtained promises, stopped the mouths of lions, quenched the violence of fire, escaped the edge of the sword, recovered strength from weakness, became valiant in battle, put to flight the armies of foreigners: women received their dead raised to life again. But others were racked, not accepting deliverance, that they might find a better resurrection. And others had trial of mockeries and stripes, moreover also of bands and prisons. They were stoned, they were cut asunder, they were tempted, they were put to death by the sword, they wandered about in sheepskins, in goatskins, being in want, distressed, afflicted: of whom the world was not worthy; wandering in deserts, in mountains, and in dens, and in caves of the earth. And all these being approved by the testimony of faith, received not the promise; God providing some better thing for us, that they should not be perfected without us. Heb. 11:32–40

PATIENCE

ENDURANCE, LONGSUFFERING, FORBEARANCE...

But [the seed that falls] on the good ground are they who in a good and perfect heart, hearing the word, keep it and bring forth fruit in patience. Luke 8:15

If you wish to remember God unceasingly, do not reject as undeserved what happens to you, but patiently accept it as your due. For patient acceptance of whatever happens kindles the remembrance of God, whereas refusal to accept weakens the spiritual purpose of the heart and so makes it forgetful. —Mark the Ascetic, *On Those who Think They are Made Righteous by Works,* 134

OUR FATHER WHO ART IN HEAVEN HALLOWED BE THY NAME

For Christ did not please himself: but, as it is written: the reproaches of them that reproached thee fell upon me. For what things soever were written were written for our learning: that, through patience and the comfort of the scriptures, we might have hope. Now the God of patience and of comfort grant you to be of one mind, one towards another, according to Jesus Christ: that with one mind and with one mouth you may glorify God and the Father of our Lord Jesus Christ. Rom. 15:3–6

THY KINGDOM COME

And we desire that every one of you shew forth the same carefulness to the accomplishing of hope unto the end: that you become not slothful, but followers of them who through faith and patience shall inherit the promises. For God making promises to Abraham, because he had no one greater by whom he might swear, swore by himself, saying: Unless blessing I shall bless thee and multiplying I shall multiply thee. And so patiently enduring he obtained the promise. Heb. 6:11–15

THY WILL BE DONE ON EARTH AS IT IS IN HEAVEN

My brethren, count it all joy, when you shall fall into divers temptations: knowing that the trying of your faith worketh patience and patience hath a perfect work: that you may be perfect and entire, failing in nothing. James 1:2–4

GIVE US THIS DAY OUR DAILY BREAD

Therefore we also, from the day that we heard it, cease not to pray for you and to beg that you may be filled with the knowledge of his will, in all wisdom and spiritual understanding: that you may walk worthy of God, in all things pleasing; being fruitful in every good work and increasing in the knowledge of God: strengthened with all might according to the power of his glory, in all patience and longsuffering with joy, giving thanks to God the Father, who hath made us worthy to be partakers of the lot of the saints in light. Col. 1:9–12

AND FORGIVE US OUR TRESPASSES AS WE FORGIVE THOSE WHO TRESPASS AGAINST US

For we know him that hath said: Vengeance belongeth to me, and I will repay. And again: The Lord shall judge his people. It is a fearful thing to fall into the hands of the living God. But call to mind the former days, wherein, being illuminated, you endured a great fight of afflictions. And on the one hand indeed, by reproaches and tribulations, were made a gazingstock; and on the other, became companions of them that were used in such sort. For you both had compassion on them that were in bands and took with joy the being stripped of your own goods, knowing that you have a better and a lasting substance. Do not therefore lose your confidence which hath a great reward. For patience is necessary for you: that, doing the will of God, you may receive the promise. Heb. 10:30–36

AND LEAD US NOT INTO TEMPTATION

We glory also in tribulation, knowing that tribulation worketh patience; and patience trial; and trial hope; and hope confoundeth not: because the charity of God is poured forth in our hearts, by the Holy Spirit who is given to us. Rom. 5:3–5

BUT DELIVER US FROM EVIL

Take, my brethren, for example of suffering evil, of labour and patience, the prophets who spoke in the name of the Lord. Behold, we account them blessed who have endured. You have heard of the patience of Job and you have seen the end of the Lord, that the Lord is merciful and compassionate. James 5:10–11

FAITH

OUR FATHER WHO ART IN HEAVEN HALLOWED BE THY NAME

And not for them only do I pray, but for them also who through their word shall believe in me, that they all may be one, as thou, Father, in me, and I in thee; that they also may be one in us; that the world may believe that thou hast sent me. John 17:20–21

THY KINGDOM COME

But, after the faith is come, we are no longer under a pedagogue. For you are all the children of God, by faith in Christ Jesus. For as many of you as have been baptized in Christ have put on Christ. There is neither Jew nor Greek; there is neither bond nor free; there is neither male nor female. For you are all one in Christ Jesus. Gal. 3:25–38

THY WILL BE DONE ON EARTH AS IT IS IN HEAVEN

Now faith is the substance of things to be hoped for, the evidence of things that appear not… By faith we understand that the world was framed by the word of God; that from invisible things visible things might be made. Heb. 11:1, 3

GIVE US THIS DAY OUR DAILY BREAD

Ask, and it shall be given you; seek, and you shall find; knock, and it shall be opened to you. For every one that asketh receiveth; and he that seeketh findeth; and to him that knocketh it shall be opened. Luke 11:9–10
Behold, I stand at the gate and knock. If any man shall hear my voice and open to me the door, I will come in to him and will sup with him; and he with me. Apoc. 3:20

AND FORGIVE US OUR TRESPASSES AS WE FORGIVE THOSE WHO TRESPASS AGAINST US

And the multitude of believers had but one heart and one soul. Neither did any one say that aught of the things which he possessed was his own; but all things were common unto them. Acts 4:32

AND LEAD US NOT INTO TEMPTATION	And Jesus saith to him: If thou canst believe, all things are possible to him that believeth. And immediately the father of the boy, crying out, with tears said: I do believe, Lord. Help my unbelief. Mark 9:22–23
BUT DELIVER US FROM EVIL	Therefore I said to you that you shall die in your sins. For, if you believe not that I am he, you shall die in your sin. They said therefore to him: Who art thou? Jesus said to them: The beginning, who also speak unto you. John 8:24–25 But yet the Son of man, when he cometh, shall he find, think you, faith on earth? Luke 18:8

SIMON PETER

MATTHEW 16:15–26

And the Lord said: Simon, Simon, behold, Satan hath desired to have you, that he may sift you as wheat. But I have prayed for thee, that thy faith fail not; and thou, being once converted, confirm thy brethren. Luke 22:31–32

OUR FATHER WHO ART IN HEAVEN HALLOWED BE THY NAME	Jesus saith to them: But who do you say that I am? Simon Peter answered and said: Thou art Christ, the Son of the Living God. And Jesus answering, said to him: Blessed art thou, Simon Bar-Jona; because flesh and blood have not revealed it to thee, but my Father who is in heaven.
THY KINGDOM COME	And I say to thee that: Thou art Peter; and upon this rock I will build my church; and the gates of hell shall not prevail against it.
THY WILL BE DONE ON EARTH AS IT IS IN HEAVEN	And I will give to thee the keys to the kingdom of heaven. And whatsoever thou shalt bind upon earth, it shall be bound also in heaven; and whatsoever thou shalt loose on earth, it shall be loosed also in heaven.
(GIVE US THIS DAY OUR DAILY BREAD)	[After His discourse on the Bread of Life] Jesus said to the twelve: Will you also go away? And Simon Peter answered him: Lord, to whom shall we go? Thou hast the words of eternal life. And we have believed and have known that thou art the Christ, the Son of God." John 6:68–70
AND FORGIVE US OUR TRESPASSES AS WE FORGIVE THOSE WHO TRESPASS AGAINST US	Then he commanded his disciples that they should tell no one that he was Jesus the Christ. From that time Jesus began to shew to his disciples that he must go to Jerusalem and suffer many things from the ancients and scribes and chief priests; and be put to death and the third day rise again.
AND LEAD US NOT INTO TEMPTATION	And Peter, taking him, began to rebuke him, saying: Lord, be it far from thee, this shall not be unto thee. Who, turning, said to Peter: Go behind me, Satan; thou art a scandal unto me, because thou savorest not the things that are of God, but the things that are of men.
BUT DELIVER US FROM EVIL	Then Jesus said to his disciples: If any man will come after me, let him deny himself and take up his cross and follow me. For he that will save his life shall lose it; and he that shall lose his life for my sake shall find it. For what doth it profit a man, if he gain the whole world and suffer the loss of his own soul? Or what exchange shall a man give for his soul?

HOPE

Why is hope so sweet, her discipline and her labors so light, and her works so easy for the soul? Because hope awakens a natural longing in the soul and gives men this cup to drink, straightway making them drunk. Thenceforth they no longer feel the wearisome toil, but become insensitive to afflictions, and throughout the whole course of their journey they think that they walk on air, and do not tread the path with human footsteps; for they see not the harshness of the way…because they fix their attention on the bosom of their Father. — Isaac the Syrian, *Ascetical Homilies*, 71

OUR FATHER WHO
ART IN HEAVEN
HALLOWED BE
THY NAME

Paul, an apostle of Jesus Christ, according to the commandment of God our Savior, and of Christ Jesus our hope: to Timothy, his beloved son in faith. Grace, mercy, and peace from God the Father, and from Christ Jesus our Lord. 1 Tim. 1:1–2

THY KINGDOM COME

Isaias saith: There shall be a root of Jesse; and he that shall rise up to rule the Gentiles, in him the Gentiles shall hope. Now the God of hope fill you with all joy and peace in believing; that you may abound in hope, and in the power of the Holy Spirit. Rom. 15:12–13

THY WILL BE DONE
ON EARTH AS IT IS
IN HEAVEN

For I know that this shall fall out to me unto salvation, through your prayer, and the supply of the Spirit of Jesus Christ, according to my expectation and hope; that in nothing I shall be confounded, but with all confidence, as always, so now also shall Christ be magnified in my body, wither it be by life, or by death. Phil. 1:19–20

GIVE US THIS DAY
OUR DAILY BREAD

But sanctify the Lord Christ in your hearts, being ready always to satisfy every one that asketh you a reason of that hope which is in you. 1 Pet. 3:15

AND FORGIVE US OUR
TRESPASSES AS WE
FORGIVE THOSE
WHO TRESPASS
AGAINST US

For the grace of God our Savior hath appeared to all men; instructing us, that, denying ungodliness and worldly desires, we should live soberly, and justly, and godly in this world, looking for the blessed hope and coming of the glory of the great God and our Savior Jesus Christ, who gave himself for us, that he might redeem us from all iniquity, and might cleanse to himself a people acceptable, a pursuer of good works. Titus 2:11–14

AND LEAD US NOT
INTO TEMPTATION
BUT DELIVER
US FROM EVIL

Hope in Affliction ~ Psalm 90

OUR FATHER WHO
ART IN HEAVEN
HALLOWED BE
THY NAME

He that dwelleth in the aid of the most High,
shall abide under the protection of the God of Jacob.
He shall say to the Lord: Thou art my protector,
and my refuge: my God, in him will I trust.

THY KINGDOM COME

For he hath delivered me from the snare of the hunters:
and from the sharp word.
He will overshadow thee with his shoulders:
and under his wings thou shalt trust.

THY WILL BE DONE
ON EARTH AS IT IS
IN HEAVEN

His truth shall compass thee with a shield:
thou shalt not be afraid of the terror of the night.
Of the arrow that flieth in the day,
of the business that walketh about in the dark:
of invasion, or of the noonday devil.
A thousand shall fall at thy side,
and ten thousand at thy right hand:
but it shall not come nigh thee.
But thou shalt consider with thy eyes:
and shalt see the reward of the wicked.

GIVE US THIS DAY
OUR DAILY BREAD

Because thou, O Lord, art my hope:
thou hast made the most High thy refuge.
There shall no evil come to thee:
nor shall the scourge come near thy dwelling.

AND FORGIVE US OUR
TRESPASSES AS WE
FORGIVE THOSE
WHO TRESPASS
AGAINST US
AND LEAD US NOT
INTO TEMPTATION

For he hath given his angels charge over thee;
to keep thee in all thy ways.
In their hands they shall bear thee up:
lest thou dash thy foot against a stone.
Thou shalt walk upon the asp and the basilisk:
and thou shalt trample under foot the lion and the dragon.

BUT DELIVER
US FROM EVIL

Because he hoped in me I will deliver him:
I will protect him because he hath known my name.
He shall cry to me, and I will hear him:
I am with him in tribulation, I will deliver him,
and I will glorify him.
I will fill him with length of days;
and I will show him my salvation.

STILLNESS

Stillness of the body is the knowledge and composure of the habits and feelings. And stillness of the soul is the knowledge of one's thoughts and an inviolable mind. A friend of stillness is a courageous and decisive thought which keeps constant vigil at the doors of the heart, and kills or repels the thoughts that come. He who practices silence with perception of heart will understand this last remark. —John Climacus, *The Ladder*, Step 27, 2–3

OUR FATHER WHO
ART IN HEAVEN
HALLOWED BE
THY NAME

Be still and see that I am God;
I will be exalted among the nations,
and I will be exalted in the earth. Psalm 45:10

THY KINGDOM COME

Let all flesh be silent at the presence of the Lord:
for he is risen up out of his holy habitation. Zech. 2:13

THY WILL BE DONE
ON EARTH AS IT IS
IN HEAVEN

But be thou, O my soul, subject to God: for from him is my patience.
For he is my God and my savior: he is my helper, I shall not be moved.
In God is my salvation and my glory:
he is the God of my help, and my hope is in God. Psalm 61:6–8

To the righteous a light is risen up in darkness:
he is merciful, and compassionate and just.
Acceptable is the man that sheweth mercy and lendeth:
he shall order his words with judgment:
Because he shall not be moved for ever. Psalm 111:4–6

GIVE US THIS DAY
OUR DAILY BREAD

[The mercies of the Lord] are new every morning, great is thy faithfulness The Lord is my portion, said my soul: therefore will I wait for him. The Lord is good to them that hope in him, to the soul that seeketh him. It is good to wait with silence for the salvation of God. It is good for a man, when he hath borne the yoke from his youth. He shall sit solitary, and hold his peace: because he hath taken it up upon himself. He shall put his mouth in the dust, if so be there may be hope. Lam. 3:23–29

AND FORGIVE US OUR
TRESPASSES AS WE
FORGIVE THOSE
WHO TRESPASS
AGAINST US

But as touching the charity of brotherhood, we have no need to write to you: for yourselves have learned of God to love one another. For indeed you do it towards all the brethren in all Macedonia. But we entreat you, brethren, that you abound more: and that you use your endeavour to be quiet: and that you do your own business and work with your own hands, as we commanded you: and that you walk honestly towards them that are without: and that you want nothing of any man's. 1 Thess. 4:9–11

AND LEAD US NOT
INTO TEMPTATION

Remove thy scourges from me.
The strength of thy hand hath made me faint in rebukes:
Thou hast corrected man for iniquity.
And thou hast made his soul to waste away like a spider:
surely in vain is any man disquieted. Psalm 38:11–12

BUT DELIVER	With me is prayer to the God of my life.
US FROM EVIL	I will say to God: Thou art my support. Why hast thou forgotten me?
	and why go I mourning, whilst my enemy afflicteth me?
	Whilst my bones are broken,
	my enemies who trouble me have reproached me;
	whilst they say to me day be day: Where is thy God?
	Why art thou cast down, O my soul?
	and why dost thou disquiet me?
	Hope thou in God, for I will still give praise to him:
	the salvation of my countenance, and my God. Psalm 41:9–12

NICODEMUS, A DOER OF THE INGRAFTED WORD

With meekness receive the ingrafted word, which is able to save your souls. But be ye doers of the word, and not hearers only, deceiving your own selves. For if a man be a hearer of the word, and not a doer, he shall be compared to a man beholding his own countenance in a glass. For he beheld himself, and went his way, and presently forgot what manner of man he was. But he that hath looked into the perfect law of liberty, and hath continued therein, not becoming a forgetful hearer, but a doer of the work; this man shall be blessed in his deed. And if any man think himself to be religious, not bridling his tongue, but deceiving his own heart, this man's religion is vain. Religion clean and undefiled before God and the Father, is this: to visit the fatherless and widows in their tribulation: and to keep one's self unspotted from this world. James 1:21–27

FAITH

Our Father who art in heaven hallowed be thy name
Thy kingdom come
Thy will be done on earth as it is in heaven

OUR FATHER WHO ART IN HEAVEN HALLOWED BE THY NAME	And there was a man of the Pharisees, named Nicodemus, a ruler of the Jews. This man came to Jesus by night, and said to him: Rabbi, we know that thou art come a teacher from God; for no man can do these signs which thou dost, unless God be with him.
THY KINGDOM COME	Jesus answered, and said to him: Amen, amen I say to thee, unless a man be born again, he cannot see the kingdom of God.
THY WILL BE DONE ON EARTH AS IT IS IN HEAVEN	Nicodemus saith to him: How can a man be born when he is old? can he enter a second time into his mother's womb, and be born again? Jesus answered: Amen, amen I say to thee, unless a man be born again of water and the Holy Spirit, he cannot enter into the kingdom of God. That which is born of the flesh, is flesh; and that which is born of the Spirit, is spirit.
GIVE US THIS DAY OUR DAILY BREAD	Wonder not, that I said to thee, you must be born again. The Spirit breatheth where he will; and thou hearest his voice, but thou knowest not whence he cometh, and whither he goeth: so is every one that is born of the Spirit.
AND FORGIVE US OUR TRESPASSES AS WE FORGIVE THOSE WHO TRESPASS AGAINST US	Nicodemus answered, and said to him: How can these things be done? Jesus answered, and said to him: Art thou a master in Israel, and knowest not these things? Amen, amen I say to thee, that we speak what we know, and we testify what we have seen, and you receive not our testimony. If I have spoken to you earthly things, and you believe not; how will you believe, if I shall speak to you

heavenly things? And no man hath ascended into heaven, but he that descended from heaven, the Son of man who is in heaven. And as Moses lifted up the serpent in the desert, so must the Son of man be lifted up: That whosoever believeth in him, may not perish; but may have life everlasting. For God so loved the world, as to give his only begotten Son; that whosoever believeth in him, may not perish, but may have life everlasting.

AND LEAD US NOT INTO TEMPTATION

For God sent not his Son into the world, to judge the world, but that the world may be saved by him. He that believeth in him is not judged. But he that doth not believe, is already judged: because he believeth not in the name of the only begotten Son of God.

BUT DELIVER US FROM EVIL

And this is the judgment: because the light is come into the world, and men loved darkness rather than the light: for their works were evil. For every one that doth evil hateth the light, and cometh not to the light, that his works may not be reproved. But he that doth truth, cometh to the light, that his works may be made manifest, because they are done in God. John 3:1–21

HOPE

Give us this day our daily bread

OUR FATHER WHO ART IN HEAVEN HALLOWED BE THY NAME

And on the last, and great day of the festivity, Jesus stood and cried, saying: If any man thirst, let him come to me, and drink.

THY KINGDOM COME

He that believeth in me, as the scripture saith, Out of his belly shall low rivers of living water.

THY WILL BE DONE ON EARTH AS IT IS IN HEAVEN

Now this he said of the Spirit which they should receive, who believed in him: for as yet the Spirit was not given, because Jesus was not yet glorified.

GIVE US THIS DAY OUR DAILY BREAD

Of that multitude therefore, when they had heard these words of his, some said: This is the prophet indeed. Others said: This is the Christ.

AND FORGIVE US OUR TRESPASSES AS WE FORGIVE THOSE WHO TRESPASS AGAINST US

But some said: Doth the Christ come out of Galilee? Doth not the scripture say: That Christ cometh of the seed of David, and from Bethlehem the town where David was? So there arose a dissension among the people because of him. And some of them would have apprehended him: but no man laid hands on him. The ministers therefore came to the chief priests and the Pharisees. And they said to them: Why have you not brought him? The ministers answered: Never did man speak like this man.

AND LEAD US NOT INTO TEMPTATION

The Pharisees therefore answered them: Are you also seduced? Hath any one of the rulers believed in him, or of the Pharisees? But this multitude, that knoweth not the law, are accursed.

Nicodemus said to them, (he that came to him by night, who was one of them:) Doth our law judge any man, unless it first hear him, and know what he doth? They answered, and said to him: Art thou also a Galilean? Search the scriptures, and see, that out of Galilee a prophet riseth not. And every man returned to his own house. John 7:37–53

CHARITY

And forgive us our trespasses as we forgive those who trespass against us
And lead us not into temptation
But deliver us from evil

OUR FATHER WHO
ART IN HEAVEN
HALLOWED BE
THY NAME

But after they were come to Jesus, when they saw that he was already dead, they did not break his legs.

THY KINGDOM COME

But one of the soldiers with a spear opened his side, and immediately there came out blood and water.

THY WILL BE DONE
ON EARTH AS IT IS
IN HEAVEN

And he that saw it, hath given testimony, and his testimony is true. And he knoweth that he saith true; that you also may believe. For these things were done, that the scripture might be fulfilled: You shall not break a bone of him.

GIVE US THIS DAY
OUR DAILY BREAD
AND FORGIVE US OUR
TRESPASSES AS WE
FORGIVE THOSE
WHO TRESPASS
AGAINST US

And again another scripture saith: They shall look on him whom they pierced.

AND LEAD US NOT
INTO TEMPTATION

And after these things, Joseph of Arimathea (because he was a disciple of Jesus, but secretly for fear of the Jews) besought Pilate that he might take away the body of Jesus. And Pilate gave leave. He came therefore, and took the body of Jesus.

BUT DELIVER
US FROM EVIL

And Nicodemus also came, (he who at the first came to Jesus by night,) bringing a mixture of myrrh and aloes, about an hundred pound weight. They took therefore the body of Jesus, and bound it in linen cloths, with the spices, as the manner of the Jews is to bury. Now there was in the place where he was crucified, a garden; and in the garden a new sepulcher, wherein no man yet had been laid. There, therefore, because of the parasceve of the Jews, they laid Jesus, because the sepulcher was nigh at hand. John 19:33–42

If the root be holy, so are the branches. And if some of the branches be broken, and thou, being a wild olive, art ingrafted in them, and art made partaker of the root, and of the fatness of the olive tree, boast not against the branches. But if thou boast, thou bearest not the root, but the root thee. Thou wilt say then: The branches were broken off, that I might be grafted in. Well: because of unbelief they were broken off. But thou standest by faith: be not highminded, but fear. For if God hath not spared the natural branches, fear lest perhaps he also spare not thee. Romans 11:16–21

AN ANTHROPOLOGY OF THE VIRTUES

OUR FATHER WHO ART IN HEAVEN, HALLOWED BE THY NAME —*Likened to the Image, Fullness of Knowledge*
THY KINGDOM COME—*A Confluence of the Virtues, A Synthesis of the Virtues, A Definition of Love, To Have the Mind of Christ*
THY WILL BE DONE ON EARTH AS IT IS IN HEAVEN—*Burden of Sin, Weight of Glory*
GIVE US THE DAY OUR DAILY BREAD—*The Seven Forms of Bodily Discipline, The Areopagites*
AND FORGIVE US OUR TRESPASSES AS WE FORGIVE THOSE WHO TRESPASS AGAINST US
AND LEAD US NOT INTO TEMPTATION—*Christian Psychology*
BUT DELIVER US FROM EVIL—*The Elements, The 'Elementary' Virtues*

THE ELEMENTS

Now the Gospels are four. These four are, as it were, the elements of the faith of the Church, out of which elements the whole world which is reconciled to God in Christ is put together. — Origin, *Commentary on John*, Book 1, 6.

OUR FATHER WHO
ART IN HEAVEN
HALLOWED BE
THY NAME

Fire

But now he promiseth, saying: Yet once more; and I will move, not only the earth, but heaven also. And in that he saith, Yet once more, he signifieth the translation of the movable things as made, that those things may remain which are immovable. Therefore, receiving an immovable kingdom, we have grace; whereby let us serve, pleasing God with fear and reverence. For our God is a consuming fire. Heb. 12:26–29

I am come to cast fire on the earth. And what will I, but that it be kindled. Luke 12:49

THY KINGDOM COME

Air

But that Jerusalem which is above is free; which is our mother. Gal. 4:26

The Spirit breatheth where he will and thou hearest his voice; but thou knowest not whence he cometh and whither he goeth. So is every one that is born of the Spirit. John 2:8

THY WILL BE DONE
ON EARTH AS IT IS
IN HEAVEN

Water

Jesus stood and cried, saying: If any man thirst, let him come to me and drink. He that believeth, as the scripture saith: Out of his belly shall flow rivers of living water. Now this he said of the Spirit which they should receive who believed in him; for as yet the Spirit was not yet given, because Jesus was not yet glorified. John 7:37–39

And I saw a new heaven and a new earth. For the first heaven and the first earth was gone; and the sea is now no more. And I, John, saw the holy city, the new Jerusalem, coming down out of heaven from God… And he [an angel] shewed me a river of water of life… proceeding from the throne of God and of the Lamb. In the midst of the street thereof, and on both sides of the river, was the tree of life… and the leaves of the tree were for the healing of the nations. Apoc. 21:1–2, 22:1–2

GIVE US THIS DAY
OUR DAILY BREAD

Earth

The sower went out to sow his seed… And other some [fell] upon good ground and, being sprung up, yielded fruit a hundred fold… That on the good ground are they who, in a good and perfect heart, hearing the word, keep it and bring forth fruit in patience. Luke 8:5, 8, 15

For God, who commanded the light to shine out of darkness, hath shined in our hearts, to give the light of the knowledge of the glory of God, in the face of Christ Jesus. But we have this treasure in earthen vessels, that the excellency may be of the power of God and not of us. 2 Cor. 4:6–7

LIVING STONES BUILT UP, A SPIRITUAL HOUSE

For certain stones, all four 'elements' participate in their making. — GJC

AND FORGIVE US OUR
TRESPASSES AS WE
FORGIVE THOSE
WHO TRESPASS
AGAINST US

And, coming, he preached peace to you that were afar off; and peace to them that were nigh. For by him we have access both in one Spirit to the Father. Now therefore you are no more strangers and foreigners; but you are fellow citizens with the saints and the domestics of God, built upon the foundation of the apostles and prophets, Jesus Christ himself being the chief corner-stone, in whom all the building, being framed together, groweth up into an holy temple in the Lord. In whom you also are built together into an habitation of God in the Spirit. Eph. 2:17–22

AND LEAD US NOT
INTO TEMPTATION

According to the grace of God that is given to me, as a wise architect, I have laid the foundation; and another buildeth thereon. But let every man take heed how he buildeth thereupon. For other foundation no man can lay, but that which is laid; which is Christ Jesus. Now if any man build upon this foundation, gold, silver, precious stones, wood, hay, stubble. Every man's work shall be manifest. For the day of the Lord shall declare it, because it shall be revealed in fire. And fire shall try every man's work, of what sort it is. If any man's work abide, which hath built thereupon, he shall receive a reward. If any man's work burn, he shall suffer loss; but he himself shall be saved, yet so as by fire. Know you not that you are the temple of God and that the Spirit of God dwelleth in you? But if any man violate the temple of God, him shall God destroy. For the temple of God is holy, which you are. 1 Cor. 3:10–17

BUT DELIVER
US FROM EVIL

So we also, when we were children, were serving under the elements of the world. But when the fulness of time was come, God sent his Son, made of a woman, made under the law, that he might redeem them who were under the law, that we might receive the adoption of sons. And because you are sons, God hath sent the Spirit of his Son into yours hearts, crying: Abba, Father. Gal. 4:3–6

For I reckon that the sufferings of this time are not worthy to be compared with the glory to come that shall be revealed in us. For the expectation of the creature waiteth for the revelation of the sons of God. For the creature was made subject to vanity; not willingly, but by reason of him that made it subject, in hope, because the creature also itself shall be delivered from the servitude of corruption, into the liberty of the glory of the children of God. For we know that every creature groaneth and travaileth in pain, even until now. And not only it, but ourselves also, who have the firstfruits of the Spirit; even we ourselves groan within ourselves, waiting for the adoption of the sons of God, the redemption of our body. Rom. 8:18–23

THE 'ELEMENTARY' VIRTUES

ACCORDING TO MAXIMUS THE CONFESSOR

There are four forms of wisdom: first, moral judgment, or the knowledge of what should and should not be done, combined with watchfulness of the intellect; second, self-restraint, whereby our moral purpose is safeguarded and kept free from all acts, thoughts and words that do not accord with God; third, courage, or strength and endurance in sufferings, trials and temptations encountered on the spiritual path; and fourth, justice, which consists in maintaining a proper balance between the first three. These four general virtues arise from the three powers of the soul in the following manner: from the intelligence, or intellect, come moral judgment and justice, or discrimination; from the desiring power comes selfrestraint; and from the incensive power comes courage... The four virtues constitute an image of the heavenly man (cf. 1 Corinthians 15:49). — Peter of Damaskos, *A Treasury of Divine Knowledge*, Book 1*

WORLD OF THE SENSES	WORLD OF THE MIND	VIRTUOUS STATE
	Our Father who art in heaven hallowed be thy name	
Fire =	Understanding (Prudence, Moral judgment)	"A state that illumines and manifests the spiritual principles particular to each created being, revealing through these principles the Cause that is present in them all, and drawing out the soul's desire for the divine."
	Thy kingdom come	
Air =	Courage (Fortitude)	"A state that quickens, sustains and activates this innate life of the spirit, and invigorates the soul's ceaseless aspiration for the divine."
	Thy will be done on earth as it is in heaven	
Water =	Self-restraint (Temperance, Sobriety)	"A state that produces a vitalizing fecundity in the spirit and generates an ever-resurgent erotic enchantment attracting the soul to the divine."

Give us this day our daily bread
and forgive us our trespasses as we
forgive those who trespass against us
and lead us not into temptation
but deliver us from evil

WORLD OF THE SENSES	WORLD OF THE MIND	VIRTUOUS STATE
Earth =	Justice	"A state that begets all the inner principles of created things according to their kind, that in spirit shares out the gifts of life to each thing in an equitable way, and that is by its own free choice rooted and established immutably in beauty and goodness."[1]

---

1. All quoted texts from *Various Texts on Theology*, Fifth Century, 95. Cf. also Nikitas Stithatos, *On Spiritual Knowledge*, 49, for a variant correspondence between elements and virtues.

CHRISTIAN PSYCHOLOGY

The Three Realms of the one Person	*Integral Prayer*	*The Three Faculties of the one Heart*
	OUR FATHER WHO	
	ART IN HEAVEN	
	HALLOWED BE THY NAME	Memory
Spirit		
	THY KINGDOM COME	Intellect
Soul		
	THY WILL BE DONE ON EARTH	Will
	AS IT IS IN HEAVEN	
Body		
	GIVE US THIS DAY	
	OUR DAILY BREAD	

Pathology

	AND FORGIVE US OUR TRESPASS-	the cure for *forgetfulness*
	ES AS WE FORGIVE THOSE	
	WHO TRESPASS AGAINST US	
	AND LEAD US NOT INTO	the cure for *distraction*
	TEMPTATION	
	BUT DELIVER	the cure for *defiance*
	US FROM EVIL	

COMMENTARY

SPIRIT "For the Spirit searches everything, even the depths of God" (1 Cor. 2:10). Because of the graced self-transcending spirit within us, it is impossible to say where the Spirit (the living immensity of God) is and where our spirit (the God-granted 'ontology' of prayer) is not— "he who is joined to the Lord is one spirit" (1 Cor. 6:17).

SOUL 'Soul' is the middle term, but this does not mean that 'soul' is separate from either 'body' or 'spirit'. All three have a share in each other, as do memory, intellect and will in 'wholeness of heart'.

BODY Even the body, once it has put on all the fulness of its resurrected flesh, will not be foreign to the Kingdom.

DISEASE OF THE MEMORY: *forgetfulness* of our oneness with God and with our fellow creatures; forget-fulness of that sovereign courtesy which reigns in "all of God's holy mountain" (Isa. 65:25).

DISEASE OF THE INTELLECT: *distraction* from the 'one thing needful'; the unwillingness to recognize (memory), welcome (intellect) and praise (will) the One Truth both in itself and in every partial truth.

DISEASE OF THE WILL: *defiance* and rejection of the life-giving antinomies of God's holy will and prov-idence for His creatures; the refusal to look up and see, despite the darkness, the stars of His innumer-able promises and fulfillments shining from the depths of heaven.

THE AREOPAGITES

The notice on the inscription of the Savior's charge clearly shows us that the one who was crucified is King and Lord of ascetic, natural and theological ways of wisdom. For we are told that the inscription was written in Latin, Greek, and Hebrew… By the Greek inscription I understand natural contemplation because the Greek nation more than anyone else devoted themselves to natural philosophy. — Maximus the Confessor, *Texts on Knowledge*, 11, 96

	Paul to the Areopagites:	*Levels of Existence* [1]
OUR FATHER WHO ART IN HEAVEN HALLOWED BE THY NAME	"For in Him…	*Theos*—(Divinity)[2]
THY KINGDOM COME	we live…	*Pneuma*—Spirit
THY WILL BE DONE ON EARTH AS IT IS IN HEAVEN	we move…	*Psyche*—Soul
GIVE US THIS DAY OUR DAILY BREAD	and have our being."	*Soma*—Body
AND FORGIVE US OUR TRESPASSES AS WE FORGIVE THOSE WHO TRESPASS AGAINST US AND LEAD US NOT INTO TEMPTATION BUT DELIVER US FROM EVIL	"Being therefore the offspring of God, we must not suppose the divinity to be like unto gold or silver or stone, the graving of art and device[4] of man."	*Sarx*—(the Flesh)[3]
	Acts 17:28, 29	

---

1. An inability to achieve a clear demarcation between levels (the 'flesh' excepted) must be kept in mind, the interplay of unity and differentiation being operative on all levels.
2. In parenthesis because superessential.
3. In parenthesis because of existential deficiency.
4. Not only something engineered externally, an idol, but also the internal 'devices' of imagination astray.

THE SEVEN FORMS OF BODILY DISCIPLINE

ACCORDING TO PETER OF DAMASKOS[1]

Then Jesus said to his disciples: If any man will come after me, let him deny himself, and take up his cross, and follow me. For he that will save his life [ψυχὴν,soul], shall lose it: and he that shall lose his life for my sake, shall find it. Matthew 16:24–25

OUR FATHER WHO ART IN HEAVEN HALLOWED BE THY NAME

7. Questioning those with experience about our thoughts and actions (recourse to a spiritual mentor in the faith) so not to "go astray because of our inexperience and self-satisfaction... imagining that we know as we should, although we still know nothing (cf. 1 Cor. 8:2)."

The ancients therefore that are among you, I beseech... Feed the flock of God which is among you, taking care of it, not by constraint, but willingly, according to God... from the heart. 1 Pet. 5:1–3

THY KINGDOM COME

6. Reading the writings and lives of the fathers: "In this way we learn from the divine Scriptures and the discrimination of the fathers how to conquer the passions and acquire the virtues... through deep communion in prayer and reading we will be able to grasp precious meanings."

Search the scriptures, for you think in them to have life everlasting; and the same are they that give testimony of me. John 5:39

THY WILL BE DONE ON EARTH AS IT IS IN HEAVEN

5. Spiritual prayer (prayer offered by the intellect and free from all thoughts): "During such prayer the intellect is concentrated within the words spoken and, inexpressibly contrite, it abases itself before God, asking only that His will be done in all its pursuits and conceptions."

He went out into a mountain to pray, and he passed the whole night in the prayer of God. Luke 6:12

GIVE US THIS DAY OUR DAILY BREAD

4. Recital of psalms (prayer expressed in a bodily way through psalms and prostrations): "To gall the body and humble the soul, so that our enemies the demons may take flight and our allies the angels come to us, and we may know from where we receive help."

Let the word of Christ dwell in you abundantly, in all wisdom: teaching and admonishing one another in psalms, hymns, and spiritual canticles, singing in grace in your hearts to God. Col. 3:16

AND FORGIVE US OUR TRESPASSES AS WE FORGIVE THOSE WHO TRESPASS AGAINST US

3. Keeping moderate vigils: "Through judicious fasting and vigil the body will become pliable to the soul, healthy and ready for every good work."

Take ye heed, watch and pray. For you know not when the time [of the Judgment] *is.* Mark 13:33

---

1. Passages in quotes from 'A Treasury of Divine Knowledge', *The Philokalia*, vol. 3, pp. 89–92.

AND LEAD US NOT INTO TEMPTATION

2. Moderate fasting: "In this way we can overcome gluttony, greed and desire, and live without distraction."

As long as [the children of the marriage] have the bridegroom with them, they cannot fast. But the days will come when the bridegroom shall be taken away from them; and then they shall fast in those days. Mark 2:19–20

BUT DELIVER US FROM EVIL

1. Stillness (living a life without distraction, far from all worldly care): "By removing ourselves from human society and distraction, we escape from turmoil… to learn about the snares of the demons and our own faults which, being more in number than the sands of the sea and like dust in their fineness, pass unrecognized by most people."

And rising very early, going out, he went into a desert place: and there he prayed. Mark 1:35

BURDEN OF SIN, WEIGHT OF GLORY

But all things that are reproved, are made manifest by the light; for all that is made manifest is light. Wherefore he saith: Rise thou that sleepest, and arise from the dead: and Christ shall enlighten thee. See therefore, brethren, how you walk circumspectly: not as unwise, But as wise: redeeming the time, because the days are evil. Wherefore become not unwise, but understanding what is the will of God. Ephesians 5:13–17

OUR FATHER WHO ART IN HEAVEN HALLOWED BE THY NAME

And the glory which thou hast given me, I have given to them; that they may be one, as we also are one: I in them, and thou in me; that they may be made perfect in one: and the world may know that thou hast sent me, and hast loved them, as thou hast also loved me. Father, I will that where I am, they also whom thou hast given me may be with me; that they may see my glory which thou hast given me, because thou hast loved me before the creation of the world. John 17:22–24

THY KINGDOM COME

And we will not have you ignorant, brethren, concerning them that are asleep, that you be not sorrowful, even as others who have no hope. For if we believe that Jesus died, and rose again; even so them who have slept through Jesus, will God bring with him. For this we say unto you in the word of the Lord, that we who are alive, who remain unto the coming of the Lord, shall not prevent them who have slept. For the Lord himself shall come down from heaven with commandment, and with the voice of an archangel, and with the trumpet of God: and the dead who are in Christ, shall rise first. Then we who are alive, who are left, shall be taken up together with them in the clouds to meet Christ, into the air, and so shall we be always with the Lord. Wherefore, comfort ye one another with these words. 1 Thess. 4:12–17

THY WILL BE DONE ON EARTH AS IT IS IN HEAVEN

Knowing that he who raised up Jesus, will raise us up also with Jesus, and place us with you. For all things are for your sakes; that the grace abounding through many, may abound in thanksgiving unto the glory of God. For which cause we faint not; but though our outward man is corrupted, yet the inward man is renewed day by day. For that which is at present momentary and light of our tribulation, worketh for us above measure exceedingly an eternal weight of glory.[1] While we look not at the things which are seen, but at the things which are not seen. For the things which are seen, are temporal; but the things which are not seen, are eternal. 2 Cor. 4:14–18

GIVE US THIS DAY
OUR DAILY BREAD

But when thou art invited, go, sit down in the lowest place; that when he who invited thee, cometh, he may say to thee: Friend, go up higher. Then shalt thou have glory before them that sit at table with thee. Because every one that exalteth himself, shall be humbled; and he that humbleth himself, shall be exalted. Luke 14:10–11

AND FORGIVE US OUR
TRESPASSES AS WE
FORGIVE THOSE
WHO TRESPASS
AGAINST US

And therefore we also having so great a cloud of witnesses over our head, laying aside every weight and sin which surrounds us, let us run by patience to the fight proposed to us: Looking on Jesus, the author and finisher of faith, who having joy set before him, endured the cross, despising the shame, and now sitteth on the right hand of the throne of God. For think diligently upon him that endured such opposition from sinners against himself; that you be not wearied, fainting in your minds. For you have not yet resisted unto blood, striving against sin:

AND LEAD US NOT
INTO TEMPTATION

...And you have forgotten the consolation, which speaketh to you, as unto children, saying: My son, neglect not the discipline of the Lord; neither be thou wearied whilst thou art rebuked by him. For whom the Lord loveth, he chastiseth; and he scourgeth every son whom he receiveth. Persevere under discipline. God dealeth with you as with his sons; for what son is there, whom the father doth not correct?

BUT DELIVER
US FROM EVIL

...But if you be without chastisement, whereof all are made partakers, then are you bastards, and not sons. Moreover we have had fathers of our flesh, for instructors, and we reverenced them: shall we not much more obey the Father of spirits, and live? Heb. 12:1–9

---

1. Properly understood asceticism is a 'resurrectional effort'; a casting off of the old man, it represents a strengthening of the inward man into the likeness of Christ. But lacking the communicated presence of Christ Himself there is no likeness, for He is that 'weight of glory', the substantiality of true God and true man that rises to meet us like the dawn, the daystar rising through our hearts (2 Pet. 1:19).

A CONFLUENCE OF THE VIRTUES

ADAPTED FROM MAXIMUS THE CONFESSOR[1]

Faculties of the Soul	Corresponding Senses[2]	Cardinal Virtues			Theological Virtues
Rational	Seeing and Hearing	Moral judgment, Prudence	unite to form }	Wisdom Humility Faith	
Vivifying	Touch	Justice		are united in } Charity	
Incensive (Irascible)	Smell	Courage, Fortitude	unite to form }	Meekness Dispassion Hope	
Appetitive (Concupiscible)	Taste	Self-restraint, Temperance			

---

1. *Ambigua* 21, Patrologia Graeca 91, 1248a–1249c. In Panayiotis Nellas, *Deification in Christ*, pp. 216–218. An alternative 'practice' of the five senses is to be found in *On the Practice of the Virtues* by Nikitas Stithatos: "Five senses characterize the ascetic life: vigilance, meditation, prayer, self-control and stillness. Once you have linked your five outward senses to them, joining sight to vigilance, hearing to meditation, smell to prayer, taste to self-control and touch to stillness, you will swiftly purify your soul's intellect: refining it by means of them, you will make it dispassionate and visionary" (*The Philokalia*, vol. 4, pp. 103–104).

2. Maximus explains the connection between the faculties of the soul and the senses in the following manner: "The senses have been called exemplary images of the faculties of the soul, since each sense with its organ... of perception, has naturally been assigned beforehand to each of the soul's faculties in an analogous manner and by a certain hidden principle" (Nellas, *op. cit.*, p. 216).

MORAL JUDGMENT / PRUDENCE[1]
Blessed are the peacemakers:
for they shall be called
children of God.

WISDOM / HUMILITY
Blessed are the poor in spirit:
for theirs is the kingdom of heaven.
Blessed are they that suffer
persecution for justice' sake:
for theirs is the kingdom of heaven.

unite to form }

JUSTICE
Blessed are they
that hunger and thirst after justice:
for they shall have their fill.

THE HEAVEN OF THE VIRTUES

━━━━━ THE DIVINE HORIZON AND AXIS OF THE VIRTUES ━━━━━

THE EARTH OF THE VIRTUES

COURAGE / FORTITUDE
Blessed are the merciful:
for they will obtain mercy.

unite to form }

MEEKNESS / DISPASSION
Blessed are the meek:
for they shall inherit the earth.

SELF-RESTRAINT / TEMPERANCE
Blessed are they that mourn:
for they shall be comforted.

GIVE US THIS DAY OUR DAILY
BREAD. AND FORGIVE US OUR
TRESPASSES AS WE FORGIVE
THOSE WHO TRESPASS AGAINST
US. AND LEAD US NOT INTO
TEMPTATION. BUT DELIVER US
FROM EVIL.

THY KINGDOM COME.
THY WILL BE DONE
ON EARTH AS IT IS
IN HEAVEN.

---

1. Informed by syneidesis, the spark of conscience. Cf. Rom. 2:14–16.

A DEFINITION OF LOVE

WISDOM / HUMILITY[1]
Blessed are the poor in spirit…
Blessed are they that suffer
persecution for justice' sake…

Learn of me for I am
━━ meek and humble of heart. ━━
Matthew 11:29

are united in }

LOVE / CHARITY / AGAPE[2]
Blessed are the clean of heart:
for they shall see God.

MEEKNESS / DISPASSION[3]
Blessed are the meek…

THY KINGDOM COME.
THY WILL BE DONE
ON EARTH AS IT IS
IN HEAVEN.

OUR FATHER WHO
ART IN HEAVEN
HALLOWED BE
THY NAME

---

1. Informed by Faith; the goal of the contemplatives, the 'quiet spirit' (ἡσυχίου πνεύματος, *hesychiou pneumatos*) of 1 Pet. 3:4, the pacification of the higher powers of the soul.

2. Informed by perichoresis, the coinherence or inner life of the Trinity. "God is charity" (1 John 4:8). "We know that when he shall appear, we shall be like to him: because we shall see him as he is" (1 John 3:2).

3. Informed by Hope, the goal of the actives, the 'meek spirit' of 1 Pet. 3:4, the pacification of the lower powers of the soul.

Speaking conjecturally Maximus has given, in *Ambigua* 21, a 'physiology' of the virtues and shown how, in their functioning, they mutually prepare each other for and are integrally united in the love that is Christ. He explains how each of the five bodily senses and their organs are analogously assigned to and, in a hidden way, partake of the soul's faculties, while soul is tied to spirit through the virtues. Although not so expressed by Maximus, if faith is counterpoised to the soul's rational aspect[1] and hope to the soul's incensive and appetitive aspects, a kind of transition zone between cardinal and theological virtues is formed, where soul looks to spirit through the cardinal virtues and spirit pervades soul through the theological virtues which, in turn, 'lighten' the body. Such is the confluence of the virtues.

Further adaptations to this Maximian 'conjecture' are made in 'A Synthesis of the Virtues, A Defintion of Love', where, along with the underlying presence of the Lord's Prayer, we see the beatitudes configured with the virtues, a possibility foreseen by Ambrose of Milan: "Just as one octave [the eighth day, the Resurrection] is the perfect fulfillment of our hope, so too another octave [the eight beatitudes] are the sum total of all virtues."[2] Lastly, just as the Lord's Prayer may be divided into 'heavenly' and 'earthly' petitions, so too the virtues are directed more to the heavenly or the earthly, with love forming the axis or horizon or center to all the rest, this love that is Christ who says: *Learn of me* (= rational power) *for I am meek* (= incensive power) *and humble* (= appetitive power[3]) *of heart* (= the union of all).[4]

---

1. The soul's vivifying aspect is said to be everywhere among the other aspects, just as touch is felt by all other senses as well as the skin.

2. *Treatise On the Gospel of Luke*, Book 5, 49.

3. Like touch among the senses, humility can stand for any virtue and represent any of the soul's aspects, but especially the appetitive power, the most 'earthy'.

4. Maximus associates this word of Christ's with His kingdom. For Maximus' explanation, see *On the Lord's Prayer* in *The Philokalia*, vol. 2, p. 297.

TO HAVE THE MIND OF CHRIST

In my opinion the person who has Christ's intellect is he whose intellection accords with that of Christ and who apprehends Christ through all things. — Maximus the Confessor, *Texts on Theology*, II, 83

OUR FATHER WHO
ART IN HEAVEN
HALLOWED BE
THY NAME

Now the God of patience and of comfort grant you to be of one mind, one towards another, according to Jesus Christ: that with one mind and with one mouth you may glorify God and the Father of our Lord Jesus Christ. Wherefore, receive one another, as Christ also hath received you, unto the honour of God. Rom. 15:5–7

THY KINGDOM COME

And in fine, be ye all of one mind, having compassion one of another, being lovers of the brotherhood, merciful, modest, humble: not rendering evil for evil, nor railing for railing, but contrariwise, blessing: for unto this are you called, that you may inherit a blessing. 1 Pet. 3:8–9

THY WILL BE DONE
ON EARTH AS IT IS
IN HEAVEN

And be not conformed to this world: but be reformed in the newness of your mind, that you may prove what is the good and the acceptable and the perfect will of God. Rom. 12:2

GIVE US THIS DAY
OUR DAILY BREAD

Wherefore, having the loins of your mind girt up, being sober, trust perfectly in the grace which is offered you in the revelation of Jesus Christ. As children of obedience, not fashioned according to the former desires of your ignorance, but according to him that hath called you, who is holy, be you also in all manner of conversation holy: because it is written: You shall be holy, for I am holy. 1 Pet. 1:13–16

AND FORGIVE US OUR
TRESPASSES AS WE
FORGIVE THOSE
WHO TRESPASS
AGAINST US

Fulfil ye my joy, that you be of one mind, having the same charity, being of one accord, agreeing in sentiment. Let nothing be done through contention: neither by vain glory. But in humility, let each esteem others better than themselves: each one not considering the things that are his own, but those that are other men's. For let this mind be in you, which was also in Christ Jesus. Phil. 2:2–5

AND LEAD US NOT
INTO TEMPTATION

Now I beseech you, brethren, by the name of our Lord Jesus Christ, that you all speak the same thing and that there be no schisms among you: but that you be perfect in the same mind and in the same judgment. 1 Cor. 1:10

BUT DELIVER
US FROM EVIL

But the sensual man perceiveth not these things that are of the Spirit of God. For it is foolishness to him: and he cannot understand, because it is spiritually examined. But the spiritual man judgeth all things: and he himself is judged of no man. For who hath known the mind of the Lord, that he may instruct him? But we have the mind of Christ. 1 Cor. 2:14–16

FULLNESS OF KNOWLEDGE

O the depth of the riches of the wisdom and of the knowledge of God! How incomprehensible are his judgments, and how unsearchable his ways! For who hath known the mind of the Lord? Or who hath been his counsellor? Or who hath first given to him, and recompense shall be made him? For of him, and by him, and in him, are all things: to him be glory for ever. Amen. Romans 11:33–36

Just as ignorance divides those who are deluded, so the presence of spiritual light draws together and unites those whom it enlightens. It makes them perfect and brings them back to what really exists; converting them from a multiplicity of opinions it unites their varied points of view—or, more accurately, their fantasies—into one simple, true and pure spiritual knowledge, and fills them with a single unifying light. —Maximus the Confessor, *Various Texts*, Fifth Century, 82

OUR FATHER WHO ART IN HEAVEN
All things are delivered to me by my Father. And no one knoweth the Son, but the Father: neither doth any one know the Father, but the Son, and he to whom it shall please the Son to reveal him. Matt. 11:27
They said therefore to him: Where is thy Father? Jesus answered: Neither me do you know, nor my Father: if you did know me, perhaps you would know my Father also. John 8:19

HALLOWED BE THY NAME
Grace to you and peace be accomplished in the knowledge[1] of God and of Christ Jesus our Lord: as all things of his divine power which appertain to life and godliness, are given us, through the knowledge* of him who hath called us by his own proper glory and virtue. 2 Pet. 1:2–3

THY KINGDOM COME
For we know in part, and we prophesy in part. But when that which is perfect is come, that which is in part shall be done away… We see now through a glass in a dark manner; but then face to face. Now I know in part; but then I shall know even as I am known. 1 Cor. 13:9–10, 12

THY WILL BE DONE ON EARTH AS IT IS IN HEAVEN
My doctrine is not mine, but his that sent me. If any man do the will of him; he shall know of the doctrine, whether it be of God, or whether I speak of myself. He that speaketh of himself, seeketh his own glory: but he that seeketh the glory of him that sent him, he is true, and there is no injustice in him. John 7:17–18

GIVE US THIS DAY OUR DAILY BREAD
Now this is eternal life: that they may know thee, the only true God, and Jesus Christ, whom thou hast sent. John 17:3
And you, employing all care, minister in your faith, virtue; and in virtue, knowledge; and in knowledge, abstinence; and in abstinence, patience; and in patience, godliness; and in godliness, love of brotherhood; and in love of brotherhood, charity. For if these things be with you and abound, they will make you to be neither empty nor unfruitful in the knowledge* of our Lord Jesus Christ. 2 Pet. 1:5–8

---

1. ἐπιγνώσει, *epignosei* = full or deep knowledge. This 'epignosis' or 'fullness of knowledge' is differentiated here from other forms of knowledge by use of the asterisk (*).

AND FORGIVE US OUR TRESPASSES AS WE FORGIVE THOSE WHO TRESPASS AGAINST US	And this I pray, that your charity may more and more abound in knowledge, and in all understanding: that you may approve the better things, that you may be sincere and without offence unto the day of Christ, filled with the fruit of justice, through Jesus Christ, unto the glory and praise of God. Phil. 1:9–11 For though we walk in the flesh, we do not war according to the flesh. For the weapons of our warfare are not carnal, but mighty to God unto the pulling down of fortifications, destroying counsels, and every height that exhalteth itself against the knowledge of God, and bringing into captivity every understanding unto the obedience of Christ. 2 Cor. 10:3–5
AND LEAD US NOT INTO TEMPTATION	Now concerning those things that are sacrificed to idols, we know that we all have knowledge. Knowledge puffeth up; but charity edifieth. And if any man think that he knoweth any thing, he hath not yet known as he ought to know. But if any love God, the same is known by him. 1 Cor. 8:1–3 But then indeed, not knowing God, you served them, who, by nature, are not gods. But now, after that you have known God, or rather are known by God: how turn you again to the weak and needy elements, which you desire to serve again? Gal. 4:8–9
BUT DELIVER US FROM EVIL	For if, flying from the pollutions of the world, through the knowledge* of our Lord and Savior Jesus Christ, they be again entangled in them and overcome: their latter state is become unto them worse than the former. For it had been better for them not to have known* the way of justice, than after they have known* it, to turn back from that holy commandment which was delivered to them. 2 Pet. 2:20–21

LIKENED TO THE IMAGE ~ THE SAINTS OF GOD

IN THE PSALMS

OUR FATHER WHO ART IN HEAVEN HALLOWED BE THY NAME	I have made a covenant with my elect: I have sworn to David my servant: Thy seed will I settle for ever. And I will build up thy throne unto generation and generation. The heavens shall confess thy wonders, O Lord: and thy truth in the church of the saints. For who in the clouds can be compared to the Lord: or who among the sons of God shall be like to God? God, who is glorified in the assembly of the saints: great and terrible above all them that are about him. O Lord God of hosts, who is like to thee? Thou art mighty, O Lord, and thy truth is round about thee. Psalm 88:4–9
THY KINGDOM COME	Sing ye to the Lord a new canticle: let his praise be in the church of the saints. Let Israel rejoice in him that made him: and let the children of Sion be joyful in their king. Let them praise his name in choir:

let them sing to him with the timbrel and the psaltery.
For the Lord is well pleased with his people:
and he will exalt the meek unto salvation.
The saints shall rejoice in glory: they shall be joyful in their beds.
Psalm 149:1–5

THY WILL BE DONE
ON EARTH AS IT IS
IN HEAVEN

O love the Lord, all ye his saints: for the Lord will require truth,
and will repay them abundantly that act proudly.
Do ye manfully, and let your heart be strengthened,
all ye that hope in the Lord. Psalm 30:24–25

GIVE US THIS DAY
OUR DAILY BREAD

O taste, and see that the Lord is sweet:
blessed is the man that hopeth in him.
Fear the Lord, all ye his saints: for there is no want to them that fear him.
The rich have wanted, and have suffered hunger:
but they that seek the Lord shall not be deprived of any good. Psalm 33:9–11

AND FORGIVE US OUR
TRESPASSES AS WE
FORGIVE THOSE
WHO TRESPASS
AGAINST US

Sing to the Lord, O ye his saints:
and give praise to the memory of his holiness.
For wrath is in his indignation; and life in his good will.
In the evening weeping shall have place, and in the morning gladness.
And in my abundance I said: I shall never be moved.
O Lord, in thy favour, thou gavest strength to my beauty.
Thou turnedst away thy face from me, and I became troubled.
To thee, O Lord, will I cry: and I will make supplication to my God.
What profit is there in my blood, whilst I go down to corruption?
Shall dust confess to thee, or declare thy truth?
The Lord hath heard, and hath had mercy on me:
the Lord became my helper. Psalm 29:5–11

AND LEAD US NOT
INTO TEMPTATION

Decline from evil and do good, and dwell for ever and ever.
For the Lord loveth judgment, and will not forsake his saints:
they shall be preserved for ever.
The unjust shall be punished, and the seed of the wicked shall perish.
Psalm 36:27–28

BUT DELIVER
US FROM EVIL

For thou art the most high Lord over all the earth:
thou art exalted exceedingly above all gods.
You that love the Lord, hate evil:
the Lord preserveth the souls of his saints,
he will deliver them out of the hand of the sinner.
Light is risen to the just, and joy to the right of heart.
Rejoice, ye just, in the Lord:
and give praise to the remembrance of his holiness. Psalm 96:9–12

LIKENED TO THE IMAGE ~ THE SAINTS OF GOD

IN THE LETTERS OF PAUL

OUR FATHER WHO
ART IN HEAVEN
HALLOWED BE
THY NAME

To the church of God that is at Corinth, to them that are sanctified in Christ Jesus, called to be saints, with all that invoke the name of our Lord Jesus Christ in every place of theirs and ours. Grace to you and peace, from God our father and from the Lord Jesus Christ. 1 Cor. 1:2–3

THY KINGDOM COME

Now therefore you are no more strangers and foreigners: but you are fellow citizens with the saints and the domestics of God, built upon the foundation of the apostles and prophets, Jesus Christ himself being the chief corner stone: in whom all the building, being framed together, groweth up into an holy temple in the Lord. Eph. 2:19–21

THY WILL BE DONE
ON EARTH AS IT IS
IN HEAVEN

And he that searcheth the hearts knoweth what the Spirit desireth: because he asketh for the saints according to God. And we know that to them that love God all things work together unto good: to such as, according to his purpose, are called to be saints. For whom he foreknew, he also predestinated to be made conformable to the image of his Son: that he might be the Firstborn amongst many brethren. Rom. 8:27–29

GIVE US THIS DAY
OUR DAILY BREAD

And God is able to make all grace abound in you: that ye always, having all sufficiently in all things, may abound to every good work, as it is written: He hath dispersed abroad, he hath given to the poor: his justice remaineth for ever. And he that ministereth seed to the sower will both give you bread to eat and will multiply your seed and increase the growth of the fruits of your justice: that being enriched in all things, you may abound unto all simplicity which worketh through us thanksgiving to God. Because the administration of this office doth not only supply the want of the saints, but aboundeth also by many thanksgivings in the Lord. 2 Cor. 9:8–12

AND FORGIVE US OUR
TRESPASSES AS WE
FORGIVE THOSE
WHO TRESPASS
AGAINST US

Dare any of you, having a matter against another, go to be judged before the unjust: and not before the saints? Know you not that the saints shall judge this world? And if the world shall be judged by you, are you unworthy to judge the smallest matters? Know you not that we shall judge angels? How much more things of this world? If therefore you have judgments of things pertaining to this world, set them to judge who are the most despised in the church. I speak to your shame. Is it so that there is not among you any one wise man that is able to judge between his brethren? But brother goeth to law with brother: and that before unbelievers. Already indeed there is plainly a fault among you, that you have law suits one with another. Why do you not rather take wrong? Why do you not rather suffer yourselves to be defrauded? But you do wrong and defraud: and that to your brethren. Know you not that the unjust shall not possess the kingdom of God? 1 Cor. 6:1–9

Therefore we were comforted, brethren, in you, in all our necessity and tribulation, by your faith. Because now we live, if you stand in the Lord. For what thanks can we return to God for you, in all the joy wherewith we rejoice for you before our God, night and day more abundantly praying that we may see your face and may accomplish those things that are wanting to your faith? Now God himself and our Father and our Lord Jesus Christ, direct our way unto you. And may the Lord multiply you and make you abound in charity towards one another and towards all men: as we do also towards you, to confirm your hearts without blame, in holiness, before God and our Father, at the coming of our Lord Jesus Christ, with all his saints. Amen. 1 Thess. 3:7–13

THE HEAVENWARD AND HEAVENLY WILL

OUR FATHER WHO ART IN HEAVEN HALLOWED BE THY NAME—*Who has the Son has life,*
Son of God, Son of Man, The Analogical Will of the Father, Born of God
THY KINGDOM COME—*The* Synergoi, *Fellow-Workers of God*
THY WILL BE DONE ON EARTH AS IT IS IN HEAVEN—*Formation of the Will, The Will of God,*
GIVE US THE DAY OUR DAILY BREAD—*Fasting, The Gate of Paradise*
AND FORGIVE US OUR TRESPASSES AS WE FORGIVE THOSE
WHO TRESPASS AGAINST US—*The Sun of Righteousness*
AND LEAD US NOT INTO TEMPTATION—*Discernment*
BUT DELIVER US FROM EVIL—*The Mustard-Seed of Conscience, The Answering Questions*
of the Lord's Prayer

THE ANSWERING QUESTIONS OF THE LORD'S PRAYER

AFTER TERTULLIAN'S *AGAINST MARCION*, BOOK IV, CHAPTER 26

OUR FATHER WHO ART IN HEAVEN HALLOWED BE THY NAME	What is this 'hallowing of the name' if not the coming of the Kingdom of Christ Incarnate and His indwelling Spirit, the Kingdom of the Father?[1]
THY KINGDOM COME	What is the coming of the kingdom if not the doing of God's holy will: the accomplishing of the kingdom and our lowly participation in deifying glory— God's 'better'[2] plan for us?
THY WILL BE DONE ON EARTH AS IT IS IN HEAVEN	What is the doing of God's will if not our reliance upon Him for all our needs?
GIVE US THIS DAY OUR DAILY BREAD	What is this request for daily bread if not the cessation of hostility with other creatures once we have recognized that everything is from God?
AND FORGIVE US OUR TRESPASSES AS WE FORGIVE THOSE WHO TRESPASS AGAINST US	What is forgiveness of trespasses if not the turning away from every temptation that assails us and towards Christ, the basis and perfection of peace?
AND LEAD US NOT INTO TEMPTATION	What is our withdrawal from temptation if not our greatest distancing from evil, the incommensurable distance between heaven and hell?
BUT DELIVER US FROM EVIL	What is deliverance from evil if not our dwelling now and for evermore in the presence of the living, thrice-holy God?

---

1. Every question implies a sacred invocation of God, since all questions imply some form of emptiness in ourselves, an emptiness which, ultimately, only God can fill. Also, is not this same God-ward insufficiency implied in the angelic names? Thus, does Michael mean 'Who is like God.' or 'Who is like God?' And, if their names do possess this interrogative quality, would not this 'embody' something of the angelic essence? Since entirely spiritual and yet creatures nonetheless, to the holy angels belong the highest degree of both certainty and perplexity, otherwise known as wonder. Wonder and love, two wings by which we draw quite near to communion in the Body and Blood of the Lord; but His is the last distance.

2. Cf. Heb. 11:40.

THE MUSTARD–SEED OF CONSCIENCE

Do not treat your conscience with contempt, for it always advises you to do what is best. It sets before you the will of God and the angels; it frees you from the secret defilements of the heart; and when you depart this life it grants you the gift of intimacy with God. — Maximus the Confessor, *Texts on Love*, Third Century, 80.

OUR FATHER WHO
ART IN HEAVEN
HALLOWED BE
THY NAME

I speak the truth in Christ, I lie not, my conscience bearing me witness in the Holy Spirit: that I have great sadness, and continual sorrow in my heart. For I wished myself to be an anathema from Christ, for my brethren, who are my kinsmen according to the flesh, who are Israelites, to whom belongeth the adoption as of children, and the glory, and the testament, and the giving of the law, and the service of God, and the promises: whose are the fathers, and of whom is Christ, according to the flesh, who is over all things, God blessed for ever. Amen. Rom. 9:1–5

THY KINGDOM COME

For not the hearers of the law are just before God, but the doers of the law shall be justified. For when the Gentiles, who have not the law, do by nature those things that are of the law; these having not the law are a law to themselves: who shew the work of the law written in their hearts, their conscience bearing witness to them, and their thoughts between themselves accusing, or also defending one another, in the day when God shall judge the secrets of men by Jesus Christ, according to my gospel. Rom. 2:13–15

THY WILL BE DONE
ON EARTH AS IT IS
IN HEAVEN

For our glory is this, the testimony of our conscience, that in simplicity of heart and sincerity of God, and not in carnal wisdom, but in the grace of God, we have conversed in this world: and more abundantly towards you. For we write no other things to you than what you have read and known. And I hope that you shall know unto the end: as also you have known us in part, that we are your glory, as you also are ours, in the day of our Lord Jesus Christ. 2 Cor. 1:12–14

GIVE US THIS DAY
OUR DAILY BREAD

For if the blood of goats and of oxen, and the ashes of an heifer being sprinkled, sanctify such as are defiled, to the cleansing of the flesh: how much more shall the blood of Christ, who by the Holy Spirit offered himself unspotted unto God, cleanse our conscience from dead works, to serve the living God? Heb. 9:13–14

AND FORGIVE US OUR
TRESPASSES AS WE
FORGIVE THOSE
WHO TRESPASS
AGAINST US

But as for the meats that are sacrificed to idols, we know that an idol is nothing in the world, and that there is no God but one. For although there be that are called gods, either in heaven or on earth (for there be gods many, and lords many); yet to us there is but one God, the Father, of whom are all things, and we unto him; and one Lord Jesus Christ, by whom are all things, and we by him. But there is not knowledge in every one. For some until this present, with conscience of the idol: eat as a thing sacrificed to an idol, and their conscience, being weak, is defiled. But meat doth not commend us to God. For neither, if we eat, shall we have the more; nor, if we eat not, shall we have the less. But take heed lest perhaps this your liberty become a stumbling block to the weak. For if a man see him that hath knowledge sit at meat in the idol's temple, shall not his conscience, being weak, be emboldened to eat those things which are sacrificed to idols? And through thy knowledge shall the weak brother perish, for whom

Christ hath died? Now when you sin thus against the brethren, and wound their weak conscience, you sin against Christ. Wherefore, if meat scandalize my brother, I will never eat flesh, lest I should scandalize my brother. 1 Cor. 8:4–13

AND LEAD US NOT
INTO TEMPTATION

Therefore, seeing we have this ministration, according as we have obtained mercy, we faint not; but we renounce the hidden things of dishonesty, not walking in craftiness, nor adulterating the word of God; but by manifestation of the truth commending ourselves to every man's conscience, in the sight of God. And if our gospel be also hid, it is hid to them that are lost, in whom the god of this world hath blinded the minds of unbelievers, that the light of the gospel of the glory of Christ, who is the image of God, should not shine unto them. 2 Cor. 4:1–4

BUT DELIVER
US FROM EVIL

A faithful saying, and worthy of all acceptation, that Christ Jesus came into this world to save sinners, of whom I am the chief. But for this cause have I obtained mercy: that in me first Christ Jesus might shew forth all patience, for the information of them that shall believe in him unto life everlasting. Now to the king of ages, immortal, invisible, the only God, be honor and glory for ever and ever. Amen. This precept I commend to thee, O son Timothy; according to the prophecies going before on thee, that thou war in them a good warfare, having faith and a good conscience, which some rejecting have made shipwreck concerning the faith. Of whom is Hymeneus and Alexander, whom I have delivered up to Satan, that they may learn not to blaspheme. 1 Tim. 1:15–20

DISCERNMENT

Among beginners, discernment is real self-knowledge; among those midway along the road to perfection, it is a spiritual capacity to distinguish unfailingly between what is truly good and what in nature is opposed to the good; among the perfect, it is knowledge resulting from divine illumination, which with its lamp can light up what is dark in others. To put the matter generally, discernment is—and is recognized to be—a solid understanding of the will of God in all times, in all places, in all things; and it is found only among those who are pure in heart, in body, and in speech.
— John Climacus, *The Ladder of Divine Ascent*, Step 26

OUR FATHER WHO
ART IN HEAVEN
HALLOWED BE
THY NAME

For God sent not his Son into the world, to judge the world, but that he world may be saved by him. He that believeth in him is not judged. But he that doth not believe, is already judged: because he believeth not in the name of the only begotten Son of God. And this is the judgment: because the light is come into the world, and men loved darkness rather than the light: for their works were evil. For every one that doth evil hateth the light, and cometh not to the light, that his works may not be reproved. But he that doth truth, cometh to the sight, that his works may be made manifest, because they are done in God. John 3:17–21

THY KINGDOM COME

But I tell you the truth: it is expedient to you that I go: for if I go not, the Paraclete will not come to you; but if I go, I will send him to you. And when he is come, he will convince the world of sin, and of justice, and of judgment. Of sin: because they believed not in me. And of justice: because I go to the Father; and you shall see me no longer. And of judgment: because the prince of this world is already judged. John 16:7–11

THY WILL BE DONE
ON EARTH AS IT IS
IN HEAVEN

But the spiritual man judgeth all things; and he himself is judged of in heaven no man. For who hath known the mind of the Lord, that we may instruct him? But we have the mind of Christ. 1 Cor. 2:15–16

GIVE US THIS DAY
OUR DAILY BREAD

For whereas for the time you ought to be masters, you have need to be taught again what are the first elements of the words of God: and you are become such as have need of milk, and not of strong meat. For every one that is a partaker of milk, is unskillful in the word of justice: for he is a little child. But strong meat is for the perfect; for them who by custom have their senses exercised to the discerning of good and evil. Heb. 5:12–14

AND FORGIVE US OUR
TRESPASSES AS WE
FORGIVE THOSE
WHO TRESPASS
AGAINST US

He that saith he is in the light, and hateth his brother, is in darkness even until now. He that loveth his brother, abideth in the light, and there is no scandal in him. 1 John 2:9–10

AND LEAD US NOT
INTO TEMPTATION
BUT DELIVER
US FROM EVIL

Dearly beloved, believe not every spirit, but try the spirits if they be of God: because many false prophets are gone out into the world. By this is the spirit of God known. Every spirit which confesseth that Jesus Christ is come in the flesh, is of God: And every spirit that dissolveth Jesus, is not of God: and this is Antichrist, of whom you have heard that he cometh, and he is now already in the world. You are of God, little children, and have overcome him. Because greater is he that is in you, than he that is in the world. 1 John 4:1–4

IN SUFFERINGS REJOICE

Blessed shall you be when men shall hate you, and when they shall separate you and shall reproach you and cast out your name as evil, for the Son of man's sake. Be glad in that day and rejoice: for behold, your reward is great in heaven. Luke 6:22–23

If God suffers in the flesh when He is made man, should we not rejoice when we suffer, for we have God to share our sufferings? This shared suffering confers the kingdom on us. For he spoke truly who said, 'If we suffer with Him, then we shall also be glorified with Him.' — Maximus the Confessor, *Various Texts*, 1, 24

OUR FATHER WHO
ART IN HEAVEN

For the Spirit himself giveth testimony to our spirit that we are the sons of God. And if sons, heirs also; heirs indeed of God and joint heirs with Christ: yet so, if we suffer with him, that we may be also glorified with him. For I reckon that the sufferings of this time are not worthy to be compared with the glory to come that shall be revealed in us. Rom. 8:16–18

HALLOWED BE
THY NAME

And calling in the apostles, after they had scourged them, they charged them that they should not speak at all in the name of Jesus. And they dismissed them. And they indeed went from the presence of the council, rejoicing that they were accounted worthy to suffer reproach for the name of Jesus. And every day they ceased not, in the temple and from house to house, to teach and preach Christ Jesus. Acts 5:40–42

But Ananias answered: Lord, I have heard by many of this man [Saul of Tarsus, the persecutor], how much evil he hath done to thy saints in Jerusalem. And here he hath authority from the chief priests to bind all that invoke thy name. And the Lord said to him: Go thy way: for this man is to me a vessel of election, to carry my name before the Gentiles and kings and the children of Israel. For I will shew him how great things he must suffer for my name's sake. Acts 9:13–16

THY KINGDOM COME

Blessed are they that suffer persecution for justice' sake: for theirs is the kingdom of heaven. Blessed are ye when they shall revile you, and persecute you, and speak all that is evil against you, untruly, for my sake: Be glad and rejoice for your reward is very great in heaven. For so they persecuted the prophets that were before you. Matt. 5:10–12

Who now rejoice in my sufferings for you and fill up those things that are wanting of the sufferings of Christ, in my flesh, for his body, which is the church: whereof I am made a minister according to the dispensation of God, which is given me towards you, that I may fulfil the word of God: the mystery which hath been hidden from ages and generations, but now is manifested to his saints, to whom God would make known the riches of the glory of this mystery among the Gentiles, which is Christ, in you the hope of glory. Whom we preach, admonishing every man and teaching every man in all wisdom, that we may present every man perfect in Christ Jesus. Col. 1:24–28

THY WILL BE DONE
ON EARTH AS IT IS
IN HEAVEN

For as the sufferings of Christ abound in us: so also by Christ doth our comfort abound. Now whether we be in tribulation, it is for your exhortation and salvation: or whether we be comforted, it is for your consolation: or whether we be exhorted, it is for your exhortation and salvation, which worketh the enduring of the same sufferings which we also suffer. That our hope for you may be steadfast: knowing that as you are partakers of the sufferings, so shall you be also of the consolation. 2 Cor. 1:5–7

For the time is, that judgment should begin at the house of God. And if at first at us, what shall be the end of them that believe not the gospel of God? And if the just man shall scarcely be saved, where shall the ungodly and the sinner appear? Wherefore let them also that suffer according to the will of God commend their souls in good deeds to the faithful Creator. 1 Pet. 4:17–19

GIVE US THIS DAY OUR DAILY BREAD

Furthermore, I count all things to be but loss for the excellent knowledge of Jesus Christ, my Lord: for whom I have suffered the loss of all things and count them but as dung, that I may gain Christ. And may be found in him, not having my justice, which is of the law, but that which is of the faith of Christ Jesus, which is of God: justice in faith. That I may know him and the power of his resurrection and the fellowship of his sufferings: being made conformable to his death, if by any means I may attain to the resurrection which is from the dead. Phil. 3:8–11

AND FORGIVE US OUR TRESPASSES AS WE FORGIVE THOSE WHO TRESPASS AGAINST US

But I say to you, Love your enemies: do good to them that hate you: and pray for them that persecute and calumniate you: that you may be the children of your Father who is in heaven, who maketh his sun to rise upon the good, and bad, and raineth upon the just and the unjust. Matt. 5:44–45

And who is he that can hurt you, if you be zealous of good? But if also you suffer any thing for justice' sake, blessed are ye. And be not afraid of their fear: and be not troubled. But sanctify the Lord Christ in your hearts, being ready always to satisfy every one that asketh you a reason of that hope which is in you. But with modesty and fear, having a good conscience: that whereas they speak evil of you, they may be ashamed who falsely accuse your good conversation in Christ. For it is better doing well (if such be the will of God) to suffer than doing ill. 1 Pet. 3:13–17

AND LEAD US NOT INTO TEMPTATION

For which cause, forbearing no longer, we thought it good to remain at Athens alone. And we sent Timothy, our brother and the minister of God in the gospel of Christ, to confirm you and exhort you concerning your faith: that no man should be moved in these tribulations: for yourselves know that we are appointed thereunto. For even when we were with you, we foretold you that we should suffer tribulations: as also it is come to pass, and you know. For this cause also, I, forbearing no longer, sent to know your faith: lest perhaps he that tempteth should have tempted you: and our labour should be made vain. 1 Thess. 3:1–5

BUT DELIVER US FROM EVIL

But thou hast fully known my doctrine, manner of life, purpose, faith, longsuffering, love, patience, persecutions, afflictions: such as came upon me at Antioch, at Iconium and at Lystra: what persecutions I endured, and out of them all the Lord delivered me. And all that will live godly in Christ Jesus shall suffer persecution. But evil men and seducers shall grow worse and worse: erring, and driving into error, but continue thou in those things which thou hast learned and which have been committed to thee. Knowing of whom thou hast learned them: And because from thy infancy thou hast known the holy scriptures which can instruct thee to salvation by the faith which is in Christ Jesus. 2 Tim. 3:10–15

THE SUN OF RIGHTEOUSNESS

But for you who fear my name the sun of righteousness shall rise, with healing in its wings. Malachi 4:2

OUR FATHER WHO
ART IN HEAVEN
HALLOWED BE
THY NAME

Righteous Father, the world hath not known thee; but I have known thee: and these have known that thou hast sent me. And I have made known thy name to them, and will make it known; that the love wherewith thou hast loved me, may be in them, and I in them. John 17:25–26

If you know, that he is righteous, know ye, that every one also, who doth righteousness, is born of him. 1 John 2:29

THY KINGDOM COME

The Son of man shall send his angels, and they shall gather out of his kingdom all scandals, and them that work iniquity. And shall cast them into the furnace of fire: there shall be weeping and gnashing of teeth. Then shall the righteous shine as the sun, in the kingdom of their Father. He that hath ears to hear, let him hear. Matt. 13:41–43

THY WILL BE DONE
ON EARTH AS IT IS
IN HEAVEN

For Christ therefore we are ambassadors, God as it were exhorting by us. For Christ, we beseech you, be reconciled to God. Him, who knew no sin, he hath made sin for us, that we might be made the righteousness of God in him. 2 Cor. 5:20–21

GIVE US THIS DAY
OUR DAILY BREAD

He that receiveth you, receiveth me: and he that receiveth me, receiveth him that sent me. He that receiveth a prophet in the name of a prophet, shall receive the reward of a prophet; and he that receiveth a righteous man in the name of a righteous man, shall receive the reward of a righteous man. And whosoever shall give to drink to one of these little ones a cup of cold water only in the name of a disciple, amen I say to you, he shall not lose his reward. Matt. 10:40–42

AND FORGIVE US OUR
TRESPASSES AS WE
FORGIVE THOSE
WHO TRESPASS
AGAINST US

Confess therefore your sins one to another: and pray one for another, that you may be saved. For the continual prayer of a righteous man availeth much. James 5:16

AND LEAD US NOT
INTO TEMPTATION

And to some who trusted in themselves as righteous, and despised others, he spoke also this parable: Two men went up into the temple to pray: the one a Pharisee, and the other a publican. The Pharisee standing, prayed thus with himself: O God, I give thee thanks that I am not as the rest of men, extortioners, unjust, adulterers, as also is this publican. I fast twice in a week: I give tithes of all that I possess. And the publican, standing afar off, would not so much as lift up his eyes towards heaven; but struck his breast, saying: O god, be merciful to me a sinner. I say to you, this man went down into his house justified rather that the other: because every one that exalteth himself, shall be humbled: and he that humbleth himself, shall be exalted. Luke 18:9–14

BUT DELIVER
US FROM EVIL

And if the righteous man shall scarcely be saved, where shall the ungodly and the sinner appear? Wherefore let them also that suffer according to the will of God, commend their souls in good deeds to the faithful Creator. 1 Pet. 4:18–19

FASTING, THE GATE OF PARADISE

ISAIAH 58:1–14

Fasting makes for purity of prayer, an enlightened soul, a watchful mind, a deliverance from blindness. Fasting is the door of compunction, humble sighing, joyful contrition, and end to chatter, an occasion for silence, a custodian of obedience, a lightening of sleep, health of the body, an agent of dispassion, a remission of sins, the gate, indeed, the delight of Paradise. — John Climacus, *Ladder of Divine Ascent*, Step 14.

BUT DELIVER
US FROM EVIL

Cry, cease not, lift up thy voice like a trumpet, and shew my people their wicked doings, and the house of Jacob their sins. For they seek me from day to day, and desire to know my ways, as a nation that hath done justice, and hath not forsaken the judgment of their God: they ask of me the judgments of justice: they are willing to approach to God.

AND LEAD US NOT
INTO TEMPTATION

Why have we fasted, and thou hast not regarded: have we humbled our souls, and thou hast not taken notice?

AND FORGIVE US OUR
TRESPASSES AS WE
FORGIVE THOSE
WHO TRESPASS
AGAINST US

Behold in the day of your fast your own will is found, and you exact of all your debtors. Behold you fast for debates and strife, and strike with the fist wickedly. Do not fast as you have done until this day, to make your cry to be heard on high. Is this such a fast as I have chosen: for a man to afflict his soul for a day? Is this it, to wind his head about like a circle, and to spread sackcloth and ashes? Wilt thou call this a fast, and a day acceptable to the Lord? Is not this rather the fast that I have chosen? loose the bands of wickedness, undo the bundles that oppress, let them that are broken go free, and break asunder every burden.

GIVE US THIS DAY
OUR DAILY BREAD

Deal thy bread to the hungry, and bring the needy and the harborless into thy house: when thou shalt see one naked, cover him, and despise not thy own flesh.

THY WILL BE DONE
ON EARTH AS IT IS
IN HEAVEN

Then shall thy light break forth as the morning, and thy health shall speedily arise, and thy justice shall go before thy face, and the glory of the Lord shall gather thee up. Then shalt thou call, and the Lord shall hear: thou shalt cry, and he shall say, Here I am. If thou wilt take away the chain out of the midst of thee, and cease to stretch out the finger, and to speak that which profiteth not.

THY KINGDOM COME

When thou shalt pour out thy soul to the hungry, and shalt satisfy the afflicted soul, then shall thy light rise up in darkness, and thy darkness shall be as the noonday. And the Lord will give thee rest continually, and will fill thy soul with brightness, and deliver thy bones, and thou shalt be like a watered garden, and like a fountain of water whose waters shall not fail. And the places that have been desolate for ages shall be built in thee: thou shalt raise up the foundation of generation and generation: and thou shalt be called the repairer of the fences, turning the paths into rest.

OUR FATHER WHO
ART IN HEAVEN
HALLOWED BE
THY NAME

If thou turn away thy foot from the sabbath, from doing thy own will in my holy day, and call the sabbath delightful, and the holy of the Lord glorious, and glorify him, while thou dost not thy own ways, and thy own will is not found, to speak a word: Then shalt thou be delighted in the Lord, and I will lift thee up above the high places of the earth, and will feed thee with the inheritance of Jacob thy father. For the mouth of the Lord hath spoken it.

FORMATION OF THE WILL

If we had determination, we should live as those Fathers did who, in olden times, shone with labors and piety; because God gives his grace and help to the faithful and to those who seek the Lord with all their heart now just as He did before.
— Seraphim of Sarov[1]

	STAGES OF VOLITIONAL ACTIVITY[2]	STAGES IN THE ACQUISITION OF THE HOLY SPIRIT
BUT DELIVER US FROM EVIL	1st: Wish (imaginative appetency)	Strive to enter by the narrow gate; for many, I say to you, shall seek to enter and shall not be able. But when the master of the house shall be gone in, and shall shut the door, you shall begin to stand without and knock at the door, saying: Lord, open to us: and he, answering, shall say to you: I know you not whence you are. Luke 13:24–25
AND LEAD US NOT INTO TEMPTATION	2nd: Enquiry (search)	A certain man, running up and kneeling before him, asked him: Good Master, what shall I do that I may receive life everlasting? And Jesus said to him: Why callest thou me good? none is good but one, that is God.[3] Thou knowest the commandments: Do not commit adultery, do not kill, do not steal… But he answering said to him: Master, all these things I have observed from my youth. And Jesus, looking on him, loved him and said to him: One thing is wanting unto thee. Go, sell whatsoever thou hast and give to the poor; and thou shalt have treasure in heaven. And come, follow me. Who, being struck sad at the saying, went away sorrowful; for he had great possessions. Mark 10:17–22 The Spirit also helpeth our infirmity. For we know not what we should pray for as we ought; but the Spirit himself asketh for us with unspeakable groanings. Rom. 8:26
AND FORGIVE US OUR TRESPASSES AS WE FORGIVE THOSE WHO TRESPASS AGAINST US	3rd: Consideration and deliberation (general survey)	From whence are wars and contentions forgive those who trespass against us among you? Are they not hence, from your concupiscences, which war in your members? You covet and have not; you kill. And envy and cannot obtain; you contend and war. And you have not because you ask not. You ask and receive not; because you ask amiss, that you may consume it on your concupiscences. James 4:1–3

---

1. Archimandrite Lazarus Moore, *St. Steraphim of Sarov, A Spiritual Biography*, p. 427.
2. According to Maximus the Confessor.
3. The Holy Spirit comes down upon us with innumerable names: Goodness of God (Might not Christ be expressing here a distinction between Himself and the Holy Spirit with whom He is only one?), the Gift of God, Living Water, the Kingdom of God and His Justice, Fulness of Joy…

STAGES OF VOLITIONAL ACTIVITY	STAGES IN THE ACQUISITION OF THE HOLY SPIRIT

GIVE US THIS DAY OUR DAILY BREAD

4th: Judgment (consent)

Ask, and it shall be given you: seek, and you shall find: knock, and it shall be opened to you. For everyone that asketh, receiveth; and he that seeketh, findeth; and to him that knocketh, it shall be opened. Or, what man is there among you, of whom if his son shall ask bread, will he reach him a stone? Or, if he shall ask him a fish, will be reach him a serpent? If you then being evil know how to give good gifts to your children; how much more will your Father who is in heaven give good things to them that ask him?" Matt. 7:7–11

Jesus answered and said to [the Samaritan woman]: If thou didst know the gift of God and who he is that saith to thee: Give me to drink; thou perhaps wouldst have asked on him, and he would have given thee living water. John 4:10

THY WILL BE DONE ON EARTH AS IT IS IN HEAVEN

5th: Choice (desire)

And this is the confidence which we have towards him: that whatsoever we shall ask according to his will, he heareth us. And we know that he heareth us whatsoever we shall ask; we know that we have the petitions which we request of him. 1 John 5:14–15

I cannot of myself do anything. As I hear, so I judge. And my judgment is just; because I seek not my own will, but the will of him that sent me. John 5:30

THY KINGDOM COME

6th: Decisive impulse (movement)

Be not solicitous therefore, saying: What shall we eat; or, What shall we drink; or, wherewith shall be clothed? For after all these things do the heathens seek. For your Father knoweth that you have need of all these things. Seek ye therefore first the kingdom of God and his justice; and all these things shall be added unto you. Matt. 6:31–33

If you then, being evil, know how to give good gifts to your children, how much more will your Father from heaven give the good Spirit to them that ask him? Luke 11:13

OUR FATHER WHO ART IN HEAVEN HALLOWED BE THY NAME

7th: Action (use of things)

If you ask the Father any thing in my name, he will give it you. Hitherto, you have not asked anything in my name. Ask, and you shall receive; that your joy may be full. John 16:23–24

THE WILL OF GOD

Therefore we also… cease not to pray for you and to beg that you may be filled with the knowledge of his will, in all wisdom and spiritual understanding. Colossians 1:9

OUR FATHER WHO
ART IN HEAVEN
Blessed be the God and Father of our Lord Jesus Christ, who hath blessed us with spiritual blessings in heavenly places, in Christ; as he chose us in him before the foundation of the world, that we should be holy and unspotted in his sight in charity. Who hath predestinated us unto the adoption of children through Jesus Christ unto himself, according to the purpose of his will; unto the praise of the glory of his grace, in which he hath graced us in his beloved Son. Eph. 1:3–6

HALLOWED BE
THY NAME
But as many as received him, he gave them power to be made the sons of God, to them that believe in his name; who are born, not of blood, nor of the will of the flesh, nor of the will of man, but of God. John 1:12–13

THY KINGDOM COME
And from the days of John the Baptist until now, the kingdom of heaven suffereth violence and the violent bear it away. Matt. 11:12
The world passeth away… but he that doth the will of God abideth for ever. 1 John 2:17

THY WILL BE DONE
ON EARTH AS IT IS
IN HEAVEN
…that he might make known unto us the mystery of his will, according to his good pleasure… to re-establish all things in Christ, that are in heaven and on earth, in him. In whom we also are called by lot, being predestinated according to the purpose of him who worketh all things according to the counsel of his will. Eph. 1:9–11

GIVE US THIS DAY
OUR DAILY BREAD
My food is to do the will of him that sent me, that I may perfect his work. John 4:34

AND FORGIVE US OUR
TRESPASSES AS WE
FORGIVE THOSE
WHO TRESPASS
AGAINST US
Glory to God in the highest; and on earth peace to men of good will. Luke 2:14

AND LEAD US NOT
INTO TEMPTATION
Wherefore let them also that suffer according to the will of God commend their souls in good deeds to the faithful Creator. 1 Pet. 4:19
Father, if thou wilt, remove this chalice from me; but yet not my will, but thine be done. Luke 22:42

BUT DELIVER
US FROM EVIL
Grace be to you, and peace from God the Father and from our Lord Jesus Christ, who gave himself for our sins, that he might us deliver from this present wicked world, according to the will of God and our Father. Gal. 1:3–4

THE *SYNERGOI*, FELLOW-WORKERS OF GOD

OUR FATHER WHO
ART IN HEAVEN
HALLOWED BE
THY NAME

But Jesus answered them: My Father worketh until now; and I work. John 5:17 Do you not believe that I am in the Father and the Father in me? The words that I speak to you, I speak not of myself. But the Father who abideth in me, he doth the works. John 14:10

THY KINGDOM COME

And I commend to you Phebe, our sister, who is in the ministry of the church, that is in Cenchrae: that you receive her in the Lord as becometh saints and that you assist her in whatsoever business she shall have need of you. For she also hath assisted many, and myself also. Salute Prisca and Aquila, my helpers [συνεργούς, *synergous*], in Christ Jesus. Rom. 16:1–3

THY WILL BE DONE
ON EARTH AS IT IS
IN HEAVEN

Wherefore, my dearly beloved, (as you have always obeyed, not as in my presence only but much more now in my absence) with fear and trembling work out your salvation. For it is God who worketh in you, both to will and to accomplish, according to his good will. Phil. 2:12–13

GIVE US THIS DAY
OUR DAILY BREAD

Therefore, neither he that planteth is any thing, nor he that watereth: but God that giveth the increase. Now he that planteth and he that watereth, are one. And every man shall receive his own reward, according to his own labor. For we are God's coadjutors [συνεργοί, *synergoi*]. You are God's husbandry. 1 Cor. 3:7–9

AND FORGIVE US OUR
TRESPASSES AS WE
FORGIVE THOSE
WHO TRESPASS
AGAINST US

Dearly beloved, thou dost faithfully whatever thou dost for the brethren: and that for strangers, who have given testimony to thy charity in the sight of the church. Whom thou shalt do well to bring forward on their way in a manner worthy of God: because, for his name they went out, taking nothing of the Gentiles. We therefore ought to receive such: that we may be fellow helpers [συνεργοὶ, *synergoi*] of the truth. 3 John 5–8

AND LEAD US NOT
INTO TEMPTATION

And we sent Timothy, our brother and the minister of God and fellow laborer [συνεργὸν, *synergon*] in the gospel of Christ, to confirm you and exhort you concerning your faith: that no man should be moved in these tribulations: for yourselves know that we are appointed thereunto. For even when we were with you, we foretold you that we should suffer tribulations: as also it is come to pass, and you know. 1 Thess. 3:2–4

BUT DELIVER
US FROM EVIL

I am the vine: you the branches. He that abideth in me, and I in him, the same beareth much fruit: for without me you can do nothing. John 15:5

BORN OF GOD

JOHN 1:13

But as many as received
him, he gave them power
to be made the sons
of God, to them that
believe in his name;
who are born:

Not of blood	The ancestral taint, the almost impotent will, the will enslaved	BUT DELIVER US FROM EVIL
Nor of the will of the flesh	The irrational will, the will astray, dispersed	AND FORGIVE US OUR TRESPASSES AS WE FORGIVE THOSE WHO TRESPASS AGAINST US AND LEAD US NOT INTO TEMPTATION
Nor of the will of man	The rational will, the recollected will	GIVE US THIS DAY OUR DAILY BREAD
But of God	The inspired will, the rightly-guided will	THY WILL BE DONE ON EARTH AS IT IS IN HEAVEN
	The divinized will, the communion of will and intellect in oneness of being	OUR FATHER WHO ART IN HEAVEN HALLOWED BE THY NAME THY KINGDOM COME

SON OF GOD, SON OF MAN
THE ANALOGICAL WILL OF THE FATHER

JOHN 5:19–30

OUR FATHER WHO ART IN HEAVEN HALLOWED BE THY NAME

Amen, amen, I say unto you, the Son cannot do any thing of himself, but what he seeth the Father doing: for what things soever he doth, these the Son also doth in like manner.

THY KINGDOM COME

For the Father loveth the Son, and sheweth him all things which himself doth: and greater works than these will he shew him, that you may wonder. For as the Father raiseth up the dead, and giveth life: so the Son also giveth life to whom he will.

THY WILL BE DONE ON EARTH AS IT IS IN HEAVEN

For neither doth the Father judge any man, but hath given all judgment to the Son. That all men may honor the Son, as they honor the Father. He who honoreth not the Son, honoreth not the Father, who hath sent him.

GIVE US THIS DAY OUR DAILY BREAD

Amen, amen I say unto you, that he who heareth my word, and believeth him that sent me, hath life everlasting; and cometh not into judgment, but is passed from death to life.

AND FORGIVE US OUR TRESPASSES AS WE FORGIVE THOSE WHO TRESPASS AGAINST US

Amen, amen I say unto you, that the hour cometh, and now is, when the dead shall hear the voice of the Son of God, and they that hear shall live. For as the Father hath life in himself, so he hath given the Son also to have life in himself:

AND LEAD US NOT INTO TEMPTATION

And he hath given him power to do judgment, because he is the Son of man.

BUT DELIVER US FROM EVIL

Wonder not at this; for the hour cometh, wherein all that are in the graves shall hear the voice of the Son of God. And they that have done good things, shall come forth unto the resurrection of life; but they that have done evil, unto the resurrection of judgment. I cannot of myself do any thing. As I hear, so I judge: and my judgment is just; because I seek not my own will, but the will of him that sent me.

WHO HAS THE SON HAS LIFE

1 JOHN 5

OUR FATHER WHO
ART IN HEAVEN
HALLOWED BE
THY NAME

Whosoever believeth that Jesus is the Christ, is born of God. And every one that loveth him who begot, loveth him also who is born of him.

THY KINGDOM COME

In this we know that we love the children of God: when we love God and keep his commandments.

THY WILL BE DONE
ON EARTH AS IT IS
IN HEAVEN

For this is the charity of God: That we keep his commandments. And his commandments are not heavy. For whatsoever is born of God overcometh the world. And this is the victory which overcameth the world: Our faith. Who is he that overcometh the world, but he that believeth that Jesus is the Son of God? This is he that came by water and blood, Jesus Christ: not by water only but by water and blood. And it is the Spirit which testifieth that Christ is the truth. And there are Three who give testimony in heaven, the Father, the Word, and the Holy Spirit. And these three are one. And there are three that give testimony on earth: the spirit and the water and the blood. And these three are one.

GIVE US THIS DAY
OUR DAILY BREAD

If we receive the testimony of men, the testimony of God is greater. For this is the testimony of God, which is greater, because he hath testified of his Son. He that believeth in the Son of God hath the testimony of God in himself. He that believeth not the Son maketh him a liar: because he believeth not in the testimony which God hath testified of his Son. And this is the testimony that God hath given to us eternal life. And this life is in his Son. He that hath the Son hath life. He that hath not the Son hath not life. These things I write to you that you may know that you have eternal life: you who believe in the name of the Son of God. And this is the confidence which we have towards him: That, whatsoever we shall ask according to his will, he heareth us. And we know that he heareth us whatsoever we ask: we know that we have the petitions which we request of him.

AND FORGIVE US OUR
TRESPASSES AS WE
FORGIVE THOSE
WHO TRESPASS
AGAINST US

He that knoweth his brother to sin a sin which is not to death, let him ask: and life shall be given to him who sinneth not to death. There is a sin unto death. For that I say not that any man ask. All iniquity is sin. And there is a sin unto death.

AND LEAD US NOT
INTO TEMPTATION
BUT DELIVER
US FROM EVIL

We know that whosoever is born of God sinneth not: but the generation of God preserveth him and the wicked one toucheth him not. We know that we are of God and the whole world is seated in wickedness. And we know that the Son of God is come. And he hath given us understanding that we may know the true God and may be in his true Son. This is the true God and life eternal. Little children, keep yourselves from idols. Amen.

BETWEEN HEAVEN AND EARTH
THE WAYS OF THE WAY

Now at that time there arose no small disturbance about the way of the Lord.
Acts 19:23

OUR FATHER WHO ART IN HEAVEN,
HALLOWED BE THY NAME—*The Blessedness of the Way*
Effects of the Spiritual Gifts
THY KINGDOM COME— *The Eight Stages of Contemplation*
THY WILL BE DONE ON EARTH AS IT IS IN HEAVEN— *The Ladder of the Cross*
GIVE US THIS DAY OUR DAILY BREAD—*Between Water and the Spirit,*
the Three Stages of the Spiritual Ascent
AND FORGIVE US OUR TRESPASSES AS WE FORGIVE THOSE WHO
TRESPASS AGAINST US—*The Ladder of Divine Ascent*
AND LEAD US NOT INTO TEMPTATION—*The Short Ladder of Spiritual Progress*
BUT DELIVER US FROM EVIL—*The Ladder of True Belief*

THE LADDER OF TRUE BELIEF

ACCORDING TO MAXIMUS THE CONFESSOR

The one who is an apostle and a disciple is also completely a believer. But the one who is a disciple is not wholly an apostle, but is wholly a believer. The one who is only a simple believer is neither disciple nor apostle. Still, by his manner of life and contemplation, the third can be moved to the rank and dignity of the second, and the second to the rank and dignity of the first. — Maximus the Confessor, *Texts on Theology,* First Century, 34.

BUT DELIVER US FROM EVIL	"The believer is seized with a holy trembling."
AND LEAD US NOT INTO TEMPTATION	"Whoever believes thus finds humility."
AND FORGIVE US OUR TRESPASSES AS WE FORGIVE THOSE WHO TRESPASS AGAINST US	"Whoever finds humility receives gentleness, and thus overcomes the influence of unnatural aggression and covetousness."
GIVE US THIS DAY OUR DAILY BREAD	"Whoever is gentle keeps the commandments."
THY WILL BE DONE ON EARTH AS IT IS IN HEAVEN	"Whoever keeps the commandments is purified."
THY KINGDOM COME	"Whoever is purified is enlightened."
OUR FATHER WHO ART IN HEAVEN HALLOWED BE THY NAME	"That person is judged worthy to enter with the Word into the nuptial chamber of the mysteries."[1]

---

1. *Texts on Theology,* First Century, 16.

THE SHORT LADDER OF SPIRITUAL PROGRESS

ACCORDING TO GREGORY OF SINAI

OUR FATHER WHO
ART IN HEAVEN
HALLOWED BE
THY NAME

God-imbued love: "By love he is led to Christ and brought into His presence. Thus by this short ladder he who is truly obedient swiftly ascends to heaven."

THY KINGDOM COME

Humility: "Thence the spiritual aspirant is embraced by humility, the great exalter, and is borne heavenwards and delivered over to love, the queen of the virtues."

THY WILL BE DONE
ON EARTH AS IT IS
IN HEAVEN

Obedience to spiritual direction: "Obedience, put into action through the practice of the commandments, builds a ladder out of various virtues and places them in the soul as rungs by which to ascend."

GIVE US THIS DAY
OUR DAILY BREAD

Submission to a religious way of life: "Submission is the discovery of Christ and the decision to serve Him."

AND FORGIVE US OUR
TRESPASSES AS WE
FORGIVE THOSE
WHO TRESPASS
AGAINST US
AND LEAD US NOT
INTO TEMPTATION
BUT DELIVER
US FROM EVIL

Renunciation: "Renunciation rises the prisoner from hell and sets him free from enslavement to material things."[1]

---

1. *On Commandments and Doctrines*, 120

THE LADDER OF DIVINE ASCENT

ACCORDING TO JOHN CLIMACUS

I

THE LADDER OF THE CHAPTERS

OUR FATHER WHO
ART IN HEAVEN
HALLOWED BE
THY NAME

Step 30. Concerning the linking together of the supreme trinity among the virtues

THY KINGDOM COME

Step 27. On holy stillness of body and soul
Step 28. On holy and blessed prayer, the mother of virtues
Step 29. concerning Heaven on earth, or Godlike dispassion and perfection, and the resurrection of the soul before the general resurrection

THY WILL BE DONE
ON EARTH AS IT IS
IN HEAVEN

Step 19. On sleep, prayer and psalmody
Step 20. On bodily vigil and how to use it to attain spiritual vigil
Step 21. On unmanly and puerile cowardice
Step 22. On the many forms of vainglory
Step 23. On mad pride
Step 24. On meekness, simplicity and guilelessness which come not from nature but from conscious effort
Step 25. On the destroyer of the passions, most sublime humility, which is rooted in spiritual perception
Step 26. On discernment of thoughts, passions and virtues

GIVE US THIS DAY
OUR DAILY BREAD

Step 13. On despondency
Step 14. On that clamorous mistress, the stomach
Step 15. On corruptible purity and chastity
Step 16. On love of money or avarice
Step 17. On non-possessiveness
Step 18. On insensibility
and forgive us our

AND FORGIVE US OUR
TRESPASSES AS WE
FORGIVE THOSE
WHO TRESPASS
AGAINST US

Step 8. On freedom from anger and on meekness
Step 9. On remembrance of wrongs
Step 10. On slander of calumny
Step 11. On talkativeness and silence
Step 12. On lying

AND LEAD US NOT
INTO TEMPTATION

Step 4. On blessed and ever-memorable obedience
Step 5. On painstaking and true repentance
Step 6. On remembrance of death
Step 7. On joy-making mourning

BUT DELIVER
US FROM EVIL

Step 1. On renunciation of the world
Step 2. On detachment
Step 3. On exile and pilgrimage

A SUMMARY

BUT DELIVER
US FROM EVIL

"The lessening of evil brings forth abstinence from evil; and abstinence from evil is the beginning of repentance; and the beginning of repentance is the beginning of salvation;

AND LEAD US NOT
INTO TEMPTATION

and the beginning of salvation is a good resolve; and a good resolve is the mother of labors.

AND FORGIVE US OUR
TRESPASSES AS WE
FORGIVE THOSE
WHO TRESPASS
AGAINST US

And the beginning of labors is the virtues; the beginning of the virtues is a flowering, and the flowering of virtue is the beginning of activity.

GIVE US THIS DAY
OUR DAILY BREAD

And the offspring of virtue is perseverance; and the fruit and offspring of persevering practice is habit, and the child of habit is character.

THY WILL BE DONE
ON EARTH AS IT IS
IN HEAVEN

Good character is the mother of fear; and fear gives birth to the keeping of commandments in which I include both heavenly and earthly. The keeping of the commandments is a sign of love; and the beginning of love is an abundance of humility;

THY KINGDOM COME

and an abundance of humility is the daughter of dispassion; and the acquisition of the latter is the fulness of love, that is to say the perfect indwelling of God in those who through dispassion are pure in heart, for they shall see God.

OUR FATHER WHO
ART IN HEAVEN
HALLOWED BE
THY NAME

And to him the glory for all eternity. Amen."[1]

---

1. *The Ladder of Divine Ascent*, Step 26, 'Brief Summary', 65.

BETWEEN WATER AND SPIRIT,
THE THREE STAGES OF THE SPIRITUAL ASCENT

UNION

OUR FATHER WHO
ART IN HEAVEN
HALLOWED BE
THY NAME
THY KINGDOM COME

Blood into fire—Pentecost:
If I go not, the Paraclete will not come to you; but if I go, I will send him to you.
John 16:7

ILLUMINATION

THY WILL BE DONE
ON EARTH AS IT IS
IN HEAVEN

Wine into blood—the Eucharist:
This is my blood of the new testament, which shall be shed for many. Amen, I say to you that I will drink no more of the fruit of the vine until that day when I shall drink it new in the kingdom of God. Mark 14:24–25

GIVE US THIS DAY
OUR DAILY BREAD

Water into wine—the marriage at Cana:
And the wine failing, the mother of Jesus saith to him: They have no wine.
John 2:3

PURIFICATION

AND FORGIVE US OUR
TRESPASSES AS WE
FORGIVE THOSE
WHO TRESPASS
AGAINST US
AND LEAD US NOT
INTO TEMPTATION
BUT DELIVER
US FROM EVIL

Water—the baptism in the Jordan:
Do penance; for the kingdom of heaven is at hand. Matt. 3:2

COMMENTARY

Just as the dove of the Spirit descends and remains upon Christ in His baptism in the Jordan, so the fiery tongues of the Spirit descend and remain upon those gathered in the upper room on Pentecost; first the Spirit descends and remains upon Christ's incarnate Body, and then, later, on His mystical Body. If, in the Christian Way, metanoia is represented by the baptism in the Jordan and theosis by Pentecost, the other scriptural 'events' thus represent successive transitions between the stages of this Way, the 'way' between water and the Spirit: "Unless a man be born again of water and the Holy Spirit, he cannot enter into the kingdom of God" (John 3:5).

THE LADDER OF THE CROSS

ACCORDING TO THE AKATHIST HYMN TO THE SPIRITUAL LADDER,
THE PRECIOUS CROSS[1]

Your passion grants dispassion to our souls.
—Holy Saturday, Lamentations, second stasis.

OUR FATHER WHO ART IN HEAVEN HALLOWED BE THY NAME	Rejoice, thou through [which] the Creator is worshipped! *Ekos 1* Rejoice, for thou art the divine footstool! *Ekos 1*
THY KINGDOM COME	Rejoice, opener of the entrance to Paradise! *Ekos 9* Rejoice, seal that men have received! *Ekos 6*
THY WILL BE DONE ON EARTH AS IT IS IN HEAVEN	Rejoice, for thou dost join together things on earth with things above! *Ekos 8* Rejoice, thou brilliant stratagem of Christ! *Ekos 12*
GIVE US THIS DAY OUR DAILY BREAD	Rejoice, food of the hungry in spirit! *Ekos 6* Rejoice, thou myriad-numbered wealth of good things! *Ekos 8*
AND FORGIVE US OUR TRESPASSES AS WE FORGIVE THOSE WHO TRESPASS AGAINST US	Rejoice, uplifting of the fallen! *Ekos 7* Rejoice, condemnation of offending mortals! *Ekos 7*
AND LEAD US NOT INTO TEMPTATION	Rejoice, thou the stern trainer of the victors! *Ekos 2* Rejoice, quencher of deception's fire! *Ekos 2*
BUT DELIVER US FROM EVIL	Rejoice, thou by which all the world was saved! *Ekos 11* Rejoice, thou that didst destroy the corrupter of souls! *Ekos 10*

---

1. *Book of Akathists* (Jordanville NY: Holy Trinity Monastery, 1994), pp. 61–71.

THE EIGHT STAGES OF CONTEMPLATION

ACCORDING TO PETER OF DAMASKOS[1]

OUR FATHER WHO ART IN HEAVEN HALLOWED BE THY NAME	8th stage: Knowledge concerning God, or what we call 'theology'.
THY KINGDOM COME	7th stage: The understanding of God's spiritual creation.
THY WILL BE DONE ON EARTH AS IT IS IN HEAVEN	6th stage: Contemplation of created beings... knowledge and understanding of God's visible creation.
GIVE US THIS DAY OUR DAILY BREAD	5th stage: Knowledge of the nature and flux of things.
	4th stage: Deep understanding of the life led by our Lord Jesus Christ in this world, and of the words and actions of the disciples and the other saints, the martyrs and the holy fathers.
AND FORGIVE US OUR TRESPASSES AS WE FORGIVE THOSE WHO TRESPASS AGAINST US	3rd stage: Knowledge of the terrible things that await us before and after death, as revealed in the Holy Scriptures.
AND LEAD US NOT INTO TEMPTATION	2nd stage: Knowledge of our own faults and God's bounty.
BUT DELIVER US FROM EVIL	1st stage: Knowledge of the tribulations and trials of this life. This fills us with grief for all the damage done to human nature by sin.

---

1. *A Treasury of Divine Knowledge*, Book 1. cf. *The Philokalia*, vol. 3, pp. 109–143 for a full explanation of these stages.

EFFECTS OF THE SPIRITUAL GIFTS

ACCORDING TO MAXIMUS THE CONFESSOR[1]

OUR FATHER WHO ART IN HEAVEN HALLOWED BE THY NAME	Wisdom: An indivisible union with God. "He who shares in wisdom becomes god by participation, and immersed in the ever-flowing, secret outpouring of God's mysteries, he imparts to those who long for it a knowledge of divine blessedness."[2]
THY KINGDOM COME	Understanding: The soul's total empathy with the things that it has come to know.
THY WILL BE DONE ON EARTH AS IT IS IN HEAVEN	Spiritual knowledge: The active grasping of the divine principles inherent in the virtues.
GIVE US THIS DAY OUR DAILY BREAD	Cognitive insight: A clear perception of what one has to do.
AND FORGIVE US OUR TRESPASSES AS WE FORGIVE THOSE WHO TRESPASS AGAINST US	Counsel: Discrimination with respect to the demons.
AND LEAD US NOT INTO TEMPTATION	Strength: The practice of goodness.
BUT DELIVER US FROM EVIL	Fear: Abstention from evil.

1. *Various Texts*, Third Century, 38.
2. *Ibid.*

THE BLESSEDNESS OF THE WAY

PSALM 118 SUMMARIZED IN ITS FIRST THREE VERSES

Since, then, nearly all the psalms which have the inscription 'alleluia' are found in the final section of the Psalms, one can clearly perceive that the final section of the Psalms, which contain for the most part praise of God or exhortation to praise God, excels every lofty ascent through the Psalms. —Gregory of Nyssa, *On the Inscriptions of the Psalms*, II, VII, 71

OUR FATHER WHO
ART IN HEAVEN
HALLOWED BE
THY NAME

Alleluia

THY KINGDOM COME
THY WILL BE DONE
ON EARTH AS IT IS
IN HEAVEN

Blessed are the undefiled in the way,
who walk in the law of the Lord.

GIVE US THIS DAY
OUR DAILY BREAD
AND FORGIVE US OUR
TRESPASSES AS WE
FORGIVE THOSE
WHO TRESPASS
AGAINST US

Blessed are they that search his testimonies:
that seek him with their whole heart.

AND LEAD US NOT
INTO TEMPTATION
BUT DELIVER
US FROM EVIL

For they that work iniquity,
have not walked in his ways.

COMMENTARY

'Way', 'whole heart' and 'ways'… Turning back from the third verse, beset by evil in many ways, many are the ways sought to live in accordance with the commandments. But once fullness of time and wholeness of heart have come, then are we attentive to but one way. As soon as the psalm begins it goes back to its beginning, and the beginning is Christ: . "They said therefore to him: Who art thou? Jesus said to them: The beginning, who also speak unto you" (John 8:25). Alleluia!

THE ANGELIC LIFE

OUR FATHER WHO ART IN HEAVEN, HALLOWED BE THY NAME—*Hosanna, The Tetramorph*
THY KINGDOM COME—*The Angels, Joy in the Holy Spirit*
THY WILL BE DONE ON EARTH AS IT IS IN HEAVEN —*The Peace Beyond Understanding,*
Set Free: the Glory of the Children of God
GIVE US THE DAY OUR DAILY BREAD—*Grace*
AND FORGIVE US OUR TRESPASSES AS WE FORGIVE THOSE
WHO TRESPASS AGAINST US—*Thy Mercy, O Lord*
AND LEAD US NOT INTO TEMPTATION
BUT DELIVER US FROM EVIL—*Born of the Spirit*
AMEN—*The Charismatic Life*

THE CHARISMATIC LIFE

THE ONENESS AND DIVERSITY OF THE GIFTS
1 CORINTHIANS 12:4–11

<table>
<tr><td>OUR FATHER WHO
ART IN HEAVEN
HALLOWED BE
THY NAME</td><td>Spirit: Now, there are diversities of graces,
but the same Spirit.
Son: And there are diversities of ministries, but the same Lord.
Father: And there are diversities of operations, but the same
God who worketh all in all.</td></tr>
<tr><td>THY KINGDOM COME</td><td>And the manifestation of the Spirit is given to every man unto profit.</td></tr>
<tr><td>THY WILL BE DONE
ON EARTH</td><td>To one indeed, by the Spirit, is given:
Our Father who art in heaven hallowed be thy name
    the word of wisdom;
Thy kingdom come
    and to another, the word of knowledge, according to the same Spirit;
Thy will be done on earth as it is in heaven
Give us this day our daily bread
    to another, faith in the same Spirit;
And forgive us our trespasses as we forgive
those who trespass against us
    to another, the grace of healing in one Spirit;
And lead us not into temptation
but deliver us from evil
    to another… the discerning of spirits.</td></tr>
<tr><td>AS IT IS
IN HEAVEN</td><td>But all these things, one and the same Spirit worketh, dividing to every one according as he will.</td></tr>
</table>

BORN OF THE SPIRIT

Created man cannot become a son of God and god by grace through deification, unless he is first through his own free choice begotten in the Spirit by means of the self-loving and independent power dwelling naturally within him. The first man neglected this divinizing, divine and immaterial birth by choosing what is manifest and delectable to the senses in preference to the spiritual blessings that were as yet unrevealed. — Maximus the Confessor, *Various Texts*, Fifth Century, 97.

<table>
<tr><td>OUR FATHER WHO
ART IN HEAVEN
HALLOWED BE
THY NAME</td><td>For whosoever are led by the Spirit of God, they are the sons of God. For you have not received the spirit of bondage again in fear: but you have received the spirit of adoption of sons, whereby we cry: Abba (Father). For the Spirit himself giveth testimony to our spirit that we are the sons of God. Rom. 8:14–15</td></tr>
<tr><td>THY KINGDOM COME</td><td>Jesus answered, and said to him: Amen, amen I say to thee, unless a man be born again, he cannot see the kingdom of God. Nicodemus saith to him: How can a man be born when he is old? can he enter a second time into his mother's womb, and be born again? Jesus answered: Amen, amen I say to thee, unless a</td></tr>
</table>

man be born again[1] of water and the Holy Spirit, he cannot enter into the kingdom of God. That which is born of the flesh, is flesh; and that which is born of the Spirit, is spirit. Wonder not, that I said to thee, you must be born again. The Spirit breatheth where he will; and thou hearest his voice, but thou knowest not whence he cometh, and whither he goeth: so is every one that is born of the Spirit. John 3:3–8

THY WILL BE DONE ON EARTH AS IT IS IN HEAVEN

But you are not in the flesh, but the spirit, if so be that the Spirit of God dwell in you. Now if any man have not the Spirit of Christ, he is none of his. And if Christ be in you, the body indeed is dead, because of sin: but the spirit liveth, because of justification. And if the Spirit of him that raised up Jesus from the dead dwell in you; he that raised up Jesus Christ, from the dead shall quicken also your mortal bodies, because of his Spirit that dwelleth in you. Rom. 8:9–11

GIVE US THIS DAY OUR DAILY BREAD

For what man knoweth the things of a man, but the spirit of a man that is in him? So the things also that are of God, no man knoweth, but the Spirit of God. Now, we have received not the spirit of this world, but the Spirit that is of God: that we may know the things that are given us from God. 1 Cor. 2:11–12

AND FORGIVE US OUR TRESPASSES AS WE FORGIVE THOSE WHO TRESPASS AGAINST US

And grieve not the holy Spirit of God: whereby you are sealed unto the day of redemption. Let all bitterness and anger and indignation and clamor and blasphemy be put away from you, with all malice. And be ye kind one to another: merciful, forgiving one another, even as God hath forgiven you in Christ. Eph. 4:30–32

AND LEAD US NOT INTO TEMPTATION

Dearly beloved, think not strange the burning heat which is to try you: as if some new thing happened to you. But if you partake of the sufferings of Christ, rejoice that, when his glory shall be revealed, you may also be glad with exceeding joy. If you be reproached for the name of Christ, you shall be blessed: for that which is of the honor, glory and power of God, and that which is his Spirit resteth upon you. 1 Pet. 4:12–14

BUT DELIVER US FROM EVIL

Now we, brethren, as Isaac was, are the children of promise. But as then he that was born according to the flesh persecuted him that was after the spirit: so also it is now. But what saith the scripture? Cast out the bondwoman and her son: for the son of the bondwoman shall not be heir with the son of the free woman. So then, brethren, we are not the children of the bondwoman but of the free: by the freedom wherewith Christ has made us free. Gal. 4:28–31

---

1. In Greek ἄνωθεν, *anothen*, means both 'again' and 'from above', a double meaning at the source of every Nicodeman perplexity, that confusion between the repetitiveness of 'this world' and the uniqueness of the 'world to come' that is 'here and now' in the Spirit.

THY MERCY, O LORD

IN THE PSALMS

OUR FATHER WHO
ART IN HEAVEN
HALLOWED BE
THY NAME
Know ye that the Lord he is God: he made us, and not we ourselves.
We are his people and the sheep of his pasture.
Go ye into his gates with praise, into his courts with hymns:
and give glory to him. Praise ye his name:
For the Lord is sweet, his mercy endureth for ever,
and his truth to generation and generation. Psalm 99:3–5

THY KINGDOM COME
Justice and judgment are the preparation of thy throne.
Mercy and truth shall go before thy face:
Blessed is the people that knoweth jubilation.
They shall walk, O Lord, in the light of thy countenance:
And in thy name they shall rejoice all the day,
and in thy justice they shall be exalted. Psalm 88:15–17

THY WILL BE DONE
ON EARTH AS IT IS
IN HEAVEN
O Lord, thy mercy is in heaven, and thy truth reacheth even to the clouds.
Thy justice is as the mountains of God, thy judgments are a great deep. Men
and beasts thou wilt preserve, O Lord:
O how hast thou multiplied thy mercy, O God! Psalm 35:6–8

For the word of the Lord is right, and all his works are done with faithfulness.
He loveth mercy and judgment;
the earth is full of the mercy of the Lord. Psalm 32:4–5

GIVE US THIS DAY
OUR DAILY BREAD
Return, O Lord, how long? and be entreated in favour of thy servants.
We are filled in the morning with thy mercy:
and we have rejoiced, and are delighted all our days. Psalm 89:13–14

AND FORGIVE US OUR
TRESPASSES AS WE
FORGIVE THOSE
WHO TRESPASS
AGAINST US
For the Lord is high, and looketh on the low: and the high he knoweth afar off.
If I shall walk in the midst of tribulation, thou wilt quicken me:
and thou hast stretched forth thy hand against the wrath of my enemies:
and thy right hand hath saved me.
The Lord will repay for me: thy mercy, O Lord, endureth for ever:
O despise not the works of thy hands. Psalm 137:6–8

AND LEAD US NOT
INTO TEMPTATION
Unless the Lord had been my helper, my soul had almost dwelt in hell.
If I said: My foot is moved: thy mercy, O Lord, assisted me.
According to the multitude of my sorrows in my heart,
thy comforts have given joy to my soul. Psalm 93:17–19

BUT DELIVER
US FROM EVIL
O Lord, rebuke me not in thy indignation, nor chastise me in thy wrath.
Have mercy on me, O Lord, for I am weak:
heal me, O Lord, for my bones are troubled.
And my soul is troubled exceedingly: but thou, O Lord, how long?
Turn to me, O Lord, and deliver my soul:
O save me for thy mercy's sake. Psalm 6:2–5

OUR FATHER WHO
ART IN HEAVEN
HALLOWED BE
THY NAME

But God (who is rich in mercy) for his exceeding charity wherewith he loved us, even when we were dead in sins, hath quickened us together in Christ (by whose grace you are saved) and hath raised us up together and hath made us sit together in the heavenly places, through Christ Jesus. Eph. 2:4–6

THY KINGDOM COME

For in Christ Jesus neither circumcision availeth any thing, nor uncircumcision: but a new creature. And whosoever shall follow this rule, peace on them and mercy: and upon the Israel of God. Gal. 6:15–16

THY WILL BE DONE
ON EARTH AS IT IS
IN HEAVEN

What shall we say then? Is there injustice with God? God forbid! For he saith to Moses: I will have mercy on whom I will have mercy. And I will shew mercy to whom I will shew mercy. So then it is not of him that willeth, nor of him that runneth, but of God that sheweth mercy. Rom. 9:14–16

GIVE US THIS DAY
OUR DAILY BREAD

Therefore seeing we have this ministration, according as we have obtained mercy, we faint not. But we renounce the hidden things of dishonesty, not walking in craftiness nor adulterating the word of God: but by manifestation of the truth commending ourselves to every man's conscience, in the sight of God. 2 Cor. 4:1–2

AND FORGIVE US OUR
TRESPASSES AS WE
FORGIVE THOSE
WHO TRESPASS
AGAINST US

What if God, willing to show his wrath and to make his power known, endured with much patience vessels of wrath, fitted for destruction, that he might show the riches of his glory on the vessels of mercy which he hath prepared unto glory? Even us, whom also he hath called, not only of the Jews but also of the Gentiles. Rom. 9:22–24

AND LEAD US NOT
INTO TEMPTATION

Blessed be the God and Father of our Lord Jesus Christ, the Father of mercies and the God of all comfort: who comforteth us in all our tribulation, that we also may be able to comfort them who are in all distress, by the exhortation wherewith we also are exhorted by God. For as the sufferings of Christ abound in us: so also by Christ doth our comfort abound. Now whether we be in tribulation, it is for your exhortation and salvation: or whether we be comforted, it is for your consolation: or whether we be exhorted, it is for your exhortation and salvation, which worketh the enduring of the same sufferings which we also suffer. That our hope for you may be steadfast: knowing that as you are partakers of the sufferings, so shall you be also of the consolation. 2 Cor. 1:3–7

BUT DELIVER
US FROM EVIL

I give him thanks who hath strengthened me, even to Christ Jesus our Lord, for that he hath counted me faithful, putting me in the ministry: who before was a blasphemer and a persecutor and contumelious. But I obtained the mercy of God, because I did it ignorantly in unbelief. Now the grace of our Lord hath abounded exceedingly with faith and love, which is in Christ Jesus. A faithful saying, and worthy of all acceptation, that Christ Jesus came into the world to save sinners, of whom I am the chief. 1 Tim. 1:12–15

PSALM 135: A PERPETUAL THANKSGIVING AND PRAISE FOR GOD'S MERCY

OUR FATHER WHO
ART IN HEAVEN
HALLOWED BE
THY NAME

Alleluia. Praise the Lord, for he is good: for his mercy endureth for ever.
Praise ye the God of gods: for his mercy endureth for ever.

THY KINGDOM COME

Praise ye the Lord of lords: for his mercy endureth for ever.

THY WILL BE DONE
ON EARTH AS IT IS
IN HEAVEN

Who alone doth great wonders: for his mercy endureth for ever.
Who made the heavens in understanding: for his mercy endureth for ever.
Who established the earth above the waters: for his mercy endureth for ever.
Who made the great lights: for his mercy endureth for ever.
The sun to rule the day: for his mercy endureth for ever.
The moon and the stars to rule the night: for his mercy endureth for ever.

GIVE US THIS DAY
OUR DAILY BREAD

Who giveth food to all flesh: for his mercy endureth for ever.[1]

AND FORGIVE US OUR
TRESPASSES AS WE
FORGIVE THOSE
WHO TRESPASS
AGAINST US

Who smote Egypt with their firstborn: for his mercy endureth for ever.
Who brought out Israel from among them: for his mercy endureth for ever.
With a mighty hand and with a stretched out arm:
for his mercy endureth for ever.
Who divided the Red Sea into parts: for his mercy endureth for ever.
And brought out Israel through the midst thereof:
for his mercy endureth for ever.
And overthrew Pharao and his host in the Red Sea:
for his mercy endureth for ever.
Who led his people through the desert: for his mercy endureth for ever.
Who smote great kings: for his mercy endureth for ever.
And slew strong kings: for his mercy endureth for ever.
Sehon king of the Amorrhites: for his mercy endureth for ever.
And Og king of Basan: for his mercy endureth for ever.
And he gave their land for an inheritance: for his mercy endureth for ever.
For an inheritance to his servant Israel: for his mercy endureth for ever.

AND LEAD US NOT
INTO TEMPTATION

For he was mindful of us in our affliction: for his mercy endureth for ever.

BUT DELIVER
US FROM EVIL

And he redeemed us from our enemies: for his mercy endureth for ever.

OUR FATHER WHO
ART IN HEAVEN
HALLOWED BE
THY NAME

Give glory to the God of heaven: for his mercy endureth for ever.
Give glory to the Lord of lords: for his mercy endureth for ever.

---

1. Verse 25 transposed between verses 9 and 10.

Psalm 135, chanted during matins at the 'polyeleos' (so named because of this psalm's repeated invocation of God's mercy), brings into high relief that continuity between the private life of prayer—the Jesus Prayer with its constant repetition of 'Lord Jesus Christ, Son of God, have mercy on me'—and the public life of the liturgy—the litanies with their constant repetition of 'Lord have mercy'. Is this some kind of monochrome spirituality where all is 'vain repetition' (Matt. 6:7)?[1] An initial answer is given by Peter of Damaskos in his *Treasury of Divine Knowledge*:

> Divine Scripture[2] often repeats the same words, yet this is not to be regarded as verbosity. On the contrary, by means of this frequent repetition it unexpectedly and compassionately draws even those who are very slow in grasping things to an awareness and understanding of what is being said; and it ensures that a particular saying does not escape notice because of its fleetingness and brevity.[3]

From this we see that repetition holds a certain benefit for ourselves. Next, turning to John Chrysostom's remarks on Matthew 6:7 we find a more complete answer:

> He seems to me to command in this place, that neither should we make our prayers long; long, I mean, not in time, but in the number and length of the things mentioned. For perseverance indeed in the same requests is our duty: His word being, 'continuing instant in prayer' (Rom. 12:12). And He Himself too, by that example of the widow, who prevailed with the pitiless and cruel ruler, by the continuance of her intercession (Luke 18:1); and by that of the friend, who came late at night time, and roused the sleeper from his bed (Luke 11:5), not for his friendship's, but for his importunity's sake; what did He, but lay down a law, that all should continually make supplication unto Him? He does not however bid us compose a prayer of ten thousand clauses, and so come to Him and merely repeat it. For this He obscurely signified when He said, 'They think that they shall be heard for their much speaking.' 'For He knows,' says He, 'what things you have need of.' And if He know, one may say, what we have need of, wherefore must we pray? Not to instruct Him, but to prevail with Him; to be made intimate with Him, by continuance in supplication; to be humbled; to be reminded of your sins.[4]

Intimacy, humility and repentance for sins: these three ensure that we have heard God's words and that God will hear ours.

But what of 'mercy' repeated and repeated? We say it often to gain entrance into the kingdom of God for, as Nicholas Cabasilas tells us in his comments on the litanies: "To beg God's mercy is to ask for his kingdom, that kingdom which Christ promised to those who seek for it, assuring them that all things else of which they have need will be added unto them (Matt. 6:33)."[5] We say it often to call down upon ourselves the gift of the Holy Spirit for, as we read in *The Philokalia*: "The mercy of God is nothing else but the grace of the Holy Spirit, the grace that we sinners must ask from God, continually saying the *Kyrie eleison*, Lord have mercy on me the sinner!"[6] Only then can we worship God in spirit and in truth. Truly, until that time all prayers are 'vain' and we rely upon the compassion, the mercy of God to supply what is lacking, while after that time "the Spirit himself asketh for us with unspeakable groanings" (Rom. 8:26).

---

1. The full passage is: "And when you pray, do not use vain repetitions as the heathen do. For they think that they will be heard for their many words."

2. And the liturgy as well.

3. 'That the Frequent Repetition Found in Divine Scripture is not Verbosity', Book 1, *A Treasury of Divine Knowledge*, in *The Philokalia*, vol. 3, p. 188.

4. *On Matthew*, Homily 19.

5. *A Commentary on the Divine Liturgy*, p. 47.

6. 'Interpretation of the *Kyrie eleison*' in *Philocalie des Pères neptiques*, fascicule 11, French trans. Bobrinskoy (Bégrolles-en-Mauges: Abbaye de Bellefontaine, 1991), p. 250.

GRACE

The whole complex of the commandments united and knit together in the Spirit (cf. Eph. 4:16) *has its analogue in man, whether his state is perfect or imperfect. The commandments are the body. The virtues—established inner qualities—are the bones. Grace is the soul that lives and vivifies, energizing the vital power of the commandments just as the soul animates the body.* —Gregory of Sinai, *On Commandments and Doctrines,* 20

OUR FATHER WHO
ART IN HEAVEN
HALLOWED BE
THY NAME

Wherefore also we pray always for you; that our God would make you worthy of his vocation, and fulfill all the good pleasure of his goodness and the work of faith in power; that the name of our Lord Jesus may be glorified in you, and you in him, according to the grace of our God, and of the Lord Jesus Christ. 2 Thess. 1:11–12

Grace be to you, and peace from God the Father, and from the Lord Jesus Christ Blessed by the God and Father of our Lord Jesus Christ, who hath blessed us with spiritual blessings in heavenly places, in Christ: as he chose us in him before the foundation of the world, that we should be holy and unspotted in his sight in charity. Eph. 1:2–4

THY KINGDOM COME

Peace be to the brethren and charity with faith, from God the Father, and the Lord Jesus Christ. Grace be with all them that love our Lord Jesus Christ in incorruption. Amen. Eph. 6:23–24

And may the God of peace himself sanctify you in all things; that your whole spirit, and soul, and body, may be preserved blameless in the coming of our Lord Jesus Christ. He is faithful who hath called you, who also will do it. Brethren, pray for us. Salute all the brethren with a holy kiss. I charge you by the Lord, that this epistle be read to all the holy brethren. The grace of our Lord Jesus Christ be with you. Amen. 1 Thess. 5:23–28

THY WILL BE DONE
ON EARTH AS IT
IS IN HEAVEN

I speak not as commanding; but by the carefulness of others, approving also the good disposition of your charity. For you know the grace of our Lord Jesus Christ, that being rich he became poor, for your sakes; that through his poverty you might be rich. 2 Cor. 8:8–9

To all that are at Rome, the beloved of God, called to be saints. Grace to you, and peace from God our Father, and from the Lord Jesus Christ. First I give thanks to my God, through Jesus Christ, for you all, because your faith is spoken of in the whole world. For God is my witness, whom I serve in my spirit in the gospel of his Son, that without ceasing I make a commemoration of you; always in my prayers making request, if by any means now at length I may have a prosperous journey, by the will of God, to come unto you. For I long to see you, that I may impart unto you some spiritual grace, to strengthen you: that is to say, that I may be comforted together in you, by that which is common to us both, your faith and mine. Rom. 1:7–12

GIVE US THIS DAY
OUR DAILY BREAD

I give thanks to my God always for you, for the grace of God that is given you in Christ Jesus, that in all things you are made rich in him, in all utterance, and in all knowledge; as the testimony of Christ was confirmed in you, so that nothing iswanting to you in any grace, waiting for the manifestation of our Lord Jesus Christ. 1 Cor. 1:4–7

And of his fulness we all have received, and grace for grace. John 1:16

Grace be unto you, and peace from God our Father, and from the Lord Jesus Christ. I give thanks to my God in every remembrance of you, always in all my prayers making supplication for you all, with joy; for your communication in the gospel of Christ from the first day until now. Being confident of this very thing, that he, who hath begun a good work in you, will perfect it unto the day of Christ Jesus. Phil. 1:2–6

Follow peace with all men, and holiness: without which no man shall see God. Looking diligently, lest any man be wanting to the grace of God; lest any root of bitterness springing up do hinder, and by it many be defiled. Heb. 12:14–15

Grace unto you, and peace from God our Father, and from the Lord Jesus Christ. We are bound to give thanks always to God for you, brethren, as it is fitting, because your faith groweth exceedingly, and the charity of every one of you towards each other, aboundeth. 2 Thess. 1:2–3

AND LEAD US NOT
INTO TEMPTATION

Therefore, brethren, stand fast; and hold the traditions which you have learned, whether by word, or by our epistle. Now our Lord Jesus Christ himself, and God and our Father, who hath loved us, and hath given us everlasting consolation, and good hope in grace, exhort your hearts, and confirm you in every good work and word. 2 Thess. 2:14–16

Grace unto you and peace from God our Father, and from the Lord Jesus Christ. Blessed be the God and Father of our Lord Jesus Christ, the Father of mercies, and the God of all comfort. Who comforteth us in all our tribulation; that we also may be able to comfort them who are in all distress, by the exhortation wherewith we also are exhorted by God. For as the sufferings of Christ abound in us: so also by Christ doth our comfort abound. 2 Cor. 1:2–5

BUT DELIVER
US FROM EVIL

Now the law entered in, that sin might abound. And where sin abounded, grace did more abound. That as sin hath reigned to death; so also grace might reign by justice unto life everlasting, through Jesus Christ our Lord. Rom. 5:20–21

Grace be to you, and peace from God the Father, and from our Lord Jesus Christ, who gave himself for our sins, that he might deliver us from this present wicked world, according to the will of God and our Father: To whom is glory for ever and ever. Amen. Gal. 1:3–5

SET FREE: THE GLORY OF THE CHILDREN OF GOD

OUR FATHER WHO
ART IN HEAVEN
HALLOWED BE
THY NAME

Now the Lord is a Spirit. And where the Spirit of the Lord is, there is liberty. But we all, beholding the glory of the Lord with open face, are transfonned into the same image from glory to glory, as by the Spirit of the Lord. 2 Cor. 3:17–18 Then Jesus said to those Jews who believed him: If you continue in 'my word, you shall be my disciples indeed. And you shall know the truth: and the truth shall make you free. They answered him: We are the seed of Abraham: and we have never been slaves to any man. How sayest thou: You shall be free? Jesus answered them: Amen, amen, I say unto you that whosoever committeth sin is the servant of sin. Now the servant abideth not in the house for ever: but the son abideth for ever. If therefore the son shall make you free, you shall be free indeed. John 8:31–36

THY KINGDOM COME

For I reckon that the sufferings of this time are not worthy to be compared with the glory to come that shall be revealed in us. For the expectation of the creature waiteth for the revelation of the sons of God. For the creature was made subject to vanity: not willingly, but by reason of him that made it subject, in hope. Because the creature also itself shall be delivered from the servitude of corruption, into the liberty of the glory of the children of God. Rom. 8:18-21 But that Jerusalem which is above is free: which is our mother. Gal. 4:26

THY WILL BE DONE
ON EARTH AS IT IS
IN HEAVEN

For if a man be a hearer of the word and not a doer, he shall be compared to a man beholding his own countenance in a glass. For he beheld himself and went his way and presently forgot what manner of man he was. But he that hath looked into the perfect law of liberty and hath continued therein, not becoming a forgetful hearer but a doer of the work: this man shall be blessed in his deed. James 1:23–25

GIVE US THIS DAY
OUR DAILY BREAD

All things are lawful for me: but all things are not expedient. All things are lawful for me: but all things do not edify. Let no man seek his own, but that which is another's. Whatsoever is sold in the shambles, eat: asking no question for conscience' sake. The earth is the Lord's and the fulness thereof. If any of them that believe not, invite you, and you be willing to go: eat of any thing that is set before you, asking no question for conscience' sake. But if any man say: This has been sacrificed to idols: do not eat of it, for his sake that told it and for conscience' sake. Conscience I say, not thy own, but the other's. For why is my liberty judged by another man's conscience? If I partake with thanksgiving, why am I evil spoken of for that for which I give thanks? Therefore, whether you eat or drink, or whatsoever else you do, do all to the glory of God. 1 Cor. 10:22–31

AND FORGIVE US OUR
TRESPASSES AS WE
FORGIVE THOSE
WHO TRESPASS
AGAINST US

For you, brethren, have been called unto liberty. Only make not liberty an occasion to the flesh: but by charity of the spirit serve one another. For all the law is fulfilled in one word: Thou shalt love thy neighbor as thyself. Gal. 5:13–14

Peter therefore was kept in prison. But prayer was made without ceasing by the church unto God for him. And when Herod would have brought him forth, the same night, Peter was sleeping between two soldiers, bound with two chains: and the keepers before the door kept the prison. And behold an angel of the Lord stood by him and a light shined in the room. And he, striking Peter on the side, raised him up, saying: Arise quickly. And the chains fell off from his hands. And the angel said to him: Gird thyself and put on thy sandals. And he did so. And he said to him: Cast thy garment about thee and follow me, and going out, he followed him. And he knew not that it was true which was done by the angel: but thought he saw a vision. And passing through the first and the second ward, they carne to the iron gate that leadeth to the city which of itself opened to them. And going out, they passed on through one street. And immediately the angel departed from him. And Peter coming to himself, said: Now I know in very deed that the Lord hath sent his angel and hath delivered me out of the hand of Herod and from all the expectation of the people of the Jews. Acts 12:5–11

For so is the will of God, that by doing well you may put to silence the ignorance of foolish men: as free and not as making liberty a cloak for malice, but as the servants of God. 1 Pet. 2:15-16

And at midnight, Paul and Silas, praying, praised God. And they that were in prison heard them. And suddenly there was a great earthquake, so that the foundations of the prison were shaken. And immediately all the doors were opened and the bands of all were loosed. And the keeper of the prison, awakening out of his sleep and seeing the doors of the prison open, drawing his sword, would have killed himself, supposing that the prisoners had been fled. But Paul cried with a loud voice, saying: Do thyself no harm, for we all are here. Then calling for a light, he went in: and trembling, fell down at the feet of Paul and Silas. And bringing them out, he said: Masters, what must I do, that I may be saved? But they said: believe in the Lord Jesus: and thou shalt be saved, and thy house. And they preached the word of the Lord to him and to all that were in his house. And he, taking them the same hour of the night, washed their stripes: and himself was baptized, and all his house immediately. And when he had brought them into his own house, he laid the table for them: and rejoiced with all his house, believing God. Acts 16:25-34

JOY IN THE HOLY SPIRIT

There are several signs that the energy of the Holy Spirit is beginning to be active in those who genuinely aspire for this to happen… In some it appears as awe arising in the heart, in others as a tremulous sense of jubilation, in others as joy, in others as joy mingled with awe, or as tremulousness mingled with joy, and sometimes it manifests itself as tears and awe. For the soul is joyous at God's visitation and mercy, but at the same time is in awe and trepidation at His presence because it is guilty of so many sins. —Gregory of Sinai, *On the Signs of Grace and Delusion*, 4

OUR FATHER WHO
ART IN HEAVEN
HALLOWED BE
THY NAME

Blessed be the God and Father of our Lord Jesus Christ, who according to his great mercy hath regenerated us unto a lively hope, by the resurrection of Jesus Christ from the dead, unto an inheritance incorruptible, and undefiled, and that can not fade, reserved in heaven for you, who, by the power of God, are kept by faith unto salvation, ready to be revealed in the last time. Wherein you shall greatly rejoice, if now you must be for a little time made sorrowful in divers temptations: that the trial of your faith (much more precious than gold which is tried by the fire) may be found unto praise and glory and honor at the appearing of Jesus Christ: whom having not seen, you love: in whom also now, though you see him not, you believe: and believing shall rejoice with joy unspeakable and glorified. 1 Pet. 1:3–8

THY KINGDOM COME

For the kingdom of God is not meat and drink; but justice, and peace, and joy in the Holy Spirit. Rom. 14:17

THY WILL BE DONE
ON EARTH AS IT IS
IN HEAVEN

Now to him who is able to preserve you without sin, and to present you spotless before the presence of his glory with exceeding joy, in the coming of our Lord Jesus Christ, to the only God our Savior through Jesus Christ our Lord, be glory and magnificence, empire and power, before all ages, and now, and for all ages of ages. Amen. Jude 24–25

GIVE US THIS DAY
OUR DAILY BREAD

Amen, amen I say to you, that you shall lament and weep, but the world shall rejoice; and you shall be made sorrowful, but your sorrow shall be turned into joy. A woman, when she is in labor, hath sorrow, because her hour is come; but when she hath brought forth the child, she remembereth no more the anguish, for joy that a man is born into the world. So also you now indeed have sorrow; but I will see you again, and your heart shall rejoice; and your joy no man shall take from you. And in that day you shall not ask me any thing. Amen, amen I say to you: if you ask the Father any thing in my name, he will give it you. Hitherto you have not asked any thing in my name. Ask, and you shall receive; that your joy may be full. John 16:20–24

AND FORGIVE US OUR
TRESPASSES AS WE
FORGIVE THOSE
WHO TRESPASS
AGAINST US
AND LEAD US NOT
INTO TEMPTATION
BUT DELIVER
US FROM EVIL

For our gospel hath not been unto you in word only, but in power also: and in the Holy Spirit and in much fulness, as you know what manner of men we have been among you for your sakes. And you became followers of us and of the Lord: receiving the word in much tribulation, with joy of the Holy Spirit: so that you were made a pattern to all that believe in Macedonia and in Achaia. For from you was spread abroad the word of the Lord not only in Macedonia and in Achaia but also in every place: your faith which is towards God, is gone forth, so that we need not to speak any thing. For they themselves relate of us, what manner of entering in we had unto you: and how you turned to God from idols to serve the living and true God. And to wait for his Son from heaven (whom he raised up from the dead), Jesus, who hath delivered us from the wrath to come. 1 Thess. 1:5–10

THE PEACE BEYOND UNDERSTANDING

And the peace of God, which surpasseth all understanding keep your minds and hearts in Christ Jesus. Philippians 4:7

As the eyes of the helmsman look to the stars, so the solitary throughout the whole course of his journey looks, with the inner eye of divine vision, to the goal which he fixed in his mind from the first day that he gave himself to voyaging over the billowy sea of stillness, until he discovers that pearl for the sake of which he set off into the unfathomable deep of the ocean of stillness. — Isaac the Syrian, *Ascetical Homily Sixty-Five.*

OUR FATHER WHO ART IN HEAVEN	Be still, and know that I am God; I will be exalted among the nations, I will be exalted in the earth. Psalm 46:11
HALLOWED BE THY NAME	Peace be to all you, who are in Christ Jesus. Amen. 1 Pet. 5:14
THY KINGDOM COME	And may the God of peace himself sanctify you in all things; that your whole spirit, and soul, and body, may be preserved blameless in the coming of our Lord Jesus Christ. 1 Thess. 5:23 For God alone my soul waits in silence; from him comes my salvation. Psalm 62:1
THY WILL BE DONE ON EARTH AS IT IS IN HEAVEN	And may the God of peace, who brought again from the dead the great pastor of the sheep, our Lord Jesus Christ, in the blood of the everlasting testament, fit you in all goodness, that you may do his will; doing in you that which is well pleasing in his sight, through Jesus Christ, to whom is glory for ever and ever. Amen. Heb. 13:20–21
GIVE US THIS DAY OUR DAILY BREAD	Now the God of hope fill you with all joy and peace in believing; that you may abound in hope, and in the power of the Holy Spirit. Rom. 15:13
AND FORGIVE US OUR TRESPASSES AS WE FORGIVE THOSE WHO TRESPASS AGAINST US	For the rest, brethren, rejoice, be perfect, take exhortation, be of one mind, have peace; and the God of peace and of love shall be with you. 2 Cor. 13:11
AND LEAD US NOT INTO TEMPTATION BUT DELIVER US FROM EVIL	But I would have you to be wise in good, and simple in evil. And the God of peace crush Satan under your feet speedily. The grace of our Lord Jesus Christ be with you. Rom. 16:19–20

THE ANGELS

But they that shall be accounted worthy of that world, and of the resurrection from the dead, shall neither be married, nor take wives. Neither can they die any more: for they are equal to the angels, and are the children of God, being the children of the resurrection. Luke 20:35–36

When he bringeth in the first begotten into the world, he saith: And let all the angels of God adore him. And to the angels indeed he saith: He that maketh his angels spirits and his ministers a flame of fire. Hebrews 1:6–7

OUR FATHER WHO ART IN HEAVEN
: And all the angels stood round about the throne and the ancients and the four living creatures. And they fell down before the throne upon their faces and adored God. Apoc. 7:11

HALLOWED BE THY NAME
: See that you despise not one of these little ones; for I say to you that their angels[1] in heaven always see the face of my Father who is in heaven. Matt. 18:10

THY KINGDOM COME
: And in the sixth month the angel Gabriel was sent from God into a city of Galilee called Nazareth, to a virgin espoused to a man whose name was Joseph, of the house of David; and the virgin's name was Mary. And the angel, being come in, said unto her: Hail, full of grace,[2] the Lord is with thee; blessed art thou among women... Fear not, Mary, for thou hast found grace with God. Behold, thou shalt conceive in thy womb and shalt bring forth a son; and thou shalt call his name Jesus. He shall be great and shall be called Son of the Most High. And the Lord God shall give unto him the throne of David his father; and he shall reign in the house of Jacob forever. And of his kingdom there shall be no end. Luke 1:28, 30–33

THY WILL BE DONE ON EARTH AS IT IS IN HEAVEN
: And he saw in his sleep a ladder standing upon the earth, and the top thereof touching heaven; the angels also of God ascending and descending upon it. Gen. 28:12

  Amen, amen, I say to you, you shall see heaven opened and the angels of God ascending and descending[3] upon the Son of man. John 1:51

GIVE US THIS DAY OUR DAILY BREAD
: And the Lord appeared to [Abraham] in the vale of Mambre as he was sitting at the door of his tent, in the very heat of the day. And when he had lifted up his eyes, there appeared to him three men standing near him; and as soon as he saw them he ran to meet them from the door of his tent, and adored them down to the ground. And he said: Lord, if I have found favor in thy sight, pass not away from thy servant: but I will fetch a little water; and wash ye your feet, and rest ye

---

1. To the extent that Christians become "one of these little ones" (i.e. born again), even in this life we share in the heaven-ward gaze of our guardian angel; and only in this contemplative and adoring gaze does our dignity triumph over our humility.

2. In this 'fulness of grace' we have a glimpse into Mary's investiture as Queen of the Angels, just as in her 'handmaid of the Lord' we have a glimpse into her servanthood, which she shares with the angels and, of itself, confers that special sway which she exercises over them.

3. Here, as in Jacob's dream, the angels first 'ascend', are first attentive to the inner counsels of God, and then 'descend' to carry out these inner counsels, either by imparting coherence and design—truth and beauty—to the goodness of the universe as God's 'conjunctive' architects, or by planting the seeds of ascensional grace in our minds and hearts, and inciting us to grow into the fullness of the stature of Christ.

under the tree. And I will set a morsel of bread, and strengthen ye your heart;[1] afterwards you shall pass on: for therefore are you come aside to your servant. And they said: Do as thou hast spoken. Gen. 18:1–5

AND FORGIVE US OUR
TRESPASSES AS WE
FORGIVE THOSE
WHO TRESPASS
AGAINST US

For as lightning cometh out of the east and appeareth even into the west; so shall the coming of the Son of man be. Wheresoever the body shall be, there shall the eagles also be gathered together… And then shall all the tribes of earth mourn; and they shall see the Son of man coming in the clouds with much power and majesty. And he shall send his angels with a trumpet and a great voice; and they shall gather together his elect from the four winds, from the farthest parts of the heavens to the utmost bounds of them. Matt. 24:27–28, 30–31

AND LEAD US NOT
INTO TEMPTATION

Then the devil took him up into the holy city and set him upon the pinnacle of the temple, and said to him: If thou be the Son of God, cast thyself down, for it is written: That he hath given his angels charge over thee, and in their hands they shall bear thee up, lest perhaps thou dash thy foot against a stone. Jesus said to him: It is written again: Thou shalt not tempt the Lord thy God… Then the devil left him. And behold, angels come and ministered to him. Matt. 4:5–7, 11

BUT DELIVER
US FROM EVIL

And, behold, there was a great earthquake. For an angel of the Lord descended from heaven and coming rolled back the stone and sat upon it. And his countenance was a lightning and his raiment as snow. And for fear of him the guards were struck with terror and became as dead men. And the angel, answering, said to the women: Fear not you; for I know that you seek Jesus who was crucified. He is not here: for he is risen, as he said. Matt. 28:2–6

---

1. Abraham at Mambre sought to strengthen with bread the heart of the three men who are but a single Lord—although called angels, they exemplify the triune God. They came to him in the heat of the day and conversed with him, just as God was wont to converse with Adam and Eve in the cool of the day, and just as Christ now reciprocates God's hospitality in the Eucharist, strengthening our hearts with his own heart.

THE ANGELIC FUNCTIONS

OUR FATHER WHO ART IN HEAVEN HALLOWED BE THY NAME	Adorers of God and guides into the depths of prayer
THY KINGDOM COME	Heralds of the kingdom
THY WILL BE DONE ON EARTH AS IT IS IN HEAVEN	Utterances of the Word, both bodiless and 'embodied' "And hospitality do not forget: for by this some, being not aware of it, have entertained angels." Heb. 13:2
GIVE US THIS DAY OUR DAILY BREAD (BOTH HEAVENLY AND EARTHLY)	Servers in the Liturgy
AND FORGIVE US OUR TRESPASSES AS WE FORGIVE THOSE WHO TRESPASS AGAINST US	Harvesters in justice and mercy of God's judgments both near and ultimate
AND LEAD US NOT INTO TEMPTATION	Consolers and healers
BUT DELIVER US FROM EVIL	Bringers of light to the darkest of places

COMMENTARY

BRINGERS OF LIGHT   Speaking of the Word of God, John declares in the prologue to his gospel: "In him was life, and the life was the light of men." Correlatively it might be said: "In him was light, and the light was the life of angels." Thus the 'Phos Zoe' (Light-Life) cryptogram becomes a symbol for the encounter of angels and men in Christ. Life and Light, that supersubstantial bread lavished by God on angels and men, that bread which is none other than Christ the Omega, the center and perfecting of all things in the Spirit, both here and in heaven.

$$\varphi$$
$$\zeta\,\omega\,\eta$$
$$\sigma$$

THE ANGELIC NAMES

You are come to mount Sion and to the city of the living God, the heavenly Jerusalem, and to the company of myriads of angels… Hebrews 12:22

Each designation of the beings far superior to us indicates ways in which God is imitated and conformed to.
—Dionysius the Areopagite, *The Celestial Hierarchy*, 8, 1.

OUR FATHER WHO ART IN HEAVEN HALLOWED BE THY NAME	Seraphim,[1] Cherubim,[2] Thrones
THY KINGDOM COME	Dominations, Virtues, Powers
THY WILL BE DONE ON EARTH AS IT IS IN HEAVEN	Principalities, Archangels, Angels
GIVE US THIS DAY OUR DAILY BREAD	Gabriel the Archangel[3]
AND FORGIVE US OUR TRESPASSES AS WE FORGIVE THOSE WHO TRESPASS AGAINST US	Michael the Archangel[4]
AND LEAD US NOT INTO TEMPTATION BUT DELIVER US FROM EVIL	Raphael the Archangel[5]

---

1. (= 'the fire-makers, carriers of warmth') the singers of the Trisagion (cf. Isaiah 6:1–3), embodiments of the supernal fire of the will.

2. (= 'fullness of knowledge, outpouring of wisdom') embodiments of the supernal light of the intellect.

3. (= 'Man of God' or 'Strength of God'), the angel of the 'image of God', of the Annunciation—the appearing of God in daily life.

4. (= 'Who is like God?'), the angel of the 'likeness of God', the guardian angel of Israel (cf. Daniel 12:1), the one who disputes and contends (Jude 9) with Satan in whom there is no forgiveness.

5. (= 'God has healed'), healer of afflictions both physical and spiritual, the guardian angel of wayfaring (cf. the Book of Tobias *passim*).

THE ANGELIC HIERARCHY AND THE STAGES OF THE SOUL'S ASSIMILATION TO GRACE

ACCORDING TO BONAVENTURE[1]

	ANGELIC HIERARCHY	STAGES OF THE SOUL'S ASSIMILATION TO GRACE
OUR FATHER WHO ART IN HEAVEN	Seraphim	Induction (the seventh day of rest, the soul enters into night, into the superluminous darkness)
HALLOWED BE THY NAME	Cherubim	Inspection (being and God stand face to face)
THY KINGDOM COME	Thrones	Admission (to participation in the supreme joys of the interior life)
THY WILL BE DONE ON EARTH AS IT IS IN HEAVEN	Dominations	Concentration (of the mind within itself)
	Virtues	Capability of doing good (through vigilance, endurance, confidence of spirit)
GIVE US THIS DAY OUR DAILY BREAD	Powers	Struggle (against the passions and for the virtues)
AND FORGIVE US OUR TRESPASSES AS WE FORGIVE THOSE WHO TRESPASS AGAINST US	Principalities	Judgment (the orienting norm)
AND LEAD US NOT INTO TEMPTATION	Archangels	Ordered election (enlightenment)
BUT DELIVER US FROM EVIL	Angels	Discernment (observation)

---

1. Cf. Etienne Gilson, *The Philosophy of St. Bonaventure*, pp. 404–416.

ACCORDING TO NIKITAS STITHATOS[1]

When our intelligence is perfected through the practice of the virtues and is elevated through the knowledge and wisdom of the Spirit and by the divine fire, it is assimilated to these heavenly powers through the gifts of God, as by virtue of its purity it draws towards itself the particular characteristic of each of them. — Nikitas Stithatos, *On Spiritual Knowledge*, 99

	ANGELIC HIERARCHY	STAGES OF THE SOUL'S ASSIMILATION TO GRACE
OUR FATHER WHO ART IN HEAVEN HALLOWED BE THY NAME THY KINGDOM COME	Seraphim Cherubim Thrones	"We are assimilated to the first rank through the fiery wisdom of the Logos and through knowledge of divine and human affairs."
THY WILL BE DONE ON EARTH AS IT IS IN HEAVEN GIVE US THIS DAY OUR DAILY BREAD	Dominations Virtues Powers	"We are assimilated to the second rank through our compassion and solidarity with our fellow-men, as well as through our ordering of matters great and divine, and through the activities of the Spirit."
AND FORGIVE US OUR TRESPASSES AS WE FORGIVE THOSE WHO TRESPASS AGAINST US AND LEAD US NOT INTO TEMPTATION BUT DELIVER US FROM EVIL	Principalities Archangels Angels	"We are assimilated to the third rank through the ministration and performance of God's commandments."

COMMENTARY

With these two gatherings of the angelic hierarchy we are reminded of those already surveyed ladders of attainment. The difference here is that we are being asked, as 'children of the resurrection', to set everything in the context of the *isangelic* life, a life both similar to and in common with the angels, the 'common life' that is not to be measured in years but from everlasting to everlasting. And so we hear the Church sing on the feast of the Synaxis of the Bodiless Powers (Nov. 8):

> *Christ, who united the things of earth with those of heaven,*
> *and brought to completion one Church of Angels and of mortals,*
> *we unceasingly magnify you.*[2]

---

1. Like the epigraph, all quoted passages, unless otherwise noted, are from Nikitas Stithatos, *On Spiritual Knowledge*, 99, in *The Philokalia*, vol. 4, pp. 172–173.
2. Matins, Ninth ode, first troparion.

THE TETRAMORPH

And in the midst of the throne, and round about the throne, were four living creatures, full of eyes before and behind. And the first living creature was like a lion; and the second living creature was like a calf; and the third living creature, having the face, as it were, of a man; and the fourth living creature was like an eagle flying. And the four living creatures had each of them six wings; and round about and within they are full of eyes. And they rested not day and night, saying: Holy, Holy, Holy, Lord God Almighty, who was, and who is, and who is to come. Apocalypse 4:6–8

Four orders of creatures… were brought into being by God on the first day, namely the empyrean heaven, the angels, matter and time. One of the chief reasons of this quadruple creation is that it was proper to produce all possible kinds of creatures at the beginning of the world: passive bodies, active bodies, spirits and the measure of them all.
— Etienne Gilson, *The Philosophy of St. Bonaventure*[1]

	THE FOUR LIVING CREATURES	ATTRIBUTES OF GOD	ATTRIBUTES OF CHRIST GOD[3]
OUR FATHER WHO ART IN HEAVEN HALLOWED BE THY NAME	"Holy!"	"Holy!"	"Holy!"
	Eagle:		
THY KINGDOM COME	empyrean heaven, space	Immensity	Giver of the Spirit
	Man:		
THY WILL BE DONE ON EARTH AS IT IS IN HEAVEN	the angels (humanity)	Pure Spirit Knowability[2]	God incarnate
	Lion:		
GIVE US THIS DAY	time, aeviternity	Eternity	Sovereign power
	Calf:		
OUR DAILY BREAD	matter	Immutability	Priestly and sacrificial power

---

1. Pp. 219–220.

2. It might be said that the Incarnation is the knowability of God. And then counterpoised to and continuous with this knowability are the unknowable attributes of 'immensity', 'pure spirit', 'eternity', and 'immutability'.

3. According to the allocation by Irenaeus of Lyons in *Against the Heresies* (III, 11, 8). Irenaeus was the first to allocate a Gospel to each of the living creatures: the Eagle to Mark, the Man to Matthew, the Lion to John and the Calf to Luke. Since Gregory the Great (540–604), it has become the norm in the West for Mark and John to exchange places. Cf. P. Péneaud, *Les Quatre Vivants* (Paris: L'Harmattan, 2007), pp. 53–71.

Humanity—work of the sixth day and the synthesis, the quintessence of the fourfold work of the first day. In this we see the appropriateness of the Incarnation, for Christ Himself is the 'work' of the seventh day of rest (cf. John 5:16–17), both the *alpha* of creation and its *omega*. And as the four living creatures can be said to represent the four orders of creatures on the first day of creation, heralds of the creating God, so these same living creatures can be said to represent the 'Gospel Beasts', heralds of the renewing Lord on the seventh day. But on the eighth day, in the resurrection, these four can be said to represent the four elements of human nature, of the individual saint fused without confusion in the Glorious and Mystical Body of Christ. Glorious because visible to all creation (Rom. 8:19–23); but mystical because simultaneously visible and invisible: as partakers of the divine nature we will share in the creature-ward attributes of God, but, as creature, our contemplation of and participation in these same attributes will be inexhaustible and more than mysterious—holy!

HOSANNA

THE TRIUMPHANT HYMN FROM THE DIVINE LITURGY OF ST. JOHN CHRYSOSTOM

There stand by Thee thousands of archangels and hosts of angels, the Cherubim and the Seraphim, six-winged, many-eyed, who soar aloft, borne on their pinions. Singing the triumphant hymn, shouting, proclaiming and saying:[1]

OUR FATHER WHO   Holy! Holy! Holy! Lord of Sabaoth![2]
ART IN HEAVEN
HALLOWED BE
THY NAME

THY KINGDOM COME   Heaven and earth are full of Thy glory! Hosanna in the highest!
THY WILL BE DONE
ON EARTH AS IT IS
IN HEAVEN

GIVE US THIS DAY   Blessed is He That comes in the name of the Lord! Hosanna in the highest!
OUR DAILY BREAD

---

1. "Singing… shouting, proclaiming and saying"—in the frescos of Cappadocia's rock-hewn churches (tenth century), these four kinds of vocalisation mentioned in preface to the Triumphant Hymn are inscribed as the proper names for each of the living creatures: to eagle is attributed singing, to the calf shouting, to the lion proclaiming, and to the man saying.

2. Germanus of Constantinople (†733) comments: 'And to one another the four-formed creatures antiphonally exclaim: the first, in the likeness of a lion, cries out "Holy"; the second, in the likeness of a calf, cries out "Holy"; the third, in the likeness of a man, cries out "Holy"; and the fourth, in the likeness of an eagle, cries out "Lord of Sabaoth"' (*On the Divine Liturgy*, p. 95).

IV

PRAYER & DEIFICATION

THE GOSPEL OF THE LORD'S PRAYER

OUR FATHER WHO ART IN HEAVEN
HALLOWED BE THY NAME
THY KINGDOM COME

INTRODUCTION

THE ETERNAL GOSPEL

OUR FATHER WHO
ART IN HEAVEN
HALLOWED BE
THY NAME

Grace be to you and peace from God our Father, and from the Lord Jesus Christ. We give thanks to God, and the Father of our Lord Jesus Christ, praying always for you. Hearing your faith in Christ Jesus, and the love which you have towards all the saints. For the hope that is laid up for you in heaven, which you have heard in the word of the truth of the gospel…

THY KINGDOM COME

…which is come unto you, as also it is in the whole world, and bringeth forth fruit and groweth, even as it doth in you, since the day you heard and knew the grace of God in truth. Col. 1:3–6
And this gospel of the kingdom, shall be preached in the whole world, for a testimony to all nations, and then shall the consummation come. Matt. 24:14

THY WILL BE DONE
ON EARTH AS IT IS
IN HEAVEN

And I saw another angel flying through the midst of heaven, having the eternal gospel, to preach unto them that sit upon the earth, and over every nation, and tribe, and tongue, and people: saying with a loud voice: Fear the Lord, and give him honor, because the hour of his judgment is come; and adore ye him, that made heaven and earth, the sea, and the fountains of waters. Apoc. 14:6–7
For our exhortation was not of error, nor of uncleanness, nor in deceit: but as we were approved by God that the gospel should be committed to us: even so we speak, not as pleasing men, but God, who proveth our hearts. 1 Thess. 2:3–4

GIVE US THIS DAY
OUR DAILY BREAD

For God hath not given us the spirit of fear: but of power, and of love, and of sobriety. Be not thou therefore ashamed of the testimony of our Lord, nor of me his prisoner: but labor with the gospel, according to the power of God, who hath delivered us and called us by his holy calling, not according to our works, but according to his own purpose and grace, which was given us in Christ Jesus before the times of the world. But is now made manifest by the illumination of our Savior Jesus Christ, who hath destroyed death, and hath brought to light life and incorruption by the gospel. 2 Tim. 1:7–10
And I do all things for the gospel's sake: that I may be made partaker thereof. 1 Cor. 9:23

AND FORGIVE US OUR
TRESPASSES AS WE
FORGIVE THOSE
WHO TRESPASS
AGAINST US

Only let your conversation be worthy of the gospel of Christ: that, whether I come and see you, or, being absent, may hear of you, that you stand fast in one spirit, with one mind laboring together for the faith of the gospel. And in nothing be ye terrified by the adversaries: which to them is a cause of perdition, but to you of salvation, and this from God: for unto youit is given for Christ, not only to believe in him, but also to suffer for him. Phil. 1:27–29

AND LEAD US NOT
INTO TEMPTATION

And you know, how through infirmity of the flesh, I preached the gospel to you heretofore: and your temptation in my flesh, you despised not, nor rejected: but received me as an angel of God, even as Christ Jesus. Gal. 4:13–14

But we renounce the hidden things of dishonesty, not walking in craftiness, nor adulterating the word of God; but by manifestation of the truth commending ourselves to every man's conscience, in the sight of God. And if our gospel be also hid, it is hid to them that are lost, in whom the god of this world hath blinded the minds of unbelievers, that the light of the gospel of the glory of Christ, who is the image of God, should not shine unto them. For we preach not ourselves, but Jesus Christ our Lord; and ourselves your servants through Jesus. 2 Cor. 4:2–5

And he said to them: Go ye into the whole world, and preach the gospel to every creature. He that believeth and is baptized, shall be saved: but he that believeth not shall be condemned. Mark 16:15–16

COMMENTARY

If Christ is the image of the invisible God, then His whole life, even the least detail, is a guidance on the way to attaining that likeness to which we are summoned. And, if prayer is the exemplary means of attaining such likeness, then what are the Commandments if not a labor of prayer, what are the Sacraments if not a sacred nurturing and ever more conscious habit of prayer, what are the Virtues if not the ever-increasing power and beauty of prayer, and what is the Gospel if we cannot 'pray' it in the love of God and neighbor with our whole heart, soul, mind and strength?

DARKNESS AND LIGHT ~ A GOSPEL PRELUDE

OUR FATHER WHO
ART IN HEAVEN
HALLOWED BE
THY NAME

Bear not the yoke with unbelievers. For what participation hath justice with injustice? Or what fellowship hath light with darkness? And what concord hath Christ with Belial? Or what part hath the faithful with the unbeliever? And what agreement hath the temple of God with idols? For you are the temple of the living God: as God saith: I will dwell in them and walk among them. And I will be their God: and they shall be my people. Where-fore: Go out from among them and be ye separate, saith the Lord, and touch not the unclean thing: and I will receive you. And will be a Father to you: and you shall be my sons and daughters, saith the Lord Almighty. 2 Cor. 6:14–18

THY KINGDOM COME

Again a new commandment I write unto you: which thing is true both in him and in you, because the darkness is passed and the true light now shineth. He that saith he is in the light and hateth his brother is in darkness even until now. He that loveth his brother abideth in the light: and there is no scandal in him. 1 John 2:8–10

THY WILL BE DONE
ON EARTH AS IT IS
IN HEAVEN

Jesus therefore said to them: Yet a little while, the light is among you. Walk whilst you have the light, and the darkness overtake you not. And he that walketh in darkness knoweth not whither be goeth. Whilst you have the light, believe in the light, that you may be the children of light. John 12:35–36

GIVE US THIS DAY
OUR DAILY BREAD

And that, knowing the season, that it is now the hour for us to rise from sleep. For now our salvation is nearer than when we believed. The night is passed And the day is at hand. Let us, therefore cast off the works of darkness and put on the armour of light. Let us walk honestly, as in the day: not in rioting and drunkenness, not in chambering and impurities, not in contention and envy. But put ye on the Lord Jesus Christ: and make not provision for the flesh in its concupiscences. Rom. 13:11–14

AND FORGIVE US OUR
TRESPASSES AS WE
FORGIVE THOSE
WHO TRESPASS
AGAINST US

At midday, O king, I saw in the way a light from heaven, above the brightness of the sun, shining round about me and them that were in company with me. And when we were all fallen down on the ground, I heard a voice speaking to me in the Hebrew tongue: Saul, Saul, why persecutest thou me? It is hard for thee to kick against the good. And I said: Who art thou, Lord? And the Lord answered: I am Jesus whom thou persecutest. But rise up and stand upon thy feet: for to this end have I appeared to thee, that I may make thee a minister and a witness of those things which thou hast seen and of those things wherein I will appear to thee, delivering thee from the people and from the nations unto which now I send thee: to open their eyes, that they may be converted from darkness to light and from the power of Satan to God, that they may receive forgiveness of sins and a lot among the saints, by the faith that is in me. Acts 26:13–18

AND LEAD US NOT
INTO TEMPTATION
BUT DELIVER
US FROM EVIL

But to me it is a very small thing to be judged by you or by man's day. But nei-ther do I judge my own self. For I am not conscious to myself of any-thing. Yet am I not hereby justified: but he that judgeth me is the Lord. Therefore, judge not before the time: until the Lord come, who both will bring to light the hid-den things of darkness and will make manifest the counsels of the hearts. And then shall every man have praise from God. 1 Cor. 4:3–5

THE COMING OF THE KINGDOM

OUR FATHER WHO ART IN HEAVEN, HALLOWED BE THY NAME—*Messiah*

THY KINGDOM COME—*The Sheepfold of the Lord's Prayer, The Invitation of the Kingdom, Similitudes of the Kingdom, The Kingdom*

THY WILL BE DONE ON EARTH AS IT IS IN HEAVEN—*The Thrice-Heard Voice of the Father*

GIVE US THIS DAY OUR DAILY BREAD—*Living Water*

AND FORGIVE US OUR TRESPASSES AS WE FORGIVE THOSE WHO TRESPASS AGAINST US— *The Sea of Galilee, the Nets of Salvation*

AND LEAD US NOT INTO TEMPTATION—*Seven Miraculous 'Signs', Amen, Amen, I say to Thee*

BUT DELIVER US FROM EVIL—*The Magnificat, The Holy Mother of God O Come, O Come, Emmanuel, Prologue to the Gospel of John, Nativity*

THE MAGNIFICAT

LUKE 1:46–55

OUR FATHER WHO
ART IN HEAVEN
    My soul doth magnify the Lord. And my spirit hath rejoiced in God my Savior.

HALLOWED BE
THY NAME
    Because he hath regarded the humility of his handmaid; for, behold, from henceforth all generations shall call me blessed. Because he that is mighty has done great things to me; and holy is his name.

THY KINGDOM COME
    And his mercy is from generation unto generations, to them that fear him.

THY WILL BE DONE
ON EARTH AS IT IS
IN HEAVEN
    He hath shewed might in his arm; he hath scattered the proud in the conceit of their heart. He hath put down the mighty from their seat and hath exalted the humble.

GIVE US THIS DAY
OUR DAILY BREAD
    He hath filled the hungry with good things; and the rich he hath sent empty away.

AND FORGIVE US OUR
TRESPASSES AS WE
FORGIVE THOSE
WHO TRESPASS
AGAINST US
AND LEAD US NOT
INTO TEMPTATION
BUT DELIVER
US FROM EVIL
    He hath received Israel his servant, being mindful of his mercy. As he spoke to Abraham and to his seed for ever.

THE HOLY MOTHER OF GOD

OUR FATHER WHO
ART IN HEAVEN

My soul doth magnify the Lord…

And a great sign appeared in heaven: a woman clothed with the sun, and the moon under her feet, and on her head a crown of twelve stars. Apoc. 12:1

HALLOWED BE
THY NAME

Hail, full of grace, the Lord is with thee; blessed art thou among women… Fear not, Mary, for thou hast found grace with God. Behold, thou shalt conceive in thy womb and shalt bring forth a son; and thou shalt call his name Jesus. He shall be great and shall be called the Son of the Most High… The Holy Spirit shall come upon thee and the power of the Most High shall overshadow thee. And therefore also the Holy which shall be born of thee shall be called the Son of God. Luke 1:28, 30–32, 35

THY KINGDOM COME

And the Lord God shall give unto to him the throne of David his father; and he shall reign in the house of Jacob forever. And of his kingdom there shall be no end. Luke 1:32–33

Behold, I come quickly… I am the root and stock of David, the bright and morning star. And the Spirit and the bride say: Come. Apoc. 22:12, 16–17

THY WILL BE DONE
ON EARTH AS IT IS
IN HEAVEN

And Mary said: Behold the handmaid of the Lord; be it done to me according to thy word. Luke 1:38

And the wine failing, the mother of Jesus saith unto him: They have no wine. And Jesus saith to her: Woman, what is that to me and to thee? My hour is not yet come. His mother saith to the waiters: Whatsoever he shall say to you, do ye. John 2:3–5

GIVE US THIS DAY
OUR DAILY BREAD

A certain woman from the crowd, lifting up her voice, said to him: Blessed is the womb that bore thee and the paps that gave thee suck. But he said: Yea, rather, blessed are they who hear the word of God and keep it. Luke 11:27–28

AND FORGIVE US OUR
TRESPASSES AS WE
FORGIVE THOSE
WHO TRESPASS
AGAINST US

Daughters of Jerusalem, weep not over me; but weep for yourselves and for your children. For, behold, the days shall come, wherein they will say: Blessed are the barren and the wombs that have not borne and the paps that have not given suck. Luke 23:28–29

And Simeon blessed them and said to Mary his mother: Behold, this child is set for the fall and for the resurrection of many in Israel and for a sign which shall be contradicted…

AND LEAD US NOT
INTO TEMPTATION

…And thy own soul a sword shall pierce, that out of many hearts thoughts may be revealed. Luke 2:34–35

BUT DELIVER
US FROM EVIL

I will put enmities between thee and the woman, and thy seed and her seed: she shall crush thy head, and thou shalt lie in wait for her heel. Gen. 4:15

… and my spirit hath rejoiced in God my Savior. Luke 1:46–47

O COME, O COME, EMMANUEL

OUR FATHER WHO ART IN HEAVEN

HALLOWED BE THY NAME

O come, our wisdom from on high, who ordered all things mightily;
To us the path of knowledge show, and teach us in her ways to go.
Rejoice! Rejoice! Emmanuel shall come to you, O Israel!

THY KINGDOM COME

O come, O Key of David, come, and open wide our heav'nly home;
Make safe the way that leads on high, and close the path to misery.
Rejoice! Rejoice! Emmanuel shall come to you, O Israel!

THY WILL BE DONE ON EARTH AS IT IS IN HEAVEN

O come, O come, our Lord of might, who to your tribes on Sinai's height
In ancient times gave holy law, in cloud and majesty and awe.
Rejoice! Rejoice! Emmanuel shall come to you, O Israel!

GIVE US THIS DAY OUR DAILY BREAD

O come, O come, Emmanuel, and ransom captive Israel,
That mourns in lonely exile here until the Son of God appear.
Rejoice! Rejoice! Emmanuel shall come to you, O Israel!

AND FORGIVE US OUR TRESPASSES AS WE

FORGIVE THOSE WHO TRESPASS AGAINST US

O come, Desire of nations, bind in one the hearts of all mankind;
O bid our sad divisions cease, and be yourself the king of Peace.
Rejoice! Rejoice! Emmanuel shall come to you, O Israel!

AND LEAD US NOT INTO TEMPTATION

O come, our Dayspring from on high, and cheer us by your drawing nigh;
Disperse the gloomy clouds of night, and death's dark shadows put to flight.
Rejoice! Rejoice! Emmanuel shall come to you, O Israel!

BUT DELIVER US FROM EVIL

O come, O rod of Jesse's stem. From every foe deliver them
That trust your mighty pow'r to save: bring them in victory through the grave.
Rejoice! Rejoice! Emmanuel shall come to you, O Israel!

THE PROLOGUE TO THE GOSPEL OF JOHN

JOHN 1:1–14

For the Father himself loveth you, because you have loved me and have believed that I have come out from God. I came forth from the Father and am come into the world; again I leave the world and I go to the Father. John 16:27–28

I CAME FORTH FROM THE FATHER AND AM COME INTO THE WORLD...		AGAIN, I LEAVE THE WORLD AND I GO TO THE FATHER
In the Beginning was the Word and the Word was with God, and the Word was God	OUR FATHER WHO ART IN HEAVEN HALLOWED BE THY NAME	And we saw his glory, the glory as it were of the only-begotten of the Father, full of grace and truth
The same was in the beginning with God	THY KINGDOM COME	And the Word was made flesh and dwelt amongst us
All things were made by him: and without him was made nothing that was made	THY WILL BE DONE ON EARTH AS IT IS IN HEAVEN	Who are born, not of blood, nor of the will of the flesh, nor of the will of man, but of God
In him was life, and the life was the light of men	GIVE US THIS DAY OUR DAILY BREAD	But as many as received him, he gave them power to be made sons of God, to them that believe in his name
And the light shineth in darkness,	AND FORGIVE US OUR TRESPASSES AS WE FORGIVE THOSE WHO TRESPASS AGAINST US AND LEAD US NOT INTO TEMPTATION	He came unto his own and his own received him not
And the darkness did not comprehend it...[1]	BUT DELIVER US FROM EVIL	...He was in the world, and the world was made by him, and the world knew him not

---

1. At the midpoint of this initial and initiating chiasmus of John's Gospel (verses 6–9) stands John the Baptist—under oath to God—bearing witness: the Lamb of God (John 1:29) and the Word of God are one and have come into the world. This Gospel begins and ends, in fact, with solemn acts of witness by John the Baptist and John the Apostle (cf. John 21:24). Also, seeded through the body of the Gospel, and even exceeding it (cf. John 21:25), are other acts of witness in the words and deeds of Christ (cf. especially John 8:14–18).

NATIVITY

OUR FATHER WHO
ART IN HEAVEN
HALLOWED BE
THY NAME

And behold there was a man in Jerusalem named Simeon, and this man was just and devout, waiting for the consolation of Israel; and…

THY KINGDOM COME

…the Holy Spirit was in him. And he had received an answer from the Holy Spirit, that he should not see death, before he had seen the Christ of the Lord. And he came by the Spirit into the temple. And when his parents brought in the child Jesus, to do for him according to the custom of the law, he also took him into his arms, and blessed God, and said: Now thou dost dismiss thy servant, O Lord, according to thy word in peace; because my eyes have seen thy salvation, which thou hast prepared before the face of all peoples: a light to the revelation of the Gentiles, and the glory of thy people Israel. Luke 2:25–32

THY WILL BE DONE
ON EARTH AS IT IS
IN HEAVEN

And there were in the same country shepherds watching, and keeping the night watches over their flock. And behold an angel of the Lord stood by them, and the brightness of God shone round about them; and they feared with a great fear. And the angel said to them: Fear not; for, behold, I bring you good tidings of great joy, that shall be to all the people: For, this day, is born to you a Savior, who is Christ the Lord, in the city of David. And this shall be a sign unto you. You shall find the infant wrapped in swaddling clothes, and laid in a manger. And suddenly there was with the angel a multitude of the heavenly army, praising God, and saying: Glory to God in the highest; and on earth peace to men of good will. Luke 2:8–14

GIVE US THIS DAY
OUR DAILY BREAD

And Joseph also went up from Galilee, out of the city of Nazareth into Judea, to the city of David, which is called Bethlehem: because he was of the house and family of David, to be enrolled with Mary his espoused wife, who was with child. And it came to pass, that when they were there, her days were accomplished, that she should be delivered. And she brought forth her firstborn son, and wrapped him up in swaddling clothes, and laid him in a manger; because there was no room for them in the inn. Luke 2:4–7

AND FORGIVE US OUR
TRESPASSES AS WE
FORGIVE THOSE
WHO TRESPASS
AGAINST US

When as his mother Mary was espoused to Joseph, before they came together, she was found with child, of the Holy Spirit. Whereupon Joseph her husband, being a just man, and not willing publicly to expose her, was minded to put her away privately. But while he thought on these things, behold the angel of the Lord appeared to him in his sleep, saying: Joseph, son of David, fear not to take unto thee Mary thy wife, for that which is conceived in her, is of the Holy Spirit. And she shall bring forth a son: and thou shalt call his name Jesus. For he shall save his people from their sins. Now all this was done that it might be fulfilled which the Lord spoke by the prophet, saying: Behold a virgin shall be with child, and bring forth a son, and they shall call his name Emmanuel, which being interpreted is, God with us. And Joseph rising up from sleep, did as the angel of the Lord had commanded him, and took unto him his wife. Matt. 1:18–24

AND LEAD US NOT INTO TEMPTATION

When Jesus therefore was born in Bethlehem of Juda, in the days of king Herod, behold, there came wise men from the east to Jerusalem. Saying, Where is he that is born king of the Jews? For we have seen his star in the east, and are come to adore him. And king Herod hearing this, was troubled, and all Jerusalem with him. And assembling together all the chief priests and the scribes of the people, he inquired of them where Christ should be born. But they said to him: In Bethlehem of Juda. For so it is written by the prophet: And thou Bethlehem the land of Juda art not the least among the princes of Juda: for out of thee shall come forth the captain that shall rule my people Israel. Then Herod, privately calling the wise men, learned diligently of them the time of the star which appeared to them; and sending them into Bethlehem, said: Go and diligently inquire after the child, and when you have found him, bring me word again, that I also may come to adore him. Who having heard the king, went their way; and behold the star which they had seen in the east, went before them, until it came and stood over where the child was. And seeing the star they rejoiced with exceeding great joy. And entering into the house, they found the child with Mary his mother, and falling down they adored him; and opening their treasures, they offered him gifts; gold, frankincense, and myrrh. And having received an answer in sleep that they should not return to Herod, they went back another way into their country. Matt. 2:1–12

BUT DELIVER US FROM EVIL

And after they were departed, behold an angel of the Lord appeared in sleep to Joseph, saying: Arise, and take the child and his mother, and fly into Egypt: and be there until I shall tell thee. For it will come to pass that Herod will seek the child to destroy him. Who arose, and took the child and his mother by night, and retired into Egypt: and he was there until the death of Herod: that it might be fulfilled which the Lord spoke by the prophet, saying: Out of Egypt have I called my son. Then Herod perceiving that he was deluded by the wise men, was exceeding angry; and sending killed all the men children that were in Bethlehem, and in all the borders thereof, from two years old and under, according to the time which he had diligently inquired of the wise men. Then was fulfilled that which was spoken by Jeremias the prophet, saying: A voice in Rama was heard, lamentation and great mourning; Rachel bewailing her children, and would not be comforted, because they are not. But when Herod was dead, behold an angel of the Lord appeared in sleep to Joseph in Egypt, saying: Arise, and take the child and his mother, and go into the land of Israel. For they are dead that sought the life of the child. Who arose, and took the child and his mother, and came into the land of Israel. But hearing that Archelaus reigned in Judea in the room of Herod his father, he was afraid to go thither: and being warned in sleep retired into the quarters of Galilee. And coming he dwelt in a city called Nazareth: that it might be fulfilled which was said by prophets: That he shall be called a Nazarene.[1] Matt. 2:13–23

---

1. And Nathanael said to [Philip]: Can any thing of good come from Nazareth? (John 1:46).

THE SEVEN MIRACULOUS 'SIGNS'

But there are also many other things which Jesus did; were every one of them to be written, I suppose that the world itself could not contain the books that would be written. John 21:25

OUR FATHER WHO ART IN HEAVEN HALLOWED BE THY NAME	1ˢᵗ Sign: The changing of water into wine at the marriage feast at Cana.[1] John 2:1–11
THY KINGDOM COME	2ⁿᵈ Sign: The healing of the official's son.[2] John 4:46–54
THY WILL BE DONE ON EARTH AS IT IS IN HEAVEN	3ʳᵈ Sign: The healing of the paralytic.[3] John 5:1–14
GIVE US THIS DAY OUR DAILY BREAD	4ᵗʰ Sign: The feeding of the five thousand. John 6:1–15
AND FORGIVE US OUR TRESPASSES AS WE FORGIVE THOSE WHO TRESPASS AGAINST US	5ᵗʰ Sign: The walking on the waters.[4] John 6:19
AND LEAD US NOT INTO TEMPTATION	6ᵗʰ Sign: The healing of the man born blind.[5] John 9:1–40
BUT DELIVER US FROM EVIL	7ᵗʰ Sign: The raising of Lazarus. John 11:1–44

---

1. "Do whatever he tells you." Not only does he tell us to take the common fare of the world and change it into the sacrificial worship of the Father in the Eucharist; he also tells how this very thing should be done: "You shall love the Lord your God with all your heart, with all your soul, with all your mind, and with all your strength" (Mark 12:30). And in so doing we fittingly partake of the great wedding feast in which we love our neighbor as ourselves (Mark 12:31).

2. The coming of the kingdom is implicit in the official's belief in Christ's words. And see how nigh this kingdom truly is for both the official and for us! Christ's words are active immediately —it just takes a while for the 'news' to reach us.

3. Here we lie paralyzed, unable to 'will' our own healing. But, if we 'sin no more', that is already the will of God, already an angel of the Lord stirring the waters of our hearts.

4. Forgiveness and love of enemies are even more miraculous than Christ's walking on the water; they too are an overcoming of the natural by the supernatural.

5. "It was not that this man sinned, or his parents, but that the works of God might be made manifest in him." The coming of the great glory of God sunders all the chains of cause and effect, attraction and repulsion, pleasure and pain, presumption and despair.

AMEN, AMEN, I SAY TO THEE

THE SEVEN JOHANNINE DISCOURSES

OUR FATHER WHO
ART IN HEAVEN
HALLOWED BE
THY NAME

After the Last Supper (John 14–17)

Do you not believe, that I am in the Father, and the Father in me? The words that I speak to you, I speak not of myself. But the Father who abideth in me, he doth the works. Believe you not that I am in the Father, and the Father in me? Otherwise believe for the very works' sake. Amen, amen I say to you, he that believeth in me, the works that I do, he also shall do; and greater than these shall he do. Because I go to the Father: and whatsoever you shall ask the Father in my name, that will I do: that the Father may be glorified in the Son. John 14:10–13

THY KINGDOM COME

Nicodemus (John 3:3–21)

Jesus answered, and said to him: Amen, amen I say to thee, unless a man be born again, he cannot see the kingdom of God. Nicodemus saith to him: How can a man be born when he is old? can he enter a second time into his mother's womb, and be born again? Jesus answered: Amen, amen I say to thee, unless a man be born again of water and the Holy Spirit, he cannot enter into the kingdom of God. That which is born of the flesh, is flesh; and that which is born of the Spirit, is spirit. Wonder not, that I said to thee, you must be born again. John 3:3–7

THY WILL BE DONE
ON EARTH AS IT IS
IN HEAVEN

At the Feast of Tabernacles (John 7–8)

My doctrine is not mine, but his that sent me. If any man do the will of him; he shall know of the doctrine, whether it be of God, or whether I speak of myself. He that speaketh of himself, seeketh his own glory: but he that seeketh the glory of him that sent him, he is true, and there is no injustice in him. Did Moses not give you the law, and yet none of you keepeth the law? …Amen, amen I say to you: If any man keep my word, he shall not see death for ever. John 7:16–19, 51

GIVE US THIS DAY
OUR DAILY BREAD

The Bread of Life (John 6:26–59)

It is written in the prophets: And they shall all be taught of God. Every one that hath heard of the Father, and hath learned, cometh to me. Not that any man hath seen the Father; but he who is of God, he hath seen the Father. Amen, amen I say unto you: He that believeth in me, hath everlasting life. John 6:45–47

AND FORGIVE US OUR
TRESPASSES AS WE
FORGIVE THOSE
WHO TRESPASS
AGAINST US

After the Healing of the Paralytic (John 5:10–47)

Amen, amen I say unto you, that the hour cometh, and now is, when the dead shall hear the voice of the Son of God, and they that hear shall live. For as the Father hath life in himself, so he hath given the Son also to have life in himself: And he hath given him power to do judgment, because he is the Son of man. John 5:25–27

AND LEAD US NOT
INTO TEMPTATION

The Good Shepherd (John 10)

Amen, amen I say to you: He that entereth not by the door into the sheepfold, but climbeth up another way, the same is a thief and a robber. But he that entereth in by the door is the shepherd of the sheep. To him the porter openeth; and the sheep hear his voice: and he calleth his own sheep by name, and leadeth them out. And when he hath let out his own sheep, he goeth before them: and the sheep follow him, because they know his voice. But a stranger they follow not, but fly from him, because they know not the voice of strangers. John 10:1–5

BUT DELIVER
US FROM EVIL

The Samaritan Woman (John 4:5–27)

Jesus saith to her: Woman, believe me, that the hour cometh, when you shall neither on this mountain, not in Jerusalem, adore the Father. You adore that which you know not: we adore that which we know; for salvation is of the Jews. But the hour cometh, and now is, when the true adorers shall adore the Father in spirit and in truth. For the Father also seeketh such to adore him. God is a spirit; and they that adore him, must adore him in spirit and in truth.[1]
John 4:21–24

THE SEA OF GALILEE, THE NETS OF SALVATION

OUR FATHER WHO
ART IN HEAVEN
HALLOWED BE
THY NAME

And Jesus returned in the power of the spirit, into Galilee: and the fame of him went out through the whole country. And he taught in their synagogues and was magnified by all. Luke 4:14–15

THY KINGDOM COME

Now those men, when they had seen what a miracle Jesus had done, said: This is of a truth the prophet, that is to come into the world. Jesus therefore, when he knew that they would come to take him by force, and make him king, fled again into the mountain himself alone. And when evening was come, his disciples went down to the sea. And when they had gone up into a ship, they went over the sea to Capharnaum; and it was now dark, and Jesus was not come unto them. And the sea arose, by reason of a great wind that blew. When they had rowed therefore about five and twenty or thirty furlongs, they see Jesus walking upon the sea, and drawing nigh to the ship, and they were afraid. But he saith to them: It is I; be not afraid. They were willing therefore to take him into the ship; and presently the ship was at the land to which they were going. John 6:14–21

THY WILL BE DONE
ON EARTH AS IT IS
IN HEAVEN

And passing by the sea of Galilee, he saw Simon and Andrew his brother, casting nets into the sea (for they were fishermen). And Jesus said to them: Come after me, and I will make you to become fishers of men. And immediately leaving their nets, they followed him. And going on from thence a little farther, he saw James the son of Zebedee, and John his brother, who also were mending their nets in the ship: and forthwith he called them. And leaving their father Zebedee in the ship with his hired men, they followed him. Mark 1:16–20
The same day Jesus going out of the house, sat by the sea side. And great multitudes were gathered unto him, so that he went up into a boat and sat: and all the multitude stood on the shore. And he spoke to them many things in parables,

---

1. In this discourse alone no "Amen, amen" is uttered. Is this because He is not speaking with a fellow Jew, or is it because, as on the second day of creation when there is no "God saw that it was good", there is a sundering: in Genesis the division between the waters above and the waters below, here between those who "know not" what they adore and those who do?

saying… The kingdom of heaven is like to a net cast into the sea, and gathering together of all kind of fishes. Which, when it was filled, they drew out, and sitting by the shore, they chose out the good into vessels, but the bad they cast forth. So shall it be at the end of the world. The angels shall go out, and shall separate the wicked from among the just. And shall cast them into the furnace of fire: there shall be weeping and gnashing of teeth. Matt. 13:1–3, 46–50

GIVE US THIS DAY
OUR DAILY BREAD

After this, Jesus shewed himself again to the disciples at the sea of Tiberias. And he shewed himself after this manner. There were together Simon Peter, and Thomas, who is called Didymus, and Nathanael, who was of Cana of Galilee, and the sons of Zebedee, and two others of his disciples. Simon Peter saith to them: I go a fishing. They say to him: We also come with thee. And they went forth, and entered into the ship: and that night they caught nothing. But when the morning was come, Jesus stood on the shore: yet the disciples knew not that it was Jesus. Jesus therefore said to them: Children, have you any meat? They answered him: No. He saith to them: Cast the net on the right side of the ship, and you shall find. They cast therefore; and now they were not able to draw it, for the multitude of fishes. That disciple therefore whom Jesus loved, said to Peter: It is the Lord. Simon Peter, when he heard that it was the Lord, girt his coat about him, (for he was naked,) and cast himself into the sea. But the other disciples came in the ship, (for they were not far from the land, but as it were two hundred cubits,) dragging the net with fishes. As soon then as they came to land, they saw hot coals lying, and a fish laid thereon, and bread. Jesus saith to them: Bring hither of the fishes which you have now caught. Simon Peter went up, and drew the net to land, full of great fishes, one hundred and fifty-three. And although there were so many, the net was not broken. Jesus saith to them: Come, and dine. And none of them who were at meat, durst ask him: Who art thou? knowing that it was the Lord. And Jesus cometh and taketh bread, and giveth them, and fish in like manner. This is now the third time that Jesus was manifested to his disciples, after he was risen from the dead. John 21:1–14

AND FORGIVE US OUR
TRESPASSES AS WE
FORGIVE THOSE
WHO TRESPASS
AGAINST US

And it came to pass, that when the multitudes pressed upon him to hear the word of God, he stood by the lake of Genesareth, and saw two ships standing by the lake: but the fishermen were gone out of them, and were washing their nets. And going into one of the ships that was Simon's, he desired him to draw back a little from the land. And sitting he taught the multitudes out of the ship. Now when he had ceased to speak, he said to Simon: Launch out into the deep, and let down your nets for a draught. And Simon answering said to him: Master, we have labored all the night, and have taken nothing: but at thy word I will let down the net. And when they had done this, they enclosed a very great multitude of fishes, and their net broke. And they beckoned to their partners that were in the other ship, that they should come and help them. And they came, and filled both the ships, so that they were almost sinking. Which when Simon Peter saw, he fell down at Jesus' knees, saying: Depart from me, for I am a sinful man, O Lord. For he was wholly astonished, and all that were with him, at the draught of the fishes which they had taken. And so were also James and John the sons of Zebedee, who were Simon's partners. And Jesus saith to Simon: Fear not: from henceforth thou shalt catch men. And having brought their ships to land, leaving all things, they followed him. Luke 5:1–11

And he saith to them that day, when evening was come: Let us pass over to the other side. And sending away the multitude, they take him even as he was in the ship: and there were other ships with him. And there arose a great storm of wind, and the waves beat into the ship, so that the ship was filled. And he was in the hinder part of the ship, sleeping upon a pillow; and they awake him, and say to him: Master, doth it not concern thee that we perish? And rising up, he rebuked the wind, and said to the sea: Peace, be still. And the wind ceased: and there was made a great calm. And he said to them: Why are you fearful? have you not faith yet? And they feared exceedingly: and they said one to another: Who is this (thinkest thou) that both wind and sea obey him? Mark 4:35–40

And forthwith Jesus obliged his disciples to go up into the boat, and to go before him over the water, till he dismissed the people. And having dismissed the multitude, he went into a mountain alone to pray. And when it was evening, he was there alone. But the boat in the midst of the sea was tossed with the waves: for the wind was contrary. And in the fourth watch of the night, he came to them walking upon the sea. And they seeing him walk upon the sea, were troubled, saying: It is an apparition. And they cried out for fear. And immediately Jesus spoke to them, saying: Be of good heart: it is I, fear ye not. And Peter making answer, said: Lord, if it be thou, bid me come to thee upon the waters. And he said: Come. And Peter going down out of the boat, walked upon the water to come to Jesus. But seeing the wind strong, he was afraid: and when he began to sink, he cried out, saying: Lord, save me. And immediately Jesus stretching forth his hand took hold of him, and said to him: O thou of little faith, why didst thou doubt? And when they were come up into the boat, the wind ceased. And they that were in the boat came and adored him, saying: Indeed thou art the Son of God.[1] Matt. 14:22–33

---

1. Jesus' multiplication of the loaves and fishes (Matt. 14:13–21) followed by his walking on the waters are thought to have occurred around the second Pasch of his three-year ministry. If this is indeed how it happened, then this diptych of miracles represents both a very precise foreshadowing of the institution of the Eucharist in the multiplication of the loaves and fishes (in the Eucharist it is Christ himself who is 'multiplied' in a way that defies mere number), and, similarly, a foreshadowing of his passion, death and resurrection in his walking on the waters. Just as the apostles are cast about by 'contrary winds' on the Sea of Galilee, so will they cower together in the upper room after the death of Christ. Just as a great fear befalls them when overtaken by an 'apparition'—the living Christ—who calms their fears and restores their faith, so our ever-living and risen Christ will return to them, walking dry-shod over the abyss of death to prove his Resurrection. On the lake the apostles cry out: "Indeed thou art the Son of God"; in the upper room Thomas cries out: "My Lord and my God" (John 20:28).

LIVING WATER

JOHN 4:9–26

The waters came down to the right side of the temple to the south part of the altar. And he led me out by the way of the north gate, and he caused me to turn to the way without the outward gate to the way that looked toward the east: and behold there ran out waters on the right side. And when the man that had the line in his hand went out towards the east, he measured a thousand cubits: and he brought me through the water up to the ankles. And again he measured a thousand, and he brought me through the water up to the knees. And he measured a thousand, and he brought me through the water up to the loins. And he measured a thousand, and it was a torrent, which I could not pass over: for the waters were risen so as to make a deep torrent, which could not be passed over. And he said to me: Surely thou hast seen, O son of man. And he brought me out, and he caused me to turn to the bank of the torrent. And when I had turned myself, behold on the bank of the torrent were very many trees on both sides. And he said to me: These waters that issue forth toward the hillocks of sand to the east, and go down to the plains of the desert, shall go into the sea, and shall go out, and the waters shall be healed. And every living creature that creepeth whithersoever the torrent shall come, shall live: and there shall be fishes in abundance after these waters shall come thither, and they shall be healed, and all things shall live to which the torrent shall come. Ezechiel 47:1–9

THY KINGDOM COME	Then that Samaritan woman saith to him: How dost thou, being a Jew, ask of me to drink, who am a Samaritan woman? For the Jews do not communicate with the Samaritans. Jesus answered, and said to her: If thou didst know the gift of God, and who he is that saith to thee, Give me to drink; thou perhaps wouldst have asked of him, and he would have given thee living water.
THY WILL BE DONE ON EARTH AS IT IS IN HEAVEN	The woman saith to him: Sir, thou hast nothing wherein to draw, and the well is deep; from whence then hast thou living water? Art thou greater than our father Jacob, who gave us the well, and drank thereof himself, and his children, and his cattle? Jesus answered, and said to her: Whosoever drinketh of this water, shall thirst again; but he that shall drink of the water that I will give him, shall not thirst for ever: But the water that I will give him, shall become in him a fountain of water, springing up into life everlasting.
GIVE US THIS DAY OUR DAILY BREAD	The woman saith to him: Sir, give me this water, that I may not thirst, nor come hither to draw.
AND FORGIVE US OUR TRESPASSES AS WE FORGIVE THOSE WHO TRESPASS AGAINST US	Jesus saith to her: Go, call thy husband, and come hither. The woman answered, and said: I have no husband. Jesus said to her: Thou hast said well, I have no husband: For thou hast had five husbands: and he whom thou now hast, is not thy husband. This thou hast said truly. The woman saith to him: Sir, I perceive that thou art a prophet.
AND LEAD US NOT INTO TEMPTATION	Our fathers adored on this mountain, and you say, that at Jerusalem is the place where men must adore. Jesus saith to her: Woman, believe me, that the hour cometh, when you shall neither on this mountain, not in Jerusalem, adore the Father.
BUT DELIVER US FROM EVIL	You adore that which you know not: we adore that which we know; for salvation is of the Jews.

OUR FATHER WHO
ART IN HEAVEN
HALLOWED BE
THY NAME
But the hour cometh, and now is, when the true adorers shall adore the Father in spirit and in truth. For the Father also seeketh such to adore him. God is a spirit; and they that adore him, must adore him in spirit and in truth. The woman saith to him: I know that the Messias cometh (who is called Christ); therefore, when he is come, he will tell us all things. Jesus saith to her: I am he, who am speaking with thee.

BEAUTIFUL UPON THE MOUNTAINS

How beautiful upon the mountains are the feet of him that bringeth good tidings and that preacheth peace, of him that sheweth forth good, that preacheth salvation, that saith to Sion: Thy God shall reign! Isaiah 52:7

OUR FATHER WHO
ART IN HEAVEN
HALLOWED BE
THY NAME

Mount Sion of the High Priestly Prayer
These things Jesus spoke; and lifting up his eyes to heaven he said: Father, the hour is come. Glorify thy Son, that thy Son may glorify thee... John 17:1ff

THY KINGDOM COME

Mount Sion of the Spirit's Descent
And when the days of the Pentecost were accomplished, they were all together in one place: and suddenly there came a sound from heaven, as of a mighty wind coming: and it filled the whole house where they were sitting. And there appeared to them parted tongues, as it were of fire: and it sat upon every one of them. And they were all filled with the Holy Spirit. Acts 2:1–4

THY WILL BE DONE
ON EARTH AS IT IS
IN HEAVEN

Mount Olivet of the Ascension
And when he had said these things, while they looked on, he was raised up:and a cloud received him out of their sight.And while they were beholding him going up to heaven, behold two men stood by them in white garments. Who also said: Ye men of Galilee, why stand you looking up to heaven? This Jesus who is taken up from you into heaven, shall so come, as you have seen him going into heaven. Then they returned to Jerusalem from the mount that is called Olivet, which is nigh Jerusalem, within a sabbath day's journey. Acts 1:9–12

Mount of the Transfiguration
And after six days, Jesus taketh with him Peter and James and John, and leadeth them up into an high mountain apart by themselves, and was transfigured before them. And his garments became shining and exceeding white as snow, so as no fuller upon earth can make white. And there appeared to them Elias with Moses: and they were talking with Jesus. And Peter answering, said to Jesus: Rabbi, it is good for us to be here. And let us make three tabernacles, one for thee, and one for Moses, and one for Elias. For he knew not what he said: for they were struck with fear. And there was a cloud overshadowing them. And a voice came out of the cloud, saying: This is my most beloved Son. Hear ye him. And immediately looking about, they saw no man any more, but Jesus only with them. And as they came down from the mountain, he charged them not to tell any man what things they had seen, till the Son of man shall be risen again from the dead. Mark 9:1–8

Mount Sion of the Last Supper
And he sent Peter and John, saying: Go, and prepare for us the pasch, that we may eat. But they said: Where wilt thou that we prepare? And he said to them: Behold, as you go into the city, there shall meet you a man carrying a pitcher of water: follow him into the house where he entereth in. And you shall say to the goodman of the house: The master saith to thee: Where is the guest chamber, where I may eat the pasch with my disciples? And he will shew you a large dining room, furnished. And there prepare. And they going, found as he had said to them and made ready the pasch. Luke 22:8–13

Mount of the Beatitudes
(Not in bread alone doth man live, but in every word that proceedeth from the mouth of God. Matt. 4:4)
And seeing the multitudes, he went up into a mountain, and when he was set down, his disciples came unto him. And opening his mouth he taught them… And it came to pass when Jesus had fully ended these words, the people were in admiration at his doctrine. For he was teaching them as one having power, and not as the scribes and Pharisees. Matt. 4:4, 5:1–2, 7:28–29

Mount Gerizim of the Reconciliation of All in the Spirit
He cometh therefore to a city of Samaria, which is called Sichar, near the land which Jacob gave to his son Joseph. Now Jacob's well was there. Jesus therefore, being wearied with his journey, sat thus on the well. It was about the sixth hour. There cometh a woman of Samaria, to draw water. Jesus saith to her: Give me to drink. For his disciples were gone into the city to buy meats. Then that Samaritan woman saith to him: How dost thou, being a Jew; ask of me to drink, who am a Samaritan woman? For the Jews do not communicate with the Samaritans. Jesus answered and said to her: If thou didst know the gift of God and who he is that saith to thee: Give me to drink; thou perhaps wouldst have asked of him, and he would have given thee living water. The woman saith to him: Sir, thou hast nothing wherein to draw, and the well is deep. From whence then hast thou living water? Art thou greater than our father Jacob, who gave us the well and drank thereof, himself and his children and his cattle? Jesus answered and said to her: Whosoever drinketh of this water shall thirst again: but he that shall drink of the water that I will give him shall not thirst for ever. But the water that I will give him shall become in him a fountain of water, springing up into life everlasting. The woman said to him: Sir, give me this water, that I may not thirst, nor come hither to draw… The woman saith to him: Sir, I perceive that thou art a prophet. Our fathers adored on this mountain: and you say that at Jerusalem is the place where men must adore. Jesus saith to her: Woman, believe me that the hour cometh, when you shall neither on this mountain, nor in Jerusalem, adore the Father. You adore that which you know not: we adore that which we know. For salvation is of the Jews. But the hour cometh and now is, when the true adorers shall adore the Father in spirit and in truth. For the Father also seeketh such to adore him. God is a spirit: and they that adore him must adore him in spirit and in truth. The woman saith to him: I know that the Messias cometh (who is called Christ): therefore, when he is come, he will tell us all things. Jesus saith to her: I am he, who am speaking with thee.
John 4:5–15, 19–26

The Garden of Gethsemane on Mount Olivet

And going out, he went, according to his custom, to the Mount of Olives. And his disciples also followed him. And when he was come to the place, he said to them: Pray, lest ye enter into temptation. And he was withdrawn away from them a stone's cast. And kneeling down, he prayed. Saying: Father, if thou wilt, remove this chalice from me: but yet not my will, but thine be done. And there appeared to him an angel from heaven, strengthening him. And being in an agony, he prayed the longer. And his sweat became as drops of blood, trickling down upon the ground. And when he rose up from prayer and was come to the disciples, he found them sleeping for sorrow. And he said to them: Why sleep you? Arise: pray: lest you enter into temptation. Luke 22:39–46

Mount of Temptation in the Desert

Again the devil took him up into a very high mountain, and shewed him all the kingdoms of the world, and the glory of them, and said to him: All these will I give thee, if falling down thou wilt adore me. Then Jesus saith to him: Begone, Satan: for it is written: The Lord thy God shalt thou adore, and him only shalt thou serve. Then the devil left him; and behold angels came and ministered to him. Matt. 4:8–11

BUT DELIVER
US FROM EVIL

Mount Calvary of the Redemption

Then therefore [Pilate] delivered him to them to be crucified. And they took Jesus and led him forth. And bearing his own cross, he went forth to the place which is called Calvary, but in Hebrew Golgotha. Where they crucified him, and with him two others, one on each side, and Jesus in the midst. John 19:16–18

THE THRICE-HEARD VOICE OF THE FATHER

The Unitive Way

OUR FATHER WHO ART IN HEAVEN

Amen, amen, I say to you, unless the grain of wheat falling into the ground die, itself remaineth alone. But if it die, it bringeth forth much fruit. He that loveth his life shall lose it; and he that hateth his life in this world keepeth it unto life eternal. If any man minister to me, let him follow me; and where I am, there also shall my minister be. If any man minister to me, him will my Father honor. Now my soul is troubled. And what shall I say? Father, save me from this hour. But for this cause came I unto this hour.

HALLOWED BE THY NAME

Father, glorify thy name. A voice therefore came from heaven: I have both glorified it and will glorify it again. The multitude therefore that stood and heard said that it thundered. Others said: An angel spoke to him.

THY KINGDOM COME

Jesus answered and said: this voice came not because of me, but for your sakes. Now is the judgment of the world; now shall the prince of this world be cast out. And I, if I be lifted up from the earth, will draw all things to myself. (Now this he said, signifying what death he should die.)

THY WILL BE DONE ON EARTH AS IT IS IN HEAVEN

The multitude answered him: We have heard out of the law that Christ abideth for ever. And how sayest thou: The Son of man must be lifted up? Who is this Son of man? Jesus therefore said to them: Yet a little while the light is among you. Walk whilst you have the light, that the darkness overtake you not. And he that walketh in darkness knoweth not whither he goeth. Whilst you have the light, believe in the light, that you may be the children of light. These things Jesus spoke; and he went away and hid himself from them. John 12:27–36

DURING THE TRANSFIGURATION

The Illuminative Way

THY KINGDOM COME

But I tell you of a truth: There are some standing here that shall not taste death till they see the kingdom of God.

THY WILL BE DONE ON EARTH AS IT IS IN HEAVEN

And it came to pass, about eight days after these words, that he took Peter and James and John and went up into a mountain to pray. And whilst he prayed the shape of his countenance was altered and his raiment became white and glittering. And, behold, two men were talking with him. And they were Moses and Elias, appearing in majesty. And they spoke of his decease that he should accomplish in Jerusalem. But Peter and they that were with him were heavy with sleep. And, waking, they saw his glory and the two men that stood with him.

GIVE US THIS DAY OUR DAILY BREAD

And it came to pass that, as they were departing from him, Peter saith to Jesus: Master, it is good for us to be here; and let us make three tabernacles, one for thee, and one for Moses, and one for Elias; not knowing what he said. And, as he spoke these things, there came a cloud and overshadowed them. And they

PRAYER AND DEIFICATION 303

were afraid when they entered into the cloud. And a voice came out of the cloud, saying: This is my beloved Son. Hear him. And, whilst the voice was uttered, Jesus was found alone. And they held their peace and told no man in those days any of these things which they had seen. Luke 9:27–36

AFTER THE BAPTISM IN THE JORDAN
The Purgative Way

GIVE US THIS DAY
OUR DAILY BREAD

John saw Jesus coming to him; and he saith: Behold the Lamb of God. Behold him who taketh away the sin of the world. John 1:29

AND FORGIVE US OUR
TRESPASSES AS WE
FORGIVE THOSE
WHO TRESPASS
AGAINST US

And [John], seeing many of the Pharisees and Sadducees coming to his baptism, he said to them: Ye brood of vipers, who hath shewed you to flee from the wrath to come? Bring forth therefore fruit worthy of penance. And think not to say within yourselves: We have Abraham for our father. For I tell you that God is able of these stones to raise up children to Abraham. For now the axe is laid to the root of the trees. Every tree therefore that doth not yield good fruit shall be cut down and cast into the fire. I indeed baptize you in water unto penance; but he that shall come after me is mightier than I, whose shoes I am not worthy to bear.

AND LEAD US NOT
INTO TEMPTATION

He shall baptize you in the Holy Spirit and fire. Whose fan is in his hand; and he will thoroughly cleanse his floor and gather his wheat into the barn. But the chaff he will burn with unquenchable fire.

BUT DELIVER
US FROM EVIL

Then cometh Jesus from Galilee to the Jordan, unto John, to be baptized by him. But John stayed him, saying: I ought to be baptized by thee, and comest thou to me? And Jesus answering said to him: Suffer it to be so now. For so it becometh us to fulfill all justice. Then he suffered him. And Jesus, being baptized, forthwith came out of the water; and lo, the heavens were opened to him, and he saw the Spirit of God descending as a dove and coming upon him. And behold, a voice from heaven, saying: This is my beloved Son, in whom I am well pleased. Then Jesus was led by the spirit into the desert, to be tempted by the devil. Matt. 3:7–4:1

COMMENTARY

This thrice-heard voice of the Father in the New Testament is foreshadowed, in the Old, by God's fourfold calling out to Samuel (1 Kings 3:1–10) "who slept in the temple of the Lord, where the ark of God was." The parallel is exact when we see the coming of the Eternal Word into the world as the first (primary and original) 'voice' of the Father, a voice as yet unheard and therefore unheeded—although present 'in the flesh'—until John's baptism of Christ in the Jordan. Once the Father has inaudibly spoken his Word within the confines of the world—"Be it done unto me according to thy word"—, each of these audible calls represent an ever-deeper summons to Christian perfection: "Rather, blessed are they who hear the word of God and keep it."(Luke 11:28) And what is this Christian perfection which beckons us? It is simply and unmistakably: "Be you therefore perfect, *as also your heavenly Father is perfect*" (Matt. 5:48). Such are the very words of Christ and such is the impossible task set before us; the imperfect are being called to put on perfection, the corruptible to put on incorruptibility. We look deeply within ourselves and at each other and, in dismay, we cry out: "Who then can be saved?" And Jesus Christ—"yesterday, and today; and the same forever"(Heb. 13:8)—repeats: "With men this is impossible; but with God all things are possible" (Matt. 19:26). But, having become imbued with the Gospel and having 'ears to hear', some have indeed understood and have cried out down through the ages: "God has become man so that man might become God." and "Man is the creature who has received the order to become God." Blasphemy for us... and yet what indescribable condescension on the part of God!

This is my beloved Son, in whom I am well pleased—in this word lies the entire mystery of the sacraments of Baptism and Confession. We come to the waters of selfreflection and see what we would not see: "If we say that we have no sin, we deceive ourselves and the truth is not in us" (1 John 1:10). That spark of conscience, which flickers how near the surface of the waters, we would extinguish; for there is a smoke of guilt, of self-accusation, of half-believed excuses which smarts our eyes. And from our eyes the half-tears of mock repentance. But the truth of the great mystery of Baptism and Confession does not leave us to face our own mystery of iniquity alone; the only way to accuse ourselves, beg forgiveness and live is that there be a 'beloved'. Only in recognizing that there is a beloved can we penetrate our own reflection: "Buried with him in baptism, in whom also you are risen again by the faith of the operation of God who hath raised him up from the dead. And you when you were dead in your sins... he hath quickened together with him, forgiving you all offenses" (Col. 2:12–13). And who more beloved than our dead and living Christ, the one who restores to us all those who have fallen asleep in him, the one who even restores us to ourselves in the bestowing of himself on us.

Wholly plunged with him in Baptism, our way begins; but there is also dust on the roads and he would wash our feet. Let us cast aside our hesitations at the sight of our loving God who would stoop to wash even our feet in the sacrament of Confession, and cry out with Peter: "Lord, not only my feet, but also my hands and my head." But, as we walk further and further with our beloved, let us also remember how Jesus answers him: "He that is washed needeth not but to wash his feet, but is clean wholly. And you are clean, but not all" (John 12:9–10). Let us therefore live our lives in fear and trembling, in peace and repentance—and love! This is how the lustral waters of Baptism and the unfeigned tears of repentance become an oil of gladness which feeds the spark of conscience. The spark of conscience bursts into flame—a fire has leapt from the waters and is cast upon the earth...

This is my beloved Son. Hear him.—From the engulfing depths of sin and repentance, we have been invited to mount the heights, with Christ and his three apostles, to view the Kingdom of God. Satan, to tempt him, had "shewed him all the kingdoms of the world in a moment of time" from one high mountain. But from this other mountain—Christ often withdrew to a mountain to pray—our view is being changed from extensive ("all the kingdoms of the world") to intensive (not the many but The One [OΩN], the 'white and glittering' Christ, himself the Kingdom of God come nigh us). And this intensity is an insight into the very meaning of life.

Moses and Elias stand as the two keys with which to unlock the meaning of the Transfiguration. Traditionally, they are said to represent the law and the prophets respectively; they are both foreshadowings, as Christ explained to the disciples at Emmaus ("Beginning at Moses and all the prophets, he expounded to them in all the scriptures the things that were concerning him." Luke 24:27), and twin radiances of the commandments to love God and neighbor ("On these two commandments dependeth the whole law and the prophets." Matt. 22:40). Both were witness to redoubtable theophanies. Moses beheld the Burning Bush on Mount Horeb and took back with him the ontological name of God; he entered into the smoke and fire of Sinai, where "all the mount was terrible," and took back with him the tables of the law. And his face became so shining from his converse with the Lord, that it had to be veiled before the children of Israel. Elias also came "unto the mount of God, Horeb," to stand before the Lord, to withstand the great and mighty wind, the earthquake and the fire which preceeded the Lord, and to receive his prophetic mission; and, with his mission complete, he went up by a whirlwind in a fiery chariot into heaven, leaving behind his 'double spirit' and his cloak to Eliseus. Such is the impact of divinity on our sight that all who behold are touched with fire and light. Mighty sounds also accompanied these theophanies. For Moses there was the sound of thunder and trumpet; for Elias the wind and earthquake.

As the two keys which unlock the enigma of the Transfiguration begin to turn, we hear the two prophets conversing with Christ about his sacrificial death in Jerusalem, and we are reminded of how Moses spoke with God "as a man is wont to speak to his friend,"[1] and of how Elias, after the clash of wind, earthquake and fire, heard the 'whistling of a gentle air' at the sound of which he covered his face and spoke with the Lord. Here, on the mount of Transfiguration, all witness and converse with open face before the Lord. Christ's transfiguration began with prayer, and Moses and Elias are two essential aspects of prayer: Moses is that spirit of meek obedience to God[2] which welcomes the *descent* of Revelation, while Elias is that fiery *ascensional* spirit—the zeal for the things of God—which provokes the incineration of our false gods and cherished idols. If Moses is the intellect at prayer, then Elias is the will at prayer. But what of Christ, who is eventually found 'alone'? In Christ, intellect and will are one, for in him we see "heaven opened and the angels of God *ascending* and *descending* upon the Son of man". Christ is both the ontology of revelation and the 'fiery chariot' of prayer. And this is why God the Father instructs us to 'hear' his beloved Son, for, being God himself, Christ's every word and deed should and will have—on the Last Day if not before—an ontological impact on each of us. 'Hearing him' is not only a sacred instinctive[3] ascent away from evil and toward the beloved; it is also a conscious reception of the Word of God, so that his word becomes our word. But, to become our word, it is not written, as of old, by the finger of God on tables of stone; it is written by the very *person* of Christ-incarnate-God in the fleshly tables of our hearts. This is how all things become transparent and dazzling to us—the First Testament of the natural world, the Old Testament of the law and the prophets and the New Testament of Christ—, this is how we worship God 'in spirit and in truth': first in the spirit of Elias and the truth of Moses, but then in the unison of Christ. Whenever and wherever we hear the Gospel, we are listening to life itself. Whenever and wherever we aspire to pray 'in Christ', and if the Holy Spirit prays with us, heaven stands open and we gaze into the meaning of Christ's sacrifice—and our own—in Jerusalem. Recognizing the very meaning of life in Christ Jesus, with him we go up to Jerusalem to experience this meaning in its fulness...

I have both glorified it and will glorify it again.—The last stage on the way to perfection has begun. But, here, those who thought that they were gaining ground find that all is lost, that the only ground to be gained is that of their 'burial in Christ'. Here, amidst the pilgrims thronging Jerusalem at Passover, Jesus comes to plant his 'grain of wheat', to have it trampled underfoot before there is time enough to send forth even a single tender shoot. All is lost and yet all is not lost, for, if we are 'in Christ', we are not alone: the Father is always with him (John 17:32). Only here does a living and true theology begin; first with the ascetic theology of the Passion and Descent into Hades, and then with the mystical theology of the Resurrection, Ascension and Pentecost;[4] first the 'falling into the ground', and then the 'bringing forth of much fruit'.

---

1. Even though he could not see the face of his 'friend' and live.

2. There were times, however, when Moses would dare to 'test' the Lord's resolve with respect to his people (Cf. Exod 32:31–32), and other times when, in his wrath, he would slay an Egyptian, or even smash the original tables of the law written by the very finger of God, having seen the idolatry of his people at the foot of Sinai.

3. "No man can come to me, unless it be given him by my Father" John 6:66.

4. Only with Pentecost, when we are ineffably 'graced' with the Holy Spirit of God, is the 'prayer' of theology complete. The liturgical theology of the Last Supper both prepares us for what is to come in Christ's passion, death and resurrection, and is ultimately a foretaste of the Mystical Banquet in the age to come, when we will be partakers of the superessential theology of the Most Holy Trinity. And, when we have put on the seamless garment of Christ both now and unto ages of ages, who would dare search for a 'seam' with which to divide any one of these theologies from the others?

But how are we to accomplish this self-sacrifice, how do we willingly embrace our own annihilation on the cross of self-sacrifice if Christ himself was 'troubled' and even 'agonized' in soul? The answer lies in Gethsemane: watch and pray[1] one hour with Christ, the 'hour' for which cause he came into the world, the 'hour' which spans the Last Supper, his agony in the garden, his trial, death and burial, his Resurrection and Ascension—the hour of glory. And, at the very brink of this hour, what is it that Christ asks of his Father? 'Father, glorify thy name.'

Christ's request of his Father strikes heaven and earth like lightning, and the Father's voice is an answering thunder: "I have both glorified it and will glorify it again." But where and when did the Father glorify his own name? All will be explained, both the past and the future of this glorification, during Christ's prayer for his disciples at the Last Supper. But, when it is explained, nowhere do we hear direct mention of the Father glorifying his own name; what we do hear is the epiclesis of this name spoken aloud: the Son has glorified the Father on earth (John 17:4) and asks glory in return so that the Father may be glorified yet again (John 17:1). We hear of 'my name' and 'thy name', but only in a continual exchange and oneness of glory, only in the unity of the Holy Spirit. But then we hear our own names mentioned (John 17:11, 21); we had been lost and even dazed in contemplating this infinite and eternal perichoresis of the Father, Son and Holy Spirit, and suddenly we are struck to the heart by amazement at what is plainly before us and within us…

Prayer: Christ's prayer for us at the Last Supper, Christ's prayer with us in the Lord's Prayer, Christ's prayer in us in the Jesus Prayer;[2] this is how we are made perfect as also our heavenly Father is perfect. In prayer, the flint of the purgative way strikes against our hardened hearts to reveal the spark of conscience. And, if this spark of conscience falls on[3] and kindles the 'tinder'[4] of the illuminative way, then the conflagration of the unitive way is set ablaze and we are 'made perfect in one' (John 17:23) in the fiery breath of the Holy Spirit.[5]

---

1. If ascetic theology is the 'work' of prayer, then mystical theology is the 'sabbath' of prayer.

2. As in the Lord's Prayer, so too in the Jesus Prayer do we find the three stages of the Christian Way: in *Lord Jesus Christ, Son of God* is the entirety of the unitive way; in *Have mercy on me* is the entirety of the illuminative way, and in the recognition of and repentance for being *A sinner* is the entirety of the purgative way.

3. Cf. the Parable of the Sower (Mark 4:3–20).

4. From the store of things both old and new, we have been well-provided with 'kindling' by the Christian tradition. Only 'a little' is needed and take fire we will.

5. Casting a glance back over the three stages of the Christian Way, we can see how each stage is appropriated to one of the three Divine Persons of the Trinity: in the purgative way we become 'begotten of the Father', in the illuminative we become 'doers of the Word', and in the unitive we become 'temples of the Holy Spirit'.

THE SHEEPFOLD OF THE LORD'S PRAYER

THE LORD IS MY SHEPHERD ~ PSALM 22 (23)

OUR FATHER WHO ART IN HEAVEN HALLOWED BE THY NAME	The Lord is my shepherd, I shall not want;
THY KINGDOM COME	He makes me lie down in green pastures.
THY WILL BE DONE ON EARTH AS IT IS IN HEAVEN	He leads me beside still waters;
GIVE US THIS DAY OUR DAILY BREAD	He restores my soul.
AND FORGIVE US OUR TRESPASSES AS WE FORGIVE THOSE WHO TRESPASS AGAINST US	He leads me in paths of righteousness for his name's sake.
AND LEAD US NOT INTO TEMPTATION	Even though I walk through the valley of the shadow of death,
BUT DELIVER US FROM EVIL	I fear no evil; for thou art with me;
AND LEAD US NOT INTO TEMPTATION	thy rod and thy staff they comfort me.
AND FORGIVE US OUR TRESPASSES AS WE FORGIVE THOSE WHO TRESPASS AGAINST US	Thou preparest a table before me in the presence of my enemies;
GIVE US THIS DAY OUR DAILY BREAD	thou anointest my head with oil, my cup overflows.
THY WILL BE DONE ON EARTH AS IT IS IN HEAVEN	Surely goodness and mercy shall follow me all the days of my life;
OUR FATHER WHO ART IN HEAVEN HALLOWED BE THY NAME THY KINGDOM COME	and I shall dwell in the house of the Lord for ever.

COMMENTARY BY MAXIMUS THE CONFESSOR[1]

OUR FATHER WHO ART IN HEAVEN
HALLOWED BE THY NAME

"The length of days [for ever] means eternal life."

THY KINGDOM COME

"The house is the kingdom in which all the saints will be restored."

THY WILL BE DONE ON EARTH
AS IT IS IN HEAVEN

"...his mercy is his Word and God. For through his incarnation he pursues us all days until he gets hold of those who are to be saved, as he did with Paul."

GIVE US THIS DAY
OUR DAILY BREAD

"The oil which anoints the mind is the contemplation of creatures, the cup of God is the knowledge of God itself."

AND FORGIVE US OUR TRESPASSES
AS WE BY FORGIVE THOSE WHO
TRESPASS AGAINST US
AND LEAD US NOT INTO TEMPTATION
BUT DELIVER US FROM EVIL

"Table here signifies practical virtue, for this has been prepared by Christ 'against those who afflict us."

---

1. *Texts on Love*, III, 2.

THE GOOD SHEPHERD

JOHN 10:1–18

BUT DELIVER
US FROM EVIL

Amen, amen I say to you: He that entereth not by the door into the sheepfold, but climbeth up another way, the same is a thief and a robber. But he that entereth in by the door is the shepherd of the sheep. To him the porter openeth; and the sheep hear his voice: and he calleth his own sheep by name, and leadeth them out.

AND LEAD US NOT
INTO TEMPTATION

And when he hath let out his own sheep, he goeth before them: and the sheep follow him, because they know his voice.

AND FORGIVE US OUR
TRESPASSES AS WE
FORGIVE THOSE
WHO TRESPASS
AGAINST US

But a stranger they follow not, but fly from him, because they know not the voice of strangers. This proverb Jesus spoke to them. But they understood not what he spoke to them. Jesus therefore said to them again: Amen, amen I say to you, I am the door of the sheep. All others, as many as have come, are thieves and robbers: and the sheep heard them not.

GIVE US THIS DAY
OUR DAILY BREAD

I am the door. By me, if any man enter in, he shall be saved: and he shall go in, and go out, and shall find pastures. The thief cometh not, but for to steal, and to kill, and to destroy. I am come that they may have life, and may have it more abundantly.

THY WILL BE DONE
ON EARTH AS IT
IS IN HEAVEN

I am the good shepherd. The good shepherd giveth his life for his sheep. But the hireling, and he that is not the shepherd, whose own the sheep are not, seeth the wolf coming, and leaveth the sheep, and flieth: and the wolf catcheth, and scattereth the sheep: And the hireling flieth, because he is a hireling: and he hath no care for the sheep. I am the good shepherd; and I know mine, and mine know me. As the Father knoweth me, and I know the Father: and I lay down my life for my sheep.

THY KINGDOM COME

And other sheep I have, that are not of this fold: them also I must bring, and they shall hear my voice, and there shall be one fold and one shepherd.

OUR FATHER WHO
ART IN HEAVEN
HALLOWED BE
THY NAME

Therefore doth the Father love me: because I lay down my life, that I may take it again. No man taketh it away from me: but I lay it down of myself, and I have power to lay it down: and I have power to take it up again. This commandment have I received of my Father.

INVITATION TO THE KINGDOM

And at midnight there was a cry made: Behold, the Bridegroom cometh. Go ye forth to meet him. Matthew 25:6

OUR FATHER WHO
ART IN HEAVEN
HALLOWED BE
THY NAME

No man came come to me, except the Father, who hath sent me, draw him. John 6:44

THY KINGDOM COME

From that time Jesus began to preach and to say: Do penance, for the kingdom of God is at hand. And Jesus walking by the sea of Galilee saw two brethren, Simon who is called Peter and Andrew his brother, casting a net into the sea (for they were fishers). And he saith to them: Come ye after me, and I will make you to be fishers of men. And they immediately leaving their nets followed him. Matt. 4:17–20

THY WILL BE DONE
ON EARTH AS IT IS
IN HEAVEN

Be thou not therefore ashamed of the testimony of our Lord, nor of me his prisoner; but labor with the gospel, according to the power of God; who hath delivered us and called us by his holy calling, not according to our works, but according to his own purpose and grace, which was given us in Christ Jesus before the times of the world. 2 Tim. 1:8–9

GIVE US THIS DAY
OUR DAILY BREAD

The kingdom of heaven is likened to a king who made a marriage for his son. And he sent his servants to call them that were invited to the marriage; and they would not come. Again he sent other servants, saying: Tell them that were invited, Behold, I have prepared my dinner; my beeves and fatlings are killed, and all things are ready. Come ye to the marriage.

AND FORGIVE US OUR
TRESPASSES AS WE
FORGIVE THOSE
WHO TRESPASS
AGAINST US

But they neglected and went their ways, one to his farm and another to his merchandise. And the rest laid hands on his servants and, having treated them contumeliously, put them to death. But, when the king had heard of it, he was angry; and sending his armies, he destroyed those murderers and burnt their city.

AND LEAD US NOT
INTO TEMPTATION

Then he saith to his servants: The marriage is indeed ready; but they that were invited were not worthy. Go ye therefore into the highways; and as many as you shall find, call to the marriage. And his servants, going forth into the ways, gathered together all that they found, both bad and good; and the marriage was filled with guests.

BUT DELIVER
US FROM EVIL

And the king went in to see the guests; and he saw there a man who had not on a wedding garment. And he saith to him: Friend, how camest thou in hither not having on a wedding garment? But he was silent. Then the king said to the waiters: Bind his hands and feet, and cast him into the exterior darkness. There shall be weeping and gnashing of teeth. For many are called, but few are chosen. Matt. 22:2–14

THE WEDDING GARMENT OF THE KINGDOM

OUR FATHER WHO
ART IN HEAVEN
HALLOWED BE
THY NAME

The night is passed and the day is at hand. Let us therefore cast off the works of darkness and put on the armor of light... Put ye on the Lord Jesus Christ; and make not provision for the flesh in its concupiscences. Rom. 13:12, 14

THY KINGDOM COME
THY WILL BE DONE
ON EARTH AS IT IS
IN HEAVEN

But let us, who are of the day, be sober, having on the breastplate of faith and charity and, for a helmet, the hope of salvation. For God in heaven hath not appointed us unto wrath; but unto the purchasing of salvation by our Lord Jesus Christ, who died for us; that, whether we watch or sleep, we may live together with him. For which cause comfort one another and edify one another, as you also do. 1 Thess. 5:8–11

GIVE US THIS DAY
OUR DAILY BREAD

Finally, brethren, be strengthened in the Lord and in the might of his power.

AND FORGIVE US OUR
TRESPASSES AS WE
FORGIVE THOSE
WHO TRESPASS
AGAINST US
AND LEAD US NOT
INTO TEMPTATION
BUT DELIVER
US FROM EVIL

Put you on the armor of God, that you may be able to stand against the deceits of the devil... Stand, therefore, having your loins girt about with truth and having on the breastplate of justice; and your feet shod with the preparation of the gospel of peace; in all things taking the shield of faith, wherewith you may be able to extinguish all the fiery darts of the most wicked one. And take unto you the helmet of salvation, and the sword of the Spirit (which is the word of God); by all prayer and supplication, praying at all times in the spirit; and in the same watching with all instance and supplication for all the saints; and for me, that speech may be given me, that I may open my mouth with confidence, to make known the mystery of the gospel. Eph. 6:10–11, 13–19

SIMILITUDES OF THE KINGDOM

MATTHEW 13

All these things Jesus spoke in parables to the multitudes; and without parables he did not speak to them; that it might be fulfilled which was spoken by the prophet; saying: I will open my mouth in parables, I will utter things hidden from the foundation of the world… And his disciples came and said to him: Why speakest thou to them in parables? Who answered and said to them: Because to you it is given to know the mysteries of the kingdom of heaven; but to them it is not given.

BUT DELIVER
US FROM EVIL

Behold, the sower went forth to sow. And, whilst he soweth, some fell by the way-side; and the birds of the air came and ate them up.
When anyone heareth the word of the kingdom, and understandeth it not, there cometh the wicked one and catcheth away that which was sown in the heart; this is he that received the seed by the wayside.

AND LEAD US NOT
INTO TEMPTATION

And other some fell upon stony ground, where they had not much earth; and they sprung up immediately, because they had no deepness of earth. And, when the sun was up, they were scorched; and, because they had no root, they withered away.
And he that received the seed upon stony ground is he that heareth the word and immediately receiveth it with joy. Yet hath he not root in himself, but is only for a time; and when there ariseth tribulation and persecution because of the word, he is presently scandalized.

AND FORGIVE US OUR
TRESPASSES AS WE
FORGIVE THOSE
WHO TRESPASS
AGAINST US

And others fell among thorns; and the thorns grew up and choked them.
And he that received the seed among thorns is he that heareth the word, and the care of this world and the deceitfulness of riches choketh up the word; and he becometh fruitless.

GIVE US THIS DAY
OUR DAILY BREAD

And others fell upon good ground; and they brought forth fruit, some an hundredfold, some sixtyfold, and some thirtyfold.
But he that received the seed upon good ground is he that heareth the word and understandeth and beareth fruit and yieldeth the one an hundredfold, and another sixty, and another thirty.

THY WILL BE DONE
ON EARTH AS IT
IS IN HEAVEN

The kingdom of heaven is likened to a man who sowed good seed in his field. But, while men were asleep, his enemy came and oversowed cockle among the wheat and went his way. And, when the blade was sprung up and had brought forth fruit, then appeared also the cockle. And the servants of the master of the house coming said to him: Sir, didst thou not sow good seed in thy field? Whence then hath it cockle? And he said to them: An enemy hath done this. And the servants said to him: Wilt thou that we go and gather it up? And he said: No, lest perhaps gathering up the cockle you root up the wheat also together with it. Suffer both to grow until the harvest, and in the time of the harvest I will say to the reapers: Gather up first the cockle and bind it into bundles to burn, but the wheat gather ye into my barn.
He that soweth the good seed is the Son of man. And the field is the world. And the good seed are the children of the kingdom. And the cockle are the children of

the wicked one. And the enemy that sowed them is the devil. But the harvest is the end of the world. And the reapers are the angels. Even as the cockle therefore is gather up and burnt with fire; so shall it be at the end of the world. The Son of man shall send his angels; and they shall gather out of his kingdom all scandals and them that work iniquity. And shall cast them into the furnace of fire. There shall be weeping and gnashing of teeth. Then shall the just shine as the sun in the kingdom of their Father.

THY KINGDOM COME

The kingdom of heaven is like to a grain of mustard seed which a man took and sowed in his field. Which is the least indeed of all seeds; but, when it is grown up, it is greater than all herbs and becometh a tree, so that the birds of the air come and dwell in the branches thereof.

OUR FATHER WHO
ART IN HEAVEN
HALLOWED BE
THY NAME

The kingdom of heaven is like to leaven which a woman took and hid in three measures[1] of meal, until the whole was leavened.

THE KINGDOM

OUR FATHER WHO
ART IN HEAVEN
HALLOWED BE
THY NAME

Therefore we also… cease not to pray for you and to beg that you may be… strengthened with all might, according to the power of his glory, in all patience and long-suffering with joy, giving thanks to God the Father, who hath made us worthy to be partakers of the lot of the saints in light; who hath delivered us from the power of darkness and hath translated us into the kingdom of the Son of his love; in whom we have redemption through his blood, the remission of sins; who is the image of the invisible God, the firstborn of every creature. For in him were all things created in heaven and on earth, visible and invisible… All things were created by him and in him. And he is before all; and by him all things consist. …in him it hath well pleased the Father that all fulness should dwell. Col. 1:9, 11–17, 19
In him dwelleth all the fulness of the Godhead corporeally. Col. 2:9

THY KINGDOM COME

The kingdom of God cometh not with observation. Neither shall they say: Behold here, or behold there. For lo, the kingdom of God is within you. And he said to his disciples: The days will come when you shall desire to see one day of the Son of man. And you shall not see it. And they shall say to you: See here, and see there. Go ye not after, nor follow them. For as the lightning that lighteneth from under heaven shineth unto the parts that are under heaven, so shall the Son of man be in his day. But first be must suffer many things and be rejected by this generation. Luke 17:20–25

---

1. Fulness of prayer, prayer in the Holy Spirit, is that leaven which permeates the 'three measures' of man—body, soul, and spirit—to the utmost. Only by this is true and complete worship possible, both now and in the resurrection.

Jesus answered: My kingdom is not of this world… Pilate therefore said to him: Art thou a king then? Jesus answered: Thou sayest that I am a king. For this was I born, and for this came I into the world. John 18:36–37

THY WILL BE DONE ON EARTH AS IT IS IN HEAVEN
And he that sat upon the throne said: Behold, I make all things new. …And he said to me: It is done. I am the Alpha and the Omega; the beginning and the end. To him that thirsteth I will give of the fountain of the water of life freely. He that shall overcome shall possess these things; and I will be his God, and he shall be my son. Apoc. 21:5–7

GIVE US THIS DAY OUR DAILY BREAD
They shall no more hunger nor thirst… For the Lamb which is in the midst of the throne, shall rule them and shall lead them to the fountains of the waters of life. Apoc. 7:16–17

AND FORGIVE US OUR TRESPASSES AS WE FORGIVE THOSE WHO TRESPASS AGAINST US
Every kingdom divided against itself shall be made desolate; and very city or house divided against itself shall not stand. Matt. 12:25

AND LEAD US NOT INTO TEMPTATION
But he said to another: Follow me. And he said: Lord, suffer me first to go and to bury my father. And Jesus said to him: Let the dead bury their dead; but go thou and preach the kingdom of God. And another said: I will follow thee, Lord; but let me first take my leave of them that are at my house. Jesus said to him: No man putting his hand to the plough and looking back is fit for the kingdom of God. Luke 9:59–62

BUT DELIVER US FROM EVIL
Unless a man be born again he cannot see the kingdom of God. John 3:3

EATING BREAD IN THE KINGDOM OF GOD

LUKE 14:7—24

OUR FATHER WHO ART IN HEAVEN HALLOWED BE THY NAME

And he spoke a parable also to them that were invited, marking how they chose the first seats at the table, saying to them:

THY KINGDOM COME

When thou art invited to a wedding, sit not down in the first place, lest perhaps one more honorable than thou be invited by him: And he that invited thee and him, come and say to thee: Give this man place. And then thou begin with shame to take the lowest place. But when thou art invited, go, sit down in the lowest place; that when he who invited thee cometh, he may say to thee: Friend, go up higher. Then shalt thou have glory before them that sit at table with thee. Because every one that exalteth himself shall be humbled: and he that humbleth himself shall be exalted.

THY WILL BE DONE ON EARTH AS IT IS IN HEAVEN

And he said to him also that had invited him: When thou makest a dinner or a supper, call not thy friends nor thy brethren nor thy kinsmen nor thy neighbors who are rich; lest perhaps they also invite thee again, and a recompense be made to thee. But when thou makest a feast, call the poor, the maimed, the lame and the blind. And thou shalt be blessed, because they have not wherewith to make thee recompense: for recompense shall be made thee at the resurrection of the just.

GIVE US THIS DAY OUR DAILY BREAD

When one of them that sat at table with him had heard these things, he said to him: Blessed is he that shall eat bread in the kingdom of God.

AND FORGIVE US OUR TRESPASSES AS WE FORGIVE THOSE WHO TRESPASS AGAINST US

But he said to him: A certain man made a great supper and invited many. And he sent his servant at the hour of supper to say to them that were invited, that they should come: for now all things are ready. And they began all at once to make excuse. The first said to him: I have bought a farm and I must needs go out and see it. I pray thee, hold me excused. And another said: I have bought five yoke of oxen and I go to try them. I pray thee, hold me excused. And another said: I have married a wife; and therefore I cannot come.[1]

AND LEAD US NOT INTO TEMPTATION

And the servant returning, told these things to his lord. Then the master of the house, being angry, said to his servant: Go out quickly into the streets and lanes of the city; and bring in hither the poor and the feeble and the blind and the lame.

BUT DELIVER US FROM EVIL

And the servant said: Lord, it is done as thou hast commanded; and yet there is room. And the Lord said to the servant: Go out into the highways and hedges, and compel them to come in, that my house may be filled. But I say unto you that none of those men that were invited shall taste of my supper.

---

1. Three excuses from the soul's three powers: the farm with its crops, an image of the concupiscible power, the yoke of oxen, an image of the soul's irascible power, and the wife, an image of the soul's rational power. Anything but the one thing needful—the supper's Lord, Christ Himself—even now in the brevity of a lifetime.

MESSIAH

We have found the Messias, which is, being interpreted, the Christ. John 1:41

OUR FATHER WHO
ART IN HEAVEN
HALLOWED BE
THY NAME

But he held his peace, and answered nothing. Again the high priest asked him, and said to him: Art thou the Christ the Son of the blessed God? And Jesus said to him: I am. And you shall see the Son of man sitting on the right hand of the power of God, and coming with the clouds of heaven. Mark 14:61–62
Jesus saith to them: But whom do you say that I am? Simon Peter answered and said: Thou art Christ, the Son of the living God. And Jesus answering, said to him: Blessed art thou, Simon Bar-Jona: because flesh and blood hath not revealed it to thee, but my Father who is in heaven. Matt. 16:15–17

THY KINGDOM COME

Now all this was done that it might be fulfilled which was spoken by the prophet, saying: Tell ye the daughter of Sion: Behold thy king cometh to thee, meek, and sitting upon an ass, and a colt the foal of her that is used to the yoke. And the disciples going, did as Jesus commanded them. And they brought the ass and the colt, and laid their garments upon them, and made him sit thereon. And a very great multitude spread their garments in the way: and others cut boughs from the trees, and strewed them in the way: And the multitudes that went before and that followed, cried, saying: Hosanna to the son of David: Blessed is he that cometh in the name of the Lord: Hosanna in the highest. Matt. 21:4–9
Jesus saith to her: Thy brother shall rise again. Martha saith to him: I know that he shall rise again, in the resurrection at the last day. Jesus said to her: I am the resurrection and the life: he that believeth in me, although he be dead, shall live: and every one that liveth, and believeth in me, shall not die for ever. Believest thou this? She saith to him: Yea, Lord, I have believed that thou art Christ the Son of the living God, who art come into this world. John 11:23–27

THY WILL BE DONE
ON EARTH AS IT IS
IN HEAVEN

The multitude answered him: We have heard out of the law, that Christ abideth for ever; and how sayest thou: The Son of man must be lifted up? Who is this Son of man? Jesus therefore said to them: Yet a little while, the light is among you. Walk whilst you have the light, that the darkness overtake you not. And he that walketh in darkness, knoweth not whither he goeth. Whilst you have the light, believe in the light, that you may be the children of light. These things Jesus spoke; and he went away, and hid himself from them. John 12:34–36
Whosoever believeth that Jesus is the Christ, is born of God. And every one that loveth him who begot, loveth him also who is born of him. In this we know that we love the children of God: when we love God and keep his commandments. 1 John 5:1–2

GIVE US THIS DAY
OUR DAILY BREAD

And behold a woman of Canaan who came out of those coasts, crying out, said to him: Have mercy on me, O Lord, thou son of David: my daughter is grievously troubled by the devil. Who answered her not a word. And his disciples came and besought him, saying: Send her away, for she crieth after us: And he answering, said: I was not sent but to the sheep that are lost of the house of Israel. But she came and adored him, saying: Lord, help me. Who answering, said: It is not good to take the bread of the children, and to cast it to the dogs. But she said: Yea, Lord; for the whelps also eat of the crumbs that fall from the table of their masters. Then Jesus answering, said to her: O woman, great is thy faith: be it done to thee as thou wilt: and her daughter was cured from that hour. Matt. 15:22–28

Then Jesus said to the twelve: Will you also go away? And Simon Peter answered him: Lord, to whom shall we go? Thou hast the words of eternal life. And we have believed and have known that thou art the Christ, the Son of God. John 6:68–70

AND FORGIVE US OUR TRESPASSES AS WE FORGIVE THOSE WHO TRESPASS AGAINST US

And behold, men brought in a bed a man, who had the palsy: and they sought means to bring him in, and to lay him before him. And when they could not find by what way they might bring him in, because of the multitude, they went up upon the roof, and let him down through the tiles with his bed into the midst before Jesus. Whose faith when he saw, he said: Man, thy sins are forgiven thee. And the scribes and Pharisees began to think, saying: Who is this who speaketh blasphemies? Who can forgive sins, is easier to say, Thy sins are forgiven thee; or to say, Arise and walk? But that you may know that the Son of man hath power on earth to forgive sins, (he saith to the sick of the palsy,) I say to thee, Arise, take up thy bed, and go into thy house. And immediately rising up before them, he took up the bed on which he lay; and he went away to his own house, glorifying God. And all were astonished; and they glorified God. And they were filled with fear, saying: We have seen wonderful things to day. Luke 5:18-26

And behold, he speaketh openly: and they say nothing to him. Have the rulers known for a truth that this is the Christ? But we know this man, whence he is: but when the Christ cometh, no man knoweth, whence he is. Jesus therefore cried out in the temple, teaching and saying: You both know me, and you know whence I am. And I am not come of myself: but he that sent me is true, whom you know not. I know him, because I am from him: and he hath sent me. They sought therefore to apprehend him: and no man laid hands on him, because his hour was not yet come. John 7:26–30

AND LEAD US NOT INTO TEMPTATION

And the Pharisees being gathered together, Jesus asked them, saying: What think you of Christ? whose son is he? They say to him: David's. He saith to them: How then doth David in spirit call him Lord, saying: The Lord said to my Lord, Sit on my right hand, until I make thy enemies thy footstool? If David then call him Lord, how is he his son? And no man was able to answer him a word; neither durst any man from that day forth ask him any more questions. Matt. 22:41–46

Of that multitude therefore, when they had heard these words of his, some said: This is the prophet indeed. Others said: This is the Christ. But some said: Doth the Christ come out of Galilee? Doth not the scripture say: That Christ cometh of the seed of David and from Bethlehem the town where David was? So there arose a dissension among the people because of him. John 7:40–43

BUT DELIVER US FROM EVIL

And they came over the strait of the sea into the country of the Gerasens. And as he went out of the ship, immediately there met him out of the monuments a man with an unclean spirit, who had his dwelling in the tombs, and no man now could bind him, not even with chains. For having been often bound with fetters and chains, he had burst the chains, and broken the fetters in pieces, and no one could tame him. And he was always day and night in the monuments and in the mountains, crying and cutting himself with stones. And seeing Jesus afar off, he ran and adored him. And crying with a loud voice, he said: What have I to do with thee, Jesus the Son of the most high God? I adjure thee by God that thou torment me not. For he said unto him: Go out of the man, thou unclean spirit. And he asked him: What is thy name? And he saith to him: My name is Legion, for we are many. And he besought him much, that he would not drive him away out of the country. And there was there near the mountain a great herd of swine, feeding. And the spirits besought him, saying: Send us into the swine, that we may enter into them. And Jesus immediately gave them leave. And the unclean spirits going out, entered into the swine: and the herd with great violence was carried headlong into the sea, being about two thousand, and were stifled in the sea. Mark 5:1–13

Who is a liar, but he who denieth that Jesus is the Christ? This is Antichrist, who denieth the Father and the Son. Whosoever denieth the Son, the same hath not the Father. He that confesseth the Son hath the Father also. As for you, let that which you have heard from the beginning abide in you. If that abide in you, which you have heard from the beginning, you also shall abide in the Son and in the Father. And this is the promise which he hath promised us, life everlasting. 1 John 2:22–25

TRANSFIGURATION

Amen I say to you, there are some of them that stand here, that shall not taste death, till they see the Son of man coming in his kingdom. Matthew 16:28

OUR FATHER WHO ART IN HEAVEN, HALLOWED BE THY NAME—*Glory*

THY KINGDOM COME—*A Life Transfigured, The Inner Man of the Heart*

THY WILL BE DONE ON EARTH AS IT IS IN HEAVEN—*All the Treasures of the Heart, Secrets of the Heart, The Unifying Grace of Prayer*

GIVE US THE DAY OUR DAILY BREAD—*The Eye of the Heart*

AND FORGIVE US OUR TRESPASSES AS WE FORGIVE THOSE WHO TRESPASS AGAINST US—*Foolishness in Christ*

AND LEAD US NOT INTO TEMPTATION—*Continual Prayer*

BUT DELIVER US FROM EVIL—*Humility of Heart*

AMEN—*The Lord's Prayer~Prayer of the Heart*

THE LORD'S PRAYER~PRAYER OF THE HEART

For as a flame increases when it is constantly fed, so prayer, made often, with the mind dwelling ever more deeply in God, arouses divine love in the heart. And the heart, set on fire, will warm all the inner man.
— Dimitri of Rostov, *The Inner Closet of the Heart*

OUR INMOST HEART THE HOLY TRINITY

Lord Jesus Christ, Son of God

If any one love me, he will keep my word, and my father will love him, and
we will come to him, and will make our abode with him. John 14:23
The kingdom of God is within you. Matt. 17:21

OUR FATHER	Father
WHO ART IN HEAVEN	
HALLOWED BE THY NAME	Son
THY KINGDOM COME	Holy Spirit

THE EYE OF THE HEART THE EUCHARIST

Have mercy on me

We shall be like him: because we shall see him as he is. 1 John 3:2
Blessed are the clean of heart: for they shall see God. Matt. 5:8

THY WILL BE DONE ON EARTH	The All-Pure Heart of Mary[1]
AS IT IS IN HEAVEN	The Theandric Heart of Jesus[2]
GIVE US THIS DAY	
OUR DAILY BREAD	The Eucharist

A HEART OF FLESH

A sinner

I will take away the stony heart out of their flesh,
and I will give them a heart of flesh. Ezech. 11:19

AND FORGIVE US OUR TRESPASSES
AS WE FORGIVE THOSE WHO TRESPASS AGAINST US
AND LEAD US NOT INTO TEMPTATION
BUT DELIVER US FROM EVIL

---

1. "And Mary said: Behold the handmaid of the Lord; be it done to me according to thy word (Luke 1:38)… And his mother kept all these words in her heart" (Luke 2:51). Mary's heart is both a mirror and a storehouse of Christian revelation; out of it the evangelists have drawn the early years, the mother's years of the Gospels and how much else beside.

2. "Who being in the form of God, thought it not robbery to be equal with God: but emptied himself, taking the form of a servant, being made in the likeness of men, and in habit found as a man" (Phil. 2:6–7). With Christ the outer man *is* the inner man of the heart, this Living Bread who "changes him who feeds on Him and transforms and assimilates him into Himself. As He is the Head and the Heart, we depend on Him for moving and living since He possesses life" (Cabasilas, *The Life in Christ*, Fourth Book, § 8).

HUMILITY OF HEART

Take my yoke upon you and learn of me, because I am meek and humble of heart; and you shall find rest to your souls. For my yoke is sweet and my burden light. Matthew 11:29–30

Love and humility make a holy team. The one exalts. The other supports those who have been exalted and never falls.
— John Climacus, *The Ladder of Divine Ascent*, Step 25, 37

BE YE THEREFORE, SIMPLE AS DOVES

OUR FATHER WHO
ART IN HEAVEN

See that you despise not one of these little ones; for I say to you that their angels in heaven always see the face of my Father who is in heaven. Matt. 18:10

HALLOWED BE
THY NAME

Whosoever shall receive this child in my name receiveth me; and whosoever shall receive me receiveth him that sent me. For he that is the lesser among you all he is the greater. Luke 9:48

THY KINGDOM COME

Amen, I say to you, unless you be converted and become as little children, you shall not enter into the kingdom of heaven. Whosoever therefore shall humble himself as this little child, he is the greater in the kingdom of heaven. Matt. 18:3–4

THY WILL BE DONE
ON EARTH AS IT IS
IN HEAVEN

The kingdom of heaven is like to a grain of mustard seed which a man took and sowed in his field. Which is the least indeed of all seeds; but, when it is grown up, it is greater than all herbs and becometh a tree, so that the birds of the air come and dwell in the branches thereof. Matt. 13:31–32

GIVE US THIS DAY
OUR DAILY BREAD

Behold the birds of the air, for they neither sow, nor do they reap nor gather into barns; and your heavenly Father feedeth them. Are not you of much more value than they? Matt. 6:26

AND WISE AS SERPENTS

And, as Moses lifted up the serpent in the desert, so must the Son of man be lifted up; that whosoever believeth in him may not perish, but may have life everlasting. John 3:14–15

For the word of the cross, to them indeed that perish, is foolishness; but to them that are saved, that is, to us, it is the power of God. 1 Corinthians 1:18

AND FORGIVE US OUR
TRESPASSES AS WE
FORGIVE THOSE
WHO TRESPASS
AGAINST US

For the weapons of our warfare are not carnal but mighty to God, unto the pulling down of fortifications, destroying counsels, and every height that exalteth itself against the knowledge of God: and bringing into captivity every understanding unto the obedience of Christ: And having in readiness to revenge all disobedience, when your obedience shall be fulfilled. 2 Cor. 10:4–6

AND LEAD US NOT
INTO TEMPTATION

And he said to me: My grace is sufficient for thee; for power is made perfect in infirmity. Gladly therefore will I glory in my infirmities, that the power of Christ may dwell in me. For which cause I please myself in my infirmities, in reproaches, in necessities, in persecutions, in distresses, for Christ. For when I am weak, then am I powerful. 2 Cor. 12:9–10

BUT DELIVER
US FROM EVIL

Be you humbled therefore under the mighty hand of God, that he may exalt you in the time of visitation; casting all your care upon him, for he hath care of you. 1 Pet. 5:6–7

CONTINUAL PRAYER

And the wine failing, the mother of Jesus saith to him: They have no wine. And Jesus saith to her: Woman, what is that to me and to thee? My hour is not yet come. His mother saith to the waiters: Whatsoever he shall say to you, do ye. John 2:3–5

OUR FATHER WHO
ART IN HEAVEN

And take unto you the helmet of salvation and the sword of the Spirit (which is the word of God); by all prayer and supplication, praying at all times in the spirit; and in the same watching with all instance and supplication for all the saints; and for me, that speech may be given me, that I may open my mouth with confidence, to make known the mystery of the gospel. Eph. 6:17–19

HALLOWED BE
THY NAME
THY KINGDOM COME

And they came to Jericho. And as he went out of Jericho with his disciples and a very great multitude, Bartimeus, the blind man, the son of Timeus, sat by the way-side begging. Who, when he had heard that it was Jesus of Nazareth, began to cry out and to say: Jesus, Son of David, have mercy on me. And many rebuked him, that he might hold his peace; but he cried a great deal the more: Son of David, have mercy on me. And Jesus, standing still, commanded him to be called. And they call the blind man, saying to him: Be of better comfort. Arise, he calleth thee. Who, casting off his garment, leaped up and came to him. And Jesus, answering, said to him: What wilt thou that I should do to thee? And the blind man said to him: Rabboni. That I may see. And Jesus said to him: Go thy way. Thy faith hath made thee whole. And immediately he saw and followed him in the way. Mark 10:46–52

THY WILL BE DONE
ON EARTH AS IT IS
IN HEAVEN

Always rejoice; pray without ceasing; in all things give thanks, for this is the will of God in Christ Jesus concerning you all. 1 Thess. 5:16–18

GIVE US THIS DAY
OUR DAILY BREAD

And, behold, a woman of Canaan, who came out of those coasts, crying out, said to him: Have mercy on me, O Lord, thou son of David; my daughter is grievously troubled by a devil. Who answered her not a word. And his disciples came and besought him, saying: Send her away, for she crieth after us. And he, answering said: I was not sent but to the sheep that are lost of the house of Israel. But she came and adored him, saying: Lord, help me. Who answering said: It is not good to take the bread of the children and cast it and to cast it to the dogs. But she said: Yea, Lord; for the whelps also eat of the crumbs that fall from the table of their masters. Then Jesus, answering, said to her: O woman, great is thy faith. Be it done to thee as thou wilt. And her daughter was cured from that hour. Matt. 15:22–28

AND FORGIVE US OUR
TRESPASSES AS WE
FORGIVE THOSE
WHO TRESPASS
AGAINST US

And it was heard that he was in the house. And many came together, so that there was no room; no, not even at the door. And he spoke to them the word. And they came to him, bringing one sick with the palsy, who was carried by four. And, when they could not offer him unto him for the multitude, they uncovered the roof, where he was; and opening it they let down the bed wherein the man sick of the palsy lay. And, when Jesus had seen their faith, he saith to the sick of the palsy: Son, thy sins are forgiven thee. And there were some of the scribes sitting there and thinking in their hearts: Why doth this man speak thus? He blasphemeth. Who can forgive sins, but God only? Which Jesus presently knowing in his spirit that they so thought within themselves, saith to them: Why think you these things in your hearts? Which is easier, to say to the sick of the palsy: Thy sins are forgiven thee; or to say: Arise, take up thy bed, and walk? But that you may know that the Son of man hath power on earth to forgive sins (he saith to the sick of the palsy), I say to thee: Arise. Take up thy bed and go into thy house. And immediately he arose and, taking up his bed, went his way in the sight of all; so that all wondered and glorified God, saying: We never saw the like. Mark 2:2–12

AND LEAD US NOT INTO TEMPTATION

And he spoke also a parable to them, that we ought always to pray and not to faint, saying: There was a judge in a certain city, who feared not God nor regarded man. And there was a certain widow in that city; and she came to him, saying: Avenge me of my adversary. And he would not for a long time. But afterwards he said within himself: Although I fear not God nor regard man, yet, because this widow is troublesome to me, I will avenge her, lest continually coming she weary me. And the Lord said: Hear what the unjust judge saith. And will God not revenge his elect who cry to him day and night? And will he have patience in their regard? I say to you that he will quickly revenge them. Luke 18:1–8

BUT DELIVER US FROM EVIL

Not every one that saith to me: Lord, Lord, shall enter into the kingdom of heaven... Many will say to me in that day: Lord, Lord, have we not prophesied in thy name and cast out devils in thy name and done many miracles in thy name? And then will I profess unto them: I never knew you; depart from me, you that work iniquity. Matt. 7:21–23

FOOLISHNESS IN CHRIST

OUR FATHER WHO
ART IN HEAVEN
HALLOWED BE
THY NAME

We are fools for Christ's sake, but you are wise in Christ; we are weak, but you are strong; you are honorable, but we without honor. Even unto this hour we both hunger and thirst and are naked and are buffeted and have no fixed abode. And we labor, working with our own hands. We are reviled, and we bless. We are persecuted, and we suffer it. We are blasphemed, and we entreat. We are made as the refuse of this world, the offscouring of all, even unto now. I write not these things to confound you; but I admonish you as my dearest children. For if you have ten thousand instructors in Christ, yet not many fathers. For in Christ Jesus, by the Gospel, I have begotten you. Wherefore, I beseech you, be ye followers of me, as I also am of Christ. 1 Cor. 4:10–16

THY KINGDOM COME

Now, we have received not the spirit of this world, but the Spirit that is of God; that we may know the things that are given us from God. Which things also we speak; not in the learned words of human wisdom, but in the doctrine of the Spirit, comparing spiritual things with spiritual. But the sensual man perceiveth not these things that are of the Spirit of God. For it is foolishness to him; and he cannot understand, because it is spiritually examined. But the spiritual man judgeth all things; and he himself is judged by no man. 1 Cor. 2:12–15

THY WILL BE DONE
ON EARTH AS IT IS
IN HEAVEN

Let no man deceive himself. If any man among you seem to be wise in this world, let him become a fool, that he may be wise. For the wisdom of this world is foolishness with God. For it is written: I will catch the wise in their own craftiness. And again: The Lord knoweth the thoughts of the wise, that they are vain. Let no man therefore glory in men; for all things are yours, whether it be Paul or Apollo or Cephas, or the world, or life, or death, or things present, or things to come. For all are yours; and you are Christ's; and Christ is God's. 1 Cor. 3:18–23

GIVE US THIS DAY
OUR DAILY BREAD

But death reigned from Adam unto Moses, even over them also who have not sinned, after the similitude of the transgression of Adam, who is a figure of him who was to come. But not as the offence, so also the gift. For if by the offence of one many died; much more the grace of God and the gift, by the grace of one man, Jesus Christ, hath abounded unto many… For if by one man's offence death reigned through one; much more they who receive abundance of grace and of the gift and of justice shall reign in life through one, Jesus Christ. Rom. 5:14–15, 17

AND FORGIVE US OUR
TRESPASSES AS WE
FORGIVE THOSE
WHO TRESPASS
AGAINST US

I speak the truth in Christ; I lie not, my conscience bearing me witness in the Holy Spirit; that I have great sadness and continual sorrow in my heart, for I wished myself to be an anathema from Christ, for my brethren; who are my kinsmen according to the flesh; who are Israelites; to whom belongeth the adoption as of children and the glory and the testament and the giving of the law and the service of God and the promises; whose are the fathers and of whom is Christ, according to the flesh, who is over all things, God blessed for ever. Amen. Rom. 9:1–5

And blessed is he that shall not be scandalized in me. Matt. 11:6

But I say to you, that whosoever is angry with his brother, shall be in danger of the judgment. And whosoever shall say to his brother, Raca, shall be in danger of the council. And whosoever shall say, Thou fool, shall be in danger of hell fire. Matt. 5:22

AND LEAD US NOT
INTO TEMPTATION

Would to God you could bear with some little of my folly! But do bear with me. For I am jealous of you with the jealousy of God. For I have espoused you to one husband, that I may present you as a chaste virgin to Christ. But I fear lest, as the serpent seduced Eve by his subtlety, so your minds should be corrupted and fall from the simplicity that is in Christ. 2 Cor. 11:1–3

BUT DELIVER
US FROM EVIL

For the word of the cross, to them indeed that perish, is foolishness; but to them that are saved, that is, to us, it is the power of God. For it is written: I will destroy the wisdom of the wise; and the prudence of the prudent I will reject… For seeing that in the wisdom of God the world, by wisdom, knew not God, it pleased God, by the foolishness of our preaching, to save them that believe. For both the Jews require signs; and the Greeks seek after wisdom. But we preach Christ crucified; unto the Jews indeed a stumbling-block, and unto the Gentiles foolishness; but unto them that are called, both Jews and Greeks, Christ, the power of God and the wisdom of God. 1 Cor. 1:18–9, 21–24

THE EYE OF THE HEART

But the path of the just, as a shining light, goeth forwards and increaseth even to perfect day. The way of the wicked is darksome: they know not where they fall. My son, hearken to my words, and incline thy ear to my sayings. Let them not depart from thy eyes, keep them in the midst of thy heart: for they are life to those that find them, and health to all flesh. With all watchfulness keep thy heart, because life issueth out from it. Proverbs 4:18–23

Keep the commandment without spot, blameless, unto the coming of our Lord Jesus Christ, which in his times he shall shew who is the Blessed and only Mighty, the King of kings, and Lord of lords; who only hath immortality, and inhabiteth light inaccessible, whom no man hath seen, nor can see: to whom be honor and empire everlasting. Amen. 1 Timothy 6:14–16

OUR FATHER WHO ART IN HEAVEN	God is light and in him there is no darkness. 1 John 1:5
HALLOWED BE THY NAME	But you are… a kingly priesthood, a holy nation… that you may declare his virtues, who hath called you out of darkness into his marvelous light. 1 Pet. 2:9
THY KINGDOM COME	Every best gift and every perfect gift is from above, coming down from the Father of lights. James 1:17
THY WILL BE DONE ON EARTH AS IT IS IN HEAVEN	For God, who commanded the light to shine out of darkness, hath shined in our hearts, to give the light of the knowledge of the glory of God, in the face of Christ Jesus. 2 Cor. 4:6 We all, beholding the glory of the Lord with open face, are transformed into the same image from glory to glory, as by the Spirit of the Lord. 2 Cor. 3:18
GIVE US THIS DAY OUR DAILY BREAD	(May) the God of our Lord Jesus Christ, the Father of glory… give unto you the spirit of wisdom and revelation, in the knowledge of him: the eyes of your heart enlightened, that you may know what the hope is of his calling, and what are the riches of the glory of his inheritance in the saints. Eph. 1:17–18
AND FORGIVE US OUR TRESPASSES AS WE FORGIVE THOSE WHO TRESPASS AGAINST US AND LEAD US NOT INTO TEMPTATION BUT DELIVER US FROM EVIL	Where thy treasure is, there is thy heart also. The light of thy body is thy eye. If thy eye be single, thy whole body will be lightsome. But if thy eye be evil, thy whole body shall be darksome. If then the light that is in thee be darkness; the darkness itself how great shalt be! Matt. 6:21–23

*And we have
the more firm prophetical word;
whereunto you do well to attend, as to a light
that shineth in a dark place, until the day dawn
and the day-star arise in your hearts.* 2 Pet. 1:19

THE UNIFYING GRACE OF PRAYER

Where there are two or three gathered together in my name, there am I in the midst of them. Matthew 18:20

Lord, teach us to pray... And he said to them: When you pray say: Father [memory], *hallowed be* [will] *thy name* [intellect]. Luke 11:1–2

Little by little, divine action grants to man increased attention and contrition of the heart in prayer. Having prepared the vessel in this manner, it touches the severed parts suddenly, unexpectedly, immaterially, and they become united in one. Who touched it? I cannot explain... but I know and feel a sudden change in myself, due to an all-powerful action. The Creator has acted now in renewal, as He acted once in creation. —Theophan the Recluse, *The Fruits of Prayer*

	THE FOUR SENSES	TWO OR THREE GATHERED
	Contemplative prayer[1]	
OUR FATHER WHO ART IN HEAVEN HALLOWED BE THY NAME	Anagogical	The perichoresis and indwelling of the Blessed Trinity
	Unceasing mind-in-heart prayer	
THY KINGDOM COME		The hypostatic union of the divine and the human in Christ and Christ in us
	Mind-in-heart prayer bestowed as a gift	
THY WILL BE DONE ONEARTH AS IT IS IN HEAVEN	Tropogogical or Moral	The recollection of the faculties of memory, will, and intellect in singleness of heart
GIVE US THIS DAY OUR DAILY BREAD	Allegorical	The eucharistic Bread and Wine in the fullness of Christ, a union of the earthly ('daily') and heavenly ('supersubstantial') and our partaking of it
	Mind-in-heart prayer produced by our own efforts	
AND FORGIVE US OUR TRESPASSES AS WE FORGIVE THOSE WHO TRESPASS AGAINST US	Literal	Memory—the blotting out of the memory of each other's personal offenses and, in its place, the remembrance of God's mercies
	Oral prayer	
AND LEAD US NOT INTO TEMPTATION		Intellect—the prayer of and for discernment
BUT DELIVER US FROM EVIL		Will—the prayer of and for repentance

---

1. Headings in italics are the stages of prayer listed by Theophan the Recluse in *The Art of Prayer*, p. 64.

ALLEGORICAL   Allegory here achieves its greatest 'livelihood', for, beyond rhetorical devices and substitutions, it is the incarnational sense of Christ assuming the life of the world for its salvation.

DAILY AND SUPERSUBSTANTIAL   As the sacrament of the love of God and neighbor, this petition is the 'gathering-place' of the preceding heavenly and the succeeding earthly petitions, the place where Christ may be truly said to be 'in the midst of'. There is a mutual symbology existing between this sacrament of love and the degrees of prayer; with the intincting of the sacred eucharistic Body in the sacred Blood, we glimpse an image of the prayer of the mind (= Body) in the heart (= Blood).

THE UNIFYING GRACE OF PRAYER~A SCRIPTURAL MIRROR

OUR FATHER WHO ART IN HEAVEN HALLOWED BE THY NAME
And not for them only do I pray, but for them also who through their word shall believe in me, that they all may be one, as thou, Father, in me, and I in thee; that they also may be one in us, that the world may believe that thou hast sent me. John 17:20–21

I know a man in Christ; above fourteen years ago (whether in the body, I know not, or out of the body, I know not; God knoweth), such a one caught up to the third heaven. And I know such a man... that he was caught up into paradise and heard secret words which it is not granted to man to utter. For such a one I will glory; but for myself I will glory nothing but in my infirmities. 2 Cor. 12:2–5

THY KINGDOM COME
Likewise, the Spirit also helpeth our infirmity. For we know not what we should pray for as we ought; but the Spirit himself asketh for us with unspeakable groanings. Rom. 8:26

But you, my beloved, building yourselves upon your most holy faith, praying in the Holy Spirit, keep yourselves in the love of God, waiting for the mercy of our Lord Jesus Christ, unto life everlasting. Jude 20

THY WILL BE DONE ON EARTH AS IT IS IN HEAVEN
Not every one that saith to me, Lord, Lord, shall enter into the kingdom of heaven; but he that doth the will of my Father who is in heaven, he shall enter into the kingdom of heaven. Matt. 7:21

GIVE US THIS DAY OUR DAILY BREAD
The harvest indeed is great, but the laborers are few. Pray ye therefore the Lord of the harvest, that he send forth laborers into his harvest. Matt. 9:37–38

AND FORGIVE US OUR TRESPASSES AS WE FORGIVE THOSE WHO TRESPASS AGAINST US
And when you shall stand to pray, forgive, if you have aught against any man; that your Father also, who is in heaven, may forgive you your sins. But, if you will not forgive, neither will your Father that is in heaven forgive you your sins. Mark 11:25–26

AND LEAD US NOT INTO TEMPTATION
Watch ye; and pray that ye enter not into temptation. The spirit is indeed willing, but the flesh weak. Matt. 26:41

And when ye pray ye shall not be as the hypocrites that love to stand and pray in the synagogues and corners of the streets, that they may be seen by men: Amen, I say to you, they have received their reward. Matt. 6:5

The Pharisee, standing, prayed thus with himself: O God, I give thee thanks that I am not as the rest of men, extortioners, unjust, adulterers, as also is this publican. I fast twice in a week; I give tithes of all that I possess. And the publican, standing afar off, would not so much as lift up his eyes towards heaven; but struck his breast, saying: O God, be merciful to me a sinner. I say to you, this man went down into his house justified rather than the other; because everyone that exalteth himself shall be humbled; and he that humbleth himself shall be exalted. Luke 18:11–14

SECRETS OF THE HEART

ACCORDING TO PAUL

For the heart directs and governs all the other organs of the body. And when grace pastures the heart, it rules over all the members and the thoughts. For there, in the heart, the mind abides as well as all the thoughts of the soul and all its hopes. This is how grace penetrates through all parts of the body. Macarius the Great, *The Spiritual Homilies*, 15, 20

OUR FATHER WHO ART IN HEAVEN HALLOWED BE THY NAME

But the sure foundation of God standeth firm, having this seal: the Lord knoweth who are his; and let every one depart from iniquity who nameth the name of the Lord. But in a great house there are not only vessels of gold and of silver, but also of wood and of earth: and some indeed unto honor, but some unto dishonor. If any man therefore shall cleanse himself from these, he shall be a vessel unto honor, sanctified and profitable to the Lord, prepared unto every good work. But flee thou youthful desires, and pursue justice, faith, charity and peace with them that call on the Lord out of a pure heart. 2 Tim. 2:19–22

THY KINGDOM COME

Wherefore tongues are for a sign, not to believers but to unbelievers: but prophecies, not to unbelievers but to believers. If therefore the whole church come together into one place, and all speak with tongues, and there come in unlearned persons or infidels, will they not say that you are mad? But if all prophesy, and there come in one that believeth not or an unlearned person, he is convinced of all: he is judged of all. The secrets of his heart are made manifest. And so, falling down on his face, he will adore God, affirming that God is among you indeed. 1 Cor. 14:22–25

THY WILL BE DONE ON EARTH AS IT IS IN HEAVEN

But God is faithful, who will strengthen and keep you from evil. And we have confidence concerning you in the Lord that the things which we command, you both do and will do. And the Lord direct your hearts, in the charity of God and the patience of Christ. 1 Thess. 3:3–5

Now the end of the commandment is charity from a pure heart, and a good conscience, and an unfeigned faith. From which things some, going astray, are turned aside unto vain babbling: desiring to be teachers of the law: understanding neither the things they say, nor whereof they affirm. But we know that the law is good, if a man use it lawfully. 1 Tim. 1:5–8

GIVE US THIS DAY OUR DAILY BREAD

Servants, be obedient to them that are your lords according to the flesh, with fear and trembling, in the simplicity of your heart, as to Christ. Not serving to the eye, as it were pleasing men: but, as the servants of Christ, doing the will of God from the heart. With a good will serving, as to the Lord, and not to men. Knowing that whatsoever good thing any man shall do, the same shall he receive from the Lord, whether he be bond or free. Eph. 6:5–8

AND FORGIVE US OUR TRESPASSES AS WE FORGIVE THOSE WHO TRESPASS AGAINST US

And may the Lord multiply you and make you abound in charity towards one another and towards all men: as we do also towards you, to confirm your hearts without blame, in holiness, before God and our Father, at the coming of our Lord Jesus Christ, with all his saints. Amen. 1 Thess. 3:12–13

AND LEAD US NOT
INTO TEMPTATION

For our exhortation was not of error, nor of uncleanness, nor in deceit. But as we were approved by God that the gospel should be committed to us: even so we speak, not as pleasing men but God, who proveth our hearts. For neither have we used at any time the speech of flattery, as you know: nor taken an occasion of covetousness (God is witness): Nor sought we glory of men, neither of you, nor of others. Whereas we might have been burdensome to you, as the apostles of Christ: but we became little ones in the midst of you, as if a nurse should cherish her children: So desirous of you, we would gladly impart unto you not only the gospel of God but also our own souls: because you were become most dear unto us. 1 Thess. 2:3–8

BUT DELIVER
US FROM EVIL

Having therefore these promises, dearly beloved, let us cleanse ourselves from all defilement of the flesh and of the spirit, perfecting sanctification in the fear of God. Receive us. We have injured no man: we have corrupted no man: we have overreached no man. I speak not this to your condemnation. For we have said before that you are in our hearts: to die together and to live together. Great is my confidence for you: great is my glorying for you. I am filled with comfort: I exceedingly abound with joy in all our tribulation. 2 Cor. 7:1–4

ALL THE TREASURES OF THE HEART

If, as St. Paul says, Christ dwells in our hearts through faith (cf. Ephesians 3:17), *and all the treasures of wisdom and spiritual knowledge are hidden in Him* (cf. Colossians 2:3), *then all the treasures of wisdom and spiritual knowledge are hidden in our hearts. They are revealed to the heart in proportion to our purification by means of the commandments. This is the treasure hidden in the field of your heart* (cf. Matthew 13:44), *which you have not yet found because of your laziness.* — Maximus the Confessor, *Texts on Love*, IV, 70 71

OUR FATHER WHO
ART IN HEAVEN
HALLOWED BE
THY NAME

No man hath seen God at any time: the only begotten Son who is in the bosom of the Father, he hath declared him. John 1:18

THY KINGDOM COME

Therefore let all the house of Israel know most certainly, that God hath made both Lord and Christ, this same Jesus, whom you have crucified. Now when they had heard these things, they had compunction in their heart, and said to Peter, and to the rest of the apostles: What shall we do, men and brethren? But Peter said to them: Do penance, and be baptized every one of you in the name of Jesus Christ, for the remission of your sins: and you shall receive the gift of the Holy Spirit. Acts 2:36–38
Now he that confirmeth us with you in Christ, and that hath anointed us, is God: Who also hath sealed us, and given the pledge of the Spirit in our hearts. 2 Cor. 1:21–22

THY WILL BE DONE
ON EARTH AS IT IS
IN HEAVEN

That their hearts may be comforted, being instructed in charity, and unto all riches of fulness of understanding, unto the knowledge of the mystery of God the Father and of Christ Jesus: in whom are hid all the treasures of wisdom and knowledge. Now this I say, that no man may deceive you by loftiness of words. For though I be absent in body, yet in spirit I am with you; rejoicing, and beholding your order, and the steadfastness of your faith which is in Christ. As therefore you have received Jesus Christ the Lord, walk ye in him; rooted and built up in him, and confirmed in the faith, as also you have learned, abounding in him in thanksgiving. Col. 2:2–6

GIVE US THIS DAY
OUR DAILY BREAD

But [the seed]that [fell] on the good ground, are they who in a good and perfect heart, hearing the word, keep it, and bring forth fruit in patience. Luke 8:15

AND FORGIVE US OUR
TRESPASSES AS WE
FORGIVE THOSE
WHO TRESPASS
AGAINST US

My little children, let us not love in word, nor in tongue, but in deed, and in truth. In this we know that we are of the truth: and in his sight shall persuade our hearts. For if our heart reprehend us, God is greater than our heart, and knoweth all things. Dearly beloved, if our heart do not reprehend us, we have confidence towards God: And whatsoever we shall ask, we shall receive of him: because we keep his commandments, and do those things which are pleasing in his sight. And this is his commandment, that we should believe in the name of his Son Jesus Christ: and love one another, as he hath given commandment unto us. And he that keepeth his commandments, abideth in him, and he in him. And in this we know that he abideth in us, by the Spirit which he hath given us. 1 John 3:18–24

AND LEAD US NOT
INTO TEMPTATION

And God, who knoweth the hearts, gave testimony, giving unto [the Gentiles] the Holy Spirit, as well as to us; and put no difference between us and them, purifying their hearts by faith. Acts 15:8–9

BUT DELIVER
US FROM EVIL

But what saith the scripture? The word is nigh thee, even in thy mouth, and in thy heart. This is the word of faith, which we preach. For if thou confess with thy mouth the Lord Jesus, and believe in thy heart that God hath raised him up from the dead, thou shalt be saved. For, with the heart, we believe unto justice; but, with the mouth, confession is made unto salvation. For the scripture saith: Whosoever believeth in him, shall not be confounded. Rom. 10:8–11

THE INNER MAN OF THE HEART

The heart is the innermost man, or spirit. Here are located self-awareness, the conscience, the idea of God and of one's complete dependence on Him, and all the treasures of the spiritual life. — Theophan the Recluse, *The Art of Prayer*

OUR FATHER WHO
ART IN HEAVEN
HALLOWED BE
THY NAME

I bow my knees to the Father of our Lord Jesus Christ, of whom all paternity in heaven and earth is named; that he would grant you, according to the riches of his glory, to be strengthened by his Spirit with might unto the inward man; that Christ may dwell by faith in your hearts; that, being rooted and founded in charity, you may be able to comprehend, with all the saints, what is the breadth and length and height and depth; to know also the charity of Christ, which surpasseth all knowledge; that you may be filled with all the fulness of God. Eph. 3:14–19

With Christ I am nailed to the cross.[1] And I live, now not I; but Christ liveth in me. Gal. 2:19–20

THY KINGDOM COME

The kingdom of God cometh not with observation... For lo, the kingdom of God is within you. Luke 17:20–21

Walk worthy of the vocation in which you are called... supporting one another in charity; careful to keep the unity of the Spirit in the bond of peace; one body and one Spirit; as you are called in one hope of your calling; one Lord, one faith, one baptism; one God and Father of all, who is above all, and through all, and in us all. But to every one of us is given grace, according to the measure of the giving of Christ... for the perfecting of the saints, for the work of the ministry, for the edifying of the body of Christ; until we all meet into the unity of faith and of the knowledge of the Son of God, unto a perfect man, unto the measure of the age of the fulness of Christ. Eph. 4:1–7, 12–13

THY WILL BE DONE
ON EARTH AS IT IS
IN HEAVEN

For God, who commanded the light to shine out of darkness, hath shined in our hearts, to give the light of the knowledge of the glory of God, in the face of Christ Jesus. But we have this treasure in earthen vessels, that the excellency may be of the power of God and not of us. 2 Cor. 4:6–7

Henceforward... walk not as also the Gentiles walk in the vanity of their mind... their understanding being darkened, being alienated from the life of God through the ignorance that is in them because of the blindness of their hearts, who, despairing, have given themselves up to lasciviousness unto the working of all uncleanness, unto covetousness. But you have not so learned Christ; if so be that you have heard him and have been taught in him, as the truth is in Jesus, to put off... the old man who is corrupted according to the desire of error, and be renewed in the spirit of your mind, and put on the new man, who according to God is created in justice and holiness of truth. Eph. 4:17–24

---

1. In *The Jesus Prayer* (p. 25) Lev Gillet notes the importance of *kiddush hashshem*, 'sanctification of the name', in Jewish spirituality. This expression "does not signify simply honor or praise rendered to God's name. It is a technical term already in use in the first century with a very strong meaning: to sanctify the name is to bear witness to God at the risk of one's own life... The sanctification of the name became almost synonymous with martyrdom."

GIVE US THIS DAY OUR DAILY BREAD If any man thirst, let him come to me and drink. He that believeth in me, as the scripture saith: out of his belly shall flow rivers of living water. Now this he said of the Spirit which they should receive who believed in him; for as yet the Spirit was not given, because Jesus was not yet glorified. John 7:37–39

For all things are for your sakes; that the grace, abounding through many, may abound in thanksgiving unto the glory of God. For which cause we faint not; but though our outward man is corrupted, yet the inward man is renewed day by day. 2 Cor. 4:15–16

AND FORGIVE US OUR TRESPASSES AS WE FORGIVE THOSE WHO TRESPASS AGAINST US Put on the new man, who according to God is created in justice and holiness of truth. Wherefore, putting away lying, speak ye the truth, every man with his neighbor; for we are members of one another. Eph. 4:24–25

Lie not to one another; stripping yourselves of the old man with his deeds, and putting on the new, him who is renewed unto knowledge [επιγνωσιν = full or deep knowledge], according to the image of him that created him; where there is neither Gentile nor Jew, circumcision nor uncircumcision, Barbarian nor Scythian, bond nor free. But Christ is all and in all. Put ye on therefore, as the elect of God, holy and beloved, the bowels of mercy, benignity, humility, modesty, patience; bearing with one another and forgiving one another, if any have a complaint against another. Even as the Lord hath forgiven you, so do you also. But, above all these things have charity, which is the bond of perfection. And let the peace of Christ rejoice in your hearts, wherein you are also called in one body. Col. 3:9–15

AND LEAD US NOT INTO TEMPTATION Try your own selves if you be in the faith; prove ye yourselves. Know you not your own selves, that Christ Jesus is in you, unless perhaps you be reprobates? 2 Cor. 13:5–6

BUT DELIVER US FROM EVIL For I am delighted with the law of God according to the inward man; but I see another law in my members, fighting against the law of my mind and captivating me in the law of sin that is in my members. Unhappy man that I am, who shall deliver me from the body of this death? The grace of God, by Jesus Christ our Lord. Rom. 7:22–25

A LIFE TRANSFIGURED

BY THE EXAMPLE OF CHRIST, TRUE GOD AND TRUE MAN	BY PRAYER TO THE FATHER	BY THE INDWELLING AND GIFTS OF THE VIRTUOUS SPIRIT
God	OUR FATHER WHO ART IN HEAVEN HALLOWED BE THY NAME	Loftiness of Faith —Faith/memory—
became man with the Incarnation[1]	THY KINGDOM COME THY WILL BE DONE ON EARTH AS IT IS IN HEAVEN	—Faith/intellect— —Faith/will—
becomes man in the Eucharist[2]	GIVE US THIS DAY OUR DAILY BREAD	All-encompassing Hope
so that man might become	AND FORGIVE US OUR TRESPASSES AS WE FORGIVE THOSE WHO TRESPASS AGAINST US AND LEAD US NOT INTO TEMPTATION	The depths of Charity[3] —love of neighbor— —love of self—
God in the Resurrection and the Life[4]	BUT DELIVER US FROM EVIL	—love of God[5] —

---

1. "I came that they may have life, and have it abundantly" John 10:10.

2. By the Eucharist I have become a particular man in you, so that you might become a universal man in me.

3. When truly lived in the spirit of the Lord's Prayer, these last three petitions are expressions of the love that overcomes all adversity.

4. John 11:25, but also: "We were buried therefore with him by baptism into death, so that as Christ was raised from the dead by the glory of the Father, we too might walk in newness of life. For if we have been united with him in a death like his, we shall certainly be united with him in a resurrection like his... You also must consider yourselves dead to sin and alive to God in Christ Jesus" (Rom. 6:4–5, 11).

5. Only in our wholehearted love for God and God's all-encompassing love for us are we truly delivered from every evil. Thus, the last petition of the Lord's Prayer mysteriously reintroduces us to the first one and 'finalizes' it.

GLORY

And whilst he prayed, the shape of his countenance was altered, and his raiment became white and glittering. And behold two men were talking with him. And they were Moses and Elias, appearing in majesty. And they spoke of his decease [exodus] that he should accomplish in Jerusalem. But Peter and they that were with him were heavy with sleep. And waking, they saw his glory, and the two men that stood with him. Luke 9:29–32

OUR FATHER WHO ART IN HEAVEN

Father And may my God supply all your want, according to his riches in glory in Christ Jesus. Now to God and our Father be glory world without end. Amen. Phil. 4:19–20

HALLOWED BE THY NAME

Son For we have not by following artificial fables, made known to you the power, and presence of our Lord Jesus Christ; but we were eyewitnesses of his greatness. For he received from God the Father, honor and glory: this voice coming down to him from the excellent glory: This is my beloved Son, in whom I am well pleased; hear ye him. And this voice we heard brought from heaven, when we were with him in the holy mount. 2 Pet. 1:16–17

THY KINGDOM COME

Holy Spirit We testified to every one of you, that you would walk worthy of God, who hath called you unto his kingdom and glory. 1 Thess. 2:2
Dearly beloved, think not strange the burning heat which is to try you, as if some new thing happened to you; but if you partake of the sufferings of Christ, rejoice that when his glory shall be revealed, you may also be glad with exceeding joy. If you be reproached for the name of Christ, you shall be blessed: for that which is of the honor, glory, and power of God, and that which is his Spirit, resteth upon you. 1 Pet. 4:12–14

THY WILL BE DONE ON EARTH AS IT IS IN HEAVEN

But the God of all grace, who hath called us into his eternal glory in Christ Jesus, after you have suffered a little, will himself perfect you, and confirm you, and establish you. To him be glory and empire for ever and ever. Amen. 1 Pet. 5:10–11

GIVE US THIS DAY OUR DAILY BREAD

But we ought to give thanks to God always for you, brethren, beloved of God, for that God hath chosen you firstfruits unto salvation, in sanctification of the spirit, and faith of the truth: whereunto also he hath called you by our gospel, unto the purchasing of the glory of our Lord Jesus Christ. 2 Thess. 2:12–13
Therefore, whether you eat or drink, or whatsoever else you do, do all to the glory of God. 1 Cor. 10:31

AND FORGIVE US OUR TRESPASSES AS WE FORGIVE THOSE WHO TRESPASS AGAINST US

Not that we are sufficient to think any thing of ourselves, as of ourselves: but our sufficiency is from God. Who also hath made us fit ministers of the new testament, not in the letter, but in the spirit. For the letter killeth, but the spirit quickeneth. Now if the ministration of death, engraven with letters upon stones, was glorious; so that the children of Israel could not steadfastly behold the face of Moses, for the glory of his countenance, which is made void: how shall not the ministration of the spirit be rather in glory? For if the ministration of condemnation be glory, much more the ministration of justice aboundeth in glory. For even that which was glorious in this part was not glorified, by reason of the glory that excelleth. For if that which is done away was glorious, much more that which remaineth is in glory. 2 Cor. 3:5–11

AND LEAD US NOT
INTO TEMPTATION

For all have sinned, and do need the glory of God. Being justified freely by his grace, through the redemption, that is in Christ Jesus, whom God hath proposed to be a propitiation, through faith in his blood, to the shewing of his justice, for the remission of former sins, through the forbearance of God, for the shewing of his justice in this time; that he himself may be just, and the justifier of him, who is of the faith of Jesus Christ. Rom. 3:23–26

BUT DELIVER
US FROM EVIL

Be mindful that the Lord Jesus Christ is risen again from the dead, of the seed of David, according to my gospel. Wherein I labor even unto bands, as an evil-doer; but the word of God is not bound. Therefore I endure all things for the sake of the elect, that they also may obtain the salvation, which is in Christ Jesus, with heavenly glory. 2 Tim. 2:8–10

DEATH, RESURRECTION AND ASCENSION INTO TRIUNE GLORY

THE FIRST PROPHECY

Obedience

OUR FATHER WHO
ART IN HEAVEN
HALLOWED BE
THY NAME
THY KINGDOM COME

And it came to pass, as he was alone praying, his disciples also were with him; and he asked them, saying: Who do the people say that am? But they answered and said: John the Baptist, but some say Elias; and others say that one of the former prophets is risen again. And he said to them: But who do you say that I am? Simon Peter, answering, said: The Christ of God. But he, strictly charging them, commanded that they should tell this to no man, saying: The Son of man must suffer many things and be rejected by the ancients and chief priests and scribes and be killed and the third day rise again. And he said to all: If any man will come after me, let him deny himself and take up his cross daily and follow me. For whosoever shall save his life shall lose it; for he that shall lose his life for my sake shall save it. Luke 9:18–24

THE SECOND PROPHECY

Chastity

THY WILL BE DONE
ON EARTH AS IT IS
IN HEAVEN

And all were astonished at the mighty power of God. But, while all wondered at all the things he did, he said to his disciples: Lay you up in your hearts these words, for it shall come to pass that the Son of man shall be delivered into the hands of men. But they understood not this word. And there entered a thought into them, which of them should be greater, but Jesus, seeing the thoughts of their heart, took a child and set him by him, and said to them: Whosoever shall receive this child in my name receiveth me; and whosoever receiveth me receiveth him that sent me. For he that is the lesser among you all is the greater. Luke 9:44–48

THE CONDITIONS FOR FOLLOWING CHRIST

THE THIRD PROPHECY

Poverty

GIVE US THIS DAY
OUR DAILY BREAD
AND FORGIVE US OUR
TRESPASSES AS WE
FORGIVE THOSE
WHO TRESPASS
AGAINST US
AND LEAD US NOT
INTO TEMPTATION
BUT DELIVER
US FROM EVIL

And a certain ruler asked him, saying: Good master, what shall I do to possess everlasting life? And Jesus said to him: Why dost thou call me good? None is good but God alone. Thou knowest the commandments: Thou shalt not kill: Thou shalt not commit adultery: Thou shalt not steal: Thou shalt not bear false witness: Honor thy father and mother. Who said: All these things I have kept from my youth. Which when Jesus had heard, he said to him: Yet one thing is wanting to thee. Sell all whatever thou hast and give to the poor; and thou shalt have treasure in heaven. And come, follow me. He, having heard these things, became sorrowful; for he was very rich. And Jesus, seeing him become sorrowful, said: How hardly shall they that have riches enter into the kingdom of God! For it is easier for a camel to pass through the eye of a needle than for a rich man to enter into the kingdom of God. And they that heard it said: Who then can be saved? He said to them: The things that are impossible with men are possible with God. Then Peter said: Behold, we have left all things and have followed thee. Who said to them: Amen, I say to you, there is no man that hath left home or parents or brethren or wife or children, for the kingdom of God's sake, who shall not receive much more in this present time, and in the world to come life everlasting. Then Jesus took unto him the twelve and said to them: Behold, we go up to Jerusalem; and all things shall be accomplished which were written by the prophets concerning the Son of man. For he shall be delivered to the Gentiles and shall be mocked and scourged and spit upon. And after they have scourged him, they will put him to death. And the third day he shall rise again. And they understood none of these things, and this word was hid from them; and they understood not the things that were said. Luke 18:18–34

THE BEATITUDES AND THE PASSION, A VERBAL ICON OF
CONFORMITY TO CHRIST

OUR FATHER WHO
ART IN HEAVEN

Blessed are they that suffer persecution for justice' sake for theirs is the kingdom of heaven. Blessed are ye when they shall revile and persecute you and speak all that is evil against you, untruly, for my sake; be glad and rejoice, for your reward is very great in heaven.

And Pilate, again answering, saith to them: What will you then that I do to the king of the Jews? But they again cried out: Crucify him. And Pilate saith to them: Why, what evil hath he done? But they cried out the more: Crucify him. Mark 15:12–14

And he said to all: If any man will come after me, let him deny himself and take up his cross daily and follow me. For whosoever will save his life shall lose it; for he that shall lose his life for my sake shall save it… For he that shall be ashamed of me and of my words, of him the Son of man shall be ashamed, when he shall come in his majesty and that of his Father and of the holy angels. Luke 9:23–24, 26

HALLOWED BE
THY NAME

Blessed be the peacemakers; for they shall be called the children of God.

And Herod with his army set him at nought and mocked him, putting on him a white garment; and sent him back to Pilate. And Herod and Pilate were made friends, that same day; for before they were enemies one to another. Luke 23:11–12

Because in him, it hath well pleased the Father that all fulness should dwell; and through him, to reconcile all things unto himself, making peace through the blood of his cross, both as to the things that are on earth and the things that are in heaven. Col. 1:19–20

THY KINGDOM COME

Blessed are the clean of heart; for they shall see God.

Then therefore Pilate took Jesus and scourged him. And the soldiers, platting a crown of thorns, put it upon his head; and they put on him a purple garment. And they came to him and said: Hail, king of the Jews. And they gave him blows. Pilate therefore went forth again and said to them: Behold, I bring him forth unto you, that you may know that I find no cause in him. (Jesus therefore came forth, bearing the crown of thorns and the purple garment.) And he saith to them: Behold the Man. John 19:1–5

And Peter said: Man, I know not what thou sayest. And immediately, as he was yet speaking, the cock crew. And the Lord turning looked on Peter. And Peter remembered the word of the Lord, as he had said: Before the cock crow, thou shalt deny me thrice. And Peter, going out, wept bitterly. Luke 22:60–62

THY WILL BE DONE
ON EARTH AS IT IS
IN HEAVEN

Blessed are the merciful; for they shall obtain mercy.

Pilate therefore said to him: Art thou a king then? Jesus answered: Thou sayest that I am a king. For this was I born, and for this came I into the world, that I should give testimony to the truth. Everyone that is of the truth heareth my voice. Pilate saith to him: What is truth? John 18:37–38

Jesus saith to him: I am the way, and the truth, and the life. No man cometh to the Father, but by me. John 14:6

I am come to cast fire on the earth. And what will I, but that it be kindled? And I have a baptism wherewith I am to be baptized. And how am I straitened until it be accomplished. Think ye that I am come to give peace on earth? I tell you, no; but separation. Luke 12:49–51

GIVE US THIS DAY
OUR DAILY BREAD

Blessed are they that hunger and thirst after justice; for they shall have their fill.

Father, if thou wilt, remove this chalice from me; but yet not my will, but thine be done. And there appeared to him an angel from heaven, strengthening him. And being in an agony, he prayed the longer. And his sweat became as drops of blood, trickling down upon the ground. Luke 22:42–44

Afterwards, Jesus knowing that all things were now accomplished, that the scripture might be fulfilled, said: I thirst. John 19:28

And Jesus said to [James and John]: You know not what you ask. Can you drink of the chalice that I drink of or be baptized with the baptism wherewith I am baptized? But they said to him: We can. And Jesus saith to them: You shall indeed drink of the chalice that I drink of; and with the baptism wherewith I am baptized you shall be baptized. Mark 10:38–39

AND FORGIVE US OUR
TRESPASSES AS WE
FORGIVE THOSE
WHO TRESPASS
AGAINST US

Blessed are the meek; for they shall inherit the earth.

Behold, Judas, one of the twelve, came, and with him a great multitude with swords and clubs, sent from the chief priests and the ancients of the people. And he that betrayed him gave them a sign, saying: Whomsoever I shall kiss, that is he. Hold him fast. And forthwith, coming to Jesus, he said: Hail, Rabbi. And he kissed him. And Jesus said to him: Friend, whereto art thou come? Then they came up and laid hands on Jesus and held him. Matt. 26:47–50

And the place of the scripture which [the eunuch] was reading was this: He was led as a sheep to the slaughter; and like a lamb without voice before his shearer, so openeth he not his mouth. In humility his judgment was taken away. His generation who shall declare, for his life shall be taken from the earth? And the eunuch, answering Philip, said: I beseech thee, of whom doth the prophet speak this? Of himself, or of some other man? Then Philip, opening his mouth and beginning at this scripture, preached unto him Jesus. Acts 8:32–35

Blessed are they that mourn; for they shall be comforted.

And there followed him a great multitude of people and of women, who bewailed and lamented him. But Jesus, turning to them, said: Daughters of Jerusalem, weep not over me; but weep for yourselves and for your children... For if in the green wood they do these things, what shall be done in the dry? Luke 23:27–28, 31

Be subject therefore to God. But resist the devil; and he will fly from you. Draw neigh to God; and he will draw neigh to you. Cleanse your hands, ye sinners, and purify your hearts, ye double-minded. Be afflicted and mourn and weep; let your laughter be turned into mourning and your joy into sorrow. Be humbled in the sight of the Lord; and he will exalt you. James 4:7–10

Blessed are the poor spirit; for theirs is the kingdom of heaven.

And they that passed by blasphemed him, wagging their heads, and saying: Vah, thou that destroyest the temple of God and in three days dost rebuild it; save thy own self. If thou be the Son of God, come down from the cross. Matt. 27:39–40

Come to me, all you that labor and are burdened; and I will refresh you. Take up my yoke upon you and learn of me, because I am meek, and humble of heart; and you shall find rest for your souls. For my yoke is sweet and my burden light. Matt. 11:28–30

THE SEVEN WORDS FROM THE CROSS

OUR FATHER WHO ART IN HEAVEN
HALLOWED BE THY NAME

And Jesus cried out with a loud voice and said, "Father, into thy hands I commend my spirit." Luke 23:46

THY KINGDOM COME

And Jesus said to (the thief), "Amen I say to thee, this day thou shalt be with me in paradise." Luke 23:43

THY WILL BE DONE ON EARTH
AS IT IS IN HEAVEN

When Jesus, therefore, saw his mother and the disciple standing by, whom he loved, he said to his mother, "Woman, behold thy son." Then said to the disciple, "Behold, thy mother." And from that hour the disciple took her into his home. John 19:26–27

GIVE US THIS DAY
OUR DAILY BREAD

Jesus, knowing that all things were now accomplished, that the Scripture might be fulfilled, said, "I thirst." John 19:28

AND FORGIVE US OUR TRESPASSES
AS WE FORGIVE THOSE WHO
TRESPASS AGAINST US

And Jesus said, "father, forgive them, for they do not know what they are doing." Luke 23:34

AND LEAD US NOT
INTO TEMPTATION

But about the ninth hour Jesus cried out with a loud voice, saying, "Eli, Eli, lema sabacthani," that is, "My God, my God, why hast thou forsaken me?"[1] Matt. 27:46

BUT DELIVER
US FROM EVIL

Therefore, when Jesus had taken the wine, he said, "It is consummated!" John 19:30

---

1. The beginning of the messianic Psalm 21 (a prayer favored in times of temptation and trial).

MYSTICAL SACRIFICE, THE KENOTIC DIMENSIONS OF THE LORD'S PRAYER

If I have spoken to you earthly things and you believe not; how will you believe, if I speak to you heavenly things? And no man hath ascended into heaven, but he that descended from heaven, the Son of man who is in heaven. And, as Moses lifted up the serpent in the desert, so must the Son of man be lifted up; that whosoever believeth in him may not perish, but have life everlasting. John 3:12–15

THE DESCENT

OUR FATHER WHO ART IN HEAVEN	1. …the lamb which was slain from the beginning of the world. Apoc. 13:8
HALLOWED BE THY NAME THY KINGDOM COME	2. For let this mind be in you, which was also in Christ Jesus, who being in the form of God, thought it not robbery to be equal with God; but emptied himself, taking the form of a servant, being made in the likeness of men, and in habit found as a man. He humbled himself, becoming obedient unto death, even to the death of the cross. For which cause, God also hath exalted him and given him a name which is above all names; that in the name of Jesus every knee should bow, of those that are in heaven, on earth, and under the earth. Phil. 2:5–10
THY WILL BE DONE ON EARTH AS IT IS IN HEAVEN	3. Father, if thou wilt, remove this chalice from me; but yet not my will, but thine be done. Luke 22:42
GIVE US THIS DAY OUR DAILY BREAD	4. I am the living bread which came down from heaven. If any man eat of this bread, he shall live forever; and the bread which I give is my flesh, for the life of the world… except you eat the flesh of the Son of man and drink his blood, you shall not have life in you. John 6:51–52, 54 I am the good shepherd. The good shepherd giveth his life for his sheep. John 10:11
AND FORGIVE US OUR TRESPASSES AS WE FORGIVE THOSE WHO TRESPASS AGAINST US	5. For why did Christ, when as yet we were weak, according to the time, die for the ungodly? For scarce for a just man will one die; yet perhaps for a good man some one would dare to die. But God commendeth his charity towards us; because, when as yet we were sinners according to the time, Christ died for us. Rom. 5:6–9
AND LEAD US NOT INTO TEMPTATION BUT DELIVER US FROM EVIL	6. Him, who knew no sin, he hath made sin for us; that we might be made the justice of God in him. 2 Cor. 5:21 Behold the Lamb of God. Behold him who taketh away the sin of the world. John 1:29

OUR FATHER WHO
ART IN HEAVEN

12. As in Adam all die, so also in Christ all shall be made alive. But everyone in his own order; the first-fruits, Christ; then they who are of Christ, who have believed in his coming. Afterwards the end; when he shall have delivered up the kingdom to God and the Father; when he shall have brought to nought all principality and power and virtue... For he must reign, until he hath put all his enemies under his feet. And, when all things shall be subdued unto him, then the Son also himself shall be subject unto him that put all things under him, that God may be all in all. 1 Cor. 15:20–28

HALLOWED BE
THY NAME
THY KINGDOM COME

11. And (that you may know) what is the exceeding greatness of his power towards us, who believe, according to the operation of the might of his power, which he wrought in Christ, raising him from the dead and setting him on his right hand in the heavenly places, above all principality and power and virtue and dominion and every name that is named, not only in this world, but also in that which is to come. And he hath subjected all things under his feet and hath made him head over all the church, which is his body and the fulness of him who is filled all in all. Eph. 1:19–23

THY WILL BE DONE
ON EARTH AS IT IS
IN HEAVEN

10. Can you drink the chalice that I shall drink? They say to him: We can. He saith to them: My chalice indeed you shall drink... Matt. 20:22–23
...with Christ I am nailed to the cross. And I live, now not I; but Christ liveth in me. Gal. 2:19–20

GIVE US THIS DAY
OUR DAILY BREAD

9. Amen, amen, I say to you, unless the grain of wheat falling into the ground die, itself remaineth alone. But if it die, it bringeth forth much fruit. He that loveth his life shall lose it; and he that hateth his life in this world keepeth it unto life eternal. John 12:24–25
This is my commandment, that you love one another, as I have loved you. Greater love than this no man hath, that a man lay down his life for his friends. John 15:12–13

AND FORGIVE US OUR
TRESPASSES AS WE
FORGIVE THOSE
WHO TRESPASS
AGAINST US

8. He must increase; but I must decrease. John 3:30
For all things are for your sakes; that the grace, abounding through many, may abound in thanksgiving unto the glory of God. For which cause we faint not; but though the outward man is corrupted, yet the inward man is renewed day by day. 2 Cor. 4:15–16

AND LEAD US NOT
INTO TEMPTATION
BUT DELIVER
US FROM EVIL

7. And if you invoke as Father him who, without respect of persons, judgeth according to every one's work; converse in fear during the time of your sojourning here; knowing that you were not redeemed with corruptible things... but with the precious blood of Christ, as of a lamb unspotted and undefiled, foreknown indeed before the foundation of the world, but manifested in the last times for you. 1 Pet. 1:17–20

THE LIFE-GIVING CROSS

ART IN HEAVEN
HALLOWED BE
THY NAME

And he shewed me a river of water of life [the Holy Spirit], clear as crystal, proceeding from the throne of God [the Father] and of the lamb [the Son]… and on both sides of the river was the tree of life…and the leaves of the tree were for the healing of the nations. And there shall be no curse any more… And they shall see his face; and his name shall be on their foreheads. Apoc. 22:1–4

For Jesus is not entered into the Holies made with hands, the patterns of the true; but into Heaven itself, that he may appear now in the presence of God for us. Nor yet that he should offer himself often, as the high priest entereth into the Holies every year with the blood of others; for then he ought to have suffered from the beginning of the world. But now once, at the end of ages, he hath appeared for the destruction of sin by the sacrifice of himself. Heb. 9:24–26

THY KINGDOM COME

And Pilate wrote a title also; and he put it upon the cross. And the writing was: Jesus of Nazareth, the King of the Jews. John 19:19

But we speak the wisdom of God in a mystery, a wisdom which is hidden, which God ordained before the world, unto our glory; which none of the princes of this world knew. For, if they had known it, they would never have crucified the Lord of glory. 1 Cor. 2:7–8

THY WILL BE DONE ON EARTH AS IT IS IN HEAVEN

Because in him, it hath well pleased the Father that all fulness should dwell; and through him, to reconcile all things unto himself, making peace through the blood of his cross, both as to the things that are on earth and the things that are in heaven. Col. 1:19–20

GIVE US THIS DAY OUR DAILY BREAD

If any man will come after me, let him deny himself and take up his cross daily and follow me. Mark 9:23

AND FORGIVE US OUR TRESPASSES AS WE FORGIVE THOSE WHO TRESPASS AGAINST US

For he is our peace, who hath made both [those near and those afar off] one, and breaking down the middle wall of partition, the enmities in his flesh, making void the law of commandments contained in decrees, that he might make the two in himself into one new man, making peace, and might reconcile both to God in one body by the cross, killing the enmities in himself. Eph. 2:14–16

AND LEAD US NOT INTO TEMPTATION

But we preach Christ crucified; unto the Jews indeed a stumbling-block, and unto the Gentiles foolishness; but unto them that are called, both Jews and Greeks, Christ, the power of God and the wisdom of God. For the foolishness of God is wiser than men; and the weakness of God is stronger than men. 1 Cor. 1:23–25

BUT DELIVER US FROM EVIL

For the word of the cross, to them indeed that perish, is foolishness; but to them that are saved, that is, to us, it is the power of God. 1 Cor. 1:18

And the Lord God brought forth of the ground all manner of trees… the tree of life also in the midst of paradise; and the tree of knowledge of good and evil. Gen. 2:9

Ye offspring of vipers, who hath shewed you to flee from the wrath to come? Bring forth therefore fruits worthy of penance… For now the axe is laid to the root of the trees. Every tree therefore that bringeth not forth good fruit shall be cut down and cast into the fire. Luke 3:7–9

DYNAMIS~THE FIVE SACRED WOUNDS,
THE POWER OF THE LIFE-GIVING CROSS

For, although he was crucified through weakness,
yet he liveth by the power (δυνάμεως, dynamis) *of God.* 2 Corinthians 13:4

OUR FATHER WHO
ART IN HEAVEN
HALLOWED BE
THY NAME
THY KINGDOM COME

The pierced side: the only wound by which Christ did not suffer. It both verified His death—in the giving up of the spirit to the Father—and proved the reality of His resurrection—in the out-pouring of blood and water—by showing that he was truly dead; and these are the three witnesses on earth spoken of by John. The power to worship the Father: "Father, the hour is come. Glorify thy Son, that thy Son may glorify thee, as thou hast given him power over all flesh, that he may give eternal life to all whom thou hast given him. Now this is eternal life: That they may know thee, the only true God, and Jesus Christ, whom thou hast sent" (John 17:1–3); and this power is conveyed in the birth of the Church (the Kingdom), seen as issuing from His side in the water (Baptism) and blood (the Eucharist) while he 'slept' in death on the cross, just as Eve was drawn from Adam's side while he slept in paradise.

THY WILL BE DONE
ON EARTH AS IT IS
IN HEAVEN
GIVE US THIS DAY
OUR DAILY BREAD

The nail-mark in the right hand: the power to both 'sow' the will of God and 'reap' the Bread of Life.

AND FORGIVE US OUR
TRESPASSES AS WE
FORGIVE THOSE
WHO TRESPASS
AGAINST US

The nail-mark in the left hand: the power to reconcile and draw His beloved friends to His heart.

AND LEAD US NOT
INTO TEMPTATION

The nail-mark in the right foot : the power to avoid evil.

BUT DELIVER
US FROM EVIL

The nail-mark in the left foot: the power to resist evil.

THE SONG OF THE PASCHAL LAMB

PSALM 21

And when the sixth hour was come, there was darkness over the whole earth until the ninth hour. And at the ninth hour, Jesus cried out with a loud voice, saying: Eloi, Eloi, lamma sabacthani? Which is, being interpreted, My God, my God, why hast thou forsaken me? Mark 15:33–34

BUT DELIVER US FROM EVIL

O God, my God, attend to me; why hast Thou forsaken me?
Far from my salvation are the words of my transgressions.
My God, I will cry by day, and wilt Thou not hearken?
and by night, and it shall not be unto folly for me.
But as for Thee, Thou dwellest in the sanctuary, O Praise of Israel.
In Thee have our fathers hoped; they hoped, and Thou didst deliver them.
Unto Thee they cried, and were saved; in Thee they hoped,
and were not brought to shame.

AND LEAD US NOT INTO TEMPTATION

But as for me, I am a worm, and not a man,
a reproach of men, and the outcast of the people.
All that look upon me have laughed me to scorn;
they have spoken with their lips and have wagged their heads:
He hoped in the Lord; let Him deliver him,
let Him save him, for He desireth him.
For Thou art He that drewest me forth from the womb;
my hope from the breasts of my mother.
On Thee was I cast from the womb;
from my mother's womb, Thou art my God.
Depart not from me, for tribulation is nigh,
for there is none to help me.

AND FORGIVE US OUR TRESPASSES AS WE FORGIVE THOSE WHO TRESPASS AGAINST US

Many bullocks have encircled me, fat bulls have surrounded me.
They have opened their mouth against me,
as might a lion ravenous and roaring.
I have been poured out like water,
and scattered are all my bones; my heart is become like wax
melting in the midst of my bowels.
My strength is dried up like a potsherd,
and my tongue hath cleaved to my throat,
and into the dust of death hast Thou brought me down.
For many dogs have encircled me,
the congregation of evildoers hath surrounded me;
they have pierced my hands and my feet.
They have numbered all my bones,
and they themselves have looked and stared upon me.
They have parted my garments amongst themselves,
and for my vesture have they cast lots.

GIVE US THIS DAY OUR DAILY BREAD	But Thou, O Lord, remove not Thy help far from me; attend unto mine aid. Rescue my soul from the sword, even this only-begotten one of mine from the hand of the dog. Save me from the mouth of the lion, and my lowliness from the horns of the unicorns.
THY WILL BE DONE ON EARTH AS IT IS IN HEAVEN	I will declare Thy name unto my brethren, in the midst of the church will I hymn Thee. Ye that fear the Lord, praise Him; all ye that are of the seed of Jacob, glorify Him; let all fear Him that are of the seed of Israel. For He hath not set at naught nor abhorred the supplications of the pauper, nor hath He turned His face from me; and when I cried unto Him, He hearkened unto me.
THY KINGDOM COME	From Thee is my praise; in the great church will I confess Thee; my vows will I pay before them that fear Thee. The poor shall eat and be filled, and they that seek the Lord shall praise Him; their hearts shall live for ever and ever. All the ends of the earth shall remember and shall turn unto the Lord, and all the kindreds of the nations shall worship before Him. For the kingdom is the Lord's and He Himself is sovereign of the nations.
OUR FATHER WHO ART IN HEAVEN HALLOWED BE THY NAME	All they that be fat upon the earth have eaten and worshipped; all they that go down into the earth shall fall down before Him. Yea, my soul liveth for Him, and my seed shall serve Him. The generation that cometh shall be told of the Lord, and they shall proclaim His righteousness to a people that shall be born, which the Lord hath made.

A THRENODY OF PRAISE

EXCERPTS FROM 'THE LAMENTATIONS' ON HOLY AND GREAT SATURDAY AT MATINS

Because Christ also died once for our sins, the just for the unjust: that he might offer us to God, being put to death indeed in the flesh, but enlivened in the spirit, in which also coming he preached to those spirits that were in prison: which had been some time incredulous, when they waited for the patience of God in the days of Noe, when the ark was a building: wherein a few, that is, eight souls, were saved by water. Whereunto baptism, being of the like form, now saveth you also: not the putting away of the filth of the flesh, but, the examination of a good conscience towards God by the resurrection of Jesus Christ. Who is on the right hand of God, swallowing down death that we might be made heirs of life everlasting.
1 Peter 3:18–22

Come, let us now sing sacred dirges to our Christ Who dieth, as once the myrrh-bearing women did sing to Him, that with them we might all hear the word: 'Rejoice!' The Lamentations, Second Stasis

Mine eyes have grown dim with waiting for Thine oracle; they say: when wilt thou comfort me? Psalm 118:82[1]

OUR FATHER WHO
ART IN HEAVEN

All the seraphim shuddered when they saw Thee, O my Savior,
Who above art with the Father insep'rable,
though Thou liest dead within the earth below.
Let the proud be put to shame, for unjustly have they transgressed against me;
but as for me I will ponder on Thy commandments. Psalm 118:78

HALLOWED BE
THY NAME

Thou that of Thine own will didst descend 'neath the earth,
and didst quicken mortal men that had died of old,
in the Father's glory Thou didst lead them forth.
Thy statutes were my songs in the place of my sojourning. Psalm 118:54

THY KINGDOM COME

Unto all creation wast Thou made known, O Christ,
as the true King of the firmament and the earth,
even though Thou wast enclosed in a small grave.
On Thy statutes will I meditate, I will not forget Thy words. Psalm 118:16

THY WILL BE DONE
ON EARTH AS IT IS
IN HEAVEN

Down to dreaded Hades, Thou descendest, O Word,
in obedience to Thy Father's will, O Lord,
and didst raise up all the race of mortal men.
I made ready, and I was not troubled:
that I might keep Thy commandments. Psalm 118:60

GIVE US THIS DAY
OUR DAILY BREAD

Even as the seed of wheat is hid in the bowels of the earth,
and thereby bringeth forth ears of grain,
thus hast Thou raised Adam's mortal sons, O Word.
I have chosen the way of truth,
and Thy judgments have I not forgotten. Psalm 118:30

---

1. This and the following passages are from *The Lamentations of Matins of Holy Saturday,* trans. Holy Transfiguration Monastery.

AND FORGIVE US OUR TRESPASSES AS WE FORGIVE THOSE WHO TRESPASS AGAINST US	Stretched upon the blest Tree, Thou, O Jesus, didst make all forgive those who trespass against us men one, and when Thy life-giving side was pierced, Thou didst shed forgiveness on the race of man. *And I walked in spaciousness, for after Thy commandments have I sought.* Psalm 118:45
AND LEAD US NOT INTO TEMPTATION	I adore Thy Passion, Thine entombing I praise, and I magnify Thy might, O Thou Friend of man; from corruptive passions have they set me free. *This hath comforted me in my humiliation, for Thine oracle hath quickened me.* Psalm 118:50
BUT DELIVER US FROM EVIL	At Thy burial, Thou, O Christ, didst shatter Hadës kingdom. Wherefore, by Thy death, hast Thou thus put death to death, to redeem out of corruption those of earth. *How many are the days of Thy servant? When wilt thou execute judgment for me on them that persecute me?* Psalm 118:84

COMMENTARY

Again the octave.[1] Here the Lord's Prayer becomes eightfold and resurrectional in honor of the eight souls 'saved by water' as they blindly navigate the Flood. Here the eightfold 'seeing' verses of Psalm 118[2] that are ebb to the flow of this 'lamentation' hymn sharpen our eyes and direct our gaze into the depths of the law of the Lord, eyes straining to glimpse the profound deeds of our vanished Christ in Hades. And the hymn: cast like a net from horizon to horizon into the dark night of the tomb of Christ and every Christian, it brings up word of the Life-giving Word where before there had been only death. Like a subtle aurora—and where two or three or eight are gathered—the Resurrection has gathered nigh.

---

1. Cf. the commentary after 'A Confluence of the Virtues'.

2. Psalm 118 is mainly composed of 'eights'. There are eight verses to every stanza, and a letter of the Hebrew alphabet is repeated at the beginning of each line in every stanza cluster. The word for law—Torah—has seven synonyms; these eight occur at least once on nearly every line of this one hundred and seventy-six verse psalm.

THE RESURRECTION

ODES FROM THE PASCHAL CANON OF ST. JOHN OF DAMASCUS[1]

OUR FATHER WHO
ART IN HEAVEN
HALLOWED BE
THY NAME

Christ appeared as a 'male' who opened the virgin womb.
As our food he is called 'lamb';
'unblemished', as our Passover without stain;
and 'perfect', for he is true God.
Ode 4

O my Savior, the living Victim unsuitable for sacrifice,
as God offering yourself willingly to the Father,
you raised with yourself all Adam's race,
in rising from the tomb.
Ode 6

For we are buried together with him by baptism into death; that, as Christ is risen from the dead by the glory of the Father, so we also may walk in newness of life. For, if we have been planted together in the likeness of his death, we shall be also in the likeness of his resurrection. Rom. 6:4–5

THY KINGDOM COME

Yesterday I was buried with you O Christ,
today I rise with you as you arise.
Yesterday I was crucified with you;
glorify me with you, Savior, in your Kingdom.
Ode 3

That I may know him, and the power of his resurrection, and the fellowship of his sufferings, being made conformable to his death, if by any means I may attain to the resurrection which is from the dead. Not as though I has already attained, or were already perfect; but I follow after, if I may by any means apprehend, wherein I am also apprehended by Christ Jesus. Brethren, I do not count myself to have apprehended. But one thing I do: forgetting the things that are behind, and stretching forth myself to those that are before, I press towards the mark, to the prize of the supernal vocation of God in Christ Jesus. Phil. 3:10–14

THY WILL BE DONE
ON EARTH AS IT IS
IN HEAVEN

The day of Resurrection, let us be radiant, O peoples!
Pascha, the Lord's Pascha;
for Christ God has brought us over from death to life,
and from earth to heaven,
as we sing the triumphal song.
Ode 1

Therefore, if you be risen with Christ, seek the things that are above; where Christ is sitting at the right hand of God: Mind the things that are above, not the things that are upon the earth. For you are dead; and your life is hid with Christ in God. When Christ shall appear, who is your life, then you also shall appear with him in glory. Col. 3:1–4

---

1. Archimandrite Ephrem Lash translation, www.anastasis.org.uk/pascha.htm.

GIVE US THIS DAY OUR DAILY BREAD	*As a yearling lamb, for us a crown of goodness,* *the Blessed One, the cleansing Passover* *has been willingly sacrificed for all;* *and from the tomb the fair Sun of justice* *has shone for us again.* Ode 4

Come let us drink a new drink,
not one marvellously brought forth from a barren rock,
but a Source of incorruption,
which pours out from the tomb of Christ,
in whom we are established.
Ode 3

Blessed are they that are called to the marriage supper of the Lamb. And he saith to me: These words of God are true. Apoc. 19:9

AND FORGIVE US OUR TRESPASSES AS WE FORGIVE THOSE WHO TRESPASS AGAINST US	*Lift your eyes around you, Sion, and see.* *For behold, like beacons shedding light divine* *your children have come to you,* *from West and North, from the Sea and from the East,* *blessing Christ in you to all the ages.* Ode 8

But all things that are reproved, are made manifest by the light; for all that is made manifest is light. Wherefore he saith: Rise thou that sleepest, and arise from the dead: and Christ shall enlighten thee. Eph. 5:13–14

AND LEAD US NOT INTO TEMPTATION	*Let us purify our senses,* *and in the unapproachable light of the resurrection* *we shall see Christ shining forth,* *and we shall clearly hear him saying 'Rejoice!',* *as we sing the triumphal song.* Ode 1

Then he saith to Thomas: Put in thy finger hither and see my hands; and bring hither thy hand and put it into my side; and be not faithless, but believing. Thomas answered and said to him: My Lord and my God. John 20:27–28
For, if the dead rise not again, neither is Christ risen again. And, if Christ be not risen again, your faith is vain; for you are yet in your sins. Then they also that are fallen asleep in Christ are perished.. If in this life only we have hope in Christ, we are of all men most miserable. But now Christ is risen from the dead, the first-fruits of them that sleep. For by a man came death; and by a man the resurrection of the dead. And, as in Adam all die, so also in Christ all shall be made alive. 1 Cor. 15:16–22

You went down to the deepest parts of the earth,
and you shattered the everlasting bars
of those that those that were fettered, O Christ.
And on the third day, like Jonas from the whale,
you arose from the tomb.
Ode 6

We feast death's slaughter, the overthrow of Hell,
the first fruits of a new eternal life:
and dancing we hymn the cause:
the only blessed and most glorious God of our Fathers.
Ode 7

Behold, I tell you a mystery. We shall all indeed rise again: but we shall not all be changed. In a moment, in the twinkling of an eye, at the last trumpet: for the trumpet shall sound, and the dead shall rise again incorruptible: and we shall be changed. For this corruptible must put on incorruption; and this mortal must put on immortality. And when this mortal hath put on immortality, then shall come to pass the saying that is written: Death is swallowed up in victory. O death, where is thy victory? O death, where is thy sting? Now the sting of death is sin: and the power of sin is the law. But thanks be to God, who hath given us the victory through our Lord Jesus Christ. 1 Cor. 15:51–57

THE PASCHAL HOMILY OF ST. JOHN CHRYSOSTOM

OUR FATHER WHO
ART IN HEAVEN
HALLOWED BE
THY NAME

If any man be devout and loveth God, let him enjoy this fair and radiant triumphal feast! If any man be a wise servant, let him rejoicing enter into the joy of his Lord.

THY KINGDOM COME

If any have labored long in fasting, let him now receive his recompense. If any have wrought from the first hour, let him today receive his just reward. If any have come at the third hour, let him with thankfulness keep the feast. If any have arrived at the sixth hour, let him have no misgivings; Because he shall in nowise be deprived therefore. If any have delayed until the ninth hour, let him draw near, fearing nothing. And if any have tarried even until the eleventh hour, let him, also, be not alarmed at his tardiness. For the Lord, who is jealous of his honor, will accept the last even as the first. He giveth rest unto him who cometh at the eleventh hour, even as unto him who hath wrought from the first hour.

THY WILL BE DONE
ON EARTH AS IT IS
IN HEAVEN

And He showeth mercy upon the last, and careth for the first; And to the one He giveth, and upon the other He bestoweth gifts. And He both accepteth the deeds, and welcometh the intention, and honoreth the acts and praises the offering.

GIVE US THIS DAY
OUR DAILY BREAD

Wherefore, enter ye all into the joy of your Lord; Receive your reward, both the first, and likewise the second. You rich and poor together, hold high festival! You sober and you heedless, honor the day! Rejoice today, both you who have fasted and you who have disregarded the fast. The table is full-laden; feast ye all sumptuously. The calf is fatted; let no one go hungry away. Enjoy ye all the feast of faith: receive ye all the riches of loving-kindness.

AND FORGIVE US OUR
TRESPASSES AS WE
FORGIVE THOSE
WHO TRESPASS
AGAINST US
AND LEAD US NOT
INTO TEMPTATION

Let no one bewail his poverty, for the universal Kingdom has been revealed. Let no one weep for his iniquities, for pardon has shown forth from the grave. Let no one fear death, for the Savior's death has set us free. He that was held prisoner of it has annihilated it.

BUT DELIVER
US FROM EVIL

By descending into Hell, He made Hell captive. He embittered it when it tasted of His flesh. And Isaiah, foretelling this, did cry: Hell, said he, was embittered when it encountered Thee in the lower regions. It was embittered, for it was abolished. It was embittered, for it was mocked. It was embittered, for it was slain. It was embittered, for it was overthrown. It was embittered, for it was fettered in chains. It took a body, and met God face to face. It took earth, and encountered Heaven. It took that which was seen, and fell upon the unseen. O Death, where is thy sting? O Hell, where is thy victory? Christ is risen, and thou art overthrown! Christ is risen, and the demons are fallen!

OUR FATHER WHO ART IN HEAVEN	Christ is risen, and the angels rejoice! Christ is risen, and life reigns!
HALLOWED BE THY NAME	Christ is risen, and not one dead remains in the grave. For Christ, being risen from the dead, is become the first-fruits of those who have fallen asleep. To Him be glory and dominion unto ages of ages. Amen.

FAITH IN THE RESURRECTION

JOHN 20: 19–31

THY KINGDOM COME	Now when it was late that same day, the first of the week, and the doors were shut, where the disciples were gathered together, for fear of the Jews, Jesus came and stood in the midst, and said to them: Peace be to you. And when he had said this, he shewed them his hands and his side. The disciples therefore were glad, when they saw the Lord.
THY WILL BE DONE ON EARTH AS IT IS IN HEAVEN	He said therefore to them again: Peace be to you. As the Father hath sent me, I also send you.
GIVE US THIS DAY OUR SUPERSUBSTANTIAL BREAD	When he had said this, he breathed on them; and he said to them: Receive ye the Holy Spirit.
AND FORGIVE US OUR TRESPASSES AS WE FORGIVE THOSE WHO TRESPASS AGAINST US	Whose sins you shall forgive, they are forgiven them; and whose sins you shall retain, they are retained.
AND LEAD US NOT INTO TEMPTATION	Now Thomas, one of the twelve, who is called Didymus, was not with them when Jesus came. The other disciples therefore said to him: We have seen the Lord. But he said to them: Except I shall see in his hands the print of the nails, and put my finger into the place of the nails, and put my hand into his side, I will not believe.
BUT DELIVER US FROM EVIL	And after eight days again his disciples were within, and Thomas with them. Jesus cometh, the doors being shut, and stood in the midst, and said: Peace be to you. Then he saith to Thomas: Put in thy finger hither, and see my hands; and bring hither thy hand, and put it into my side; and be not faithless, but believing.
OUR FATHER WHO ART IN HEAVEN	Thomas answered, and said to him: My Lord, and my God.
HALLOWED BE THY NAME	Jesus saith to him: Because thou hast seen me, Thomas, thou hast believed: blessed are they that have not seen, and have believed. Many other signs also did Jesus in the sight of his disciples, which are not written in this book. But these are written, that you may believe that Jesus is the Christ, the Son of God: and that believing, you may have life in his name.

WHEN THE MORNING WAS COME

JOHN'S SEVEN WORDS OF THE RESURRECTED CHRIST

OUR FATHER WHO
ART IN HEAVEN
HALLOWED BE
THY NAME

But Mary stood at the sepulcher without, weeping. Now as she was weeping, she stooped down, and looked into the sepulcher, And she saw two angels in white, sitting, one at the head, and one at the feet, where the body of Jesus had been laid. They say to her: Woman, why weepest thou? She saith to them: Because they have taken away my Lord; and I know not where they have laid him. When she had thus said, she turned herself back, and saw Jesus standing; and she knew not that it was Jesus. Jesus saith to her: Woman, why weepest thou? whom seekest thou? She, thinking it was the gardener, saith to him: Sir, if thou hast taken him hence, tell me where thou hast laid him, and I will take him away. Jesus saith to her: Mary. She turning, saith to him: Rabboni (which is to say, Master). Jesus saith to her: Do not touch me, for I am not yet ascended to my Father. But go to my brethren, and say to them: I ascend to my Father and to your Father, to my God and your God. John 20:11–17

THY KINGDOM COME

Peter turning about, saw that disciple whom Jesus loved following, who also leaned on his breast at supper, and said: Lord, who is he that shall betray thee? Him therefore when Peter had seen, he saith to Jesus: Lord, and what shall this man do? Jesus saith to him: So I will have him to remain till I come, what is it to thee? follow thou me. This saying therefore went abroad among the brethren, that that disciple should not die. And Jesus did not say to him: He should not die; but, So I will have him to remain till I come, what is it to thee? John 21:20–23

THY WILL BE DONE
ON EARTH AS IT IS
IN HEAVEN

When therefore they had dined, Jesus saith to Simon Peter: Simon son of John, lovest thou me more than these? He saith to him: Yea, Lord, thou knowest that I love thee. He saith to him: Feed my lambs. He saith to him again: Simon, son of John, lovest thou me? He saith to him: Yea, Lord, thou knowest that I love thee. He saith to him: Feed my lambs. He said to him the third time: Simon, son of John, lovest thou me? Peter was grieved, because he had said to him the third time: Lovest thou me? And he said to him: Lord, thou knowest all things: thou knowest that I love thee.[1] He said to him: Feed my sheep.[2] John 21:15–17

GIVE US THIS DAY
OUR DAILY BREAD

But when the morning was come, Jesus stood on the shore: yet the disciples knew not that it was Jesus. Jesus therefore said to them: Children, have you any meat? They answered him: No. He saith to them: Cast the net on the right side of the ship, and you shall find. They cast therefore; and now they were not able to draw it, for the multitude of fishes. That disciple therefore whom Jesus loved, said to Peter: It is the Lord. Simon Peter, when he heard that it was the Lord, girt his coat about him, (for he was naked,) and cast himself into the sea. But the other disciples came in the ship, (for they were not far from the land, but as it were two hundred cubits,) dragging the net with fishes. As soon then as they came to land, they saw hot coals lying, and a fish laid thereon, and bread. Jesus saith to them: Bring hither of the fishes which you have now caught. Simon

---

1. Love of God.
2. Love of neighbor.

Peter went up, and drew the net to land, full of great fishes, one hundred and fifty-three. And although there were so many, the net was not broken. Jesus saith to them: Come, and dine. And none of them who were at meat, durst ask him: Who art thou? knowing that it was the Lord. And Jesus cometh and taketh bread, and giveth them, and fish in like manner. John 21:4–13

AND FORGIVE US OUR TRESPASSES AS WE FORGIVE THOSE WHO TRESPASS AGAINST US

Now when it was late that same day, the first of the week, and the doors were shut, where the disciples were gathered together, for fear of the Jews, Jesus came and stood in the midst, and said to them: Peace be to you. And when he had said this, he shewed them his hands and his side. The disciples therefore were glad, when they saw the Lord. He said therefore to them again: Peace be to you. As the Father hath sent me, I also send you. When he had said this, he breathed on them; and he said to them: Receive ye the Holy Spirit. Whose sins you shall forgive, they are forgiven them; and whose sins you shall retain, they are retained. John 20:19–23

AND LEAD US NOT INTO TEMPTATION

Now Thomas, one of the twelve, who is called Didymus, was not with them when Jesus came. The other disciples therefore said to him: We have seen the Lord. But he said to them: Except I shall see in his hands the print of the nails, and put my finger into the place of the nails, and put my hand into his side, I will not believe. And after eight days again his disciples were within, and Thomas with them. Jesus cometh, the doors being shut, and stood in the midst, and said: Peace be to you. Then he saith to Thomas: Put in thy finger hither, and see my hands; and bring hither thy hand, and put it into my side; and be not faithless, but believing. Thomas answered, and said to him: My Lord, and my God. Jesus saith to him: Because thou hast seen me, Thomas, thou hast believed: blessed are they that have not seen, and have believed. John 20:24–29

BUT DELIVER US FROM EVIL

Amen, amen I say to thee, when thou wast younger, thou didst gird thyself, and didst walk where thou wouldst. But when thou shalt be old, thou shalt stretch forth thy hands, and another shall gird thee, and lead thee whither thou wouldst not. And this he said, signifying by what death he should glorify God. And when he had said this, he saith to him: Follow me. John 21:18–19

SON OF GOD, SON OF MAN

THE THEANDRIC DIMENSIONS OF THE LORD'S PRAYER

OUR FATHER WHO ART IN HEAVEN	For he received from God the Father honor and glory, this voice coming down to him from the excellent glory: This is my beloved Son, in whom I am well pleased. Hear ye him. 2 Pet. 1:17

HALLOWED BE THY NAME
He that believeth in the Son of God hath the testimony of God in himself… And this is the testimony: that God hath given us eternal life. And this life is in his Son. He that hath the Son hath life; he that hath not the Son hath not life. These things I write to you that you may know that you have eternal life; you who believe in the name of the Son of God. 1 John 5:10–13

THY KINGDOM COME
Behold what manner of charity the Father hath bestowed upon us, that we should be called and should be the sons of God… Dearly beloved, we are now the sons of God; and it hath not yet appeared what we shall be. We know that when he shall appear we shall be like to him; because we shall see him as he is. 1 John 3:1–2
As all things of his divine power, which appertain to life and godliness, are given us through the knowledge of him who hath called us by his own proper glory and virtue; by whom he hath given us most great and precious promises, that by these you may be made partakers of the divine nature. 2 Pet. 1:3–4

THY WILL BE DONE ON EARTH AS IT IS IN HEAVEN
And we know that to them that love God all things work together unto good; to such as, according to his purpose, are called to be saints. For whom he foreknew, he also predestinated to be made conformable to the image (εἰκόνος—the icon) of his Son. Rom. 8:28–29

GIVE US THIS DAY OUR DAILY BREAD
Amen, amen, I say to you; except you eat the flesh of the Son of man and drink his blood, you shall not have life in you. He that eateth my flesh and drinketh my blood hath everlasting life; and I will raise him up in the last day. For my flesh is meat indeed; and my blood is drink indeed. He that eateth my flesh and drinketh my blood abideth in me and I in him. As the living Father hath sent me and I live by the Father; so he that eateth me, the same also shall live by me. This is the bread that came down from heaven. Not as your fathers did eat manna and are dead. He that eateth this bread shall live for ever. John 6:54–59

IN THE IMAGE AND LIKENESS OF GOD

Let us make man to our image and likeness… Genesis 1:26

GIVE US THIS DAY OUR DAILY BREAD
Of every tree of paradise thou shalt eat: but of the tree of knowledge of good and evil, thou shalt not eat. For in what day soever thou shalt eat of it, thou shalt die the death.[1] Gen. 2:16–17

---

1. "For that tree was, to my mind, the tree of contemplation, which only those could enter into without harm whose spiritual preparation had reached sufficient perfection. On the other hand, that tree could only be a source of misfortune for souls as yet too coarse, endowed with too bestial an appetite, just as solid food is harmful to babies who still need milk." Gregory Nazianzen, *Oration 45*, For Easter, 8 (*Patrologia Graeca* 36, 850).

AND FORGIVE US OUR TRESPASSES AS WE FORGIVE THOSE WHO TRESPASS AGAINST US	And Adam said: The woman, whom thou gavest to be my companion, gave me of the tree, and I did eat... And she: The serpent deceived me, and I did eat. Gen. 3:12–13
AND LEAD US NOT INTO TEMPTATION	And the serpent said to the woman: No, you shall not die the death. For God doth know that in what day soever you shall eat thereof, your eyes shall be opened: and you shall be as Gods, knowing good and evil. Gen. 3:4–5
BUT DELIVER US FROM EVIL	For the law of the spirit of life, in Christ Jesus, hath delivered me from the law of sin and of death... God, sending his own Son in the likeness of sinful flesh and of sin, hath condemned sin in the flesh... For the wisdom of the flesh is death; but the wisdom of the spirit is life and peace... For if you live according to the flesh, you shall die; but if by the Spirit you mortifythe deeds of the flesh, you shall live; for whosoever are led by the Spirit of God, they are the sons of God. Rom. 8:2–3, 6, 13–14

In these days (God) hath spoken to us by his Son, whom he hath appointed heir of all things, by whom also he made the world. Who, being the brightness of his glory and the figure of his substance and upholding all things by the word of his power, making purgation of sins, sitteth on the right hand of the majesty on high. Heb. 1:2–3

OUR FATHER WHO ART IN HEAVEN HALLOWED BE THY NAME THY KINGDOM COME THY WILL BE DONE ON EARTH AS IT IS IN HEAVEN	The call to an increasing similarity, the perfecting of the image.
GIVE US THIS DAY OUR DAILY BREAD	Our share, God's image and likeness in the created—Son of God and Son of Man
AND FORGIVE US OUR TRESPASSES AS WE FORGIVE THOSE WHO TRESPASS AGAINST US AND LEAD US NOT INTO TEMPTATION BUT DELIVER US FROM EVIL	The antidotes to increasing dissimilarity.

THE ASCENSION

OUR FATHER WHO
ART IN HEAVEN
HALLOWED BE
THY NAME

In that day, you shall ask in my name; and I say not to you that I will ask the Father for you, for the Father himself loveth you, because you have loved me and have believed that I came out from God. I came forth from the Father and am come into the world; again I leave the world and I go to the Father. John 16:26–8

THY KINGDOM COME

They therefore who were come together asked him, saying: Lord, wilt thou at this time restore again the kingdom of Israel? But he said to them: It is not for you to know the times or moments, which the Father hath put in his own power; but you shall receive the power of the Holy Spirit coming upon you, and you shall be witnesses unto me in Jerusalem, and in all Judea and Samaria, and even to the uttermost part of the earth. And when he had said these things, while they looked on, he was raised up; and a cloud received him out of their sight. And while they were beholding him going up to heaven, behold, two men stood by them in white garments. Who also said: Ye men of Galilee, why stand you looking up to heaven? This Jesus who is taken up from you into heaven shall so come as you have seen him going into heaven. Acts 1:6–11

THY WILL BE DONE
ON EARTH AS IT IS
IN HEAVEN

But these things I have told you, that when the hour shall come you may remember that I told you of them. But I told you not these things from the beginning, because I was with you. And now I go to him that sent me, and none of you asketh me: Whither goest thou? But because I have spoken these things to you, sorrow hath filled your heart. But I tell you the truth; it is expedient to you that I go. For if I go not, the Paraclete will not come to you; but if I go, I will send him to you. And, when he is come, he will convince the world of sin and of justice and of judgment. Of sin, because they believed not in me. And of justice; because I go to the Father; and you shall see me no longer. And of judgment; because the prince of this world is already judged. John 16:4–11

GIVE US THIS DAY
OUR DAILY BREAD

Many therefore of his disciples, hearing it, said: This saying1 is hard; and who can hear it? But Jesus, knowing in himself that his disciples murmured at this, said to them: Doth this scandalize you? If then you shall see the Son of man ascend up where he was before? It is the spirit that quickeneth; the flesh profiteth nothing. The words that I have spoken to you are spirit and life. John 6:61–64

AND FORGIVE US OUR
TRESPASSES AS WE
FORGIVE THOSE
WHO TRESPASS
AGAINST US

Jesus saith to her: Mary. She turning saith to him: Rabboni (which is to say, Master). Jesus saith to her: Do not touch me; for I am not yet ascended to my Father. But go to my brethren and say to them: I ascend to my Father and to your Father, to my God and to your God. John 20:16–17

---

1. "For my flesh is meat indeed; and my blood is drink indeed. He that eateth my flesh and drinketh my blood abideth in me; and I in him. As the living Father hath sent me and I live by the Father; so he that eateth me, the same also shall live by me" (John 6:56–58).

AND LEAD US NOT INTO TEMPTATION	Peace I leave with you; my peace I give unto you. Let not your heart be troubled; nor let it be afraid. You have heard that I said to you: I go away, and I come unto you. If you loved me, you would indeed be glad, because I go to the Father; for the Father is greater than I. And now I have told you before it come to pass; that, when it shall come to pass, you may believe. John 14:27–29
BUT DELIVER US FROM EVIL	And no man hath ascended into heaven, but he that descended from heaven, the Son of man who is in heaven. And, as Moses lifted up the serpent in the desert, so must the Son of man be lifted up; that whosoever believeth in him may not perish, but may have life everlasting. John 3:13–15

INVOCATION TO THE HOLY SPIRIT

THY KINGDOM COME	Come, Holy Ghost, Creator blest, and in our hearts take up Thy rest; come with Thy grace and heav'nly aid, To fill the hearts which Thou hast made.
THY WILL BE DONE ON EARTH AS IT IS IN HEAVEN	O Comforter, to Thee we cry, Thou heav'nly gift of God most high, Thou Fount of life, and Fire of love, and sweet anointing from above.
	O Finger of the hand divine, the sevenfold gifts of grace are thine; true promise of the Father thou, who dost the tongue with power endow.
GIVE US THIS DAY OUR DAILY BREAD	Thy light to every sense impart, and shed thy love in every heart; thine own unfailing might supply to strengthen our infirmity.
AND FORGIVE US OUR TRESPASSES AS WE FORGIVE THOSE WHO TRESPASS AGAINST US AND LEAD US NOT INTO TEMPTATION BUT DELIVER US FROM EVIL	Drive far away our ghostly foe, and thine abiding peace bestow; if thou be our preventing Guide, no evil can our steps betide.
OUR FATHER WHO ART IN HEAVEN HALLOWED BE THY NAME	Praise we the Father and the Son and Holy Spirit with them One; and may the Son on us bestow the gifts that from the Spirit flow.[1]

---

1. Traditional English translation of the hymn, *Veni Creator Spiritus*, attributed to Rabanus Maurus (776–856), sung at vespers on Pentecost by the Latin Church.

PENTECOST

OUR FATHER WHO ART IN HEAVEN HALLOWED BE THY NAME

And while staying with them he charged them not to depart from Jerusalem, but to wait for the promise of the Father, which, he said, "you heard from me, for John baptized with water, but before many days you shall be baptized with the Holy Spirit."...

THY KINGDOM COME

So when they had come together they asked him, "Lord, will you at this time restore the kingdom to Israel?" He said to them, "It is not for you to know times or seasons which the Father has fixed by his own authority. But you shall receive power when the Holy Spirit has come upon you; and you shall be my witnesses in Jerusalem and in all Judea and Samaria and to the end of the earth." Acts 1:4–8

THY WILL BE DONE ON EARTH AS IT IS IN HEAVEN

When the day of Pentecost had come, they were all together in one place. And suddenly a sound came from heaven like the rush of a mighty wind, and it filled the house where they were sitting....

GIVE US THIS DAY OUR DAILY BREAD

And there appeared to them tongues of fire, distributed and resting on each one of them. And they were all filled with the Holy Spirit and began to speak in other tongues, as the Spirit gave them utterance....

AND FORGIVE US OUR TRESPASSES AS WE FORGIVE THOSE WHO TRESPASS AGAINST US

Now there were dwelling in Jerusalem Jews, devout men from every nation under heaven. And at this sound the multitude came together, and they were bewildered, because each one heard them speaking in his own language....[1]

AND LEAD US NOT INTO TEMPTATION

But Peter... lifted up his voice and addressed them, "...Let all the house of Israel therefore know assuredly that God has made him both Lord and Christ, this Jesus whom you crucified." Now when they heard this they were cut to the heart, and said to Peter and the rest of the apostles, "Brethren, what shall we do?"...

BUT DELIVER US FROM EVIL

And Peter said to them, "Repent, and be baptized every one of you in the name of Jesus Christ for the forgiveness of your sins; and you shall receive the gift of the Holy Spirit.... Save yourselves from this crooked generation." Acts 2:1–7, 14, 36–40

---

1. This 'gift of languages' represents the restoration of our humanity from the trespass, temptation and evil of the tower of Babel.

PNEUMATIC DIMENSIONS OF THE LORD'S PRAYER

Without the air to prolong its vibrations, the most striking word is a mute explosion. In principle and at origin, the revelatory Word produces its own 'atmosphere' which purifies and transmits its salvific vibrations to our human substance. This is the function of the Holy Spirit, of the Holy Breath which the Father exhales in pronouncing his Word.
—Jean Borella, *Love and Truth.*

SPIRIT OF THE FATHER, SPIRIT OF THE SON

OUR FATHER WHO
ART IN HEAVEN

But, when the fullness of time was come, God sent his Son, made of a woman, made under the law, that he might redeem them that were under the law, that we might receive the adoption of sons. And, because you are sons, God hath sent the Spirit of his Son into your hearts, crying: Abba, Father. Gal. 4:4–6

But the hour cometh, and now is, when the true adorers shall adore the Father in spirit and in truth.[1] For the Father also seeketh such to adore him. God is a spirit; and they that adore him must adore him in spirit and in truth. John 4:23–24

HALLOWED BE
THY NAME

But the Paraclete, the Holy Spirit, whom the Father will send in my name, he will teach you all things and bring all things to your mind, whatsoever I shall have said to you. John 14:26

Wherefore, I give you to understand that no man, speaking by the Spirit of God, saith Anathema to Jesus. And no man can say The Lord Jesus, but by the Holy Spirit. 1 Cor. 12:3

THY KINGDOM COME

But when the Paraclete cometh, whom I will send you from the Father, the Spirit of truth, who proceedeth from the Father, he shall give testimony of me. John 15:26

For the kingdom of God is not meat and drink; but justice and peace and joy in the Holy Spirit. Rom. 14:17

GIVER OF LIFE, GIFT OF GOD

THY WILL BE DONE
ON EARTH AS IT IS
IN HEAVEN

Eye hath not seen, nor ear hear, neither hath it entered into the heart of man, what things God hath prepared for them that love him. But to us, God hath revealed them, by his Spirit. For the Spirit searcheth all things, yea, the deep things of God. For what man knoweth the things of a man, but the spirit of a man that is in him? So the things also that are of God, no man knoweth, but the Spirit of God. Now, we have received not the spirit of this world, but the Spirit that is of God; that we may know the things that are given us from God. 1 Cor. 2:9–12

I am come to cast fire on the earth. And what will I, but that it be kindled. Luke 12:49

---

1. That is, we must adore the Father in the Holy Spirit, who "fillest all things", and in the Son, who is "the way, and the truth, and the life" John 14:6

And when the days of the Pentecost were accomplished they were all together in one place. And suddenly there came a sound from heaven, as of a mighty wind coming; and it filled the whole house where they were sitting. And there appeared to them parted tongues, as it were of fire; and it sat upon every one of them. And they were all filled with the Holy Spirit. Acts 2:1–4

GIVE US THIS DAY OUR DAILY BREAD

Grace to you and peace be accomplished in the knowledge of God and of Christ Jesus our Lord… by whom he hath given us most great and precious promises, that by these you may be made partakers of the divine nature. 2 Pet. 1:2, 4
Know you not that your members are the temple of the Holy Spirit, who is in you, whom you have from God; and you are not your own? For you are bought with a great price. Glorify and bear God in your body. 1 Cor. 6:19–20

PARACLETE

AND FORGIVE US OUR TRESPASSES AS WE FORGIVE THOSE WHO TRESPASS AGAINST US

My dearest, if God has so loved us, we also ought to love one another. No man hath seen God at any time. If we love one another, God abideth in us; and his charity is perfected in us. In this we know that we abide in him, and he in us: because he hath given us of his spirit. 1 John 4:11–13
And, coming, he preached peace to you that were afar off; and peace to them that were nigh. For by him we have access both in one Spirit to the Father. Eph. 2:17–18
He breathed on them; and he said to them: Receive ye the Holy Spirit; whose sins you shall forgive, they are forgiven them; and whose sins you shall retain, they are retained. John 20:22–23
Every sin and blasphemy shall be forgiven men, but the blasphemy of the Spirit shall not be forgiven. And, whosoever shall speak a word against the Son of man, it shall be forgiven him; but he that shall speak against the Holy Spirit, it shall not be forgiven him, neither in this world, nor in the world to come. Matt. 12:31–32

AND LEAD US NOT INTO TEMPTATION

Dearly beloved, believe not every spirit; but try the spirits if they be of God; because many false prophets are gone out into the world. By this is the spirit of God known. Every spirit which confesseth that Jesus Christ is come in the flesh is of God. And every spirit that dissolveth Jesus is not of God; and this is Antichrist, of whom you have heard that he cometh; and he is now already in the world. You are of God, little children, and have overcome. Because greater is he that is in you, than he that is in the world. 1 John 4:1–4

BUT DELIVER US FROM EVIL

Not by the works of justice which we have done, but according to his mercy, he saved us, by the laver of regeneration and renovation of the Holy Spirit. Titus 3:5

THE IDENTITIES OF CHRIST

OUR FATHER WHO
ART IN HEAVEN
HALLOWED BE
THY NAME

Before Abraham was made I am. John 8:58

I am Alpha and Omega, the beginning and the end, saith the Lord God, who is and who was and who is to come, the Almighty. Apoc. 1:8

THY KINGDOM COME

Thou sayest that I am a king. For this was I born, and for this came I into the world, that I should give testimony to the truth. Every one that is of the truth heareth my voice. John 18:37

I am the door. By me, if any man enter in, he shall be saved; and he shall go in and out, and shall find pastures. John 10:9

THY WILL BE DONE
ON EARTH AS IT IS
IN HEAVEN

I am the light of the world. He that followeth me walketh not in darkness, but shall have the light of life. John 8:12

I am the way the truth and the life. No man cometh to the Father but by me. John 14:6

GIVE US THIS DAY
OUR DAILY BREAD

He that believeth in me hath everlasting life. I am the bread of life. John 6:47–48

AND FORGIVE US OUR
TRESPASSES AS WE
FORGIVE THOSE
WHO TRESPASS
AGAINST US

I am the true vine; and my Father is the husbandman. Every branch in me that beareth not fruit, he will take away; and every one that beareth fruit, he will purge it, that it may bring forth more fruit… I am the vine; you the branches. John 15:1–2, 5

AND LEAD US NOT
INTO TEMPTATION

I am the good shepherd. The good shepherd giveth his life for his sheep… My sheep hear my voice; and I know them; and they follow me. And I give them life everlasting. John 10:11, 27–28

BUT DELIVER
US FROM EVIL

I am the resurrection and the life; he that believeth in me, although he be dead, shall live; and every one that liveth and believeth in me shall not die forever. John 11:25–26

PREFACE TO 'THE NAME'

"IN THE NAME OF"[1]

"Unfortunately the English expression 'in the name of', like the Latin *in nomine*, is powerless to render the rich complexity of the Greek terms. The Greek text, when referring to the name of Jesus, uses three formulas… These three formulas are not equivalent, but each one expressed a special attitude toward the name."

UNION

OUR FATHER WHO ART IN HEAVEN HALLOWED BE THY NAME

ἐν τῷ ὀνόματι, in the name[2]—
"the attitude is static; it expresses the repose which follows the attainment of the goal and a certain interiorization or immanence."

ILLUMINATION

THY KINGDOM COME THY WILL BE DONE ON EARTH AS IT IS IN HEAVEN GIVE US THIS DAY OUR DAILY BREAD

εἰς τὸ ὄνομα, into the name[3]—
"there is movement 'toward' the name, a dynamic relationship of finality which sees the name as the goal to be attained, the terminus *ad quem*."

PURIFICATION

AND FORGIVE US OUR TRESPASSES AS WE FORGIVE THOSE WHO TRESPASS AGAINST US AND LEAD US NOT INTO TEMPTATION BUT DELIVER US FROM EVIL

ἐπὶ τῷ ὀνόματι, on the name[4]—
"one leans 'on' the name; it is the foundation on which one builds, the terminus a quo, the point of departure toward a subsequent action, the start of a new advance."

---

1. All quotations from Lev Gillet's *The Jesus Prayer*, p. 27.
2. John 5:43, 10:25, 16:23–24; Acts 9:27, 16:18; 1 Cor. 5:4, 6:11; Col. 3 :17.
3. Matt. 28:19, John 3:18, Acts 19:5.
4. Acts 2:38.

THE NAME

OUR FATHER WHO ART IN HEAVEN	In the beginning was the Word, and the Word was with God, and the Word was God. John 1:1
HALLOWED BE THY NAME	Father, glorify thy name. A voice therefore came from heaven: I have both glorified it and will glorify it again. John 12:28
THY KINGDOM COME	Blessed be the king who cometh in the name of the Lord! Peace in heaven and glory on high! Luke 19:38
THY WILL BE DONE ON EARTH AS IT IS IN HEAVEN	And I have made known thy name to them and will make it known; that the love wherewith thou hast loved me may be in them, and I in them. John 17:26
GIVE US THIS DAY OUR DAILY BREAD	But what saith the scripture? The word is nigh thee, even in thy mouth and in thy heart. This is the word of faith, which we preach. For, if thou confess with thy mouth the Lord Jesus and believe in thy heart that God hath raised him up from the dead, thou shalt be saved... For whosoever shall call upon the name of the Lord shall be saved. Rom. 10:8–9, 13
AND FORGIVE US OUR TRESPASSES AS WE FORGIVE THOSE WHO TRESPASS AGAINST US	And there entered a thought into them, which of them should be greater, but Jesus, seeing the thoughts of their heart, took a child and set him by him, and said to them: Whosoever shall receive this child in my name receiveth me; and whosoever shall receive me receiveth him that sent me. For he that is the lesser among you all he is the greater. And John, answering, said: Master, we saw a certain man casting out devils in thy name; and we forbade him, because he followeth not with us. And Jesus said to him: Forbid him not, for he that is not against you is for you. Luke 9:46–50
AND LEAD US NOT INTO TEMPTATION	And I saw heaven opened; and, behold, a white horse. And he that sat upon him was called faithful and true... and he had a name written, which no man knoweth but himself. And he was clothed with a garment sprinkled with blood. And his name is called: The Word of God... And out of his mouth proceedeth a sharp two-edged sword, that with it he may strike the nations... and he hath on his garment and on his thigh written: King of Kings and Lord of Lords. Apoc. 19:11–16 For the word of God is living and effectual and more piercing than any two-edged sword and reaching unto the division of the soul and the spirit, of the joints also and the marrow; and is a discerner of the thoughts and intents of the heart. Heb. 4:12
BUT DELIVER US FROM EVIL	And the seventy-two returned with joy, saying: Lord, the devils also are subject to us in thy name. And he said to them: I saw Satan like lightning falling from heaven. Behold, I have given you power to tread upon serpents and scorpions and upon all the power of the enemy, and nothing shall hurt you. But yet rejoice not in this, that spirits are subject unto you; but rejoice in this, that your names are written in heaven. Luke 10:17–20

THE NAMES OF GOD

ACCORDING TO JOHN OF DAMASCUS

From *An Exact Exposition of the Orthodox Faith*, Book 1, Chapter 9

The Deity is simple and uncompound. But that which is composed of many and different elements is compound. If, then, we should speak of the qualities of being uncreate and without beginning and incorporeal and immortal and everlasting and good and creative and so forth as essential differences in the case of God, that which is composed of so many qualities will not be simple but must be compound. But this is impious in the extreme. Each then of the affirmations about God should be thought of as signifying not what He is in essence, but either something that it is impossible to make plain, or some relation to some of those things which are contrasts or some of those things that follow the nature, or an energy.

OUR FATHER WHO ART IN HEAVEN HALLOWED BE THY NAME

Essence

It appears then that the most proper of all the names given to God is "He that is". as He Himself said in answer to Moses on the mountain, Say to the children of Israel, HE WHO IS hath sent Me (Exod. 3:14). For He keeps all being in His own embrace, like a sea of essence infinite and unseen. Or as the holy Dionysius says, "He that is good ." For one cannot say of God that He has being in the first place and goodness in the second.

THY KINGDOM COME

Energy

The second name of God is θεός, derived from θέειν, to run, because He courses through all things, or from αἴθω, to burn: For God is a fire consuming all evil (Deut. 4:24): or from ue˙suai because He is all-seeing (2 Macc. 10:5): for nothing can escape Him, and over all He keeps watch. For He saw all things before they were, holding them timelessly in His thoughts; and each one conformably to His voluntary and timeless thought, which constitutes predetermination and image and pattern, comes into existence at the predetermined time.

THY WILL BE DONE ON EARTH AS IT IS IN HEAVEN

Further, the terms 'without beginning,' 'incorruptible,' 'unbegotten,' as also 'uncreate,' 'incorporeal,' 'unseen,' and so forth, explain what He is not: that is to say, they tell us that His being had no beginning, that He is not corruptible, nor created, nor corporeal, nor visible . Again, goodness and justice and piety and such like names belong to the nature , but do not explain His actual essence.

GIVE US THIS DAY OUR DAILY BREAD

Finally, Lord and King and names of that class indicate a relationship with their contrasts: for the name Lord has reference to those over whom the lord rules, and the name King to those under kingly authority, and the name Creator to the creatures, and the name Shepherd to the sheep he tends.

AND FORGIVE US OUR TRESPASSES AS WE FORGIVE THOSE WHO TRESPASS AGAINST US AND LEAD US NOT INTO TEMPTATION BUT DELIVER US FROM EVIL

…or from αἴθω, to burn: For God is a fire consuming all evil…

JESUS

ADAPTED FROM THE AKATHIST TO OUR SWEETEST LORD JESUS CHRIST[1]

Thou, O Lord, art our Father, our Redeemer: from everlasting is thy name. Isaiah 63:16
Thou shalt call his name Jesus: for he shall save his people from their sins. Matthew 1:23

OUR FATHER WHO
ART IN HEAVEN
HALLOWED BE
THY NAME

Jesus, Eternal God! Jesus, True God! Jesus, Lord of Lords! Jesus, my Almighty God! Jesus, Supreme Strength! Jesus, Eternal Power! Jesus, Incomprehensible Power! Jesus, my Immortal Lord! Jesus, the Light above all lights! Jesus, my most glorious Creator! Jesus, Inscrutable Intelligence! Jesus, Undepictable Deity! Jesus, Uncontainable Word! Jesus, Inconceivable Wisdom! Jesus, High Praise! Jesus, my most exalted Glory! Jesus, Son of David! Jesus, Son of the Living God! Jesus, Memory Eternal!

THY KINGDOM COME

Jesus, Eternal King, have mercy on me! Jesus, King of Kings! Jesus, All-Powerful King! Jesus, Boundless Dominion! Jesus, Invincible Kingdom! Jesus, Unending Sovereignty! Jesus, Glorious King! Jesus All-Glorious, Kings' Stronghold! Jesus, my All-powerful King! Jesus, Eternal Temple, shelter me! Jesus, Radiant Beauty! Jesus, my Light, enlighten me! Jesus, Gladness of my heart! Jesus, Unspeakable Love! Jesus, Son of God, have mercy on me!

THY WILL BE DONE
ON EARTH AS IT IS
IN HEAVEN

Jesus, Invincible Power! Jesus, Creator of those on high! Jesus, Redeemer of those below! Jesus, Adorner of every creature! Jesus, Garment of Light, adorn me! Jesus, Pearl of great price, beam on me! Jesus, precious Stone, illumine me! Jesus, Sun of Righteousness, shine on me! Jesus, holy Light, make me radiant! Jesus All-Beloved, Prophets' Fulfillment! Jesus, Enlightener of my mind! Jesus, Brightness of the mind! Jesus, Gladness of the conscience! Jesus, enlighten the thoughts of my heart! Jesus, Purity of the soul! Jesus, my most kind Teacher and Guide! Jesus, my most compassionate Shepherd! Jesus, Wonderful Shepherd! Jesus, my most gracious Master! Jesus, Son of God, have mercy on me.

GIVE US THIS DAY
OUR DAILY BREAD

Jesus, Strong Food! Jesus, Inexhaustible Drink! Jesus, Bread of Life, fill me who am hungry! Jesus, Source of Knowledge, refresh me who am thirsty! Jesus, Sweetness of the heart! Jesus, Strength of the body! Jesus, Health of my body! Jesus, Glory of the poor! Jesus, Treasurer Incorruptible! Jesus, Unfailing Wealth! Jesus, Garment of the poor! Jesus, Garment of Gladness, clothe my nakedness! Jesus, Defender of widows! Jesus, Protector of orphans! Jesus, Helper of toilers! Jesus, Guide of pilgrims! Jesus, Pilot of voyagers! Jesus, Finder of those who seek, find my soul! Jesus, Opener to those who knock, open my wretched heart! Jesus All-Merciful, Fasters' Abstinence! Jesus, Veil of Joy, cover my unworthiness! Jesus, Giver to those who ask, give me sorrow for my sins! Jesus, Son of God, have mercy on me!

---

1. *Book of Akathists*, pp. 33–43.

| AND FORGIVE US OUR TRESPASSES AS WE FORGIVE THOSE WHO TRESPASS AGAINST US | Jesus, Innocent Lamb! Jesus, Infinite Mercy! Jesus, God, constant in Mercy! Jesus, All-Merciful Savior! Jesus, my Creator, have compassion on me! Jesus, Long-suffering Master! Jesus, take away my iniquities! Jesus, pardon my unrighteousness! Jesus, my Hope, forsake me not! Jesus, my Helper, reject me not! Jesus, my Creator, forget me not! Jesus, my Shepherd, lose me not! Jesus, cleanse my sins! Jesus, Judge of the living and the dead! Jesus, my Comfort at Thy Judgment! Jesus, condemn me not according to my deeds! Jesus, my Savior, save me! |

AND FORGIVE US OUR TRESPASSES AS WE FORGIVE THOSE WHO TRESPASS AGAINST US

Jesus, Innocent Lamb! Jesus, Infinite Mercy! Jesus, God, constant in Mercy! Jesus, All-Merciful Savior! Jesus, my Creator, have compassion on me! Jesus, Long-suffering Master! Jesus, take away my iniquities! Jesus, pardon my unrighteousness! Jesus, my Hope, forsake me not! Jesus, my Helper, reject me not! Jesus, my Creator, forget me not! Jesus, my Shepherd, lose me not! Jesus, cleanse my sins! Jesus, Judge of the living and the dead! Jesus, my Comfort at Thy Judgment! Jesus, condemn me not according to my deeds! Jesus, my Savior, save me!

AND LEAD US NOT INTO TEMPTATION

Jesus, my gracious Guardian! Jesus, the Truth, dispelling falsehood! Jesus, teach me who am worthless! Jesus, enlighten my darkness! Jesus, enlighten my senses darkened by passions! Jesus, cleanse my mind from vain thoughts! Jesus, keep my heart from evil desires! Jesus, purify me who am unclean! Jesus, heal my body scabbed with sins! Jesus, cleanse me according to Thy mercy! Jesus, take from me despondency! Jesus, Hope of the hopeless! Jesus, Comforter of the mournful! Jesus, Comforter of my soul! Jesus, Calmer of tempests! Jesus, my Savior, save me!

BUT DELIVER US FROM EVIL

Jesus everlasting, Sinners' Salvation! Jesus, Sure Hope! Jesus, my Hope at death! Jesus, make me ever mindful of death! Jesus, my Life after death! Jesus, raise me who am fallen! Jesus, my Shepherd, recover me! Jesus, restore me, a prodigal! Jesus, save me despite my unworthiness! Jesus, Redeemer of sinners, wash away my sins! Jesus, deliver me from sickness of soul and body! Jesus, my Desire, reject me not! Jesus, rescue me from the hands of the adversary! Jesus, Vanquisher of the powers of hell! Jesus, save me from the unquenchable fire and from the other eternal torments! Jesus, deliver me from all torments! Jesus, my most merciful Savior! Jesus, my Savior, save me!

THREE AS WITH ONE MOUTH

DANIEL 3:51–90

<table>
<tr><td>OUR FATHER WHO
ART IN HEAVEN</td><td>Then these three, as with one mouth,
praised and glorified and blessed God, in the furnace:
Blessed art thou, O Lord, the God of our fathers;
and worthy to be praised, and glorified,
and exalted above all for ever:</td></tr>
<tr><td>HALLOWED BE
THY NAME</td><td>and blessed is the holy name of thy glory:
and worthy to be praised and exalted above all, in all ages.</td></tr>
<tr><td>THY KINGDOM COME</td><td>Blessed art thou in the holy temple of thy glory:
and exceedingly to be praised and exalted above all for ever.
Blessed art thou that beholdest the depths, and sittest upon
the cherubim: and worthy to be praised
and exalted above all for ever.
Blessed art thou in the firmament of heaven: and worthy of
praise, and glorious for ever. All ye works of the Lord, bless
the Lord: praise and exalt him above all for ever.
O ye angels of the Lord, bless the Lord: praise and exalt him
above all for ever.</td></tr>
<tr><td>THY WILL BE DONE
ON EARTH AS IT IS
IN HEAVEN</td><td>O ye heavens, bless the Lord:
praise and exalt him above all for ever.
O all ye waters that are above the heavens, bless the Lord:
praise and exalt him above all for ever.
O all ye powers of the Lord, bless the Lord:
praise and exalt him above all for ever.
O ye sun and moon, bless the Lord:
praise and exalt him above all for ever.
O ye stars of heaven, bless the Lord:
praise and exalt him above all for ever.
O every shower and dew, bless ye the Lord:
praise and exalt him above all for ever.
O all ye spirits of God, bless the Lord:
praise and exalt him above all for ever.
O ye fire and heat, bless the Lord:
praise and exalt him above all for ever.
O ye cold and heat, bless the Lord,
praise and exalt him above all for ever.
O ye dews and hoar frost, bless the Lord:
praise and exalt him above all for ever.
O ye frost and cold, bless the Lord:
praise and exalt him above all for ever.
O ye ice and snow, bless the Lord:
praise and exalt him above all for ever.</td></tr>
</table>

O ye nights and days, bless the Lord:
praise and exalt him above all for ever.
O ye light and darkness, bless the Lord:
praise and exalt him above all for ever.
O ye lightnings and clouds, bless the Lord:
praise and exalt him above all for ever.
O let the earth bless the Lord:
let it praise and exalt him above all for ever.

GIVE US THIS DAY
OUR DAILY BREAD

O all ye things that spring up in the earth, bless the Lord:
praise and exalt him above all for ever.
O ye fountains, bless the Lord:
praise and exalt him above all for ever.
O ye seas and rivers, bless the Lord:
praise and exalt him above all for ever.
O ye whales, and all that move in the waters, bless the Lord:
praise and exalt him above all for ever.
O all ye fowls of the air, bless the Lord:
praise and exalt him above all for ever.
O all ye beasts and cattle, bless the Lord:
praise and exalt him above all for ever.

AND FORGIVE US OUR
TRESPASSES AS WE
FORGIVE THOSE
WHO TRESPASS
AGAINST US

O ye sons of men, bless the Lord:
praise and exalt him above all for ever.
O let Israel bless the Lord: let them
praise and exalt him above all for ever.
O ye priests of the Lord, bless the Lord:
praise and exalt him above all for ever.
O ye servants of the Lord, bless the Lord:
praise and exalt him above all for ever.
O ye spirits and souls of the just, bless the Lord:
praise and exalt him above all for ever.

AND LEAD US NOT
INTO TEMPTATION

O ye holy and humble of heart, bless the Lord:
praise and exalt him above all for ever.

BUT DELIVER
US FROM EVIL

O Ananias, Azarias, Misael, bless ye the Lord:
praise and exalt him above all for ever.
For he hath delivered us from hell,
and saved us out of the hand of death,
and delivered us out of the midst of the burning flame,
and saved us out of the midst of the fire.
O give thanks to the Lord, because he is good:
because his mercy endureth for ever and ever.
O all ye religious, bless the Lord, the God of gods:
praise him, and give him thanks,
because his mercy endureth for ever and ever.

THE SIGN OF THE CROSS, THE CRUCIFORM NAME

What is this mystery in which the sign of Christ's life-giving death is joined to the blessing of the triune name as a seal that covers the body and discloses the heart? GJC

A SCRIPTURAL SIGN OF THE CROSS

OUR FATHER WHO
ART IN HEAVEN
HALLOWED BE
THY NAME
THY KINGDOM COME

In the name of the Father... [1]
And I beheld, and lo, a Lamb stood upon mount Sion, and with him a hundred and forty-four thousand, having his name and the name of his Father written on their foreheads. Apoc. 14:1

THY WILL BE DONE
ON EARTH AS IT IS
IN HEAVEN
GIVE US THIS DAY
OUR DAILY BREAD

and of the Son... [2]
I am the living bread which came down from heaven. If any man eat of this bread, he shall live for ever; and the bread that I will give is my flesh, for the life of the world. John 6:51–52

AND FORGIVE US OUR
TRESPASSES AS WE
FORGIVE THOSE
WHO TRESPASS
AGAINST US
AND LEAD US NOT
INTO TEMPTATION
BUT DELIVER
US FROM EVIL

and of the Holy Spirit [3]
Peace be to you. As the Father hath sent me, I also send you. When he said this, he breathed on them; and he said to them: Receive ye the Holy Spirit; whose ins you shall forgive, they are forgiven them; and whose sins you shall retain, they are retained. John 20:21–22

AMEN

Amen
These things saith the Amen, the faithful and true witness, who is the beginning of the creation of God. Apoc. 3:14

---

1. The forehead is touched with the hand, its first two fingers joined to the thumb to signify the Holy Trinity, the two remaining fingers joined to the palm to signify Christ both true God and true man.
2. The hand is brought down to the abdomen.
3. The hand is brought up to and traverses the chest from right to left, ending on the side of the heart.

A SIGNATURE TO THE WORK OF THE TRINITY

OUR FATHER WHO ART IN HEAVEN	In the name of the Father	Creator
HALLOWED BE THY NAME	and of the the Son	Redeemer and Savior
THY KINGDOM COME	and of the Holy Spirit	Sanctifier and Renewer of Creation

A SIGNATURE TO THE MYSTERY OF THE INCARNATION

THY WILL BE DONE, AS IT IS IN HEAVEN	In the name of the Father	"God… (begotten in eternity without mother)
…ON EARTH	and of the the Son	became man… (conceived in time without father)
GIVE US THIS DAY OUR DAILY BREAD	and of the Holy Spirit	so that man might become God" (by the power of the Holy Spirit).

A SIGNATURE TO THE MYSTERY OF THE EUCHARIST

A Prosphora Seal

GIVE US THIS DAY OUR DAILY BREAD	In the name of the Father	IC (Jesus, consubstantial with the Father)
AND FORGIVE US OUR TRESPASSES AS WE FORGIVE THOSE WHO TRESPASS AGAINST US	and of the the Son	XC (Christ, anointed by a repentant sinner before ascending his throne on the Cross)
AND LEAD US NOT INTO TEMPTATION BUT DELIVER US FROM EVIL	and of the Holy Spirit	NI KA (Victor, overcoming all things, even death, with the power of humility and the liberating Spirit of Truth,)

THE LORD'S PRAYER ~ THE OUR FATHER

But, thou, when thou shalt pray, enter into thy closet and, having shut the door, pray to thy Father in secret; and thy Father who seeth in secret will repay thee. Matthew 6:6

The material closet of a man who is silent embraces only the man himself, but the inner spiritual closet also holds God and all the Kingdom of Heaven, according to the Gospel words of Christ Himself: 'The kingdom of God is within you' (Luke 17:21)… Man needs to enclose himself in the inner closet of his heart more often than he need go to church: and collecting all his thoughts there, he must place his mind before God, praying to Him in secret with all warmth of spirit and with living faith. At the same time he must also learn to turn his thoughts to God in such a manner as to be able to grow into a perfect man. — Dimitri of Rostov, *The Inner Closet of the Heart*

OUR FATHER WHO ART IN HEAVEN

And no one knoweth who the Son is, but the Father; and who the Father is, but the Son and to whom the Son will reveal him. Luke 10:22

Philip saith to him: Lord, shew us the Father; and it is enough for us. Jesus saith to him: Have I been so long a time with you and you have not known me? Philip, he that seeth me seeth the Father also. John 14:8–9

I and the Father are one. John 10:30

HALLOWED BE THY NAME

I have manifested thy name to the men whom thou hast given me out of the world… Holy Father keep them in thy name whom thou hast given me; that they may be one, as we also are. John 17:6, 11

THY KINGDOM COME

Seek ye first the kingdom of God and his justice; and all these things shall be added unto you. Fear not, little flock, for it hath pleased your Father to give you a kingdom. Luke 12:31–32

Then shall the just shine as the sun in the kingdom of their Father. Matt. 13:43

THY WILL BE DONE ON EARTH AS IT IS IN HEAVEN

I came down from heaven, not to do my own will but the will of him that sent me. Now this is the will of the Father who sent me that of all that he hath given me I should lose nothing; but should raise it up again in the last day. And this is the will of my Father that sent me: that everyone who seeth the Son and believeth in him may have life everlasting; and I will raise him up on the last day. John 6:38–40

GIVE US THIS DAY OUR DAILY BREAD

Moses gave you not bread from heaven, but my Father giveth you the true bread from heaven. For the bread of God is that which cometh down from heaven and giveth life to the world. They said therefore unto him: Lord, give us always this bread. And Jesus said to them: I am the bread of life. John 6:32–35

AND FORGIVE US OUR TRESPASSES AS WE FORGIVE THOSE WHO TRESPASS AGAINST US

And Jesus said: Father, forgive them, for they know not what they do. Luke 23:34

That they all may be one, as thou, Father, in me, and I in thee; that they also may be one in us; that the world may believe that thou hast sent me. John 17:21

AND LEAD US NOT INTO TEMPTATION

Father, if thou wilt, remove this chalice from me; but yet not my will, but thine be done. Luke 22:42

BUT DELIVER US FROM EVIL

And Jesus, crying with a loud voice, said: Father, into thy hands I commend my spirit. Luke 23:46

UNTO AGES OF AGES

OUR FATHER WHO ART IN HEAVEN HALLOWED BE THY NAME— *The Thrice-Holy*
THY KINGDOM COME—*Children of the Adoption*
THY WILL BE DONE ON EARTH AS IT IS IN HEAVEN—*Unto the Praise of His Glory*
GIVE US THE DAY OUR DAILY BREAD—*Many Mansions, Eternal Life*
AND FORGIVE US OUR TRESPASSES AS WE FORGIVE THOSE WHO TRESPASS AGAINST US—
Reward and Punishment
AND LEAD US NOT INTO TEMPTATION—*The Last Things*
BUT DELIVER US FROM EVIL—*The Sign of the Son of Man*

THE SIGN OF THE SON OF MAN

MATTHEW 24:3–31

Woe to them who say: "When will the day of the Lord come?" and make no effort to grasp it. For the coming of the Lord has already taken place and is ever taking place in the faithful, and is at hand for all who desire it. If He is the light of the world and said to His disciples that He would be with us until the consummation of the age, then how, being with us, shall He come again? In no way! For we are not sons of the darkness and of the night, that the light should take us by surprise, but are sons of the light and of the Lord's day. — Symeon the New Theologian, *Ethical Discourses*, 10

BUT DELIVER
US FROM EVIL

What shall be the sign of thy coming, and of the consummation of the world? And Jesus answering, said to them: Take heed that no man seduce you: For many will come in my name saying, I am Christ: and they will seduce many.

AND LEAD US NOT
INTO TEMPTATION

And you shall hear of wars and rumors of wars. See that ye be not troubled. For these things must come to pass, but the end is not yet. For nation shall rise against nation, and kingdom against kingdom; and there shall be pestilences, and famines, and earthquakes in places: Now all these are the beginnings of sorrows.

AND FORGIVE US OUR
TRESPASSES AS WE
FORGIVE THOSE
WHO TRESPASS
AGAINST US

Then shall they deliver you up to be afflicted, and shall put you to death: and you shall be hated by all nations for my name's sake. And then shall many be scandalized: and shall betray one another: and shall hate one another. And many false prophets shall rise, and shall seduce many. And because iniquity hath abounded, the charity of many shall grow cold. But he that shall persevere to the end, he shall be saved.

GIVE US THIS DAY
OUR DAILY BREAD

And this gospel of the kingdom, shall be preached in the whole world, for a testimony to all nations, and then shall the consummation come. When therefore you shall see the abomination of desolation, which was spoken of by Daniel the prophet, standing in the holy place: he that readeth let him understand.

THY WILL BE DONE
ON EARTH AS IT
IS IN HEAVEN

Then they that are in Judea, let them flee to the mountains: And he that is on the housetop, let him not come down to take any thing out of his house: And he that is in the field, let him not go back to take his coat. And woe to them that are with child, and that give suck in those days. But pray that your flight be not in the winter, or on the sabbath. For there shall be then great tribulation, such as hath not been from the beginning of the world until now, neither shall be. And unless those days had been shortened, no flesh should be saved: but for the sake of the elect those days shall be shortened.

THY KINGDOM COME

Then if any man shall say to you: Lo here is Christ, or there, do not believe him. For there shall arise false Christs and false prophets, and shall show great signs and wonders, insomuch as to deceive (if possible) even the elect. Behold I have told it to you, beforehand. If therefore they shall say to you: Behold he is in the desert, go ye not out: Behold he is in the closets, believe it not. For as lightning cometh out of the east, and appeareth even into the west: so shall the coming of the Son of man be. Wheresoever the body shall be, there shall the eagles also be gathered together.

And immediately after the tribulation of those days, the sun shall be darkened and the moon shall not give her light, and the stars shall fall from heaven, and the powers of heaven shall be moved: And then shall appear the sign of the Son[1] of man in heaven: and then shall all tribes of the earth mourn: and they shall see the Son of man coming in the clouds of heaven with much power and majesty. And he shall send his angels with a trumpet, and a great voice: and they shall gather together his elect from the four winds, from the farthest parts of the heavens to the utmost bounds of them.

---

1. Patristic tradition identifies this 'sign' with the Cross of Christ: "The glorious cross will also be the first to appear at the second coming of Christ as the glorious, life-giving, adorable and holy scepter of Christ our King, according to the word of the Lord" —Ephrem the Syrian, *Sermon on the Glorious Cross* (cited in Macarius of Moscow, *Orthodox Dogmatic Theology*, vol. 2, p. 742 [French ed.]).

THE LAST THINGS

HEAVEN

OUR FATHER WHO
ART IN HEAVEN
HALLOWED BE
THY NAME

Dearly beloved, we are now the sons of God; and it hath not yet appeared what we shall be. We know that when he shall appear we shall be like to him; because we shall see him as he is. 1 John 3:2

That they all may be one, as thou, Father, in me, and I in thee; that they also may be one in us... that they may be one as we also are one. John 17:21–22

THE SECOND COMING OF CHRIST

THY KINGDOM COME

Again the high priest asked him and said to him: Art thou the Christ, the Son of the Blessed God? And Jesus said to him: I am. And you shall see the Son of man sitting on the right hand of the power of God and coming with the clouds of heaven. Mark 14:61–62

For the Lord himself shall come down from heaven with commandment and with the voice of an archangel and with the trumpet of God; and the dead who are in Christ will rise first. Then we who are alive, who are left, shall be taken up together with them in the clouds to meet Christ, into the air; and so shall we be always with the Lord. 1 Thess. 4:15–16

NEW HEAVENS AND A NEW EARTH

THY WILL BE DONE
ON EARTH AS IT IS
IN HEAVEN

But we look for new heavens and a new earth, according to his promises, in which justice dwelleth. Wherefore, dearly beloved, waiting for these things, be diligent that you may be found before him unspotted and blameless in peace. 1 Pet. 3:13–14

THE GENERAL RESURRECTION

GIVE US THIS DAY
OUR DAILY BREAD

The hour cometh wherein all that are in the graves shall hear the voice of the Son of God. And they that have done good things shall come forth unto the resurrection of life: but they that have done evil, unto the resurrection of judgment. John 5:28–29

For as lightning cometh out of the east and appeareth even into the west; so shall the coming of the Son of man be. Wheresoever the body shall be, there shall the eagles also be gathered together. Matt. 24:27–28

THE LAST JUDGMENT

AND FORGIVE US OUR
TRESPASSES AS WE
FORGIVE THOSE
WHO TRESPASS
AGAINST US

And I saw a great white throne and one sitting upon it, from whose face the earth and heaven fled away; and there was no place found for them. And I saw the dead, great and small, standing in the presence of the throne. And the books were opened; and another book was opened, which was the book of life. And the dead were judged by those things which were written in the books, according to their works. And the sea gave up the dead that were in it; and death and hell gave up their dead that were in them. And they were judged, every one according to their works. Apoc. 19:11–13

Amen, amen, I say unto you that he who heareth my word and believeth him that sent me hath life everlasting: and cometh not into judgment, but is passed from death to life. John 5:24

AND LEAD US NOT
INTO TEMPTATION

The Lord delayeth not his promise, as some imagine, but dealeth patiently for your sake, not willing that any should perish, but that all should return to penance. But the day of the Lord shall come as a thief, in which the heavens shall pass away with great violence and the elements shall be melted with heat and the earth and the works which are in it shall be burnt up. Seeing, then, that all these things are to be dissolved, what manner of people ought you to be in holy conversation and godliness? 2 Pet. 3:9–11

GEHENNA

BUT DELIVER
US FROM EVIL

And hell and death were cast into the pool of fire. This is the second death. And whosoever was not found written in the book of life was cast into the pool of fire... the fearful and unbelieving, and the abominable and murderers, and whoremongers and sorcerers, and idolaters and all liars, they shall have their portion in the pool burning with fire and brimstone, which is the second death. Apoc. 20:14–15, 21:8

REWARD AND PUNISHMENT

OUR FATHER WHO ART IN HEAVEN HALLOWED BE THY NAME Take heed that you do not your justice before men, to be seen by them; otherwise you shall not have reward of your Father who is in heaven.

Almsgiving. Therefore, when thou dost an almsdeed, sound not a trumpet before thee, as the hypocrites do in the synagogues and in the streets, that they may be honored by men: Amen, I say to you, they have received their reward. And when thou dost alms, let not thy left hand know what thy right hand doth, that thy alms may be in secret; and thy Father who seeth in secret will repay thee.

Prayer. And when ye pray ye shall not be as the hypocrites that love to stand and pray in the synagogues and corners of the street, that they may be seen by men: Amen, I say to you,, they have received their reward. But, thou, when thou shalt pray, enter into thy chamber and, having shut the door, pray to thy Father in secret; and thy Father who seeth in secret will repay thee.

Fasting. And, when you fast, be not as the hypocrites, sad; for they disfigure their faces, that they may appear unto men to fast. Amen, I say to you, they have received their reward. But thou, when thou fastest, anoint thy head and wash thy face; that thou appear not to men to fast, but to thy Father who is in secret; and thy Father who seeth in secret will repay thee. Lay not up to yourselves treasures on earth; where the rust and moth consume and where thieves break through and steal. But lay up to yourselves treasures in heaven; where neither the rust nor moth doth consume, and where thieves do not break through and steal. For, where thy treasure is, there is thy heart also. Matt. 6:1–6, 16–21

THY KINGDOM COME And seek not what you shall eat and what you shall drink; and be not lifted up on high. For all these things do the nations of the world seek. But your Father knoweth that you have need of these things. But seek ye first the kingdom of God and his justice; and all these things shall be added unto you. Fear not, little flock, for it hath pleased your Father to give you a kingdom. Sell what you possess and give alms. Make to yourselves bags which grow not old, a treasure in heaven which faileth not; where no thief approacheth, nor moth corrupteth. For where your treasure is, there will your heart be also. Luke 12:29–34

THY WILL BE DONE ON EARTH AS IT IS IN HEAVEN For what doth it profit a man, if he gain the whole world and suffer the loss of his own soul? For the Son of man shall come in the glory of his Father with his angels; and then will he render to every man according to his works. Matt. 16:26–27

GIVE US THIS DAY OUR DAILY BREAD And when the Son of man shall come in his majesty, and all the angels with him, then shall he sit upon the seat of his majesty. And all nations shall be gathered together before him; and he shall separate them one from another, as the shepherd separates the sheep from the goats; and he shall set the sheep on his right hand, but the goats on his left. Then shall the king say to them that shall be on his right hand: Come, ye blessed on my Father, possess you the kingdom prepared for you from the foundation of the world. For I was hungry, and you gave me to eat; I was thirst, and you gave me to drink; I was a stranger, and you took me in; naked, and you covered me; sick, and you visited me; I was in prison, and you came to me. Then the just shall answer him, saying: Lord, when did we see thee hungry and fed thee; thirsty and gave thee drink? And when did we see thee a stranger and take thee in? Or naked and covered thee? Or when did we see thee sick or in prison and came to thee? And the king answering shall say to them: Amen, I say to you, as long as you did it to one of these my least brethren, you did it to me. Then he shall say to them also that shall be on his left hand: Depart from me, you cursed, into everlasting fire, which was prepared for the devil and his angels. For I was hungry and you gave me not to eat; I was thirsty and you gave me not to drink. I was a stranger and you took me not in; naked and you covered me not; sick and in prison and you did not visit me. Then they also shall answer him, saying: Lord, when did we see thee hungry or thirsty or a stranger or naked or sick or in prison and did not minister to thee? Then he shall answer them, saying: Amen, I say to you, as long as you did it not to one of these least, neither did you do it to me. And these shall go into everlasting punishment; but the just, into life everlasting. Matt. 25:31–46

AND FORGIVE US OUR TRESPASSES AS WE FORGIVE THOSE WHO TRESPASS AGAINST US

And I say to you: Whosoever shall confess me before men, him shall forgive the Son of man also confess before the angels of God. But he that shall deny me before men shall be denied before the angels of God. And whosoever speaketh a word against the Son of man, it shall be forgiven him; but to him that shall blaspheme against the Holy Spirit, it shall not be forgiven. Luke 12:8–10

AND LEAD US NOT INTO TEMPTATION BUT DELIVER US FROM EVIL

And, if thy hand scandalize thee, cut it off; it is better for thee to enter But into life, maimed, than having two hands to go into hell, into unquenchable fire; where the worm dieth not, and the fire is not extinguished. And, if thy foot scandalize thee, cut it off; it is better for thee to enter lame into life everlasting than having two feet to be cast into the fire of unquenchable fire; where the worm dieth not, and the fire is not extinguished. And, if thy eye scandalize thee, pluck it out; it is better for thee with one eye to enter into the kingdom of God than having two eyes to be cast into the hell of fire; where the worm dieth not, and the fire is not extinguished.[1] Mark 9:42–47

---

1. This thrice-repeated refrain is analogous to that of Matt. 6 above, for those hands not occupied with warding off the surfeit of earthly things, with fasting, are busy elsewhere; those feet not occupied with visiting the needy, with almsgiving, are busy elsewhere; and those eyes not occupied with gazing On High, in prayer, are busy elsewhere.

MANY MANSIONS

They say, moreover, that there is this distinction between the habitation of those who produce an hundred-fold, and that of those who produce sixty-fold, and that of those who produce thirty-fold: for the first will be taken up into the heavens, the second will dwell in paradise, the last will inhabit the city; and that was on this account the Lord declared, "In My Father's house are many mansions. (John 14:2). For all things belong to God, who supplies all with a suitable dwelling-place; even as His Word says, that a share is allotted to all by the Father, according as each person is or shall be worthy.
—Irenaeus, *Against the Heresies*, v. 36. 2

OUR FATHER WHO ART IN HEAVEN HALLOWED BE THY NAME THY KINGDOM COME	The Heavens	the hundredfold yield
THY WILL BE DONE ON EARTH AS IT IS IN HEAVEN	Paradise	the sixtyfold yield
GIVE US THIS DAY OUR DAILY BREAD	The City	the thirtyfold yield
AND FORGIVE US OUR TRESPASSES AS WE FORGIVE THOSE WHO TRESPASS AGAINST US AND LEAD US NOT INTO TEMPTATION BUT DELIVER US FROM EVIL	For to every one that hath shall be given, and he shall abound; but, from him that hath not, that also which he seemeth to have shall be taken away. And the unprofitable servant cast ye out into the exterior darkness. Matt. 25:29–30	

You see then that there are different stages of perfection, and that we are called by the Lord from high things to still higher in such a way that he who has become blessed and perfect in the fear of God; going as it is written 'from strength to strength' (Psalm 83:8), and from one perfection to another, i.e., mounting with keenness of soul from fear to hope, is summoned in the end to that still more blessed stage, which, is love, and he who has been 'a faithful and wise servant' (Matt. 24:45) will pass to the companionship of friendship and to the adoption of sons. So then our saying also must be understood according to this meaning: not that we say that the consideration of that enduring punishment or of that blessed recompense which is promised to the saints is of no value, but because, though they are useful and introduce those who pursue them to the first beginning of blessedness, yet again love, wherein is already fuller confidence, and a lasting joy, will remove them from servile fear and mercenary hope to the love of God, and carry them on to the adoption of sons, and somehow make them from being perfect still more perfect. For the Savior says that in His Father's house are 'many mansions' (John 14:2). John Cassian, The Conferences, Eleventh, XII, 5–6.

ETERNAL LIFE

<table>
<tr><td>OUR FATHER WHO ART IN HEAVEN HALLOWED BE THY NAME</td><td>Now this is eternal life: That they may know thee, the only true God, and Jesus Christ, whom thou hast sent. John 17:3</td></tr>
</table>

OUR FATHER WHO ART IN HEAVEN HALLOWED BE THY NAME

Now this is eternal life: That they may know thee, the only true God, and Jesus Christ, whom thou hast sent. John 17:3

THY KINGDOM COME

That as sin hath reigned to death: so also grace might reign by justice unto life everlasting, through Jesus Christ our Lord. Rom. 5:21

THY WILL BE DONE ON EARTH AS IT IS IN HEAVEN

For I have not spoken of myself: but the Father who sent me, he gave me commandment what I should say and what I should speak. And I know that his commandment is life everlasting. John 12:49–50

GIVE US THIS DAY OUR DAILY BREAD

Do not you say: There are yet four months, and then the harvest cometh? Behold, I say to you, lift up your eyes, and see the countries. For they are white already to harvest. And he that reapeth receiveth wages and gathereth fruit unto life everlasting: that both he that soweth and he that reapeth may rejoice together. John 4:35–36

Jesus answered them and said: Amen, amen, I say to you, you seek me, not because you have seen miracles, but because you did eat of the loaves and were filled. Labour not for the meat which perisheth, but for that which endureth unto life everlasting, which the Son of man will give you. For him hath God, the Father, sealed. They said therefore unto him: What shall we do, that we may work the works of God? Jesus answered and said to them: This is the work of God, that you believe in him whom he hath sent. John 6:26–29

AND FORGIVE US OUR TRESPASSES AS WE FORGIVE THOSE WHO TRESPASS AGAINST US

But now being made free from sin and become servants to God, you have your fruit unto sanctification, and the end life everlasting. For the wages of sin is death. But the grace of God, life everlasting in Christ Jesus our Lord. Rom. 6:22–23

We know that we have passed from death to life, because we love the brethren. He that loveth not abideth in death. Whosoever hateth his brother is a murderer. And you know that no murderer hath eternal life abiding in himself. In this we have known the charity of God, because he hath laid down his life for us: and we ought to lay down our lives for the brethren. 1 John 3:14–16

AND LEAD US NOT INTO TEMPTATION

Amen, amen, I say to you, unless the grain of wheat falling into the ground die, itself remaineth alone. But if it die it bringeth forth much fruit. He that loveth his life shall lose it and he that hateth his life in this world keepeth it unto life eternal. John 12:24–25

BUT DELIVER US FROM EVIL

My sheep hear my voice. And I know them: and they follow me. And I give them life everlasting: and they shall not perish for ever. And no man shall pluck them out of my hand. That which my Father hath given me is greater than all: and no one can snatch them out of the hand of my Father. John 10:27–29

UNTO THE PRAISE OF HIS GLORY

EPHESIANS 1

In the heaven of our soul let us be praises of glory of the Holy Trinity, praises of love of our Immaculate Mother. One day the veil will fall, we will be introduced into the eternal courts, and there we will sing in the bosom of infinite Love. And God will give us 'the new name promised to the Victor.' What will it be? Laudem Gloriae. —Sister Elizabeth of the Holy Trinity, *I Have Found God*

OUR FATHER WHO ART IN HEAVEN HALLOWED BE THY NAME
Grace be to you and peace, from God the Father and from the Lord Jesus Christ. Blessed be the God and Father of our Lord Jesus Christ, who hath blessed us with spiritual blessings in heavenly places, in Christ; as he chose us in him before the foundation of the world, that we should be holy and unspotted in his sight in charity.

THY KINGDOM COME
Who hath predestinated us unto the adoption of children through Jesus Christ unto himself, according to the purpose of his will; unto the praise of the glory of his grace, in which he hath graced us in his beloved Son.

THY WILL BE DONE ON EARTH AS IT IS IN HEAVEN
In whom we have redemption through his blood, the remission of sins, according to the riches of his grace. Which hath superabounded in us, in all wisdom and prudence, that he might make known unto us the mystery of his will, according to his good pleasure, which he hath purposed in him. In the dispensation of the fulness of times, to re-establish all things in Christ, that are in heaven and on earth, in him.

GIVE US THIS DAY OUR DAILY BREAD
In whom we also are called by lot, being predestinated according to the purpose of him who worketh all things according to the counsel of his will; that we may be unto the praise of his glory; we who before hoped in Christ; in whom you also, after you had heard the word of truth (the gospel of your salvation), in whom also believing, you were signed with the holy Spirit of promise, who is the pledge of our inheritance, unto the redemption of acquisition, unto the praise of his glory.

AND FORGIVE US OUR TRESPASSES AS WE FORGIVE THOSE WHO TRESPASS AGAINST US
Wherefore, I also, hearing of your faith that is in the Lord Jesus and of your love towards all the saints, cease not to give thanks for you, making commemoration of you in my prayers,

AND LEAD US NOT INTO TEMPTATION
That the God of our Lord Jesus Christ, the Father of glory, may give unto you the spirit of wisdom and of revelation, in the knowledge of him; the eyes of your heart enlightened, that you may know what the hope is of his calling and what are the riches of the glory of his inheritance in the saints,

BUT DELIVER US FROM EVIL
And what is the exceeding greatness of his power towards us, who believe, according to the operation of the might of his power, which he wrought in Christ, raising him up from the dead and setting him on his right hand in the heavenly places, above all principality and power and virtue and dominion and every name that is named, not only in this world, but also in that which is to come. And he hath subjected all things under his feet and hath made him head over all the church, which is his body and the fulness of him who is filled all in all.

CHILDREN OF THE ADOPTION

Jesus of Nazareth, the Son of God, the adopted son of Joseph the carpenter, became man so that we might become the adopted children of God. — GJC

OUR FATHER WHO ART IN HEAVEN	For whosoever are led by the Spirit of God, they are the sons of God. For you have not received the spirit of bondage again in fear: but you have received the spirit of adoption of sons, whereby we cry: Abba (Father). For the Spirit himself giveth testimony to our spirit that we are the sons of God. And if sons, heirs also; heirs indeed of God and joint heirs with Christ: yet so, if we suffer with him, that we may be also glorified with him. Rom. 8:14–15
HALLOWED BE THY NAME	But as many as received him, he gave them power to be made the sons of God, to them that believe in his name. John 1:12
THY KINGDOM COME	Behold what manner of charity the Father hath bestowed upon us, that we should be called and should be the sons of God. Therefore the world knoweth not us, because it knew not him. Dearly beloved, we are now the sons of God: and it hath not yet appeared what we shall be. We know that when he shall appear we shall be like to him: because we shall see him as he is. 1 John 3:1–2
THY WILL BE DONE ON EARTH AS IT IS IN HEAVEN	For whom he foreknew, he also predestinated to be made conformable to the image of his Son: that he might be the Firstborn amongst many brethren. Rom. 8:29 For you are all the children of God, by faith in Christ Jesus. Gal. 3:26
GIVE US THIS DAY OUR DAILY BREAD	And this is the testimony that God hath given to us eternal life. And this life is in his Son. He that hath the Son hath life. He that hath not the Son hath not life. 1 John 5:11–12 He that shall overcome shall possess these things. And I will be his God: and he shall be my son. Apoc. 21:7
AND FORGIVE US OUR TRESPASSES AS WE FORGIVE THOSE WHO TRESPASS AGAINST US	Blessed be the God and Father of our Lord Jesus Christ… Who hath predestinated us unto the adoption of children through Jesus Christ unto himself: according to the purpose of his will: unto the praise of the glory of his grace, in which he hath graced us, in his beloved son. In whom we have redemption through his blood, the remission of sins, according to the riches of his, grace. Eph. 1:3–7
AND LEAD US NOT INTO TEMPTATION	But when it pleased him who separated me from my mother's womb and called me by his grace, to reveal his Son in me, that I might preach him among the Gentiles: immediately I condescended not to flesh and blood. Gal. 1:15–16
BUT DELIVER US FROM EVIL	But when the fulness of the time was come, God sent his Son, made of a woman, made under the law: that he might redeem them who were under the law: that we might receive the adoption of sons. And because you are sons, God hath sent the Spirit of his Son into your hearts, crying: Abba, Father. Therefore, now he is not a servant, but a son. And if a son, an heir also through God. Gal. 4:4–7

THE THRICE-HOLY

And the four living creatures… rested not day and night, saying: Holy, Holy, Holy, Lord God Almighty, who was, and who is, and who is to come. Apocalypse 4:8

OUR FATHER WHO ART IN HEAVEN	Holy God	Lord God
HALLOWED BE THY NAME	Holy mighty	Almighty
THY KINGDOM COME	Holy Immortal	Who was, and who is, and who is to come

We hold the words 'Holy God' to refer to the Father, without limiting the title of divinity to Him alone, but acknowledging also as God the Son and the Holy Spirit: and the words 'Holy and Mighty' we ascribe to the Son, without stripping the Father and the Holy Spirit of might: and the words 'Holy and Immortal' we attribute to the Holy Spirit, without depriving the Father and the Son of immortality. For, indeed, we apply all the divine names simply and unconditionally to each of the subsistences in imitation of the divine Apostle's words. But to us there is but one God, the Father, of Whom are all things, and we in Him: and one Lord Jesus Christ by Whom are all things, and we by Him (1 Cor. 8:5). And, nevertheless, we follow Gregory the Theologian when he says, "But to us there is but one God, the Father, of Whom are all things, and one Lord Jesus Christ, through Whom are all things, and one Holy Spirit, in Whom are all things:" for the words 'of Whom' and 'through Whom' and 'in Whom' do not divide the natures (for neither the prepositions nor the order of the names could ever be changed), but they characterize the properties of one unconfused nature. And this becomes clear from the fact that they are once more gathered into one, if only one reads with care these words of the same Apostle, Of Him and through Him and in Him are all things: to Him be the glory for ever and ever. Amen (Rom. 11:36). John of Damascus, An Exact Exposition of the Orthodox Faith, 3, 10

HYMNS TO THE HOLY TRINITY

OUR FATHER WHO ART IN HEAVEN	O uncreated Nature, Maker of all things, open our lips that we may proclaim Thy praises, crying: Holy, holy, holy art Thou, our God; at the prayers of all Thy saints have mercy upon us.[1]
HALLOWED BE THY NAME	O Gladsome Light of the holy glory of the immortal Father, heavenly holy, blessed Jesus Christ, now that we have come to the setting of the sun and behold the Light of Evening, we praise God, Father, Son and Holy Spirit. For meet it is at all times to worship Thee with voices of praise O Son of God and Giver of Life. Therefore all the world doth glorify Thee.[2]
THY KINGDOM COME	Come, O people, and let us worship the Godhead in three Persons, the Son in the Father, with the Holy Spirit. For the Father, outside time, begot the Son Co-eternal and Coenthroned, and the Holy Spirit who is in the Father and is glorified together with the Son: One Power, one Essence, one Godhead, Whom worshipping we all say: Holy God, Who hast created all things by the Son

---

1. From 'Hymns to the Trinity', Tone 2; *Lenten Triodion*, p. 664.
2. This vespers hymn, the *Phos Hilaron*, is one of the oldest Christian hymns (third century or earlier) outside of the Bible.

through the operation of Holy Spirit; Holy Mighty, by Whom we have come to know the Father, and by Whom the Holy Spirit camest into the world; Holy Immortal, the Comforting Spirit, Who proceedeth from the Father, and resteth in the Son. O Holy Trinity, glory to Thee![1]

THY WILL BE DONE
ON EARTH AS IT IS
IN HEAVEN

As the angelic hosts in heaven, we men on earth, standing now with fear, offer unto Thee, O loving Lord, a hymn of victory: Holy, holy, holy art Thou, our God; at the prayers of all Thy saints, have mercy upon us.[2]

GIVE US THIS DAY
OUR DAILY BREAD

Holy, Holy, Holy art Thou, our Lord God, Who in Thy Tri-Personal Counsel didst decide to create man, and into his body taken from earth, didst breathe the breath of life from Thy lips![3]

AND FORGIVE US OUR
TRESPASSES AS WE
FORGIVE THOSE
WHO TRESPASS
AGAINST US

Having risen from sleep, I thank Thee, the Holy Trinity. In the abundance of Thy kindness and long patience, Thou hast not been angry with me for my laziness and sinfulness, nor hast Thou destroyed me in my lawlessness. Instead, in Thy usual love for mankind, Thou hast raised me as I lay in despair, that I might rise early and glorify Thy Reign. Enlighten now the eyes of my mind and open my lips, that I might learn of Thy words, understand Thy commandments, accomplish Thy will, hymn Thee in heart-felt confession and praise Thy all-holy name, the Father and the Son, and the Holy Spirit, now and ever and unto ages of ages. Amen.[4]

AND LEAD US NOT
INTO TEMPTATION

Behold! The bridegroom approaches in the middle of the night, and blessed is that servant whom He shall find watching; but unworthy he whom He shall find careless. Beware, therefore, O my soul. Be not overcome with sleep, lest thou be given over to death and shut outside the kingdom. But arise and cry: Holy, holy, holy art Thou, O God! Through the Theotokos have mercy on us.[5]

BUT DELIVER
US FROM EVIL

The Judge will come suddenly and the acts of every man will be revealed; but in the middle of the night we cry with fear: Holy! Holy! Holy! art Thou. O God; through the Theotokos, have mercy on us.[6]

1. From 'The Order for the Blessing and Sanctification of Icons of the Most-Holy Life-Originating Trinity', Sticheron, Tone 8; *The Great Book of Needs*, Vol. 2, p. 213.
2. From 'Hymns to the Trinity', Tone 4; *The Lenten Triodion*, p. 665.
3. From 'Akathist to the Holy Trinity', Ekos 5; *Book of Akathists,* p. 15.
4. 'Prayer of St. Basil the Great to the Holy Trinity', Morning Prayers; *Orthodox Daily Prayers*, pp. 7–8.
5. 'Troparion of the Bridegroom', Matins, Monday of Holy Week.
6. From 'Troparia to the Trinity', Morning Prayers; *Orthodox Daily Prayers,* p. 7.

V

THE APOCALYPSE

OUR FATHER WHO ART IN HEAVEN HALLOWED BE THY NAME—*A New Canticle*
THY KINGDOM COME— *The Lamb as it Were Slain*
The Seven 'Blesseds' of the Apocalypse, The Holy City,
THY WILL BE DONE ON EARTH AS IT IS IN HEAVEN—*Come Up Hither*
GIVE US THIS DAY OUR DAILY BREAD—*The Seven Promises of Christ*
AND FORGIVE US OUR TRESPASSES AS WE FORGIVE
THOSE WHO TRESPASS AGAINST US—*The Book with Seven Seal*s
AND LEAD US NOT INTO TEMPTATION
BUT DELIVER US FROM EVIL— *A Sinner's Bestiary*
AMEN —*A Vista on the Apocalypse*

INTRODUCTION

Throughout Christian history the Apocalypse has been called upon to prove the near approach of time's end. But for all the mysteries of its numbers, outlandish beasts, and angelic interventions, it is actually a naked book: in two bold strokes, the solving of all the riddles occurs immediately at the beginning—"I am the Alpha and the Omega, the beginning and the end" (Apoc. 1:8)—and almost as a parting caress at the end—"I am the Alpha and the Omega, the beginning and the end" (Apoc. 22:13).[1] Between these two eternalizing parentheses the whole working out of salvation occurs in a torrent of sevens: churches, golden candlesticks, stars, eyes, spirits of God, letters (admonitions and promises), angels, seals, trumpets, thunders, heads, diadems, bowls, crowns, plagues, golden vials, mountains, kings. Such numberings and repetitions have a way of eliciting either bewilderment or ecstasy. But what if the Lord's Prayer, the Alpha and Omega's own prayer, were to appear in the midst of these visionary sentences? Would there be a stilling of the tumult, as Christ did for his apostles on the Sea of Galilee, so that we might enter the safe harbor of the New Jerusalem? World-stunning events may be foreshadowed in the Apocalypse, but what of the human heart in all this; what if the Bible's last book can be seen as an ascetic treatise, a verbal icon of the ascetic life as liturgy, the drama of salvation vividly enacted in the soul of the Christian here and now?

---

1. A third instance of this declaration occurs at the center (Apoc. 21:6) of the chiastic introduction (Apoc. 21:1–11) to the descent of the Holy City. Since we do not know how John numbered the verses, might this not be a twelve-fold introduction to the twelve-fold city?

A VISTA ON THE APOCALYPSE

PROLOGUE

OUR FATHER WHO
ART IN HEAVEN
HALLOWED BE
THY NAME

I am Alpha and Omega, the beginning and the end, saith the Lord God, who is, and who was, and who is to come, the Almighty.

THY KINGDOM COME

I John, your brother and your partner in tribulation, and in the kingdom, and patience in Christ Jesus, was in the island, which is called Patmos, for the word of God, and for the testimony of Jesus. I was in the spirit on the Lord's day, and heard behind me a great voice, as of a trumpet, Saying:

THY WILL BE DONE
ON EARTH AS IT IS
IN HEAVEN

What thou seest, write in a book, and send to the seven churches which are in Asia, to Ephesus, and to Smyrna, and to Pergamus, and to Thyatira, and to Sardis, and to Philadelphia, and to Laodicea.

GIVE US THIS DAY
OUR DAILY BREAD

And I turned to see the voice that spoke with me. And being turned, I saw seven golden candlesticks: And in the midst of the seven golden candlesticks, one like to the Son of man, clothed with a garment down to the feet, and girt about the paps with a golden girdle. And his head and his hairs were white, as white wool, and as snow, and his eyes were as a flame of fire, and his feet like unto fine brass, as in a burning furnace. And his voice as the sound of many waters. And he had in his right hand seven stars. And from his mouth came out a sharp two edged sword: and his face was as the sun shineth in his power. And when I had seen him, I fell at his feet as dead. And he laid his right hand upon me, saying: Fear not. I am the First and the Last, And alive, and was dead, and behold I am living for ever and ever, and have the keys of death and of hell. Write therefore the things which thou hast seen, and which are, and which must be done hereafter. The mystery of the seven stars, which thou sawest in my right hand, and the seven golden candlesticks. The seven stars are the angels of the seven churches. And the seven candlesticks are the seven churches. Apoc. 1:8–20

AND FORGIVE US OUR
TRESPASSES AS WE
FORGIVE THOSE
WHO TRESPASS
AGAINST US
AND LEAD US NOT
INTO TEMPTATION
BUT DELIVER
US FROM EVIL

The seven letters to the seven churches. Apoc. 2–3

OUR FATHER WHO ART IN HEAVEN HALLOWED BE THY NAME	The vision of the throne of God. Apoc. 4
THY KINGDOM COME	The book sealed with seven seals opened by the Lamb. Apoc. 5
THY WILL BE DONE ON EARTH AS IT IS IN HEAVEN	The opening of the seals. Apoc. 6–9
GIVE US THIS DAY OUR DAILY BREAD	John given a book to eat. The woman clothed with the sun. Apoc. 10–12:2
AND FORGIVE US OUR TRESPASSES AS WE FORGIVE THOSE WHO TRESPASS AGAINST US	The red dragon and Saint Michael. Apoc. 12:3–18
AND LEAD US NOT INTO TEMPTATION	The beasts[1] and the Lamb. Apoc. 13–15
BUT DELIVER US FROM EVIL	The seven vials/plagues. The fall of Babylon. Apoc. 16–20
OUR FATHER WHO ART IN HEAVEN HALLOWED BE THY NAME	The new Jerusalem. Apoc. 21–22:16
THY KINGDOM COME	Invocation of the Spirit and the Bride. Apoc. 22:17–21

---

1. If the dragon and the other beasts are seen as the different classes of sin (cf. below 'A Sinner's Bestiary'), they can also be seen as the different 'justifications' for war, which is only, after all, one of sin's many exaggerated consequences. Thus, from the 'rational' power of the dragon comes every conflict motivated by ideology (including dynastic hostilities); from the 'irascible' power of the beast risen from the sea comes every conflict motivated by impatience, anger or the fear that a enemy might strike first; and from the 'concupiscible' power of the beast with the whore of Babylon upon its back comes every conflict motivated by greed or deprivation.

A SINNER'S BESTIARY

Just as St. John affirms that we shall be like God because we shall see him as he is (1 John 3:2), so one of hell's greatest torments is to see Satan as he really is, that Great Beast who draws all the damned into the bottom-most of alienation and dissimilarity forever. —GJC

Two Wings of a Great Eagle—That Which Ever Evades the Sinner

OUR FATHER WHO
ART IN HEAVEN
HALLOWED BE
THY NAME

And a great sign appeared in heaven: A woman clothed with the sun and the moon under her feet, and on her head a crown of twelve stars: And being with child, she cried travailing in birth, and was in pain to be delivered. ... And she brought forth a man child, who was to rule all nations with an iron rod. And her son was taken up to God and to his throne. And the woman fled into the wilderness, where she had a place prepared by God, that there they should feed her, a thousand two hundred sixty days. And there was a great battle in heaven: Michael and his angels fought with the dragon, and the dragon fought, and his angels. And they prevailed not: neither was their place found any more in heaven. And that great dragon was cast out, that old serpent, who is called the devil and Satan, who seduceth the whole world. And he was cast unto the earth: and his angels were thrown down with him. And I heard a loud voice in heaven, saying: Now is come salvation and strength and the kingdom of our God and the power of his Christ: because the accuser of our brethren is cast forth, who accused them before our God day and night. And they overcame him by the blood of the Lamb and by the word of the testimony: and they loved not their lives unto death. Therefore, rejoice, O heavens, and you that dwell therein. Woe to the earth and to the sea, because the devil is come down unto you, having great wrath, knowing that he hath but a short time. And when the dragon saw that he was cast unto the earth, he persecuted the woman who brought forth the man child. And there were given to the woman two wings of a great eagle, that she might fly into the desert, unto her place, where she is nourished for a time and times, and half a time, from the face of the serpent. And the serpent cast out of his mouth, after the woman, water, as it were a river: that he might cause her to be carried away by the river. And the earth helped the woman: and the earth opened her mouth and swallowed up the river which the dragon cast out of his mouth. And the dragon was angry against the woman: and went to make war with the rest of her seed, who keep the commandments of God and have the testimony of Jesus Christ. Apoc. 12:1–2, 5–17

The Sinful 'Look' of the Rational Power

THY KINGDOM COME

... And there was seen another sign in heaven: and behold a great red dragon, having seven heads, and ten horns: and on his head seven diadems: And his tail drew the third part of the stars of heaven, and cast them to the earth: and the dragon stood before the woman who was ready to be delivered; that, when she should be delivered, he might devour her son. Apoc. 11:19–12:4

The Sinful 'Look' of the Irascible Power

THY WILL BE DONE ON EARTH AS IT IS IN HEAVEN

And I saw a beast coming up out of the sea, having seven heads and ten horns, and upon his horns ten diadems, and upon his heads names of blasphemy. And the beast, which I saw, was like to a leopard, and his feet were as the feet of a bear, and his mouth as the mouth of a lion. And the dragon gave him his own strength, and great power. And I saw one of his heads as it were slain to death: and his death's wound was healed. And all the earth was in admiration after the beast. And they adored the dragon, which gave power to the beast: and they adored the beast, saying: Who is like to the beast? and who shall be able to fight with him? And there was given to him a mouth speaking great things, and blasphemies: and power was given to him to do two and forty months. And he opened his mouth unto blasphemies against God, to blaspheme his name, and his tabernacle, and them that dwell in heaven. And it was given unto him to make war with the saints, and to overcome them. And power was given him over every tribe, and people, and tongue, and nation. And all the dwell upon the earth adored him, whose names are not written in the book of life of the Lamb, which was slain from the beginning of the world. Apoc. 13:1–8

The Sinful 'Look' of the Concupiscible Power

GIVE US THIS DAY OUR DAILY BREAD

And I saw a woman sitting upon a scarlet colored beast, full of names of blasphemy, having seven heads and ten horns. And the woman was clothed round about with purple and scarlet, and gilt with gold, and precious stones and pearls, having a golden cup in her hand, full of the abomination and filthiness of her fornication. And on her forehead a name was written: A mystery; Babylon the great, the mother of the fornications, and the abominations of the earth. And I saw the woman drunk with the blood of the saints, and with the blood of the martyrs of Jesus. Apoc. 17:3–6

The White Horse and Its Rider—That Which Ever Confronts the Sinner

AND FORGIVE US OUR TRESPASSES AS WE FORGIVE THOSE WHO TRESPASS AGAINST US AND LEAD US NOT INTO TEMPTATION BUT DELIVER US FROM EVIL

And I saw heaven opened: and behold a white horse. And he that sat upon him was called faithful and true: and with justice doth he judge and fight. And his eyes were as a flame of fire: and on his head were many diadems. And he had a name written, which no man knoweth but himself. And he was clothed with a garment sprinkled with blood. And his name is called: The Word of God. And the armies that are in heaven followed him on white horses, clothed in fine linen, white and clean. And out of his mouth proceedeth a sharp two-edged sword, that with it he may strike the nations. And he shall rule them with a rod of iron: and he treadeth the winepress of the fierceness of the wrath of God the Almighty. And he hath on his garment and on his thigh written: King of Kings and Lord of Lords. Apoc. 19:11–16

THE BOOK WITH SEVEN SEALS

APOCALYPSE 6:1–7:4

And they sung a new canticle, saying: Thou art worthy, O Lord, to take the book, and to open the seals thereof; because thou wast slain, and hast redeemed us to God, in thy blood, out of every tribe, and tongue, and people, and nation. And hast made us to our God a kingdom and priests, and we shall reign on the earth. Apocalypse 5:9–10

BUT DELIVER
US FROM EVIL

And I saw that the Lamb had opened one of the seven seals, and I heard one of the four living creatures, as it were the voice of thunder, saying: Come, and see. And I saw: and behold a white horse, and he that sat on him had a bow, and there was a crown given him, and he went forth conquering that he might conquer.

AND LEAD US NOT
INTO TEMPTATION

And when he had opened the second seal, I heard the second living creature, saying: Come, and see. And there went out another horse that was red: and to him that sat thereon, it was given that he should take peace from the earth, and that they should kill one another, and a great sword was given to him.

AND FORGIVE US OUR
TRESPASSES AS WE
FORGIVE THOSE
WHO TRESPASS
AGAINST US

And when he had opened the third seal, I heard the third living creature saying: Come, and see. And behold a black horse, and he that sat on him had a pair of scales in his hand. And I heard as it were a voice in the midst of the four living creatures, saying: Two pounds of wheat for a penny, and thrice two pounds of barley for a penny, and see thou hurt not the wine and the oil.

GIVE US THIS DAY OUR
DAILY BREAD

And when he had opened the fourth seal, I heard the voice of the fourth living creature, saying: Come, and see. And behold a pale horse, and he that sat upon him, his name was Death, and hell followed him. And power was given to him over the four parts of the earth, to kill with sword, with famine, and with death, and with the beasts of the earth.

GIVE US THIS DAY OUR
SUPERSUBSTANTIAL
BREAD (THY
KINGDOM COME)

And when he had opened the fifth seal, I saw under the altar the souls of them that were slain for the word of God, and for the testimony which they held. And they cried with a loud voice, saying: How long, O Lord (holy and true) dost thou not judge and revenge our blood on them that dwell on the earth? And white robes were given to every one of them one; and it was said to them, that they should rest for a little time, till their fellow servants, and their brethren, who are to be slain, even as they, should be filled up.

THY WILL BE DONE
ON EARTH AS IT
IS IN HEAVEN

And I saw, when he had opened the sixth seal, and behold there was a great earthquake, and the sun became black as sackcloth of hair: and the whole moon became as blood: and the stars from heaven fell upon the earth, as the fig tree casteth its green figs when it is shaken by a great wind: and the heaven departed as a book folded up: and every mountain, and the islands were moved out of their places. And the kings of the earth, and the princes, and tribunes, and the rich, and the strong, and every bondman, and every freeman, hid themselves in the dens and in the rocks of mountains: And they say to the mountains and the rocks: Fall upon us, and hide us from the face of him that sitteth upon the throne and from the wrath of the Lamb: For the great day of their wrath is come, and who shall be able to stand?

OUR FATHER WHO
ART IN HEAVEN
HALLOWED BE
THY NAME
THY KINGDOM COME

And when he had opened the seventh seal, there was silence in heaven, as it were for half an hour. And I saw seven angels standing in the presence of God; and there were given to them seven trumpets. And another angel came, and stood before the altar, having a golden censer; and there was given to him much incense, that he should offer of the prayers of all saints upon the golden altar, which is before the throne of God. And the smoke of the incense of the prayers of the saints ascended up before God from the hand of the angel.

THE SEVEN PROMISES OF CHRIST

OUR FATHER WHO
ART IN HEAVEN
HALLOWED BE
THY NAME

He that shall overcome shall be clothed in white garments, and I will not blot out his name out of the book of life; and I will confess his name before my Father and before his angels. Apoc. 3:5

THY KINGDOM COME

To him that overcometh I will give the hidden manna and a white stone; and in the stone, a new name written, which no man knoweth but he that receiveth it. Apoc. 2:17

THY WILL BE DONE
ON EARTH AS IT IS
IN HEAVEN

He that shall overcome, I will make him a pillar in the temple of my God; and he shall go out no more. And I shall write upon him the name of my God, and the name of the city of my God, the new Jerusalem, which cometh down out of heaven from my God, and my new name. Apoc. 3:12

GIVE US THIS DAY
OUR DAILY BREAD

To him that overcometh I will give to eat of the tree of life, which is in the paradise of my God. Apoc. 2:6

AND FORGIVE US OUR
TRESPASSES AS WE
FORGIVE THOSE
WHO TRESPASS
AGAINST US

To him that shall overcome, I will give to sit with me in my throne; as I also have overcome and am sat down with my Father in his throne. Apoc. 3:21

AND LEAD US NOT
INTO TEMPTATION

And he that shall overcome and keep my works until the end, I will give him power over the nations. And he shall rule them with a rod of iron; and as the vessel of a potter they shall be broken; as I also have received of my Father. And I will give him the morning star. Apoc. 2:26–27

BUT DELIVER
US FROM EVIL

He that shall overcome shall not be hurt by the second death. Apoc. 2:11

COME UP HITHER

APOCALYPSE 11:3–14

He who endures suffering for the sake of virtue, without being shaken in his resolve, is inspired by the first advent of the Logos, which cleanses him from all defilement. He who through contemplation has raised his intellect to the angelic state possesses the power of the second advent, which produces dispassion and incorruptibility. — Maximus the Confessor, *Text on Theology*, First Century, 98

THY KINGDOM COME

And I will give unto my two witnesses,[1] and they shall prophesy a thousand two hundred sixty days, clothed in sackcloth. These are the two olive trees, and the two candlesticks, that stand before the Lord of the earth. And if any man will hurt them, fire shall come out of their mouths, and shall devour their enemies. And if any man will hurt them, in this manner must he be slain.

THY WILL BE DONE
ON EARTH AS IT IS
IN HEAVEN
GIVE US THIS DAY
OUR DAILY BREAD

These have power to shut heaven, that it rain not in the days of their prophecy: and they have power over waters to turn them into blood, and to strike the earth with all plagues as often as they will.

AND FORGIVE US OUR
TRESPASSES AS WE
FORGIVE THOSE
WHO TRESPASS
AGAINST US

And when they shall have finished their testimony, the beast, that ascendeth out of the abyss, shall make war against them, and shall overcome them, and kill them. And their bodies shall lie in the streets of the great city, which is called spiritually, Sodom and Egypt, where their Lord also was crucified. And they of the tribes, and peoples, and tongues, and nations, shall see their bodies for three days and a half: and they shall not suffer their bodies to be laid in sepulchers.

AND LEAD US NOT
INTO TEMPTATION

And they that dwell upon the earth shall rejoice over them, and make merry: and shall send gifts one to another, because these two prophets tormented them that dwelt upon the earth. And after three days and a half, the spirit of life from God entered into them. And they stood upon their feet, and great fear fell upon them that saw them.

BUT DELIVER
US FROM EVIL

And they heard a great voice from heaven, saying to them: Come up hither. And they went up to heaven in a cloud: and their enemies saw them. And at that hour there was made a great earthquake, and the tenth part of the city fell: and there were slain in the earthquake names of men seven thousand,

OUR FATHER WHO
ART IN HEAVEN
HALLOWED BE
THY NAME

and the rest were cast into a fear, and gave glory to the God of heaven.

---

1. These two witnesses, olive trees, or candlesticks have been interpreted in Church tradition as Enoch and Elijah, both of whom were 'taken by God' while yet alive, Enoch who "began to call upon the name of the Lord" (Gen. 4:26) and Elijah whose name means 'Yaweh is God'. Inwardly, they can be seen as intellect and will (resolve) laboring together in a holy unison.

THE LAMB AS IT WERE SLAIN

~THE CHURCH OF THE FIRST-BORN FROM AMONG THE DEAD~

OUR FATHER WHO ART IN HEAVEN

And I saw no temple therein. For the Lord God Almighty is the temple thereof, and the Lamb. And the city hath no need of the sun, nor of the moon, to shine in it. For the glory of God hath enlightened it: and the Lamb is the lamp thereof. Apoc. 21:22–23

HALLOWED BE THY NAME

And I beheld: and lo a Lamb stood upon mount Sion, and with him an hundred forty-four thousand, having his name and the name of his Father written on their foreheads. Apoc. 14:1

THY KINGDOM COME

And I heard as it were the voice of a great multitude, and as the voice of many waters, and as the voice of great thunders, saying: Alleluia: for the Lord our God, the Almighty, hath reigned. Let us be glad and rejoice and give glory to him. For the marriage of the Lamb is come: and his wife hath prepared herself. And it is granted to her that she should clothe herself with fine linen, glittering and white. For the fine linen are the justifications of saints. And he said to me: Write: Blessed are they that are called to the marriage supper of the Lamb. And he saith to me: These words of God are true. Apoc. 19:6–9

THY WILL BE DONE ON EARTH AS IT IS IN HEAVEN

And I saw, in the right hand of him that sat on the throne, a book, written within and without, sealed with seven seals. And I saw a strong angel, proclaiming with a loud voice: Who is worthy to open the book and to loose the seals thereof? And no man was able, neither in heaven nor on earth nor under the earth, to open the book, nor to look on it. And I wept much, because no man was found worthy to open the book, nor to see it. And one of the ancients said to me: Weep not: behold the lion of the tribe of Juda, the root of David, hath prevailed to open the book and to loose the seven seals thereof. And I saw: and behold in the midst of the throne and of the four living creatures and in the midst of the ancients, a Lamb standing, as it were slain, having seven horns and seven eyes: which are the seven Spirits of God, sent forth into all the earth. Apoc. 5:1–6

GIVE US THIS DAY OUR DAILY BREAD

They shall no more hunger nor thirst: neither shall the sun fall on them, nor any heat. For the Lamb, which is in the midst of the throne, shall rule them and shall lead them to the fountains of the waters of life: and God shall wipe away all tears from their eyes. Apoc. 7:16–17

AND FORGIVE US OUR TRESPASSES AS WE FORGIVE THOSE WHO TRESPASS AGAINST US

And I saw as it were a sea of glass mingled with fire: and them that had overcome the beast and his image and the number of his name, standing on the sea of glass, having the harps of God: And singing the canticle of Moses, the servant of God, and the canticle of the Lamb, saying: Great and wonderful are thy works, O Lord God Almighty. Just and true are thy ways, O King of ages. Who shall not fear thee, O Lord, and magnify thy name? For thou only art holy. For all nations shall come and shall adore in thy sight, because thy judgments are manifest. Apoc. 15:2–4

AND LEAD US NOT INTO TEMPTATION	And one of the ancients answered and said to me: These that are clothed in white robes, who are they? And whence came they? And I said to him: My Lord, thou knowest. And he said to me: These are they who are come out of great tribulation and have washed their robes and have made them white in the blood of the Lamb. Therefore, they are before the throne of God: and they serve him day and night in his temple. And he that sitteth on the throne shall dwell over them. Apoc. 7:13–15
BUT DELIVER US FROM EVIL	And the ten horns which thou sawest are ten kings, who have not yet received a kingdom: but shall receive power as kings, one hour after the beast. These have one design: and their strength and power they shall deliver to the beast. These shall fight with the Lamb. And the Lamb shall overcome them because he is Lord of lords and King of kings: and they that are with him are called and elect and faithful. Apoc. 17:12–14

THE SEVEN 'BLESSEDS' OF THE APOCALYPSE

A blessing to open the Book	Blessed is he, that readeth and heareth the words of this prophecy; and keepeth those things which are written in it; for the time is at hand. Apoc. 1:3
OUR FATHER WHO ART IN HEAVEN HALLOWED BE THY NAME	Blessed and holy is he that hath part in the first resurrection. In these the second death hath no power; but they shall be priests of God and of Christ; and shall reign with him a thousand years. Apoc. 20:6
THY KINGDOM COME	Blessed are they that do his commandments: that they may have a right to the tree of life, and may enter in by the gates into the city. Apoc. 22:14
THY WILL BE DONE ON EARTH AS IT IS IN HEAVEN	Blessed are the dead, who die in the Lord. From henceforth now, saith the Spirit, that they may rest from their labors; for their works follow them. Apoc. 14:13
GIVE US THIS DAY OUR DAILY BREAD	Blessed are they that are called to the marriage supper of the Lamb. Apoc. 19:9
AND FORGIVE US OUR TRESPASSES AS WE FORGIVE THOSE WHO TRESPASS AGAINST US AND LEAD US NOT INTO TEMPTATION BUT DELIVER US FROM EVIL	Blessed is he that watcheth, and keepeth his garments, lest he walk naked, and they see his shame. Apoc. 16:15
A blessing to close the book	Blessed is he that keepeth the words of the prophecy of this book. Apoc. 22:7

THE HOLY CITY

FROM CHAPTERS 21 & 22

OUR FATHER WHO
ART IN HEAVEN
HALLOWED BE
THY NAME

He that shall overcome shall possess these things. And I will be his God: and he shall be my son. Apoc. 21:7

And they shall see his face: and his name shall be on their foreheads. Apoc. 22:4

THY KINGDOM COME

I saw a new heaven and a new earth. For the first heaven and the first earth was gone: and the sea is now no more. And I, John, saw the holy city, the new Jerusalem, coming down out of heaven from God, prepared as a bride adorned for her husband. And I heard a great voice from the throne, saying: Behold the tabernacle of God with men: and he will dwell with them. And they shall be his people: and God himself with them shall be their God. Apoc. 21:1–3

And I saw no temple therein. For the Lord God Almighty is the temple thereof, and the Lamb. Apoc. 21:22

And night shall be no more. And they shall not need the light of the lamp, nor the light of the sun, because the Lord God shall enlighten then. And they shall reign for ever and ever. Apoc. 22:5

THY WILL BE DONE
ON EARTH AS IT IS
IN HEAVEN

And the city hath no need of the sun, nor of the moon, to shine in it. For the glory of God hath enlightened it: and the Lamb is the lamp thereof. And the nations shall walk in the light of it: and the kings of the earth shall bring their glory and honor into it. Apoc. 21:23–24

GIVE US THIS DAY
OUR DAILY BREAD

To him that thirsteth, I will give of the fountain of the water of life, freely. Apoc. 21:6

And he shewed me a river of water of life, clear as crystal, proceeding from the throne of God and of the Lamb. In the midst of the street thereof, and on both sides of the river, was the tree of life, bearing twelve fruits, yielding its fruits every month: the leaves of the tree for the healing of the nations. Apoc. 22:1–2

AND FORGIVE US OUR
TRESPASSES AS WE
FORGIVE THOSE
WHO TRESPASS
AGAINST US

There shall not enter into it any thing defiled or that worketh abomination or maketh a lie: but they that are written in the book of life of the Lamb. Apoc. 21:27

AND LEAD US NOT
INTO TEMPTATION

And God shall wipe away all tears from their eyes: and death shall be no more. Nor mourning, nor crying, nor sorrow shall be any more, for the former things are passed away. Apoc. 21:4

BUT DELIVER
US FROM EVIL

And there shall be no curse any more: but the throne of God and of the Lamb shall be in it. And his servants shall serve him. Apoc. 22:3

A NEW CANTICLE

APOCALYPSE 5:9–14

<table>
<tr><td>OUR FATHER WHO
ART IN HEAVEN
HALLOWED BE
THY NAME</td><td>And they sung a new canticle, saying: Thou art worthy, O Lord, to take the book and open the seals thereof; because thou wast slain and hast redeemed us to God, in thy blood, out of every tribe and tongue and people and nation;</td></tr>
<tr><td>THY KINGDOM COME</td><td>And hast made us to our God a kingdom and priests; and we shall reign on the earth.</td></tr>
<tr><td>THY WILL BE DONE
IN HEAVEN</td><td>*The praise of glory by invisible creation*
And I beheld, and I heard the voice of many angels round about the throne and the living creatures and the ancients (and the number of them was myriads of myriads), saying with a loud voice: The Lamb that was slain is worthy to receive power and wealth and wisdom and strength and honor and glory and benediction.</td></tr>
<tr><td>THY WILL BE DONE
ON EARTH</td><td>*The praise of glory by visible creation*
And every creature which is in heaven and on the earth and under the earth, and such as are in the sea, and all that are in them, I heard all saying: To him that sitteth on the throne and to the Lamb, benediction and honor and glory and might, for ever and ever.</td></tr>
<tr><td>GIVE US THIS DAY
OUR DAILY BREAD</td><td>And the four living creatures said: Amen.[1] And the four and twenty ancients fell down on their faces and adored[2] him that liveth for ever and ever.</td></tr>
</table>

---

1. In early Christian times 'to take the Amen' meant 'to receive Communion'. Cf. Apoc. 3:14.

2. In the age to come and even here and now there is the Eucharist, at once 'daily' and 'supersubstantial' , there is the Lamb of God, at once slain and redemptively alive, to communicate the Spirit's everlasting life, which we in turn offer back to God in the great mystery of adoration. Adoration is the very life-blood and marrow of the deified creature.

VI

PSALMIC MUSIC

OUR FATHER WHO ART IN HEAVEN HALLOWED
BE THY NAME—*An Alphabet for the Praise of God,*
The Six Psalms of Christic Prayer
THY KINGDOM COME—*Learning Scripture by Heart,*
Going up to Jerusalem
THY WILL BE DONE ON EARTH AS IT IS
IN HEAVEN—*An Alphabet for the Will of God*
GIVE US THIS DAY OUR DAILY BREAD—*The 'Hallel' of the Mystical Supper*
AND FORGIVE US OUR TRESPASSES AS WE FORGIVE THOSE
WHO TRESPASS AGAINST US—*The Seven Penitential Psalms*
AND LEAD US NOT INTO TEMPTATION—*Converting the soul, rejoicing the heart*
BUT DELIVER US FROM EVIL—*Coming to Judgment*

INTRODUCTION

Attunement to the word of God hidden everywhere in daily life proceeds from the singing of psalms. What a commandment St Paul has decreed for us: "Be ye filled with the Holy Spirit, speaking to yourselves in psalms and hymns and spiritual canticles, singing and making melody in your hearts to the Lord" (Eph. 5:18–19)—the eleventh commandment, the commandment of the singing heart. Psalms! They pervade the sacramental mysteries, even when not quoted directly; since earliest Christian times they pervade and are the 'liturgy of the hours': daily, weekly, yearly, century after century. At first hearing they seem to ramble; when viewed as a whole, they seem haphazard, with strange inconsistencies. Thus we read in the midrash on Psalm 3:

> As to the exact order of David's Psalms, Scripture says elsewhere: *Man knoweth not the order thereof* (Job 28:13). R[abbi] Eleazar taught: The sections of Scripture are not arranged in their proper order. For if they were arranged in their proper order, and any man so read them, he would be able to resurrect the dead and perform other miracles. For this reason the proper order of the sections of Scripture is hidden from mortals and known only to the Holy One.[1]

If this is so, then Christ, who worked untold miracles, raised the dead and even Himself,[2] knew the proper order, He who is the fulfillment of Scripture, He who is (John 8:58). This same Christ has said (John 14:10–12):

> But the Father who abideth in me, he doth the works. Believe you not that I am in the Father and the Father in me? Otherwise believe for the very works' sake. Amen, amen, I say to you, he that believeth in me, the works that I do, he also shall do: and greater than these shall he do.

Extravagant as this word may seem, we see it enacted again and again by priests in the holy mystery of the Eucharist, and perhaps—God alone knows—in this present rearrangement of psalms sung in the key of the Lord's Prayer.

Before entering this chapter, though, we must first contemplate David, the singer of psalms, and his musical instrument, the ten-stringed lyre. Two lessons in the playing of the lyre, as interpreted by Maximus the Confessor in his *Mystagogia*, follow.

---

1. *The Midrash on Psalms*, Vol. 1, p. 49.
2. Nowhere in scripture does it say that Christ raised Himself from the dead, and yet Paul informs us that Christ was raised 'by the glory of the Father' (Rom. 6:4), that same glory that is native to Christ in his oneness with the Father (John 10:30). How unbounded the intratrinitarian latitude! There is even a suggestion and more than a suggestion when Christ declares: "Therefore doth the Father love me: because I lay down my life, that I may take it again. No man taketh it away from me: but I lay it down of myself. And I have power to lay it down: and I have power to take it up again. This commandment have I received of my Father" (John 10:17–18). And yet always begotten of the Father: eternally, in the world, and lastly from realm of *sheol*—the firstborn from the dead (Col. 1:18).

THE LYRE OF DAVID'S HEART

PSALM 32

OUR FATHER WHO
ART IN HEAVEN
HALLOWED BE
THY NAME

Rejoice in the Lord, O ye just: praise becometh the upright.
Give praise to the Lord on the harp;
sing to him with the lyre, the instrument of ten strings.
Sing to him a new canticle, sing well unto him with a loud noise.

THY KINGDOM COME

For the word of the Lord is right,
and all his works are done with faithfulness.
He loveth mercy and judgment; the earth is full of the mercy of the Lord.

THY WILL BE DONE
ON EARTH AS IT IS
IN HEAVEN

By the word of the Lord the heavens were established;
and all the power of them by the spirit of his mouth:
Gathering together the waters of the sea, as in a vessel;
laying up the depths in storehouses.
Let all the earth fear the Lord,
and let all the inhabitants of the world be in awe of him.
For he spoke and they were made: he commanded and they were created.
The Lord bringeth to nought the counsels of nations;
and he rejecteth the devices of people,
and casteth away the counsels of princes.
But the counsel of the Lord standeth for ever:
the thoughts of his heart to all generations.
Blessed is the nation whose God is the Lord:
the people whom he hath chosen for his inheritance.

GIVE US THIS DAY
OUR DAILY BREAD

The Lord hath looked from heaven: he hath beheld all the sons of men.
From his habitation which he hath prepared,
he hath looked upon all that dwell on the earth.
He who hath made the hearts of every one of them:
who understandeth all their works.

AND FORGIVE US OUR
TRESPASSES AS WE
FORGIVE THOSE
WHO TRESPASS
AGAINST US
AND LEAD US NOT
INTO TEMPTATION

The king is not saved by a great army:
nor shall the giant be saved by his own great strength.
Vain is the horse for safety:
neither shall he be saved by the abundance of his strength.
Behold the eyes of the Lord are on them that fear him:
and on them that hope in his mercy.

BUT DELIVER
US FROM EVIL

To deliver their souls from death; and feed them in famine.
Our soul waiteth for the Lord: for he is our helper and protector.

OUR FATHER WHO
ART IN HEAVEN
HALLOWED BE
THY NAME

For in him our heart shall rejoice: and in his holy name we have trusted.
Let thy mercy, O Lord, be upon us, as we have hoped in thee.

THE 'THREADING' OF THE LYRE STRINGS

"That I might learn the meaning of the ten which sing and the ten [divine commandments] which are sung and how the ten are mystically attuned and united to the other ten… We should know that every soul by the grace of the Holy Spirit and his own works and diligence can unite these things and weave them into each other."[1]

Our Father who art in heaven
Hallowed be thy name

GOD

1 TRUTH   GOODNESS 2

'Somewhat' reveals the divine in   Reveals God when it manifests
its essence   Him in its activities

Thy kingdom come

CAUSES   —Grace—   EFFECTS

3 ENDURING KNOWLEDGE   FAITH 4
"Perpetual and unceasing movement   "The ingrained and unchanging
toward the knowable which transcends   stability in prudence, action, and
knowledge whose term is truth,   virtue (i.e. in one's powers,
the ultimate knowable"   habits, and activity)"

Thy will be done on earth as it is in heaven

5 KNOWLEDGE   —Act—   VIRTUE 6

Give us this day our daily/supersubstantial bread

7 CONTEMPLATION   —Habit—   ACTION 8
(supersubstantial)   (daily)

And forgive us our trespasses as we
forgive those who trespass against us
And lead us not into temptation
But deliver us from evil

9 WISDOM   —Potency—   PRUDENCE 10

MIND   **REASON**
(the soul's contemplative aspect)   (the soul's active aspect)

---

1. All quotes are from Chapter Five of Maximus the Confessor's *Mystagogia*, one of the most complex and rewarding chapters in Christian literature. Both Stead and Berthold translations are used.

THE 'TETRADIC' PLAYING OF THE LYRE

The 'tetradic' playing of the lyre "conveys to God the effects wisely joined to their causes and the acts to their potencies, and in exchange for these it receives a deification which creates simplicity."[1]

OUR FATHER WHO ART IN HEAVEN
HALLOWED BE THY NAME
10 Deification, the bestowal of God's beauty,[2] through His truth and goodness

THY KINGDOM COME
4 An enduring knowledge both faithful and unchanging

THY WILL BE DONE ON EARTH
AS IT IS IN HEAVEN
3 A virtuous knowledge

GIVE US THIS DAY
OUR DAILY BREAD
2 An active contemplation

AND FORGIVE US OUR TRESPASSES
AS WE FORGIVE THOSE WHO
TRESPASS AGAINST US
AND LEAD US NOT
INTO TEMPTATION
BUT DELIVER
US FROM EVIL
1 A prudent wisdom

COMMENTARY

For the Pythagoreans the 'tetrad', the first four numbers, possesses an especially sacred character; added together, these numbers produce 10, the number of completion (1+2+3+4=10), the 10 which can be reduced again to the '1' (1+0=1), as reiterated by Maximus.[3] What, then, is to be heard in this tetradic playing of the lyre? Essentially this: the inner man of the heart (1), through knowledge and love or intellect and will (2), harmonizes the soul's three aspects (3), and so gives unquavering voice to the four cardinal virtues (4). If this effort finds favor with God, instead of proceeding further in the series there is wrought, by the gift of grace, a change from 'progression' to 'conversion'—the first four numbers become 'wedded' to each other in the miracle of deification (10). Miracles that heal the body, heal the soul, or raise the dead to life pale before this miracle of 'the saints in light'.

---

1. *Ibid.*
2. Hence the title 'Philokalia', 'love of the beautiful', given to the Orthodox Church's collection of ascetic texts.
3. *The Church's Mystagogy*, Chapter 5 (Berthold, p. 193).

COMING TO JUDGMENT

PSALM 49

When Scripture speaks of rod and staff (cf. Psalm 23:4), *you should take these to signify in the prophetic sense judgment and providence, and in the moral sense psalmody and prayer. For when we are chastened by the Lord with the rod of correction* (cf. 1 Cor. 11:32)*, this is so that we may learn how to mend our ways. And when we chasten our assaiiants wilh the rod of dauntless psalmody, we become established in prayer. Since we thus wield the rod and stuff of spiritual action, let us not cease to chasten and be chastened until we are wholly in the hands of providence and escape judgment both now and hereafter.* —Gregory of Sinai, *On Commandments and Doctrines,* 161

OUR FATHER WHO
ART IN HEAVEN
HALLOWED BE
THY NAME

The God of gods, the Lord, hath spoken, and He hath called the earth
from the rising of the sun and unto the setting thereof.

THY KINGDOM COME

Out of Sion is the magnificence of His comeliness.
God shall come visibly, yea, our God,
and shall not keep silence.
Fire shall blaze before Him,
and roundabout Him shall there be a mighty tempest.

THY WILL BE DONE
ON EARTH AS IT IS
IN HEAVEN

He shall summon heaven above and the earth
that He may judge His people.
Gather together unto Him His holy ones
who have established His covenant upon sacrifices.
And the heavens shall declare His righteousness, for God is judge.
Hear, O my people, and I will speak unto thee, O Israel,
and I will testify against thee; I am God, thy God.

GIVE US THIS DAY
OUR DAILY BREAD

Not for sacrifices will I reprove thee;
nay, thy whole-burnt offerings are continually before Me.
I will not welcome bullocks out of thy house,
nor he-goats out or thy flocks.
For Mine are all the beasts of the field,
cattle on the mountains, and oxen.
I know all the fowls of the air,
and with Me is the beauty of the field.
If I hunger, not to thee will I tell it;
for Mine is the world, and the fullness thereof.
Shall I eat of the flesh of bulls?
Or the blood of goats, shall I drink it?

AND FORGIVE US OUR
TRESPASSES AS WE
FORGIVE THOSE
WHO TRESPASS
AGAINST US

Sacrifice unto God a sacrifice of praise,
and pay unto the Most High thy vows.
And call upon Me in the day or thine affliction,
and I will deliver thee,
and thou shalt glorify Me.
But unto the sinner God hath said:
Why declarest thou My statutes
and takest up My covenant in thy mouth?

AND LEAD US NOT
INTO TEMPTATION

Thou hast hated instruction,
and hast cast out My words behind thee.
If thou sawest a thief, thou didst run with him;
and with the adulterer thou hast set thy portion.
Thy mouth hath abounded with evil,
and thy tongue hath woven deceits.
Thou didst sit down and speak against thy brother,
and against thine own mother's son
didst thou lay a stumbling-block;
these things thou didst, and I kept silence.

BUT DELIVER
US FROM EVIL

Thou didst think an iniquity,
that I should be like unto thee;
I will reprove thee, and bring thy sins berore thy race.
Wherefore, understand these things, ye that forget God,
lest He snatch you away and there be none to deliver you.
A sacrifice of praise shall glorify Me,
and there is the way wherein I shall show unto him My salvation.

CONVERTING THE SOUL, REJOICING THE HEART

PSALM 18

OUR FATHER WHO ART IN HEAVEN HALLOWED BE THY NAME

The heavens shew forth the glory of God,
and the firmament declareth the work of his hands.
Day to day uttereth speech, and night to night sheweth knowledge.
There are no speeches nor languages,
where their voices are not heard.

THY KINGDOM COME

Their sound hath gone forth into all the earth:
and their words unto the ends of the world.
He hath set his tabernacle in the sun:
and he as a bridegroom coming out of his bridechamber,
hath rejoiced as a giant to run the way:

THY WILL BE DONE ON EARTH AS IT IS IN HEAVEN

Our Father who art in heaven, hallowed be thy name
His going out is from the end of heaven,
and his circuit even to the end thereof:

Thy kingdom come
and there is no one that can hide himself from his heat.

Thy will be done on earth as it is in heaven
The law of the Lord is unspotted, converting souls:
the testimony of the Lord is faithful, giving wisdom to little ones.

Give us this day our daily bread
The justices of the Lord are right, rejoicing hearts:
the commandment of the Lord is lightsome, enlightening the eyes.

And forgive us our trespasses as we forgive those who trespass against us
And lead us not into temptation
But deliver us from evil
The fear of the Lord is holy, enduring for ever and ever:
the judgments of the Lord are true, justified in themselves.

GIVE US THIS DAY OUR DAILY BREAD

More to be desired than gold and many precious stones:
and sweeter than honey and the honeycomb.
For thy servant keepeth them, and in keeping them there is a great reward.

AND FORGIVE US OUR TRESPASSES AS WE FORGIVE THOSE WHO TRESPASS AGAINST US

Who can understand sins? from my secret ones cleanse me, O Lord:
And from those of others spare thy servant.

AND LEAD US NOT INTO TEMPTATION BUT DELIVER US FROM EVIL

If they shall have no dominion over me, then shall I be without spot:
and I shall be cleansed from the greatest sin.
And the words of my mouth shall be such as may please:
and the meditation of my heart always in thy sight.
O Lord, my helper and my Redeemer.

THE SEVEN PENITENTIAL PSALMS

OUR FATHER WHO ART IN HEAVEN
HALLOWED BE THY NAME

PSALM 50

BUT DELIVER
US FROM EVIL

Have mercy on me, O God, according to thy great mercy. And according to the multitude of thy tender mercies blot out my iniquity. Wash me yet more from my iniquity, and cleanse me from my sin. For I know my iniquity, and my sin is always before me. To thee only have I sinned, and have done evil before thee: that thou mayst be justified in thy words, and mayst overcome when thou art judged. For behold I was conceived in iniquities; and in sins did my mother conceive me.

AND LEAD US NOT
INTO TEMPTATION

For behold thou hast loved truth: the uncertain and hidden things of thy wisdom thou hast made manifest to me. Thou shalt sprinkle me with hyssop, and I shall be cleansed: thou shalt wash me, and I shall be made whiter than snow.

AND FORGIVE US OUR
TRESPASSES AS WE
FORGIVE THOSE
WHO TRESPASS
AGAINST US

To my hearing thou shalt give joy and gladness: and the bones that have been humbled shall rejoice. Turn away thy face from my sins, and blot out all my iniquities.

GIVE US THIS DAY
OUR DAILY BREAD

Create a clean heart in me, O God: and renew a right spirit within me.

THY WILL BE DONE
ON EARTH AS IT
IS IN HEAVEN

Cast me not away from thy face; and take not thy holy spirit from me. Restore unto me the joy of thy salvation, and strengthen me with a perfect spirit. I will teach the unjust thy ways: and the wicked shall be converted to thee. Deliver me from blood, O God, thou God of my salvation: and my tongue shall extol thy justice.

THY KINGDOM COME

O Lord, thou wilt open my lips: and my mouth shall declare thy praise. For if thou hadst desired sacrifice, I would indeed have given it: with burnt offerings thou wilt not be delighted. A sacrifice to God is an afflicted spirit: a contrite and humbled heart, O God, thou wilt not despise.

OUR FATHER WHO
ART IN HEAVEN
HALLOWED BE
THY NAME

Deal favorably, O Lord, in thy good will with Sion; that the walls of Jerusalem may be built up. Then shalt thou accept the sacrifice of justice, oblations and whole burnt offerings: then shall they lay calves upon thy altar.

PSALM 101

Hear, O Lord, my prayer: and let my cry come to thee.
Turn not away thy face from me: in the day when I am in
trouble, incline thy ear to me.
In what day soever I shall call upon thee, hear me speedily.
For my days are vanished like smoke,
and my bones are grown dry like fuel for the fire.
I am smitten as grass, and my heart is withered:
because I forgot to eat my bread.
Through the voice of my groaning,
my bone hath cleaved to my flesh.
I am become like to a pelican of the wilderness:
I am like a night raven in the house.
I have watched, and am become as a sparrow
all alone on the housetop.
All the day long my enemies reproached me:
and they that praised me did swear against me.
For I did eat ashes like bread,
and mingled my drink with weeping.
Because of thy anger and indignation:
for having lifted me up thou hast thrown me down.
My days have declined like a shadow,
and I am withered like grass.
But thou, O Lord, endurest for ever:
and thy memorial to all generations.
Thou shalt arise and have mercy on Sion: for it is time to
have mercy on it, for the time is come.
For the stones thereof have pleased thy servants: and they
shall have pity on the earth thereof.
All the Gentiles shall fear thy name, O Lord,
and all the kings of the earth thy glory.
For the Lord hath built up Sion:
and he shall be seen in his glory.
He hath had regard to the prayer of the humble:
and he hath not despised their petition.
Let these things be written unto another generation:
and the people that shall be created shall praise the Lord:
Because he hath looked forth from his high sanctuary:
from heaven the Lord hath looked upon the earth.
That he might hear the groans of them that are in fetters:
that he might release the children of the slain:
That they may declare the name of the Lord in Sion:
and his praise in Jerusalem;
When the people assemble together, and kings,
to serve the Lord.
He answered him in the way of his strength:
Declare unto me the fewness of my days.

Call me not away in the midst of my days:
thy years are unto generation and generation.
In the beginning, O Lord, thou foundedst the earth:
and the heavens are the works of thy hands.
They shall perish but thou remainest:
and all of them shall grow old like a garment:
And as a vesture thou shalt change them,
and they shall be changed.
But thou art always the selfsame,
and thy years shall not fail.
The children of thy servants shall continue and their seed
shall be directed for ever.

THY WILL BE DONE ON EARTH AS IT IS IN HEAVEN

PSALM 142

Hear, O Lord, my prayer: give ear to my supplication
in thy truth: hear me in thy justice.
And enter not into judgment with thy servant:
for in thy sight no man living shall be justified.
For the enemy hath persecuted my soul:
he hath brought down my life to the earth.
He hath made me to dwell in darkness
as those that have been dead of old:
And my spirit is in anguish within me:
my heart within me is troubled.
I remembered the days of old, I meditated on all thy works:
I meditated upon the works of thy hands.
I stretched forth my hands to thee:
my soul is as earth without water unto thee.
Hear me speedily, O Lord: my spirit hath fainted away.
Turn not away thy face from me,
lest I be like unto them that go down into the pit.
Cause me to hear thy mercy in the morning;
for in thee have I hoped.
Make the way known to me, wherein I should walk:
for I have lifted up my soul to thee.
Deliver me from my enemies, O Lord, to thee have I fled:
teach me to do thy will, for thou art my God.
Thy good spirit shall lead me into the right land:
for thy name's sake,
O Lord, thou wilt quicken me in thy justice.
Thou wilt bring my soul out of trouble:
And in thy mercy thou wilt destroy my enemies.
And thou wilt cut off all them that afflict my soul:
for I am thy servant.

Rebuke me not, O Lord, in thy indignation;
nor chastise me in thy wrath.
For thy arrows are fastened in me:
and thy hand hath been strong upon me.
There is no health in my flesh, because of thy wrath:
there is no peace for my bones, because of my sins.
For my iniquities are gone over my head:
and as a heavy burden are become heavy upon me.
My sores are putrefied and corrupted,
because of my foolishness.
I am become miserable,
and am bowed down even to the end:
I walked sorrowful all the day long.
For my loins are filled with illusions;
and there is no health in my flesh.
I am afflicted and humbled exceedingly:
I roared with the groaning of my heart.
Lord, all my desire is before thee,
and my groaning is not hidden from thee.
My heart is troubled, my strength hath left me,
and the light of my eyes itself is not with me.
My friends and my neighbors have drawn near,
and stood against me.
And they that were near me stood afar off:
And they that sought my soul used violence.
And they that sought evils to me spoke vain things,
and studied deceits all the day long.
But I, as a deaf man, heard not:
and as a dumb man not opening his mouth.
And I became as a man that heareth not:
and that hath no reproofs in his mouth.
For in thee, O Lord, have I hoped:
thou wilt hear me, O Lord my God.
For I said: Lest at any time my enemies rejoice over me:
and whilst my feet are moved,
they speak great things against me.
For I am ready for scourges:
and my sorrow is continually before me.
For I will declare my iniquity: and I will think for my sin.
But my enemies live, and are stronger than I:
and they that hate me wrongfully are multiplied.
They that render evil for good, have detracted me,
because I followed goodness.
Forsake me not, O Lord my God:
do not thou depart from me.
Attend unto my help, O Lord, the God of my salvation.

PSALM 31

Blessed are they whose iniquities are forgiven,
and whose sins are covered.
Blessed is the man to whom the Lord hath not imputed sin,
and in whose spirit there is no guile.
Because I was silent my bones grew old;
whilst I cried out all the day long.
For day and night thy hand was heavy upon me:
I am turned in my anguish, whilst the thorn is fastened.
I have acknowledged my sin to thee,
and my injustice I have not concealed.
I said I will confess against
my self my injustice to the Lord:
and thou hast forgiven the wickedness of my sin.
For this shall every one that is holy
pray to thee in a seasonable time.
And yet in a flood of many waters,
they shall not come nigh unto him.
Thou art my refuge from the trouble
which hath encompassed me:
my joy, deliver me from them that surround me.
I will give thee understanding, and I will instruct thee in
this way, in which thou shalt go:
I will fix my eyes upon thee.
Do not become like the horse and the mule,
who have no understanding.
With bit and bridle bind fast their jaws,
who come not near unto thee.
Many are the scourges of the sinner, but mercy shall
encompass him that hopeth in the Lord.
Be glad in the Lord, and rejoice,
ye just, and glory, all ye right of heart.

AND LEAD US NOT INTO TEMPTATION

PSALM 6

O Lord, rebuke me not in thy indignation,
nor chastise me in thy wrath.
Have mercy on me, O Lord, for I am weak:
heal me, O Lord, for my bones are troubled.
And my soul is troubled exceedingly:
but thou, O Lord, how long?
Turn to me, O Lord, and deliver my soul:
O save me for thy mercy's sake.
For there is no one in death, that is mindful of thee:
and who shall confess to thee in hell?
I have labored in my groanings,
every night I will wash my bed:

I will water my couch with my tears.
My eye is troubled through indignation:
I have grown old amongst all my enemies.
Depart from me, all ye workers of iniquity: for the Lord
hath heard the voice of my weeping.
The Lord hath heard my supplication:
the Lord hath received my prayer.
Let all my enemies be ashamed,
and be very much troubled:
let them be turned back, and be ashamed very speedily.

BUT DELIVER US FROM EVIL

PSALM 129

Out of the depths I have cried to thee, O Lord:
Lord, hear my voice.
Let thy ears be attentive to the voice of my supplication.
If thou, O Lord, wilt mark iniquities:
Lord, who shall stand it.
For with thee there is merciful forgiveness:
and by reason of thy law, I have waited for thee, O Lord.
My soul hath relied on his word:
my soul hath hoped in the Lord.
From the morning watch even until night,
let Israel hope in the Lord.
Because with the Lord there is mercy:
and with him plentiful redemption.
And he shall redeem Israel from all his iniquities.

THE 'HALLEL' OF THE MYSTICAL SUPPER

The group 112–117 form the Hallel *or* Hymn of Praise, *which was embodied in the Hebrew liturgy for the great festivals. At the paschal meal 112–113:8 were sung before, and 113:9–117 after the supper.* — T. E. Bird, 'The Psalms'

OUR FATHER WHO ART IN HEAVEN
HALLOWED BE THY NAME

PSALM 112

OUR FATHER WHO
ART IN HEAVEN
HALLOWED BE
THY NAME

Praise the Lord, ye children; praise ye the name of the Lord.
Blessed be the name of the Lord: from henceforth now and forever.

THY KINGDOM COME

From the rising of the sun unto the going down of the same,
the name of the Lord is worthy of praise.

THY WILL BE DONE
ON EARTH AS IT IS
IN HEAVEN

The Lord is high above all nations:
and his glory above the heavens.
Who is as the Lord our God, who dwelleth on high,
and looketh down on the low things in heaven and in earth?

GIVE US THIS DAY
OUR DAILY BREAD
AND FORGIVE US OUR
TRESPASSES AS WE
FORGIVE THOSE
WHO TRESPASS
AGAINST US
AND LEAD US NOT
INTO TEMPTATION
BUT DELIVER
US FROM EVIL

Raising up the needy from the earth:
and lifting up the poor out of the dunghill:
that he may place him with princes;
with the princes of his people.
Who maketh a barren woman to dwell in a house;
the joyful mother of children.

THY KINGDOM COME

PSALM 115

I have believed, therefore have I spoken;
but I have been humbled exceedingly.
I said in my excess: Every man is a liar.
What shall I render to the Lord,
for all the things that he hath rendered to me?
I will take the chalice of salvation;
and I will call upon the name of the Lord.
I will pay my vows to the Lord before all his people:
Precious in the sight of the Lord is the death of his saints.
O Lord, for I am thy servant: I am thy servant, and the son
of thy handmaid. Thou hast broken my bonds:

I will sacrifice to thee the sacrifice of praise,
and I will call upon the name of the Lord.
I will pay my vows to the Lord in the sight of all his people:
In the courts of the house of the Lord,
in the midst of thee, O Jerusalem.

THY WILL BE DONE ON EARTH AS IT IS IN HEAVEN

PSALM 113

When Israel went out of Egypt,
the house of Jacob from a barbarous people:
Judea was made his sanctuary, Israel his dominion.
The sea saw and fled: Jordan was turned back.
The mountains skipped like rams,
and the hills like the lambs of the flock.
What ailed thee, O thou sea, that thou didst flee: and thou,
O Jordan, that thou wast turned back?
Ye mountains, that ye skipped like rams,
and ye hills, like lambs of the flock?
At the presence of the Lord the earth was moved,
at the presence of the God of Jacob:
Who turned the rock into pools of water,
and the stony hill into fountains of waters.
Not to us, O Lord, not to us; but to thy name give glory.
For thy mercy, and for thy truth's sake: lest the Gentiles
should say: Where is their God?
But our God is in heaven:
he hath done all things whatsoever he would.
The idols of the Gentiles are silver and gold,
the works of the hands of men.
They have mouths and speak not:
they have eyes and see not.
They have ears and hear not:
they have noses and smell not.
They have hands and feel not: they have feet and walk not:
neither shall they cry out through their throat.
Let them that make them become like unto them:
and all such as trust in them.
The house of Israel hath hoped in the Lord:
he is their helper and their protector.
The house of Aaron hath hoped in the Lord:
he is their helper and their protector.
They that fear the Lord have hoped in the Lord:
he is their helper and their protector.
The Lord hath been mindful of us, and hath blessed us.
He hath blessed the house of Israel:
he hath blessed the house of Aaron.
He hath blessed all that fear the Lord, both little and great.
May the Lord add blessings upon you:

upon you, and upon your children.
Blessed be you of the Lord, who made heaven and earth.
The heaven of heaven is the Lord's:
but the earth he has given to the children of men.
The dead shall not praise thee, O Lord:
nor any of them that go down to hell.
But we that live bless the Lord:
from this time now and for ever.

GIVE US THIS DAY OUR DAILY BREAD

PSALM 116

O Praise the Lord, all ye nations: praise him, all ye people.
For his mercy is confirmed upon us:
and the truth of the Lord remaineth for ever.

AND FORGIVE US OUR TRESPASSES AS WE FORGIVE THOSE WHO TRESPASS AGAINST US

PSALM 117

Give praise to the Lord, for he is good: for his mercy endureth for ever.
Let Israel now say, that he is good: that his mercy endureth for ever.
Let the house of Aaron now say, that his mercy endureth for ever.
Let them that fear the Lord now say, that his mercy endureth for ever.
In my trouble I called upon the Lord:
and the Lord heard me, and enlarged me.
The Lord is my helper: I will not fear what man can do unto me.
The Lord is my helper: and I will look over my enemies.
It is good to confide in the Lord,
rather than to have confidence in man.
It is good to trust in the Lord,
rather than to trust in princes.
All nations compassed me about; and, in the name of the
Lord I have been revenged on them.
Surrounding me they compassed me about: and in the
name of the Lord I have been revenged on them.
They surrounded me like bees,
and they burned like fire among thorns:
and in the name of the Lord I was revenged on them.
Being pushed I was overturned that I might fall:
but the Lord supported me.
The Lord is my strength and my praise:
and he is become my salvation.
The voice of rejoicing and of salvation
is in the tabernacles of the just.
The right hand of the Lord hath wrought strength: the
right hand of the Lord hath exalted me:
the right hand of the Lord hath wrought strength.
I shall not die, but live:
and shall declare the works of the Lord.

The Lord chastising hath chastised me:
but he hath not delivered me over to death.
Open ye to me the gates of justice:
I will go in to them, and give praise to the Lord.
This is the gate of the Lord, the just shall enter into it.
I will give glory to thee because thou hast heard me:
and art become my salvation.
The stone which the builders rejected; t
he same is become the head of the corner.
This is the Lord's doing, and it is wonderful in our eyes.
This is the day which the Lord hath made:
let us be glad and rejoice therein.
O Lord, save me: O Lord, give good success.
Blessed be he that cometh in the name of the Lord. We
have blessed you out of the house of the Lord.
The Lord is God, and he hath shone upon us.
Appoint a solemn day, with shady boughs,
even to the horn of the altar.
Thou art my God, and I will praise thee:
thou art my God, and I will exalt thee.
I will praise thee, because thou hast heard me,
and art become my salvation.
O praise ye the Lord, for he is good:
for his mercy endureth for ever.

AND LEAD US NOT INTO TEMPTATION BUT DELIVER US FROM EVIL

PSALM 114

I have loved,
because the Lord will hear the voice of my prayer.
Because he hath inclined his ear unto me:
and in my days I will call upon him.
The sorrows of death have compassed me:
and the perils of hell have found me.
I met with trouble and sorrow:
And I called upon the name of the Lord.
O Lord, deliver my soul.
The Lord is merciful and just, and our God sheweth mercy.
The Lord is the keeper of little ones:
I was humbled, and he delivered me.
Turn, O my soul, into thy rest:
for the Lord hath been bountiful to thee.
For he hath delivered my soul from death:
my eyes from tears, my feet from falling.
I will please the Lord in the land of the living.
I will be well-pleasing before the Lord
in the land of the living.

AN ALPHABET FOR THE WILL OF GOD

PSALM 118

Psalm 118, accompanied as it is by a constant repetition of words such as, 'commandments', 'statutes', and 'law', represents a psalmic rosary invoking the holy will of God. The longest psalm is simplicity itself: a single word of many facets. GJC

The simple and humble believer frees himself from the domination of the imagination by a wholehearted aspiration to live according to God's will. This is so simple, and at the same time so 'hid from the wise and the prudent' that there are no words to explain it. Archimandrite Sophrony, *Saint Silouan the Athonite*

Aleph Blessed are the undefiled in the way, who walk in the law of the Lord.[2]
Blessed are they that search his testimonies: that seek him with their whole heart.[3]
For they that work iniquity, have not walked in his ways.[7]
Thou hast commanded thy commandments to be kept most diligently.[3]
O! that my ways may be directed to keep thy justifications.[3]
Then shall I not be confounded, when I shall look into all thy commandments.[6]
I will praise thee with uprightness of heart, when I shall have learned the judgments of thy justice.[3]
I will keep thy justifications: O! do not thou utterly forsake me.[7]

Beth By what doth a young man correct his way? By observing thy words.[6]
With my whole heart have I sought after thee: let me not stray from thy commandments.[7]
Thy words have I hidden in my heart, that I may not sin against thee.[6]
Blessed art thou, O Lord: teach me thy justifications.[1]
With my lips I have pronounced all the judgments of thy mouth.[4]
I have been delighted in the way of thy testimonies, as in all riches.[2]
I will meditate on thy commandments: and I will consider thy ways.[3]
I will think of thy justifications: I will not forget thy words.[5]

Gimel Give bountifully to thy servant, enliven me: and I shall keep thy words.[4]
Open thou my eyes: and I will consider the wondrous things of thy law.[2]
I am a sojourner on the earth: hide not thy commandments from me.[2]
My soul hath coveted to long for thy justifications, at all times.[3]
Thou hast rebuked the proud: they are cursed who decline from thy commandments.[7]
Remove from me reproach and contempt: because I have sought after thy testimonies.[3]
For princes sat, and spoke against me: but thy servant was employed in thy justifications.[6]
For thy testimonies are my meditation: and thy justifications my counsel.[3]

---

1. Our Father who art in heaven, hallowed be thy name.
2. Thy kingdom come.
3. Thy will be done on earth as it is in heaven.
4. Give us this day our daily bread.
5. And forgive us our trespasses as we forgive those who trespass against us.
6. And lead us not into temptation.
7. But deliver us from evil.

Daleth My soul hath cleaved to the pavement: quicken thou me according to thy word.[4]
I have declared my ways, and thou hast heard me: teach me thy justifications.[3]
Make me to understand the way of thy justifications: and I shall be exercised in thy wondrous works.[4]
My soul hath slumbered through heaviness: strengthen thou me in thy words.[6]
Remove from me the way of iniquity: and out of thy law have mercy on me.[7]
I have chosen the way of truth: thy judgments I have not forgotten.[3]
I have stuck to thy testimonies, O Lord: put me not to shame.[7]
I have run the way of thy commandments, when thou didst enlarge my heart.[2]

He Set before me for a law the way of thy justifications, O Lord: and I will always seek after it.[1]
Give me understanding, and I will search thy law; and I will keep it with my whole heart.[2]
Lead me into the path of thy commandments; for this same I have desired.[3]
Incline my heart into thy testimonies and not to covetousness.[4]
Turn away my eyes that they may not behold vanity: quicken me in thy way.[5]
Establish thy word to thy servant, in thy fear.[6]
Turn away my reproach, which I have apprehended: for thy judgments are delightful.[7]
Behold I have longed after thy precepts: quicken me in thy justice.[4]

Vau Let thy mercy also come upon me, O Lord: thy salvation according to thy word.[1]
So shall I answer them that reproach me in any thing; that I have trusted in thy words.[6]
And take not thou the word of truth utterly out of my mouth:
for in thy words, I have hoped exceedingly.[7]
So shall I always keep thy law, for ever and ever.[2]
And I walked at large: because I have sought after thy commandments.[3]
And I spoke of thy testimonies before kings: and I was not ashamed.[6]
I meditated also on thy commandments, which I loved.[1]
And I lifted up my hands to thy commandments, which I loved,
and I was exercised in thy justifications.[5]

Zain Be thou mindful of thy word to thy servant, in which thou hast given me hope.[5]
This hath comforted me in my humiliation: because thy word hath enlivened me.[6]
The proud did iniquitously altogether: but I declined not from thy law.[5]
I remembered, O Lord, thy judgments of old: and I was comforted.[1]
A fainting hath taken hold of me, because of the wicked that forsake thy law.[6]
Thy justifications were the subject of my song, in the place of my pilgrimage.[2]
In the night I have remembered thy name, O Lord: and have kept thy law.[1]
This happened to me: because I sought after thy justifications.[3]

---

1. Our Father who art in heaven, hallowed be thy name.
2. Thy kingdom come.
3. Thy will be done on earth as it is in heaven.
4. Give us this day our daily bread.
5. And forgive us our trespasses as we forgive those who trespass against us.
6. And lead us not into temptation.
7. But deliver us from evil.

Heth O Lord, my portion, I have said, I would keep thy law.[4]
I entreated thy face with all my heart: have mercy on me according to thy word.[1]
I have thought on my ways: and turned my feet unto thy testimonies.[5]
I am ready, and am not troubled: that I may keep thy commandments.[6]
The cords of the wicked have encompassed me: but I have not forgotten thy law.[7]
I rose at midnight to give praise to thee; for the judgments of thy justification.[1]
I am a partaker with all them that fear thee, and that keep thy commandments.[4]
The earth, O Lord, is full of thy mercy: teach me thy justifications.[3]

Teth Thou hast done well with thy servant, O Lord, according to thy word.[5]
Teach me goodness and discipline and knowledge; for I have believed thy commandments.[3]
Before I was humbled I offended; therefore have I kept thy word.[7]
Thou art good; and in thy goodness teach me thy justifications.[3]
The iniquity of the proud hath been multiplied over me:
but I will seek thy commandments with my whole heart.[6]
Their heart is curdled like milk: but I have meditated on thy law.[7]
It is good for me that thou hast humbled me, that I may learn thy justifications.[6]
The law of thy mouth is good to me, above thousands of gold and silver.[1]

Yod Thy hands have made me and formed me: give me understanding,
and I will learn thy commandments.[3]
They that fear thee shall see me, and shall be glad: because I have greatly hoped in thy words.[2]
I know, O Lord, that thy judgments are equity: and in thy truth thou hast humbled me.[6]
O! let thy mercy be for my comfort, according to thy word unto thy servant.[5]
Let thy tender mercies come unto me, and I shall live: for thy law is my meditation.[4]
Let the proud be ashamed, because they have done unjustly towards me:
but I will be employed in thy commandments.[7]
Let them that fear thee turn to me: and they that know thy testimonies.[5]
Let my heart be undefiled in thy justifications, that I may not be confounded.[6]

Caph My soul hath fainted after thy salvation: and in thy word I have very much hoped.[4]
My eyes have failed for thy word, saying: When wilt thou comfort me?[7]
For I am become like a bottle in the frost: I have not forgotten thy justifications.[7]
How many are the days of thy servant: when wilt thou execute judgment on them that persecute me?[7]
The wicked have told me fables: but not as thy law.[6]
All thy statutes are truth: they have persecuted me unjustly, do thou help me.[7]
They had almost made an end of me upon earth: but I have not forsaken thy commandments.[7]
Quicken thou me according to thy mercy: and I shall keep the testimonies of thy mouth.[4]

---

1. Our Father who art in heaven, hallowed be thy name.

2. Thy kingdom come.

3. Thy will be done on earth as it is in heaven.

4. Give us this day our daily bread.

5. And forgive us our trespasses as we forgive those who trespass against us.

6. And lead us not into temptation.

7. But deliver us from evil.

Lamed For ever, O Lord, thy word standeth firm in heaven.[1]
Thy truth unto all generations: thou hast founded the earth, and it continueth.[3]
By thy ordinance the day goeth on: for all things serve thee.[2]
Unless thy law had been my meditation, I had then perhaps perished in my abjection.[7]
Thy justifications I will never forget: for by them thou hast given me life.[4]
I am thine, save thou me: for I have sought thy justifications.[2]
The wicked have waited for me to destroy me: but I have understood thy testimonies.[7]
I have seen an end of all perfection: thy commandment is exceeding broad.[2]

Mem O how have I loved thy law, O Lord! it is my meditation all the day.[1]
Through thy commandment, thou hast made me wiser than my enemies: for it is ever with me.[2]
I have understood more than all my teachers: because thy testimonies are my meditation.[2]
I have had understanding above ancients: because I have sought thy commandments.[4]
I have restrained my feet from every evil way: that I may keep thy words.[7]
I have not declined from thy judgments, because thou hast set me a law.[6]
How sweet are thy words to my palate! more than honey to my mouth.[4]
By thy commandments I have had understanding: therefore have I hated every way of iniquity.[7]

Nun Thy word is a lamp to my feet, and a light to my paths.[3]
I have sworn and am determined to keep the judgments of thy justice.[5]
I have been humbled, O Lord, exceedingly: quicken thou me according to thy word.[4]
The free offerings of my mouth make acceptable, O Lord: and teach me thy judgments.[1]
My soul is continually in my hands: and I have not forgotten thy law.[1]
Sinners have laid a snare for me: but I have not erred from thy precepts.[6]
I have purchased thy testimonies for an inheritance for ever: because they are the joy of my heart.[2]
I have inclined my heart to do thy justifications for ever, for the reward.[3]

Samech I have hated the unjust: and have loved thy law.[7]
Thou art my helper and my protector: and in thy word I have greatly hoped.[4]
Depart from me, ye malignant: and I will search the commandments of my God.[6]
Uphold me according to thy word, and I shall live: and let me not be confounded in my expectation.[4]
Help me, and I shall be saved: and I will meditate always on thy justifications.[7]
Thou hast despised all them that fall off from thy judgments; for their thought is unjust.[7]
I have accounted all the sinners of the earth prevaricators: therefore have I loved thy testimonies.[7]
Pierce thou my flesh with thy fear: for I am afraid of thy judgments.[5]

---

1. Our Father who art in heaven, hallowed be thy name.
2. Thy kingdom come.
3. Thy will be done on earth as it is in heaven.
4. Give us this day our daily bread.
5. And forgive us our trespasses as we forgive those who trespass against us.
6. And lead us not into temptation.
7. But deliver us from evil.

Ain I have done judgment and justice: give me not up to them that slander me.[5]
Uphold thy servant unto good: let not the proud calumniate me.[6]
My eyes have fainted after thy salvation: and for the word of thy justice.[2]
Deal with thy servant according to thy mercy: and teach me thy justifications.[3]
I am thy servant: give me understanding that I may know thy testimonies.
It is time, O Lord, to do: they have dissipated thy law.[4]
Therefore have I loved thy commandments above gold and the topaz.[1]
Therefore was I directed to all thy commandments: I have hated all wicked ways.[3]

Pe Thy testimonies are wonderful: therefore my soul hath sought them.[3]
The declaration of thy words giveth light: and giveth understanding to little ones.[2]
I opened my mouth, and panted: because I longed for thy commandments.[4]
Look thou upon me, and have mercy on me according to the judgment of them that love thy name.[5]
Direct my steps according to thy word: and let no iniquity have dominion over me.[6]
Redeem me from the calumnies of men: that I may keep thy commandments.[7]
Make thy face to shine upon thy servant: and teach me thy justifications.[1]
My eyes have sent forth springs of water: because they have not kept thy law.[5]

Tzade Thou art just, O Lord: and thy judgment is right.[5]
Thou hast commanded justice thy testimonies: and thy truth exceedingly.[3]
My zeal hath made me pine away: because my enemies forgot thy words.[7]
Thy word is exceedingly refined: and thy servant hath loved it.[6]
I am very young and despised; but I forget not thy justifications.[6]
Thy justice is justice for ever: and thy law is the truth.[2]
Trouble and anguish have found me: thy commandments are my meditation.[6]
Thy testimonies are justice for ever: give me understanding, and I shall live.[4]

Koph I cried with my whole heart, hear me, O Lord: I will seek thy justifications.[6]
I cried unto thee, save me: that I may keep thy commandments.[7]
I prevented the dawning of the day, and cried: because in thy words I very much hoped.[4]
My eyes to thee have prevented the morning: that I might meditate on thy words.[3]
Hear thou my voice, O Lord, according to thy mercy: and quicken me according to thy judgment.[4]
They that persecute me have drawn nigh to iniquity; but they are gone far off from thy law.[6]
Thou art near, O Lord: and all thy ways are truth.[1]
I have known from the beginning concerning thy testimonies:
that thou hast founded them for ever.[2]

---

1. Our Father who art in heaven, hallowed be thy name.
2. Thy kingdom come.
3. Thy will be done on earth as it is in heaven.
4. Give us this day our daily bread.
5. And forgive us our trespasses as we forgive those who trespass against us.
6. And lead us not into temptation.
7. But deliver us from evil.

Resh See my humiliation and deliver me for I have not forgotten thy law.[7]
Judge my judgment and redeem me: quicken thou me for thy word's sake.[5]
Salvation is far from sinners; because they have not sought thy justifications.[7]
Many, O Lord, are thy mercies: quicken me according to thy judgment.[4]
Many are they that persecute me and afflict me; but I have not declined from thy testimonies.[6]
I beheld the transgressors, and pined away; because they kept not thy word.[7]
Behold I have loved thy commandments, O Lord; quicken me thou in thy mercy.[4]
The beginning of thy words is truth: all the judgments of thy justice are for ever.[2]

Shin Princes have persecuted me without cause: and my heart hath been in awe of thy words.[6]
I will rejoice at thy words, as one that hath found great spoil.[2]
I have hated and abhorred iniquity; but I have loved thy law.[5]
Seven times a day I have given praise to thee, for the judgments of thy justice.[1]
Much peace have they that love thy law, and to them there is no stumbling block.[3]
I looked for thy salvation, O Lord: and I loved thy commandments.[2]
My soul hath kept thy testimonies and hath loved them exceedingly.[3]
I have kept thy commandments and thy testimonies: because all my ways are in thy sight.[1]

Tav Let my supplication, O Lord, come near in thy sight:
give me understanding according to thy word.[4]
Let my request come in before thee; deliver thou me according to thy word.[7]
My lips shall utter a hymn, when thou shalt teach me thy justifications.[1]
My tongue shall pronounce thy word: because all thy commandments are justice.[5]
Let thy hand be with me to save me; for I have chosen thy precepts.[7]
I have longed for thy salvation, O Lord; and thy law is my meditation.[2]
My soul shall live and shall praise thee: and thy judgments shall help me.[1]
I have gone astray like a sheep that is lost: seek thy servant,
because I have not forgotten thy commandments.[7]

---

1. Our Father who art in heaven, hallowed be thy name.
2. Thy kingdom come.
3. Thy will be done on earth as it is in heaven.
4. Give us this day our daily bread.
5. And forgive us our trespasses as we forgive those who trespass against us.
6. And lead us not into temptation.
7. But deliver us from evil.

LEARNING SCRIPTURE *BY HEART*

A DISTILLATION OF PSALM 118

OUR FATHER WHO
ART IN HEAVEN
HALLOWED BE
THY NAME

I entreated thy face with all my heart: have mercy on me according to thy word. 118:58

THY KINGDOM COME

I have purchased thy testimonies for an inheritance for ever: because they are the joy of my heart. I have inclined my heart to do thy justifications for ever, for the reward. 118:111–112

THY WILL BE DONE
ON EARTH AS IT IS
IN HEAVEN

Blessed are they that search his testimonies: that seek him with their whole heart. 118:2
I will praise thee with uprightness of heart, when I shall have learned the judgments of thy justice. 118:7
I have run the way of thy commandments, when thou didst enlarge my heart. 118:32

GIVE US THIS DAY
OUR DAILY BREAD

Give me understanding, and I will search thy law; and I will keep it with my whole heart. 118:34
Incline my heart into thy testimonies and not to covetousness. 118:36

AND FORGIVE US OUR
TRESPASSES AS WE
FORGIVE THOSE
WHO TRESPASS
AGAINST US

Let my heart be undefiled in thy justifications, that I may not be confounded. 118:80

AND LEAD US NOT
INTO TEMPTATION

I cried with my whole heart, hear me, O Lord: I will seek thy justifications. 118:145
Princes have persecuted me without cause: and my heart hath been in awe of thy words. 118:161

BUT DELIVER
US FROM EVIL

With my whole heart have I sought after thee: let me not stray from thy commandments. Thy words have I hidden in my heart, that I may not sin against thee. 118:10–11
The iniquity of the proud hath been multiplied over me: but I will seek thy commandments with my whole heart. Their heart is curdled like milk: but I have meditated on thy law. 118:69–70

COMMENTARY

Much attention has been focused on the eightfoldness of this psalm, both in its structure (see p. 355) and in the repetition of the word 'Torah' or 'law' and its synonyms. But what of 'heart', a word that is said to encompass the five books of Moses?[1] There are fifteen occurrences—the fifteen steps to the Lord's Temple—and the one that is lacking to make 'twice-eight' is ours to supply.

---

1. In Hebrew, the *Pentateuch* begins with *beith* and ends with *lamed*, the two consonants that form the word 'heart', 'lev'.

GOING UP TO JERUSALEM

A PILGRIMAGE THROUGH THE ASCENSIONAL PSALMS[1]

Behold, we go up to Jerusalem, and all things shall be accomplished which were written by the prophets concerning the Son of man. Luke 18:31

OUR FATHER WHO ART IN HEAVEN HALLOWED BE THY NAME

PSALM 133

Behold now bless ye the Lord, all ye servants of the Lord:
Who stand in the house of the Lord,
in the courts of the house of our God.
In the nights lift up your hands to the holy places,
and bless ye the Lord.
May the Lord out of Sion bless thee,
he that made heaven and earth.

HALLOWED BE THY NAME THY KINGDOM COME

PSALM 131

O Lord, remember David, and all his meekness.
How he swore to the Lord,
he vowed a vow to the God of Jacob:
If I shall enter into the tabernacle of my house:
if I shall go up into the bed wherein I lie:
If I shall give sleep to my eyes, or slumber to my eyelids,
Or rest to my temples: until I find out a place for the Lord,
a tabernacle for the God of Jacob.
Behold we have heard of it in Ephrata:
we have found it in the fields of the wood.
We will go into his tabernacle:
We will adore in the place where his feet stood.
Arise, O Lord, into thy resting place:
thou and the ark, which thou hast sanctified.
Let thy priests be clothed with justice:
and let thy saints rejoice.
For thy servant David's sake,
turn not away the face of thy anointed.
The Lord hath sworn truth to David,
and he will not make it void:
Of the fruit of thy womb I will set upon thy throne.
If thy children will keep thy covenant, and these my
testimonies which I shall teach them:
Their children also for evermore shall sit upon thy throne.
For the Lord hath chosen Sion:

---

1. It is conjectured that the ascensional or gradual psalms were recited along the pilgrim way leading up to Jerusalem or on the fifteen steps leading up to the Temple.

he hath chosen it for his dwelling.
This is my rest for ever and ever:
here will I dwell, for I have chosen it.
Blessing, I will bless her widow:
I will satisfy her poor with bread.
I will clothe her priests with salvation:
and her saints shall rejoice with exceeding great joy.
There will I bring forth a horn to David:
I have prepared a lamp for my anointed.
His enemies I will clothe with confusion:
but upon him will my sanctification flourish.

THY KINGDOM COME

PSALM 132

Behold how good and how pleasant
it is for brethren to dwell in unity.
Like the precious ointment on the head,
that ran down upon the beard, the beard of Aaron,
Which ran down to the skirt of his garment:
As the dew of Hermon,
which descendeth upon mount Sion.
For there the Lord hath commandeth blessing,
and life for evermore.

PSALM 121

I rejoiced at the things that were said to me:
We shall go into the house of the Lord.
Our feet were standing in thy courts, O Jerusalem.
Jerusalem, which is built as a city,
which is compact together.
For thither did the tribes go up, the tribes of the Lord: the
testimony of Israel, to praise the name of the Lord.
Because their seats have sat in judgment,
seats upon the house of David.
Pray ye for the things that are for the peace of Jerusalem:
and abundance for them that love thee.
Let peace be in thy strength: and abundance in thy towers.
For the sake of my brethren, and of my neighbors,
I spoke peace of thee.
Because of the house of the Lord our God,
I have sought good things for thee.

THY KINGDOM COME THY WILL BE DONE ON EARTH AS IT IS IN HEAVEN

PSALM 124

They that trust in the Lord shall be as mount Sion:
He shall not be moved for ever that dwelleth in Jerusalem.

Mountains are round about it: so the Lord is round about
his people from henceforth now and for ever.
For the Lord will not leave the rod of sinners
upon the lot of the just:
That the just may not stretch forth their hands to iniquity.
Do good, O Lord, to those that are good,
and to the upright of heart.
But such as turn aside into bonds,
the Lord shall lead out with the workers of iniquity:
peace upon Israel.

THY WILL BE DONE ON EARTH AS IT IS IN HEAVEN

PSALM 120

I have lifted up my eyes to the mountains, from whence
help shall come to me.
My help is from the Lord, who made heaven and earth.
May he not suffer thy foot to be moved:
neither let him slumber that keepeth thee.
Behold he shall neither slumber nor sleep,
that keepeth Israel.
The Lord is thy keeper,
the Lord is thy protection upon thy right hand.
The sun shall not burn thee by day:
nor the moon by night.
The Lord keepeth thee from all evil:
may the Lord keep thy soul.
May the Lord keep thy going in and thy going out; from
henceforth now and for ever.

THY WILL BE DONE ON EARTH AS IT IS IN HEAVEN GIVE US THIS DAY OUR DAILY BREAD

PSALM 126

Unless the Lord build the house,
they labor in vain that build it.
Unless the Lord keep the city,
he watcheth in vain that keepeth it.
It is vain for you to rise before light,
rise ye after you have sitten,
you that eat the bread of sorrow.
When he shall give sleep to his beloved,
Behold the inheritance of the Lord are children:
the reward, the fruit of the womb.
As arrows in the hand of the mighty,
so the children of them that have been shaken.
Blessed is the man that hath filled the desire with them;
He shall not be confounded when he shall speak to his
enemies in the gate.

GIVE US THIS DAY OUR DAILY BREAD

PSALM 125

When the lord brought back the captivity of Sion,
we became like men comforted.
Then was our mouth filled with gladness;
and our tongue with joy.
Then shall they say among the Gentiles:
The Lord hath done great things for them.
The Lord hath done great things for us:
we are become joyful.
Turn again our captivity, O Lord, as a stream in the south.
They that sow in tears shall reap in joy.
Going they went and wept, casting their seeds.
But coming they shall come with joyfulness,
carrying their sheaves.

GIVE US THIS DAY OUR DAILY BREAD AND FORGIVE US OUR TRESPASSES AS WE FORGIVE THOSE WHO TRESPASS AGAINST US

PSALM 127

Blessed are all they that fear the Lord: that walk in his ways.
For thou shalt eat the labors of thy hands: blessed art thou,
and it shall be well with thee.
Thy wife as a fruitful vine, on the sides of thy house.
Behold, thus shall the man be blessed that feareth the Lord.
May the Lord bless thee out of Sion:
And mayest thou see the good things of Jerusalem
all the days of thy life.
And mayest thou see thy children's children,
peace upon Israel.

AND FORGIVE US OUR TRESPASSES AS WE FORGIVE THOSE WHO TRESPASS AGAINST US

PSALM 129

Out of the depths I have cried to thee, O Lord:
Lord, hear my voice. Let thy ears be attentive
to the voice of my supplication.
If thou, O Lord, wilt mark iniquities:
Lord, who shall stand it.
For with thee there is merciful forgiveness:
and by reason of thy law, I have waited for thee,
O Lord. My soul hath relied on his word:
my soul hath hoped in the Lord.
From the morning watch even until night,
let Israel hope in the Lord.
Because with the Lord there is mercy:
and with him plentiful redemption.
And he shall redeem Israel from all his iniquities.

AND FORGIVE US OUR TRESPASSES AS WE FORGIVE THOSE WHO TRESPASS AGAINST US
AND LEAD US NOT INTO TEMPTATION

PSALM 130

Lord, my heart is not exalted: nor are my eyes lofty.
Neither have I walked in great matters,
nor in wonderful things above me.
If I was not humbly minded, but exalted my soul:
As a child that is weaned is towards his mother,
so reward in my soul.
Let Israel hope in the Lord,
from henceforth now and for ever.

AND LEAD US NOT INTO TEMPTATION

PSALM 122

To thee have I lifted up my eyes,
who dwellest in heaven.
Behold as the eyes of the servants
are on the hands of their masters,
As the eyes of the handmaid
are on the hands of her mistress:
So are our eyes unto the Lord our God,
until he have mercy on us.
Have mercy on us, O Lord, have mercy on us:
for we are greatly filled with contempt.
For our soul is greatly filled: we are a reproach to the rich,
and contempt to the proud.

AND LEAD US NOT INTO TEMPTATION BUT DELIVER US FROM EVIL

PSALM 128

Often have they fought against me
from my youth, let Israel now say.
Often have they fought against me from my youth:
but they could not prevail over me.
The wicked have wrought upon my back:
they have lengthened their iniquity.
The Lord who is just will cut the necks of sinners:
Let them all be confounded
and turned back that hate Sion.
Let them be as grass on the tops of houses:
which withered before it be plucked up:
Wherewith the mower filleth not his hand:
nor he that gathereth sheaves his bosom.
And they that have passed by have not said:
The blessing of the Lord be upon you:
we have blessed you in the name of the Lord.

BUT DELIVER US FROM EVIL

PSALM 119

In my trouble I cried to the Lord: and he heard me.
O Lord, deliver my soul from wicked lips,
and a deceitful tongue.
What shall be given to thee, or what shall be added to thee,
to a deceitful tongue.
The sharp arrows of the mighty, with coals that lay waste.
Woe is me, that my sojourning is prolonged!
I have dwelt with the inhabitants of Cedar:
my soul hath been long a sojourner.
With them that hate peace I was peaceable: when I spoke to
them they fought against me without cause.

BUT DELIVER US FROM EVIL

OUR FATHER WHO ART IN HEAVEN HALLOWED BE THY NAME

PSALM 123

If it had not been that the Lord was with us,
let Israel now say:
If it had not been that the Lord was with us,
When men rose up against us perhaps
they had swallowed us up alive.
When their fury was enkindled against us,
perhaps the waters had swallowed us up.
Our soul hath passed through a torrent: perhaps our soul
had passed through a water insupportable.
Blessed be the Lord,
who hath not given us to be a prey to their teeth.
Our soul hath been delivered as a sparrow
out of the snare of the followers.
The snare is broken, and we are delivered.
Our help is in the name of the Lord,
who made heaven and earth.

THE SIX PSALMS OF CHRISTIC PRAYER

The meaning of the Six Psalms is very deep; it is the prayer of the Son to God the Father. — Elder Nektary of Optina[1]

OUR FATHER WHO ART IN HEAVEN, HALLOWED BE THY NAME, THY KINGDOM COME

PSALM 102

OUR FATHER WHO ART IN HEAVEN HALLOWED BE THY NAME

Bless the Lord, O my soul: and let all that is within me bless his holy name. Bless the Lord, O my soul, and never forget all he hath done for thee.

THY KINGDOM COME THY WILL BE DONE ON EARTH AS IT IS IN HEAVEN

Who forgiveth all thy iniquities: who healeth all thy diseases. Who redeemeth thy life from destruction: who crowneth thee with mercy and compassion.

GIVE US THIS DAY OUR DAILY BREAD

Who satisfieth thy desire with good things: thy youth shall be renewed like the eagle's.

AND FORGIVE US OUR TRESPASSES AS WE FORGIVE THOSE WHO TRESPASS AGAINST US

The Lord doth mercies, and judgment for all that suffer wrong. He hath made his ways known to Moses: his wills to the children of Israel.

AND LEAD US NOT INTO TEMPTATION

The Lord is compassionate and merciful: longsuffering and plenteous in mercy. He will not always be angry: nor will he threaten for ever.

BUT DELIVER US FROM EVIL

He hath not dealt with us according to our sins: nor rewarded us according to our iniquities.

AND LEAD US NOT INTO TEMPTATION

For according to the height of the heaven above the earth: he hath strengthened his mercy towards them that fear him.

AND FORGIVE US OUR TRESPASSES AS WE FORGIVE THOSE WHO TRESPASS AGAINST US

As far as the east is from the west, so far hath he removed our iniquities from us.

GIVE US THIS DAY OUR DAILY BREAD

As a father hath compassion on his children, so hath the Lord compassion on them that fear him: for he knoweth our frame. He remembereth that we are dust:

---

1. I. M. Kontzevitch, *Elder Nektary of Optina*, p. 185. The Six Psalms are read daily at the beginning of Matins.

THY WILL BE DONE ON EARTH AS IT IS IN HEAVEN	Man's days are as grass, as the flower of the field so shall he flourish. For the spirit shall pass in him, and he shall not be: and he shall know his place no more. But the mercy of the Lord is from eternity and unto eternity upon them that fear him: And his justice unto children's children, to such as keep his covenant, and are mindful of his commandments to do them.
THY KINGDOM COME	The lord hath prepared his throne in heaven: and his kingdom shall rule over all.
OUR FATHER WHO ART IN HEAVEN HALLOWED BE THY NAME	Bless the Lord, all ye his angels: you that are mighty in strength, and execute his word, hearkening to the voice of his orders. Bless the Lord, all ye his hosts: you ministers of his that do his will. Bless the Lord, all his works: in every place of his dominion, O my soul, bless thou the Lord.

THY WILL BE DONE ON EARTH AS IT IS IN HEAVEN

PSALM 142

Hear, O Lord, my prayer: give ear to my supplication
in thy truth: hear me in thy justice.
And enter not into judgment with thy servant:
for in thy sight no man living shall be justified.
For the enemy hath persecuted my soul:
he hath brought down my life to the earth.
He hath made me to dwell in darkness as
those that have been dead of old:
And my spirit is in anguish within me:
my heart within me is troubled.
I remembered the days of old, I meditated on all thy works:
I meditated upon the works of thy hands.
I stretched forth my hands to thee:
my soul is as earth without water unto thee.
Hear me speedily, O Lord: my spirit hath fainted away.
Turn not away thy face from me,
lest I be like unto them that go down into the pit.
Cause me to hear thy mercy in the morning;
for in thee have I hoped.
Make the way known to me, wherein I should walk:
for I have lifted up my soul to thee.
Deliver me from my enemies, O Lord, to thee have I fled:
teach me to do thy will, for thou art my God.
Thy good spirit shall lead me into the right land:
for thy name's sake,
O Lord, thou wilt quicken me in thy justice.
Thou wilt bring my soul out of trouble:
And in thy mercy thou wilt destroy my enemies.
And thou wilt cut off all them that afflict my soul:
for I am thy servant.

GIVE US THIS DAY OUR DAILY BREAD

PSALM 62

O God, my God, to thee do I watch at break of day.
For thee my soul hath thirsted;
for thee my flesh, O how many ways!
In a desert land, and where there is no way, and no water:
so in the sanctuary have I come before thee,
to see thy power and thy glory.
For thy mercy is better than lives: thee my lips will praise.
Thus will I bless thee all my life long:
and in thy name I will lift up my hands.
Let my soul be filled as with marrow and fatness:
and my mouth shall praise thee with joyful lips.
If I have remembered thee upon my bed,
I will meditate on thee in the morning:
Because thou hast been my helper.
And I will rejoice under the covert of thy wings:
My soul hath stuck close to thee:
thy right hand hath received me.
But they have fought my soul in vain,
they shall go into the lower parts of the earth:
They shall be delivered into the hands of the sword,
they shall be the portions of foxes.
But the king shall rejoice in God,
all they shall be praised that swear by him:
because the mouth is stopped of them
that speak wicked things.

AND FORGIVE US OUR TRESPASSES AS WE FORGIVE THOSE WHO TRESPASS AGAINST US

PSALM 37

Rebuke me not, O Lord, in thy indignation;
nor chastise me in thy wrath.
For thy arrows are fastened in me:
and thy hand hath been strong upon me.
There is no health in my flesh, because of thy wrath:
there is no peace for my bones, because of my sins.
For my iniquities are gone over my head:
and as a heavy burden are become heavy upon me.
My sores are putrefied and corrupted,
because of my foolishness.
I am become miserable, and am bowed down
even to the end: I walked sorrowful all the day long.
For my loins are filled with illusions;
and there is no health in my flesh.
I am afflicted and humbled exceedingly:
I roared with the groaning of my heart.
Lord, all my desire is before thee,

and my groaning is not hidden from thee.
My heart is troubled, my strength hath left me,
and the light of my eyes itself is not with me.
My friends and my neighbors have drawn near,
and stood against me.
And they that were near me stood afar off:
And they that sought my soul used violence.
And they that sought evils to me spoke vain things,
and studied deceits all the day long.
But I, as a deaf man, heard not:
and as a dumb man not opening his mouth.
And I became as a man that heareth not:
and that hath no reproofs in his mouth.
For in thee, O Lord, have I hoped:
thou wilt hear me, O Lord my God.
For I said: Lest at any time my enemies rejoice over me:
and whilst my feet are moved,
they speak great things against me.
For I am ready for scourges:
and my sorrow is continually before me.
For I will declare my iniquity: and I will think for my sin.
But my enemies live, and are stronger than I: and they that
hate me wrongfully are multiplied.
They that render evil for good, have detracted me,
because I followed goodness.
Forsake me not, O Lord my God:
do not thou depart from me.
Attend unto my help,
O Lord, the God of my salvation.

AND LEAD US NOT INTO TEMPTATION

PSALM 3

Many say to my soul:
There is no salvation for him in his God.
But thou, O Lord, art my protector,
my glory, and the lifter up of my head.
I have cried to the Lord with my voice:
and he hath heard me from his holy hill.
I have slept and have taken my rest:
and I have risen up, because the Lord hath protected me.
I will not fear thousands of the people surrounding me:
arise, O Lord; save me, O my God.
For thou hast struck all them who are my adversaries
without cause: thou hast broken the teeth of sinners.
Salvation is of the Lord:
and thy blessing is upon thy people.

PSALM 87

O Lord, the God of my salvation: I have cried in the day,
and in the night before thee.
Let my prayer come in before thee:
incline thy ear to my petition.
For my soul is filled with evils:
and my life hath drawn nigh to hell.
I am counted among them that go down to the pit:
I am become as a man without help,
Free among the dead.
Like the slain sleeping in the sepulchers,
whom thou rememberest no more:
and they are cut off from thy hand.
They have laid me in the lower pit:
in the dark places, and in the shadow of death.
Thy wrath is strong over me:
and all thy waves thou hast brought in upon me.
Thou hast put away my acquaintance far from me:
they have set me an abomination to themselves.
I was delivered up, and came not forth:
My eyes languished through poverty. All the day I cried to
thee, O Lord: I stretched out my hands to thee.
Wilt thou shew wonders to the dead? or shall physicians
raise to life, and give praise to thee?
Shall any one in the sepulcher declare thy mercy:
and thy truth in destruction?
Shall thy wonders be known in the dark;
and thy justice in the land of forgetfulness?
But I, O Lord, have cried to thee:
and in the morning my prayer shall prevent thee.
Lord, why castest thou off my prayer:
why turnest thou away thy face from me?
I am poor, and in labors from my youth: and being exalted
have been humbled and troubled.
Thy wrath hath come upon me:
and thy terrors have troubled me.
They have come round about me like water all the day:
they have compassed me about together.
Friend and neighbor thou hast put far from me:
and my acquaintance, because of misery.

AN ALPHABET FOR THE PRAISE OF GOD

PSALM 144

OUR FATHER WHO
ART IN HEAVEN
HALLOWED BE
THY NAME

Aleph I will extol thee, O God my king:
and I will bless thy name forever; yea, for ever and ever.
Beth Every day will I bless thee:
and I will praise thy name for ever; yea, for ever and ever.
Gimel Great is the Lord, and greatly to be praised:
and of his greatness there is no end.

THY KINGDOM COME

Daleth Generation and generation shall praise thy works:
and they shall declare thy power.
He They shall speak of the magnificence of the glory of thy holiness:
and shall tell thy wondrous works.
Vav And they shall speak of the might of thy terrible acts:
and shall declare thy greatness.
Zain They shall publish the memory of the abundan ce of thy sweetness:
and shall rejoice in thy justice.
Heth The Lord is gracious and merciful: patient and plenteous in mercy.
Teth The Lord is sweet to all: and his tender mercies are over all his works.
Yod Let all thy works, O Lord, praise thee: and let thy saints bless thee.
Caph They shall speak of the glory of thy kingdom:
and shall tell of thy power:
Lamed to make thy might known to the sons of men:
and the glory of the magnificence of thy kingdom.
Mem Thy kingdom is a kingdom of all ages:
and thy dominion endureth throughout all generations.

THY WILL BE DONE
ON EARTH AS IT IS
IN HEAVEN

Nun The Lord is faithful in all his words: and holy in all his works.
Samech The Lord lifteth up all that fall:
and setteth up all that are cast down.

GIVE US THIS DAY
OUR DAILY BREAD

Ain The eyes of all hope in thee, O Lord:
and thou givest them meat in due season.
Pe Thou openest thy hand:
and fillest with blessing every living creature.

AND FORGIVE US OUR
TRESPASSES AS WE
FORGIVE THOSE
WHO TRESPASS
AGAINST US

Tzade The Lord is just in all his ways: and holy in all his works.
Koph The Lord is nigh unto all them that call upon him:
to all that call upon him in truth.

AND LEAD US NOT
INTO TEMPTATION

Resh He will do the will of them that fear him:
and he will hear their prayer and save them.

BUT DELIVER
US FROM EVIL

Shin The Lord keepeth all them that love him:
but all the wicked he will destroy.

OUR FATHER WHO
ART IN HEAVEN
HALLOWED BE
THY NAME

Tav My mouth shall speak the praise of the Lord:
and let all flesh bless his holy name for ever;
yea, for ever and ever.

VII

RECAPITULATIONS

OUR FATHER WHO ART IN HEAVEN, HALLOWED BE THY NAME—*Christ Jesus, the Fulfillment of the Lord's Prayer,*
Christ Jesus, The Power of God
THY KINGDOM COME—*Seven Deifying Blessings Contained in the Lord's Prayer,*
Partakers of the Ever-Lasting Kingdom,
Wisdom Found, Scripture Fulfilled
THY WILL BE DONE ON EARTH AS IT IS IN HEAVEN—*Humility and Glory,*
All Things
GIVE US THE DAY OUR DAILY BREAD—*The Five Incarnations of Christ*
AND FORGIVE US OUR TRESPASSES AS WE FORGIVE THOSE WHO TRESPASS AGAINST US—
The Five Mediations of Christ
AND LEAD US NOT INTO TEMPTATION
BUT DELIVER US FROM EVIL—
The Jesus Prayer~A Messianic Prayer~A Summary of the Lord's Prayer

INTRODUCTION

Coming to this last chapter with 'Recapitulations' as a heading, some form of summary might be expected, and such is the case in at least one instance: 'The Jesus Prayer, A Messianic Prayer'. Then there is 'Humility and Glory' offered in symmetrical contrast to the sin and humiliation dealt with in Chapter 1. But, for the rest, the sense of 'summary' proves to be a temporary kernel from which something vast has sprung. An effort at synthesis that exceeds itself, we see it begin in Paul's letter to the Ephesians and be taken up again by Irenaeus of Lyons, who shapes it into a multifaceted concept:[1]

> Into this paradise [the Church] the Lord has introduced those who obey His call, "summing up in Himself all things which are in heaven, and which are on earth" (Eph. 1:10); but the things in heaven are spiritual, while those on earth constitute the dispensation in human nature. These things, therefore, He recapitulated in Himself: by uniting man to the Spirit, and causing the Spirit to dwell in man, He is Himself made the head of the Spirit, and gives the Spirit to be the head of man: for through Him (the Spirit) we see, and hear, and speak.[2]

From Paul and Irenaeus this lineage passes through Clement of Alexandria and Athanasius down to Maximus the Confessor:

> At the center of Maximus' theological and christological universe is the doctrine of Recapitulation… In terms of preeminence it means that Christ is both the presupposition, the method, the paradigm, and the summit of whatever might be said either about God or about man. God is truly, uniquely, ultimately and finally revealed in The Word Incarnate. And man, perfect humanity, is also only understood properly in union with the Word.[3]

To illustrate, three of the chapter's meditations and one representative statement from Maximus will suffice, this statement chosen because it is, like the one from Irenaeus, so full of echoes from Paul: "We are his members and his body, and the fullness of Christ God who fills all things in every way according to the plan hidden in God the Father before the ages. And we are being recapitulated in him through his Son our Lord Jesus the Christ of God."[4]

But perhaps it is better to introduce all of the above and the remaining four more 'scriptural' meditations in this way:

FILLED WITH ALL THE FULLNESS OF GOD

OUR FATHER WHO ART IN HEAVEN HALLOWED BE THY NAME

But when the fulness of the time was come, God sent his Son, made of a woman, made under the law: that he might redeem them who were under the law: that we might receive the adoption of sons. And because you are sons, God hath sent the Spirit of his Son into your hearts, crying: Abba, Father. Gal. 4:4–6

THY KINGDOM COME

For in him were all things created in heaven and on earth, visible and invisible, whether thrones, or dominations, or principalities, or powers. All things were created by him and in him. And he is before all: and by him all things consist. And he is the head of the body, the church: who is the beginning, the firstborn from the dead, that in all things he may hold the primacy: because in him, it hath well pleased the Father that all fulness should dwell. Col. 1:16–19

---

1. Eric Osborn lists 'at least' eleven ideas as present in Irenaeus' understanding of the concept (*Irenaeus of Lyons*, p. 97).
2. *Against the Heresies*, v, 20, 2.
3. Joseph P. Farrell, *The Disputation with Pyrrhus*, pp. iii, iv.
4. *Ambiguua* 7 [1097 a], in *On the Cosmic Mystery of Christ*, p. 70.

THY WILL BE DONE ON EARTH AS IT IS IN HEAVEN	Wherefore I pray you not to faint at my tribulations for you, which is your glory. For this cause I bow my knees to the Father of our Lord Jesus Christ, of whom all paternity in heaven and earth is named: that he would grant you, according to the riches of his glory, to be strengthened by his Spirit with might unto the inward man: that Christ may dwell by faith in your hearts: that, being rooted and founded in charity, you may be able to comprehend, with all the saints, what is the breadth and length and height and depth, to know also the charity of Christ, which surpasseth all knowledge: that you may be filled unto all the fulness of God. Eph. 3:13–19
GIVE US THIS DAY OUR DAILY BREAD	Of his fulness we all have received: and grace for grace. John 1:16
AND FORGIVE US OUR TRESPASSES AS WE FORGIVE THOSE WHO TRESPASS AGAINST US	For I would not have you ignorant, brethren, of this mystery (lest you should be wise in your own conceits) that blindness in part has happened in Israel, until the fulness of the Gentiles should come in. And so all Israel should be saved, as it is written: There shall come out of Sion, he that shall deliver and shall turn away ungodliness from Jacob. And this is to them my covenant: when I shall take away their sins. Rom. 11:25–27
AND LEAD US NOT INTO TEMPTATION	And he gave some apostles, and some prophets, and other some evangelists, and other some pastors and doctors: for the perfecting of the saints, for the word of the ministry, for the edifying of the body of Christ: until we all meet into the unity of faith and of the knowledge of the Son of God, unto a perfect man, unto the measure of the age of the fulness of Christ: that henceforth we be no more children tossed to and fro and carried about with every wind of doctrine, by the wickedness of men, by cunning craftiness by which they lie in wait to deceive. But doing the truth in charity, we may in all things grow up in him who is the head, even Christ. Eph. 4:11–15
BUT DELIVER US FROM EVIL	And what is the exceeding greatness of his power towards us, who believe according to the operation of the might of his power, which he wrought in Christ, raising him up from the dead and setting him on his right hand in the heavenly places. Above all principality and power and virtue and dominion and every name that is named, not only in this world, but also in that which is to come. And he hath subjected all things under his feet and hath made him head over all the church, which is his body and the fulness of him who is filled all in all. Eph. 1:19–23

THE JESUS PRAYER~A MESSIANIC PRAYER

For beginners prayer is like a joyous fire kindled in the heart; for the perfect it is like a vigorous sweet-scented light. Or again, prayer is… the Gospel of God… baptism made manifest… a pledge of the Holy Spirit, the exultation of Jesus, the soul's delight… the disclosure of reconciliation with God, God's grace, God's wisdom, or, rather, the origin of true and absolute Wisdom… Why say more? Prayer is God, who accomplishes everything in everyone (cf. 1 Cor. 12:6), for there is a single action of Father, Son and Holy Spirit, activating all things through Christ Jesus. —Gregory of Sinai, *On Commandments and Doctrines*, 113.

Lord Jesus Christ, Son of God, have mercy on me a sinner.

'Lord' refers to the Father, the Anointer (= "Our Father who art in heaven")
'Jesus' refers to the Son , the Anointed (= "thy name")
'Christ' refers to the Holy Spirit, the Unction (= "hallowed be")

OUR FATHER WHO ART IN HEAVEN	*Lord Jesus Christ, Son of God*
HALLOWED BE THY NAME	
THY KINGDOM COME	*have mercy on me*
THY WILL BE DONE ON EARTH	
AS IT IS IN HEAVEN	
GIVE US THIS DAY	
OUR DAILY BREAD	
AND FORGIVE US OUR TRESPASSES	
AS WE FORGIVE THOSE WHO	
TRESPASS AGAINST US	
AND LEAD US NOT	
INTO TEMPTATION	
BUT DELIVER	*a sinner.*
US FROM EVIL	

COMMENTARY

All commandments, sacraments, virtues, and the scriptures have been poured into the Lord's Prayer. Now, here, a perfect miniature of the Lord's Prayer is beheld in the Jesus Prayer, that horn of oil by which 'the spirit of the Lord' comes down upon us (cf. 1 Kings 2:13), that by which the grace of filial adoption anoints us "a royal priesthood, a holy nation" (1 Pet. 2:9), and therefore a messianic people, a Christendom.

THE JESUS PRAYER~A SUMMARY OF THE LORD'S PRAYER

	THE JESUS PRAYER	SCRIPTURE & CONTEMPLATIONS
OUR FATHER WHO ART IN HEAVEN HALLOWED BE THY NAME	*Lord*	*No one can say The Lord Jesus, but by the Holy Spirit.* 1 Cor. 12:3
		On Sinai's Height, p. 21
	Jesus *Christ*	*Every spirit which confesseth that Jesus Christ is come in the flesh is of God.* 1 John 4:2
		Jesus, p. 374
	Son of God	*Thou art Christ, the Son of the living God.* Matt. 16:16
		Messiah, p. 317 Son of God, Son of Man, p. 249
THY KINGDOM COME THY WILL BE DONE ON EARTH AS IT IS IN HEAVEN GIVE US THIS DAY OUR DAILY BREAD AND FORGIVE US OUR TRESPASSES AS WE FORGIVE THOSE WHO TRESPASS AGAINST US AND LEAD US NOT INTO TEMPTATION	*have mercy on me*	*Jesus, Son of David, have mercy on me.* Mark 10:47
		Thy Mercy, O Lord, p. 264 The Lord's Prayer~Prayer of the Heart, p. 322
BUT DELIVER US FROM EVIL	*a sinner.*	*O God, be merciful to me a sinner.* Luke 18:13
		Sin, p. 41

COMMENTARY

If the Jesus Prayer can be imbued with the entire cosmos of the Lord's Prayer, so too there is a re-blossoming of the Lord's Prayer from the Jesus Prayer as indicated by the above analogies. The co-presence of these two prayers is surely a 'great sign' of the oneness of Christian life in Christ, fruit of the much-saying of sincere entreaty: the Lord's Prayer from Christ for us and the Jesus Prayer from us in the divine-humanity of the Church.

And now do but this:

Stand with your mind in the *Our Father who art in heaven, hallowed be thy name* and look down, all along the other petitions, until you come to *Deliver us from evil*, to your own heart. And, with your mind in your heart, look up, all the way back to the prayer's beginning, and see

THE FIVE MEDIATIONS OF CHRIST

ACCORDING TO MAXIMUS THE CONFESSOR[1]

OUR FATHER WHO ART IN HEAVEN HALLOWED BE THY NAME	Mediator between God and His creation *As Word, he cannot be separated in any way at all from the Father; as man, he has fulfilled, in word and truth, with unchangeable obedience, everything that, as God, he has predetermined is to take place, and has accomplished the whole will of God the Father on our behalf.*
THY KINGDOM COME	…between the intelligible and the sensible *By passing with his body and soul, that is, the whole of our nature, through all the divine and intelligible ranks of heaven, he united the sensible and intelligible and showed the convergence of the whole of creation with the One according to its most original and universal logos, which is completely undivided and at rest in itself.*
THY WILL BE DONE ON EARTH AS IT IS IN HEAVEN	…between heaven and earth *By his ascension he clearly united heaven and earth, and with his earthly body that is of the same nature and consubstantial with ours he entered into heaven and showed that the whole nature that can be perceived through the senses is, by the most universal logos of its being, one, thus obscuring the peculiar nature of the division which cuts it into two.*
GIVE US THIS DAY OUR DAILY BREAD	…between paradise and the inhabited world *Having sanctified the world we inhabit by his own humanly-fitting way of life he opened a clear way into paradise after his death* [Luke 23:43]… *showing that the world is one and not divided in itself.*
AND FORGIVE US OUR TRESPASSES AS WE FORGIVE THOSE WHO TRESPASS AGAINST US	…between the sexes *He united us in himself by removing the difference between male and female, and instead of men and women, in whom above all this manner of division is beheld, he showed us as properly and truly to be simply human beings, thoroughly transfigured in accordance with him.*

---

1. All quotes in italics from Maximus the Confessor, *Difficulty* [*Ambigua*] 41, Patrologia Graeca 91, 1309 B–1312 A; Andrew Louth, *Maximus the Confessor* (London and New York: Routledge, 1996), pp. 159–160. Cf. Lars Thunberg, *Microcosm and Mediator*, 2nd ed. (Peru IL: Open Court, 1995), pp. 373–427.

THE FIVE INCARNATIONS OF CHRIST

ACCORDING TO MAXIMUS THE CONFESSOR

The soul that through the grace of its calling resembles God keeps inviolate within itself the Substance of the blessings bestowed upon it. In souls such as this Christ always desires to be born in a mystical way, becoming incarnate in those who attain salvation, and making the soul that gives birth to Him a Virgin Mother. — Maximus the Confessor, *On the Lord's Prayer*

OUR FATHER WHO ART IN HEAVEN HALLOWED BE THY NAME

Christ incarnate
In becoming incarnate, the Word of God teaches us the mystical knowledge [theology] of God because he shows us in himself the Father and the Holy Spirit. For the full Father and the full Holy Spirit are essentially and completely in the full Son, even the incarnate Son, without being themselves incarnate.[1]

THY KINGDOM COME

Christ incarnate in the Eucharist
[The Eucharist] *transforms into itself and renders similar to the causal good by grace and participation those who worthily share in it. To them is there lacking nothing of this good that is possible and attainable for men, so that they also can be and be called gods by adoption through grace because all of God entirely fills them and leaves no part of them empty of his presence.*[2]

THY WILL BE DONE ON EARTH AS IT IS IN HEAVEN

Christ incarnate through the virtues
The Mother of the Word is truth, pure and spotless faith, she who He had made mother by accepting through love of man to be born of her as man. And so the Word within us first creates faith, then he becomes son of this faith within us, 'embodied' of it through the practice of the virtues.[3]

GIVE US THIS DAY OUR DAILY BREAD

Christ incarnate through creatures
He is hidden in the words of visible beings, ineffably and analogically in each of them as if He were being signified there with written letters, fully altogether in all, integrally in each without being diminished, invariable in their variety, always similar to Himself, simple and without composition in the composite, without beginning in things begun, invisible in the visible, intangible in the tangible.[4]

AND FORGIVE US OUR TRESPASSES AS WE FORGIVE THOSE WHO TRESPASS AGAINST US

Christ incarnate through the commandments
Those who truly believed Christ and, through the commandments, made Him to dwell wholly within themselves spoke in this fashion: And I live, now not I; but Christ liveth in me.[5]

---

1. *On the Lord's Prayer* (Berthold, p. 103).
2. *The Church's Mystagogy*, 21 (Berthold, p. 203).
3. *Questions to Thalassius*, 40.
4. *Ambigua* 33, 214 A.
5. *The Ascetic Life*, p. 123.

ALL THINGS

He [the Spirit of truth] shall glorify me: because he shall receive of mine and shall shew it to you. All things whatsoever the Father hath are mine. Therefore I said that he shall receive of me and shew it to you. John 16:14–15

Of him, and by him, and in him, are all things: to him be glory for ever. Amen. Rom. 11:36

In these days, [God] hath spoken to us by his Son, whom he hath appointed heir of all things, by whom also he made the world. Who being the brightness of his glory and the figure of his substance and upholding all things by the word of his power, making purgation of sins, sitteth on the right hand of the majesty on high: being made so much better than the angels as he hath inherited a more excellent name than they. For to which of the angels hath he said at any time: thou art my Son, today have I begotten thee? And again: I will be to him a Father, and he shall be to me a Son? And again, when he bringeth in the first begotten into the world, he saith: And let all the angels of God adore him. Heb. 1:2–6

Again he sent other servants, saying: Tell them that were invited, Behold, I have prepared my dinner: my beeves and fatlings are killed, and all things are ready. Come ye to the marriage. Matt. 22:4

And again I say to you: It is easier for a camel to pass through the eye of a needle, than for a rich man to enter into the kingdom of heaven. And when they had heard this, the disciples wondered much, saying: Who then can be saved? And Jesus beholding, said to them: With men this is impossible: but with God all things are possible. Matt. 19:24–26

That he might make known unto us the mystery of his will, according to his good pleasure, which he hath purposed in him, in the dispensation of the fulness of times, to re-establish all things in Christ, that are in heaven and on earth, in him. Eph. 1:9–10

And Jesus saith to him: If thou canst believe, all things are possible to him that believeth. And immediately the father of the boy crying out, with tears said: I do believe, Lord. Help my unbelief. Mark 9:22–23

And all things whatsoever you shall ask in prayer believing, you shall receive. Matt. 21:22

He said to him the third time: Simon, son of John, lovest thou me? Peter was grieved because he had said to him the third time: Lovest thou me? And he said to him: Lord, thou knowest all things: thou knowest that I love thee. John 21:17

AND LEAD US NOT
INTO TEMPTATION

[Charity] beareth all things, believeth all things, hopeth all things, endureth all things. 1 Cor. 13:7

But prove all things: hold fast that which is good. From all appearance of evil refrain yourselves. 1 Thess. 5:21–22

BUT DELIVER
US FROM EVIL

All things are delivered to me by my Father. Matt. 11:27

Furthermore, I count all things to be but loss for the excellent knowledge of Jesus Christ, my Lord: for whom I have suffered the loss of all things and count them but as dung, that I may gain Christ. Phil. 3:8

HUMILITY AND GLORY

OUR FATHER WHO
ART IN HEAVEN
HALLOWED BE
THY NAME And the four and twenty ancients and the four living creatures fell down and adored God that sitteth upon the throne, saying: Amen. Alleluia. And a voice came out from the throne, saying: Give praise to our God, all ye his servants; and you that fear him, little and great. And I heard as it were the voice of a great multitude, and as the voice of many waters, and as the voice of great thunders, saying: Alleluia; for the Lord our God, the Almighty, hath reigned. Let us be glad and rejoice and give glory to him; for the marriage of the Lamb is come, and his wife hath prepared herself. And it is granted to her that she should clothe herself with fine linen, glittering and white; for the fine linen are the justifications of the saints. Apoc. 19:4–8

COMMENTARY

AMEN ALLELUIA If the Lord's Prayer can be summarized by the Jesus Prayer, so too can the Jesus Prayer (and, by inference, the Lord's Prayer) be summarized in just two words: Amen and Alleluia.

Lord Jesus Christ, Son of the living God,	Alleluia (glory)
Have mercy on us.	Amen (humility)

On earth it is meet to glorify God first and then take cognizance of our lowliness, as we are taught by both the Lord's Prayer and the Jesus Prayer. However, in heaven, in the life of glory, we see these prayers to be the mirror images of the Prayer of the Blessed. In the 'Amen' is the nothingness of the creature totally accomplished at last and continually; an immense peace reigns in the creature extinguished before the almightiness of its God. But by what unfathomable miracle is this nothingness able to say 'Amen'? By an even greater miracle which, if it had a name, might be called 'the perichoresis of the Alleluia'. In this 'Alleluia' is to be found the creation and re-creation of the creature, the praise of God's great and superluminous glory. So great is this Alleluia that the Amen becomes wholly one with it—the lion of the Alleluia lies down with the lamb of the Amen, the Lion who is Christ and the Lamb who is Christ, Christ's divine and human natures. And in our oneness with Christ has dawned the daystar that rises in our hearts: the perichoresis of the Blessed Trinity—the true mystery of love; the indwelling of Father, Son and Holy Spirit in each other—has come to dwell within us: Amen. Alleluia.

HALLOWED BE
THY NAME
THY KINGDOM COME
THY WILL BE DONE
ON EARTH AS IT
IS IN HEAVEN

And on the next day, a great multitude that was come to the festival day, when they had heard that Jesus was coming to Jerusalem, took branches of palmtrees and went forth to meet him and cried: Hosanna.[1] Blessed[2] is he that cometh in the name of the Lord, the king of Israel. And Jesus found a young ass and sat upon it, as it is written: Fear not, daughter of Sion; behold thy king cometh, sitting on an ass's colt.[3] These things his disciples did not know at first; but when Jesus was glorified, then they remembered that these things were written of him and that they had done these things to him. John 12:12–16

HALLOWED BE THY
NAME
THY KINGDOM COME
THY WILL BE DONE
ON EARTH AS IT
IS IN HEAVEN
GIVE US THIS DAY
OUR DAILY BREAD
AND FORGIVE US OUR
TRESPASSES AS WE
FORGIVE THOSE
WHO TRESPASS
AGAINST US
AND LEAD US NOT
INTO TEMPTATION
BUT DELIVER
US FROM EVIL

And there were in the same country shepherds watching and keeping the night-watches over their flock. And, behold, an angel of the Lord stood by them and the brightness[4] of God shone round about them; and they feared with a great fear.[5] And the angel said to them: Fear not; for, behold, I bring to you good tidings of great joy that shall be to all the people; for this day is born to you a Savior, who is Christ the Lord, in the city of David. And this shall be a sign unto you: You shall find the infant wrapped in swaddling clothes[6] and laid in a manger.[7] And suddenly there was with the angel a multitude of the heavenly army, praising God[8] and saying: Glory[9] to God in the highest; and on earth peace[10] to men of good will. Luke 2:8–14

1. Alleluia
2. Alleluia
3. Amen
4. Alleluia
5. Amen
6. Amen
7. Amen
8. Alleluia
9. Alleluia
10. Amen

WISDOM FOUND, SCRIPTURE FULFILLED

Just as soul and body combine to produce a human being, so practice of the virtues and contemplation together constitute a unique spiritual wisdom, and the Old and New Testaments together form a single mystery. —Maximus the Confessor, *Various Texts*, Fourth Century, 90.

OUR FATHER WHO
ART IN HEAVEN
HALLOWED BE
THY NAME

Now to him that is able to establish you, according to my gospel, and the preaching of Jesus Christ, according to the revelation of the mystery, which was kept secret from eternity, (which now is made manifest by the scriptures of the prophets, according to the precept of the eternal God, for the obedience of faith,) known among all nations; to God the only wise, through Jesus Christ, to whom be honor and glory for ever and ever. Amen. Rom. 16:25–27

Jesus answered them: Is it not written in your law: I said you are gods? If he called them gods, to whom to word of God was spoken, and the scripture cannot be broken; do you say of him whom the Father hath sanctified and sent into the world: Thou blasphemest, because I said, I am the Son of God? John 10:34–36

THY KINGDOM COME

Let the word of Christ dwell in you abundantly, in all wisdom: teaching and admonishing one another in psalms, hymns, and spiritual canticles, singing in grace in your hearts to God. Col. 3:16

And when they drew nigh to Jerusalem, and were come to Bethphage, unto mount Olivet, then Jesus sent two disciples, saying to them: Go ye into the village that is over against you, and immediately you shall find an ass tied, and a colt with her: loose them and bring them to me. And if any man shall say anything to you, say ye, that the Lord hath need of them: and forthwith he will let them go. Now all this was done that it might be fulfilled which was spoken by the prophet, saying: Tell ye the daughter of Sion: Behold thy king cometh to thee, meek, and sitting upon an ass, and a colt the foal of her that is used to the yoke. And the disciples going, did as Jesus commanded them. Matt. 21:1–6

THY WILL BE DONE
ON EARTH AS IT IS
IN HEAVEN

For I would have you know, what manner of care I have for you and for them that are at Laodicea, and whosoever have not seen my face in the flesh: that their hearts may be comforted, being instructed in charity, and unto all riches of fulness of understanding, unto the knowledge of the mystery of God the Father and of Christ Jesus: in whom are hid all the treasures of wisdom and knowledge. Col. 2:1–3

And he came to Nazareth, where he was brought up: and he went into the synagogue, according to his custom, on the sabbath day; and he rose up to read. And the book of Isaias the prophet was delivered unto him. And as he unfolded the book, he found the place where it was written: The Spirit of the Lord is upon me. Wherefore he hath anointed me to preach the gospel to the poor, he hath sent me to heal the contrite of heart, to preach deliverance to the captives, and sight to the blind, to set at liberty them that are bruised, to preach the acceptable year of the Lord, and the day of reward. And when he had folded the book, he restored it to the minister, and sat down. And the eyes of all in the synagogue were fixed on him. And he began to say to them: This day is fulfilled this scripture in your ears. Luke 4:16–21

GIVE US THIS DAY
OUR DAILY BREAD

But if any of you want wisdom, let him ask of God, who giveth to all men abundantly, and upbraideth not; and it shall be given him. But let him ask in faith, nothing wavering. For he that wavereth is like a wave of the sea, which is moved and carried about by the wind. Therefore let not that man think that he shall receive any thing of the Lord. James 1:5–7

And the Father himself who hath sent me, hath given testimony of me: neither have you heard his voice at any time, nor seen his shape. And you have not his word abiding in you: for whom he hath sent, him you believe not. Search the scriptures, for you think in them to have life everlasting; and the same are they that give testimony of me. And you will not come to me that you may have life. John 5:37–40

AND FORGIVE US OUR
TRESPASSES AS WE
FORGIVE THOSE
WHO TRESPASS
AGAINST US

For I would not have you ignorant, brethren, of this mystery, (lest you should be wise in your own conceits), that blindness in part has happened in Israel, until the fulness of the Gentiles should come in. And so all Israel should be saved, as it is written: There shall come out of Sion, he that shall deliver, and shall turn away ungodliness from Jacob. And this is to them my covenant: when I shall take away their sins. As concerning the gospel, indeed, they are enemies for your sake: but as touching the election, they are most dear for the sake of the fathers. For the gifts and the calling of God are without repentance. For as you also in times past did not believe God, but now have obtained mercy, through their unbelief; so these also now have not believed, for your mercy, that they also may obtain mercy. For God hath concluded all in unbelief, that he may have mercy on all. O the depth of the riches of the wisdom and of the knowledge of God! How incomprehensible are his judgments, and how unsearchable his ways! Rom. 11:27–33

And the Pharisees going out made a consultation against him, how they might destroy him. But Jesus knowing it, retired from thence: and many followed him, and he healed them all. And he charged them that they should not make him known. That it might be fulfilled which was spoken by Isaias the prophet, saying: Behold my servant whom I have chosen, my beloved in whom my soul hath been well pleased. I will put my spirit upon him, and he shall shew judgment to the Gentiles. He shall not contend, nor cry out, neither shall any man hear his voice in the streets. The bruised reed he shall not break: and smoking flax he shall not extinguish: till he send forth judgment unto victory. And in his name the Gentiles shall hope. Matt. 12:14–21

AND LEAD US NOT
INTO TEMPTATION

For I judged not myself to know anything among you, but Jesus Christ, and him crucified. And I was with you in weakness, and in fear, and in much trembling. And my speech and my preaching was not in the persuasive words of human wisdom, but in shewing of the Spirit and power; that your faith might not stand on the wisdom of men, but on the power of God. Howbeit we speak wisdom among the perfect: yet not the wisdom of this world, neither of the princes of this world that come to nought. 1 Cor. 2:2–6

And whereas he had done so many miracles before them, they believed not in him: that the saying of Isaias the prophet might be fulfilled, which he said: Lord, who hath believed our hearing? and to whom hath the arm of the Lord been revealed? Therefore they could not believe, because Isaias said again: He hath blinded their eyes, and hardened their heart, that they should not see with their eyes, nor understand with their heart, and be converted, and I should heal them. These things said Isaias, when he saw his glory, and spoke of him. However, many of the chief men also believed in him; but because of the Pharisees they did not confess him, that they might not be cast out of the synagogue. John 12:37–42

BUT DELIVER US FROM EVIL	For professing themselves to be wise, they became fools. And they changed the glory of the incorruptible God into the likeness of the image of a corruptible man, and of birds, and of four-footed beasts, and of creeping things. Wherefore God gave them up to the desires of their heart, unto uncleanness, to dishonor their own bodies among themselves. Who changed the truth of God into a lie; and worshipped and served the creature rather than the Creator, who is blessed for ever. Amen. Rom. 1:22–25

And after they were departed, behold an angel of the Lord appeared in sleep to Joseph, saying: Arise, and take the child and his mother, and fly into Egypt: and be there until I shall tell thee. For it will come to pass that Herod will seek the child to destroy him. Who arose, and took the child and his mother by night, and retired into Egypt: and he was there until the death of Herod: that it might be fulfilled which the Lord spoke by the prophet, saying: Out of Egypt have I called my son. Matt. 2:13–15

PARTAKERS OF THE EVER-LASTING KINGDOM

2 Peter 1:2–11

OUR FATHER WHO ART IN HEAVEN HALLOWED BE THY NAME	Grace to you and peace be accomplished in the knowledge of God and of Christ Jesus our Lord. As all things of his divine power which appertain to life and godliness are given us through the knowledge of him who hath called us by his own proper glory and virtue.
THY KINGDOM COME	By whom he hath given us most great and precious promises: that by these you may be made partakers of the divine nature: flying the corruption of that concupiscence which is in the world.
THY WILL BE DONE ON EARTH AS IT IS IN HEAVEN	And you, employing all care, minister in your faith, virtue: And in virtue, knowledge: and in knowledge, abstinence: and in abstinence, patience: and in patience, godliness: and in godliness, love of brotherhood: and in love of brotherhood, charity.
GIVE US THIS DAY OUR DAILY BREAD	For if these things be with you and abound, they will make you to be neither empty nor unfruitful in the knowledge of our Lord Jesus Christ.
AND FORGIVE US OUR TRESPASSES AS WE FORGIVE THOSE WHO TRESPASS AGAINST US	For he that hath not these things with him is blind and groping, having forgotten that he was purged from his old sins.

AND LEAD US NOT INTO TEMPTATION	Wherefore, brethren, labor the more, that by good works you may make sure your calling and election. For doing these things, you shall not sin at any time.
BUT DELIVER US FROM EVIL	For so an entrance shall be ministered to you abundantly into the ever-lasting kingdom of our Lord and Savior Jesus Christ.

SEVEN DEIFYING BLESSINGS CONTAINED IN THE LORD'S PRAYER

ACCORDING TO MAXIMUS THE CONFESSOR[1]

If then the realization of the divine counsel is the deification of our nature, and if the aim of the divine thoughts is the successful accomplishment of what we ask for in life, then it is profitable to recognize the full import of the Lord's prayer, to put it into practice and to write about it properly… Indeed this prayer contains in outline, mysteriously hidden, or to speak more properly, openly proclaimed for those whose understanding is strong enough, the whole scope of what the words deal with. For the words of the prayer make request for whatever the Word of God himself wrought through the flesh in his self-abasement. — Maximus the Confessor, *On the Lord's Prayer*, 1.

OUR FATHER WHO ART IN HEAVEN HALLOWED BE THY NAME	Theology[2]
THY KINGDOM COME	Adoption in grace
THY WILL BE DONE ON EARTH AS IT IS IN HEAVEN	Equality of honor with the angels
GIVE US THIS DAY OUR DAILY BREAD	Participation in eternal life
AND FORGIVE US OUR TRESPASSES AS WE FORGIVE THOSE WHO TRESPASS AGAINST US	The restoration of nature inclining toward itself to a tranquil state
AND LEAD US NOT INTO TEMPTATION	Abolition of the law of sin
BUT DELIVER US FROM EVIL	Overthrow of the tyranny of evil

---

1. Cf. the prologue to Maximus' *Commentary on the Lord's Prayer* (*The Philokalia*, vol. 2, pp. 287–289 or Berthold, *Maximus Confessor, Selected Writings*, pp. 102–105) for a condensed description of these seven keys to blessedness.

2. *Theologia*—which Maximus "most often understands at its loftiest point and in its strictest sense… when it constitutes 'supreme knowledge'… (knowledge in the broad sense including at once *theoria* and *theologia*), 'veritable gnosis', 'mystical gnosis', 'divine gnosis', 'ineffable gnosis', or again 'unforgettable gnosis'. It corresponds to the knowledge of God independent of His creatures, to the knowledge and illumination of the Holy Trinity, to knowledge of the divine mysteries" (Jean-Claude Larchet, *La divinisation de l'homme selon saint Maxime le Confesseur* (Paris: Cerf, 1996), p. 496.

CHRIST JESUS, THE POWER OF GOD

But we preach Christ crucified… Christ, the power of God and the wisdom of God. 1 Corinthians 1:23–24

OUR FATHER WHO ART IN HEAVEN HALLOWED BE THY NAME

But as many as received him, he gave them power to be made the sons of God, to them that believe in his name. John 1:12

THY KINGDOM COME

That you may walk worthy of God, in all things pleasing; being fruitful in every good work and increasing in the knowledge of God: strengthened with all might according to the power of his glory, in all patience and longsuffering with joy, giving thanks to God the Father, who hath made us worthy to be partakers of the lot of the saints in light. Col. 1:10–12

THY WILL BE DONE ON EARTH AS IT IS IN HEAVEN

And Jesus coming, spoke to them, saying: All power is given to me in heaven and in earth. Matt. 28:18
Wherefore also we pray always for you: that our God would make you worthy of his vocation and fulfil all the good pleasure of his goodness and the work of faith in power: that the name of our Lord Jesus may be glorified in you, and you in him, according to the grace of our God and of the Lord Jesus Christ. 2 Thess. 1:11–12

GIVE US THIS DAY OUR DAILY BREAD

That the Gentiles should be fellow heirs and of the same body: and copartners of his promise in Christ Jesus, by the gospel of which I am made a minister, according to the gift of the grace of God, which is given to me according to the operation of his power. To me, the least of all the saints, is given this grace, to preach among the Gentiles the unsearchable riches of Christ. Eph. 3:6–8

AND FORGIVE US OUR TRESPASSES AS WE FORGIVE THOSE WHO TRESPASS AGAINST US

Do you seek a proof of Christ that speaketh in me, who towards you is not weak, but is mighty in you? For although he was crucified through weakness, yet he liveth by the power of God. For we also are weak in him: but we shall live with him by the power of God towards you. Try your own selves if you be in the faith: prove ye yourselves. Know you not your own selves, that Christ Jesus is in you, unless perhaps you be reprobates? 2 Cor. 13:3–5

AND LEAD US NOT INTO TEMPTATION

For God hath not given us the spirit of fear: but of power and of love and of sobriety. Be not thou therefore ashamed of the testimony of our Lord, nor of me his prisoner: but labor with the gospel, according to the power of God. 2 Tim. 1:7–8

BUT DELIVER US FROM EVIL

For the word of the cross, to them indeed that perish, is foolishness: but to them that are saved, that is, to us, it is the power of God. 1 Cor. 1:18

CHRIST JESUS, THE FULFILLMENT OF THE LORD'S PRAYER

ACCORDING TO PAUL

OUR FATHER WHO
ART IN HEAVEN
HALLOWED BE
THY NAME

For let this mind be in you, which was also in Christ Jesus: who being in the form of God, thought it not robbery to be equal with God: but emptied himself, taking the form of a servant, being made in the likeness of men, and in habit found as a man. He humbled himself, becoming obedient unto death, even to the death of the cross. For which cause God also hath exalted him, and hath given him a name which is above all names: that in the name of Jesus every knee should bow, of those that are in heaven, on earth, and under the earth: and that every tongue should confess that the Lord Jesus Christ is in the glory of God the Father. Phil. 2:5–11

THY KINGDOM COME

I charge thee before God, who quickeneth all things, and before Christ Jesus, who gave testimony under Pontius Pilate, a good confession, that thou keep the commandment without spot, blameless, unto the coming of our Lord Jesus Christ, which in his times he shall shew who is the Blessed and only Mighty, the King of kings, and Lord of lords; who only hath immortality, and inhabiteth light inaccessible, whom no man hath seen, nor can see: to whom be honor and empire everlasting. Amen. 1 Tim. 6:13–16

THY WILL BE DONE
ON EARTH AS IT IS
IN HEAVEN

Grace be to you, and peace from God the Father, and from the Lord Jesus Christ. Blessed by the God and Father of our Lord Jesus Christ, who hath blessed us with spiritual blessings in heavenly places, in Christ: as he chose us in him before the foundation of the world, that we should be holy and unspotted in his sight in charity. who hath predestinated us unto the adoption of children through Jesus Christ unto himself: according to the purpose of his will: unto the praise of the glory of his grace, in which he hath graced us in his beloved son. In whom we have redemption through his blood, the remission of sins, according to the riches of his grace, which hath superabounded in us in all wisdom and prudence, that he might make known unto us the mystery of his will, according to his good pleasure, which he hath purposed in him, in the dispensation of the fulness of times, to re-establish all things in Christ, that are in heaven and on earth, in him. Eph. 1:2–10

GIVE US THIS DAY
OUR DAILY BREAD

The chalice of benediction, which we bless, is it not the communion of the blood of Christ ? And the bread, which we break, is it not the partaking of the body of the Lord ? For we, being many, are one bread, one body, all that partake of one bread. 1 Cor. 10:16–17

AND FORGIVE US OUR
TRESPASSES AS WE
FORGIVE THOSE
WHO TRESPASS
AGAINST US

And you, when you were dead in your sins, and the uncircumcision of your flesh; he hath quickened together with him, forgiving you all offences: blotting out the handwriting of the decree that was against us, which was contrary to us. And he hath taken the same out of the way, fastening it to the cross: and despoiling the principalities and powers, he hath exposed them confidently in open shew, triumphing over them in himself. Col. 2:13–15

AND LEAD US NOT INTO TEMPTATION	For we have not a high priest, who can not have compassion on our infirmities: but one tempted in all things like as we are, without sin. Let us go therefore with confidence to the throne of grace: that we may obtain mercy, and find grace in seasonable aid. Heb. 4:15–16
BUT DELIVER US FROM EVIL	For Christ, we beseech you, be reconciled to God. Him, who knew no sin, he hath been made sin for us, that we might be made the justice of God in him. 2 Cor. 5:20–21

CONCLUSION

Amen, Amen and Amen

AMEN, AMEN AND AMEN

THE HIGH PRIESTLY PRAYER OF JESUS
OUR LORD'S OWN COMMENTARY ON THE LORD'S PRAYER
JOHN 17:1–26

The new Scripture is greater than the old; the four Gospels are greater than the new Scripture as a whole; the fourth Gospel is greater than the other three; and the Lord's Testament (chap. 13–17) is greater than the Gospel of St. John as a whole. — Nicodemos of the Holy Mountain, *A Handbook of Spiritual Counsel*

CHRIST'S PRAYER FOR HIMSELF

OUR FATHER WHO ART IN HEAVEN HALLOWED BE THY NAME

These things Jesus spoke; and lifting up his eyes to heaven he said: Father, the hour is come. Glorify thy Son, that thy Son may glorify thee,[1] as thou hast given him power over all flesh, that he may give eternal life to all whom thou hast given him.[3&4] Now this is eternal life: that they may know thee, the only true God, and Jesus Christ, whom thou hast sent.[2] I have glorified thee on the earth; I have finished the work which thou gavest me to do.[3] And now glorify thou me, O Father, with thyself, with the glory which I had, before the world was, with thee.[2]

CHRIST'S PRAYER FOR THE APOSTLES

THY KINGDOM COME

I have manifested thy name to the men whom thou hast given me out of the world.[1] Thine they were; and to me thou gavest them. And they have kept thy word.[3] Now they have known that all things which thou hast given me are from thee;[1] because the words which thou gavest me, I have given to them.[4] And they have received them and have known in very deed that I came out from thee; and they have believed that thou didst send me.[3] I pray for them. I pray not for the world, but for them whom thou hast given me; because they are thine.[2&6] And all my things are thine, and thine are mine; and I am glorified in them.[2] And now I am not in the world, and these are in the world, and I come to thee. Holy Father, keep them in thy name whom thou hast given me; that they may be one, as we also are.[1&3] While I was with them, I kept them in thy name. Those whom thou gavest me I have kept; and none of them is lost, but the son of perdition, that the scripture might be fulfilled.[7] And now I come to thee; and these things I speak in the world, that they may have my joy filled in themselves.[2&3] I have given them thy word, and the world hath hated them; because they are not of the world, as I also am not of the world.[5] I pray not that thou shouldst take them out of the world, but that thou shouldst keep them from evil.[7] They are not of the world, as I also am not of the world.[2] Sanctify them in truth. Thy word is truth.[2&3] As thou hast sent me into the world, I also have sent them into the world.[3] And for them do I sanctify myself, that they also may be sanctified in truth.[3&4]

---

1. Our Father who art in heaven, hallowed be thy name.
2. Thy kingdom come.
3. Thy will be done on earth as it is in heaven.
4. Give us this day our daily bread.
5. And forgive us our trespasses as we forgive those who trespass against us.
6. And lead us not into temptation.
7. But deliver us from evil.

CHRIST'S PRAYER FOR THE CHURCH

THY WILL BE DONE
ON EARTH AS IT
IS IN HEAVEN
GIVE US THIS DAY
OUR DAILY BREAD

And not for them only do I pray, but for them also who through their word shall believe in me,[3] that they all may be one, as thou, Father, in me, and I in thee; that they also may be one in us;[1, 3&5] that the world may believe that thou hast sent me. And the glory which thou hast given me, I have given to them; that they may be one, as we also are one,[2&4] I in them, and thou in me; that they may be made perfect in one;[5] and the world may know that thou hast sent me and hast loved them, as thou hast also loved me.[2]

CHRIST'S PRAYER FOR ALL

AND FORGIVE US OUR
TRESPASSES AS WE
FORGIVE THOSE
WHO TRESPASS
AGAINST US
AND LEAD US NOT
INTO TEMPTATION
BUT DELIVER
US FROM EVIL

Father, I will that where I am, they also whom thou hast given me may be with me;[3] that they may see my glory which thou hast given me,[2] because thou hast loved me before the creation of the world. Just Father, the world hath not known thee;[6] but I have known thee;[1] and these have known that thou hast sent me. And I have made know thy name to them and will make it known; that the love wherewith thou hast loved me may be in them, and I in them.[1&2]

COMMENTARY

Of the four gospels, only John's makes no mention of the Transfiguration. But then, at the Mystical Supper in the upper room, are not the Lord's transfigured and transfiguring words of His high-priestly prayer the verbal equivalent of the light that so dazzled the three apostles' eyes on the high mountain? There, on the high mountain—the apostles caught between brightness and brightness: the brightness of Christ and the brightness of an overshadowing cloud (Matt. 17:5)—the voice of the Father had asked that His beloved Son be heard; here, in the upper room, Christ now speaks words of glory, beginning with the unitary glory of Father and Son and ending with the glory shared between God and those who believe in His Name, who have become children of the light (Eph. 5:8).

---

1. Our Father who art in heaven, hallowed be thy name.
2. Thy kingdom come.
3. Thy will be done on earth as it is in heaven.
4. Give us this day our daily bread.
5. And forgive us our trespasses as we forgive those who trespass against us.
6. And lead us not into temptation.
7. But deliver us from evil.

EPILOGUE

FOR THE GRACE OF A SPIRITUAL MENTOR

Because we all have passions we ought not to have faith in our own goodness of heart, for a crooked rule makes the crooked straight and the straight crooked. — Dorotheos of Gaza, *Maxims on the Spiritual life*, 2

CHARACTERISTICS OF THE SPIRITUAL MENTOR ACCORDING TO
JOHN CLIMACUS AND SYMEON THE NEW THEOLOGIAN[1]

OUR FATHER WHO
ART IN HEAVEN
HALLOWED BE
THY NAME
THY KINGDOM COME

Mediator (*mesites*)
But all things are of God, who hath reconciled us to himself by Christ and hath given to us the ministry of reconciliation. For God indeed was in Christ, reconciling the world to himself, not imputing to them their sins. And he hath placed in us the word of reconciliation. For Christ therefore we are ambassadors, God as it were exhorting by us, for Christ, we beseech you, be reconciled to God. 2 Cor. 5:18–20

THY WILL BE DONE
ON EARTH AS IT IS
IN HEAVEN

Counsellor (*sumboulos*)
[Of the Church] I am made a minister according to the dispensation of God, which is given me towards you, that I may fulfil the word of God: the mystery which hath been hidden from ages and generations, but now is manifested to his saints, to whom God would make known the riches of the glory of this mystery among the Gentiles, which is Christ, in you the hope of glory. Whom we preach, admonishing every man and teaching every man in all wisdom, that we may present every man perfect in Christ Jesus. Col. 1:25–28

GIVE US THIS DAY
OUR DAILY BREAD

Intercessor (*prebeutes*)
I desire therefore, first of all, that supplications, prayers, intercessions and thanksgivings be made for all men... For this is good and acceptable in the sight of God our Savior, who will have all men to be saved and to come to the knowledge of the truth. 1 Tim. 2: 1, 3–4

AND FORGIVE US OUR
TRESPASSES AS WE
FORGIVE THOSE
WHO TRESPASS
AGAINST US

Sponsor, Burden-Bearer (*anadochos*)
Brethren, and if a man be overtaken in any fault, you, who are spiritual, instruct such a one in the spirit of meekness, considering thyself, lest thou also be tempted. Bear ye one another's burdens: and so you shall fulfil the law of Christ. For if any man think himself to be some thing, whereas he is nothing, he deceiveth himself. Gal. 6:1–3

AND LEAD US NOT
INTO TEMPTATION
BUT DELIVER
US FROM EVIL

Physician (*iatros*)
[G]rant unto thy servants that with all confidence they may speak thy word, by stretching forth thy hand to cures and signs and wonders, to be done by the name of thy holy Son, Jesus. And when they had prayed, the place was moved wherein they were assembled: and they were all filled with the Holy Spirit: and they spoke the word of God with confidence. Acts 4:29–31

---

1. See Bishop Kallistos Ware's Foreward to *Spiritual Direction in the Early Christian East*. pp. xii–xvii.

APPENDIX

THREE WORLDS

Approaches other than a sequential reading or a random sampling of this book are possible. Below are three thematic rearrangements of the book's contents to create other worlds of meaning and understanding: a second 'epitome' of the Lord's Prayer, a rendering of the Nicene-Constantinopolitan Creed, and, lastly, a 'cruciform' view of the ascetic path. GJC

1

THE WORLD OF THE LORD'S PRAYER

Our Father who art in heaven
Hallowed be thy name

2

THE WORLD OF THE CREED

Thy kingdom come
Thy will be done on earth as it is in heaven
Give us this day our daily bread

I believe in — Faith, p. 207

one God, the Father Almighty, — Creation, p. 12
Maker of heaven and earth,
and of all things visible and invisible;

And in one Lord, Jesus Christ, — Prologue to the Gospel of John, p. 291
the Son of God, the Only-begotten,
begotten of the Father before all ages,
Light of Light, True God of True God,
begotten, not made,
of one essence with the Father,

by Whom all things were made: — Christ Jesus, the Power of God, p. 468
All Things, p. 460

Who for us men and for our salvation — Mystical Sacrifice, The Kenotic Dimensions
came down from heaven, — of the Lord's Prayer, p. 348

and was incarnate of the Holy Spirit and — The Holy Mother of God, p. 289
the Virgin Mary, and was made man; — The Nativity, p. 292

And was crucified also for us under — The Beatitudes and the Passion, p. 344
Pontius Pilate, and suffered — The Seven Words from the Cross, p. 347

and was buried; — A Threnody of Praise, p. 354

And the third day He rose again, — When Morning Was Come, p. 361
according to the Scriptures;

And ascended into heaven, and — The Ascension, p. 365
sitteth at the right hand of the Father;

And He shall come again with glory — The Sign of the Son of Man, p. 384
to judge the living and the dead, — Glory, p. 338

whose kingdom shall have no end. — The Holy City, p. 409
Eternal Life, p. 391

And we believe in the Holy Spirit, the Lord, and Giver of Life, Who proceedeth from the Father,	The Pneumatic Dimensions of the Lord's Prayer, p. 368
Who with the Father and the Son together is worshipped and glorified,	The Thrice-Holy, p. 394
Who spoke by the Prophets;	Messianic Prophecy Fulfilled in the Lord's Prayer, p. 32
And I believe in One, Holy, Catholic and Apostolic Church.	The Apostles' Creed, p. 168 The Mystical Body of Christ according to Paul, p. 108 The Mystical Body of Christ according to John, p. 109
We acknowledge one Baptism for the remission of sins.	Baptism, p. 90
We look for the Resurrection of the dead, And the Life of the age to come. Amen.	The Last Things ,p. 386

3

CRUCIFIED TO THE WORLD ~ THE WORLD OF ASCETIC ENDEAVOR

And forgive us our trespasses as we forgive those who trespass against us
And lead us not into temptation
But deliver us from evil

CALLED TO BEAR THE CROSS

A VISTA ON THE BEATITUDES

Blessed are the poor in spirit: for theirs is the kingdom of heaven.	The Poverty of the Rich, the Wealth of the Poor, p. 198 Foolishness in Christ, p. 326
Blessed are the meek: for they shall possess the land.	Humility of Heart, p. 323 Humility and Glory, p. 462
Blessed are they that mourn: for they shall be comforted.	The Gift of Tears, p. 56 Repentance, p. 52
Blessed are they that hunger and thirst after justice: for they shall have their fill.	The Sun of Righteousness, p. 242 Love Justice, p. 200
Blessed are the merciful: for they shall obtain mercy.	Seventy Times Seven Times, p. 51 Reward and Punishment, p. 388
Blessed are the clean of heart: they shall see God.	To Have the Mind of Christ, p. 229 Set Free, the Glory of the Children of God, p. 270
Blessed are the peacemakers: for they shall be called the children of God.	The Peace Beyond Understanding, p. 273 Stillness, p. 211
Blessed are they that suffer persecution for justice' sake: for theirs is the kingdom of heaven.	Scrutiny by the Deep Things of God, p. 24 In Sufferings Rejoice, p. 240

SHOW US THE FATHER

THE SATOR-ROTAS ENIGMA, A CHRISTIAN SOLUTION

Every emblem thus possesses one or several meanings proper to it, but meanings can be remarkably changed or amplified with respect to an emblem's use by the circumstances of locale, group, or time period: hence the astonishing wealth of thought hidden beneath the enigmatic appearance of these ideographic signs.
—Louis Charbonneau-Lassay, *The Bestiary of Christ*

INTRODUCTION

SATOR, THE SOWER, AND THE VARYING CIRCUMSTANCES of the seed he casts are the subjects of one of the few parables fully interpreted by Christ for His baffled disciples (Matt. 13:3–23, Mark 4:3–20, Luke 8:5–15). But another "sower" is yet to receive a full interpretation. This sower is the initial word of the so-called "magic square", composed of five five-letter Latin words, that forms either an intelligible or unintelligible sentence, that yields either bland statements about farming or intriguing hints about some deep mystery. After reviewing the massive literature on the subject, several authors are even convinced that it means whatever anyone would like it to mean. Although fully cognizant of others' efforts and grateful for their many insights, while blithely ignoring the threat of wasting my time, my own efforts will go into building up an interpretive field out of an assumed Christian origin; next, applying the square to Christian contemplative practice, and ultimately showing how the square can shed unexpected light on a "kinetic" reading of *The Way to Our Heavenly Father*. Also, as will become apparent soon, there is yet another reason why such a subject is included in a book about the Lord's Prayer.

PART ONE

S A T O R
A R E P O
T E N E T
O P E R A
R O T A S

FIVE WORDS WITH UNDERSTANDING

But in the church I had rather speak five words with my under-
standing, that I may instruct others also: than ten thousand
words in a tongue.

—1 Corinthians 14:19

Corresponding to the Roman Empire's geographical reach in the first centuries of the Christian era we find, in a number of its remote outposts (to the east at Dura Europa on the border with the Persian Empire, to the west at Cirencester in Britain, to the north at Aquincum, part of present-day Budapest, Hungary), and even at center—buried under volcanic rubble in Pompeii—the presence of an enigmatic palindrome that even today retains its *allure*.[1] All early examples of these palindromes go from ROTAS down to SATOR, but, since the sixth century, the reverse ordering beginning with SATOR has become normative.

Mithraic, Pythagorean, Stoic, Jewish, Gnostic, Orphic, and local Italian, as well as Christian origins have been claimed for the word square, but, despite considerable effort and ingenuity, no clear evidence has emerged from the cultural strata of Roman antiquity. And its interpretations are even more abundant than its conjectured origins, with interpreters finding AREPO especially vexing and elusive, this word being seen variously as a Celtic loan word, a proper name, an "Ephesian word" (i. e. a magical but ultimately meaningless word), or a shortened form of *arrepo* (Lat.), meaning "I creep". The first recorded attempt to decipher the word-square seems to have occurred in fourteenth century Byzantium when a writer listed (in Greek) what he thought were the equivalents for each Latin word: SATOR = sower, AREPO = plough, TENET = holds, OPERA = works, ROTAS = wheels. C. W. King,[2] in 1873, took this to mean: "the laborer

---

1. See Rose Mary Sheldon's exhaustive annotated bibliography in "The Sator Rebus: An Unsolved Cryptogram?" (*Cryptologia* 27, no. 3, July 2003, pp. 233–287). Much of the information in the first part of this study will be found there.

2. *Ibid.*, p. 241.

holds the plough wheels and I the sower creep after him." By the early 1880s the square had entered the world of scholarly journals in a major way, and hardly a year has passed since without some new contribution or solution. The latest solution (2010) would have it be an address to the god Asclepius: "O Creator, you cause [all] to rotate. With effort I crawl toward [you]." Followed by a repeated mantra: "Maintain."[1]

The next watershed event in the square's history occurred with the apparently separate discoveries (1924–1927) made by Christian Frank, Felix Grosser and Sigurd Agrell: rearranged, the twenty-five letters were found to be an anagram, a PATER NOSTER ("our father") cross, with two A's and two O's left over to frame the T's, just as they do in the original version. The A's and O's were seen as Latin stand-ins for the *Alpha* and *Omega* of the Apocalypse. Since then, however, a host of alternative messages have been deduced — Sheldon lists twenty-four as a sampling. Among the

```
                    P
                    A
      A             T             O
                    E
                    R
P  A  T  E  R  N  O  S  T  E  R
                    O
                    S
      O             T             A
                    E
                    R
```

messages are more that call on the Father, while others invoke Satan or repudiate him, or even address a certain "Nestor". None of these other messages, though, possess the geometric elegance so akin to the original square or share the selfsame central "N". Is not part of the "magic" of magic squares, after all, the way in which they are inextricably bound together?

For a time the discovery of this concealed PATER NOSTER assured many scholars that the cryptogram was indeed of Christian inspiration. But the last great watershed event was soon to follow. At this point, all examples of the SATOR square were dated to the Middle Ages or later; the claim that the one example uncovered at Cirencester in England (1868) dated from Roman times was seen as highly unlikely by most scholars. Then the excavations at Pompeii yielded two examples (in 1929 and 1936), both of which would have to be prior to the 79 AD eruption of Vesuvius, and a 1931–1932 archaeological expedition to Dura Europa on the Euphrates in Syria uncovered yet another, this one dating from around 200 AD. With these finds everything was back in play and the debate over origins continues even now, eighty years later.

Conflicting origins and word meanings are one thing, but it is simply astounding to see what use people have made of these five five-letter words through the centuries, and this despite four of the five words having quite unambiguous entries in the Latin dictionary. Here we enter that vast penumbra of spells, charms, talismans and amulets. The earliest Roman use might just as well have been a word or letter-game, like tic-

---

1. J. H. Charlesworth, *The Good and Evil Serpent, How a Universal Symbol Became Christianized* (New Haven and London: Yale University Press, 2010), p. 483.

tack-toe, or a kind of chess, the pieces and rules for which no longer survive, or simply a most clever and geometrically complex palindrome invented by some Roman matron late one autumn evening sitting at leisure by the hearth. Sooner or later, though, seeing the favor in which palindromes were held by antiquity's sorcerers and folk healers, the word-square was applied to more subtle ends. Thus, among the bric-a-brac of the waning Roman Empire we find the SATOR-square associated with magic sigils and words of power and, as a distant echo down to our own times, we read in sixteenth century annals as well as nineteenth century folklore collections of remedies, recipes and protective spells using this same square: by it the bite of a rabid dog loses its potency,[1] by it safe childbirth is assured, by it the presence of witches is detected, pestilence turned back, toothache relieved, snake bite cured, and the devil cast out. Nor were fires immune to its charms, especially in eighteenth century Germany where wooden disks with the square emblazoned on either side were kept handy — they were simply tossed at a fire to extinguish it. In 1743 Duke Ernst August of Saxe-Weimar even decreed that all homes should have one for emergencies.[2] And scholars have suggested further uses. Wolfgang Christian Schneider sees in it a pattern reflecting Roman augural practice and a Stoic blueprint for harmonizing man and cosmos.[3] Couchard and Audin declare it a kind of wind-sextant or stationary wind-sock — a device for determining wind direction.[4] Then there are the Christian uses or, if one prefers a different origin, the *Christianized* uses.

Those inclined to see in the square a Christian origin reason that the squares found in a house and on a column in Pompeii were cryptic signs with a Christian message, like the fish symbol, to alert passers-by to the presence of fellow Christians in town.[5] But purely Christian uses are confined mostly to the iconological and didactic which, for lack of intervening evidence, we can begin to trace only five centuries later. But, with the inscriptions found at Dura Europa, we witness at least a transition point from the Latin-speaking world, where the palindrome "makes sense" (however challenging), to the Greek-speaking world and beyond. And perhaps even by this time its original

---

1. Sheldon, *op. cit.*, p. 267. Sheldon refers to an incident recorded by Jerome Cardan in his *De rerum varietate* (1558, bk. 8, chap. 54, pp. 427–428) in which the cryptogram was used to cure a case of rabies. The victim ate three crusts of bread, each inscribed with the cryptogram, while saying the Lord's Prayer five times in honor of Christ's five wounds and the five nails. Was it a chance piety that brought SATOR-square, Christ's wounds and the Lord's Prayer together over three hundred years before the discovery of the PATER NOSTER anagram, or were they together since the square's invention?

2. Sheldon, *op. cit.*, pp. 266–267. In seventeenth century Russia and later a similar efficacy was attributed to the icon of the *Mother of God of the Burning Bush*. Like the cryptogram, it contained a complex geometry, with sixteen "facets" to the burning bush itself, if both points and petal-like features are counted. Kept in the home (despite the official ban on the image in 1722), it was said to ward off fire, lightning and the raging of the elements in general.

3. "Sator Opera Tenet - Poras Aras. 'Der Sämann erhält die Werke - Du aber pfliigst Eine Deutung des Sator-Quadrats," *Castrum Peregrini* 189/90 (1989), pp. 113–116.

4. Sheldon, *op. cit.*, p. 255.

5. Father Jean Carmignac (*Recherches sur le «Notre Père»* [Paris: Letouzey & Ané, 1969], pp. 453–460) has stoutly defended the Christian origin thesis, answering in turn each invalidating argument, including a supposed lack of Christians in Pompeii prior to 79 AD.

FIGURE 1.
Drawing of the mosaic floor in the church of the Beheading of St. John at Pieve Terzagni (11th century).
Reproduced from H. Sökeland, *Zeitschrift des Vereins für Volkskunde* 20, 1915.

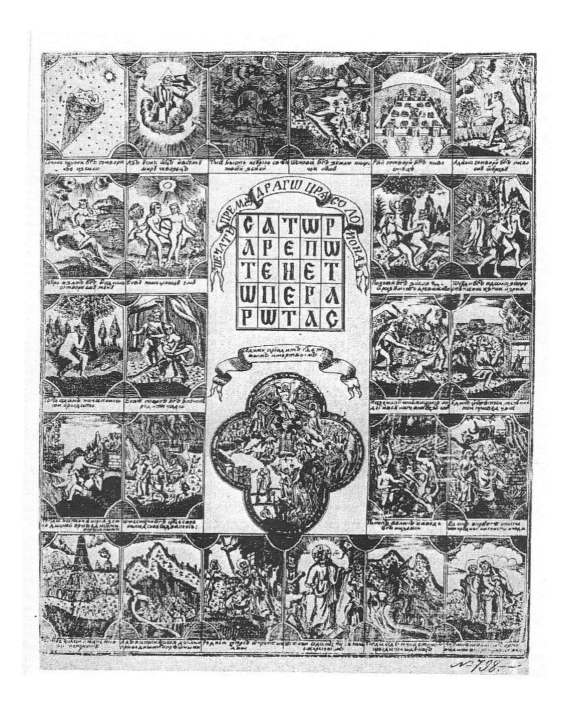

FIGURE 2.
Lubok with illuminated acrostic based on the SATOR square
from D. Rovinsky, *Russki narodnye kartinki*. Atlas iii (Spb., 1881), no. 798.

use or sense is already buried beneath tales of its reputed efficacy, judging by the presence of a number of magic signs and texts elsewhere on the walls of the same chamber. Thus one of the inscriptions reads: POTAC-OPEPA-TENET-APEPO-CATOP, where the equivalent Greek letters are substituted for the Latin ones. From this point the five words begin to disaggregate until, rather than an interlocking square, they become a string of words with adopted meanings.

Only in the fourth or fifth century, though, do we encounter a clear Christian association.[1] With this association we have for the first time SATOR in the top position. As Jerphanion has suggested,[2] the close resemblance of *sator* to *soter* ("Savior" in Greek) might have led to a reverse ordering of the words at this point. By the sixth or seventh century Coptic inscriptions identify the five words with the names of the nails used at Christ's crucifixion. From Coptic areas this identification spread to Nubia and Ethiopia. The five words also became the names for Christ's wounds: *sador, aroda, danad, adem, rodas* in sixteenth-century Ethiopia. Meanwhile, in the Greek world, in the rock-hewn churches of tenth century Cappadocia, we find the names of the shepherds at the Nativity inscribed on frescos as either: *Sator, Aprepo, Tenete, Opera, Rotas*, or: *Sator, Apepon, Teneton*.[3] Then, about a century later, the square is represented on the mosaic flooring behind the altar of a parish church near Cremona, Italy (see FIGURE 1). This square, surrounded by the four "gospel beasts", is set in a position usually reserved for an image of the luminous and triumphant cross. Thus, the square's TENET-cross seems to be the focus of this iconographic program. And one last example, this time from eighteenth or nineteenth century Russia, brings out the square's didactic possibilities. In a *lubok* or "folk picture" (see FIGURE 2) each of the SATOR square's letters are used acrostically to recount the story of Genesis, then Christ's coming in the flesh, His resurrection, and His return in glory to judge the living and the dead.[4] Of all the accompanying illustrations, the Last Judgment shares the central panel with the SATOR square—perhaps yet another reference to Christ's luminous and triumphant cross.

Lastly, we should endeavor to understand the square *as it is*, ahistorically. And here the literature is just as extensive as with its other aspects. First to meet the eye is the five word "sentence' that reads the same from above to below and from left to right, with the palindrome of TENET forming an equal-branched or "Greek" cross at center. However, if the sentence is seen to have only three words, we are faced with what might be

1. A SATOR-square from Cappadocia, accompanied by an image of a fish and the Greek word *ichthus* (Wulff and Volbach, 1909, in Sheldon, p. 253). Father Carmignac argues (*op. cit.*, pp. 463–464) that the early second century tile found at Aquincum is a Christian artifact, since its striated bands are in the form of a St. Andrew's cross and frame the square. St. Andrew's cross is a combination of I and X, the initial Greek letters of *Iesous Christos*.

2. *La Voix des Monuments, Études d'archeologie. nouvelle serie* (Paris: les Éditions d'Art et d'Histoire, 1938), pp. 88–89.

3. C. Picard, "Sur le carré magique à l'église odorante, (Kokar Kilise, Cappadoce)", *Revue archéologique* 1 (1965), 101–102.

4. *Cf.* W. F. Ryan, "Solomon, Sator, Acrostics, and Leo the Wise in Russia," *Oxford Slavonic Papers*, n.s. 19 (1986), pp. 46-61.

called a "total" palindrome. The SATOR AREPO TENET or the ROTAS OPERA TENET read the same top to bottom, bottom to top, right to left and left to right with an interplay of mirror images. This "locked-in" quality was thought to imbue words with heightened potency, hence the frequency of palindromes among the spells and incantations of the ancient world. An alternative view of this "locked-in" or "hall of mirrors" quality can be gained if these twenty-five letters are exchanged for twenty-five numbers, that is, the numbers from one to twenty-five, and these numbers rearranged to form what is called a "magic square". When added up, every row, every column and every diagonal is found to equal the same number, 65 in this case. In itself this is just an interesting piece of mathematical

11	24	7	20	3
4	12	25	8	16
17	5	13	21	9
10	18	1	14	22
23	6	19	2	15

symmetry, that is unless numbers are qualitative as well as quantitative notions.[1] Now, like the N, the 13 is at the center of its square, which has led one researcher[2] to point to a happy convergence of number and letter: N is the thirteenth letter of the classical Latin alphabet! The number thirteen, besides falling midmost according to the demands of a fivefold square, is also the midmost number between one and twenty-five. This focus on the thirteen is even carried through to the PATERNOSTER anagram — if the "free-floating" A's and O's take up positions at the beginning and end of the PATERNOSTER sequences, there will be thirteen letters to the horizontal and thirteen letters to the vertical segments of the cross, with N once more entitled to be acclaimed thirteenth letter. These particular number and letter squares betray, then, a kind of qualitative or mystical coexistence through their centers. Next, observe how twelve vowels and twelve consonants are arranged in an alternating pattern around the central N,[3] which would be, in this case — in the logic of things, in the spirit of the square — the thirteenth consonant.

As interesting as all this debate and discovery might be, are we really any closer to extracting five words of understanding from the square? So far there is little to distinguish this particular five from that tangled myriad of words to which St. Paul alludes. At least the PATERNOSTER anagram is in clear focus, even though some have argued that this was unintended and was only revealed for the first time nearly two thousand years after the square's invention. Now, if the square is an artifact of early Jewish Christians, like the *titulus* on the cross of Christ, they would have had three languages at their disposal: Latin, Greek and *Hebrew*. As a sign of recognition, what can be made of the N central to both the entire square and the TENET-cross? After all, we do see it given

---

1. The Pythagorean school, founded by Pythagoras at Crotona in southern Italy about 500 BC, stressed the qualitative aspect of numbers. Crotona is on the instep, Pompeii on the shin of Italy's boot. After a revival, the school disappeared around 200 AD.

2. Jren Paulsen, "Du carré SATOR au palindrome de Raban Maur: un ésoterisme arithmologique chrétien", *Connaissance des religions*, 51–52, Juli–Dec. 1997, p. 93.

3. Cf. J. Vassel, "A propos des «Études d'histoire chrétienne»", *Études traditionnelles* 56, 1955, pp. 31–32.

separate treatment on the Pompeii column, inscribed after an A and before an O. Father Carmignac sees in it a key to unlock the cryptogram.[1] Besides being the "kernel" out of which the PATERNOSTER anagram blossoms, in Phoenician, Aramaic and Hebrew the N is equivalent to the letter *nun*, seen as the pictograph for a snake—the brazen serpent of Numbers (21:9) and John (3:14)—or a fish. If the square's inventor had a fish in mind, we might be well on our way to discovering five words with understanding, for early Christians understood the Greek word *ichthus*, "fish", to be an acronym for Christ, its five Greek letters being the initials for the five words: *Jesus Christ Son* [of] *God Savior.*

But there is another approach, one in which both Paul's five words with understanding and a possible Christian reading of the cryptogram seem to be found in unison. For this we must examine the writings of one of the early Church Fathers.

Irenaeus of Lyons was born of Christian parents in Smyrna, Asia Minor (present-day Izmir, Turkey) in the first half of the second century. In his youth he was a "hearer" of Polycarp who was in turn a hearer of John the Evangelist. He emigrated to Lugdunum in Roman Gaul (present-day Lyons) and eventually became its second bishop. He died a martyr in the early years of the third century. His major work, *Adversus haereses* (*Against the Heresies*), was mainly a refutation of the various schools of Gnosticism

---

1. *Op. cit.*, pp. 450–451.

prevalent at the time. Because of Cardan's previously mentioned account of a rabies cure in sixteenth century Lyons involving the SATOR-square and a five-fold recitation of the Lord's Prayer in honor of the five nails and Christ's five wounds, Jérôme Carcopino[1] sought to trace a line of descent—however tenuous—from the 1550s back to the Rhone valley at the time of Irenaeus. As evidence, Carcopino points to the presence of AREPO in the square, which he sees as a variant of the Celtic loan word *arepennis*, "acre" and by inference "plough".[2] The second piece of evidence he offers is Irenaeus' devotion to the "fivefold" Cross of Christ as expressed in *Against the Heresies* [II, 24, 4][3]: "The very form of the cross, too, has five extremities, two in length, two in breadth, and one in the middle, on which [last] the person rests who is fixed by the nails."[4] In light of this evidence, Father Jean Daniélou will soon chide Carcopino for emphasizing these two items without connecting them. Daniélou himself sees a confirmation of Irenaeus' familiarity with the SATOR-square in a later passage from *Against the Heresies* [IV, 34, 4], where the plough, taken as a symbol of the Cross, is associated with "sowing" (and therefore with SATOR), as well as the A and the O, that is to say, "beginning" and "end"[5]:

> It is He Himself who has made the plough, and introduced the pruning-hook, that is, the first semination of man, which was the creation exhibited in Adam, and the gathering in of the produce in the last times by the Word; and, for this reason, since He joined the beginning to the end, and is the Lord of both, He has finally displayed the plough [i. e. the Cross], in that the wood has been joined on to the iron, and has thus cleansed His land; because the Word, having been firmly united to flesh, and in its mechanism fixed with pins, has reclaimed the savage earth.[6]

If, despite the evidence of the two foregoing Irenaean passages, the presence of the SATOR-square still remains tenuous, there is something else to consider in *Against the Heresies*: the context of the earlier passage on the Cross.

As part of a general refutation of the heretics' use of numbers to bolster their arguments, and their predilection for finding instances of the ogdoad (8), the decad (10) and the duodecad (12) throughout Scripture, Irenaeus counters with a number ill-fitted to their system but occurring there with notable frequency: the number *five*.[7] The number is introduced in paragraph three with two examples, but nearly the entirety of paragraph four is an extensive listing of fives, biblical and otherwise. Coming from the SATOR-square to this list, besides the passage about the fivefold Cross, there are three other possible links to consider. First, the passage about the Cross occurs at mid-list, just as the TENET is mid-square; next, the list includes twenty-six examples of the five,

1. *Études d'histoire chrétienne*, new ed. (Paris: Albin Michel, 1963), p. 23.

2. *Ibid.*, pp. 34–35, 79–80.

3. *Ibid.*, p. 23.

4. *The Ante-Nicene Fathers*, Roberts and Donaldson ed. (New York: Charles Scribner's Sons, 1913), vol, 1, p. 395.

5. *Primitive Christian Symbols*, trans D. Attwater (London: Burns & Oates, 1964), pp. 100–101.

6. *Op. cit.*, p. 512. This passage assails the Valentinian Gnostic interpretation of John 4:37 in which the God who sows (the Demiurge) is set in opposition to the Christ who redeems and reaps.

7. *Ibid.*, II, 24, 3–4; pp. 394–395.

just as the square consists of twenty-five letters, with a possible twenty-sixth if the *n* is doubled. The third is not, however, so readily perceived.

Initially the list seems a random affair, with entries taken from both Old and New Testaments, as well as mankind's natural life. But there are, in fact, very distinct and meaningful clusters. The introductory cluster is composed of two sacred substances, each having five ingredients: anointing oil and incense, one that descends and one that ascends. At the beginning of the list proper are three five-letter words, words that are barely disguised references to the Trinity: *Soter* or "Savior" is the Son, *Pater* is of course the Father, and *Agape* or "Love" is the Holy Spirit. The next eight examples are all from the New Testament. (A reference to Christ's resurrection on the "eighth day" of the week?[1]) Then comes the Cross: solitary, a stark dividing line between what precedes and succeeds it. The Cross is followed significantly by a cluster of five examples drawn from natural life, at the foot of the Cross so to speak. Last in order come seven examples drawn from the Old Testament. (A reference to the Jewish Sabbath? the seven "first" days of Creation and rest?) So, taking the list in reverse order, we have the Old Testament shepherding the fallen life of our "natural" humanity until the Cross. The Cross in turn opens the way to the "kingdom" of the New Testament and, ultimately, the Trinity. Leaving aside the two introductory examples, we have in the body of the list four clusters balanced almost evenly on either side of the Cross, with twelve examples below and eleven above. Two more will tip the scales if we include with the latter number incense and the anointing oil, in other words, prayer and fasting (cf. Matt. 6:17), or, at the very deepest level, the Christian's participation in Christ's prayer to the Father and Christ's anointing with the Holy Spirit.

See how deftly Irenaeus, while speaking of the five, has hidden away the number five among these four clusters and the Cross for our delight and instruction. See how five themes dear to Paul are brought together: God (Father, Son and Spirit), the old man (and by inference the new man), the Law (the Old Testament), the Gospel, and the Cross of Christ. And see how the Christian provenance of the SATOR-square at such an early date becomes a little less tenuous, a little more credible.

But what of the more hidden PATER NOSTER? For this we shall read the entire list in this way, a way that shows us the Father:

---

1. Cf. Jean Daniélou, *The Bible and the Liturgy* (Notre Dame IN: Notre Dame University Press, 1966), pp. 262–286.

FIVE WITH UNDERSTANDING

NUMBERING THE FIVES OF IRENAEUS

Two Sacred Substances: One that Descends and One that Ascends

ENTER INTO THY
CHAMBER,
AND HAVING SHUT
THE DOOR,
PRAY [INCENSE]
TO THY FATHER IN
SECRET,
AND THY FATHER
WHO SEETH IN
SECRET
WILL REPAY THEE
[ANOINTING OIL]

1.) The anointing oil, which sanctified the whole tabernacle... consisting, as it did, of five hundred shekels of myrrh, five hundred of cassia, two hundred and fifty of cinnamon, two hundred and fifty of calamus, and oil in addition, so that it was composed of five ingredients. Exod. 30:23–25
2.) The incense also, in like manner, [was compounded] of stacte, onycha, galbanum, mint, and frankincense. Exod. 30:34

Three Sacred Words

OUR FATHER WHO
ART IN HEAVEN
HALLOWED BE
THY NAME

3.) *Soter* is a name of five letters; (= Son)
4.) *Pater*, too, contains five letters; (= Father)
5.) *Agape* (love), too, consists of five letters; (= Holy Spirit)

New Testament Examples

THY KINGDOM COME

6.) Our Lord, after blessing the five loaves,
7.) fed with them five thousand men. Matt. 14:19–21
8.) Five virgins were called wise by the Lord;
9.) and, in like manner, five were styled foolish. Matt. 25:2
10.) Again, five men are said to have been with the Lord when He obtained testimony from the Father—namely, Peter, and James, and John, and Moses, and Elias. Matt. 17:1
11.) The Lord also, as the fifth person, entered into the apartment of the dead maiden, and raised her up again... Peter and James, and the father and mother of the maiden. Luke 8:51
12.) The rich man in hell declared that he had five brothers, to whom he desired that one rising from the dead should go. Luke 16:28
13.) The pool from which the Lord commanded the paralytic man to go into his house, had five porches. John 5:2

The Only Cross

THY WILL BE DONE
ON EARTH AS IT IS
IN HEAVEN

14.) The very form of the cross, too, has five extremities, two in length, two in breadth, and one in the middle, on which [last] the person rests who is fixed by the nails.

The Natural Life

GIVE US THIS DAY
OUR DAILY BREAD

15.) Each of our hands has five fingers;

16.) we have also five senses;

17.) our internal organs may also be reckoned as five, viz., the heart, the liver, the lungs, the spleen, and the kidneys.

18.) the whole person may be divided into this number [of parts]—the head, the breast, the belly, the thighs, and the feet.

19.) The human race passes through five ages first infancy, then boyhood, then youth, then maturity, and then old age.

Old Testament Examples

AND FORGIVE US OUR
TRESPASSES AS WE
FORGIVE THOSE
WHO TRESPASS
AGAINST US
AND LEAD US NOT
INTO TEMPTATION
BUT DELIVER
US FROM EVIL

20.) Moses delivered the law to the people in five books.

21.) Each table which he received from God contained five commandments.

22.) The veil covering the holy of holies had five pillars. Exod. 26:37

23.) The altar of burnt-offering also was five cubits in breadth. Exod. 27:1

24.) Five priests were chosen in the wilderness—namely, Aaron, Nadab, Abiud, Eleazar, Ithamar. Exod. 28:1

25.) The ephod and the breastplate, and other sacerdotal vestments, were formed out of five materials; for they combined in themselves gold, and blue, and purple, and scarlet, and fine linen. Exod. 28:5

26.) And there were five kings of the Amorites, whom Joshua the son of Nun shut up in a cave, and directed the people to trample upon their heads. Josh. 10:17

PART TWO

ROTAS
OPERA
TENET
AREPO
SATOR

WHERE THREE ARE GATHERED

Following this general survey, we will step back and approach the square as presented in its earliest version, with ROTAS on top. But this does not mean simply a reversal of word order. From this point forward SATOR and AREPO will be seen as mirror images of ROTAS and OPERA, and no longer as discrete words. From this perspective we will briefly attempt a phenomenological approach to the words; screening out cultural backgrounds and scholarly conjectures, only Latin definitions and letter or word positions will be of interest—a kind of initial *ascesis* or cleansing. The far greater share of this part, though, will be an attempt to imbed the square, both retrospectively and prospectively, in Christian tradition, that is, we will endeavor to see how the square is "at home" in Christian tradition and especially Christian contemplative practice.

Before reading further, spend a few minutes following ROTAS, OPERA and TENET about the square, alternating each word between foreground and background… Are not two of the ROTAS square's three words actually performing their meanings?

— ROTAS, meaning "wheels" or "you revolve" is actually a wheeling or revolving backwards and forwards along the periphery; square in shape but round in meaning, this is at once a circling of the square and a squaring of the circle. And all this time we thought the solution had something to do with geometry…

—TENET, meaning "he (she or it) holds" or "maintains", pushes from the center outwards, erect and stiff, at right angles to the world — righteous. And then there are the terminal letters, replicas or microcosms or performers of the figure to which they belong. Like Atlas supporting the weight of the globe.

But what of OPERA? It seems to depict a net or mesh, something woven, at once porous and retentive, something that knits together, an "interstitial" something. It is a disconcerting figure, with the wind of the vowels whispering on the outside and whistling on the inside. Although shared with the other two words, all twelve of the square's vowels are woven into the fourfold OPERA. Looking back to ROTAS, there are clearly four words, to TENET, there are even more clearly two. But the OPERA's… they are everywhere and restless; they form into straight lines, they bend into L-shapes, they curve into C-shapes. And on the way to sixteen, their maximum, they seem fugitive and constantly multiplied. Inwardly, only the E's about the center seem resolved upon stillness, the turning keys of their shapes locking down to silence, while instantly their sound is the axle's scream. Outwardly in the meantime, the o's and A's are furled and unfurled wings, open and unopened eyes.

—OPERA, meaning "works", "labor", or "with effort", is the centripetal force that keeps the ROTAS from dissipating into the empty spaces, into meaninglessness, the centrifugal reach that, bending, keeps the TENET upright, unbent. OPERA is then a kind of "bedding" for the clarity of the other forms, itself on the very edge of the visible, the palpable.

```
R   O   T   A   S               T               O       A

O               A               E           O   P   E   R   A

T               T   T   E   N   E   T        E       E

A               O               E           A   R   E   P   O

S   A   T   O   R               T               A       O
```

Having observed the cryptogram's "dry bones",[1] it is time now to clothe it with its Christian possibilities. A prologue from Ezechiel will abruptly usher us into the courts of heaven and prepare those who sigh and mourn to be marked with the mark of the *Tau*. Two contemplations follow that are indeed the *Tau*, otherwise known as the sign of the cross: the naming of the Holy Trinity and a placing of the Cross "squarely" upon ourselves both for our lack of Paradise and for its restoration. Beyond these, three more contemplations follow on the call of God (*Burning Bush*), the call from our neighbor (*Church*) and the recall to our true self (*Three Motions*)—"Thou shalt love the Lord thy God... and thy neighbor as thyself."

---

1. *Cf.* Ezech. 37.

A CONTEMPLATION ON EZECHIEL

Noted historian and philologist Franz Cumont[1] was one of the first to suggest a possible link between the square and Ezechiel's throne vision (the bracketed words are my own interpolations[2]):

> And I saw, and behold a whirlwind [ROTAS] came out of the north: and a great cloud, and a fire infolding it, and brightness was about it: and out of the midst thereof, that is, out of the midst of the fire [IGNIS[3]], as it were the resemblance of amber: And in the midst thereof the likeness of four living creatures: and this was their appearance: there was the likeness of a man in them. Every one had four faces, and every one four wings… and they had faces, and wings on the four sides, and the wings of one were joined to the wings of another [ROTAS]. They turned not when they went: but every one went straight forward [TENET]… And their faces, and their wings were stretched upward [TENET]: two wings of every one were joined, and two covered their bodies: And every one of them went straight forward [TENET]: whither the impulse [OPERA] of the spirit was to go, thither they went: and they turned not when they went [TENET]. And as for the likeness of the living creatures, their appearance was like that of burning coals of fire [IGNIS], and like the appearance of lamps. This was the vision running to and fro [ROTAS] in the midst of the living creatures, a bright fire [IGNIS], and lightning going forth from the fire. And the living creatures ran and returned like flashes of lightning. Now as I beheld the living creatures, there appeared upon the earth by the living creatures one wheel with four faces [ROTAS]. And the appearance of the wheels [ROTAS], and the work [OPERA] of them was like the appearance of the sea: and the four had all one likeness: and their appearance and their work [OPERA] was as it were a wheel in the midst of a wheel [ROTAS]. When they went, they went by their four parts: and they turned not when they went.… And the glory of the Lord of Israel went up from the cherub, upon which he was, to the threshold of the house: and he called to the man that was clothed with linen, and had a writer's inkhorn at his loins. And the Lord said to him: Go through the midst [OPERA] of the city, through the midst [OPERA] of Jerusalem: and mark Thau [TENET] upon the foreheads of the men that sigh, and mourn for all the abominations that are committed in the midst thereof.… And he spoke to the man, that was clothed with linen, and said: Go [OPERA] in between the wheels [ROTAS] that are under the cherubims and fill thy hand with the coals of fire [IGNIS] that are between the cherubims, and pour them out [OPERA] upon the city. And he went in, in my sight… And when he had commanded the man that was clothed with linen, saying: Take [OPERA] fire [IGNIS] from the midst of the wheels

---

1. *Rendiconti Pontificia Accademia di Archeologia* 13 (1937), pp. 7–8.

2. Most of these interpolations—set in brackets—are allusive within the bounds of the word's definition (cf. *Cassell's Latin Dictionary*) and only rarely represent an exact equivalence or actual word in the Latin Vulgate.

3. Although not part of the cryptogram, this five-letter Latin word for "fire" with its central "n" may not be so completely arbitary. In the present instance it serves as a stand-in for the N, the square's only unrepeated letter—"I am come to cast fire [*ignem*] on the earth. And what will I, but that it be kindled?" (Luke 12:49) and "Our God is a consuming fire [*ignis*]" (Heb. 12:29).

[ROTAS] that are between the cherubims: he went in and stood beside the wheel. And one cherub stretched out his arm [TENET] from the midst of the cherubims to the fire [IGNIS] that was between the cherubims: and he took [OPERA], and put [OPERA] it into the hands [TENET] of him that was clothed with linen: who took it and went forth [OPERA]. And there appeared in the cherubims the likeness of a man's hand [TENET] under their wings. And I saw, and behold there were four wheels [the fourfold ROTAS] by the cherubims: one wheel by one cherub, and another wheel [ROTAS] by another cherub: and the appearance of the wheels [ROTAS] was to the sight like the chrysolite stone: And as to their appearance, all four were alike [as in a four-way palindrome]: as if a wheel were in the midst of a wheel [ROTAS]. And when they went, they went by four ways [ROTAS]: and they turned not when they went [OPERA]: but to the place whither they first turned, the rest also followed, and did not turn back (Ezech. 1:4–17, 9:3–4, 10:2, 6–11).

As Rino Cammilleri has noted,[1] a possible connection with Ezechiel does not preclude a Christian origin for the square. After all, the New Testament abounds in references to both Moses and the *prophets*. In fact, reading the "transcripts" of the early apostolic preaching in the Book of Acts, a case can be made for the young Church actually *owning*—in Christ— the prophets.

A CONTEMPLATION ON THE HOLY TRINITY

Our Father who art in heaven

Surprisingly, immediately above the ROTAS inscription on the Pompeii column we find a Greek *delta* (Δ). Although no other corroboration for the *delta* as a sign for the Holy Trinity seems to exist at this early date, it might be well worth considering, especially if, as I am suggesting, the original cryptogram was composed of only three words.

ROTAS — You, heavenly Father, to whom the Son will hand over all things, because He upholds (TENET) all things, that at the last you might be all in all (1 Cor. 15:28), You that even now encompass more than the universe itself, You revolve. Yet to create, you have created; in the very act of Creation You have entered into Your rest, into your holy Sabbath. At rest, and yet You and your Son are at work (OPERA). This is how you circle. You are the motionlessness beyond stillness, and this is why we say: "ROTAS", "You revolve". But we say this only because of the measure of our stuttering love, we who have heard with joy Your urgent summons: "ROTAS", "you, you personally, turn around", and—yesterday, today and tomorrow—behold "the light of the knowledge of the glory of God in the face of Jesus Christ" (2 Cor. 4:6).

TENET — Standing before the TENET-cross these words from Gregory of Nyssa come to mind:

This is the very thing we learn from the figure of the Cross; it is divided into four parts, so that there are the projections, four in number, from the central point where the

---

1. *Il quadrato magico* (Milan: Rizzoli, 1999), p. 37.

whole converges upon itself; because He Who at the hour of His pre-arranged death was stretched upon it is He Who binds together all things into Himself, and by Himself brings to one harmonious agreement the diverse natures of actual existences.... Since, then, all creation looks to Him, and is about and around Him, and through Him is coherent with itself, things above being through Him conjoined to things below and things lateral to themselves, it was right that not by hearing only we should be conducted to the full understanding of the Deity, but that sight also should be our teacher in these sublime subjects for thought.[1]

Gregory's "hearing" and "sight" become simultaneously perceptible with the image of the cross imbedded in the cryptogram. The sight of a fivefold cross (the overall TENET-cross plus the four T's at its extremities) is the likely source for the naming of the nails as well as Christ's wounds with the cryptogram's five words, while the word TENET—spoken, heard and understood—is itself rich with allusions to the Crucified. By the Incarnation He has arrived at (TENET) the human condition and, in His final hours on Calvary, He endures (TENET) the cross, despising its shame (Heb. 12:2). He perseveres (TENET) to the end in love for his friends and forgiveness for His tormentors, and does not swerve from (TENET) His Father's will, He who alone grasps (TENET) perfectly the Father's will because He is the Son and only one with His Father. He submits to the destitution of the cross even though, as the Son, He contains (TENET) all things and all things belong to (TENET) Him. Dying, He reaches (TENET) the utter depths of the human condition—except for sin—and, as in the icon of the *Anastasis*, grasps (TENET) with His life-giving hands the life-given hands of Adam and Eve.

This appreciation of the TENET, which began with Gregory's geometrical insights on the cross, should end on John's very personal and hymnic remembrance of the Son of God:

That which was from the beginning, which we have heard, which we have seen with our eyes, which we have looked upon and our hands have handled [TENET], of the word of life. For the life was manifested [TENET]: and we have seen and do bear witness and declare unto you the life eternal, which was with the Father and hath appeared to us. That which we have seen and have heard, we declare unto you: that you also may have [TENET] fellowship with us and our fellowship may be with the Father and with his Son Jesus Christ. And these things we write to you, that you may rejoice and your joy may be full (1 John 1:1–4).

John's seeing, hearing and especially touching are not casual affairs, a brief encounter in a jostling crowd, or even that single healing touch of the Savior leaving a deep interior trace for the rest of one's life. For John, Christ's three year ministry was a time of unbroken fellowship with the Savior. But even more than that, he was "one of his disciples, whom Jesus loved" (John 13:23). And, of the all the apostles, he alone stood by the Cross. If John the Baptist was another Elias, John the Evangelist was another Eli-

---

1. *The Great Catechism*, trans. W. Moore and H. A. Wilson (1934), pp. 21, 42.

seus. Eliseus refused to "tarry" behind in Bethel, Jericho or at the Jordan (2 Kings 2:1–8) but continued with Elias until the end, to see Elias taken up from the earth in a fiery chariot. For this he asked for and was granted the "double spirit" of Elias. John stood by the fiery chariot of the Cross and—without asking—received a double gift. First, the gift of Christ's own mother into his home (John 19:25–27) and then, at Pentecost, the Holy Spirit. (Is it any wonder that John's Gospel is so distinct from the other three?) Such, then, are the personal dimensions of the Son of God from His cross, tenderly coextensive with His Church.

OPERA — Speaking of the Holy Spirit, John Damascene declares: "Having learned that there is a Spirit of God, we conceive of Him as associated with the Word and making the operation [OPERA] of the Word manifest".[1] With this manner of cooperation between Word and Spirit where the Father is ever-present in the oneness of the Trinity, we are confronted by this passage concerning work on the Sabbath from the Gospel of John: "My Father worketh [OPERA] until now; and I work [OPERA]" (John 5:17). What is this "work" if not the Holy Spirit? This work and the power to accomplish it: "You shall receive the power [OPERA] of the Holy Spirit coming upon you, and you shall be witnesses unto me in Jerusalem, and in all Judea, and Samaria, and even to the uttermost part of the earth" (Acts 1:8). And this work, this power not only sweeps through the outer world, but even to the utmost recesses of the inner world: "For this cause I bow my knees to the Father of our Lord Jesus Christ... that he would grant you, according to the riches of his glory, to be strengthened [OPERA] by his Spirit with might [OPERA] unto the inward man" (Eph. 3:14, 16). And, with the Spirit's saturation of these outer and inner worlds, carrying everything before it, there comes that great explosion of gifts:

> To one indeed, by the Spirit, is given the word of wisdom: and to another, the word of knowledge, according to the same Spirit: to another, faith in the same spirit: to another, the grace of healing in one Spirit: to another the working [OPERA] of miracles: to another, prophecy: to another, the discerning of spirits: to another, diverse kinds of tongues: to another, interpretation of speeches. But all these things, one and the same Spirit worketh [OPERA], dividing to every one according as he will (1 Cor. 12:8–11).

Lastly, gathering together every gift before God in thanksgiving, we should acknowledge that through the Trinity we "live [OPERA] and move [ROTAS] and have [TENET] our being" (Acts 17:28).

---

1. *An Exact Eposition of the Orthodox Faith*, I, 7; F. H. Chase trans., p. 175.

And lead us not into temptation
But deliver us from evil

Captured in the TENET-cross is a fleeting glimpse of the four rivers of paradise—the Pishon, Gihon, Tigris and Euphrates[1]—issuing from their fontal source in the N. God had placed Adam in this abundantly watered garden to till (OPERA) and keep (TENET) it. The TENET-cross is also an image of the tree of the knowledge of good and evil and the tree of life, both laden with fruit—together, on the tree of life, the A's and O's represent the everlastingness of everlasting life; apart, on the tree of the knowledge of good and evil, they represent the separation of beginning from end, death. Adam and Eve might have lived forever had they persevered (TENET) in keeping (TENET) the one commandment. But they fell head long (ROTAS) from their original state and did not repent (ROTAS), did not *revert*,[2] placing blame elsewhere rather than face the shame of self-accusation. Now an angel guards the way back against them with a "flaming sword, turning every way [ROTAS] to keep [TENET] the way of the tree of life" (Gen. 3:24) until the days be accomplished.

But the days are and will be accomplished when the source of these paradise rivers erupts into time. This source is a river of prophecy; like the Jordan in the days of Joshua, it flows backwards. This backwards flow into the distant past was impelled by Christ's life, death, resurrection and ascension that are ever-present—even to the past—because accomplished "once for all" (Heb. 10:10). These rivers gush reunited in their common source from the rock that is Christ (1 Cor. 10:4) struck by Moses to quench the desert thirst of Israel; as witnessed by Ezechiel, they pour reunited and in full spate from the right side of the Temple, a living and life-giving water (47:1–10). And this water is also Christ, for as Cyril of Alexandria declares:

> That He is and is called spiritually a Brook, the most wise Psalmist too will testify to us, saying to God the Father about us, *The children of men shall hope in the shadow of Thy wings: they shall be inebriated with the fatness of Thy House, and Thou shalt give them drink of the Brook of Thy delights* [Psalm 35:8–9]. And the Lord Himself somewhere in the prophets says, *Behold, I am inclining to them as a river of peace and as an overflowing brook* [Isa. 66:12].[3]

Christ indeed, but also the Holy Spirit as John informs us after Christ's own words: "If any man thirst, let him come to me and drink. He that believeth in me, as the scripture saith: Out of his belly shall flow rivers of living water. Now this he said of the Spirit

---

1. *Cf.* Gen. 2:11–14. The Tigris and Euphrates are known, the Gihon is mostly identified as the Nile, while the Pishon is variously identified as the Danube (Ephrem the Syrian) or the Ganges (Ambrose of Milan). Following Philo of Alexandria, Ambrose allegorizes the rivers into the four cardinal virtues: the Pishon is prudence, the Gihon temperance, the Tigris fortitude and the Euphrates justice (*Paradise*, Chap. 3, 15–18, in *Fathers of the Church, A New Translation*, vol. 42, trans. J. J. Savage [New York: Fathers of the Church Inc., 1961], pp. 296–298.

2. *Cf.* Cammillieri, pp. 184–185.

3. *Commentary on the Gospel according to St. John*, v, 37, (Oxford: James Parker & Co., 1874) vol. 1, p. 543–544.

which they should receive who believed in him: for as yet the Spirit was not given, because Jesus was not yet glorified" (John 7:37–39). Compared to earlier prophecies, this one was nearly contemporaneous with its fulfillment on Calvary where:

> …after they were come to Jesus, when they saw that he was already dead, they did not break his legs. But one of the soldiers with a spear opened his side: and immediately there came out blood and water. John 19:33–34

And immediately there opened the floodgates of the Christian dispensation. Earlier Christ had seen Satan fall like lightning from heaven (Luke 10:18). So now Christ in His turn falls like an all-dazzling bolt into the uttermost depths of death and hell, where, deeper than death and hell, He has burst open the promise of universal resurrection. From the days of His cross and empty tomb even until now, those who listen intently can hear these deep uprushing waters on their way to us. These ultimate waters, yes, but also in the meantime: Christ's and the Spirit's unstinting waters of Paradise issuing from the Holy Theotokos, the Church, and, by God's grace, anyone.

The Holy Theotokos:

> Most sincerely do we call thee the manna of heaven and the divine wellspring of paradise, O Virgin Mistress; for the grace of thy spring, which covereth the four parts of the earth, hath ever poured forth a stream of strange miracles, and is become the water requested and imbibed by all. Wherefore, in gladness, O ye who bear the name of Christ, let us hasten with faith, ever drawing forth sweetly flowing holiness…
>
> O ye faithful, with wondrous songs let us hymn the heavenly cloud, which hath incorruptibly let fall upon the earth the celestial Rain-drop — Christ, the Bestower of life — which giveth rise to life and poureth forth immortality, the divine water, ambrosia, nectar, which never corrupteth after it hath been drunk, and dispelleth the thirst which afflicteth men's souls. Unto those who drink thereof with understanding divine streams shall come forth from thy noetic womb, pouring forth abundant grace upon all.[1]

The Church:

> Awful in truth are the Mysteries of the Church, awful in truth is the Altar. A fountain went up out of Paradise sending forth material rivers, from this table springs up a fountain which sends forth rivers spiritual…. If any be scorched with heat, let him come to the side of this fountain and cool his burning. For it quenches drought, and comforts all things that are burnt up, not by the sun, but by the fiery darts [of temptation and sin]. For it has its beginnings from above, and its source is there, whence also its water flows. Many are the streams of that fountain which the Comforter sends forth, and the Son is the Mediator, not holding mattock to clear the way, but opening our minds. This fountain is a fountain of light, spouting forth rays of truth… Fiercer than fire the river boils up, yet burns not, but only baptizes that on which it lays hold. This Blood was ever typified of old in the altars and sacrifices of righteous men, This is the price of the world, by This Christ purchased to Himself the Church, by This He

---

1. Bright Thursday at Vespers, in *The Pentecostarion of the Orthodox Church*, trans. I. E. Lambertsen (Liberty TN: St. John of Kronstadt Press, 2010), p. 42.

has adorned Her all. For as a man buying servants gives gold for them, and again when he desires to deck them out does this also with gold; so Christ has purchased us with His Blood, and adorned us with His Blood. They who share this Blood stand with Angels and Archangels and the Powers that are above, clothed in Christ's own kingly robe, and having the armor of the Spirit. Nay, I have not as yet said any great thing: they are clothed with the King Himself.[1]

And now he has said a great thing: clothed with Christ Himself, the deified Christian is plunged deeper than thirst into the confluence of the Church, that voice of many waters (Ezech. 43:2), to become one stream among all the *personalized* streams of salvation, one of the Savior's rivers among all the rivers of Paradise.

Anyone:
> He who does not disbelieve shall revel in richest graces from God. For he shall be so replete with the gifts through the Spirit, as not only to fatten his own mind, but even to be able to overflow into others' hearts, like the river stream gushing forth the God-given good upon his neighbor too. This very thing used He to enjoin the holy Apostles, saying, *Freely ye received, freely give* [Matt. 10:8].[2]

Mindful of the rivers that flow from Paradise, we should also be mindful of the word, the two-edged sword (cf. Heb. 4:12, but also Eph. 6:17 and Apoc. 1:16) "turning every way" that keeps the entry to the paradise of the scriptures: "The letter killeth [TENET]: but the spirit [ROTAS] quickeneth [OPERA]" (2 Cor. 3:6). Turning every way, it is also like those four rivers that come out of Paradise to water the earth, it is a word that bathes the source of the manifold rivers of interpretation which flood the ages for our deliverance.

Killeth-TENET: Once upon a time a mysterious series of intersections occurred that were not once upon a time. As vouched for by a host of eyewitnesses who became believers and believers who became eyewitnesses by the power of their faith—"Blessed are they that have not seen and have believed" (John 20:29) —, the all-holy Mother of God foremost among them, God was made man in the Person of Jesus Christ the Word— "Blessed are they who hear the word of God and keep it" (Luke 11:28)—from whom all the other intersections follow: earth and heaven in His incarnation and ascension, life and death and Life in His crucifixion and resurrection, God and man in Himself and in His Church. Sentenced to death by upholders of the much-interpreted "letter of the law", He is and always is the letter that gives meaning to everything, for, as Maximus the Confessor explains:

---

1. *Homilies of St. John Chrysostom on the Gospel of St. John* 46.4; vol. 2 (Oxford: John Henry Parker, 1852), pp. 400–401. Reminiscent of his Paschal homily, Chrysostom's hymn to the Holy Mysteries in his *Homilies on John*, is an wondrous verbal icon of the Church.

2. Cyril of Alexandria, *op.cit.*, p. 544.

The mystery of the incarnation of the Logos is the key to all the arcane symbolism and typology in the Scriptures, and in addition gives us knowledge of created things, both visible and intelligible. He who apprehends the mystery of the cross and the burial apprehends the inward essences of created things; while he who is initiated into the inexpressible power of the resurrection apprehends the purpose for which God first established everything.[1]

...two strands cross at a barely specified and unique angle as the knotting of a prayer-rope begins.[2]

Quickeneth-OPERA: Seizing upon the facts of the Incarnation—every article of faith—, the believer interprets them into the quickening arts and sciences. Here is the well-spring for the practices of asceticism, iconography, hymnography, theology, liturgics; all celebrating each in their own way, according to particular or multiple senses conjoined to the deep recesses of the heart, the solemn proclamation of God come in the flesh to save us, all drinking deeply of scripture's clear, immaterial waters. Nourished and cleansed and swept away by the tradition and calling of the saints... we become, we *are* according to Christ.

Once more Maximus the Confessor comes forward to explain, this time from the mid-torrent of interpretation to those on the shore:

> Jacob's well (cf. John 4:5-15) is Scripture. The water is the spiritual knowledge found in Scripture. The depth of the well is the meaning, only to be attained with great difficulty, of the obscure sayings in Scripture. The bucket is learning gained from the written text of the word of God, which the Lord did not possess because He is the Logos Himself; and so He does not give believers the knowledge that comes from learning and study, but grants to those found worthy ever-flowing waters of wisdom that spill from the fountain of spiritual grace and never run dry. For the bucket—that is to say, learning—can only grasp a very small amount of knowledge and leaves behind all that it cannot lay hold of, however it tries. But the knowledge which is received through grace, without study, contains all the wisdom that man can attain, springing forth in different ways according to his needs.[3]

...the two strands are folded and interwoven. The hand, having become enmeshed in a single knot, feels the outline of the prayer-knot from within. This is how it is to be gripped by prayer....

Spirit-ROTAS: Scripture, instilled over a lifetime, gradually or sometimes even suddenly permeates the very substance of our minds, until that day when we ourselves are interpreted into the grace of the Spirit to become God's own living scripture. And here

---

1. *Centuries on Theology* 1, 66; *The Philokalia*, vol. 2, p. 127.

2. This and the following two italicized continuous but non-contiguous threads of text are "interpretations" of the major stages in the knotting of an Orthodox prayer-rope, that highly recommended *nexus* between prayer and daily life, with every prayer yet another chance to interpet our lives into God. *Cf.* R. M. Deed, "The Sword of the Spirit, the Making of an Orthodox Rosary" (*Studies in Comparative Religion*, vol. 1 num. 3), pp. 376–385; *Comboschini (The Prayer Rope): Meditations of a Monk of the Holy Mountain Athos* (Florence, AZ.: St. Anthony's Monastery, nd).

3. *Various Texts*, 2, 29; *The Philokalia*, vol. 2, pp. 193–194.

Maximus, to complete this circle of considerations, offers a final word with some salient advice about misinterpreting scripture in however worthy a manner:

> So long as we only see the Logos of God as embodied multifariously in symbols in the letter of Holy Scripture, we have not yet achieved spiritual insight into the incorporeal, simple, single and unique Father as He exists in the incorporeal, simple, single and unique Son, according to the saying, 'He who has seen Me has seen the Father . . . and I am in the Father and the Father in Me' (John 14:9-10). We need much knowledge so that, having first penetrated the veils of the sayings which cover the Logos, we may with a naked intellect see—in so far as men can—the pure Logos, as He exists in Himself, clearly showing us the Father in Himself. Hence a person who seeks God with true devotion should not be dominated by the literal text, lest he unwittingly receives not God but things appertaining to God; that is, lest he feel a dangerous affection for the words of Scripture instead of for the Logos. For the Logos eludes the intellect which supposes that it has grasped the incorporeal Logos by means of His outer garments, like the Egyptian woman who seized hold of Joseph's garments instead of Joseph himself (cf. Gen. 39:7-13).[1]

. . . After a lesser or greater multitude of knots, each composed of seven crosses, each one tightened or rounded *to itself, the two ends of the prayer-rope are rounded to each other and relinquished into the form of a cross, an eighth and glorious cross:* "...PATER NOSTER..."[2]

According to the pattern of the-letter-killeth-but-the-spirit-quickeneth, the "interpretive" reading of Scripture has been bound together here with the running commentaries from Maximus and the stages in the knotting of a prayer-rope. Together, such disparate things are a symbol of the Christian's praying with scripture in the tradition of the apostles and all the saints, that is to say, in the Church. And such is the fullness of Christ in His Church that, wherever scripture falls open, this word of Christ stands sentinel over every reading: *Today this scripture is fulfilled in your hearing* (Luke 4:21).

---

1. *Centuries on Theology*, 2, 73; *The Philokalia*, vol. 2, p. 155.

2. The stages in the knotting of a prayer-rope reflect the way of the Way (Heb. 10:20), a way with no known borders between *catharsis*, *photismos* and *theosis*, that is, between purification, illumination and deification or ethical philosophy, natural contemplation and mystical theology.

KNIT TOGETHER IN LOVE

OUR FATHER WHO
ART IN HEAVEN
HALLOWED BE
THY NAME

That their hearts may be comforted, being instructed [knit together] in charity and unto all riches of fulness of understanding, unto the knowledge of the mystery of God the Father and of Christ Jesus: in whom are hid all the treasures of wisdom and knowledge. Col. 2:2–3

THY KINGDOM COME

And we know that to them that love God all things work together unto good: to such as, according to his purpose, are called to be saints. Rom. 8:28

THY WILL BE DONE
ON EARTH AS IT IS
IN HEAVEN

For the Lord himself shall come down from heaven with commandment and with the voice of an archangel and with the trumpet of God: and the dead who are in Christ shall rise first. Then we who are alive, who are left, shall be taken up together with them in the clouds to meet Christ, into the air: and so shall we be always with the Lord. 1 Thess. 4:15–16

GIVE US THIS DAY
OUR DAILY BREAD

And we beseech you, brethren, by the coming of our Lord Jesus Christ and of our gathering together unto him: that you be not easily moved from your sense nor be terrified, neither by spirit nor by word nor by epistle as sent from us, as if the day of the Lord were at hand. 2 Thess 2:1–2

AND FORGIVE US OUR
TRESPASSES AS WE
FORGIVE THOSE
WHO TRESPASS
AGAINST US

Buried with him in baptism: in whom also you are risen again by the faith of the operation of God who hath raised him up from the dead. And you, when you were dead in your sins and the uncircumcision of your flesh, he hath quickened together with him, forgiving you all offences. Col. 2:12–13

AND LEAD US NOT
INTO TEMPTATION

Only let your conversation be worthy of the gospel of Christ: that, whether I come and see you, or, being absent, may hear of you, that you stand fast in one spirit, with one mind labouring together for the faith of the gospel. And in nothing be ye terrified by the adversaries: which to them is a cause of perdition, but to you of salvation, and this from God. For unto you it is given for Christ, not only to believe in him, but also to suffer for him. Phil. 1:27–29

BUT DELIVER
US FROM EVIL

But God (who is rich in mercy) for his exceeding charity wherewith he loved us, even when we were dead in sins, hath quickened us together in Christ (by whose grace you are saved), and hath raised us up together and hath made us sit together in the heavenly places, through Christ Jesus. Eph. 2:4–6

A CONTEMPLATION ON THE BURNING BUSH

Hallowed be thy name

God conversed with Moses from the burning bush on Mount Horeb. At length Moses asked (Exod. 3:13): "If [the children of Israel] shall say to me: What is his name? What shall I say to them?", and was answered with an unprecedented outpouring of names (Exod. 3:14–15): "I am who am", "He who is",[1] "The Lord God of your fathers, the God of Abraham, the God of Isaac, and the God of Jacob". To this last name God affixed a special seal: "This is my name for ever, and this is my memorial unto all generations." Lastly, to the Egyptians, He would have himself known as "the Lord God of the Hebrews" (Exod. 3:18). Now mindful that in Hebrew, as in Greek, there are no numerals, this function being served by letters, each letter having its assigned number, we should dwell for a moment on the numerical "properties" given by Jewish tradition[2] to these most sacred of names: "I am that I am" (*ehyeh asher eyeh*) = 543, "He who is" (*eyeh*) = 21, "God" (*elohim*) = 86, "the Lord God" (*Yahweh elohe*) = 72, with "Lord" = 26 and "God" = 46. To these should be added another form of "Lord": *Adonai* = 65, usually substituted for *Yahweh* when a text is read aloud.[3]

Turning directly from these considerations to the appearance of the cryptogram, we find there an image of the Burning Bush, with the TENET-cross forming the Bush's stem and branches, the ROTAS-circle its silhouette, and the OPERA its twigs and foliage. There too even and especially the Names. And—resolving the letters of the cryptogram back into the numbers of a magic square[4] —what an overwhelming host of Names! As stated earlier, 65 is the sum of all rows of numbers, horizontally, vertically and diagonally, a total of 12 rows, and therefore a twelve-fold utterance of *Adonai*, "The Lord." Nicolas Vinel, who argues that the SATOR square is Jewish in origin, draws out two more significant numbers: 13 and 26.[5] At center, 13 has *ehad*, "one", a divine attribute, as its verbal equivalent,[6] and this central 13 is encompassed by an inner and an outer ring

---

1. *Am* and *am* and *is* (in transliterated Hebrew: *'eh-yeh* thrice repeated), a most personal revelation and foreshadowing of the Trinity.

2. This process of assigning numbers to letters and then gaining insights from coordinating scriptural words or phrases that share the same numbers, or of simply working from the "raw material" of the numbers themselves—the "number of the beast" in the Apocalypse—first becomes evident during the "Tannaic" period of Judaism (10–220 AD). This discipline of verbal numerology is called *gematria* in the Jewish tradition (*isopsephy* among the Greeks).

3. To remind readers of the Hebrew Bible, YHVH (the consonants of the Holy Name termed the *Tetragammaton* or "four-lettered word") is written with the vowels of *Adonai*. Much has been made of such name and number equivalences, even too much, as might be judged from the great swarm of meanings disclosed by Kabbalists and their Christian counterparts. Here, we will consider only numbers as discrete and simple reflections at one remove from these names.

4. Admittedly, this affinity between cryptogram and magic square has no basis in what is known about the first century. The earliest mention of magic squares occurs in the ninth century Islamic world of Baghdad (Jacques Sesiano, "Les carrés magiques de Manuel Moschopoulos", *Archive for History of Exact Sciences*, Vol. 53, No. 5 [Nov. 1998], p. 379). But this would not be the first time later, unintended discoveries sprang from an earlier inspiration.

5. "Le judaïsme caché du carré SATOR de Pompéi", *Revue de l'histoire des religions*, vol. 223, no. 2 (2006), p. 179.

6. Significantly *ahabah*, "love" and *Jeshuah*, "Jesus", are also equivalent to this 13. *Jeshuah* is actually equivalent to 391 which then becomes 13 by reduction: 3+9+1 = 13 (cf. N. Boon, *Au coeur de l'écriture*, pp. 261–262.).

of 26s linked in a symmetrical "skipping stone" fashion; thus on the inner ring we have: 12+14, 8+18, 5+21 and 25+1, while on the outer ring: 11+15, 3+23, 4+22, etc. In sum there are twelve pairs of numbers equaling 26 and therefore equivalent to the other name for Lord: *Yahweh*. Next, seeing that 26 is composed of two 13's and 65 of five 13's, we discover that, in the logic of this arithmology, a oneness undergirds, emphasizes and intensifies the presence of *Adonai* and *Yahweh* twenty-five times.[5] Lastly, with the N at the junction of the two TENET's, we might well consider it a double N, and so bring the number of the cryptogram's letters to 26: the all-pervasiveness of the Lord.

Retaining the above mentioned concentric pattern, when numbers are once more exchanged for letters we discover a concentric reading of the square: ROTAS on the outer ring, PER ("through", "during" or "by") on the inner, and N at the center. In other words: "You turn around, change from a downward to an upward path, through... N." Several authors suggest that this N stands for *nomen*, "name" in Latin,[2] the double N parting to reveal *nomen*. Indeed, through the Burning Bush, through the recognition of being known and knowing *by name*—God addresses Moses by name and begins to reveal His own name—a converse of friend with friend is established (Exod. 33:11), the familiar yet fearsome converse with the living God, the very basis of all true prayer. But this is the Lord's initiative: He provides the circumstances that turn us aside from our—however serene, however atrocious—daily lives, as in the prodigy of the Burning Bush (Exod. 3:2); He calls out to us so that we too may speak (Exod. 3:4); He even solemnly confirms that this is so in the words of Christ: "No man can come to me, except the Father, who hath sent me, draw him" (John 6:44).

God discloses His name to Moses, but also His purposes: "I have seen the affliction of my people in Egypt, and I have heard their cry because of the rigor of them that are over the works; and knowing their sorrow, I am come down to deliver them out of the hands of the Egyptians, and to bring them out of that land into a good and spacious land" (Exod. 3:7–8). Moses leads the exodus out of Egypt, but it is Joshua, the son of Nun, who leads Israel into the Promised Land. Once more the central N of the square becomes evident in Joshua (equivalent to Jesus) and *Nun*. Then, in the fullness of time, there comes another Joshua who held within Himself both the powers of deliverance: "Thou shalt call his name Jesus. For he shall save his people from their sins" (Matt. 1:21), and the very name of the God of the Burning Bush: "Before Abraham was made, I AM" (John 8:58). Was it not the Burning Bush in fully human form, both mother and child,[3] that the aged Simeon encountered in the Temple when he exclaimed: "Now thou dost dismiss thy servant, O Lord, according to thy word in peace: because my eyes

---

1. *Cf.* Eph. 4:3–6.

2. Marcel Simon, *Verus Israel,* trans. H. McKeating (Oxford: Oxford University Press, 1986). Simon makes it a Latin equivalent for *shem*, the divine name (pp. 352–353). See also Cammilleri, *op. cit.*, pp. 52, 58.

3. Sacred typology has held that the unburnt bush foreshadowed the Holy Virgin, while the fire and light foreshadowed Christ. (Cf. Gregory of Nyssa, *The Life of Moses*, II, 20–21; p. 59.) But the Burning Bush can just as well foreshadow Christ himself, unburnt by being at once true God and true Man.

have seen thy salvation, which thou hast prepared before the face of all peoples: a light to the revelation of the Gentiles and the glory of thy people Israel" (Luke 2:29–32)?

After contemplating such a unison between cryptogram, names of God and numbers, we should pause for a moment over the history of the so-called "magic squares" in general and the square of the fifth order (i.e. a square with five numbers per side) in particular.

Knowledge of the construction of magic squares in the Islamic world was already well developed by the tenth century, the date of the earliest extant manuscripts. At that time such squares were termed "the harmonious arrangement [of numbers]". Although solely the province of mathematicians at first, by the thirteenth century this knowledge became increasingly associated with magic and divination. And it is under this form, in the following century, that the "lore" of the squares—stripped of its mathematical foundations—entered into the Latin world.[1] This lore percolated through the Italian Renaissance, and we see it first presented by the Franciscan friar, Luca Pacioli, a friend of Leonardo Da Vinci. In Pacioli's *De viribus quantitatis* (1498) the then known magic squares, in ascending order, are assigned to each of the then known planets in descending order, starting with Saturn. According to this schema the square of the fifth order is assigned to Mars, although almost a half century later Cardan, in his *Practica Arithmetica* (1539), will reverse the order of the planetary assignments, giving Venus the fifth order square. Thus, keeping in mind that astrology and astronomy were hardly distinguished at that time, each magic square in these systems was the bearer of a potency similar to that of the assigned planet.

Is not this cultural history of magic squares reminiscent of an episode from early Church history? Just as, "with itching ears", the inventors and followers of the various gnosticisms turned aside from sound doctrine to fables,[2] so too, in the Islamic world, a mathematical discipline was diverted from its original beauty—the harmony of numerical arrays—to serve unwarranted ends. Now, to cleanse the fifth-order square of its culturally accumulated flaws and ready it for theological use, it would be well to listen to Irenaeus as he gives closing arguments against the numerology (or allegorical arithmetic) of Marcus the Magician:

> Nor should they seek to prosecute inquiries respecting God by means of numbers, syllables, and letters. For this is an uncertain mode of proceeding, on account of their varied and diverse systems, and because every sort of hypothesis may at the present day be, in like manner, devised by any one; so that they can derive arguments against the truth from these very theories, inasmuch as they may be turned in many different directions. But, on the contrary, they ought to adapt the numbers themselves, and those things which have been formed, to the true theory lying before them. For system

---

1. Sesiano, *op. cit.*, p. 379. During those same years, and in contrast to the rage for things magical in the West, the Byzantine scholar Manuel Moschopoulos will publish a work of purely mathematical interest based on the Arabic treatises available to him.

2. *Cf.* 2 Tim. 4:3–4.

does not spring out of numbers, but numbers from a system; nor does God derive His being from things made, but things made from God. For all things originate from one and the same God. [1]

Heeding the words of Irenaeus, the contemplative "system" of the Burning Bush presented above, with its mingling of numbers, letters and biblical passages should also be viewed as an "uncertain mode of proceeding". But, to this general rule, Irenaeus has added a surprising qualification:

> The Hebrew letters do not correspond in number with the Greek, although these [i.e. the Hebrew letters] especially, as being the more ancient and unchanging, ought to uphold the reckoning connected with the names.[2]

By this statement he has validated, at least in part, the application of Hebrew divine names to the cryptogram's numerical array. And so, after encountering the fire and light of the Burning Bush, the fifth order square should be set apart in an utterly unique category: conjoined, or rather fused without confusion, these particular letter and number squares should best be called the *Enclosure of the Blessed Names*.

Yet another Irenaean surprise is to be found in *On the Apostolic Preaching*,[3] as well as another possible shred of evidence for his awareness of the cryptogram and its meaning. Examining the book's one hundred chapters, the clear parallels evident between the book's beginning and end are a sign that the reader should be alert for a chiastic process at work.[4] Thus, at the very beginning (chap. 2), we find interpolated into the first verse of the first psalm—"Blessed is the man who walks not in the counsel of the ungodly"…"nor stands in the way of sinners"—the God of the Burning Bush:

> They are the ungodly who do not worship Him Who Is, true God, and for this reason the Word says to Moses "I Am HE-WHO-IS accordingly, those who do not worship the God Who IS, are the ungodly.[5]

Then, near the end (chap. 97), we have a similar declaration, but this time in terms of the "godly", the believer, and in terms of that other burning bush, the Cross:

> Through the invocation of the name of Jesus Christ, who was crucified under Pontius Pilate, [the apostasy] is cast out from men, and wherever anyone of those who believe in Him and do His will shall call upon Him, He is present, fulfilling the petitions of those who call upon Him with a pure heart.[6]

---

1. *Against the Heresies*, II. 25, 1.

2. *Ibid.*, II, 24, 2.

3. Trans. J. Behr (Crestwood NY: St. Vladimir's Seminary Press, 1997. As Father Behr notes, this work, rediscovered in the nineteenth century, "is the earliest summary of Christian teaching, presented in a non-polemical or apologetic manner, that we now have" (p. 7).

4. See below p. 531 for a discussion on the chiastic process.

5. *Ibid.*, p. 40.

6. *Ibid.*, p. 99. *Cf.* Emmanuel Lanne "Le nom de Jésus-Christ et son invocation chez saint Irénée de Lyon", *Irénikon* 48, 1975, pp. 447–467 and 49, 1976, pp. 34–53.

At the "crossing" of this book-length chiasmus, and therefore at the book's center, is a new mention of Moses before the Burning Bush (chap. 46). But this time, instead of the blazing forth of "He Who Is", it is the light of Christ we see refracted into five-fold radiance (chaps. 47–52): *Father and Son are both Lord and God* (= ROTAS, betokening the trinitarian perichoresis); *the Son is God* (= SATOR, betokening the sower of the worlds, by whom all things were made); *the Son is Lord* (= OPERA, betokening the immediacy and effortlessness of Christ's word in His miracles); *Christ is the Son and King* (AREPO, betokening the reverse of OPERA, of overt power; Christ's willingness to rule with the power of love from the extreme humility and throne of His Cross), and *Christ, in being Servant of God* (= TENET, betokening the suffering servant, He who came not to be served but to serve), *is the Savior of man* (= TENET, betokening the power of Christ's redeeming sacrifice that entirely suffuses the reach of His Cross).[1] Could this be the way in which Irenaeus understood the cryptogram? And could he have seen in the mysterious dual N at center the revealed name *Jesus*, the Jesus who leads us to the hidden Father—"He Who Is"—and is only one with Him: PATER NOSTER?

A CONTEMPLATION ON THE CHURCH

Thy kingdom come
Thy will be done on earth as it is in heaven
Give us this day our daily bread

But what is the other name for this enclosure that is at once Paradise and Burning Bush and excessively filled with trinitarian life? Reading the cryptogram with new eyes now, is it not an enactment of Christ's word: "Where there are… three gathered together in my name, there am I in the midst of them" (Matt. 18:20)? Wherever Christ is, there is the Church; wherever the Church is, there is Christ. The three words of the square, viewed as a four-way palindrome, converge on the N, *nomen*, His name. And this N is the pivot—"he that seeth me seeth the Father also" (John 14:9)—by which we discover the anagram, discover how to say PATERNOSTER, "Our Father". But first the three words and then the letter:

ROTAS — This word stands for all the cycles of time within the Church year: the daily, weekly and yearly liturgical observances, as well as the rhythms of one's personal prayer life.

OPERA —This word is synonymous with "liturgy", a Greek word composed of *laos*, "people", and *ergon*, "work". In the Church such work combines both the personal asceticism that readies the individual to fitly participate in worship, and the aesthetic struggle, shared by iconographer, choir and liturgist, to raise the purified hearts of the faithful in beauty to God.

---

1. This list, with some minor changes, is drawn from the convenient headings provided by Father Behr for these central chapters (*op. cit.*, pp. 71–74) and throughout his translation of *The Demonstration of the Apostolic Teaching*.

TENET — Not only the trophy of the Cross, Christ's victory over death, persists at the core of the liturgy, but, along with it, all those who share in the life of His body, standing firm in faith through all the days, weeks, seasons and ages of their lives, "no more strangers and foreigners: but… fellow citizens with the saints and the domestics of God, built upon the foundation of the apostles and prophets, Jesus Christ himself being the chief corner stone: in whom all the building, being framed together, groweth up into an holy temple in the Lord… built together into an habitation of God in the Spirit" (Eph. 2:19–22). In this temple Christ—the chief corner stone—is N; the apostles and prophets—the foundation—are the E's or evangelists, and all the faithful without exception are the outer T's: "If any man will come after me, let him deny himself and take up his cross daily and follow me" (Luke 9:23).

N — This unique and central letter is twice doubled. There is an outer doubling at the crossing of the two TENET's, but there is also an inner or hidden doubling. With a touch the word square with its central cross becomes *all* cross. Through this N, the *nodus*, the knot that binds the outer world of meaning together in Christ's name, we pass through to, or rather are permeated by[1] an inner world where we dare to say "our Father" because we belong fervently to Christ and to each other: *Thine own of Thine own we offer unto Thee, on behalf of all and for all!*[2]

Even a Latin dictionary can be of assistance in understanding this mysterious dual N that ushers in *our* Father and, with Him, the Lord's Prayer:

OUR FATHER WHO ART IN HEAVEN	*nuncupo* = to call by name, to nominate as heir
HALLOWED BE THY NAME	*nomen* = name
THY KINGDOM COME	*numen* = divine command, divine might or majesty
THY WILL BE DONE ON EARTH AS	*nuntio* = announce (the Gospel)
IT IS IN HEAVEN	*enuntio* = pronounce (the utterance of the Word through the Incarnation)
GIVE US THIS DAY OUR DAILY BREAD	*nunc* = now
AND FORGIVE US OUR TRESPASSES AS WE FORGIVE THOSE WHO TRESPASS AGAINST US	*nona* = the ninth hour (when Christ died on the Cross)
AND LEAD US NOT INTO TEMPTATION BUT DELIVER US FROM EVIL	*non* = no, not (all negations and their resolutions, that is to say the negating of negations)

---

1. "Pass through to", "permeated by", but also "raised up to", for truly this is the *anaphora* at the heart of the liturgy.
2. *Liturgy of St. John Chrysostom*, prayer at the elevation of the Holy Gifts.

One last consideration on the Church has to do with its orientation both physically and theologically, for here is to be seen how closely temple and contemplation are tied together. Several authors see a Stoic influence in the cryptogram, chiefly through the ROTAS circle and the crossing avenues of the TENET.[1] In antiquity the practice of augury would divide up the sky in an attempt to glimpse the will of the gods according to which birds passed or what weather occurred in any given portion. Likewise the land could be divided for the purpose of founding a settlement or siting a temple. *Templum* was the term for a location from which such surveys were taken, as well as the center of a measured site which would serve as consecrated ground. *Contemplatio* was the attentive viewing of the land- or skyscape by which all these determinations were made.[2] (A rule of silence was generally observed during these contemplations, in accord with the hush that seems to fall naturally over anyone in a contemplative state.) A site was selected at the crossing of an East-West line aligned on a particular sunrise or sunset, called the *decumanus*, and a North-South line aligned on the North Star (at least in Roman usage), called the *cardo*.[3]

With the Christian temple, however, everything is founded in and by the light of Christ. East-West is a preferred alignment for the Christian temple too, but this is to honor the direction of His expected return in glory: "For as lightning cometh out of the east and appeareth even into the west: so shall also the coming of the Son of man be" (Matt. 24:27). This is expressed on the iconostasis by an icon of Christ holding an open book, the book of judgment, the book of life. The North-South axis has been transposed into a zenithal one, in accord with the angels' declaration after Christ's ascension: "Ye men of Galilee, why stand you looking up to heaven? This Jesus who is taken up from you into heaven, shall so come as you have seen him going into heaven" (Acts 1:11). This in turn is expressed by the mosaics or frescos of Christ Pantocrator in church cupolas.

Christian churches receive their orientation then—ideally, if not in fact—from the light of Christ's Second Coming. So too does the cryptogram, for the TENET-cross, with the A's and O's displayed about the T's, mirrors the hidden or yet-to-appear PATERNOSTER cross. Again, with an *Alpha* and *Omega* at the beginnings and endings of each PATERNOSTER, this cross expresses even more forcefully the birth of eternity in time and its consequences. Two candles, one bearing the light from the first day of creation, one bearing the light from the last day and Christ's glorious return, quietly illumine and sacredly welcome our saying of the Our Father.

---

1. Wolfgang Christian Schneider, *op. cit.*, pp. 113–116 and Hildebrecht Hommel, *Schöpher und Erhalter* (Berlin: Lettner Verlag, 1956), p. 48–58.

2. It should be noted that the Greek world does not share its vocabulary of contemplation with such augural roots, even though the Latin *templum* is derived from the Greek *temenos*.

3. Adrian Snodgrass, *Architecture, Time and Eternity*, vol. 1 (New Delhi: International Academy of Indian Culture and Aditya Prakashan, 1990), pp. 225–230; A. L. Frothingham, "Ancient Orientation Unveiled", *American Journal of Archaeology*, Vol. 21, No. 2 (Apr.–Jun., 1917), pp. 187-201.

THE THREE CONTEMPLATIVE MOTIONS —
A reading of the ROTAS-square for a reading of the book

*And forgive us our trespasses as we
forgive those who trespass against us*

How is it that contemplation is repentance and repentance contemplation? If contemplation means seeing things as they are, apart from our personal desires and intentions, then parting from these personal desires and intentions is somewhere to begin. We have heard the rumor—so swiftly spoken that the memory of it barely outlasts the saying—that there is a desire and intention coeval with our very being, that there is a "kingdom of God" within us, and that this is why we in our ignorance relentlessly pursue these other desires, these other intentions. But for two thousand years we have constantly forgotten and are forgetting that "the time is fulfilled, and the kingdom of God is at hand". And what are the conditions for realizing this? "Repent, and believe in the Gospel" (Mark 1:15); faith that there is somewhere to begin and repentance. Faith that Someone from the very center of our being became man and stood before us, and we did not and do not hear Him… repentance! When He told us everything, we stood and stand there unmoved… repentance! But to take only a first tottering step is soon to be walking even as He walked (see opposite page).

As this meditation on "walking in the Lord" shows, the physical act of walking is only incidental to what is important: the moral and—increasingly—unitary act of walking "as he walked", the inner life set in motion. In his treatise, *The Divine Names*, Dionysius the Areopagite identifies three spiritual motions: the straight, the spiral and the circular[1] (the spiral being a composite of the straight and circular) and describes how they unfold in God,[2] angels ("divine intelligences") and the human soul (see table on page 322).

---

1. On the three motions see: E. Hugueny, "Circulaire, réctiligne, helicoïdal", *Revue des sciences philosophique et théologique*, 1924, pp. 327–331; A. Gardeil, "Les mouvements direct, en spiral, circulaire de l'âme et les oraisons mystiques", *Revue thomiste*, 30 (1925), pp. 321–340; C.-A. Bernard, "Les formes de la Théologie chez Denys l'Areopagite", *Gregorianum* 59/1 (Roma: Pontifica Universitas Gregoriana, 1978), pp. 45–47; L. Chvátal, "Mouvement circulaire, rectiligne et spiral. Une contribution à la recherche des sources philosophiques de Maxime le Confesseur", *Freiburger Zeitschrift für Philosophie und Theologie*, vol. 54, issue 1/2, 2007, pp. 189–206; W. Riordan, *Divine Light, the Theology of Denys the Areopagite* (San Francisco: Ignatius Press, 2008), pp. 202–206.

2. Dionysius cautions that, in God, such motions must be understood in a "befitting" way. Cf. *Divine Names*, Chap. 9, 9 (Luibheid, p. 118).

WALK EVEN AS HE WALKED

BUT DELIVER
US FROM EVIL

Wherein in time past you walked according to the course of this world, according to the prince of the power of this air, of the spirit that now worketh on the children of unbelief: In which also we all conversed in time past, in the desires of our flesh, fulfilling the will of the flesh and of our thoughts, and were by nature children of wrath, even as the rest: But God (who is rich in mercy) for his exceeding charity wherewith he loved us, even when we were dead in sins, hath quickened us together in Christ (by whose grace you are saved). Eph 2:2–5

AND LEAD US NOT
INTO TEMPTATION

I say then: Walk in the spirit: and you shall not fulfill the lusts of the flesh. For the flesh lusteth against the spirit: and the spirit against the flesh: For these are contrary one to another: so that you do not the things that you would. Gal. 5:16–17

AND FORGIVE US OUR
TRESPASSES AS WE
FORGIVE THOSE
WHO TRESPASS
AGAINST US

I know, and am confident in the Lord Jesus, that nothing is unclean of itself: but to him that esteemeth any thing to be unclean, to him it is unclean. For if, because of thy meat, thy brother be grieved, thou walkest not now according to charity. Destroy not him with thy meat, for whom Christ died. Rom. 14:14–15

GIVE US THIS DAY
OUR DAILY BREAD

As therefore you have received Jesus Christ the Lord, walk ye in him: Rooted and built up in him and confirmed in the faith, as also you have learned: abounding in him in thanksgiving. Col. 2:6–7

THY WILL BE DONE
ON EARTH AS IT IS
IN HEAVEN

Therefore having always confidence, knowing that while we are in the body we are absent from the Lord. (For we walk by faith and not by sight.) But we are confident and have a good will to be absent rather from the body and to be present with the Lord. And therefore we labor, whether absent or present, to please him. For we must all be manifested before the judgment seat of Christ, that every one may receive the proper things of the body, according as he hath done, whether it be good or evil. 2 Cor. 5:6–10

THY KINGDOM COME

For we are buried together with him by baptism into death: that, as Christ is risen from the dead by the glory of the Father, so we also may walk in newness of life. Rom. 6:4

OUR FATHER WHO
ART IN HEAVEN
HALLOWED BE
THY NAME

But he that keepeth his word, in him in very deed the charity of God is perfected. And by this we know that we are in him. He that saith he abideth in him ought himself also to walk even as he walked. 1 John 2:5–6
Walk then as children of the light. Eph. 5:8.

THE THREE MOTIONS

	STRAIGHT	SPIRAL	CIRCULAR
GOD *DIVINE NAMES 9, 9*	"…the unswerving procession of his activities, the coming-to-be of all things from him."	"…the continuous procession from him together with the fecundity of his stillness."	"…has to do with his sameness, to the grip he has on the middle range as well as on the outer edges of order, so that all things are one and all things that have gone forth from him may return to him once again."
DIVINE INTELLIGENCES *DIVINE NAMES 4, 8*	"…when, out of Providence, they come to offer unerring guidance to all those below them."	"…even while they are providing for those beneath them they continue to remain what they are and they turn unceasingly around the Beautiful and the Good from which all identity comes."	"…while they are at one with those illuminations which, without beginning and without end, emerge from the Good and the Beautiful."
THE SOUL *DIVINE NAMES 4, 9*	"…instead of circling in upon its own intelligent unity… it proceeds to the things around it, and is uplifted from external things, as from certain variegated and pluralized symbols, to the simple and united contemplations."	"…whenever [it] receives, in accordance with its capacities, the enlightenment of divine knowledge and does so not by way of the mind nor in some mode arising out of its identity, but rather through discursive reasonings, in mixed and changeable activities."	…when "it turns within itself and away from what is outside and there is an inner concentration of its intellectual powers. A sort of fixed revolution causes it to return from the multiplicity of externals, to gather in upon itself and then, in this undispersed condition, to join those [the angels] who are themselves in a powerful union. From there the revolution brings the soul to the Beautiful and the Good, which is beyond all things."[1]

---

1. Quoted passages from *Pseudo-Dionysius, The Complete Works*, trans. Luibheid, pp. 78, 118–119.

Following Dionysius a few—but significant—theologians have commented on these motions: Maximus the Confessor (sixth–seventh century), Gregory Palamas (early fourteenth century), Callistus Cataphygiotes (late fourteenth century), and, closest to our own time, Nicodemos the Hagiorite (eighteenth century). Maximus, in his *Ambigua 10*, speaks of these three motions as converging into one and providing a path of ascent to God, with straight motion first, then spiral motion, and lastly circular motion:

> In a noble manner, by these [motions] [the Fathers] pass beyond this present age of trials in accordance with the true and immutable forms of [each] natural motion, so that they make sense, which possesses the spiritual reasons of things perceived through the senses, ascend by means of reason up to mind, and, in a singular way, they unite reason, which possesses the meaning of beings, to mind in accordance with one, simple and undivided sagacity.[1]

But to what end this whole unified expanse of knowledge? In a stunning passage later in the paragraph, Maximus reveals the doxological essence of all knowledge:

> If, however, the Saints are moved by visions of beings, they are not moved, as with us, in a material way principally to behold and know those things, but in order to praise in many ways God, who is and appears through all things and in all things, and to gather together for themselves every capacity for wonder and reason for glorying.[2]

This is the orthodox (right-glorifying) vocation, this is what it means to *be Orthodox*.

After this lengthy introduction, it is now time to return to our contemplation of the cryptogram, to discover that these three motions are to be found there as well. Two of them are easily discerned, with ROTAS representing a circle and TENET being either two crossing or a bundle of four straight lines. But how are we to derive a spiral from OPERA? With a spiral being the composite of curved and straight lines, OPERA satisfies this definition quite admirably, that is, once we perceive its two horizontally and two vertically linear OPERA's, and the circular PER:

O	P	E	R	A		O		A		P	E	R
						P		R			E		E
A	R	E	P	O		E		E		R	E	P
						R		P				
						A		O				

1. *Patrologiae Graeca* XCI, 1113A; Andrew Louth, *Maximus the Confessor* (New York/London: Routledge, 1996, pp. 100–101.

2. *Ibid.*, 1115D–1116A; Louth, p. 101.

When we attempt to see how these linear and circular elements of OPERA fit in with the other two words, we discover a mirroring or echoing effect. With the linear elements we see a "ghost" of the TENET-cross, especially when they seem to pass through the arms of the cross at the E's, seem to act as a subtle escort, either bringing the cross into high relief or giving it an unexpected depth. For its part, the circular element acts like an inner reverberation of the outer ROTAS-circle, either as a recurrent wave originally propagated from the center, or as a wave mysteriously propagated all along the outermost reaches of this "verbal ocean" and sweeping inwards. Under this particular guise of the cryptogram we discern theology in motion. Not the systematic theology written down in books, which has its place and value, but what Justin of Chelije calls the "praying theology of the Church."[1] Dionysius and Maximus have already set before us such a theology, articulating it into these three—straight, spiral and circular—simple motions, the motions of symbolic, discursive and mystical theology respectively, each in turn another rung of the ascent to God, yet each one availing itself of the other two at every rung until, he declares:

> they raise the mind, freed and pure of any motion around any existing thing and at rest in its own activity, to God, so that in this way it is wholly gathered to God, and made wholly worthy through the Spirit of being united with the whole Godhead, for it bears the whole image of the heavenly, so far as is humanly possible, and draws down the divine splendor to such a degree, if it is permitted to say this, that it is drawn to God and united with Him.[2]

In light of these theological analogies, we should also see the cryptogram as an image of St. Paul's "tablets of the heart" (2 Cor. 3:3) upon which the Spirit writes theological "psalms and hymns and spiritual canticles" so that we might sing and make melody in our hearts to the Lord (Eph. 5:19). Maximus equates this "tableted" heart to the pure heart that sees God:

> A pure heart is perhaps one which has no natural propulsion towards anything in any manner whatsoever. When in its extreme simplicity such a heart has become like a writing-tablet beautifully smoothed and polished, God comes to dwell in it and writes there His own laws. A pure heart is one which offers the mind to God free of all image and form, and ready to be imprinted only with His own archetypes, by which God Himself is made manifest.[3]

Extending this analogy, these three motions condensed into the word-square are images of the finding and guarding of the heart, depending upon whether one's standpoint is outside or from within the square, and, beyond all standpoints, an image of the prayer of the heart itself.

---

1. *Philosophie orthodoxe de la vérité*, vol. IV, p. 219.

2. *Ambigua* 10, P. G. XCI, 1113B; Louth, p. 101.

3. *On Theology and the Incarnate Dispensation of the Son of God*, 2nd century, 81–82; *The Philokalia*, vol. 2, p. 158.

FINDING THE HEART Mere physical anatomy offers no guarantee of ever finding that heart about which scripture and tradition speak.[1] The ascetic Fathers urge us to "strive [OPERA] to preserve [TENET] a pure [ROTAS] conscience"[2] so that, calling upon Jesus Christ (N = *nomen*) and His mercy, we might win through at last to the heart. Gregory Palamas gives the merest outline of a method for accomplishing this feat by the grace of God; merest because it implies a steadfast participation in the sacraments of the Church (TENET), a humble practicing of the virtues (OPERA) and the daily cycle of prayer (ROTAS):

> [Whoever] seeks to make his mind return to itself needs to propel it not only in a straight line [TENET] but also in the circular motion [ROTAS] that is infallible. How should such a one not gain great profit if, instead of letting his eye roam hither and thither, he should fix it [N = *nodus*, "knot"; *nexus*, "a binding together"] on his breast or on his navel, as a point of concentration? For in this way, he will not only gather himself together externally, conforming as far as possible to the inner movement he seeks for his mind; he will also, by disposing his body in such a position, recall into the interior of the heart a power which is ever flowing outwards through the faculty of sight.[3]

Here we see body and mind—the body a symbol but also a fellow worker for the mind—bound together to find the inmost sanctuary of our person. As for this power that flows outward through the faculty of sight, even the blind possess it. When it comes into focus at last in the heart, it becomes the power of spiritual perception by which the pure of heart see God. Even though we find ourselves standing outside the square, the way to the center is now clearly marked.

GUARDING THE HEART Spiral motion, as the middle term, is particularly suitable for the human endeavor. Maximus writes:

> There are three general ways, accessible to human beings, in which God has made all things — for giving us existence He has constituted it as being, well being and eternal being — and the two ways of being at the extremes [being and eternal being] are God's alone, as the cause, while the other one in the middle [well being],[4] depending on our inclination and motion, through itself makes the extremes what they are, properly speaking, for if the middle term is not present and 'well' is not added, the extremes are designated in vain, and the truth that is in the extremes cannot otherwise accrue to them or be preserved, or even come to be, if the well being in the middle is not mixed in with the extremes, or rather intended by eternal movement towards God.[5]

---

1. Tradition includes even those in our own time who speak with the mind (*phronema*) of the Fathers, of the Church, of Christ.

2. Symeon the New Theologian, "The Three Methods of Prayer"; *The Philokalia*, vol. 4, p. 72.

3. *Triads*, I, ii, 8; pp. 46–47.

4. We are reminded here of Dionysius' words about the "grip [God] has on the middle range as well as on the outer edges of order."

5. *Ambigua* 10, *P. G.* XCI, 1116B; Louth, p. 102.

Our well being depends then on finding a way to the center of our being—the descent of the mind into the heart—and, from there, beginning to pray in spirit and in truth; this prayer is indeed the dawning of that day star of eternal being spoken of by the Apostle Peter (2 Pet. 1:19).

But there is at first only a narrow foothold here, because ignorance of our own narrowness is just beginning to clear, because we are just starting to remember our own very particular gift of being and how precarious it is, and because the lethargy that we did not even know we had is beginning to fall from us. These are the three "giants of the Philistines"—ignorance, forgetfulness and laziness—about which Mark the Ascetic speaks.[1] Ignorance that isolates us in the circle of our own self-centeredness—ROTAS, you revolve, you revolve in emptiness: the voiding of the soul's rational power. Forgetfulness that witnesses how so much of spiritual value is pulverized into finest dust and passes out of our hands, beyond our ken—TENET, he or she holds, he or she holds onto nothing: the voiding of the soul's concupiscible power. Laziness that "weaves the dark shroud enveloping the soul in murk",[2] that refuses to recognize that life itself is passing away without the least true accomplishment—OPERA, with effort, with futile effort: the voiding of the soul's irascible power. Here on this narrow foothold at the very center of our being we realize how acute and perilous is our situation and we take up arms, the arms of ceaseless prayer. Abruptly we realize, even though we had heard it said many times before, that the devil is a roaring lion going about (ROTAS) seeking someone to devour. But, steadfast in faith, we are to resist him (TENET) with sobriety and vigilance,[3] we are to take up the shield of faith (ROTAS) so to extinguish all the fiery darts (TENET) of the most wicked one,[4] who is the prince of the power of this air, of the spirit that now works (OPERA) on the children of unbelief. But God has quickened us together in Christ by whose grace (OPERA) we are saved.[5]

As ascetic literature attests, this struggle for purity of heart is beset with snares and pitfalls, especially since the spiral mode of meditation used to guard the heart is a varying mixture of ours and God's. Nicodemos of the Holy Mountain addresses this problem in *A Handbook of Spiritual Counsel*:

> St. Gregory Palamas has noted that it is possible for deception to enter the direct and spiral meditations, but not into the circular meditation.... Spiral meditation occurs when the mind is illumined by divine knowledge, not entirely spiritually and apophatically, but rather intellectually and cataphatically, combining direct and some circular meditation. Therefore, those who love to meditate without deception must occupy themselves more with the circular meditation of the mind, which is accomplished by the return of the mind to the heart and the spiritual prayer of the heart.

---

1. Mark the Ascetic, "Letter to Nicolas the Solitary"; *The Philokalia*, vol. 1, p. 158 ff.
2. *Ibid.*, p. 159.
3. *Cf.* 1 Pet. 5:8–9.
4. *Cf.* Eph. 6:16.
5. *Cf.* Eph. 2:2–5.

The more this prayer is difficult and painful the more fruitful it becomes because it is free of deception.[1]

Heedful of this advice, we turn now to the circular mode of meditation.

PRAYER OF THE HEART For Maximus the current of circular motion begins with God alone and His virtues:

Therefore [the three general ways of being, well being and eternal being] teach the mind to…

OUR FATHER WHO ART IN HEAVEN HALLOWED BE THY NAME	…concern itself with God alone and His virtues, and to cast itself with unknowing into the ineffable glory of His blessedness;
THY KINGDOM COME	reason to become the interpreter of things intelligible and a singer of hymns, and to reason rightly about the forms that bring things to unity;
THY WILL BE DONE ON EARTH AS IT IS IN HEAVEN	sense ennobled by reason to imagine the different powers and activities in the universe
GIVE US THIS DAY OUR DAILY BREAD	and to communicate, so far as possible, the meanings that are in beings to the soul.[2]

God alone and His virtues—this is important, for virtue cannot be emphasized enough. Why this is so we learn from Maximus:

There can be no doubt that the one Word of God is the substance of virtue in each person. For our Lord Jesus Christ is the substance of all the virtues… since he is wisdom and righteousness and sanctification itself. They are not, as in our case, simply attributed to him.[3]

If in baptism we have put on the whole Christ and in the Eucharist we receive the whole Christ, so with the virtues we put on the whole Christ and in prayer we receive the whole Christ. Only by virtue can we enter fully into the life of prayer, and only by virtue and prayer can we give back to the Church what the Church has given us—Christ Jesus.

From Maximus, we turn now to Callistos Cataphygiotes. After instructing us on the three motions, Callistos shows that the so called three theological virtues, the trinal summit of all the virtues, impart a motion parallel but in the opposite direction to that presented by Maximus where, instead of beginning with "ineffable glory", we begin with faith, which even in its embryonic state is already god-like:

The *nous*, which avails itself of its own imagination to contemplate the invisible, is led by faith. When grace illuminates it is strengthened with hope. But when it is enraptured by the divine light it becomes a treasure-house of love for men, and even more for the love of God. Thus the triple order of the *nous*, its movement in faith, hope, and

---

1. P. A. Chamberas trans. (New York & Mahwah: Paulist Press, 1989), p. 158.

2. Louth, p. 102.

3. *Ambiguum 7*, Blowers p. 58.

love is perfect and deifying, sure and steadfast. Once this vast space of the acropolis is attained, the *nous* is itself secured in the citadel of love.[1]

Abruptly, the narrow foothold that we struggled to reach and struggled to defend has become "this vast space of the acropolis"—acropolis meaning literally "the heights of the city". With the three motions translated into the virtues, we have gone instantly from the deep recesses of the inner man to the mystical heights of heaven, we have "come to mount Sion and to the city of the living God, the heavenly Jerusalem, and to the company of many thousands of angels, and to the church of the firstborn who are written in the heavens, and to God the judge of all, and to the spirits of the just made perfect, and to Jesus the mediator of the new testament" (Heb. 12:22–24). The still-point at the center is where the prayer of the heart and the in-gathering of the heavenly Jerusalem are one, and this is why the term hesychast, "one who dwells in stillness", is so favored by those who practice the prayer. And this, in turn, brings us back to the cryptogram's central N, for the hesychast is also someone who has become *no* one, a *null*-point, someone who has become meek and humble of heart yoked to a daily cross (TENET).[2] And, through constantly beseeching from the heart God's mercy in the name of Jesus, so that not just the words but the meaning of the words become second nature, we pass, by the power of the Holy Spirit, from our daily cross to His eternal, glorious and supersubstantial cross, from the withheld center of our being to the outpouring of the Holy Spirit.[3] Set plainly before us, we read in Paul's epistles how and why the Jesus Prayer becomes a deifying prayer:

THE JESUS PRAYER, A DEIFYING PRAYER

LORD JESUS CHRIST	No man can say The Lord Jesus, but by the Holy Spirit (1 Cor. 12:3).
SON OF GOD	You have received the spirit of adoption of sons, whereby we cry: Abba (Father). For the Spirit himself giveth testimony to our spirit that we are the sons of God. And if sons, heirs also; heirs indeed of God and joint heirs with Christ (Rom. 8:15–17).
HAVE MERCY ON ME	And because you are sons, God hath sent the Spirit of his Son into your hearts, crying: Abba, Father (Gal. 4:6).[4]

---

1. Callistos Cataphygiotes, *On Divine Union and the Contemplative Life*, 8. A light-imagery of the three virtues akin to the imagery of the three motions is presented in *Directions to the Hesychasts* by Callistus and Ignatius of Xanthopoulos: "As I understand it, the first of them [faith] is a ray, the second [hope] light, the third [love] a disc; but all three together are one brilliant radiance" (§ 90; *Writings from the Philokalia on the Prayer of the Heart*, p. 257).

2. No one, yet one in Christ (*cf.* Gal. 2:19–20) and therefore all things to all people (*cf.* 1 Cor. 9:22).

3. *Cf.* John 4:14 and 7:38–39.

4. A variant chain of passages is considered the scriptural basis for the Jesus Prayer: "No man can say The Lord Jesus, but by the Holy Spirit" (1 Cor. 12:3)—"Every spirit which confesseth that Jesus Christ is come in the flesh is of God" (1 John 4:2)—"Simon Peter answered and said: Thou art Christ, the Son of the living God." (Matt. 16:16). Cf. *Writings from the Philokalia on the Prayer of the Heart*, pp. 225–226 and *Philocalie des pères neptiques*, fasc. 11, pp. 240–246.

By the Spirit and with the Son, we are caught away into the moving stillness of trinitarian life where Person speaks to person and person to Person, where we can say in spirit and in truth: "Our Father", *Pater noster*. From this perspective the cryptogram's PATER-NOSTER was necessarily first and only then anagramatically transposed into ROTAS OPERA TENET.

JOHN'S GOSPEL AND THE THREE MOTIONS   Both displayed at once, the two interlocking, mutually anagramatic fields of the cryptogram remind us of the portrait page from the Gospel of John in the *Book of Kells* (eighth century). There we see the Gospel writer enthroned at the center of the page, holding book and stylus as if they were orb and scepter, signifying his authority as inspired writer. He is framed by a rectangular

border containing three differing panels of interlacings (the spiral element) with each panel repeated four times, thus twelve in all, signifying that he shares the throne with Christ[1] at the center of the New Jerusalem, the Church. The cross-shaped panels (the rectilinear element) we find situated at the very points held by the T's in the cryptogram. Encompassing John's head is one of the most complex halos (the circular element) in all of Christian art, made up of three regions, the third of these regions being the central point concentrated on John's forehead, while, on the halo's first and outermost rim, shedding their more than luminous rays, are three discs representing the energies of the Holy Trinity. It is as if the energies of the Holy Trinity were coming to a stable

but burning focus in John's mind, signifying his inspiration. We see three discs, but a fourth is implied. Making free to trace the outer rim of the halo to the place where a fourth disc would be, we find this precisely at the center of John's chest. A hint or framing of the place can even be seen in the slight gatherings of his tunic, this place signifying the most hidden, deified heart, known only to the one who receives it.[2] Indeed, this is the compositional center of the entire page, for all major diagonals, horizontals and verticals converge here, just as with the central N of the cryptogram. And lastly, just as the PATERNOSTER-cross exceeds the square of the cryptogram, so, jutting beyond the

---

1. *Cf.* Apoc. 3:21.
2. *Cf.* Apoc. 2:17.

portion of each cross that extends into the margin, we see the extremities and head of a mysterious person, mysterious yet closely associated with the Cross. If Christ, then the entire image would symbolize Christ's mystical body with John representing the deified Christian. If John, then the inside image would symbolize the inner man of the heart. Or, if the unseen Father, then… "the glory which thou hast given me, I have given to them: that, they may be one, as we also are one. I in them, and thou in me: that they may be made perfect in one: and the world may know that thou hast sent me and hast loved them, as thou hast also loved me" (John 17:22–23).

Turning now from John's image to his words, we find evidence of straight, spiral and circular verbal motions throughout his gospel. Rectilinear movement is of course in the narrative line, beginning with the eternal "birth" of the *Logos* and ending with Christ's post-resurrection appearances and John's final testimony. Thus the Gospel begins with *the* Word and ends either with an infinite number of possible books or with *the* Book, depending on how the last verse is interpreted: "There are also many other things which Jesus did which, if they were written every one, the world itself. I think, would not be able to contain the books that should be written" (21:25). The pivotal phrase here is "if they were written every one", which could mean either rectilinearly "one by one" and hence as an inexhaustible and exhausting number of books, or *not* one by one but circularly and hence exactly as this gospel has been written already, with the whole of it wondrously present in the least of its parts. Some sense of how John has achieved this all-pervasiveness of his gospel with itself will become clear when we delve into its spiral and circular elements.

Included among the spiral elements are all statements about the fulfilling of scripture: prophetic lines from the past are joined into the circle of Christ's all-fulfilling presence; there is also in the background of John's gospel the assumed presence of the other evangelical accounts which, as the last living eye-witness, he brings to completion. Then there is the shape of Christ's journeys once His public life begins. As a first century Jew, He would of course "go up to Jerusalem" if possible for major yearly festivals. But during His ministry He truly had no fixed abode—"the Son of man hath not where to lay his head" (Luke 9:5). And so He journeyed to various regions, yet always *circled* back to Jerusalem until He took the cross to the center of the world. Lastly, there is a spiral factor in the rhetorical device known as parallelism. Parallels are sequences in the narrative flow that reflect earlier sequences, but in reverse order. Scholars usually designate components of the parallel by capital letters, with reversed elements having a prime mark (′) added. Thus the sequence John 1:19–50 is mirrored by John 20:19–21:24, with 1:19–28 bringing forward John the Baptist as witness and 21:24 John the Beloved Disciple (A and A′). At the center of this parallel Christ tells His disciples they will see greater things: heaven open and angels descending and ascending on the Son of Man

---

1. John Breck, in *The Shape of Biblical Language*, gives a more detailed explanation of the entire sequence (pp. 229–232).

(1:50–51); this is juxtaposed (G and G´) with the risen Lord's appearance to His disciples and His bestowal of the Holy Spirit (20:19–23).[1] The two sequences are divided in this fashion:

A: 1:19–28	B: 1:29–34	C: 1:35–39	D: 1:40–42	E: 1:43–46	F: 1:47–49	G: 1:50–51
A´: 21:24	B´: 21:20–23	C´: 21:18f	D´: 21:15–17	E´: 21:1–14	F´: 20:24–31	G´: 20:19–23

From the initial and final acts of witness by John the Baptist and John the Evangelist, we spiral inward between beginning and end of the Gospel to arrive at the flesh and blood *and spirit* appearance of the risen Lord, along with His imparting of those descending and ascending angels—the Holy Spirit—to the disciples. Following Father John Breck's division of the two sequences, however, we see that the Gospel's first eighteen verses and final verse are passed over in silence, presumably because of their apparent lack of parallelism. But they are parallel, as stated earlier in connection with this Gospel's rectilinear movement. Running parallel to the effortless work of the Logos—"All things were made by him: and without him was made nothing that was made" (1:3)—is either the unremitting toil of the human scribe—"if [the many other things which Jesus did] were written every one, the world itself, I think, would not be able to contain the books that should be written" (21:25)—, or a participation of the writer in the words of the Word, writing that in both style and substance conveys the Logos in an unprecedented manner. Despite appearances, the world itself can not contain the Gospel of John. To verify this last statement, we turn now to the Gospel's circular movement.

Although John's gospel is, as a whole, framed by parallel sequences, it is also brimming with *chiasmi*.[1] The chiasmus—a parallel sequence sharing a common center— is a rhetorical device favored in the ancient world as an aid to memory due to its symmetrical and repetitive elements, its beauty. It was also a habit of mind for both writer and reader—especially in the Semitic world—prior to the invention of punctuation, when books were an unbroken thread of letters from beginning to end. It was a way for the author to mark and the reader to recognize the core meaning in any given passage.[2] But what if the above mentioned parallels were actually part of a giant chiasmus? Where might its pivotal theme be found?

While the bible has been divided into chapter and verse only since the sixteenth century, let us assume the currently accepted verse division approximates a unit of measure possibly employed by John. So, since our two parallel sequences are at the beginning and end of John's Gospel, what passage would stand at center, and how significant would it be for the entirety of the gospel? And there it stands, suddenly risen from the midst of the well-thumbed pages, familiar and yet, in this context, nearly as

---

1. *Cf.* Breck, *ibid.*, pp. 191–232 and Peter F. Ellis, *The Genius of John* (Collegeville, MN: The Liturgical Press, 1984). The entirety of Ellis' book is devoted to examining twenty-one chiasmic sequences in John's gospel.

2. *Cf.* Breck, *op. cit.*, pp. 59–61.

frighteningly strange as it was for those who, at His words, took up stones to strike Him down: "I and the Father are one" (10:30).

> *Christ in the holy Virgin's womb and as an infant, one with the Father.*
> *Christ teaching, healing and performing all manner of miracles, one with the Father.*
> *Christ plotted against, betrayed and condemned, one with the Father.*
> *Even Christ on the cross, still one with the Father.*[1]
> *Christ risen, ascended and seated at the right hand of the Father, one with the Father.*
> *Christ in the sacred writings of the evangelists and in every*
> *Christian made worthy of that name, intelligibly one with the Father.*

Not only is this passage central to John's gospel, it is also the first of eight declarations of oneness, six of which are clustered in Christ's Last Supper discourse.[2] This series of declarations begins with the oneness of Father and Son (10:30), proceeds to include "in one" the diaspora of Israel (11:52), then all believers (17:21), and ends with the wish that all believers be perfected in one as witness to the living out of that oneness (17:23). These and other oneness sayings, such as "I am the resurrection and the life" (11:23)—Christ, the renewal of life and life itself—, are all eddies of the gospel's circular motion.

One last circular element needs to be considered. Attempting to perceive an overall design, biblical scholars have divided John's gospel into a "Book of Signs" (1:19–12:50) and a "Book of Glory" (13:1–20:31). But another possible "two book" solution would name chapters 1–5 the "Book of the Baptist" and chapters 6–21 the "Book of Feastings", the first book framed and centered on a round of testimonies involving John the Baptist, the second on a round of meals according to their daily pattern. In the *Book of the Baptist*, John's witnessing to Christ is scattered through the first chapter (1:7, 15, 32, 34); then, midway through the book, John speaks of the need to receive the testimony of Jesus (3:32–33); concluding the book, Christ honors the testimony of John in the context of the testimony of His own works and the Father's witness to Him (5:33–37). Baptismal themes are also prevalent: Nicodemus and rebirth, the Samaritan woman by the well, the healing of the paralytic by the pool. All the *firsts* of Christ's ministry are here too, so that it might also be called the *Book of Inaugurals*. The *Book of Feastings* manifests eucharistic themes in a similar way. Chapter 6 opens, at the approach of Passover, with a noon meal of miraculously multiplied bread and fish—manna in the wilderness; midway, at chapter 13, falls the beginning of the Last Supper—the evening meal before Passover—with its five-chapter account of Christ's discourse, an inexhaustible feast of the words of the Word; while, at the end, we come to a post-Passover morning meal, with the risen Christ again providing food for his disciples from a miraculously multiplied catch of fishes. Bread and fish are presented here in a reverse order to that of

---

1. When we finally come to perceive, or rather are known of the everlasting Father through the lattices of the cross, or rather the nail-marks and His side (John 20:27), we will discover that we have finally verified, or rather solved the enigma of the PATERNOSTER-cross as it takes the cryptogram to itself.

2. John 10:30, 11:52, 17:11, 17:21 (twice), 17:22 (twice), 17:23.

chapter 6. A chiastic indication? And, if a chiasmus, what passage stands at the center of the book? Just this one: "A new commandment I give unto you: That you love one another, as I have loved you, that you also love one another" (13:34). Not simply "love", but "as I have loved you": only by taking up the daily cross of sacrifice, leading resurrectional lives *from the cross*, will we truly love God and each other as Christ has loved us.

A READER'S GUIDE These straight, spiral and circular motions are—in unison—that summary means by which *The Way to Our Heavenly Father* is shaped into a verbal icon, or rather into a complete verbal iconostasis that includes walls, ceiling and even floor—yes, like Moses before the Burning Bush, we too must remove the sandals or shoes of whatever is not according to God to enter fully here.

Passing straight through the book, the Lord's Prayer is followed from end (Chapter I) to beginning (Chapter IV), and from there back to the end (Chapter VII), for "The Apocalypse" (Chapter V) is a scriptural fleshing out of "The Virtues", a liturgical narrative of the inner struggle for the gifts and Gift of God; "Psalmic Music" (Chapter VI) is a scriptural fleshing out of "The Sacraments", the psalms being the prayer from the heart that "arises like incense" before God through the sacraments and especially the liturgy; while "Recapitulations" (Chapter VII) shows the complete healing of all divisions for which "The Commandments" are only an emergency first aid. Thus, viewed as a whole, the book's straight path actually forms a macro-chiasmus, which represents in this case a paradox, confronted as we are by a straight line that is also a circle, the greatly merciful paradox of the Lord Jesus, the God-Man and the prayer He would have us pray.

Spiraling through the book are the myriad transverse threads linking each contemplation to all the others through a particular phrase of the Lord's Prayer. For instance, if you would know something and more than something of "hallowed be thy name", go, collect everything associated with this phrase and you will see what a full measure will be measured to you by the end. Entire contemplations can also be nested into further themes, as exemplified by the material found in the appendix. Viewed from a spiral perspective *The Way to Our Heavenly Father* is kaleidoscopic and should come with a companion volume, a loose-leaf version so that any contemplation can be reset in any order.

As for circular motion, the Lord's Prayer is center and circumference, turning all things in between to itself.

Growing accustomed to the flickering of each contemplation through the latticework of the Lord's Prayer, sooner or later the inner eye is "tricked" into perceiving unities, that is, the intercommunion of the Christian tradition with itself: scripture, ascetic effort, hymns, icons, theology, sacraments and liturgy all in full communion among themselves, made so by the full communion of believers—through the Church—with God and each other in the joy-bringing sorrow of repentance and in humility of wisdom.

Finally, to those wearied by the book's *perhaps* over-zealous use of scripture, I will say this: proceeding from everlasting to everlasting, with the self-same movement never to be identified as straight, spiral or circular, the Holy Spirit both inspires the "variegated and pluralized" scriptures and brings scripture back to the unity of our Father, to Father, Son and Holy Spirit.

GENERAL BIBLIOGRAPHY

Ambrose of Milan. *Traité sur l'évangile de S. Luc*, tome 1. Trans. G. Tissot. Paris: Éditions du Cerf, 1956.

———. *Paradise*, in *Fathers of the Church, A New Translation*, vol. 42. Trans. J. J. Savage. New York: Fathers of the Church Inc., 1961.

Anonymous. *Comboschini (The Prayer Rope): Meditations of a Monk of the Holy Mountain Athos.* Florence, AZ.: St. Anthony's Monastery, nd.

The Art of Prayer, An Orthodox Anthology. Compiled by Igumen Chariton of Valamo. Trans. E. Kadloubovsky and E. M. Palmer. London: Faber and Faber, 1966.

Athanasius. *On the Incarnation*. Vol. IV, Nicene and Post-Nicene Fathers, series II, P. Schaff and H. Wace (eds.). New York: Christian Literature Publishing Co., 1890.

Augustine. *The Lord's Sermon on the Mount*. Westminster: Newman, 1948.

———. *Sermons on the Liturgical Seasons*. Trans. M. S. Muldowney. New York: Fathers of the Church, 1959.

Balthasar, Hans Urs von. *Cosmic Liturgy, The Universe According to Maximus the Confessor*. Trans. B. E. Daley. San Francisco, CA: Ignatius Press/Communio Book, 2003.

Bernard, Charles-André. "Les formes de la Théologie chez Denys l'Areopagite", *Gregorianum* 59/1 (Roma: Pontifica Universitas Gregoriana, 1978), pp. 39–68.

Bird, T. E. 'The Psalms', in *A Catholic Commentary on Holy Scripture*. London, etc.: Thomas Nelson and Sons, 1953.

Boethius. *The Consolation of Philosophy*. Trans. R. Green. Indianapolis, IN: Bobbs-Merrill Company, 1962.

Bonaventure. Trans. and introduction E. Cousins. New York: Paulist Press, 1978.

Book of Akathists. Jordanville, NY: Holy Trinity Monastery, 1994.

Boon, Nicolas. *Au coeur de l'écriture*. Paris: Dervy Livres, 1987.

Borella, Jean. *Amour et Vérité, La voie chrétienne de la charité*. Paris: L'Harmattan, 2011.

———. *Guénonian Esoterism and Christian Mystery*. Trans. G. J. Champoux. Hillsdale, NY: Sophia Perennis, 2004.

Brooke, G. J. 'The Lord's Prayer Interpreted Through John and Paul,' *Downside Review*, 98 (1980) pp. 298–311.

Bulgakov, Sergius. *The Friend of the Bridegroom*. Trans. Boris Jakim. Grand Rapids MI/Cambridge UK: William B. Eerdmans Publishing Co., 2003.

———. *Jacob's Ladder: On Angels*. Trans. T. A. Smith.Grand Rapids MI: Eerdmans, 2010.

Bovenmars, Jan G. *A Biblical Spirituality of the Heart*. New York: Alba House, 1991.

Breck, John. *The Shape of Biblical Liturgy*. Crestwood, NY: St. Vladimir's Seminary Press, 1994.

Buchan, Thomas. *"Blessed Is He Who Has Brought Adam From Sheol". Christ's Descent to the Dead in the Theology of Saint Ephrem the Syrian*. Piscataway, NJ: Gorgias Press, 2004.

Cabasilas, Nicholas. *Commentary on the Divine Liturgy*. Trans. J. M. Hussey and P. A. McNulty, London: SPCK, 1960.

———. *Life in Christ*. Trans. C. J. deCatanzaro. Crestwood, NY: St. Vladimir's Seminary Press, 1974.

Caldecott, Stratford. *The Seven Sacraments, Entering the Mysteries of God*. New York: Crossroad Publishing Company, 2006.

Callistos Cataphygiotes, *On Divine Union and the Contemplative Life* in *Philocalie des Pères neptique*, fascicule 11. Trans. Boris Bobrinskoy. Bégrolles-en-Mauges: Abbaye de Bellefontaine, 1991, pp. 145–228.

Callistus and Ignatius of Xanthopoulos. *Directions to the Hesychasts* in *Writings from the Philokalia on the Prayer of the Heart*, London: Faber & Faber, 1951, pp. 164–270.

Champoux, G. John (ed. and trans.). *The Secret of the Christian Way, A Contemplative Ascent Through the Writings of Jean Borella*. Albany, NY: SUNY Press, 2001.

Chase, Frederic Henry. *The Lord's Prayer in the Early Church* (collection: Texts and Studies, vol. 1, num. 3). Cambridge: Cambridge University Press, 1891.

Chvátal, Ladislav. "Mouvement circulaire, rectiligne et spiral. Une contribution à la recherche des sources philosophiques de Maxime le Confesseur", *Freiburger Zeitschrift für Philosophie und Theologie*, vol. 54, issue 1/2, 2007, pp. 189–206.

Clément, Olivier. *The Roots of Christian Mysticism*. Trans. T. Berkeley. New York: New City Press, 1995.

Cyril of Alexandria. *Commentary on the Gospel according to St.John*, vol. 1. Oxford: James Parker & Co., 1874.

Cyril of Jerusalem. *On the Mysteries*. Vol. VII, Nicene and Post-Nicene Fathers, series II, P. Schaff and H. Wace (eds.). New York: Christian Literature Publishing Co., 1890.

Daniélou, Jean. *The Bible and the Liturgy*. Notre Dame, IN: University of Notre Dame Press, 1956.

———. *Primitive Christian Symbols*. Trans D. Attwater. London: Burns & Oates, 1964.

Deed, R. M. "The Sword of the Spirit, the Making of an Orthodox Rosary", *Studies in Comparative Religion*, vol. 1 num. 3.

Deseille, Archimandrite Placide. 'Hesychast Prayer in the Orthodox Church', in Rama Coomaraswamy, *The Invocation of the Name of Jesus*, pp. 217–254. Louisville: Fons Vitae, 1999.

Dimitri of Rostov. 'The Inner Closet of the Heart', in *The Art of Prayer*.

Dorotheos of Gaza. *Discourses and Sayings*. Trans. E. P. Wheeler. Kalamazoo: Cistercian Publications, 1977.

Elizabeth of the Holy Trinity. *I Have Found God*, Complete Works, vol. 1. Trans. A. Kane. Washington, DC: ICS Publications, 1984.

Evagrius of Pontus. *Talking Back. A Monastic Handbook for Combatting Demons*. Trans. D. Brakke.Collegeville MN: Cistercian Publications/Liturgical Press, 2009.

Evdokimov, Paul. *Ages of the Spiritual Life*. Trans. Sister Gertrude, rev. trans. M. Plekon and A. Vinogradov. Crestwood, NY: St Vladimir's Seminary Press, 1998.

———. *L'Orthodoxie*. Neuchatel and Paris: Delachaux et Niestlé, 1959.

The Festal Menaion. Trans. Mother Mary and Kallistos Ware. London: Faber & Faber, 1969.

Gardeil, A. "Les mouvements direct, en spiral, circulaire de l'âme et les oraisons mystiques", *Revue thomiste*, 30 (1925), pp. 321–340.

Germanus of Constantinople, St. *On the Divine Liturgy*. Trans. P. Meyendorff. Crestwood, NY: St. Vladimir's Seminary Press, 1984.

Gilson, Etienne. *The Philosophy of St. Bonaventure*. Trans. Dom I. Trethowan and F. J. Sheed. Patterson, NJ: St. Anthony Guild Press, 1965.

Grace for Grace, The Psalter and the Holy Fathers. Compiled and edited by Johanna Manley. Crestwood, NY: St. Vladimir's Seminary Press, 2003.

The Great Book of Needs. Trans. St. Tikhon's Monastery. South Canaan, PA: St. Tikhon's Seminary Press, 1998.

Gregory the Great. *Forty Gospel Homilies*. Trans. D. Hurst. Kalamazoo, MI: Cistercian Publications, 1990.

Gregory of Nyssa. *Against Eunomius*. Vol. V, Nicene and Post-Nicene Fathers, series II, P. Schaff and H. Wace (eds.). New York: Christian Literature Publishing Co., 1890.

———. *The Great Catechism*. Trans. W. Moore and H. A. Wilson. Nicene and Post-Nicene Fathers, series II, vol. v. P. Schaff and H. Wace (eds.). New York: Christian Literature Publishing Co., 1893.

———. *The Life of Moses*. Trans. A. J. Malherbe and E. Ferguson. New York/Ramsey/Toronto: Paulist Press, 1978.

———. *The Lord's Prayer, The Beatitudes*. Trans. H. C. Graef. New York: Paulist, 1954.

———. *Treatise on the Inscriptions of the Psalms*. Trans. R. E. Heine. Oxford: Clarendon Press, 1995.

Gregory of Sinai. 'On Commandments and Doctrines', *The Philokalia*, vol. 4, pp. 212–252.

————. 'On the Signs of Grace and Delusion', *The Philokalia*, vol. 4, pp. 257–262.

Gregory Palamas. *Mary the Mother of God. Sermons by Saint Gregory Palamas.* C. Veniamin (ed.). South Canaan PA: Mount Thabor Publishing, 2005.

Guardini, Romano. *The Lord's Prayer.* Manchester: Sophia, 1996.

Hausherr, Irénée. *The Name of Jesus.* Trans. C. Cummings. Kalamazoo, MI: Cistercian Publ., 1978.

————. *Spiritual Direction in the Early Christian East*, Trans. A. P. Gythiel. Kalamazoo, MI: Cistercian Publ. 1990.

Hugueny, Etienne. "Circulaire, réctiligne, helicoïdal", *Revue des sciences philosophique et théologique*, 1924, pp. 327–331.

Irenaeus of Lyons. *Against the Heresies.* The Writings of the Apostolic Fathers, Ante-Nicene Fathers, vol. I. A. Roberts and J. Donaldson (eds.). Edinburgh: T & T Clark, 1867.

————. *On the Apostolic Preaching.* Trans. J. Behr. Crestwood NY: St. Vladimir's Seminary Press, 1997.

Isaac the Syrian. *The Ascetical Homilies.* Boston, MA: Holy Transfiguration Monastery, 1984.

John Cassian. *The Conferences.* Vol. XI, Nicene and Post-Nicene Fathers, series II, P. Schaff and H. Wace (eds.). New York: Christian Literature Publishing Co., 1894.

John Chrysostom, *Homilies of St. John Chrysostom on the Gospel of St. John,* vol. 2. Oxford: John Henry Parker, 1852.

John Climacus. *The Ladder of Divine Ascent.* New York: Paulist Press, 1982.

————. *The Ladder of Divine Ascent*, rev. ed.. Boston, MA: Holy Transfiguration Monastery, 2001.

John of Damascus. *An Exact Eposition of the Orthodox Faith.* Trans. S. D. F. Salmond. Vol. IX, Nicene and Post-Nicene Fathers, series II, P. Schaff and H. Wace (eds.). New York: Christian Literature Publishing Co., 1890.

Florensky, Pavel. *Iconostasis.* Trans. D. Sheehan and O. Andrejev. Crestwood: St. Vladimir's Seminary Press, 1996.

Klein, G. "Die ursprüngliche Gestalt des Vaterunsers" in *Zeitschrift für die neutestamentliche Wissenschaft*, vol. 7, num. 1 (Feb. 1906), pp. 34–50.

Kontzevitch, I. M. *Elder Nektary of Optino.* Platina, CA: St. Herman of Alaska Brotherhood, 1998.

Kreeft, Peter. *Back to Virtue.* San Francisco: Ignatius, 1992.

Lamentations of Matins of Holy and Great Saturday. Trans. Holy Transfiguration Monestary. Boston: Holy Transfiguration Monestary, 1981.

Lanne, Emmanuel. "Le nom de Jésus-Christ et son invocation chez saint Irénée de Lyon", *Irénikon 48*, 1975, pp. 447–467 and 49, 1976, pp. 34–53.

Larchet, Jean-Claude. *La divinisation de l'homme selon Maxime le Confesseur.* Paris: Éditions du Cerf, 1996.

————. *L'inconscient spirituel.* Paris: Éditions du Cerf, 2005.

————. *Mental Disorders and Spiritual Healing, Teachings from the Early Christian East.* Trans. G. J. Champoux and R. P. Coomaraswamy. Hillsdale, NY: Sophia Perennis, 2005.

Lash, Archimandrite Ephrem. www.anastasis.org.uk/pascha.htm

The Lenten Triodion. Trans. Mother Mary and Archimandrite K. Ware. South Canaan PA: St. Tikhon's Seminary Press, 1994.

Lossky, Vladimir. *In the Image and Likeness of God.* Crestwood, NY: St Vladimir's Seminary Press, 1974.

————. *The Mystical Theology of the Eastern Church.* Cambridge & London: James Clarke & Co., 1957.

Louth, Andrew. *Maximus the Confessor.* New York/London: Routledge, 1996.

Lubac, Henri de. *Medieval Exegesis*, Vol. 1. Trans. M. Sebanc. Grand Rapids, MI: Wm. B. Eerdmans Publishing Co. and Edinburgh, Scotland: T & T Clark Ltd., 1998.

————. *Medieval Exegesis*, Vol. 2. Trans. E. M. Macierowski. Grand Rapids, MI: Wm. B. Eerdmans Publishing Co. and Edinburgh, Scotland: T & T Clark Ltd., 2000.

Macarius, Starets of Optino. *Russian Letters of Spiritual Direction 1834-1860.* Selected and trans. I. De Beausobre. Crestwood: St. Vladimir's Seminary, 1994.

Mark the Ascetic, "Letter to Nicolas the Solitary"; *The Philokalia*, vol. 1, p. 147–160.

Maximus the Confessor. *Ambigua*. Trans. E. Ponsoye. Paris-Suresnes: Les Éditions de l'Ancre, 1994.

———. *The Ascetic Life*. Trans. P. Sherwood. New York, NY/Ramsey, NJ: Newman Press, 1955.

———. *The Church, the Liturgy and the Soul of Man, The Mystagogia of St. Maximus the Confessor.* Trans. Dom J. Stead. Still River, MA: St. Bede's Publications, 1982.

———. *The Disputation with Pyrrhus of Our Father Among the Saints Maximus the Confessor.* Trans. J. P. Farrell. South Canaan, PA, 1990.

———. *On the Cosmic Mystery of Jesus Christ. Selected Writings from St Maximus the Confessor.* Trans. P. Blowers and R. L. Wilken. Crestwood, NY: St Vladimir's Seminary Press, 2003.

———. 'On the Lord's Prayer', *The Philokalia*, vol. 2, pp. 285–305 and *Selected Writings*, pp. 101–119.

———. *Selected Writings*. Trans. G. Berthold. New York: Paulist Press, 1985.

———. 'Texts on Love', *The Philokalia*, vol. 2, pp. 52–113 and *Selected Writings*, pp. 35–87.

———. 'Texts on Theology', *The Philokalia*, vol. 2, pp. 114–163 and *Selected Writings*, pp 129–170.

———. 'Various Texts', *The Philokalia*, vol. 2, pp. 164–284.

The Midrash on Psalms, Vol. 1. Trans. W. G. Baude. New Haven: Yale University Press, 1959.

Monk of the Eastern Church. (Archimandrite Lev Gillet), *The Jesus Prayer*. Crestwood, NY: St. Vladimir's Seminary Press, 1987.

Moore, Archimandrite Lazarus. *St. Seraphim of Sarov, A Spiritual Biography.* Blanco, TX: New Sarov Press, 1994.

Nellas, Panayiotis. *Deification in Christ*. Trans. N. Russell. Crestwood, NY: St. Vladimir's Seminary Press, 1987.

Nikitas Stithatos. 'On Spiritual Knowledge', *The Philokalia*, vol. 4, pp. 139–174.

Nikodemos the Hagiorite. *Concerning Frequent Communion. Of the Immaculate Mysteries of Christ.* Trans. Fr. G. Dokos. The Dalles, Oregon: Uncut Mountain Press, 2006

———. *Exomologetarion, A Manual of Confession*. Trans. Fr. G. Dokos. The Dalles, Oregon: Uncut Mountain Press, 2006.

———. *A Handbook of Spiritual Counsel*. Trans. P. A. Chamberas. New York/Mahwah: Paulist Press, 1989.

———. *Nea Klimax* (New Ladder). Volos, 1956.

Origen. Trans. R. A. Greer. New York: Paulist Press, 1979.

Orthodox Daily Prayers. South Canaan, PA: St. Tikhon's Seminary Press, 1982.

Osborn, Eric. *Irenaeus of Lyons*. Cambridge: Cambridge University Press, 2001.

Ouspensky, Leonid. *Theology of the Icon*, 2 vols. Trans. A. Gythiel and E. Meyendorff (vol. 1 only). Crestwood, NY: St. Vladimir's Seminary, 1992.

Ouspensky, Leonid and Vladimir Lossky. *The Meaning of Icons*. Trans. G. E. H. Palmer and E. Kadloubovsky. Crestwood, NY: St Vladimir's Seminary Press, 1983.

Péneaud, Philippe. *Les Quatre Vivants*. Paris: L'Harmattan, 2007.

The Pentecostarion of the Orthodox Church. Trans. I. E. Lambertsen. Liberty TN: St. John of Kronstadt Press, 2010.

Peter of Damaskos. 'A Treasury of Divine Knowledge', in *The Philokalia*, vol. 3, pp. 74–210.

Philocalie des Pères neptique, fascicule 11. Trans. B. Bobrinskoy. Bégrolles-en-Mauges: Abbaye de Bellefontaine, 1991.

The Philokalia, 4 vols. Compiled by St Nikodimos of the Holy Mountain and St Makarios of Corinth. Trans. G.E.H. Palmer, P. Sherrard, K. Ware. London: Faber and Faber, 1979-1995.

Pieper, Josef. *The Four Cardinal Virtues*. Notre Dame: University of Notre Dame, 1966.

Pomazansky, Protopresbyter Michael. *Orthodox Dogmatic Theology*, 2nd editon. Trans. Hieromonk Seraphim Rose. Platina, CA: Saint Herman of Alaska Brotherhood, 1997.

Popovitch, Père Justin, *Philosophie orthodoxe de la vérité*, 5 vols. Fr. trans. J.-L. Palierne. Lausanne, Switzerland: L'Age d'Homme, 1992–1997

Pseudo-Dionysius. *The Complete Works*. Trans. C. Luibheid and N. Russell. New York: Paulist Press, 1987.

Riordan, William. *Divine Light, the Theology of Denys the Areopagite*. San Francisco: Ignatius Press, 2008.

Schmemann, Alexander. *The Eucharist*. Crestwood, NY: St. Vladimir's Seminary Press, 1988.

———. *Great Lent, Journey to Pascha*. Crestwood, NY: St. Vladimir's Seminary Press, 1990).

———. Of Water and the Spirit. Crestwood, NY: St. Vladimir's Seminary,1974.

Sendler, Egon. *The Icon, Image of the Invisible*. Trans. Fr. S. Bigham. Torrance, CA: Oakwood Publications, 1988.

Sluzebnic (priest's). www.orthodox.net/services/sluzebnic-vespers-lamplighting-prayers.html

Symeon the New Theologian, "The Three Methods of Prayer"; *The Philokalia*, vol. 4, pp. 67–75.

Snodgrass, Adrian. *Architecture, Time and Eternity*, vol. 1. New Delhi: International Academy of Indian Culture and Aditya Prakashan, 1990.

Sophrony, Archimandrite. *Saint Silouan the Athonite*. Trans. R. Edmonds. Crestwood, NY: St. Vladimir's Seminary Press, 1999.

Spidlik, Tomas. *Prayer, The Spirituality of the Christian East*, vol. 2. Trans. A. P. Gythiel. Kalamazoo: Cistercian Publ., 2005.

———. *The Spirituality of the Christian East*. Trans. A. P. Gythiel. Kalamazoo: Cistercian Publ., 1986.

Staniloae, Dumitru. *The Experience of God, Orthodox Dogmatic Theology*, 5 vols. Trans. I. Ionita and R. Barringer. Brookline MA: Holy Cross Orthodox Press, 1994–2012.

———. *Orthodox Spirituality*. Trans. Archimandrite J. Newville and O. Kloos. South Canaan, PA: St. Tikhon's Seminary Press, 2002.

Stevenson, Kenneth W. *The Lord's Prayer, A Text in Tradition*. Minneapolis: Fortress Press, 2004.

Stithatos, Nikitas. *On Spiritual Knowledge* in *The Philokalia*, vol. 4, pp. 139–174.

Theophan the Recluse. 'The Fruits of Prayer', in *The Art of Prayer*.

———. *Kindling the Divine Spark*. Trans. Valentina Lyovin. Platina: St Herman of Alaska Brotherhood/Wildwood, CA: St. Xenia Skete, 1994.

———. *The Path to Salvation*. Trans. Fr. Seraphim Rose. Platina: St Herman of Alaska Brotherhood, 1996.

Thunberg, Lars. *Microcosm and Mediator*. Second ed.. Peru: Open Court, 1995.

Tugwell, Simon, *The Beatitudes: Soundings in Christian Tradition*. Springfield, IL: Templegate, 1980.

Vasileios, Archimandrite. *Hymn of Entry*. Trans. E.Briere. Crestwood, NY: St. Vladimir's Seminary Press, 1984.

Vlachos, Archimandrite Hierotheos S. *Orthodox Psychotherapy, The Science of the Fathers*. Trans. E. Williams. Levadia: Birth of the Theotokos Monastery, 1994.

von Hildebrand, Dietrich, *Transformation in Christ*. San Francisco, CA: Ignatius Press, 2001.

Ware, Timothy. *The Orthodox Church*, 2nd, rev. ed. London/New York: Penguin Books, 1993.

Weil, Simone. 'Concerning the Our Father', *Waiting for God*, pp. 216–227. Trans. E. Craufurd. New York: Capricorn, 1959.

Zacharias, Archimandrite. *The Hidden Man of the Heart*. Waymart, PA: Mount Tabor Publishing/Essex, UK: The Stavropegic Monastery of St. John the Baptist, 2008.

———. *Remember Thy First Love*. Dalton, PA: Mount Tabor Publishing/Essex, UK: The Stavropegic Monastery of St. John the Baptist, 2010.

SATOR-ROTAS BIBLIOGRAPHY

Boris, Roland and May, Louis Philippe. "Le Pythagorisme Secret du SATOR AREPO, Lettres et nombres", *Recueil des notices et mémoires de la Société Archéologique, Historique, et Géographique de Département de Constantine*, vol. 69, 1955–1956, pp. 95–117.

Cammilleri, Rino. *Il quadrato magico*. Milan: Rizzoli, 1999.

Carcopino, Jérôme. *Études d'histoire chrétienne*, new ed. Paris: Albin Michel, 1963.

Carmignac, Jean. *Recherches sur le «Notre Père»*. Paris: Letouzey & Ané, 1969.

Charlesworth, James H. *The Good and Evil Serpent, How a Universal Symbol Became Christianized* (New Haven and London: Yale University Press, 2010),

Couchard, Paul-Louis and Audin, Amable.. "Le carré magique: Une interprétation graphique." *Latomus*, tome 17, fasc. 3 (juilliet-septembre 1958), pp. 518-527.

Cumont, Franz. *Rendiconti Pontificia Accademia di Archeologia* 13 (1937) pp. 7–8.

Jerphanion, Guillaume de. *La Voix des Monuments, Études d'archeologie. nouvelle serie*. Paris: les Éditions d'Art et d'Histoire, 1938.

Paulsen, Jren. "Du carré SATOR au palindrome de Raban Maur: un ésoterisme arithmologique chrétien", *Connaissance des religions*, 51–52 (juilliet–décembre), 1997, pp. 92–102.

Picard, Charles. "Sur le carré magique à l'église odorante, (Kokar Kilise, Cappadoce)", *Revue archéologique* 1 (1965), 101–102.

Ryan, W. F.. "Solomon, Sator, Acrostics, and Leo the Wise in Russia," *Oxford Slavonic Papers*, n.s. 19 (1986).

Schneider, Wolfgang Christian. "Sator Opera Tenet - Poras Aras. 'Der Sämann erhält die Werke - Du aber pfliigst Eine Deutung des Sator-Quadrats'," *Castrum Peregrini* 189/90, 1989.

Sesiano, Jacques. "Les carrès magiques de Manuel Moschopoulos", *Archive for History of Exact Sciences*, Vol. 53, No. 5, Nov. 1998, pp. 377-397.

Sheldon, Rose Mary. "The Sator Rebus: An Unsolved Cryptogram?". *Cryptologia* 27, no. 3, July 2003, pp. 233–287.

Simon, Marcel. *Verus Israel*. Trans. H. McKeating. Oxford: Oxford University Press, 1986.

Vassel, Jean. "A propos des «Études d'histoire chrétienne»", *Études traditionnelles* 56, 1955, pp. 28–37.

Vinel, Nicolas. "Le judaïsme caché du carré SATOR de Pompéi", *Revue de l'histoire des religions*, vol. 223, no. 2, 2006, pp. 173–194.

Index of Scriptural References

Printed in Great Britain
by Amazon

75601535R00343